MAURICE HINSON is Professor of Church Music at the Southern Baptist Theological Seminary and an authority on piano literature and pedagogy. He is a frequent lecturer at teachers' meetings and clinics and has been guest-lecturer in piano at the National Music Camp in Interlochen, Michigan, for eight summers. He is author of numerous publications on keyboard literature.

IRWIN FREUNDLICH was a member of the piano faculty of the Juilliard School and visiting faculty member at the North Carolina School of the Arts. He originated and developed the classes in piano repertoire at the Juilliard School, and was coauthor (with the late James Friskin) of *Music for the Piano.*

Guide to the Pianist's Repertoire

MAURICE HINSON

GUIDE TO THE PIANIST'S REPERTOIRE

EDITED BY IRWIN FREUNDLICH

INDIANA UNIVERSITY PRESS
Bloomington / London

TO THE MEMORY OF MY TEACHERS,

Joseph Brinkman

(1901-1960)

AND

Olga Samaroff-Stokowski

(1882-1948)

WHOSE INTEGRITY AND DEVOTION TO

THE ART OF MUSIC WERE INSPIRING

MODELS FOR COUNTLESS ASPIRING PIANISTS

M. H.

Published in Canada by Fitzhenry & Whiteside Limited, Don Mills, Ontario
Library of Congress catalog card number: 72-75983
ISBN: 0-253-32700-8
Manufactured in the United States of America
5 79 78

Contents

Preface

No single musician can successfully encompass the entire piano repertoire. It is, in fact, by far the largest devoted to any instrument, second only in scope to that for voice. Not only is it beyond the capability of any single pianist to master more than a very limited segment of the repertoire but it is also equally difficult to have even a cursory acquaintance with its scope and be able to sift out material for study and performance from the mass of works accumulated over the years without some organized guiding hand to lead the way. It is, indeed, a lengthy path to travel from the earlier keyboard works to the present creations of the *avant-garde* especially if, as in the present volume, one chooses to include works for harpsichord, clavichord and organ suitable for performance on the modern piano. A practicable *Guide to the Pianist's Repertoire* is, then, a necessity for student, performer and teacher alike.

The key questions for the reader are: What is there? What it is like? Where can I get it? To date the most useful efforts in English to provide answers to these questions have been attempted in Ernest Hutcheson's *The Literature of the Piano* (1948, revised by Rudolph Ganz, 1964), *Music for the Piano* (1954) by James Friskin and Irwin Freundlich, and the *Short History of Keyboard Music* (1966) by F. E. Kirby. The main interest in Hutcheson's book lies in the personal viewpoints of that distinguished Australian pianist. However, it is short on the earlier and more modern repertoire since it concentrates on the traditional pianistic literature. These gaps are only partially repaired by Ganz's interesting additions. The Friskin-Freundlich handbook is organized by periods and style groupings and has as its point of departure 1590, its cut-off date 1952. It includes not only the solo repertoire but also works for four hands at one and two pianos, and concertos. Kirby's more recent volume is an historical, chronological approach concerned with the development of style and although not a handbook (in the sense of the Hutcheson and Friskin-Freundlich volumes) contains a wealth of material for the practical keyboardist even though clothed in a musicological garb.

Two rather unusual volumes in German must be mentioned:

The *Geschichte der Klaviermusik* (1941, fourth edition 1965) of Walter Georgii and the almost unbelievable *Handbuch der Klavierliteratur* (1967) of Klaus Wolters. The Georgii work was in a class by itself in terms of completeness, clarity, scope and scholarship until the appearance of Wolters' monumental volume. But it was, in fact, a history of the repertoire comparable to Kirby's opus. Wolters produced a genuine handbook of unparalleled scope in which, *e.g.,* one can find all the variant readings in all the Beethoven Sonatas in all the major editions! It also devotes much space to instructional material, methods, technical treatises and anthologies, and attempts to grade the difficulty of the material in a scale ranging from 1 to 15.

The present volume is organized along completely different lines. First of all, it is devoted completely to the solo literature. It is alphabetical instead of chronological or stylistic in emphasis, taking on somewhat the aspect of a catalogue of catalogues supplemented by a listing of anthologies, collections and bibliographical material inserted into the text and running over into an additional appendix. The bibliography includes not only books and articles but also doctoral dissertations (both published and unpublished) pertaining to the composers and works mentioned. The inclusion of such material is unique to this volume and should prove invaluable for purposes of further self-study. The problem of style groupings and national groupings (*e.g.,* what works are there by Canadian or Bulgarian or American composers?) has been met by an indexing system aimed to solve this problem most expeditiously for the reader. It is also hoped that the inclusion of a generous number of *avant-garde* works and listings of more than two hundred and fifty American composers will fill an obvious gap. Similar attention has been lavished on the entire spectrum of the contemporary repertoire as well as countless earlier composers never before included in any volume on the pianist's repertoire.

The huge amount of research needed to compile this book has been the responsibility of Dr. Maurice Hinson, whose indefatigable energy and industry have been exemplary and most impressive. My own contribution has been as consultant, helping to organize the material, edit it as thoroughly as possible, reformulating and rephrasing to ensure a felicitous text with, here and there, some additional contributions inserted from my own special knowledge of the repertoire. It goes without saying that even with the greatest care it is impossible to avoid an occasional error. Dr. Hinson and I would both be grateful for communications to help eliminate errata in future editions.

IRWIN FREUNDLICH
New York, September, 1971

Introduction

Guide to the Pianist's Repertoire purports to make available in one practical listing the important solo piano literature. Part I of the book is a list of solo piano compositions by individual composers and a list of anthologies and collections of solo piano music. Part II consists of: (1) an extension of the bibliography listed with composers and compositions in Part I, (2) an appendix listing outstanding historical recital programs and (3) indexes to composers by nationality, to black composers, to women composers, and to editors, arrangers, and transcribers.

Selection. Criteria used in selecting composers were: (1) to make sure all standard composers were thoroughly covered and (2) to introduce contemporary composers of merit, especially composers of the United States. In addition, music is included that was composed before the invention of the piano in the hope that more thorough exploration of some unfamiliar treasures will be encouraged. Arrangements of music originally written for other instruments have, as a rule, been excluded. Exceptions have been made in the case of outstanding transcribers such as Bach, Busoni, Liszt, etc.

Special effort has been made to examine as many contemporary works as possible. Recent *avant-garde* works are difficult to judge since most of the pieces and techniques have not met the test of time. Many *avant-garde* composers are using the piano as a sound-source rather than identifying the instrument with its past history. This may be a transitional stage or it may be, as some musicians feel, the end of piano literature as we have known it for so many years (John Tilbury, Musical Times, 110, February 1969, 150-2).

A certain amount of subjectivity is unavoidable in a book of this nature but the attempt has been made to be as fair and objective as possible. Composers wishing to submit compositions for possible inclusion in future editions are encouraged to do so.

Because of constant change in the publishing world it is impossible to list only music currently in print. Some works were known to be out-of-print but were listed because of their merit.

If a work has been published and is not in print today, it can often be located at second-hand music stores, one of the larger university or municipal libraries, or, more especially, the Library of Congress.

Acknowledgments. Many people in many places have generously given me their help. Acknowledgments for assistance are gratefully made to Miss Martha Powell, Music Librarian of The Southern Baptist Theological Seminary; Mr. Rodney Mill of the Library of Congress; Dr. Donald Krummell, formerly of the Newberry Library, Chicago, Illinois; Miss Marian Korda, Music Librarian of the University of of Louisville; to my graduate assistant, Richard Shadinger; and to the Southern Baptist Theological Seminary for making possible the typing of the manuscript and graduate assistants through the years. The American Music Center, American Composers' Alliance Library, Canadian Music Centre and Composers Autograph Publications have been most helpful. Without the generous assistance of numerous publishers this volumc would not have been possible. Special appreciation goes to John Bice of Boosey and Hawkes, Judith Hemstreet of Music Corporation of America, Norman Auerback of Theodore Presser, John Sweeney of Belwin-Mills, Gertrud Mathys of C. F. Peters, Mike Warren of Oxford University Press, Ronald Freed of Peer International Corporation, Karl Bradley of G. Schirmer, Don Malin of E. B. Marks and Donald Hinshaw of Carl Fischer. I am especially grateful to my highly esteemed editor, Professor Irwin Freundlich of The Juilliard School. His encouragement, wisdom and friendship have been a constant source of inspiration throughout the years. Finally, I wish to express appreciation to my children, Jane and Susan, for living with the inconvenience necessarily caused by the preparation of this book. Special gratitude to my wife, Peggy, who has understood, in her remarkable way, a musician.

MAURICE HINSON

Louisville, Kentucky, September, 1971

Using the Guide

Arrangement of entries. In the "Individual Composers" section, all composers are listed alphabetically. Sometimes biographical or stylistic comments follow the composer's name and dates of birth and death. Under each composer's name, individual compositions are listed, by opus number, or by title, or by musical form, or by a combination of the three.

The "Anthologies and Collections" section (beginning on p. 694) is divided into five groupings: "General," "General: Contemporary," "Tombeau, Hommage," and "Separate Countries." The entries in this section include the editor or compiler, the publisher, the composers and sometimes the titles represented in the collection. (See p. xiv for further explanation of entries.)

Grading. An effort has been made to grade representative works of each composer. Four broad categories of grading are used: Easy, Intermediate (Int.), Moderately Difficult (M-D), and Difficult (D). To provide a more thorough understanding of this grading, the following standard works will serve as guide.

Easy: Bach, dance movements from the *Anna Magdalena Notebook*
Leopold Mozart, *Notebook for Wolfgang*
Schumann, easier pieces from *Album for the Young*
Bartók, *Mikrokosmos,* Vols. I-II

Int.: Bach, *Twelve Little Preludes and Fugues*
Beethoven, *Ecossaises*
Mendelssohn, *Children's Pieces* Op. 72
Bartók, *Rumanian Folk Dances* 1-5

M-D: Bach, *French Suites (English)*
Mozart, *Sonatas*
Brahms, *Rhapsody* Op. 79/2
Debussy, *La Soirée dans Grenade*

D: Bach, *Partitas*
Beethoven, *Sonata* Op. 57
Chopin, *Etudes*
Barber, *Sonata*

Description. Descriptions have been limited to style, form, interpretative suggestions and pianistic problems inherent in the music. Editorial procedures found in a particular edition are mentioned.

Details of entries. The publisher's name is frequently abbreviated. Editors, arrangers and/or transcribers are listed preceding the publisher. When more than one edition is available, the editions are listed in order of preference, with the most desirable listed first. Approximate date of composition, when known, is given; "c." refers to copyright date. Timing and number of pages are frequently listed. Spelling of composers' names and compositions were retained as they were found on the music or collection being described. Specifically related bibliographic entries of books and periodical articles have been incorporated into the main body of the text, at the listing of a specific composition or at the conclusion of the discussion of a composer's works.

Other assistance. A list of "Abbreviations" (pp. xvi-xx) including terms, publishers, books and periodicals precedes the main body of the text. An index of "American Agent, Parent Company, or Location of Music Publishers" (pp. xxi-xlv) will assist the reader in locating the publishers' addresses. Titles of anthologies and collections are listed with their page numbers in a "Title Index" (pp. 758-765) immediately following the "Anthologies and Collections" section.

Explanation of Entries

INDIVIDUAL COMPOSER ENTRIES

JOHANNES BRAHMS

2 Rhapsodies Op. 79/1 g, 2 b (1879). (Georgii-Henle) (Klasen-UE).

Op. 79/1 indicates Op. 79 No. 1; g indicates the key of G minor; 2 b indicates Op. 79 No. 2 in B minor. The date of composition is 1879. Georgii is editor for the Henle edition. Klasen is editor for the Universal Edition publisher.

CARMARGO GUARNIERI

Sonatina No. 3 (AMP 1937). Written in G clef only. Allegro: eighth-note motion, 3 voices; grazioso melody over broken-chord figuration in the Con tenerezza; Two-part Fugue: rhythmic, moving sixteenth notes, forte conclusion. M-D.

This work is published by Associated Music Publishers and was composed in 1937. Written in G clef only refers to complete work. The titles of individual movements are separated by semi-colons. Allegro is the first movement, followed by general description. Con tenerezza is the second movement, also briefly described. Two-part Fugue is the final movement, with its description. The entire work is classified as Moderately Difficult.

ARTHUR FARWELL

Sourwood Mountain (GS). In *51 Piano Pieces from the Modern Repertoire*. A "Rip-snorting development of a good old American tune." Virtuoso treatment.

This work is published by G. Schirmer and is contained in the collection *51 Piano Pieces from the Modern Repertoire*. This collection is not listed in the "Anthologies and Collections" section as the wording reads "In *51 Piano Pieces*" instead of "See *51 Piano Pieces.*"

ANTHOLOGIES AND COLLECTIONS SECTION ENTRY

Thirteen Keyboard Sonatas of the 18 and 19th Centuries (W. S. Newman-UNC c. 1947).

A fine collection of unfamiliar sonatas with critical commentaries. Includes sonatas by Jean Barrière (flourished 1720-50), Platti, Alberti, Georg Benda (1722-95), J. J. Agrell (1701-65), C. G. Neefe (1748-98), Manuel Blasco de Nebra (ca. 1750-84), Dittersdorf (1739-99), Joseph Wölfl (1773-1812), E. T. A. Hoffman (1776-1822), J. F. Reichardt, Loewe, Moscheles.

W. S. Newman is the editor; UNC indicates the University of North Carolina is the publisher; copyright in 1947. Composers are listed.

Abbreviations

A	Allemande
ABRSM	Associated Board of the Royal Schools of Music
ACA	American Composers Alliance
ACA-CFE	American Composers Alliance—Composers Facsimile Edition
AL	Abr. Lundquist AB Stockholm
AM	Acta Musicologia
AMC	American Music Center
AME	American Music Editions
AMP	Associated Music Publishers
AMS	American Musicological Society
AMT	American Music Teacher
B	Bourrée
B&VP	Broekmans & Van Poppel
BB	Broude Brothers
BBD	*A Bio-Bibliographical Dictionary of Twelve-Tone and Serial Composers.* Effie B. Carlson. Metuchen, N.J.: Scarecrow Press, 1970.
Bk(s)	Book(s)
BMC	Boston Music Co.
BMI	Broadcast Music, Inc.
Bo&Bo	Bote & Bock
Bo&H	Boosey & Hawkes
Br	Bärenreiter
Br&H	Breitkopf & Härtel
c.	copyright
ca.	circa
C	Courante
CAP	Composers' Autograph Publications
CeBeDeM	CeBeDeM Foundation
CF	Carl Fischer
CFE	Composers Facsimile Edition
CFP	C. F. Peters
CMC	Canadian Music Center
CMP	Consolidated Music Publishing
cols.	columns

D	Difficult
DDT	Denkmäler deutscher Tonkunst
Der	Derry Music Co.
Dob	Doblinger
DTB	Denkmäler der Tonkunst in Bayern
DTOe	Denkmäler der Tonkunst in Oesterreich
EAM	Editorial Argentina de Música
EB	Editions J. Buyst
EBM	E. B. Marks
EC	Edizioni Curci
ECIC	Editorial Cooperativa Interamericana de Compositores
ECo	Edition Cotta'sche
ECS	E. C. Schirmer
EGZ	Editore Gugliemo Zanibon
EHM	Edwin H. Morris
ELK	Elkan & Schildknecht
EMB	Editio Musica Budapest
EMH	Editions Musikk-Huset
EMM	Ediciones Mexicanas de Música
EMT	Editions Musicales Transatlantiques
ESC	Max Eschig
EV	Elkan-Vogel
FSF	Fast Slow Fast
FVB	Fitzwilliam Virginal Book
G	Gigue
Gau	Gaudiosi
GD	*Grove's Dictionary of Music and Musicians.* 5th ed. New York: St. Martin's Press Inc., 1955.
Gen	General Music Publishing Co.
GM	Gehrmans Musikförlag
GS	G. Schirmer
GZ	Gugliemo Zanibon
HF	High Fidelity
Hin	Hinrichsen

HV	Heinrichshofen's Verlag
HWG	H. W. Gray
ICM	*Introduction to Contemporary Music.* Joseph Machlis. New York: Norton & Co., 1961.
IEM	Instituto de Extension Musicale, Calle Compañia
IMC	International Music Company
IMI	Israel Music Institute
Int.	Intermediate difficulty
JAMS	Journal of the American Musicological Society
JF	J. Fischer
JR	Juilliard Review
JWC	J. W. Chester
K	Kalmus
K&S	Kistner and Siegel
Ku	Kultura
LG	Lawson-Gould
l'OL	l'Oiseau-Lyre
LOT	Lottermoser S.A.C.I.
M	Minuet
M&M	Music and Musicians
MAB	Musica Antiqua Bohemica (Artia)
MC	Mildly Contemporary
MCA	M.C.A. Music (Music Corporation of America)
M-D	Moderately Difficult
Mer	Mercury Music Corp.
MFTP	*Music for the Piano.* James Friskin and Irwin Freundlich. New York: Rinehart & Co., 1954.
MJ	Music Journal
MK	Musikaliska Konstföreningen
ML	Music and Letters
MM	Modern Music
MMR	Monthly Musical Record
MO	Musical Opinion
MQ	Musical Quarterly
MR	Music Review

MS	Music-Survey
ms, mss	manuscript(s)
MT	Musical Times
MTC	*Music in the Twentieth Century.* William W. Austin. New York: Norton & Co., 1966.
MTNA	Music Teachers National Association
MTP	Music Treasure Publications
MVH	Musica Viva Historica (Artia)
Nag	Nagel's Musik-Archiv
NME	New Music Editions
NMO	Norsk Musikförlag
NMS	Nordiska Musikförlaget
Nov	Novello
NV	Noetzel Verlag
OBV	Oesterreichischer Bundesverlag
OD	Oliver Ditson
OUP	Oxford University Press
p(p)	page(s)
P	Polonaise
PAU	Pan American Union
PIC	Peer International Corporation
PMP	Polish Music Publications
PNM	Perspectives of New Music
PQ	Piano Quarterly
PQN	Piano Quarterly Newsletter
PRMA	Proceedings of the Royal Musical Association
PSM	Pennsylvania State Music Series (Pennsylvania State University Press)
PWM	Polskie Wydawnictwo Muzyczne
R&E	Ries & Erler
Rev.	Revised
Ric	Ricordi
S	Sarabande
SA	Sonata-Allegro
Sal	Salabert
S&B	Stainer and Bell
SB	Summy-Birchard

SBE	*Sonata in the Baroque Era.* W. S. Newman. Chapel Hill, N. C.: University of N. C. Press, 1959.
SCE	*Sonata in the Classic Era.* W. S. Newman. Chapel Hill, N. C.: University of N. C. Press, 1963.
SFS	Slow Fast Slow
SHKY	*A Short History of Keyboard Music.* Frank E. Kirby. New York: The Free Press, 1966.
SHV	Státní hudbení vydavatelství
SIMG	Sammelbände der Internationalen Musikgesellschaft
SKABO	Skandinavisk og Borups Musikforlag
SM	Skandinavisk Musikförlag
SP	Shawnee Press
SPDM	Society for Publishing Danish Music
SSB	*Sonata Since Beethoven.* W. S. Newman. Chapel Hill, N. C.: University of N. C. Press, 1969.
SZ	Suvini Zerboni
TP	Theodore Presser
TPA	*Antologia di musica antica e moderna per il pianoforte* (Gino Tagliapietra), 18 Vols., Ricordi, 1931-32.
UE	Universal Edition
UME	Unión Musical Española
UMP	United Music Publishers
UNC	University of North Carolina Press
UNL	Universidad Nacional del Litoral
USSR	Mezhdunarodnaya Kniga (Music Publishers of the USSR)
Var.	Variation(s)
vol(s)	volume(s)
VU	Vienna Urtext Edition (UE)
WH	Wilhelm Hansen
YMP	Yorktown Music Press
ZV	Zenemükiadó Vállalat

American Agent or Parent Company of Music Publishers

1. Associated Music Publishers, Inc.
   609 Fifth Ave., New York, N. Y. 10017
2. Barnhouse, C. L. Co.
   110 B Avenue East, Oskaloosa, Iowa 52577
3. Baron, M. Co.
   Box 149, Oyster Bay, N. Y. 11771
4. Belwin-Mills Publishing Corp.
   25 Deshon Drive, Melville, N. Y. 11746
5. Big 3 Music Corp.
   1350 Avenue of the Americas, New York, N. Y. 10019
6. Boosey & Hawkes, Inc.
   Oceanside, N. Y. 11572
7. Brodt Music Co.
   1409 East Independence Blvd., Charlotte, N. C. 28201
8. Broude, Alexander, Inc.
   120 West 57th St., New York, N. Y. 10019
9. Broude Bros., Inc.
   56 West 45th St., New York, N. Y. 10036
10. Chappell & Co., Inc.
    609 Fifth Ave., New York, N. Y. 10017
11. Concordia Music Publishing House
    3558 South Jefferson Ave., St. Louis, Mo. 63118
12. Elkan, Henri Music Publisher
    1316 Walnut St., Philadelphia, Pa. 19107
13. Elkan-Vogel Co., Inc. (see Presser, Theodore)
    Presser Place, Bryn Mawr, Pa. 19010
14. Fischer, Carl, Inc.
    56-62 Cooper Sq., New York, N. Y. 10003
15. Foster Music Co., Mark
    P.O. Box 783, Marquette, Michigan 49855
16. Fox, Sam, Publishing Co.
    1841 Broadway, New York, N. Y. 10023
17. Frank Distributing Corp.
    116 Boylston St., Boston, Mass. 02116
18. Galaxy Music Corp.
    2121 Broadway, New York, N. Y. 10023

19. Hansen Publications, Inc.
250 Carol Place, Moonachie, N. J. 07074
20. M. C. A. Music
445 Park Avenue South, New York, N. Y. 10022
21. Magna Music
Sharon, Connecticut 06069
22. Marks, Edward B. Music Corp.
136 West 52nd St., New York, N. Y. 10019
23. Music Sales Corp.
33 West 60th St., New York, N. Y. 10023
24. Oxford University Press, Inc.
200 Madison Ave., New York, N. Y. 10016
25. Peters, C. F. Corporation
373 Park Avenue South, New York, N. Y. 10016
26. Presser, Theodore
Presser Place, Bryn Mawr, Pa.
27. Rubank, Inc.
16215 N. W. 15th Ave., Miami, Fla. 33169
28. Schirmer, E. C. Music Co.
600 Washington St., Boston, Mass. 02111
29. Schirmer, G., Inc.
609 Fifth Ave., New York, N. Y. 10017
30. Shapiro-Bernstein & Co., Inc.
666 Fifth Ave., New York, N. Y. 10019
31. Shawnee Press Inc.
Delaware Water Gap, Pa. 18327
32. Southern Music Pub. Co., Inc.
1619 Broadway, New York, N. Y. 10019
33. Southern Music Co.
P.O. Box 329, 1100 Broadway, San Antonio, Texas 78206
34. Summy-Birchard Company
1834 Ridge Ave., Evanston, Ill. 60204
35. Warner Bros., Seven Arts Music
488 Madison Ave., New York, N. Y. 10022
36. World Library Publications, Inc.
2145 Central Parkway, Cincinnati, Ohio 45214
37. Location or American agent unverified.

LOCATION OF MUSIC PUBLISHERS

Abraham Lundquists Musikforlag
Drottninggatan 26, Stockholm, Sweden

Ahn & Simrock
Meinekestrasse 10, 1 Berlin 15, West Germany

Akadémiai Kiadó
Budapest, Hungary

Akademische Druck-und Verlagsanstalt
Graz, Austria

Albersen
The Hague, Netherlands

Alfred Music Co.
75 Channel Drive, Port Washington, N. Y. 11050

Alpeg Editions (USA) 25

Alsbach 25
Amsterdam, Netherlands

American Composers Alliance—Composers Facsimile Edition
170 West 74th Street, New York, N. Y. 10023

American Institute of Musicology
P.O. Box 30665, Dallas, Texas 75230

American Music Center
2019 Broadway (15-79), New York, N. Y. 10023

American Music Editions
263 East 7th St., New York, N. Y. 10009

Amici della Musica da Camera, Gli
Via Bocca di Leone 25, Rome, Italy

Amphion Editions Musicales 4

Andrew Music Corp. 17

Anglo-French Music Co. 24

Araujo (see Valentin de Carvalho)

Arcadia Music Publishing Co., Ltd.
10 Sherlock Mews, Baker St., London, W. 1, England

Belmont Music Publishers
P.O. Box 49961, Los Angeles, Calif. 90049

Bender, C. C.
Amsterdam, Netherlands

Berandol Music Ltd. (Canada) 1

Bessel et Cie. (France) 4

Biblioteca Central, Sección de música
17 Barcelona, Spain

Birnbach, Richard
45 Lichterfelde, Berlin, Germany

BMI Canada, Ltd. 1
16 Gould St., Toronto 2, Ontario

Bomart Music Publications 1

Bongiovanni, F. 4
Bologna, Italy

Boston Music Co. 17
116 Boylston St., Boston, Mass. 02116

Bosworth & Co., Ltd. 4

Bote and Bock 1
Schutzenhofstrasse 4, Wiesbaden, West Germany

Bratti
Florence, Italy

Breitkopf und Härtel 1
Burgstrasse 6, 6200 Wiesbaden, Germany

British and Continental Music Agencies 20
64 Dean St., London, W. 1, England

Broadcast Music, Inc. 1

Broadcast Music Canada 1

Broekmans & Van Poppel 25
Amsterdam, Netherlands

Broude Bros., Inc.
56 West 45th St., New York, N. Y. 10036

Brown, Robert B.
1815 North Kenmore Ave., Hollywood, Calif. 90027

Bruzzichelli, Aldo, Editore (Italy) 8

Camara Music Publishers
229 West 52nd St., New York, N. Y. 10019

Cambridge University Press
32 East 57th St., New York, N. Y. 10022

Cameo Music
1527½ North Vine Street, Los Angeles, Calif. 90028

Canadian Music Center
33 Edward Street, Toronto 101, Ontario, Canada

Carisch, S. P. A. 4
Via General Fara 39, Milan, Italy

Carminignani Fondazione Rossini
Pesaro, Italy

Casa Amarilla
San Diego 128, Santiago, Chile

Casa Moreira de Sá (see Valentin de Carvalho)

CeBeDem (Centre Belge de Documentation Musicale) 12
4, Boulevard de l'Empereur, Brussels 1, Belgium

Centro di estudios historicos
Madrid, Spain

Century Music Publishing Co.
39 West 60th St., New York, N. Y. 10023

Chant du Monde, Le (France) 20

Chester, J. W.
Eagle Court, London, E. C. 1, England

Chopin Institute Edition (see Polish Music Publications) 22
Warsaw, Poland

Choudens 25
38 Rue Jean Mermos, Paris 8e, France

Cnudde
Ghent, Belgium

Coleman, see Sprague-Coleman

Combre, Marcel 13
Paris, France

Composers' Autograph Publications
P.O. Box 7103, Cleveland, Ohio 44128

Composers Facsimile Edition (see American Composers Alliance)

Composers Music Corp. 14

Composers Press 33

Consolidated Music Publishing, Inc. 23

Consortium Musical (formerly Phillipo) 13

Costallat 33

Cotta'sche, G.
Stuttgart and Berlin, Germany

Cramer, J. B. & Co., Ltd. 7
99 St. Martin's Lane, London, W. C. 2, England

Cranz, A. 27
Brussels, Belgium

Cserépfalvi (see Editio Musica Budapest)
Budapest, Hungary

Curci, Edizioni (see Edizioni Curci) 5

Curwen & Son, J. (England) 29

Dan Fog Musikforlag
Graabrødretorv 1, 1154 Copenhagen K, Denmark

De Ring
17 Laurierstraat, Antwerp, Belgium

De Santis, Edizioni
Via Cassia 13, 00191 Rome, Italy

Deiss 4
Paris, France

Delrieu & Cie., Georges 18
45, Avenue de la Victoire, Nice, France

Derry Music Co.
1240 Stockton St., San Francisco, Calif. 94133

Dessain (Belgium) 25

Ditson Co., Oliver 26

Doblinger, Ludwig 1
Dorotheergasse 10, A-1010, Vienna 1, Austria

Donemus 25
Jacob Obrechtstraat 51, Amsterdam-Z., Holland

Dotesio (Spain)

Dover
180 Varick St., New York, N. Y. 10014

Dow 20

Drago, A.
Magenta, Italy

Drustvo Slovenskih Skladateljev
Ljubljana, Yugoslavia

Durand & Co. 13
Paris, France

Dutch Society for Musicology
c/o Heer A.Creyghton, Lassuslaan 45, Bilthoven, Netherlands

Eastman School of Music Publications 14

Ediciones 'Los Diez"
Santiago, Chile

Ediciones Mexicanas de Música A. C. (Mexico) 32

Fischer, J. & Bro. 4
Harristown Road, Glen Rock, N. J. 07452

Foetisch (Switzerland) 28

Foley, Charles, Inc. 4

Fondazione Eugenio Bravi
Milan, Italy

Fondazione Rossini
Pesaro, Italy

Föreningen Svenska Tonsättare
Stockholm, Sweden

Forlivesi & Co., A. (Italy) 4

Forni
40132 Bologna, Italy

Forsyth Brothcrs, Ltd. 4

Francis, Day & Hunter, Ltd. (England) 5

Franco Colombo 4

Fritzsch

Fundação Calouste Gulbenkian
Parque de Sta. Gertrudes à Avda. de Berna, Lisbon, Portugal

Fürstner, Adolph
55 Iverna Court, London, W. 8, England

Galliard, Ltd. (England) 18

Gaudiosi
Buenos Aires, Agentina

Gehrmans, Carl Musikförlag 13
Post Fack 505, Vasagatan 46, Stockholm 1, Sweden

General Labor Federation, Cultural Department
Tel Aviv, Israel

General Music Publishing Co., Inc. 17
P.O. Box 267, Hastings-on-Hudson, N. Y. 10706

Israel Music Institute 6
P.O. Box 11253, Tel-Aviv, Israel

Israeli Music Publications (Israel) 32

Japanese Society of Rights of Authors & Composers
Tameike Meisan Bldg., 30 Akasaka Tameikecho, Minato-Ku, Tokyo, Japan

Jobert, Jean 13
Paris, France

Johnson Reprint Corp.
111 Fifth Avenue, New York, N. Y. 10003

Jürgenson, P.
Moscow 200, Russia

Kahnt, C. F. 25
Hofstatt 8, Lindau, Germany

Kalmus, Edwin F.
P.O. Box 1007, Commack, N. Y. 11725

Kalnajs, A.
719 W. Willow St., Chicago, Ill. 60614

Kistner & Siegel 11
Postfach 267, 478 Lippstadt, Germany

Körlings Förlag
Stockholm, Sweden

Krompholz
Bern, Switzerland

Kultura 6
P.O. Box 149, Budapest 62, Hungary

Lauweryns, F.
Brussels, Belgium

Lawson-Gould Music Publishers, Inc. 29

Lea Pocket Scores 26

Leduc, Alphonse 2, 3, 7, 13, 33
175, Rue Saint Honoré, Paris Ier, France

Lee Roberts 29

Leeds Music (Canada) Ltd. 20
Willowdale, Ontario, Canada

Leeds Music Corp. (see M. C. A. Music) 20

Lehman Foundation, Robert Owen
One William St., New York, N. Y. 10004

Lemoine, Henry & Cie. 13
17, rue Pigalle, 75 Paris 9, France

Lengnick & Co., Ltd., Alfred 4
421a Brighton Road, South Croydon, Surrey, England

Lerolle
Paris, France

Leuckart, F. E. C. 1
Munich, Germany

Lienau 25

Litolff, Collection 25
Frankfurt, Germany

L'Oiseaux-Lyre, Editions de
Les Ramparts, Monaco

London & Continental Publishing Co.
London, England

Lottermoser S. A. C. I.
Rivadavia 851, Buenos Aires, Argentina

Lyche, Harald & Co.'s Musikkforlag 25
Kongensgaten 2, Oslo, Norway

Magyar Kórus
Budapest, Hungary

Maurri, Edizioni R.
Florence, Italy

Musica Islandica (Menningarsjodur) 37

Musica Obscura
  410 South Michigan Avenue #730, Chicago, Ill. 60605

Musica Viva (Periodical)
  Rio de Janeiro, Brazil

Musical Americana
  c/o Harry Dichter, Apartment 808, Brighton Towers,
    Atlantic City, N. J. 08401

Musical Scope Publishers
  Box 125, Audubon Station, New York, N. Y. 10032

Musikaliska Konstföreningen (Swedish Society for Musical Art)
  Stockholm, Sweden

Musikk-Huset, Editions 25
  Karl Johans gate 45, Oslo 1, Norway

Musikverlag Schwann (see Schwann)

Muziekuitgeverij
  Amsterdam, Netherlands

Nagel's Musik-Archiv 1

Napoleão, Arthur
  Casa Napoleão, Sampaio Araujo & Cia.,
    122 Avenida Rio Branco, Rio de Janeiro, Brazil

Nederlandse Muziekgeschiedenis
  (see Dutch Society for Musicology)

Neuparth & Carneiro (see Valentin de Carvalho)

New Music Editions 26

New Valley Press
  Sage Hall, Smith College, Northampton, Mass. 01060

New World Music Corp. 35

Noel, Pierre 3
  Paris, France

Rahter 1

Reid Bros., Ltd.
16 Mortimer Street, London, W. 1, England

Reinhardt, Edition (Switzerland) 25

Remick Music Corp. 35

Revue Musicale
(Periodical) Paris, France

Ricordi & Co. (International) 4

Ricordi Americana (see Ricordi & Co.) 4

Ries & Erler (Germany) 25

Robbins Music Corp. 5
1540 Broadway, New York, N. Y. 10036

Rogers, Winthrop
295 Regent Street, London, W. 1, England

Rongwen Music, Inc. 9

Rouart, Lerolle & Co., E. (see Salabert, Editions)
Paris, France

Rózsavölgyi
P.O. Box 149, Budapest, Hungary

Russell, G. D.
Boston, Mass.

Russian State Publishers 20

Ryûnginsha
Tokyo, Japan

Salabert, Editions
22, Rue Chauchat, Paris 9e, France
575 Madison Avenue, New York, N. Y. 10022

Sassetti & Cia., Editores de Musica
R. Nova do Almada, 60, Lisbon 2, Portugal

Savez Kompozitora Jugoslavije Drustvo Slovenskih Skladateljev
(see Drustvo Slovenskih Skladateljev)

Schaum Publications, Inc.
2018 East North Avenue, Milwaukee, Wisconsin 53202

Schlesinger, Schemusikhandlung 25
Lankwitzerstrasse 9, Berlin-Lichterfelde-Ost, Germany

Schmidt Co., A. P. 34

Schneider
Paris, France

Schneider, P. 37

Schott 4
Schott and Co., Ltd.
48 Green Marlborough St., London, W. 1, England
B. Schott's Söhne
Mainz, West Germany

Schott Frères 25
Brussels, Belgium

Schroeder & Gunther 1

Schultheiss Musikverlag, C. L.
Stuttgart, Germany

Schwann Musikverlag
Charlottenstrasse 80-86, Düsseldorf, Germany

Seesaw Music
241½ East 84th Street, New York, N. Y. 10028

Selbstverlag des Komponisten
(Composer himself serves as publisher)

Sikorski, Hans
Hamburg, Germany

Simon, C.
Berlin, Germany

Simon and Schuster
630 Fifth Avenue, New York, N. Y. 10020

Simrock, N. 1
London, England

Skandinavisk Musikförlag
Borgergade 2, Copenhagen, Denmark

Skandinavisk og Borups Musikforlag (see Dan Fog)
Copenhagen, Denmark

Società Anonima Notari (see Notari, Società Anonima)

Société des Auteurs, Compositeurs et Editeurs de Musique
10 Rue Chaptal, Paris 9, France
15 East 48th Street, New York, N. Y. 10020

Société Francaise de Musicologie
Paris, France

Société pour la Publication de Musique Classique et Moderne
Paris, France

Society for Publishing Danish Music (see Dan Fog)

Sprague-Coleman 20

Stainer & Bell 18

State University of New York 18
Binghampton, N. Y. 13901

Státní hudbení vydavatelství (State Music Publishers—
now Supraphon) 6
Prague, Czechoslovakia

Státní Nakladtelstvi Krasne Literatury, Hudby Umeni
Prague, Czechoslovakia

Steingräber Verlag
Postfach 471, Wiesbaden, Germany

Stella Verlag 37

Süddeutscher Musikverlag (Willy Müller) 25
Heidelberg, Germany

Suvini Zerboni, Edizioni 4
Galaria del Corso 4, Milan, Italy

Swan & Co.
10 Sherlock Mews, Baker Street, London, W. 1, England

Part I

Individual Composers, Their Solo Piano Works in Various Editions

and Facsimile Reproductions

A

JEAN ABSIL (1893-   ) Belgium

Presently teaching at the Brussels Conservatory, Absil was one of the founders of the "Revue Internationale de Musique." Many of his earlier works were written in a conventional idiom but in recent years he has turned to a more personal, austere style. Unconventional rhythmic procedure is the norm in his writing.

3 Impromptus Op. 10 (Schott, Bruxelles 1932).

Sonatine Op. 36 (Schott, Bruxelles 1939).

2nd Sonatine: Suite Pastorale Op. 37 (Cnudde). Pastourelle, Musette, Berceuse, Gavotte, Toccata.

5 Bagatelles Op. 61 (Schott, Bruxelles 1944).

Grand Suite Op. 62 (Schott, Bruxelles 1944). Prélude, Scherzetto, Nocturne, Toccata. 22 p.

Homage à Schumann Op. 67 (Schott, Bruxelles 1946).

Esquisses sur les sept Pêches Capitaux Op. 83 (CeBeDeM 1954).

Variations Op. 93 (CeBeDeM 1956). M-D.

Echecs: Suite Op. 96 (CeBeDeM 1957). 16 minute set. Much variety and contrast. No. 6 is an effective toccata. M-D.

1. Le roi.
2. La reine
3. Le fou
4. La tour
5. Les pions
6. Les cavaliers.

6 Bulgarian Dances Op. 102 (Lemoine). Dances in ternary or variation form, Bartók influence. Driving rhythms, unusual dissonances over stable tonalities, whimsical. See especially No. 6. Int.

Pastourelle (Lemoine 1958). 2 pages, accompanied melody, MC writing. Int.

GEORGE ADAMS (1917-   ) USA

Adams studied composition at the Eastman School of Music.

Sonata b (CFP 1959). A three-movement (FSF) work written by a versatile hand. Tonal, dramatic, full sonorities. Dedicated to Howard Hanson. M-D.

SAMUEL ADLER (1928-   ) USA, born Germany

Adler came to the USA in 1939. He received degrees from Boston and Harvard Universities and studied with Walter Piston, Randall Thompson and Paul Hindemith.

Incantation See Anthologies and Collections USA, *New Music for the Piano* (LG).

Sonata brève (OUP 1967). Dedicated to Stefan Bardas. Allegro grazioso; Adagio con delicatezza; Allegro di bravura. Large span, mature pianism required.

Triptych for Dancing (AMC 1958). Large span required (many 10ths) for this three-sectional polytonal conception. Changing meters, colorful.

DENES AGAY (1911-   ) USA

Agay came to USA 1939. He is an editor, arranger and lecturer presently living in New York City.

2 Country Sketches (GS 1966). The Shepherds Night Song. Frolic.

Dance Scherzo (GS 1969). Int.

Mosaics (MCA 1968). 21 p. (6 Piano Pieces on Hebrew Folk Themes). Beautifully laid out for the piano. First 5 pieces are short while the last piece is a set of 11 variations over an 8 bar melody that progresses to a brilliant but not demanding climax. M-D.

Prelude to a Fairy Tale (GS 1969). Int.

3 Recital Dances (TP). 9 p. Parade Polka. Waltz Serenade. Mardi Gras Bolero.

Serenata Burlesca (Bo&H 1968). 7 p. Cross rhythms, chromatic lines, brilliant closing. Int.

Sonatina Hungarica (MCA 1967). 19 p.
Scena; Serenata; Rondo. Int.
Changing meters, quartal harmony, cadenza passages, well put together, attractive.

Sonatina Toccata (Bo&H 1964). 4 p.

GUIDO AGOSTI (1901-) Italy

Cinque Bagatelle Op. 5 (SZ 1941). 10 p.
Scorrevole, Lento, Presto, Marcia Funebre per Bobolino, Allegro vivace. Grateful tonal writing, impressionistic, varied moods. M-D.

Prelude and Toccata Op. 7 (SZ 1942). A slow, expressive Prelude e, PP closing leads to a short, brilliant Toccata E, somewhat in Ravel's style. D.

JULIÁN AGUIRRE (1868-1924) Argentina

Aguirre taught at the Buenos Aires Conservatory for a number of years. Some of his piano works are based on Argentine idioms while others show Spanish and French influences.

Intima No. 2, Op. 11/2 (Ric).

2 Books of Argentine National Airs (Ric). Book I: Op. 17, 5 Tristes. Book II; Op. 36, 5 Cançiones. No. 5 has text and melody. Unusual rhythms and haunting melodies. M-D.

Zamba: danza Argentina Op. 40 (Ric).

Huella Op. 49 (Ric). Tricky but effective rhythms. M-D.

Aires Criollos (Ric 1948).

Gato (Ric). Very rhythmic Argentine dance. Int.

EMIL G. AHNELL (1925-) USA

Ahnell received his training at the New England Conservatory,

Northwestern University and the University of Illinois. He teaches at Kentucky Wesleyan College.

Passacaglia (CAP 1970). 15 p. M-D.
Varied pianistic treatment including full chords, running figuration, repeated octaves. Tonal, changing meters, freely chromatic.

Sonatina (CAP 1969). 14 p. M-D.
Somewhat Fast: triplet figure generates main interest, impressionistic; Slowly: contemporary "Alberti bass" treatment, quartal harmony, atmospheric; Fast: active rhythms, toccata-like figuration, dynamic contrasts.

Ten Pieces for Two Girls (CAP 1970). Easy to Int.
Short, varied moods, colorful titles (Scary House, Dancing Feet, etc.), MC.

HUGH AITKEN (1924-) USA

Aitken studied composition with Bernard Wagenaar, Robert Ward and Vincent Persichetti. He teaches at Patterson State College, Wayne, New Jersey where he is chairman of the music department.

Piano Fantasy (OUP 1969). 20 p. 15 minutes. Complex, large-scale work in two movements demanding virtuosity and mature musicianship. D.

Three Connected Pieces for Piano (OUP 1968). 4 p. Thirds; Melody; Fifths. Changing meters. Melody uses ostinato figures. Fifths displays attractive contrasting writing. M-D.

JÉHAN ALAIN (1911-1940) France

Alain's style is characterized by rhythmic and metric flexibility, and colorful, highly individualized writing. Rhythm and melody are emphasized. The music contains great variety, ranging in difficulty from the two-line *Choral* in *Mythologies Japonaises* to the *Etude on a Four-Note-Theme* and the driving rhythms of *Taras Boulba*. The easiest works are: *Suites faciles* I-II, *Nocturne, Romance Etude de Sonorité.*

Works for Piano (Leduc). Three volumes.

Vol. I: Chorale, Etude de sonorité, Un cercle d'argent souple, Heureusement la bonne fée, Mythologies japonaises, Romance, Nocturne, Suite facile I, Suite facile II.

Vol. II: Thème varié, Ecce ancille Domine, Etude, Togo, Lumière qui tombe d'un vasistas, Historie d'un homme, Prélude, Il pleura toute la journée.

Vol. III: Etude sur un thème de 4 notes, Petite rapsodie, Dans le rêve laissé par, Taras Boulba.

ISAAC ALBENIZ (1860-1909) Spain

Albeniz, a prolific composer for the piano, was one of Spain's finest pianists. His works are a composite of Lisztian pianistic techniques and the idioms and rhythms of Spanish popular music. He wrote about 250 pieces for his instrument, mostly in small form. Only a portion is listed below.

Album of 8 Pieces (BMC). Cadiz, Cuba, Tango, Seguidilla, Curranda, Leyenda, Mazurka, Zortzico.

Album of Isaac Albeniz Masterpieces (EBM).
Contains: Cadiz from *Suite Espagnole,* El Puerto from *Iberia Suite,* Evocation from *Iberia Suite,* Fête-Dieu à Seville from *Iberia* Suite, Seguidillas, Op. 232 No. 5, Sevilla, Tango, Triana from *Iberia Suite.*

Alhambra Suite No. 1 Op. 47 (ESC).

Barcarolle Catalane Op. 23 (UME).

Cantos de España Op. 232 (UME). Prelude, Orientale, Sous le palmier, Cordoba, Seguidillas.

España Op. 165 (6 Album Leaves) (UME) (Weitzmann-CFP) (IMC). Prelude, Tango, Malagueña, Serenata, Capricho catalan, Zortzico.

Iberia (UME) (K) (Sal) (EBM No. 1-9). Albeniz's masterpieces. 12 pieces, 4 books: Evocation, El Puerto, Fête-Dieu à

Seville, Rondeña, Almeria, Triana, El Albaicin, El Polo, Lavapies, Malaga, Jerez, Eritana.

Mallorca: barcarola Op. 202 (UME).

Navarra Op. Posthumous. (EBM) (Sal) (UME). The last 26 bars were completed by Déodat de Sévérac (1872-1921).

Pavana-Capricho Op. 12 (UME).

Pavana Muy Facil: para manos pequeñas, Op. 83 (UME).

12 Piezas Caracteristicas Op. 92 (UME). Gavotte; Minuetto à Sylvia; Barcarolle; Prière; Conchita: Polka; Pilar: Waltz; Zambra; Pavana; Polonesa; Majurka; Staccato: Caprice; Torre Bermeja: Serenade. Published separately.

Rapsodia Cubaña Op. 66 (UME).

Recuerdos de Viaje (Travel Impressions) (IMC) (UME). En el mar, Leyenda, Alborada, En la Alhambra, Puerta de Tierra, Rumores de la Caleta, En la Playa.

Rêves Op. 201 (Leduc). Berceuse.

Ricordatta Op. 96, Salon Mazurka (UME).

Les Saisons (Leduc).

Serenata Arabe (UME).

Serenata Española (UME).

3 Sonatas: No. 3, Op. 68 A♭, No. 4 Op. 72 A, No. 5 Op. 82 G♭. (UME) separately. For a thorough discussion of these three sonatas see Newman: SSB, 652-4.

2 Spanish Dancers Op. 164 (Schott). Jota aragonesa, Tango.

6 Spanish Dances (K) (UME). Some of the easier works.

7 Studies Op. 65 (UME).

Suite Ancienne No. 2 (UME). Sarabande, Chaconne.

Suite Ancienne No. 3 (UME). Only Minuet published.

Suite Española No. 1 Op. 47 (Salvat-UME) (K) (IMC) (Ric)

(Schott). Granada, Cataluña, Sevilla, Cadiz, Asturias, Aragon, Castilla, Cuba.

Suite Española No. 2 (UME). Zaragoza, Sevilla.

Zambra Granadina. Oriental Dance (UME).

See: Sydney Grew, "The Music for Pianoforte of Albeniz," Chesterian, 6, November 1924, 43-8.

EUGEN D'ALBERT (1864-1932) Germany, born Scotland

D'Albert, an outstanding pianist, left a few early works, eminently pianistic and well-grounded in a late 19th-century idiom. He is better known for his operas and editions of keyboard works by Bach and Beethoven.

Suite d Op. 1 (Bo&Bo). A, C, S, Gavotte, Musette and G. (GS) has reprinted the A, Gavotte and Musette. M-D.

Acht Klavierstücke Op. 5 (c. 1886) (Bo&Bo).

Sonata f♯ Op. 10 (1892) (Bo&Bo). 31 p. Brahms influence in all three movements. Cyclic construction.

4 Klavierstücke Op. 16 (CFP Nos. 3 and 4). Waltz A♭, Scherzo f♯, Intermezzo B, Ballade b.

5 Bagatelles Op. 29 (Bo&Bo). Ballade, Humoresque, Nocturne, Intermezzo, Scherzo.

Transcriptions:
Bach: *Prelude and Fuge* D (Bo&Bo); *Passacaglia c* (Bo&Bo).

DOMENICO ALBERTI (ca. 1710-ca. 1740) Italy

Although Alberti probably did not invent the "Alberti Bass" he used it with such prominence that his name has become invariably linked with this technique. The sonata listed below is from a set of eight published by Walsh in London. He wrote about 36 works in this genre.

Sonata G Op. 1 No. 8. (W. S. Newman-UNC) *Thirteen Keyboard Sonatas of the 18th and 19th Centuries.* Thin textures, Alberti bass, elaborate ornamentation.

Toccata G (Boghen-Ric) *Toccatas by Old Italian Masters.*

WILLIAM ALBRIGHT (1944-) USA

Albright studied at the Eastman School of Music and the University of Michigan. He also studied in Paris with Oliver Messiaen for one year as the recipient of a Fulbright Scholarship. He is presently a member of the composition department in the School of Music at the University of Michigan.

Pianoagogo (Jobert 1965). 8 p. 8 minutes.
Suggestions for performance, spatial notation, dynamic range PPPPP-FFF. Jazz element gradually becomes more important throughout. Pianistic for both hand and instrument. D.

RAFFAELE D'ALESSANDRO (1911-1959) Switzerland

In addition to study in Zürich, d'Alessandro studied with Nadia Boulanger and Marcel Dupré in Paris. He gave organ recitals in Switzerland and lived in Lausanne a number of years.

Introduction et Toccata. Op. 2a (Foetisch 1952). D.

24 Préludes Op. 30 (Foetisch 1940). M-D to D.

Fantaisie Op. 59 (Bo&Bo 1950). 17 p. 12-13 minutes.
Improvisation: introduction, recitative-like.
Marcato: driving rhythmic punctuation.
Lirico (Lent)
Con brio Toccata: brilliant figuration with exciting close. M-D.

12 Etudes Op. 66 (Foetisch 1949). D.

Sonate (Henn). M-D.

HAIM ALEXANDER (1915-) Israel

Alexander, a graduate of the Israeli Conservatory of Music, has won several important competitions.

6 Israeli Dances (Israeli Music Publications). Suite of short pieces of moderate difficulty inspired by Israeli folk material. Could be played as a group or individually. Climactic ending.

Soundfigures (IMI 1968). 12 cyclic pieces in variation form. A 12-tone row and a cantus firmus form the basis of the work.

Profuse use of the melodic interval of a minor second. This work won the Israel Music Institute's competition for a piano composition. D.

JOSEF ALEXANDER (1910-   ) USA

Alexander studied at both Harvard University and the New England Conservatory.

12 Bagatelles for Piano (Gen 1967).
These thin textured "trifles" demand a well-developed technique. Wide variety of moods employing a liberal sprinkling of dissonances. All pieces are tonal. Seconds are exploited in No. 1. Most are no longer than 2 pages each. M-D.

ANATOLY ALEXANDROW (1888-   ) USSR

Scriabin influenced Alexandrow's early works but native folk song took on more importance in later compositions.

Sonata No. 5 g Op. 22 (UE 1922). 2 movements: Scriabin influence in first movement. Second movement is a set of 10 variations and a fugue. M-D.

Sonata No. 6 Op. 26 (USSR 1925). A lyric, serene opening leads to an Adagio and closes with a rhythmic Foxtrot. M-D.

Eight Pieces on USSR Folksongs Op. 46 (USSR 1938). Simple settings of Armenian, Kirghiz, Russian and Tchouvach folktunes. Int.

Sonata No. 8 B♭ Op. 50 (USSR 1946). Employs tunes from Op. 46 in transparent writing. A buoyant Allegretto giocoso opening, a serious Andante cantabile and a concluding exuberant finale make this a well-balanced work. M-D.

Sonata No. 9 Op. 61 (USSR 1946). 3 movements: Allegro moderato; Andante; Allegro. M-D.

Six Pieces of Medium Difficulty (USSR). Short character pieces in varied moods.

HUGO ALFVEN (1872-1960) Sweden

Alfven served as musical director of the University of Uppsala from 1910 until 1939.

The first 4 works are published by (NMS).

Menuette Op. 2

Triumfmarsch Op. 10

Sorg Op. 14

Skargärdsbilder 3 pianostycken Op. 17.

Midsommervaka (WH).

Swedish Rhapsody (WH).

Synnöve Solbakken (WH).

CHARLES HENRI VALENTIN ALKAN (1813-1888) France

Much interest has been generated recently in this unknown contemporary of Chopin, Liszt, Anton Rubinstein, César Franck, etc. Busoni placed him among "the greatest of the post-Beethoven piano composers."

The Piano Music of Alkan (Raymond Lewenthal-GS c. 1964). D. In this collection Lewenthal gives a brief biography of Alkan, a Preface "On Recreating a Style," General Remarks on Alkan's Style as it Affects the Interpreter, Alkan's Treatment of the Piano, Athletic Form, and extensive suggestions on performing the music. The works included are: *Le Festin D'Esope* Op. 39/12 (the last Etude in a 275 p. set of studies published in 1857); *Symphonie* Op. 39 (comprising Nos. 4, 5, 6, 7 of the *Etudes* Op. 39); *Fa* Op. 38/2; *Barcarolle* Op. 65/6; *Le Tambour Bat Aux Champs* Op. 50/2; *Etude* Op. 35/8; *Quasi-Faust* Op. 33 (second movement of the "Grande Sonate"); *Esquisses* Op. 63 (11 pieces from this set of 48 short pieces through all the major and minor keys). The 11 *Esquisses* are: *La Vision* No. 1, *Le Staccatissimo* No. 2, *Le Legatissimo* No. 3, *Les Soupirs* No. 11, *Barcarolette* No. 12, *Scherzettino* No. 37. *Héraclite et Démocrite* No. 39, *Les Enharmoniques* No. 41,

Les Diablotins No. 45, *Le Premier Billet Doux* No. 46, *Scherzetto* No. 47. Virtuoso techniques required for this orchestral approach to the piano.

A few separate pieces are available: *Allegro Barbaro* (Leeds); *The Wind* (GS); *13 Selected Works for the Piano* (George Beck-Heugel), with notes in French, German and English. The Beck collection does not duplicate any composition in the Lewenthal album. *Bourée D'Auvergne; Etude* Op. 29 (Schott); *Grande Sonate* No. 1 (Les quatres âges) Op. 33 (Jobert); *Sonatine* a Op. 61 (Costallat), described by Bellamann as "classic" in its "purity of form" and "what a piano sonata by Berlioz might have sounded like".

See: Henry H. Bellamann, "The Piano Works of C. V. Alkan," MQ, 10, April 1924, 251-62.

Joseph Bloch, "Charles-Valentin Alkan," unpub. thesis, Harvard University. (Indianapolis: privately printed for the author, 1941).

DOUGLASS ALLANBROOK (1921-) USA

Allanbrook studied composition with Walter Piston and Nadia Boulanger.

40 Changes (Bo&H c. 1971). 22 minutes.

Large-scale set of variations, exploits the piano's possibilities. The composer states: "Its form could be thought of as a jeweled sphere with many facets which wheels before the ear and the mind — its intensity increases until the end where it reveals itself as a song." Mature pianism required. D.

P. HUMBERTO ALLENDE (1885-1959) Chile

An impressionistic nationalism pervades the work of Allende. Unusual metric structure also appeals to him.

6 Etudes (Sal). French influence, melodic in emphasis. M-D.

6 Miniatures Grecques (Sal). All on white keys except No. 5.

2 Preludes (Sal).

Tempo di Minuetto (Sal). Short, chromatic, lyric. Int.

12 Tonadas (Sal 1918-22). Based on popular Chilean tunes, these short pieces go through a circle of major and minor keys. Each piece begins in a minor key followed by a parallel major key in a faster tempo. Some of the finest piano music inspired by folk music of this region. Int. to M-D.

WILLIAM ALWYN (1905-) Great Britain

Alwyn was trained at the Royal Academy of Music in London where he later became professor of composition.

Fantasy-Waltzes (Lengnick). These 11 pieces of varying difficulty have an affinity with Ravel. No. 9 is a virile "valse triste" and No. 11 is a fine display work with a short cadenza.

3 Movements (JWC). Allegro appassionato; Evocation; The Devil's Reel. Pianistic writing of moderate difficulty.

12 Preludes (Lengnick 1959). Short, chromatic pieces requiring above-average technique. Varied moods. Nos. 1, 3, 4, 5, 6, and 12 make a satisfactory group if the complete set is not played.

Sonata alla Toccata (Lengnick 1951). 3 movements preceded by a 3-bar Maestoso introduction. Allegro ritmico e jubilante; Andante con moto e semplice; Molto vivace. Vigorous rhythmic drive in the outer movements is essential to a successful performance. Mature pianism required throughout.

RENÉ AMENGUAL (1911-1954) Chile

Amengual wrote evocative piano works that show sylistic influences of the modern French school.

Sonatina (ECIC 1945). Three highly dissonant movements. The second movement contains effective melodic writing. M-D.

DAVID AMRAM (1930-) USA

Amram, trained at Oberlin College and George Washington University, is equally at home with classical music and jazz. He has written music for over 30 dramatic productions and several movies.

Sonata (CFP 1965). 18 minutes. Requires first-class pianism.
Overture: rhythmic with quiet ending.
Lullaby: song-like, requires span of ninth.
Theme and Variations: variety of moods, brilliant climax, quiet close.

See: David Amram, *Vibrations; the Adventures and Musical Times of David Amram.* New York: Macmillan, 1968.

GILBERT AMY (1936-) France

Amy studied with Messiaen and Milhaud but Messiaen influenced him most. The two seemingly opposed principles of serial and aleatoric techniques exist side by side in his piano works. "Amy seeks continually to develop the musical possibilities these two techniques generate. His goal is to achieve what he calls 'champs sonores'." BBD, 36.

Cahiers d'Epigrammes pour Piano (Heugel 1966). Contains Formant A, Formant B, Formant B, second part. Dircctions given. Serial and aleatoric. D.

Epigramme pour piano (Heugel 1962). Issued in an envelope with one large score printed on both sides. Performance directions are listed on outside cover. Serial and aleatoric. D.

Sonate pour piano (Heugel 1961). Within its aleatoric limits this is extraordinarily fashioned music. D.

See: André Hodeir, *Since Debussy: A View of Contemporary Music.* New York: Grove, 1961.

H. Riley, "Aleatoric Procedures in Contemporary Piano Music," MT, 107, April 1966, 311-12.

K. Stone, "The Piano and the Avant-Garde," PQ, Summer 1965, No. 52, 14-28.

CARL-OLOF ANDERBERG (1914-1972) Sweden

Anderberg was active in Malmö, Sweden as composer, conductor and writer on music. He studied in Salzburg and London. During the middle of the 1950's Anderberg adopted serial technique. Gradually there came a reaction to strict serial technique, and a freer, more "geometric" formation of the musical structure developed. In later works, his style became more radical.

A New York Sonata (ms). Manuscript copies are available through Eriks Musikhandel.

Fantasia (ms). *Fyra piano stycken* (ms 1956). *Skimachia, fantasi* (ms). *Soldiers Music: Sonat* (ms). *Solo für Marco Polo* (ms). *Tre stycken* (ms 1959). *Tscherkessische Juxerei* (ms). *Trois bagatelles* (ms). *Varianter* (ms).

KARL ANDERSEN (1903-) Norway

Andersen is one of Norway's leading cellists. His style is thoroughly contemporary, logically thought out and developed.

Columbine and the Annoyed Harlequin (Lyche). Serial technique handled in a highly personal manner. D.

HENDRIK ANDRIESSEN (1892-) The Netherlands

The elder Andriessen's style incorporates influences of both Debussy and popular music. From 1937 to 1949 he was director of the conservatory at Utrecht, and occupied the same position at the Royal Conservatorium in The Hague from 1949 to 1957.

The Convex Looking Glass (Alsbach 1954). 2 minutes.

Pavane (B&VP 1937). 8 minutes.

Serenade (Bender 1950). 4 minutes.

Sonate (Van Rossum 1934). 10 minutes. Oriented towards Hindemith, polytonal. M-D.

JURRIAAN ANDRIESSEN (1925-) The Netherlands

Andriessen studied with his father Hendrik. Later, in Paris, he studied film music and met Olivier Messiaen, who influenced him. However he writes in a neoclassic style and is oriented toward Stravinsky.

Astrazione (Donemus 1957).

Complainte (Alsbach 1955). 2 minutes.

Deux études (Donemus 1948). 6 minutes.

Drie dansen (B&VP 1942). 3 minutes.

Pavane e Passamezzo for harpsichord (Donemus 1962).

Sonate No. 2 (Donemus 1955). 15 minutes.

LOUIS ANDRIESSEN (1939-) The Netherlands

Andriessen studied with his father Hendrik and later with Kees van Baaren. During 1962-63 he worked with Luciano Berio in Milano, Italy and again with Berio in Berlin in 1964 and 1965. Cage and Stockhausen have influenced Andriessen considerably.

Registers (Donemus 1963). 7 minutes.
Written in spatial or time-notation i.e., the duration is fixed by the space on the paper. Andriessen says this piece "is more an indication for action than a composition." *Avant-garde,* fascinating sonorities. D.

WILLEM ANDRIESSEN (1887-1964) The Netherlands

Willem, brother of Hendrik, was director of the conservatory at Amsterdam for many years, was very active as a pianist and was one of his country's most important composers.

Praeludium (B&VP 1942). 2 minutes.

Praeludium (Bender 1950). 2 minutes.

Sonata (Alsbach). 10 minutes.

Sonatine (Muziekuitgeverij).

JEAN-HENRI D'ANGLEBERT (1635-1691) France

"D'Anglebert's own music is surpassed in 17th-century quality only by that of Chambonnières and Louis Couperin. D'Anglebert is always a good, and occasionally a great composer, as in his *Tombeau de M. Chambonnières.*" Ralph Kirkpatrick, Notes, 24, September 1967, 141.

Pièces de Clavecin (Roesgen-Champion-Société Française de Musicologie c. 1934). Urtext edition containing all the keyboard works.

Pièces de Clavecin (BB c. 1965) Facsimile of the 1689 Paris edition. Contains a Preface and a detailed Table of Ornaments. Harpsichord Suites in G, g, d, and D; five fugues and a short contrapuntal Kyrie for the organ; Principles of Accompaniment; six pages of theoretical treatise, chords, intervals, etc. The harpsichord suites usually contain a prelude, A, C, S, and G. Other compositions, including works by Lully (transcriptions) follow. The final piece is d'Anglebert's tribute to his teacher, Chambonnières.

ISTVAN ANHALT (1919-   ) Canada, born Hungary

Anhalt studied in Hungary with Kodály and in France with L. Fourestier and Nadia Boulanger. He is presently chairman of the theory department and director of the electronic music studio at McGill University.

Fantasia for piano (CMC). Eloquent serial writing. D.

GEORGE ANTHEIL (1900-1959) USA

Antheil shocked audiences in the twenties with his "machine music." His style changed remarkably since the early experimental days and he finally seemed at home in the area of neoromantic and impressionist surroundings. A sense of humor often permeates his writing.

Piano Pastels (Weintraub). 15 varied short pieces, mildly dissonant. First-rate teaching pieces. Int.

Sonata No. 2 "The Airplane" (NME 1931).

3rd Piano Sonata (AMC 1947).
Allegro marcato (Heroic): chordal, dramatic, syncopated, bitonal writing, large gestures. Coda based on opening material. Adagio molto expressivo (Romantic): accompanied melody in tripartite form. Nocturne-like. Sensitive pedaling needed. Some bitonality. Presto (Diabolic): full chords at fast tempo. Changing meters, large skips. Sardonic, ironic, humorous. C major pounded out in last 18 bars. Effective virtuoso writing.

Sonata No. 4 (Weintraub 1951).

Suite (GS). 3 short pieces that provide an introduction to the contemporary idiom. M-D.

2 Toccatas (GS 1951). Published separately. No. 2 B♭, constant 8th-note motion, alternating chords and octaves. M-D.

See: Ezra Pound, *Antheil and the Treatise on Harmony*. New York: Da Capo, 1968, reprint of the 1927 edition.

HANS ERIC APOSTEL (1901-) Austria

Apostel's early works were highly chromatic and thick textured. After studying with Schönberg and Berg, more linear writing and thinner textures appeared in his compositions. For a while he was interested in combining traditional principles with serial technique but since the mid-fifties he has shown more interest in exploiting possibilities of 12-tone writing.

Sonatina Ritmica Op. 5 (Dob 1934). 3 movements. Changing meters plus thick textures. Slow movement is most effective. M-D.

Klavierstücke Op. 8 (Dob). Thick chromatic textures. M-D.

Kubiniana Op. 13 (UE). 10 short pieces after drawings of Alfred Kubin. Variety of moods, serial. Some use of harmonics. D.

Suite "Concise" Op. 24 (UE 1956). Descriptive serial writing. Switzerland is the inspiration for this work in 7 movements. About 11 minutes. M-D.

1. L'arrivée
2. La promenade

3. La maison
4. Les salutations
5. Problème dodecaphonique
6. Le vin et les poissons
7. Le départ

Vier Kleine Klavierstücke Op. 31A (Dob 1962) bound with *Fantasie* Op. 31B. The 4 pieces (Promenade, Walzer, Fantasie, and Marsch) are each one page long. Imitation, some chromaticism. Serial. 6½ minutes. M-D.
The *Fantasie* Op. 31B is more involved but employs the same techniques. 4 minutes. M-D.

VIOLET ARCHER (1913-) Canada

Archer studied with Douglas Clarke and Claude Champagne at the McGill Conservatorium in Montreal, with Béla Bartók in New York City and Paul Hindemith at Yale University. She teaches composition and orchestration at the University of Alberta, Canada.

Habitat Sketches (TP).

6 Preludes (CMC). Variety of moods and idioms, of average difficulty. All are tonal, tend toward lean textures.

Rondo (PIC 1964).

11 Short Pieces (PIC 1964). Pedagogic material much above average. Fertile ideas, varied moods and techniques. Int.

Sonata for Pianoforte (CMC). A large-scale three-movement work demanding mature pianism. D.

Sonatina No. 2 (Bo&H 1948). 14 p. 3 movements in neoclassic style. Final movement, Fughetta, is difficult but attractive. M-D.

JOSÉ ARDÉVOL (1911-) Cuba, born Spain

Seis Piezas (Southern 1949). Preludio, Danzon, Invencion, Habanera, Son, Rumba. Short, folk-like melodies, tricky rhythms. Int. to M-D.

Sonata No. 3 (ECIC 1944). Moderato: 3 basic contrasting textures alternate; Invenciones en Rondo: lengthy allegretto, 2- and 3-part linear treatment, deceptive rhythms; Differencias sobre la cantiga "Entre Ave et Eva" del Rey Sabio: theme and nine variations, theme da capo, homophonic and linear treatment of modal tune, quiet. D.

Sonatina (NME 1934). Two short dissonant movements: Larghetto: linear and lyric; Allegro: in 2 and 3 voices. M-D.

ANTON ARENSKY (1861-1906) Russia

Excellent material in salon style.

6 Morceaux Op. 6 No. 5 Basso ostinato D (Augener).

3 Esquisses Op. 24 No. 2 A♭ (Bosworth).

Sketches on Forgotten Rhythms Op. 28 No. 1 Logades (Siloti-UE), No. 2 Peacocks (CF).

24 Morceaux Caractéristiques Op. 36. No. 13 Etude F♯ only (Osterle-GS).

Près de la Mer: 6 Esquisses Op. 52. No. 4 Allegro moderato (CF).

12 Preludes Op. 63 (Jurgenson). No. 1 a, No. 3 g♯, No. 7 E (JWC).

RODOLFO ARIZAGA (1926-) Argentina

Arizaga studied with Luis Gianneo, Olivier Messiaen and Nadia Boulanger. He is Secretary of the National Symphony Orchestra in Buenos Aires.

Preludio y Arietta (EAM 1946).

Serranillas del Jaque Op. 17 (EAM 1956). 8 minutes.

Toccata Op. 5 (Southern 1947). 4 p. In Prokofieff Toccata style, chromatic, driving rhythm, large span required, tonal, exciting. Program closer. M-D.

PAUL ARMA (1905-) France, born Hungary

Arma studied with Béla Bartók. He has given piano recitals in Europe and the USA. In 1945 he organized the Folklore de la Résistance at the Radiodiffusion Française in Paris.

Sonata da Ballo (EMT 1940). 11 minutes. A three-movement work based on popular French themes from Bourgogne, Savoie, Auvergne and Bretagne. First movement is longest, rhythmic drive, attractive melodic construction. Second movement contains orchestral-like coloring. Third movement builds to a tremendous climax. An appealing, unusual work. M-D.

Le Tour du Monde en 20 Minutes (Galaxy). Varied styles incorporated, clever. Int.

Transparence (EMT 1969). 8 p. 11½ minutes.

Trois epitaphes (EMT 1969). 9 p. 15 minutes.

Two Sonatinas

THOMAS ARNE (1710-1778) Great Britain

Arne was no mere imitator of the Handelian style but, nevertheless, italianate ornamental melody is characteristic of his *Sonatas* or *Lessons*. These suite-like compositions, dating from about 1756, were the first works entitled Sonatas to be published in England. They contain lively dance movements, vigorous toccatas and simple airs.

8 Sonatas or Lessons for the Harpsichord (E. Pauer-Augener) (K). (S&B) have a facsimile reproduction of the first edition (1756) with an introductory note by Gwilym Beechey and Thurston Dart.
No. 1 F; 2 e; 3 G; 4 d, has a fine fugue; 5 B♭; 6 g; 7 a; 8 G. No. 8 is a set of variations on a minuet of Rameau.

Suite per Clavicembalo (Gubitosi-Ric). One of the above-listed sonatas.

See: A. E. F. Dickinson, "Arne and the Keyboard Sonata," MMR, 85, May 1955, 88-95.
A. M. Henderson, "Old English Keyboard Music (Byrd to Arne)," PRMA, 64, 1937-38.

RICHARD ARNELL (1917-   ) Great Britain

Arnell writes in an eclectic style and has composed in almost all forms. He has described his approach to music: "I simply believe that it is mere prejudice and unclear thinking which rejects a work of art that has attached to it the stigma of 'programme music.' Music is a complicated amalgam of meanings, an expression of man himself, and cannot be abstracted from him without becoming 'un-music' or sheer noise. Theorists and academicians who try to tear them apart would doom us to sterility and death." BMI Brochure.

Siciliana and Furiante Op. 8 (Music Press c. 1947). 2 p. Siciliana in a smoothly-flowing style. 8 p. Furiante (Poco presto), imitative, thin textures, some ostinato-like writing, hand crossings, MC. M-D.

22 Variations on an Original Theme Op. 24 (Belwin-Mills 1948). Eight-bar theme, short variations, transparent writing. Int. to M-D.

Sonata No. 1 Op. 32 (Hin).

Recitative and Aria Op. 53 (Schott 1951).

Impromptu Op. 66 (PIC 1960). Four pages of essentially diatonic, modern writing. M-D.

Fox Variations Op. 75 (Belwin-Mills 1958). Eight variations, colorful and dexterous: Prelude, Chorale, Staccato, Nocturne, Courante, Note-spinning, Theme, and Farewell. M-D.

6 Pieces for Harpsichord (Hin). 15 minutes. Exposition, Vivace, Aria, Siciliana, Voluntary and Researches, Invention.

Suite of Five (Hin).

JUAN CRISOSTOMO ARRIAGA (1806-1826) Spain

Precocious Spanish violinist and composer who left some astonishing works: three string quartets, a symphony, an overture and many unpublished works.

Estudios o Caprichos (UME).

Tres Estudios de Caracter (Dotesio).

KURT ATTERBERG (1887-) Sweden

One of Sweden's most productive composers, Atterberg was an engineer until he was 42 years old. He writes in a colorful romantic style.

Menuett Op. 9/2 (WH). From "Per Svineherde."

Prinsens frieri Op. 9/4 (WH 1915). 5 p. A pantomime ballet, romantic harmonies. Good octave technique required.

Höstballader (Ballades d'Automne) Op. 15 (NMS 1919). 11 p. No. 1, b requires big octave technique. No. 2, c lyric. Both are written in a post-Brahmsian idiom.

Kungahyllning (ms). Available from Eriks Musikhandel.

TONY AUBIN (1907-) France

Aubin writes in a neoclassic style and "aims at liveliness rather than originality." GD, 1, 256. Since 1946 he has taught composition at the Paris Conservatory.

Prélude, Récitatif et Final (Heugel 1931). In Franckian tradition. Utilizes full resources of the keyboard. D.

Le Sommeil d'Iskender (Revue Musicale 1936).

Sonata b (Heugel 1930). A large three-movement (FSF) work in romantic character. Effective pianistic writing. D.

GEORGES AURIC (1899-) France

Auric is the youngest member of the group known as "Les Six." He was influenced early in his career by Satie and wrote in a style that would produce "auditory pleasure without demanding a disproportionate effort from the listener."

Adieu, New York (Edition de la Sirène 1919). Exciting foxtrot with a ragtime bass.

3 Impromptus (ESC 1940). Each exploits clear ideas.

3 Pastorales (Sal 1920). No. 2 is serene, No. 3 spirited. All are short.

Petite Suite (Heugel 1927). Five movements of 2- and 3-part writing in varied moods: Prélude, Danse, Vilanelle et Entrée, Sarabande and Voltes. Int. to M-D.

Rondeau from Ballet "L'Eventail de Jeanne" (Heugel 1927). Very rhythmic with a waltz for the mid-section.

La Seine, au Matin (Sal 1937). From the album *A l'Exposition.* Short and jazzy.

9 Short Pieces (ESC 1941).

Sonata F (Sal 1931). A large virtuoso work in improvisatory style. Mature pianism required. D.

Sonatine G (Sal 1922). A three-movement work with clear, thin textures. Allegro has much rhythmic vitality; a flowing Andante; and a brisk Presto. M-D.

CHARLES AVISON (1710-1770) Great Britain

Harpsichord Sonata B♭ (A. Carse-Augener). Op. 5 No. 3 (from the composer's six sonatas for the harpsichord, with accompaniments for two violins and violoncello, arranged for solo keyboard by Adam Carse).

JACOB AVSHALOMOV (1919-) USA, born China

"Here, then is the music of Avshalomov: lyric, harmonically rather uncomplicated, subtly and authentically aware of worlds which are not the usual ones". . . William Bergsma, Bulletin of the American Composers Alliance, Fall 1956.

One-Two-Three for David (ACA-CFE 1957). 5 minutes.

Theme and Variations Miniature (ACA-CFE 1942).

Vision (ACA-CFE 1942).

EMIL AXMAN (1887-1949) Czechoslovakia

Axman was a prolific composer and wrote in all forms except opera. He was highly respected by his contemporaries. His romantic style is based on folksong.

Sonata Appassionata (Hudební Matice 1922). 36 p.
Warm, romantic, virtuoso writing. This is the first of three piano sonatas, all written in the early twenties. D.

Sonatina (Hudební Matice c. 1947).

B

KEES VAN BAAREN (1906-1970) The Netherlands

Van Baaren was a pupil of Pijper and, since 1957, director of the Royal Conservatory in The Hague. He occupied a major role in Dutch musical life.

Sonatina in memoriam Willem Pijper (B&VP 1948).

MILTON BABBITT (1916-) USA

Babbitt is on the music faculty at Princeton University and head of the Columbia University Electronic Institute. He is also a professional mathematician whose analytical mind probes all aspects of complete serialization. He is also one of the most important leaders in the field of electronic music.

3 Compositions for Piano (Bomart 1947). 7 minutes. "Probably the earliest serialization of non-pitch elements occurs in these pieces. They are based on a computational system that is analogous to 12-tone pitch ordering." BBD, 39.

Duet (EBM 1956). See album *American Composers of Today.*

Partitions (LG 1963). See album *New Music for the Piano.* Serial, pointillistic writing, subtle use of sostenuto pedal, complex rhythmic treatment. D.

Post Partitions (CFP 1966).

Semi-Simple Variations (TP 1956). Five variations in 12-tone technique. Explanatory notes.
See: Elaine Barkin, "A Simple Approach to Milton Babbitt's Semi-Simple Variations," MR, 28/4, November 1967, 316-22.

STANLEY BABIN (1932-) Israel, born Latvia

Babin received his musical training in Israel and at the Curtis Institute of Music.

Dance Around the World (MCA 1969). Twenty countries represented by characteristic dances. Mood of each nation cleverly captured. Int.

Four Piano Studies (Waldwick 1969). All written in treble clef. Excellent pieces for hands close together. Int. to M-D.
Legato-Staccato: bitonal
Canon on a Hassidic Tune
Legato-Staccato (2)
Ten Finger Exercises (d'après M. Debussy): Bitonal, scalar.

Three Piano Pieces (MCA 1968). A mildly-modern triptych. M-D.
Musette: ostinato in 7/8 meter.
Fugue: modal subject, Hindemithian treatment.
Presto: dramatic closing, Prokofieff-inspired.

Two Sonatinas (MCA). No. 1 (c. 1965). 3 movements: Comodo; Lento; Allegro molto; requires span of ninth. Int. No. 2 published separately.

VICTOR BABIN (1908-1972) USA, born Russia

Babin studied with Artur Schnabel and performed as a duo team with his wife Vitya Vronsky. He was Director of the Cleveland Institute of Music.

Deux Mouvements Dansants (Augener). Triste, Gai. D.

Fantasia, Aria and Capriccio (Augener 1932).

Variations on a Theme of Beethoven (Augener 1960). Five variations, closing with a fugue and coda. Contains some brilliant idiomatic writing. D.

VYTAUTAS BACEVIČIUS (1905-   ) Poland, born Lithuania

Poems are short single movements in rhapsodic style. M-D.

Poem contemplation Op. 5 (Mer).

Poem mystique Op. 6 (Mer).

Poem astral Op. 7 (Mer).

Poem No. 4 Op. 10 (Mer).

Premier mot Op. 11 (UE 1938).

Deux grotesques Op. 20 (UE 1938).

4 Lithuanian Dances Op. 35 (Paragon 1945).

Sonata No. 2 Op. 37 (Mer 1960). 3 movements, with introduction to first movement. Traditional harmonic and tonal treatment, chromatic embellishment. Thick textures, thematic material well-defined. D.

Sonata No. 3 Op. 52 (Mer 1960). 3 movements (FSF), chromatic, dramatic, tonal writing. 23 p. D.

Poem cosmique Op. 65 (Mer).

Sixième mot Op. 72 (UE). In 4 parts, no bar lines. More tightly unified than the early works. D.

Trois pensées musicales Op. 75 (Mer). Serious atonal works requiring sensitive pedaling. D.

6 Preludes (Paragon).

GRAZYNA BACEWICZ (1913-1969) Poland

Bacewicz, a fine violinist, was Poland's outstanding woman composer in her generation.

Sonata No. 2 (PWM 1955). 21 p. 14 minutes.
Maestoso; Largo; Toccata. Many chromatics, much rhythmic interest. A sonorous Largo, virtuoso writing in the Toccata. This work is a good example of mid-20th-century Polish piano writing by a moderately conservative composer. D.

Suita Dziecieca (Suite Enfantine) (PWM 1966). Preludium, Marsz, Walc, Kolysanka, Burleska, Menuet, Gawat, Scherzino. A clever 14 p. suite sparkling with charm, MC. No key signatures, chromatic. Composed in 1934. Int. to M-D.

Zehn Etuden (PWM 1958).

CARL PHILIPP EMANUEL BACH (1714-1788) Germany

The keyboard contribution of this most talented son of J.S. Bach contains over 400 works, including some 143 sonatas, approximately 50 concerti and many separate pieces. Alfred Wotquenne compiled a thematic catalogue of Bach's works. Although there is no complete edition of his works, a comprehensive listing is to be found in MGG, I, cols. 930-5. The most extensive collection of the sonatas is to be found in *Le Trésor des Pianistes* which contains 65 sonatas and 4 rondos.

Indispensible to studying this composer is his *Essay on the True Manner of Playing Keyboard Instruments*, available in a fine English translation by William J. Mitchell, W. W. Norton, 1949. Numbers preceded by W. refer to Wotquenne's *Thematisches Verzeichnis der Werke von C.P.E. Bach* (Br&H 1905).

SONATAS:

Clavier Sonaten und freien Fantasien, nebst einigen Rondos für Fortepiano für Kenner und Liebhaber (Krebs-Br&H) 6 volumes, Vol. I: W. 55, 1-6. Vol. II: W. 56, 1-6. Vol. III: W. 57, 1-6. Vol. IV: W. 58, 1-7. Vol. V: W 59, 1-6. Vol. VI: W. 61, 1-6. Urtext.

From the 6 volumes *Für Kenner und Liebhaber* (Connoisseurs and Amateurs, 1779-1787), the most grandiose among Bach's creation in the sonata form (in spite of the title!) the sonatas C and A (W. 55, Nos. 1 and 3) deserve special mention. These large-scale works are eminently suitable for recitals. The fantasies contain some of Bach's most original writing. Of special interest are the Fantasia E♭ from volume 6, and the Fantasia C from volume 5. The other genre is the rondo, which is to be found in all but volume 1. The Rondos b and G are also in *Klavierwerke* (H. Schenker-UE) Volume II, while those in B♭ and c from volumes 4 and 5 are contained in Georgii, *Keyboard Music of the Baroque and Rococo* III.

4 Leichte Sonaten (O. Vrieslander-Nag). W. 65, Nos. 22, 33, 11, and 14 in G, a, g and D. These easy sonatas were not published during Bach's life. They show more buoyancy in style than many of the other sonatas.

The Prussian Sonatas 1742, W. 48 (R. Steglich-Nag) 2 volumes, (K). 6 sonatas dedicated to Frederick the Great.
From *The Prussian Sonatas:* Sonata F No. 1 contains an Andante f, parts of which are modelled after operatic recitative. Numerous dynamic indications. Sonata B♭ No. 2 has a slow movement, Adagio g, with a cadenza near the end. Sonata A No. 6 contains an Adagio movement with a cadenza and recitative-like passages.

Sonata G, W. 62 (H. Albrecht-K&S) Organum, Series 5 No. 2. A delightful FSF arrangement of movements. The last movement, a short Allegro, sparkles.

Sonatas and Pieces (K. Herrmann-CFP). 4 sonatas, Variations on *La Folia,* Rondo E♭, and short pieces.

6 Sonatas for Keyboard (Philip Friedheim-State University of New York, Editions in Music, Series 2, No. 1 available through Galaxy).

The Württemberg Sonatas 1744, W. 49 (R. Steglich-Nag) 2 volumes, (K). 6 sonatas dedicated to the Duke of Württemberg.

MISCELLANEOUS PIECES:

Keyboard Pieces with Varied Reprises (O. Jonas-UE). 22 easy pieces.

Klavierwerke (H. Schenker- UE) 2 volumes. 9 sonatas, 4 single movements and a rondo. A superb, interesting edition.

24 Kleine Stücke für Klavier (O. Vrieslander-Nag). Menuets, Fantasias, Polaccas, 4 Solfeggi, and Arioso con Variazione (W. 118 No. 4, 1747) and other pieces.

Kurze und Leichte Clavierstücke (O. Vrieslander-UE). Also edited by O. Jonas (UE c. 1962) in Vienna Urtext Edition. 22 small pieces, Int.

Miscellaneous Pieces: Abschied von meinem Silbermannschen Clavier (1781). Poignant rondo, liberally laced with rubato, unusual harmonic treatment and florid melodies. See *The Character Piece* (Anthology of Music Series), and *The Bach Family* (UE).

Musikalisches Mancherlei (Musical Diversities) (Kranz-NV). 6 pieces. See the collections *Sons of Bach* for other separate pieces.

18 Probestücke (E. Döflein-Schott). Example pieces for Bach's *Essay,* organized into 6 sonatas, each sonata in three movements.
From the *18 Probestücke* (1753): Allegro siciliano e scherzando, a short, graceful piece in f♯ and Allegro di molto f, fast, etude-like with contrasting lyric sections are choice selections.

The Second Bach (O. Jonas-SB). Unusual choice and variety of material.

12 Variationen auf die "Folie d'Espagne" (Herrmann-CFP). Unusual modulations and changes of key, brilliant and expressive keyboard treatment make for heightened interest throughout.

Many short character pieces exist (*La Bach, La Stahl, Les Langueurs tendres,* etc). and are to be found in various collections.

See: Philip Barford, *The Keyboard Music of C.P.E. Bach.* London: Barrie and Rockliff, 1965.
"C.P.E. Bach, A Master of the Clavichord," MO, 76, July 1953, 601-3.

Paz Corazon G. Canave, *A Re-Evaluation of the Role Played by C.P.E. Bach in the Development of the Clavier Sonata.* Washington: Catholic University Press, 1956.

Kathleen Dale, "C.P.E. Bach and the Keyboard," MMR, October, 76, 1946, 187-92.

Frank E. Lorince, "A Study of Musical Texture in Relation to Sonata-Form as Evidenced in Selected Keyboard Sonatas from

C.P.E. Bach through Beethoven," unpub. diss., University of Rochester, 1966.

Emily R. Daymond, "C.P.E. Bach," PRMA, 33, 1907.

William J. Mitchell, "C.P.E. Bach's 'Essay': an Introduction," MQ, 33, 1947, 460-480.

Dragan Plamenac, "New Light on the Last Years of C.P.E. Bach," MQ, 35, 1949, 565-587.

Eduard Reeser, *The Sons of Bach.* Stockholm: Continental Book Co., 1949.

Alfred Wotquenne, *Thematisches Verzeichnis der Werke von Carl Philipp Emanuel Bach.* Leipzig: Br&H, 1905. Reprint, 1964.

JAN BACH (1937-) USA

Bach received his graduate training at the University of Illinois and teaches at Northern Illinois University.

Three Bagatelles (CAP 1963). 21 p.

1. Emilia (for unprepared piano)
2. Lauretta
3. Pamfilo

All are thorny mazes to cut through. Contain unusual sonorities — expressionist in style. Helpful suggestions to the performer e.g.: "Use all or none depending on tightness in R.H." D.

JOHANN CHRISTIAN BACH (1735-1782) Germany

The youngest and most successful son of J. S. Bach is one of the most important representatives of italianate lyricism in the early development of the piano sonata. A student of Padre Martini during his stay in Italy, J. C. Bach soon became a major musical influence in London after his arrival in that world capital. Thin textures, Alberti basses, sequences, passage work and smooth "singing melodies" are all found in abundance in his works which are of moderate difficulty. In 1768, J. C. Bach was the first musician to perform in solo on the pianoforte, and with his friend Carl Friedrich Abel, gave concerts in London for seventeen years.

J. C. Bach greatly influenced Mozart whose admiration for this youngest son of Johann Sebastian is well known. He composed 24 solo keyboard sonatas but only about half of them are readily available in modern editions.

10 Sonatas (L. Landschoff-CFP) 2 Vols.
Excellent introductory remarks.

Sonata G Op. 5/3 (F. Goebels-Schott).

Le Trésor des Pianistes contains Op. 5 Nos. 3-6, and Op. 17 Nos. 2, 3, and 6 (as Op. 12).

Sonata B♭ Op. 17 No. 6 (W. Newman-Mer) in *Sons of Bach.*

Sonata c Op. 17 No. 2 (W. Georgii-Arno Volk Verlag) in Vol. III *Keyboard Music of the Baroque and Rococo.*

See: Beth Mekota, "The Solo and Ensemble Keyboard Works of J. C. Bach,"unpub. diss., University of Michigan, 1969.

Charles S. Terry, *John Christian Bach.* London: Oxford University Press, 1929.

JOHANN CHRISTOPH BACH (1732-1795) Germany

Known as the "Bückeburg Bach" (since he was active at the Bückeburg court), this ninth son of J. S. Bach wrote 15 solo sonatas and smaller works for the keyboard. His style combines German and Italian elements with a compositional technique characteristic of both baroque and classic styles.

Sechs leichte Sonaten (H. Ruf and H. Bemmann-Schott).
Originally published in 1785, all in three movements, simple and attractive.

Sonatas A, D, and A (Schunemann-K&S).

Sonata C (Cesi-Ric).

Variations on "Ah, vous dirai-je Maman" (Barbe-Hug).

Musikalische Nebenstunden (A. Kreutz-Schott). 15 varied short pieces; Marche, Menuet, Polonaise, etc.

Le Trésor des Pianistes Vol. 15 contains sonatas in F, C, G, F, and various pieces.

See: Karl Geiringer, *The Bach Family,* New York: Oxford University Press, 1954.

Eduard Reeser, *The Sons of Bach,* translated by W.A.G. Doyle-Davidson. Stockholm: The Continental Book Co., 1949.

Hannsdieter Wohlfarth, "Neues Verzeichnis der Werke von Johann Christoph Friedrich Bach," Die Musikforschung, 13, 1960, 404-17.

JOHANN SEBASTIAN BACH (1685-1750) Germany

The pianist must have a thorough knowledge of the keyboard works of this great master. The Hans Bischoff edition (published by Kalmus) still has many positive features. If tempo, dynamic and articulation marks are disregarded, this edition is remarkable considering the date of its publication (1891). The original Bach-Gesellschaft edition is now available in Lea Pocket Scores, and, in regular size, from J. W. Edwards (Ann Arbor, Michigan). See volumes 3, 13, 14, 36 and 45 for the keyboard works. When the *Neue Ausgabe Sämtliche Werke* (Br) is complete, the latest scholarly thinking will be available. Henle Verlag of Munich, Germany has produced some remarkable urtext editions for practical use. Peters publishes many fine editions of the individual works. It is best to request specific editors or individual volume numbers of Peters for many works are available by this publisher in more than one edition. S. numbers refer to Wolfgang Schmieder's *Thematisch-systematisches Verzeichnis der musikalischen Werke von Johann Sebastian Bach.* Leipzig: Br&H, 1950.

Helpful to the pianist is "The Execution of Bach's Keyboard Works on the Piano" by Erwin Bodky in his book *The Interpretation of Bach's Keyboard Works,* Cambridge, Mass.: Harvard University Press, 1960 pp. 90-99, and the preface to Rosalyn Tureck's *An Introduction to the Performance of Bach,* New York: Oxford University Press, 1962. Consult the bibliography (pp. 44-6, 769) for other specific references to the performance of Bach on the modern piano.

Fifteen Two-Part and Fifteen Three-Part Inventions S. 772-801. A fine scholarly and performing edition is published by Alfred Music Co. (edited by Willard A. Palmer).

Differences in the autograph copies of 1720 and 1725 are

noted. A table of tempo indications by Bischoff and Czerny as well as tempi of recordings by Glenn Gould, Martin Galling, Ralph Kirkpatrick, Wanda Landowska, George Malcolm and Rosalyn Tureck are listed.

(Landshoff-CFP) urtext, with a fine preface. CFP also publishes a facsimile of the 1723 autograph with a foreward by Ralph Kirkpatrick. See also the fine edition of (Steglich and Lampe-Henle). Yale University Press publishes a facsimile (reproduced from the holograph) of the *Notebook for Wilhelm Friedemann Bach* with a preface by Ralph Kirkpatrick. It contains the first version of the two and three-part inventions. (W. Newman-SB) (Bischoff-K) (E. Fischer-WH) (Röntgen-UE) (Kreutz-Schott) (J. Friskin-JF) (I. Friedman-WH). (E. Simon-Dover) has a facsimile of the autograph with a reprint of the Bach-Gesellschaft edition.

See: John Satterfield, "Dissonance and Emotional Content in the Bach Two-Part Inventions," MR, 17, November 1956, 273-81; 19, August 1958, 173-9.

Six French Suites S. 812-817.

The form Allemande, Courante, Sarabande, Optional Dances, and Gigue is followed throughout this set. (Bischoff-K) (Steglich and Lampe-Henle) based on the autographs and copies in the *Notebook for Anna Magdalena* of 1725, (Keller-CFP) (Petri-Br&H) (E. Fischer-WH) (Mugellini-Ric) (Röntgen-UE).

No. 1 d (S. 812) A, C, S, M I & II, G.
No. 2 c (S. 813) A, C, S, Air, M. G: technically the easiest of the set.
No. 3 b (S. 814) A, C, S, M & Trio, Anglaise, G.
No. 4 E♭ (S. 815) A, C, S, Gavotte, Air, G.
No. 5 G (S. 816) A, G, S, Gavotte, B, Loure, G.
No. 6 E (S. 817) A, C, S, Gavotte, P, B, M, G.

Six English Suites S. 806-811.

These suites begin with a Prelude, are generally on a larger scale, and are more imposing than the French Suites. (Bischoff-K), (Steglich and Lampe-Henle) in 2 volumes based on copies by Bach's pupils. (A. Kreutz-Mitteldeutscher Verlag) (CFP)

(E. Fischer-WH) (Röntgen-UE) (Mugellini-Ric) (Petri-Br&H).

No. 1 A (S. 806) Prelude, A, C I & II with 2 Doubles, S, B 1 & II, G.

No. 2 a (S. 807) Prelude, A, C, S, B I & II, G.

No. 3 g (S. 808) Prelude, A, C, S, Gavotte I & II, G.

No. 4 F (S. 809) Prelude, A, C, S, M I & II, G.

No. 5 e (S. 810) Prelude, A, C, S, Passepied I & II, G.

No. 6 d (S. 811) Prelude, A, C, S and Double, Gavotte I & II, G.

See: J. Fuller-Maitland, *The Keyboard Suites of J. S. Bach.* London: Oxford University Press, 1925.

James W. McConkie, "The Keyboard Suites of Bach; A Consideration of the Horizontal and Vertical Elements Found Therein," unpub. diss., Columbia University, 1950.

Klavierübung. This set was one of the few works of Bach published during his lifetime. It was divided into four parts. Bach's complete title was:

"Keyboard Practice consisting of Preludes, Allemandes, Courantes, Sarabandes, Gigues, Minuets, and other Galanteries, composed for Music Lovers, to Refresh their Spirits."

Part I *Six Partitas* (1731) S. 825-830.

(Bischoff-K) (Steglich and Lampe-Henle) in one or two volumes, based on the original edition of 1731, (Soldan-CFP) (Petri-Br&H) (Röntgen-UE) (E. Fischer-WH). Separately (CFP).

No. 1 B♭ (S. 825) Praeludium, A, C, S, M I & II, G.

No. 2 c (S. 826) Sinfonia, A, C, S, Rondeau, Capriccio.

No. 3 a (S. 827) Fantasia, A, C, S, Burlesca, Schergo, G.

No. 4 D (S. 828) Overture, A, C, Aría, S, M, G.

No. 5 G (S. 829) Praeambulum, A, C, S, Tempo di Minuetto, Passepied, G.

No. 6 e(S. 830)Toccata, A, C, Air, S, Tempo di Gavotta, G.

Published as Bach's Opus I, these grand suites have greater diversity than the French and English Suites. The dance movements become more free, as in the fifth suite where Bach uses "Tempo di Minuetto" and in the sixth, "Tempo di Gavotta." The standard form as used in the other two sets of suites is changed in the second partita; a Capriccio is substituted for the Gigue. The introductory movements vary in each partita: Praeludium, Sinfonia, Fantasia, Overture, Praeambulum, Toccata. Bach's first biographer, Forkel, expressed his appreciation for these suites in the following words: "This work made in its time a great noise in the musical world. Such excellent compositions for the clavier had never been seen and heard before. Anyone who had learnt to perform well some pieces out of them could make his fortune in the world thereby; and even in our times, a young artist might gain acknowledgment by doing so, they are so brilliant, well-sounding, expressive, and always new." Hans David and Arthur Mendel, *The Bach Reader*. New York: Norton, 1945, pp. 337-8.

See: Walter Emery, "Bach's Keyboard Partitas: a set of Composer's Corrections?," MT, 93, November 1952, 495-99.

Arthur A. Lambert, "The Keyboard Partitas of J. S. Bach, A Study of Background, Text, and Interpretation," unpub. diss., State University of Iowa, 1961.

Joseph Ponte, "Problems in the Performance of J. S. Bach's Clavierübung", Part I, unpub. thesis, Harvard University, 1952.

Part II (1735) S. 831 *Overture nach französischer Art* b, and S. 971 *Concerto nach italienischem Gusto* F.

(Steglich and Lampe-Henle) (Bischoff-K) (Hans T. David-Schott); (Soldan-CFP) has an early version in c, S. 831a, (Petri-Br&H). Petri's edition is nearly a transcription of S. 971. He tries to reproduce pitches the harpsichord produced via 16′ 8′ and 4′ stops. The "forte" and "piano" markings are original, indicating it was written for a two-manual harsichord. The movements are an Overture in the French manner with a majestic introduction, gigue-like mid-section and a return to the opening idea, C, Gavotte I and II, Passepied I and II, S, B I and II, G and an Echo that makes clever use of the two manuals. This Echo is very effective on the piano; it is published separately by CFP. Paired dances take on greater importance than in any of the other suites.

The *Concerto in the Italian Manner* F S. 971. (Bischoff-K), (Steglich and Lampe-Henle) based on first edition and manuscript copies of Bach's pupils, (E. Fischer-WH) (Kruetz-Schott) (Petri-Br&H) published with *The French Overture,* (Röntgen-UE) (Schungeler-Heinrichshofen) published with *Chromatic Fantasia and Fugue,* (Soldan-CFP) published with *The French Overture.* Designed for a two-manual harpsichord, this work was also provided with a few dynamic marks by Bach. Written in the style of an Italian Concerto (concerto grosso), the dynamic marks "forte" and "piano" represent the alternation of large (grosso) and small (concertino) groups. Three movements, Allegro; Andante; and Presto, bear out the normal design of the concerto grosso.

Part III (1739) *Four Duets* S. 802-805 in e, F, G and a.

(Steglich and Lampe-Henle) published separately and also with the rest of the *Klavierübung,* (Bischoff-K) (Soldan-CFP) (Petri-Br&H). These are not pieces for two players! Bach intended one part for the right hand and one part for the left hand. Other works in Part III are intended for the organ, and perhaps these Duets were also, but they sound well on the piano. Even though they are short and similar in character to the *Two-Part Inventions,* they are mature Bach and their construction is much more elaborate.

Part IV (1742) *The Goldberg Variations* S. 988.

(R. Kirkpatrick-GS) excellent scholarly edition that contains information on many performance problems. (Soldan-CFP) (Busoni & Petri-Br&H) (Bischoff-K), (Steglich and Lampe-Henle) published with the rest of the Klavierübung. This towering set of 30 variations, based on a majestic sarabande, was written for a harpsichord with two keyboards, but performances on the piano are frequent today. Wanda Landowska called this work, along with *The Art of Fugue* and *The Musical Offering,* "a dazzling secular temple erected in honor of absolute music." It is Bach's most highly organized set of variations. See bibliography (pp. 45-6) for numerous writings on this work.

The Well-Tempered Clavier S. 846-893.

(von Irmer and Lampe-Henle) (Kroll-CFP), (Tovey & Samuel-ABRSM) contains an excellent introduction and separate notes for each Prelude and Fugue. (Busoni-Br&H) contains interesting phrasing and is published in 8 volumes. (K) has the Fugues in open score. (GS) and (K) have Busoni edition of Volume I only. (Mugellini-Br&H) contains judicious fingering. (Bischoff-K) (Hughes-GS) (Kreutz & Keller-CFP) (Röntgen-UE) (Brooke-Nov) (Bartók-EMB).

(Bartók-EMB) is arranged in two vols. in progressive order as follows:

Example: 15/II indicates Prelude and Fugue No. 15, Book II of the "48"; 6 indicates Prelude and Fugue, No. 6 Book I of the "48."

Volume I	*Volume II*
15/II	15
6	12/II
21	1/II
10	24/II
20/II	10/II
11	16
2	5/II
9	18/II
13	24
21/II	9/II
6/II	4/II
19/II	23
11/II	3/II
19	12
14	3
18	8/II
2/II	22
5	17/II
7	4
14/II	8
7/II	20
1	22/II
17	16/II
13/II	23/II

"The Well-Tempered Clavier or Preludes and Fugues through all the tones and semitones, both as regards the 'tertia major' or 'Ut Re Mi,' and as concerns the 'tertia minor' or 'Re Mi Fa.' For the

Use and Profit of the Musical Youth Desirous of Learning, drawn up and written by Johann Sebastian Bach, Capellmeister to His Serene Highness the Prince of Anhalt-Cothen, etc. and Director of His Chamber Music. Anno 1722." Hans David and Arthur Mendel *The Bach Reader*. New York: Norton, 1945, 85. This title illustrates the instructional emphasis Bach placed on this work, yet the musical world has chosen to place both volumes among the loftiest of his creations. Thorough discussions of each work are found in the following books listed in the bibliography: MFTP (p. xviii); Bodky (p. 32); Landowska, Rothschild (p. 46); Gray (p. 780); Iliffe (p. 783).

Volume I (1722), Cöthen

Prelude and Fugue

No. 1 C	S. 846
No. 2 c	S. 847
No. 3 C♯	S. 848
No. 4 c♯	S. 849
No. 5 D	S. 850
No. 6 d	S. 851
No. 7 E♭	S. 852
No. 8 e♭	S. 853
No. 9 E	S. 854
No. 10 e	S. 855
No. 11 F	S. 856
No. 12 f	S. 857
No. 13 F♯	S. 858
No. 14 f♯	S. 859
No. 15 G	S. 860
No. 16 g	S. 861
No. 17 A♭	S. 862
No. 18 g♯	S. 863
No. 19 A	S. 864
No. 20 a	S. 865
No. 21 B♭	S. 866
No. 22 b♭	S. 867
No. 23 B	S. 868
No. 24 b	S. 869

Volume II (1744), Leipzig.

Prelude and Fugue

No. 1 C	S. 870
No. 2 c	S. 871
No. 3 C♯	S. 872
No. 4 c♯	S. 873
No. 5 D	S. 874
No. 6 d	S. 875
No. 7 E♭	S. 876
No. 8 d♯	S. 877
No. 9 E	S. 878
No. 10 e	S. 879
No. 11 F	S. 880
No. 12 f	S. 881
No. 13 F♯	S. 882
No. 14 f♯	S. 883
No. 15 G	S. 884
No. 16 g	S. 885
No. 17 A♭	S. 886
No. 18 g♯	S. 887
No. 19 A	S, 888
No. 20 a	S. 889
No. 21 B♭	S. 890
No. 22 b♭	S. 891
No. 23 B	S. 892
No. 24 b	S. 893

Seven Toccatas S. 910-916.
f♯ S. 910, c S. 911, D S. 912, d S. 913, e S. 914, g S. 915, G S. 916. Urtext (Keller-CFP); (Bischoff-K) (Busoni, Petri-Br&H) (Steglich and Lampe-Henle) (Hughes-GS). D, S. 912 (Kreutz-Schott) and (Bauer-GS); d, S. 913 (Donath-Mitteldeutscher Verlag). The toccatas are multi-sectional works of a free and rhapsodic character employing diverse moods, rhythms and textures. All contain at least one slow movement and one fugue. The fugues are more improvisatory than those in the *Well-Tempered Clavier.* The f♯ and c Toccatas are later than the others. All seven toccatas make fine opening numbers for programs.

See: J. Fuller-Maitland, "The Toccatas of Bach," SIMG, 14, 1912-13, 578-82. Published separately, London, 1913.
Sidney Grew, "The Clavier Toccatas of J. S. Bach," MT, 60, 1919, 17-20.

The Little Notebook for Anna Magdalena Bach. Neue Ausgabe Sämtlicher Werke (Dadelsen-Br). Contains both the 1722 and 1725 editions. (A. Schering-K) based on the 1725 edition; (Keller-CFP) (O. Mortensen-WH). Selections are offered by (Sauer-CFP) *Twenty Easy Pieces;* (Sauer-Augener) *Twenty Easy Pieces;* (Philipp-IMC) *Twelve Selected Pieces; Twenty Easy Pieces* (Ludwig-Schott); (Anson-Willis) *Eighteen Pieces* . The two editions of 1722 and 1725 published in the *Neue Ausgabe Sämtlicher Werke* contain: 1722: Suite d S. 812 A, C, S, M I & II, G. Suite c S. 813 A, C, S, Air, G. Suite b S. 814 A, C, S, Gavotte, G. Suite E♭ S. 815 A, C, S, Gavotte, Air, G. Suite G S. 816 A, C, S, Gavotte, B, Loure, G. Fantasia for Organ S. 573. Air c S. 991. Chorale "Jesu, meine Zuversicht" S. 728. Menuet c from Suite S. 813. Menuet and Trio b from Suite S. 814. Menuet G S. 814.

1725: Partita a S. 827 Prelude, A, C, S, M, G. Partita e S. 830 Prelude, A, C, S, Tempo di Gavotta, G. Suite I pour le Clavessin d S. 812 A, C, S, M I & II, G. Suite II pour le Clavessin c S. 813 A, C, S. Smaller works by Bach and other composers such as Couperin, C. P. E. Bach, Stoelzel (?) and Boehm. Some of the small dance movements (so popular with many piano teachers) are not by Bach.

The Little Notebook for Wilhelm Friedemann Bach (1720). *Neue Ausgabe Sämtlicher Werke* (Wolfgang Plath-Br). A scholarly edition that includes Bach's only table of ornaments and 62 pieces. (K) also has the complete work. 16 selections are offered by (H. Trede-Schott). A facsimile reproduced from the holograph of the complete work with editorial commentary by Ralph Kirkpatrick is published by Yale University Press (1959). This notebook contains first versions of 11 preludes from *The Well Tempered Clavier, 15 Two-Part Inventions* (Praeambulums), *14 Three-Part Inventions* (Fantasias), and miscellaneous pieces by Bach, W. F. Bach, Richter, Telemann and J. G. Stoelzel. These miscellaneous pieces are: Applicatio C S. 994, Prelude C S. 924a, "Wir nur den lieben Gott" S. 691, Prelude d S. 926, "Jesu meine Freude" S. 753, 2 Allemandes g S. 836 and 837, Prelude F S. 927, Prelude g S. 928, Minuet G S. 841, Minuet g S. 842, Minuet G S. 843. Different S. numbers appear on earlier versions of two preludes from *The Well Tempered Clavier*: Prelude No. I C S. 846a, and Prelude No. 5 e S. 855a. Other pieces: Prelude C S. 924, Prelude D S. 925, Prelude e S. 932, Prelude a S. 931, Fugue C S. 953. Suite by Telemann S. 824, Partita by Stoelzel with minuet trio by Bach S. 824.

See: Trevor Fischer, "The Little Clavier Book for W. F. Bach," MT, 101, February 1960, 87-8.

SEPARATE PIECES:

Chromatic Fantasia and Fugue d S. 903 (1720-3).
(Keller-CFP) (Busoni-Br&H) (Bischoff-K) (Kreutz-Schott) (E. Fischer-WH) (Röntgen-UE) (Huber-UE), (Schungeler-Heinrichshofen) published with the *Italian Concerto.* This work, characterized by an expansive harmonic language, is highly sectionalized, and free in construction. The three-voice fugue is a magnificent example of dramatic cumulative effect. A splendid edition of S. 903 is the Vienna Urtext (H. Schenker, revised O. Jonas-UE).

Fantasia and Fugue a S. 904 (CFP-No. 208) (Br&H).
Fantasia is written in organ style while the double Fugue is one of Bach's most majestic compositions.

Fugue a S. 944 (CFP-No. 9009) (Br&H) (Durand). Opening arpeggiated introduction leads to one of Bach's longest fugues (198 bars) in "perpetual motion" style.

Fantasia c S. 906 (CFP-No. 9009) (Br&H) (Henle) (Schott) (JF) (K). Brilliant, short, Scarlatti-like.

Prelude and Fugue a S. 894 (CFP-No. 9009) (Br&H). This large work, later transformed into the opening and closing movement of the *Triple Concerto* in a S. 1044, requires the utmost finger dexterity. The Prelude is in the style of a huge fantasy while the fugue is gigue-like in character. Difficult and impressive.

Adagio G S. 968 (CFP-No. 9091). A beautiful transcription by Bach of the first movement of the *Sonata* C for unaccompanied violin S. 1005. Very effective on the keyboard.

Two Fugues on themes by Albinoni. A S. 950, b S. 951 (Bischoff-K) (Kreutz-Schott) (Friskin-JF).

Capriccio, On the Departure of a Beloved Brother S. 992. (Bischoff-K) (Kreutz-Henle) (Busoni-Br&H) (Friskin-JF) (CFP). An early (1704?) work. Bach's only example of programmatic keyboard music. In 6 sections with programmatic titles.

Three Fugues on Themes by Reinken S. 965 a, 966 C, 954 Bb. Keller-Br). S. 965 a and S. 966 C are from Reinken's *Hortus Musicus.*

Sonata D S. 963 (CFP) (Br&H). Two untitled movements (125 bars and 41 bars respectively), an Adagio introduction to a fugue "all' Imitatio Gallina Cucca", imitation of a hen and cuckoo.

Sonata d S. 964 (CFP) (Br&H). A transcription of a solo violin sonata a S. 1003. Adagio, Fuga, Andante, Allegro.
See: Kenwyn G. Boldt, "The Solo Clavier Sonatas Attributed to J. S. Bach," unpub. DM paper, Indiana University, 1967.

Suite a S. 818. (CFP-No. 214 and No. 9007). A, C, S Simple, S Double, G. S. 818a (Busoni, Mugellini-Br&H) includes a

Prelude, a different version of the C, a different S, M and the same A and G as S.818. In the style of the *French Suites.*

Suite E♭ S 819. (CFP-No. 214, No. 9007), (Busoni, Petri-Br&H). Two separate A's, C, S, B and a M with a Trio in e♭.

Suite f S. 823. (CFP-No. 9007) (Busoni, Petri-Br&H), (Tureck-OUP) in Volume III of *An Introduction to the Performance of Bach.* P, S, G. Lute influence.

Suite A S. 824. (Busoni, Petri-Br&H), (Tureck-OUP) in Volume III *An Introduction to the Performance of Bach.* A, C, G. This suite is contained in the *Notebook for W. F. Bach.* Difficulty of *French Suites.*

Ouverture F (Suite) S. 820. (CFP-No. 9007) (Busoni, Petri-Br&H). An untitled opening movement in the style of a French Overture, Entrée, M (Trio), B, G.

Suite B♭ S. 821. (Busoni, Petri-Br&H). Praeludium, A, C, S, Echo.

Suite g S. 822. (CFP-No. 1959). Overture, Aria, Gavotte en Rondeau, M I & II (Trio), G. An early work.

Partita c S. 997. (CFP-No. 9007) (Busoni, Petri-Br&H) (H. Ferguson-Schott). Preludio, Fuga, S, G, Double.

Suite F S. Anhang 80. (J. Werner-Ascherberg). Dates from around 1701 and contains an A, C, S, G. Easier than any of the French or English Suites. The autograph is at Stanford University.

Aria with Variations in the Italian Manner S. 989. (Tureck-OUP) in Volume III *An Introduction to the Performance of Bach,* (CFP-No. 9043) (Br&H) (Bischoff-K) (Frotscher-Mitteldeutscher Verlag). An early work (1709): Aria with 10 variations.

COLLECTIONS for the Early Grades of Piano Study:

Bach I (Anson-Willis). 18 pieces from the *Anna Magdalena Bach Note Book.*

Selections from Anna Magdalena Note Book (Palmer-Alfred). 22 pieces in scholarly edition.

12 Little Preludes (Anson-Willis).

Dance Forms from the Suites (Anson-Willis). 13 dances from the Suites and Partitas.

Bach—26 Easy Pieces in Progressive Order (O. Beringer-Augener). Two volumes.

Bach Collection (Berlinger, Jonas-SB). 15 Pieces mainly from the suites, and one G by Telemann.

Various Short Preludes and Fugues (Bischoff-K).

The Young Bach (E. H. Davies-OUP). 20 pieces from the two notebooks and 5 preparatory canonic studies.

The First Bach Book (Lipsky-K).

An Introduction to the Performance of Bach (R. Tureck-OUP c. 1960). A graded series of three volumes on Bach performance. Contains both text and music.
Vol. I discusses fingering, phrasing, dynamics, touch, pedaling, ornamentation, instruments (harpsichord, clavichord, piano), and a section on playing Bach on the piano. Eight pieces from the notebooks plus Miss Tureck's realization of the Applicatio from the W. F. Bach notebook.
Vol. II. Further notes on ornamentation, fingering, phrasing, practical uses of the sustaining pedal and suggestions for the study of contrapuntal music, especially 2-, 3-, and 4-part counterpoint. Music includes: Invention C S. 722 with its inversion, Fantasia g S. 917 and Prelude and Fugue a S. 895.
Vol. III. Manuscripts, editions, repeats, the Baroque dot, Bach's table of ornaments, and further discussion of ornamentation. Music includes Suite f S. 823, Suite A S. 824, Aria and Ten Variations in the Italian Style S. 989. A first-rate series by one of our foremost Bach interpreters.

Bach verklärt (P. Cox-E. C. Schirmer).

Bach. Die kleinen Klavierstücke (Döflein-Br). 33 pieces, mainly little preludes.

Short Preludes and Fugues:

Unedited: *Little Preludes and Fugues* (Steglich-Henle). Based on the *Wilhelm Friedemann Bach Note Book.*
24 Little Preludes and Fugues (Keller-CFP).
Little Preludes (Edwin Fischer-WH).
12 Little Preludes (Kreutz-Schott). S. 924-930; 939-942; 999.
6 Little Preludes (Kreutz-Schott). S. 933-938.
6 Little Preludes (Bischoff-K).

Edited: *Little Preludes, Fughetta c, Four Duets (*Busoni-Br&H).
24 Little Preludes and Fugues (Czerny-CFP).
24 Little Preludes and Fugues (Röntgen-UE).

MORE DIFFICULT COLLECTIONS

Bach Collection (CFP-No. 1959).
Praeludium a S. 923a. Scherzo d S. 844. Andante g S. 969. Presto d S. 970.

Supplement to the Piano Works (CFP-No. 9043).
Capriccio B♭ on the Departure of His Beloved Brother S. 992. Aria Variata alla Maniera Italiana S. 989. Fantasia c S. 919. Fugue on a Theme of Reinken S. 954. Four Preparatory Studies to the Second part of *The Well Tempered Clavier* S. 972a, 901, 902, 902a. Three Minuets and Applicatio from the *Note Book for W. F. Bach* S. 841, 842, 843. Capriccio E S. 993. Fantasia a S. 922. Fugue a S. 947. 2 Fugues by Albinoni S. 950, 951. Fugue e S. 945.

See: Warren D. Allen, "Bach's Teaching Pieces," MTNA Proceedings, 1949, 252-54.

Sol Babitz, "On Using J. S. Bach's Keyboard Fingerings," ML, 43, April 1962, 123-28.

L. S. Barnard, "Philip Dore's Bach Clavier Lectures," MO, 76 May, June 1953, 491-93, 557-59.

Malcolm Boyd, *Bach's Instrumental Counterpoint.* London: Barrie and Rockliff, 1967.

Conrad Bruderer, "A Comparison of the Preludes Found in Common in the *Clavier-Büchlein vor Wilhelm Friedemann Bach, The Well-Tempered Clavier,* and the Forkel Edition of *The*

Well-Tempered Clavier," unpub. DM paper, Indiana University, 1968.

Diane Carliner, *The Bach Sinfonias: History and Performance.* Baltimore: Musicolor Publication, 1968. In color. Different color for each voice; historical and performance commentary.

Jan Chiapusso, "Editions of the Piano Works of Johann Sebastian Bach," MTNA Proceedings, 1944, 349-56. "Bach for Purists," MTNA Proceedings, 1940, 380-87.
Bach's World. Bloomington: Indiana University Press, 1968. See especially chapter 15, 160-76 "Compositions for the Keyboard."

James Ching, "On the Playing of Bach's Clavier Music," MT, 91, August 1950, 299-301.

Frances E. Cole, "Bach's 'Goldberg Variations': A Descriptive Study and Analysis," unpub. diss., Columbia University, 1966.

A. E. F. Dickinson, *The Art of J. S. Bach.* London: Hinrichsen, 1936. 2nd revised edition, 1950.

Robert Donington, *Tempo and Rhythm in Bach's Organ Music.* London: Hinrichsen, 1960.

Robert C. Ehle, "Comments on the Goldberg Variations," AMT, 19, November-December 1969, 20-2.

Walter Emery, "The London Autograph of 'The Forty-Eight'," ML, 34, April 1953, 106-23.
"An Introduction to the Textual History of Bach's Clavierübung, Part II," MT, 92, May 205-9, June 260-2, 1951.
Bach's Ornaments. London: Novello, 1953.

Edwin Fischer, *Reflections on Music.* London: Williams and Norgate, 1951. See chapter on Bach.

J. Fuller-Maitland, *The "48": Bach's Wohltemperiertes Clavier.* Two volumes. London: Oxford University Press, 1925.

Karl Geiringer, *The Bach Family.* London: Allen and Unwin, 1954. *Johann Sebastian Bach.* Oxford University Press, 1966.

Edwin Hughes, " 'Forty-Eight' from the Player's Standpoint," MQ, 11, July 1925, 444-53.

Frederick Iliffe, "The Constitution as to Form of Bach's Forty-Eight Preludes," PRMA XXIII, 1896-97.

Alfred Kreutz, "Ornamentation in J. S. Bach's Keyboard Works," London: *Hinrichsen's Musical Yearbook,* VII, 1952, 358-79.

Wanda Landowska, *Landowska on Music.* Edited by Denise Restout. New York: Stein & Day, 1964.

Fred Lape, "An Amateur's Life with the Goldbergs," Cornell University Music Review, 5, 1962, 14-17. Discussion of playing the *Goldberg Variations* on the piano.

Gustav M. Leonhardt, *The Art of Fugue, Bach's Last Harpsichord Work. An Argument.* The Hague: M. Nijhoff, 1952, 58 pp.

Ray McIntyre, "On the Interpretation of Bach's Gigues," MQ, 51, July 1965, 478-92.

Yella Pessl, "French Patterns in Bach's Secular Keyboard Music," MTNA Proceedings, 1941, 210-24.

Hugo Riemann, *Analysis of J. S. Bach's Well-Tempered Clavier.* London: Augener, 1900.

Albert Riemenschneider, "A List of Editions of Bach's Well-Tempered Clavier," Notes (Ser. I), 14, August 1942, 38-45.

Fritz Rothschild, *A Handbook of the Performance of the Forty-eight Preludes and Fugues of Bach According to the Rules of the Old Tradition.* Two volumes. London: Adam and Charles Black, 1955.

Hugo Schwarzschild, "New Light on the Forty-Eight," MT, 97, April 1956, 182-4.

Liselotte Selbiger, "Bach on the Piano," MR, 11, May 1950, 98-108.

Sidney J. Tretick, "An Analysis of Performance Practices for the Johann Sebastian Bach Chaconne Based upon the Anna Magdalena Manuscript," unpub. diss., University of Colorado, 1957.

Rosalyn Tureck, "Bach in the Twentieth Century," MT, 103, February 1962, 92-4.

WILHELM FRIEDEMANN BACH (1710-1784) Germany

The oldest son of J. S. Bach combines both contrapuntal and homophonic styles in his keyboard writing. His musical language is very expressive and represents the "Empfindsamkeit" style, so popular during this age of stylistic overlapping. His keyboard works consist of sonatas, fantasias, fugues, concerti, polonaises and short pieces. A thematic index by Martin Falck, *W. F. Bach.* Leipzig, Kahnt, 1913 serves as the accepted catalogue of this composer's works. The numbers preceded by F. refer to this index.

Nine Sonatas (F. Blume-Nag) in 3 volumes (1744-1754). Each sonata is in three movements FSF.

Vol. I: Sonatas G (F. 7), A (F. 8), B♭ (F. 9).
Vol. II: Sonatas D (F. 3), D (F. 4), E♭ (F. 5).
Vol. III: Sonatas C (F. 1), C (F. 2), F (F. 6).

The 2nd and 3rd movements of F. 1 and F. 2 were revised and appear in a Fantasia c of 1784. (K) also publishes all nine sonatas in three volumes. Sonata E♭ (F. 5) is to be found in the Newman collection *Sons of Bach* (see Collections). Sonata G (F. 7) is contained in the collection *The Bach Family* edited by Geiringer (see Collections: German: Bach Family).

Twelve Polonaises (CFP) (J. Epstein-UE) (F. Wührer-OBV) F. 12 (c. 1765). Varied moods, these Polonaises are arranged according to key and are excellent examples of idealized dances. In the keys of C, c, D, d, E♭, e♭, E, e, F, f, G, and g.

Eight Fugues (CFP) F. 31 (1778). No. 1 C, No. 2 c, No. 3 D, No. 4 d, No. 5 E♭, No. 6 e, No. 7 B♭ and No. 8 f. No. 2 is contained in *Alte Meister* (see collections) and No. 4 is contained in Volume II of *Harvard Anthology of Music* (Harvard University Press). *Six Little Fugues* (F. Koschinsky-NV).

Ten Fantasias (1778). Not all are available in performing editions. *A Fantasia* C is No. 31 in *Organum,* Series V (K&S). *Fantasia* e is contained in the *Alte Meister* (see Collections) and a *Fantasie* e is found in Georgii *400 Years of European Keyboard Music* (see Collections).

Solo Concerto G (K&S-No. 31 Series V *Organum*). In the same category as *The Italian Concerto* of J. S. Bach. Three movements, FSF.

Four Fantasias and a *Suite* are contained in Volume X of *Le Trésor des Pianistes.*

SVEN-ERIK BÄCK (1919-) Sweden

Bäck studied with both Hilding Rosenberg and Goffredo Petrassi. He has developed from his early works in a post-Nielsen style to a vital modern idiom. Bäck is fundamentally an intellectual with a strong feeling towards mysticism.

Sonata alla ricercare (WH 1950). The first movement is both exuberant and humorous.

Expansive Preludes (WH 1949). Three atonal pieces. D.

Impromptu (WH).

ERNST BACON (1898-) USA

Flight (Bo&H c. 1948). Rhumba rhythm, perpetual motion, virtuoso writing. D.

Sombrero (MCA). In *USA 1946,* album of piano music. Short, light, humorous, 5/8. M-D.

Byways (GS). 24 pieces based on folktunes from various countries. Easy to Int.

My World (SB). 14 pieces, good introduction to contemporary sounds. Easy.

Maple Sugaring (GS). Arrangements of New England folktunes. Easy.

The Pig-Town Fling. See Anthologies and Collections, USA, *New Music for the Piano* (LG).

HENK BADINGS (1907-) The Netherlands, born Java

Badings first studied engineering and was not professionally involved with music until he was 24 years old. He became director of the Royal Conservatory in The Hague in 1941. He is a prolific composer and has written in many musical genres. His sonatas, written in a style that has been referred to as romantic modernism, are modelled on Beethoven's motivic procedures in a harmonic system very much his own but oriented toward the Brahms-Reger-Hindemith tradition.

Sonata I (Schott 1934). 15½ minutes.

Sonata II (Schott 1941).

Sonata III (Donemus).

Sonata IV (WH)

Sonata V (Alsbach).

Sonatine I (Schott 1936).

Sonatine II (Donemus).

Sonatine III (Bender).

Tema con variazioni (UE 1938).

Suite (Donemus 1943).

Suite No. 4 on Netherland Folk Dances (Donemus 1953). Four dances, MC. Written for a 3-octave carillon. Int.

Arcadia VII (Schott 1945). 3 vols. 10 short pieces in each volume.

5 Little Piano Pieces (Donemus 1940).

8 Short Pieces (Schott 1940).

RAYMOND BAERVOETS (1930-) Belgium

Baervoets studied at the Conservatoire Royal de Musique de Bruxelles with François de Bourguignon, René Barbier and Jean Absil. He also studied with Goffredo Petrassi at the Santa Cecilia Academia in Rome.

Invensioni (CeBeDeM 1964). 26 p. 12 minutes.
6 pieces, pointillistic writing, wide range of dynamics. Photocopy of autograph. D.

Flemish Sonatina (Dessain).

LEONARDO BALADA (1933-) Spain, living in USA

Balada is head of the music department at the United Nations International School in New York City. He studied with Bernard Wagenaar and Vincent Persichetti.

Musica en Cuatro Tiempos (Gen. c. 1967). A suite. D.
- Lento: one page, quiet mood builds to climax.
- Energico: changing meters, vigorous, fist and forearm clusters.
- Scherzando: eighth notes in continuous motion, changing meters.
- Tiempos variados: expressive, cross rhythms, accents, ends fast, climactic closing.

MILI BALAKIREV (1837-1910) Russia

Balakirev was the guiding spirit behind the Russian group known as "The Five." He was a competent pianist but could never perform his own *Islamey*.

Complete Piano Works (USSR) 3 Vols. edited by Sorokin. Volumes I and III contain two books each. Vol. III, book 2, contains the two-piano works.

Au jardin (GS).

Berceuse D♭ (Zimmermann).

The Lark (GS) Arrangement of Glinka song.

L'alouette (GS) (JWC).

Islamey (1869) (CF) (Simrock) (Montes-Ric). His most famous work for piano, based on Lisztian technique. D.

Scherzo No. 2 b♭ (Zimmermann). One of his finest works; pianistically superb and much easier than *Islamey*.

Sonata b♭ (Zimmermann). Reached its final form after two revisions in 1905. A four-movement work, 34 pages, in Liszt traditional. Well-unified. Andante, Alegro assai feroce, Maestoso; Mazurka; Intermezzo; Finale. See: SSB, pp. 728-29. D.

See: Gerald Abraham, "A Remarkable Piano Sonata," Sackbut, 1931, 11, 330-34. Discusses the Balakirev b♭ Sonata.

In addition to the above, the *Complete Piano Works* contain Esquisses (Sonatina); Fantasiestück D♭; Humoresque b; 7 Mazurkas A♭, c♯, b, G♭, D, A♭, e♭; 3 Nocturnes b♭, b, d; Novelette; Polka; Reverie; 3 Scherzi b, b♭, F♯; Tarantella B; Toccata c♯; Tyrolienne; 7 Waltzes, G, F, b, B♭, D♭, f♯, g♯.

See: Edward Garden, *Balakirev: A Critical Study of His Life and Music*. New York: St. Martin's Press, 1968. An unannotated Catalogue of Works (pp. 330-39) and a large bibliography (pp. 321-25) are of special interest.

CLAUDE BALBASTRE (1729-1799) France

Noël with Variations (J. Ohl-SB). Serves as excellent preparation for the Haydn or Mozart easier sets of variations.

GERALD BALES (1919-) Canada

Toccata (BMI Canada 1947).
Tempo and texture changes, contemporary recital piece. Solid technical equipment necessary.

ESTHER WILLIAMSON BALLOU (1915-) USA

Presently teaching at American University in Washington, D.C.

Sonata (ACA 1955). 3 movements, 11 minutes. D.
Allegro quasi Fantasia: effective use of trill, melodic sevenths, complete range of keyboard, harmonics.
Andante sostenuto: bitonal.
Chorale Variations: chorale in unison 5 octaves apart. 4 variations.

Variations, Scherzo and Fugue on a Theme by Lou Harrison (ACA 1959). 12 minutes. D.
This is Ballou's second sonata, a large work. Contains 4 variations on a 2-part theme, each variation well defined.
Scherzo exploits percussive effects, good octave technique required. Plaintive trio using ostinato-like effect before Scherzo idea returns.
Fugue is excitingly worked out and leads to a frenetic climax. Mature pianism required. Ballou knows the capabilities of the piano thoroughly.

DON BANKS (1932-   ) Great Britain

Pezzo Drammatico (Schott). In Album *Contemporary British Piano Music.*

GEORGE BARATI (1913-   ) USA, born Hungary

Barati studied at the Budapest Conservatory and was first cellist at the Budapest Opera. He came to the USA in 1939 and taught at Princeton University. From 1950-1967 he was conductor of the Honolulu Symphony.

2 Piano Pieces (ACA 1948). Small tone poems.
Andantino: tonal, ABA, accompanied melody, succulent sonorities.
Andante: harmonic preference for 2nds, 7ths, and 9ths. Piquant sonorities, builds to climax then ends *mezzo forte.* Rather diffuse in style but effective.

Musical Chairs (ACA 1958).

Rolling Wheels (TP 1956).

SAMUEL BARBER (1910-   ) USA

Barber's accessible idiom is based on a lyrical, neoclassical style.

Excursions (GS 1944). Barber says "These are 'Excursions' in small classical forms into regional American idioms. Their rhythmic characteristics, as well as their source in folk material and their scoring, reminiscent of local instruments are easily recognized." Un poco Allegro, (boogie-woogie style); In slow blues tempo; Allegretto, (western song with variations over ostinato harmonies); Allegro molto, (square dance). M-D.

Sonate e♭ Op. 26 (GS 1949). One of the most important American piano sonatas of this century. Four movements: Allegro energico: energetic, rhythmic vitality; Allegro vivace e leggiero: quick waltz vacillating between double and triple meter (hemiola); Adagio mesto: impressive ostinato treatment involving use of all 12 tones in a unique way; Allegro con spirito: demanding fugue. D.

Nocturne (GS 1959). Inscribed "Homage to John Field." Some reference to the Field Nocturne e, No. 10. A flexible rhythmic pattern is combined with a nineteenth-century melody and twentieth-century harmonies. M-D.

See: James P. Fairleigh, "Serialism in Barber's Solo Piano Music," PQ, 72, Summer 1970, 13-17.

Hans Tischler, "Barber's Piano Sonata, Opus 26," ML, 33, 1952, 352-4.

JAN BARK (1934-) Sweden

Bark began his musical career as a jazz trombonist. His attitude toward composing is colored by his experiences in jazz, especially with regard to the improvisatory character of the music.

Sonata (NM 1957).
In four short movements. Atonal writing with strong tonal final cadence. Economical use of material, clear style. A misprint at opening of second movement: bass clef should obviously be a treble clef. M-D.

DAVID BARLOW (1927-) Great Britain

Genesis (Nov 1953).
A short fantasy in four contrasting sections built on a basic motif of four ascending notes. Sombre contrapuntal writing, neoromantic style. M-D.

ELSA BARRAINE (1910-) France

Barraine studied with Paul Dukas and won the Prix de Rome in 1929. "She is one of the few romanticists of her generation . . ." GD, 1, 454.

Fantasie pour clavecin ou piano (EMT 1961). 11 p. Neoclassic writing in one movement with contrasting sections. A piano addenda is included for certain passages. Effective on the piano; lean textures.

La Nuit dans les chemins du rêve (Enoch).

Prélude pour piano (Durand).

JEAN BARRAQUÉ (1928-   ) France

A student of Jean Langlais and Olivier Messiaen, Barraqué developed a unique modification of 12-tone technique. Certain elements of tonal and atonal writing are highly synthesized in his writing.

Sonate pour Piano (Bruzzichelli 1950-52). A 40-minute work of enormous dimensions, to be played without interruption. It is divided into two large parts. The composer warns in his preface that too fast a tempo will mar the clarity of the polyphony. Extreme organization of material: rhythm, melody and dynamics. Silence is an integral part of the form. One writer has described this work as "one of the most important works for piano in recent French music alongside the sonatas of Boulez."[1] Few pianists will be able to handle this work successfully.

See: G. W. Hopkins, "Jean Barraqué," MT, 107, November 1966, 952-4.

Andre Hodeir, *Since Debussy: A View of Contemporary Music.* New York: Grove, 1961. pp. 193-96 contain a fine discussion of this work.

[1]Antoine Goléa, "French Music Since 1945," MQ, 51, January 1965, 22-37.

HENRI BARRAUD (1900-   ) France

"Technically an avowed eclectic, he (Barraud) takes the view that a composer's originality lies in the expressive content of his music, not in his harmonic or contrapuntal devices." GD, 1, 455.

6 Impromptus (Amphion).
Souple et Calme: short, chordal.
Rapide: long melodic line with flowing eighths as substructure.
Lent et Grave: quiet opening, contrasting sections, large climax, quiet close.
Modéré: short, melody in tenor.
Sans Trainer: bass ostinato rhythms, dirgelike.
Cursif: 2 voices.

Histoires pour les Enfants (Durand 1930).
Four simple pieces.

Premiers Pas (ESC).
Five pieces for young people.

HANS BARTH (1897-1956) USA, born Germany

Barth came to the USA as a child. He experimented with the quarter-tone piano, his own invention, and was active in Jacksonville, Florida many years before his death.

Sonata No. 2 Op. 14 (AMP 1937). 20 p. Two movements, short, fugal texture in first movement, big octave technique required. D.

Sonata No. 4 Op. 30 (Belwin-Mills 1954).

Sonata No. 5 Op. 31 (Belwin-Mills 1954).

Sonata No. 6 Op. 32 (Belwin-Mills 1954).
In the 4th, 5th and 6th sonatas, Barth uses the traditional three movements (FSF). In addition, he closely unifies each work by using the first theme of the first movement in the second movement in contrasting tempo, and the second theme of the first movement in the third movement. While the theme can be recognized in its second appearance, the rhythmic and harmonic treatment is changed. All three sonatas are short.

BÉLA BARTÓK (1881-1945) Hungary

Bartók was one of the musical giants of this century. He was an outstanding pianist and his piano works mirror this great talent. "The piano music of Bartók exhibits a variety of styles. The early *Rhapsody* takes its departure from Liszt. The *Bagatelles* show a preoccupation with the treatment of various characteristic sonorities and musical ideas in miniature. The mass of folk-song arrangements often use block chordal accompaniments, other homophonic settings or occasional light contrapuntal textures. The drone bass is frequent, especially in "bagpipe" effects. Octaves and chords are often heavy, demanding and unorthodox. Stretches become a technical problem of importance (*Musettes, Etude No. 1*) and the treatment of characteristic sonorities achieves prominence (*Night's Music*). Wide skips also abound (*Sonata, Improvisations*) and the clever balancing of harsh sounds is important to proper projection of the music (*Diary of a Fly*). Irregular meters are plentiful (*Dances in Bulgarian Style*) and rapid ostinato figures offer problems in endurance and control (*The Chase, Suite Op. 14,* third movement). Asymmetrical phrase groupings constantly add to the interest and vitality of the music.

Since Bartók's music is built primarily on the melodic, harmonic and rhythmic vocabulary of Central and Eastern European folk music (on which he was an outstanding authority), it is well to begin study of his piano works with some of the folk-tune and folk-dance arrangements that occupied much of his attention. Although pedalings, phrasings, fingerings and metronome marks are almost too finicky (he uses subdivisions applicable to the electric metronome), they are all authentic and, if carefully considered, will lead to greater comprehension of his musical intent." MFTP, 187.

Bartók recorded about 12 long playing records of his own works. These are of inestimable value when studying his music.

(Bo&H) publish all the piano music. Other publishers are also listed.

4 Pieces (1905) (K). *Study for the LH* (sonata-rondo); wistful *First Phantasy; Second Phantasy;* zestful *Scherzo.* All show harmonic experimentation.

Rhapsody Op. 1 (1904). Lisztian style. Later arranged for piano and orchestra.

3 Popular Hungarian Songs (1907) (K). Simple treatment of the tunes.

14 Bagatelles Op. 6 (1908) (K). Short, original treatment of sonorous materials. No. 13 "Elle est morte"; No. 14 "Valse. Ma mie qui danse." Others are unnamed.

Young People at the Piano. 2 volumes. Pieces for the second and third years of instruction.
12 pieces in Vol. I, 10 pieces in Vol. II.

10 Easy Piano Pieces (1908) (MCA) (Schott). (17 minutes). Supplementary to Op. 6

1. Paraszti nota (Peasant song)
2. Lassú vergödés (Painful wrestling)
3. Tót legényak tánca (Slovak dance)
4. Sostenuto
5. Este a székelyeknél (Evening in the country)
6. 'Gödölle! piactérre leesett a hó' (Hungarian folk song)
7. Hajnal (aurora)
8. 'Azt mondják, nem adnak' (Folksong)
9. Ujjgyakorlat (Finger exercise)
10. Medvetánc (Bear dance)

2 Rumanian Dances Op. 8a (1909-10) (K). Thick textures, skips, D.

2 Elegies Op. 8b (1908-9) (Schott) (K). Related stylistically to Op. 1.

3 Burlesques Op. 8c (1908-10) (K). Querelle, Un peu gris, Molto vivo. Varied moods, impressionist, no folk influence.

For Children (1908-9). 2 volumes. (GS) has the first edition that contains 85 pieces. 79 pieces without octaves, ingenious treatment of folk materials.

See: Denes Agay, "Bartók's 'For Children' Which Edition? Original? . . . Revised?," Clavier 10, March 1971, 18-23.

Vol. 1 (based on Hungarian Folk tunes)

1.	Children at play	32″seconds
2.	Children's song	48″
3.	Quasi adagio (andante)	45″
4.	Pillow dance	58″
5.	Play	1′05″
6.	Study for the left hand	50″
7.	Play song	26″
8.	Children's game	1′30″
9.	Song	
10.	Children's dance	40″
11.	Lento	56″
12.	Allegro	1′20″

13.	Ballad				52″
14.	Allegretto				32″
15.	Allegro moderato				28″
16.	Old Hungarian tune				
17.	Round dance				1′00″
18.	Soldiers' song				1′02″
19.	Allegretto				40″
20.	Drinking song				25″-35″
21.	Allegro robusto				21″
22.	Allegretto				52″
23.	Dance song				50″
24.	Andante sostenuto				52″
25.	Parlando	no. 28 in original version			37″
26.	Moderato				40″
27.	Jest				50″
28.	Choral				1′30″
29.	Pentatonic tune	no. 31 in original version			50″
30.	Jeering song	32 "	"	"	36″-40″
31.	Andante tranquillo	33 "	"	"	1′30″
32.	Andante	34 "	"	"	1′15″
33.	Allegro non troppo	35 "	"	"	45″
34.	Allegretto	36 "	"	"	30″
35.	Con moto	37 "	"	"	27″
36.	Drunkard's song	38 "	"	"	35″-40″
37.	Swineherd's song	39 "	"	"	36″
38.	Winter solstice song	40 "	"	"	1′07″
39.	Allegro moderato	41 "	"	"	1′35″
40.	Swineherd's song	42 "	"	"	1′45″

Vol. 2 (based on Slovakian folk tunes)

1.	Allegro	30″
2.	Andante	43″
3.	Allegretto	28″
4.	Wedding song (Lakodalmas)	30″
5.	Variations (Váltonzatok)	2′15″
6.	Round dance (Játékdal)	40″-1′00″
7.	Sorrow (Betyárnóta)	50″
8.	Dance (Táncdal)	37″
9.	Round dance 2 (Gyermekdal)	30″

10.	Funeral song (Temetésre)		1′12″
11.	Lento		1′00″
12.	Andante rubato		40″
13.	Allegro		40″
14.	Moderato		34″
15.	Bagpipe 1 (Dudanóta)		55″
16.	Lament (Panasz)		50″
17.	Andante		45″
18.	Teasing song (Gúnydal)		36″
19.	Romance		1′25″
20.	Game of tag (Kergetödzö)		25″
21.	Pleasantry (Tréfa)		1′00″
22.	Revelry (Duhajkodó)		50″
23.	Andante (Tranquillo)	no. 24 in original	40″
24.	Andante	25 " "	50″
25.	Scherzando	26 " "	45″
26.	Peasant's flute (Furulassó)	28 in original	1′00″
27.	Pleasantry 2 (Még egy tréfa)		50″
28.	Andante molto rubato	30 in original	55″
29.	Canon	31 " "	52″
30.	Bagpipe 2 (Szól a Duda)	32 " "	57″
31.	The highway robber (Nóta egy másik betyárról	no. 35 in original	42″
32.	Pesante	36 " "	55″
33.	Andante tranquillo	37 " "	45″
34.	Farewell (Púcsû)	38 " "	1′35″
35.	Ballad	39 " "	1′30″
36.	and	40 " "	
37.	Rhapsody (Rapszódia)	41 " "	2′05″
38.	Dirge (Sirató ének)	42 " "	1′30″
39.	Mourning song (Halotti ének)	45 in original	2′05″

7 *Sketches* Op. 9 (1908-10) (EBM) (K) (Augener). 11 minutes. Short, M-D.

1. Andante (Portrait d'une jeune fille)
2. Commodo (Balançoire)
3. Lento
4. Non troppo lento
5. Andante (Mélodie populaire Roumaine)

6. Allegretto (A la manière valaque)
7. Poco lento

4 Nénies (Dirges) (1910) (K). 9 minutes. Short, stark, deceptively simple, refined pedaling required, impressionistic. M-D.

Allegro Barbaro (1911) (UE). Dancelike, barbaric, bravura and strength demanded. Phrygian and lydian modes mixed. M-D.

First Term at the Piano (1913) (K). 18 pieces from the Bartók-Reschofsky *Piano Method.* All by Bartók. Easy.

15 Hungarian Peasant Songs and Dances (1914-17) (UE). 12 minutes. A connected cycle of short folktunes, simply harmonized. Boisterous "Bagpipe" concludes set.

Sonatine (1915) (IMC) (GS in collection *Selected Works for the piano*). Bagpipe, Bear Dance, Finale.

Rumanian Folk Dances (1915) (UE). 4 minutes. 6 short pieces.

1. Bot-tánc (The dance with the staff)
2. Brâul (Braul)
3. Topogó (The stamper)
4. Bucsumi tánc (Dance from Bucsum)
5. Roman (Rumanian polka)
6. Aprozó (Lively dance)

Rumanian Christmas Songs (1915) (UE) 2 series, 10 in each to be played as connected cycles. Modal, asymmetrical phrasing.

Suite Op. 14 (1916) (UE). 4 varied movements: jesting Allegretto, sturdy Scherzo, driving Allegro molto, short impressionistic Sostenuto. M-D.

3 Etudes Op. 18 (1918). Virtuoso works, much dissonance, highly original. D.

Allegro molto: expansion and contraction of the hand, ninths and tenths.

Andante sostenuto: impressionistic sonorities, double notes in cadenza.

Tempo giusto: LH figuration against staccato chords, irregular meters.

Improvisations on Hungarian Peasant Songs Op. 20 (1920). 12 minutes. 8 tunes in a connected cycle, very dissonant, highly individual. The end point of Bartók's folksong settings. No. 7 in memory of Debussy. D.

Dance Suite (1923) (UE). 18 minutes. Originally written for orchestra, transcribed for piano by Bartók. Consists of 6 sections: Moderato, Allegro molto, Allegro vivace, Molto tranquillo, Commodo, Finale (Allegro). Contains some of Bartók's most arresting and invigorating writing.

Sonata (1926) (UE). 13 minutes. 3 movements: Allegro moderato; Sostenuto e pesante; Allegro molto. Bartók's most lengthy work for solo piano, has become a classic of this century. Requires brittle tone, power, rhythmic drive, virtuosity. D.

Out of Doors (1926) (UE). 13 minutes. Cycle of 5 descriptive pieces. D.

With Drums and Pipes: percussive, rhythmic, short.

Barcarolla: plastic, chromatic, linear, swaying barcarolle figure.

Musettes: major-minor sonorities mixed, drone decorated with trills.

Night's Music: hypnotic in effect, a nocturnal picture that includes crickets, croaking frogs, twittering, chirping, cluster chords.

The Chase: wild ostinato, wide skips, octaves, parallel ninths, dissonant.

9 Little Pieces (1926) (UE). In 3 books. 4 short dialogues in 2- and 3-part counterpoint, Bachlike.
Also a Menuetto, Air, Marcia delle Bestie, Tambour de Basque, Preludío — All'Ungherese.

3 Rondos on Folk Tunes (1916-1927) (UE). 7 minutes. No. 1 is the easiest. Light, clever, playful.

Little Suite (1936) (UE). 6 minutes. 6 adaptations from *44 Duos for 2 Violins:* Slow Melody; Walachian Dance; Whirling Dance; Quasi Pizzicato; Ukrainian Song; Bagpipe.

Mikrokosmos, 153 progressive piano pieces (1926-37), in 6 volumes. Bartók began writing these pieces for his son Peter. When completed, they comprised one of the most comprehensive collections of contemporary techniques and idioms for the piano ever assembled.

See: Benjamin Suchoff, *Guide to the Mikrokosmos.* New York: Boosey and Hawkes, 1971.

Vol. 1, 1-36: Hands in unison. Independence developed by simple 2-part counterpoint, including canon. Modal melodies.

1-6.	Unison melodies	2′30″seconds
7.	Dotted notes	30″
8.	Repetition	30″
9.	Syncopation	35″
10.	With alternate hands	40″
11.	Parallel motion	27″
12.	Reflection	25″
13.	Change of position	1′30″
14.	Question & answer	40″
15.	Village song	25″
16.	Parallel motion & change of position	45″
17.	Contrary motion	30″
18.-21.	Unison melodies	1′52″
22.	Imitation & counterpoint	28″
23.	Imitation & inversion	30″
24.	Pastorale	35″
25.	Imitation & inversion	57″
26.	Repetition	30″
27.	Syncopation	35″
28.	Canon at the octave	30″
29.	Imitation reflected	30″
30.	Canon at the lower fifth	43″
31.	Little dance in canon form	35″
32.	In Dorian mode	52″
33.	Slow dance	45″
34.	In Phrygian mode	45″
35.	Chorale	1′13″
36.	Free canon	42″

Mikrokosmos — Continued

Vol. 2, 37-66: 2-part writing, varied homophonic accompaniments, legato and staccato dynamics, pieces for 2 pianos, some chromaticism, more difficult key signatures. Technical exercises.

37.	In Lydian mode	40″
38.	Staccato & legato	15″
39.	Staccato & legato	30″
40.	In Yugoslav mode	1′40″
41.	Melody with accompaniment	40″
42.	Accompaniment in broken triads	1′20″
43.	In Hungarian style (duet 2 pianos)	30″
44.	Contrary motion ” ”	17″
45.	Méditation	37″
46.	Increasing — diminishing	58″
47.	Big fair	35″
48.	In Mixolydian mode	1′00″
49.	Crescendo — diminuendo	24″
50.	Minuetto	17″
51.	Waves	1′00″
52.	Unison divided	17″
53.	In Transylvanian style	36″
54.	Chromatic	15″
55.	Triplets in Lydian mode (duet 2 pianos)	30″
56.	Melody in tenths	15″
57.	Accents	67″
58.	In oriental style	55″
59.	Major & minor	42″
60.	Canon with sustained notes	42″
61.	Pentatonic melody	50″
62.	Minor sixths in parallel motion	40″
63.	Buzzing	37″
64.	Line & point	1′00″
65.	Dialogue: song	37″
66.	Melody divided	1′08″

Vol. 3, 67-96: Double notes, chord studies, irregular rhythmic groupings, inventions, changing meters, technical exercises.

67.	Thirds against a single voice	35″
68.	Hungarian dance (2 pianos, 4 hands)	30″

69.	Chord study	1'00"
70.	Melody against double notes	1'08"
71.	Thirds	1'15"
72.	Dragon's dance	30"
73.	Sixths & triads	37"
74.	Hungarian song	38"
75.	Triplets	54"
76.	In three parts	27"
77.	Little study	36"
78.	Five-tone scale	27"
79.	Hommage à J.S.B.	50"
80.	Hommage à R. Sch.	37"
81.	Wandering	1'00"
82.	Scherzo	30"
83.	Melody with interruptions	45"
84.	Merriment	45"
85.	Broken chords	1'17"
86.	Two major pentachords	1'18"
87.	Variations	1'20"
88.	Duet for pipes	1'00"
89.	In four parts	53"
90.	In Russian style	37"
91.	Chromatic invention	55"
92.	Chromatic invention	40"
93.	In four parts	37"
94.	Tale	55"
95.	Song of the fox	40"
96.	Stumblings	45"

Vol. 4, 97-121: More complicated problems, studies in clashing dissonances, Bulgarian rhythms.

97.	Notturno	1'40"
98.	Thumb under	35"
99.	Crossed hands	1'00"
100.	In the style of a folksong	45"
101.	Diminished fifths	57"
102.	Harmonies	1'21"
103.	Minor & major	1'15"
104.	Through the keys	30"

Mikrokosmos — Continued

105.	Playsong	1′00″
106.	Children's song	1′05″
107.	Melody in the mist	1′05″
108.	Wrestling	1′00″
109.	From the island of Bali	1′58″
110.	Clashing sounds	1′08″
111.	Intermezzo	1′38″
112.	Variations on a folk tune	1′00″
113.	Bulgarian rhythm	1′00″
114.	Theme & inversion	1′15″
115.	Bulgarian rhythm	23″
116.	Melody	1′30″
117.	Bourrée	1′00″
118.	Triplets in 9/8 time	57″
119.	Dance in 3/4 time	50″
120.	Fifth chords	55″
121.	Two-part study	1′15″

Vol. 5, 122-139: Double notes, chord studies, thirds, fourths, major and minor seconds, whole tone scales, syncopations, changing meters.

122.	Chords together & opposed	55″
123.	Staccato & legato	50″
124.	Staccato	1′08″
125.	Boating	1′20″
126.	Change of time	40″
127.	New Hungarian folksong	55″
128.	Peasant dance	1′13″
129.	Alternating thirds	47″
130.	Village joke	45″
131.	Fourths	45″
132.	Major seconds broken & together	1′30″
133.	Syncopation	1′05″
134.	Studies in double notes	
135.	Perpetuum mobile	30″
136.	Whole-tone scale	1′35″
137.	Unison	1′40″
138.	Bagpipe	1′10″
139.	Merry Andrew	58″

Vol. 6, 140-153: More extended treatment of the foregoing problems, culminating in 6 dances in Bulgarian rhythms. Volumes 5 and 6 are suitable for concert use.

140.	Free variations	1′40″
141.	Subject & reflection	1′16″
142.	From the diary of a fly	1′45″
143.	Divided arpeggios	2′05″
144.	Minor seconds, major sevenths	3′55″
145.	Chromatic invention	1′15″
146.	Ostinato	2′10″
147.	March	1′35″
148-153.	Six dances in Bulgarian rhythm	9′00″

TRANSCRIPTIONS: (CF)

Fugue G (Falsely ascribed to Frescobaldi)
Toccata C (M. Rossi)
Toccata a (M. Rossi)
Tre Correnti (M. Rossi)
These transcriptions are the result of Bartók's great interest in the pre-Bach repertoire.

Bartók Album (Bo&H) Two Volumes

Vol. 1 14 works: Bagatelles Nos. 2, 3, 5, 10 and 14, Burlesque No. 1 and 2, Danse roumaine, Esquisses Nos. 1, 2, 5 and 6, Soir à la campagne, Danse de l'ours.

Vol. 2 14 works: Aurora, Bagatelles Nos. 1, 6, 8 and 11, Dirge No. 3, Folksong, Rumanian Dance No. 2, Sketch No. 7, Slovak Peasant's Dance, Sostenuto, Three Folksongs from the Country of Csik, Village Dance.

Selected works for the piano (GS). Funeral march from the symphonic poem "Kossuth"; Rhapsody Op. 1; 14 Bagatelles Op. 6; 2 Elegies Op. 8b; Sketches Op. 9; 4 Dirges; 2 Rumanian Dances Op. 8a; 3 Burlesques Op. 8c; Sonatina.

Bartók Album (K). 3 Hungarian Folksongs; Fantasy (1903); 2 Rumanian Dances; Scherzo (1903); Sonatina; Sketches Op. 9; 14 Bagatelles Op. 6; Bear Dance.

See: William D. Dustin, "Two-Voiced Textures in The Mikrokosmos of Béla Bartók," unpub. diss., Cornell University, 1959.

Thomas Fenyo, 'The Piano Music of Béla Bartók," unpub. diss., University of California at Los Angeles, 1956.

Herbert Alvin Horn, "Idiomatic Writing in the Piano Music of Béla Bartók," unpub. diss., University of Southern California, 1963.

Colin Mason, "Bartók's Rhapsodies," ML, 30, 1949, 26-36.

Carolyn Walton Rosse, "An analysis of *Improvisations,* Opus 20 by Béla Bartók," unpub. thesis, San Diego State College, 1968.

Halsey Stevens, *The Life and Music of Béla Bartók*. New York: Oxford University Press, 1953; 2d edition, 1963.

Benjamin Suchoff, "Errata in the 'Mikrokosmos' Publication," PQN, 16, 1956, 11, 24.

Guide to the Mikrokosmos. Rev. ed. New York: Boosey and Hawkes, 1971.

Stuart Thyne, "Bartók's Improvisations," ML, 31/1, 1950, 30-45.

JAN Z. BARTOŠ (1908-) Czechoslovakia

Bartoš is a prolific and gifted composer. Contemporary events in his country have inspired some recent compositions. His educational work with children is commendable.

Sonata Op. 70 (Artia 1953).
Allegro — Piu animato
Adagio
Tarantella (Presto)

Sonata Op. 82 (Artia 1959).
Allegro molto
Largo
Allegro molto

Both sonatas display a fine compositional technique and could only have been written by a pianist. Both are tonal, yet liberally sprinkled with dissonance. Highly effective. M-D.

LESLIE BASSETT (1923-) USA

Bassett is a member of the Composition Department of the School of Music, University of Michigan. Manuscript copies are available from the composer.

Six Piano Pieces (ACA 1951).

1. Allegro moderato: mainly 2 voices, imitative, tonal.
2. Allegro: thin textures, melodic, chromatic coloring.
3. Andante cantabile: long melodic idea well developed, unusual sonorities.
4. Allegro brilliante: bitonal, perpetual motion, breathless.
5. Adagio, ma non troppo: ethereal, melodic.
6. Allegro assai: Toccata-like, moving freely into closely related tonalities.

A refreshing set, effective as a group. M-D.

Hommage à Arthur Honegger (ACA 1951).
Andantino: a 2-voice Nocturne employing linear writing with a quote from Honegger's *King David.* Piquant. M-D.

Elaborations (CFP 1966). 4 pieces for piano. 11 p. Wide range of keyboard and dynamics exploited throughout in these facile works. Basic patterns unfold inconspicuously.

Fast: scalar passages punctuated by chordal gestures, thin textures, ornamented by trills, PP close.

Slow: great freedom, long crescendo leads to a dynamic climax.

Quiet: more harmonically treated, incisive rhythmic punctuation relaxes to a calm close.

Brilliant: broad chromatic line, martellato effects, trill produces stunning sonorities. Dramatic close. D.

STANLEY BATE (1913-1959) Great Britain

Bate's works reveal the direct influence of his teacher Hindemith and also Vaughan Williams.

7 Pieces (AMP 1940).
Prelude
Romance
Chanson Populaire
Moment Musical
Polka
Valse
Short works of moderate difficulty, influenced by Shostakovitch.

6 Pieces for an Infant Prodigy Op. 13 (Mer).
Short, unpretentious.

Sonatina No. 1 (MCA).

Sonatina No. 2 (MCA).

Sonatina No. 6 E♭ (AMP 1943). 3 movements: Moderato; Andante; Allegro. Quartal and quintal harmonies; clear, facile writing.

Sonatina No. 7 C (AMP 1949). Bright, smaller in dimensions than No. 6.

Sonatina No. 8 C (AMP 1945). 3 short movements: Prelude; Valentine; Toccata. Alternating hands, tremolos, repeated notes and scales.

YVES BAUDRIER (1906-) France

Baudrier was one of the group of "La Jeune France," formed in 1936. This group also included O. Messiaen, A. Jolivet and D. Lesur.

La Dame à la Licorne (Amphion 1935).
The title refers to the tapestries "The Lady and the Unicorn" in the Musée de Cluny in Paris.

MARION BAUER (1887-1955) USA

Turbulence Op. 17/2 (EBM). Octaves, vigorous, brief motives, sonorous. M-D.

A Fancy (Axelrod). Short, impressionistic.

Eight Diversions (Chappell). Varied moods, styles. Int.

Four Piano Pieces Op. 21 (Arrow Music Press). Chromaticon, Ostinato, Toccata, Syncope. Short, varied compositional techniques. M-D.

Dance Sonata Op. 24 (ACA). Three gracefully-written movements. Allegro Appassionata: very chromatic; Sarabande: 5 variations; Allegretto giocoso. M-D.

Patterns Op. 41 (ACA). Five 12-tone pieces. Allegretto in 2 voices; quick Waltz; Scherzo; eloquent slow movement; Toccata. M-D.

JÜRG BAUR (1918-) Germany

Baur studied under Philipp Jarnach at the University of Cologne. He taught at the Robert Schumann Conservatory in Düsseldorf since 1946 and became director in 1965. In his serial writing he is fond of mirror structures.

Aphorismen (Br&H) 1957). 17 minutes.
12 pieces. M-D.

Capriccio (Br&H 1953). 5 minutes.
One of his earliest serial works. M-D.

Suite für Cembalo oder Klavier (Br&H 1956).

Heptameron (Br&H 1964-65). Dedicated to Anton von Webern. 7 pieces in serial technique with well-contrasted, attractive sonorities. M-D.

ARNOLD BAX (1883-1953) Great Britain

Bax wrote prolifically for the piano. His style always shows great facility and a romantic temperament. A love of the great Irish poets and Celtic folklore plus an early visit to Russia proved to be major influences.

2 Russian Tone Poems (J. Williams).
Nocturne (May night in the Ukraine). Imaginative writing requiring keyboard facility.
Gopak (National Dance). Strong rhythmic drive.

Country Tune (Murdoch). Needs careful balance of tone. Easy.

Lullaby (Murdoch). Melody treated with varied harmonies.

Toccata (Murdoch 1920). Double-note technique in RH, brilliant.

Nereid (JWC). Poetical, flowing, recurring rhythmic figure. M-D.

Winter Waters (JWC). "Tragic Landscape" achieved by a 4-note ground bass. Effective.

Whirligig (JWC 1919). Ostinato passed between RH and LH. Clever, needs digital facility.

Sonata No. 1 f♯ (Murdoch 1922). One movement, varied moods and tempi. Advanced pianism required.

Sonata No. 2 G (Murdoch 1921). One movement, rhapsodic in character. 5 themes, folksong influence, thick textures. Large span required.

Sonata No. 3 g♯ (Murdoch 1929). 3 movements, not easy for performer or audience. Advanced pianism required.

Sonata No. 4 (Chappell 1934). Perhaps the most attractive of the sonatas.

7 Selected Piano Solos (Chappell 1915-43). A fine varied album including: Lullaby, Mediterranean Country-Tune, A Hill Tune, Serpent Dance, In a Vodka Shop.

IRWIN BAZELON (1922-　　) USA

Sonatina (Weintraub 1952). 11 p. 3 movements.
Outside movements are quick, without clearly defined tonal centers. Shifting tonality in middle movement. D.

Five Pieces for Piano (Weintraub 1956).
Miniatures with disjunct melody, much dissonance and complex rhythmic ideas. Polyphonic texture. Difficult for performer and listener.

Suite for Young People (PIC 1954). 2 parts. Part 1 is easier. Part 2 is for more advanced pianists.

Part 1: Little Serenade, Christmas Carol, Dance for a Tomboy, Lullaby, Cowboy Tune, Prayer.

Part 2: Prelude, The Clown and the Puppet, Circus Parade, The Haunted Chateau, Dance of an Elf, Goblins and Ghosts.

"The purpose in writing these pieces was to acquaint young pianists with style and character of contemporary music as early as possible in their musical training."

JAMES BEALE (1924-   ) USA

Presently teaching at the University of Washington, Seattle. All the sonatas are well-written for the piano by a composer who obviously knows the possibilities and limitations of the instrument.

Sonata No. 2 Op. 8 (University of Washington Press 1953).
Contains five movements that exploit a wide range of sonorities and techniques. Lyrical aspects and fluid handling of the instrument emphasized.

Sonata No. 3 Op. 9 (ACA 1952). 15 minutes.
Allegretto espressivo
Allegro pesante
Allegro misterioso: exploits extreme ranges. Prestissimo coda.
Some use of harmonics, neoclassic style.

Sonata No. 6 Op. 13 (ACA 1956). Least involved of the 4 piano sonatas.
Adagietto
Presto
Andante
Presto con impeto.

Sonata No. 7 Op. 20 (ACA 1956). 23 minutes.

Slow-Moderate-Slow Fast Moderate-Slow Slow-Fast-Slow	This tempo chart is suggested for program printing. Few tempo marks are actually used in the work, usually only metronome marks. Many "start and stopping" effects. Tremolandos and long pedal effects are effectively used.

6 Bagatelles (ACA 1960).

GUSTAVO BECERRA-SCHMIDT (1925-   ) Chile

Becerra-Schmidt studied composition with Pedro Humberto Allende and Domingo Santa Cruz. He teaches composition, music analysis and musicology at the National Conservatory and is a member of the electronic music workshop at the Catholic University of Chile.

Sonata para Piano (IEM 1950). 24 minutes.
Allegro
Allegro
Lento
Allegro

Variaciones para Piano (IEM 1958). 8 minutes.

CONRAD BECK (1901-) Switzerland

Beck lived in Paris from 1925 to 1933 and was closely acquainted with Roussel, Ibert and Honegger. Many of his works show their influence.

Sonatine I (Schott 1922).

Klavierstücke (Schott 1920-30). Books I and II contain 11 pieces.

Dance (ESC 1929).

Sonatine II (Schott 1947).

Prélude (Heugel 1948). This work and the *Sonatine II* show more emphasis on a unified French-German style. Contrapuntal texture underlies both these works. M-D.

JOHN BECKER (1886-1961) USA

Becker developed a personal harmonic style and was quite adventurous as a composer. He wrote articles for numerous music journals and was associate editor of the quarterly "New Music."

2 Architectural Impressions (ACA 1924). 4 minutes.

2 Chinese Miniatures (GS 1926). 4 minutes.

Soundpiece No. 5 (NME 1937). 8 minutes. (Short Sonata for Piano). A one-movement work in four contrasting sections utilizing arpeggio figuration, chorale and toccata treatment plus a fugue, MC. M-D.

4 Modern Dances (CFE). 5 minutes.

JOHN BECKWITH (1927-   ) Canada

Beckwith studied piano with Alberto Guerrero at the Royal Conservatory of Music in Toronto, and composition with Nadia Boulanger in Paris. He is the music critic for the *Toronto Daily Star,* associate editor of the *Canadian Music Journal,* and on the music faculty at the University of Toronto.

4 Conceits (CMC 1945-48).
Contrasting short pieces in impressionistic style. M-D.

Novelette (BMI Canada 1954).
Requires broad span and good sense of driving rhythmic syncopation. Pungent sonorities. M-D.

DAVID BEDFORD (1937-   ) Great Britain

Bedford studied with both Lennox Berkeley and Luigi Nono.

Piano Piece I (UE).
Bars lasting 5 seconds are marked off. Values are only approximate and much is left to the performer to decide. Staccato and legato elements are cleverly used, dramatic. D.

LUDWIG VAN BEETHOVEN (1770-1827) Germany

The piano works occupy a unique place in keyboard literature and demand the detailed attention of both the teacher and serious student. Works without opus number (WoO) are numbered in accordance with Georg Kinsky, *Das Werk Beethovens, thematisch-bibliographisches Verzeichnis seiner sämtlichen vollendeten Kompositionen,* completed by Hans Halm, Munich: G. Henle Verlag, 1955.

EDITIONS OF THE SONATAS:

There have been more editions of the sonatas than almost any other works in keyboard literature. Urtext editions include (B. Wallner-Henle). (GS) and (K) reprint the old (Br&H) which is also available in 5 volumes in Lea Pocket Scores (LPS 11-15). (Heinrich Schenker-UE) newly revised by Erwin Ratz, in 4 volumes is very reliable and based on solid research and scholarship.

A very personal conception is the Artur Schnabel (Simon and Schuster) edition. Compare this with Schnabel's recordings! The fingering is one of the finest attributes of this edition. (Tovey, Craxton-ABRSM) contains much illuminating commentary. Other editions with merit are: (Martienssen-CFP) (Koehler, Ruthardt-CFP) (Lamond-Br&H) (d'Albert-CF) (Casella-Ric) (Dukas-Durand) (L. Weiner-EMB). Expected soon is an edition by Claudio Arrau (CFP).

Facsimilies of the following sonatas are available: Op. 53 (Beethovenhaus, Bonn, Germany), Op. 57 (prepared by H. Piazza-GS), Op. 109 (Robert O. Lehman Foundation), Op. 111 (CFP) and (Dover).

Separate copies of the sonatas are available in the following editions:

Op. 2/1 (Hoehn-Schott) (Wallner-Henle) (J. Ching-Prowse) (d'Albert-CF) (K) (Heugel).

Op. 2/2 (Hoehn-Schott).

Op. 2/3 (Hoehn-Schott) (d'Albert-CF).

Op. 10/1 (Hoehn-Schott) (Wallner-Henle) (J. Ching-Prowse) (d'Albert-CF) (K).

Op. 10/2 (Hoehn-Schott) (d'Albert-CF) (K).

Op. 10/3 (Hoehn-Schott).

Op. 13 (Hoehn-Schott) (Wallner-Henle) (Schenker, Ratz-UE) (J. Ching-Prowse) (d'Albert-CF) (K) (Heugel).

Op. 14/1 (Hoehn-Schott) (Wallner-Henle) (K).

Op. 14/2 (Hoehn-Schott) (Wallner-Henle) (K) (J. Ching-Prowse).

Op. 26 (Hoehn-Schott) (Wallner-Henle) (Heugel).

Op. 27/1 (Hoehn-Schott) (K).

Op. 27/2 (Hoehn-Schott) (Wallner-Henle) (Schenker, Ratz-UE) (J. Ching-Prowse) (K).

Op. 28 (Hoehn-Schott) (Schenker, Ratz-UE) (K).

Op. 31/2 (Hoehn-Schott) (Heugel).

Op. 49/1 and 2 (Hoehn-Schott) (J. Ching-Prowse) (K) (d'Albert-CF for No. 2) also (K).

Op. 53 (Hoehn-Schott) (Schenker, Ratz-UE) (Wallner-Henle) (K) (Heugel).

Op. 57 (Hoehn-Schott) (Schenker, Ratz-UE) (Wallner-Henle) (K) (Heugel).

Op. 79 (Hoehn-Schott) (Wallner-Henle) (K).

Op. 81a (Hoehn-Schott) (K) (Heugel).

Op. 90 (K) (Heugel).

Op. 106 (Hoehn-Schott).

Op. 109 (K).

Op. 110 (K).

Op. 111 (Hoehn-Schott) (K).

(GS) has all the sonatas individually and in 2 volumes edited by Bülow and Lebert. Use with care; notes are changed.

An order of progressive difficulty in the sonatas might be: Op 49, 2/1, Op. 79, Op. 14/1, Op. 2/1 (last movement more difficult), Op. 14/2, Op. 10/2, Op. 10/1, Op. 10/3, Op. 13, Op. 26, Op. 27/1, Op. 28, Op. 22, Op. 2/2, Op. 2/3, Op. 78, Op. 90, Op. 7, Op. 31/3, Op. 54, Op. 31/2, Op. 27/2 ,Op. 31/1, Op. 109, Op. 110, Op. 81a, Op. 53, Op. 57, Op. 101, Op. 111, Op. 106.

SONATAS BY OPUS NUMBER, Date of Composition and Tempo Indication of Each Movement: (based on Wallner-Henle edition):

Sonata f Op. 2/1 (1795) Allegro; Adagio; Minuetto: Allegretto; Prestissimo.

Sonata A Op. 2/2 (1795) Allegro vivace; Largo appassionato; Scherzo: Allegretto; Rondo: Grazioso.

Sonata C Op. 2/3 (1796) Allegro con brio; Adagio; Scherzo: Allegro; Allegro assai.

Sonata E♭ Op. 7 (1796) Allegro molto e con brio; Largo, con gran espressione; Allegro; Rondo: Poco Allegretto e grazioso.

Sonata c Op. 10/1 (?1796) Allegro molto e con brio; Adagio Molto; Finale: Prestissimo.

Sonata F Op. 10/2 (?1797) Allegro; Allegretto; Presto.

Sonata D Op. 10/3 (1798) Presto; Largo e mesto; Menuetto: Allegro; Rondo: Allegro.

Sonata c Op. 13 (?1789) Grave—Allegro di molto e con brio; Adagio cantabile; Rondo: Allegro.

Sonata E Op. 14/1 (1799) Allegro; Allegretto; Rondo: Allegro commodo.

Sonata G Op. 14/2 (1799) Allegro; Andante; Scherzo: Allegro assai espressione.

Sonata B♭ Op. 22 (1800) Allegro con brio; Adagio con molta espressione; Menuetto; Rondo: Allegretto.

Sonata A♭ Op. 26 (1801) Andante con Variazioni; Scherzo: Allegro molto; (Marcia funebre sulla morte d'un Eroe); Allegro.

Sonata E♭ Op. 27/1 (1801) Andante—Allegro—Tempo primo; Allegro molto e vivace; Adagio con espressione; Allegro vivace.

Sonata c♯ Op. 27/2 (1801) Adagio sostenuto; Allegretto; Presto.

Sonata D Op. 28 (1801) Allegro; Andante; Scherzo: Allegro vivace; Rondo: Allegro, ma non troppo.

Sonata G Op. 31/1 (1802) Allegro vivace; Adagio grazioso; Rondo: Allegretto.

Sonata d Op. 31/2 (1802) Largo—Allegro; Adagio; Allegretto.

Sonata E♭ Op. 31/3 (1802) Allegro; Scherzo: Allegretto vivace; Menuetto: Moderato e grazioso; Presto con fuoco.

Sonata g Op. 49/1 (1795-6) Andante; Rondo: Allegro.

Sonata G Op. 49/2 (1795-6) Allegro, ma non troppo; Tempo di Menuetto.

Sonata C Op. 53 (1804) Allegro con brio; Introduzione: Adagio molto; Rondo: Allegretto moderato.

Sonata F Op. 54 (1804) In tempo d'un menuetto; Allegretto.

Sonata f Op. 57 (1804-5) Allegro assai; Andante con moto; Allegro ma non troppo.

Sonata F♯ Op. 78 (1809) Adagio cantabile—Allegro ma non troppo; Allegro vivace.

Sonata G Op. 79 (1809) Presto alla tedesca; Andante; Vivace.

Sonata E♭ Op. 81a (1809) Adagio—Allegro; Andante espressivo; Vivacissimamente.

Sonata e Op. 90 (1814) Mit Lebhaftigkeit und durchaus mit Empfindung und Ausdruch; Nicht zu geschwind und sehr singbar vorgetragen.

Sonata A Op. 101 (1816) Etwas lebhaft, und mit der innigsten Empfindung (Allegretto, ma non troppo); Lebhaft, marschmässig (Vivace alla marcia); Langsam und sehnsuchtsvoll (Adagio, ma non troppo, con affetto); Geschwind, doch nicht zu sehr, und mit Entschlossenheit (Allegro).

Sonata B♭ Op. 106 (1817-18) Allegro; Scherzo: Assai vivace; Adagio sostenuto; Largo; Allegro risoluto.

Sonata E Op. 109 (1820) Vivace, ma non troppo; Prestissimo; Gesangvoll, mit innigster Empfindung (Andante molto cantabile ed espressivo).

Sonata A♭ Op. 110 (1821) Moderato cantabile molto espressivo; Allegro molto; Adagio ma non troppo; Fuga: Allegro ma non troppo.

Sonata c Op. 111 (1822) Maestoso—Allegro con brio ed appassionato; Arietta: Adagio molto semplice e cantabile.

See: Tovey (p. 85) and MFTP (p. xviii) for analysis of each sonata.

An arrangement entitled *Grande Sonata für Klavier* Op. 3 based on the String Trio Op. 3 (Eugene Hartzell-Dob) became available in 1968. This work is an arrangement of 5 of the 6 movements from the trio and it is questionable whether Beethoven transcribed all or part of it, but most of the work is expertly pianistic.

EDITIONS OF THE VARIATIONS:

22 sets of variations make up another large group of Beethoven's keyboard writing. They date from 1782 to 1823 and cover even a larger span of years than the sonatas (1782-1822). Opus numbers were used with only a few sets. Interpretative problems vary from easy to the most formidable.

(Joseph Schmidt-Görg-Henle) 22 sets including: 9 Variations on a March of E. Chr. Dressler WoO 63; 6 Variations on a Swiss Air WoO 64; 24 Variations on "Vieni Amore" by V. Righini WoO 65; 13 Variations on "Es war einmal" by K. Ditters von Dittersdorf WoO 66; 12 Variations on the Minuett à la Vigano by J. Haibel WoO 68; 9 Variations on "Quant' è più bello" by G. Paisiello WoO 69; 12 Variations on a Russian Dance by P. Wranitzky WoO 71; 8 Variations on "Une fièvre brûlante" by A. E. M. Gretry WoO 72; 10 Variations on "La stessa la stessissima" by A. Salieri WoO 73; 7 Variations on "Kind, willst du ruhig schlafen" by P. Winter WoO 75; 8 Variations on "Tändeln und Scherzen" by F. X. Sussmayr WoO 76; 6 Easy Variations G WoO 77; 6 Variations F Op. 34; 15 Variations and Fugue E♭ Op. 35; 7 Variations on "God Save the King" WoO 78; 5 Variations on "Rule Britannia" WoO 79; 32 Variations c WoO 80; 6 Variations D Op. 76; 33 Variations on a Waltz by A. Diabelli Op. 120; 9 Variations on a March of E. Chr. Dressler (2nd version) WoO 63; 8 Variations on "Ich hab' ein kleines Hüttchen nur" Anhang 10.

(Ratz, Holl-UE) 2 volumes. Vol. I: Op. 34, 35, 76, 120; Wo0 65, 70, 64, 77, 71; Vol. II in preparation. (Ruthardt-CFP) 2 volumes. (Ruthardt-K) 2 volumes.

Other collections include: (Henle) Selected Variations WoO 70, 64, 77. (von Irmer-Edition Stella) WoO 69, 70, 64, 71, 72, 77, Op. 34, 4 variations from Op. 105/107. (K. Herrmann-Hug)

The Unknown Beethoven contains Variations on Folksongs Op. 105/107. (Br&H) 10 Variations from Op. 107.

Single editions of: Variations c WoO 80 (Henle) (Schott) (Ric) (Agosti-Curci). "Nel cor più non mi sento" WoO 70 (Schott) (Heinrichshofen) (Ric) (WH). Op. 120 C (Kuhlmann-CFP) (Schnabel-CF). Variations F Op. 34 (Schott). Swiss Air Variations WoO 64 (Heinrichshofen). 6 Easy Variations G WoO 77 (Schott). Variations Op. 105/3 and 4 (Schott). Variations on a Russian Folksong Op. 107 (Schott). 10 Variierte Themen Op. 107 (Br&H) 2 volumes.

PIANO PIECES:

Collections containing miscellaneous works such as bagatelles, rondos, ecossaises, etc. (Brendel-UE) *Klavierstücke*: Rondo G Op. 129, Rondo C Op. 51/1, Allegretto c WoO 53, Rondo G Op. 51/2, 7 Bagatelles Op. 33, Andante F WoO 57, 6 Ecossaisen WoO 83, Fantasie Op. 77, "Für Elise" WoO 59, Polonaise Op. 89, Klavierstück B♭ WoO 60, 11 Bagatelles Op. 119, 6 Bagatelles Op. 126. Excellent scholarship evident; part of the Wiener Urtext Ausgabe. (von Irmer-Henle) *Klavierstücke* Vol. I: Rondo C (1782), 2 movements from an unknown Sonatina F, Allegretto c (1796), 2 Bagatelles c and C (1797), "Lustig-Traurig", Menuett E♭, Klavierstück g, Menuett F, Andante C, "Für Elise," Klavierstück B♭ (1818). Vol. II: Op. 77, 89, 119, 126, Klavierstücke B♭ and b, "Letzter Gedanke" C.

(H. Keller-CFP) *Klavierstücke* Vol. I: Bagatelles and Rondos. Vol. II: Andante F WoO 57, Fantasie Op. 77, Polonaise Op. 89, Allegretto c (1797), Presto C (1797), Allegretto C (1804), "Lustig und traurig", Für Elise, Klavierstück B♭, Allegretto for F. Piringer, Menuette E♭, Allemande A, Walzer D E♭, Ecossaisen, Fuge D (1817; Op. 137 original for string quartet), Praeludium f, 2 Praeludien through all keys.

(Kohler, Ruthardt-CFP) *Klavierstücke:* Op. 33, 39, 51/1-2, 77, 89, 119, 126, 129, Andante F WoO 57. Also same volume (K). Bagatelles Op. 119 (CFP) (IMC); Op. 126 (IMC); Op. 33 (Henle). *Complete Bagatelles* (von Irmer-Henle). *14 Bagatelles* (Frickert-CFP) in progressive order, Op. 33/1-6, Op. 119/1, 3-4, 9-11, Op. 126/2, 5. *7 Bagatelles* Op. 33 (von Irmer-

Henle) (Hoehn-Schott) (Scholz-Dob) (WH) (Ric). *6 Bagatelles* Op. 126 (Hoehn-Schott). *Andante favori* F, WoO 57 (von Irmer-Henle) (Hoehn-Schott) (WH). *Rondo* C G, Op 51/1-2 (Hoehn-Schott). *Rondo* C Op. 51/1 (Henle) (Ric) (Dob). *Rondo* a *Capriccio* G Op. 129 (Henle) (Hoehn-Schott) (Dob) (Ric) (Hertzmann-CF).

Two interesting volumes (d'Albert-OD) contain a broad survey: Vol. I Sonatas Op. 2/3, 13, 26, 27/2, 31/3 and Bagatelles, Op. 33; Vol. II Variations c WoO 80, Rondo G Op. 51/2, Sonatas Op. 53, 57, 90, 111, Bagatelles Op. 119.

EASIER COLLECTIONS AND PIECES:

6 Sonatinas WoO 47 No. 1 E♭, No. 2 F, No. 3 D; WoO 51 G, 2 others in G and F, (authentic?) (Hoehn-Schott) (Kohler-CFP) (K) (Heinrichschofen) (Frugatta-Ric) (ABRSM). WoO 47 Nos. 1, 2, and 3 published separately (Mills).

Albumblatt "Für Elise" WoO 59 (Henle). *14 Easy Pieces* (Schott). *Easy Pieces* (Br&H), Sonatine for Mandoline and Klavier (arranged), Lustig-Traurig, Für Elise, Dances, Bagatelles F E♭ Op. 33/3, 1, Rondos C G Op. 51/1-2. *The Easiest Original Pieces* (A. Rowley-Hin), Dance, Adagio/Sonatine C WoO 51, Op. 33/3, Op. 119/2-4, 9, 10, Variations on "God Save the King" WoO 78. *Pieces for the Young* (Ric) Bagatelles Op. 33, Rondo 51/1, Variations G WoO 77, Variations G WoO 70, Sonatas Op. 49, 1/2, Op. 79. *Beethoven for the Young Musician* (EBM) 6 Country & 6 German Dances, 6 Minuets, Sonatinas G, E♭, 6 Easy Variations on a Swiss Song.

DANCE COLLECTIONS:

6 Ecossaises (Georgii-Schott) (Parlow-WH) (Ric) (Busoni-Br&H). *Ecossaises and German* Dances (Niemann-CFP). *12 German Dances* (Lutz-Schott). *6 German Dances* (K).

Contradances (WH). Kleine Tänze (Frey-Schott) 20 Menuette, Ländler, Ecossaises, Kontretänze. *11 Little Dances* (Schott) (Br&H).

6 Contretänze (Frickert-Schott). *15 Walzer* (Kuhlstrom- Schott). *6 Walzer* (Vitali-Ric). *Allemandes, Waltzes and Songs* (BMC).

6 Allemandes, Allemande (1800), Ecossaise, 2 Waltzes, Lustig-Traurig, 7 Variations from Op. 107.

BEETHOVENS SÄMTLICHE WERKE, SUPPLEMENTE:

In 1957 under the editorial direction of Willy Hess, Breitkopf and Härtel began issuing *Supplemente zur Gesamtausgabe,* supplements to the first and only "critical" and "complete" edition of *Ludwig van Beethovens Werke* (1864-90). Hess has listed some 335 items not included in the first critical edition. Two volumes of piano works have so far come out in the series: one volume (VIII) 1964, contains arrangements for piano by Beethoven of works for 2 and 4 hands originally written for other media. Works for 2 hands include: Musik zu einem Ritterballet WoO 1 (1791) (8 sections), Scherzo from Klaviertrio Op. 1/2 (Fragment), Menuett A♭ for String Quartet (ca. 1794), 12 German Dances for Orchestra WoO 8, 12 Menuette for Orchestra WoO 7, 12 German Dances for Orchestra WoO 13, 6 Contradances for Orchestra (1802), The Creatures of Prometheus Op. 43—Ballet music (Overture and 18 numbers), Wellington's Victory Op. 91.

Another volume (IX) 1965, contains solo piano works and chamber works with piano. Many of these are not listed in Kinsky/Halm (p. 74). 23 piano works comprise this section and include: Rondo C WoO 48, Sonatine F WoO 50, Zwei Klavierübungen C B♭, Menuett C, Drei kleine Nachahmungssätze, Dreistimmige Fuge, Allegretto WoO 53, Allegretto (ca. 1797), Zwei Bagatellen C E♭ (1800), Anglaise, Zweistimmiger Kanon G (1802), Ländler c, Zweistimmiger Kanon A♭, Thema mit Variationen A (1803), Zwei "Deutsche" F f (1811-12), Thema für Erzherzog Rudolph (1818), Kleines Konzertfinale (1820), Allegretto (18 Febr. 1821), Bagatelle C (1823-24), Bagatelle g (27 Sept. 1825).

See: Claudio Arrau, "The (Beethoven) Piano Sonatas—Performance Insights," as told to Dean Elder. Clavier, 9, January 1970, 18-23.

Philip Barford, "Beethoven's Last Sonata," ML, 35, October 1954, 320-31. "Bagatelles or Variations?" MO, 76, February 1953, 277-9. A discussion of the origin of Beethoven's Bagatelles Op. 119, Nos. 7 and 8.

Malcolm Bilson, "The Emergence of the Fantasy-Style in the

Beethoven Piano Sonatas of the Early and Middle Periods," unpub. diss., University of Illinois, 1968.

Eric Blom, "Beethoven's Diabelli Variations," in *Classics Major and Minor*. London: J. M. Dent, 1958, 48-78. *Beethoven's Pianoforte Sonatas Discussed*. London: J. M. Dent, 1927. Reprint Da Capo, 1968.

Howard Chase, "Tonality and Tonal Factors in the Piano Sonatas of Beethoven," unpub. diss., University of Michigan, 1953.

John V. Cockshoot, *The Fugue in Beethoven's Piano Music*. London: Routledge and Paul, 1959.

Anthony J. Crain, "Problems in the Beethoven Literature," Clavier, 9, January 1970, 30-36. Mainly a discussion of trouble spots with special reference to Sonata C Op. 53.

Carl Czerny, *On The Proper Performance of All Beethoven's Works for the Piano*. Edited and with a Commentary by Paul Badura-Skoda. Vienna: Universal Edition, 1970.

George Dyson, "Beethoven and the Piano," ML, 8/2, 1927, 206-10.

Edwin Fischer, *Beethoven's Piano Sonatas*. London: Faber, 1959.

Irwin Fischer, "A Note in Opus 27, No. 2," (Beethoven Sonata), ML, 32, January 1951, 45-6.

Watson Forbes, "Beethoven's Op. 14, No. 1," MT, 86, 1945, 108-11. Discusses Beethoven's own arrangement of Op. 14 No. 1 for string quartet.

Allen Forte, *The Compositional Matrix*. Cincinnati: Music Teachers National Association, 1961. On the sketches for Beethoven's Op. 109.

J. A. Fuller-Maitland, "Random Notes on the (Beethoven Piano) Sonatas and Their Interpreters," ML, 8/2, 1927, 218-23.

Karl Geiringer, "The Structure of Beethoven's Diabelli Variations," MQ, 50, October 1964, 496-503.

William Glock, "A Note on Beethoven's Pedal Marks," Score, 2, January 1950, 24-5.

Eric Hertzmann, "Newly Discovered Autograph of Beethoven's 'Rondo Capriccio, Opus 129'," MQ, 32, April 1946, 171-95.

Rudolf Kastner, *Beethoven's Piano Sonatas.* London:Reeves, 1935. A descriptive commentary on the sonatas in the light of Schnabel's interpretations; gives an aesthetic appreciation of each sonata, with an outline of the development of the sonata form in Beethoven's hands. Also contains a biographical sketch of Schnabel and an account of his activity as an executant, composer and teacher. Translated by Gerald Abraham.

George Kochevitsky, "Controversial Pedaling in Beethoven's Piano Sonatas," PQ, 40, Summer 1962, 24-28.

Rudolf Kolisch, "Tempo and Character in Beethoven's music," MQ, 29, 1943, 169-87, 291-312.

George Langley, "The Triune Element in Beethoven as Specially Exemplified in his Piano Sonatas," PRMA, 23, 1896-7, 67-84.

E. H. W. Meyerstein, "The Problem of Evil and Suffering in Beethoven's Piano Sonatas," MR, 5, 1944, 96-111.

Ludwig Misch, *Beethoven Studies.* Norman: University of Oklahoma Press, 1953. Deals only partly with the piano works but contains fine observations. "Fugue and Fugato in Beethoven's Variation Form," MQ, 42, 1956, 14-27.

William S. Newman, "Some 19th-Century Consequences of Beethoven's 'Hammerklavier' Sonata, Op. 106," PQ, 67, Spring, 12-18; 68, Summer, 12-17, 1969. *Performance Practices in Beethoven's Piano Sonatas.* New York: Norton, 1971.

Cecil B. Oldman, "Beethoven's Variations on National Themes; Their Composition and First Publication," MR, 12, February 1951, 45-51.

Ates Orga, "An Authentic Beethoven Transcription," M&M, December 1968, 30-3. Discusses a piano transcription of the String Trio in E♭, Op. 3 as a piano sonata.

David Ossenkop, "Editions of Beethoven's Easy Piano Pieces," PQ, 38, 1961-62, 17-20.

Ernst Oster, "The Fantasie-Impromptu—A Tribute to Beethoven," Musicology, 1/4, 1947, 407-29.

Rudolph Reti, *Thematic Patterns in Sonatas of Beethoven. New* York: Macmillan, 1967.

Donald Francis Tovey, *A Companion to Beethoven's Pianoforte Sonatas.* London: Associated Board of the Royal Schools of Music, 1948. A measure by measure analysis of each sonata.

NICOLAS ANTOINE LE BÈGUE (1631-1702) France

Oeuvres de Clavecin (N. Dufourcq-l'OL 1956) Two Books. Livre I (1677), II (1687).

Livre I contains 5 suites in D, G, A, C, F, and Livre II contains 6 suites in d, g, a, A, F, and G. All the suites but two include an unmeasured prelude. Le Bègue is considered the first French composer to maintain the order of the suite as A, C, S, G with optional dances added. Norbert Dufourcq's description of Le Bègue as "the man had little genius, but a great knowledge and talent" is a terse summation. (Norbert Dufourcq, *La Musique d'Orgue Française.* Paris: Librarie Fleury, 1949, 70.)

Nöels variés (Br). These variations on Christmas carols resemble folksongs in their simplicity.

See: John Edward Gillespie, "The Harpsichord Works of Nicolas Le Bègue," unpub. diss., University of Southern California, 1951.

JACK BEHRENS (1935-) Canada, born Lancaster, Pa.

Events for Piano Op. 28 b (CMC 1961-63). 5 short character pieces, mostly one page each, in clear, tonal writing: Celebration, Meditation, Anticipation, Joy, Praise.

Passacaglia Op. 36 (CMC).
Approximate difficulty of Copland *Passacaglia.*

VICTOR BELYI (1904-1968) USSR

3 Miniatures (MCA 1939). 2 lyric, 1 dancelike. M-D.

Sonata No. 3 (MCA 1942). One movement of energetic, dissonant writing.

Sonata No. 4 (MCA 1947). Advanced pianism required.
Allegretto semplice
Moderato sostenuto
Andante con moto—Allegro appassionato.

ANTON BEMETZRIEDER (1743-1817) Germany

Leçons de Clavecin, et Principes d'Harmonie Paris 1771 (BB). In "Monuments of Music and Music Literature in Facsimile," Second Series—Music Literature, XVIII.

The above collection was written for Denis Diderot's daughter, a pupil of Bemetzrieder. Numerous examples of fingering are helpful in this *Music Made Easy,* published by this title in an English translation (1778).

GEORG BENDA (1722-1795) Bohemia (Czechoslovakia)

Although born and trained in Bohemia, much of Benda's adult life was spent in Germany, especially in Berlin. He was a close friend of C. P. E. Bach whose influence can be seen in many of Benda's keyboard works. Mozart appreciated Benda who wrote at least 55 sonatas.

Sonatas I-XVI (MAB Vol. 24-Artia).

34 Sonatinen (MAB Vol. 37-Artia).

See collection *German Keyboard music of the 17th and 18th Centuries* (Fischer, Oberdoerffer-Vieweg), Vol. 6.

PAUL BEN-HAIM (1897-) Israel

Ben-Haim writes a colorful folkloristic music that is especially well adapted for the keyboard.

5 Country Dances (MCA).

5 Pieces for Piano Op. 34 (MCA 1948).
Pastorale: improvisational exotic melody.
Intermezzo: siciliano rhythms.
Capriccio agitato: bravura writing.
Canzonetta: melodic.
Toccata: repeated note figuration, similar to the Prokofieff and Ravel Toccatas.

Sonatina a Op. 38 (MCA 1946).
Allegretto grazioso: varied moods.
Improvisazione: melodic.
Molto vivo: driving rhythms culminating in a rigorous finale based on the national dance, Hora.

Sonata (MCA).

Music for the Piano (MCA 1957).
Dedication
Melody
Rhythm
Movement
Epilogue

ARTHUR BENJAMIN (1893-1960) Great Britain, born Australia

Benjamin, a prolific composer in many forms, taught in Sidney, Australia for a few years before moving to London where he was on the faculty of the Royal College of Music.

Tambourin (Bo&H 1927). Quartal and quintal harmonies.

3 Little Pieces (Bo&H 1929). Easy.

Fantasies (Bo&H 1933). Moderately easy. 2 books, 3 pieces each book.

Let's go Hiking (Bo&H 1936).

Chinoiserie (Bo&H 1936). Gavotte and Musette.

3 New Fantasies (Bo&H 1938).

Jamaican Rumba (Bo&H 1938). His most popular piano work.

Pastorale, Arioso and Finale (Bo&H 1943). 14 minutes. Virtuoso but unpretentious writing.

Suite (OUP). 14 minutes.
Prelude
Air
Tambourin
Toccata
Epilogue in canon

RICHARD RODNEY BENNETT (1936-) Great Britain

Bennett studied composition with Lennox Berkeley and Howard Ferguson, and worked with Pièrre Boulez from 1957 to 1960. Total serialization appeals to Bennett and much use of this technique appears in his piano works. Jazz elements show some influence from time to time.

3 Diversions (UE).
Outstanding works for children, excellent for small hands.

5 Studies (UE 1965). Fluent ideas, many time signature changes, rich textures, serial. Demand a complete pianism.

Fantasy for Piano (Belwin-Mills 1962).
3-movement serial work with some delicate and unusual sonorities. D.

Sonata (UE 1954).
A 3-movement serial work that produces unusual sonorities and fine pianistic writing. The Grave is extremely expressive. Barkókian influence is felt in the percussive quality and clear-cut rhythmic figures. Inventive and vital. D.

A Week of Birthdays (Mills 1961). 7 short pieces. Int.

WILLIAM STERNDALE BENNETT (1816-1875) Great Britain

Bennett studied in Leipzig and later was the director of the Royal Conservatory of Music. His style of writing was greatly influenced by Felix Mendelssohn.

The Lake Op. 10/1 (GS) (Augener).

The Millstream Op. 10/2 (GS) (Augener).

The Fountain Op. 10/3 (Augener).

6 Studies in the form of Capriccios Op. 11 (McFarren-Ashdown). (O'Leary-J. Williams) No. 1 c; 2 E; 3 B♭; 4 f; 5 D; 6 g.

Sonata f Op. 13 (1836-37) (Ashdown). 4 movements, the 2 inner movements of more interest than the outer movements.

Suite de Pièces Op. 24 (McFarren-Ashdown). 6 contrasting movements in c♯, E, e, A, f♯, B.

Toccata c Op. 38 (Augener). Abundance of right-hand figuration.

Theme and Variations Op. 31 (O'Leary-J. Wiliams).

JØRGEN BENTZON (1897-1951) Denmark

A pupil of Carl Nielsen, Bentzon wrote in a modern contrapuntal style tempered with an expressive lyric quality.

Sonata No. 1 Op. 43 (SKABO 1946). 3 movements. M-D.
First movement: SA design, chromatically colored, PP ending.
Second movement: ABA design with B section containing some dramatic writing.
Third movement: changing meters, many octaves, brilliant ending.

NIELS VIGGO BENTZON (1919-) Denmark

Bentzon is probably the most prolific composer in all of Scandinavia. The major influences in Bentzon's music are Brahms, Nielsen and Hindemith. In fact, his large piano works can be regarded as direct successors of Carl Nielsen's big keyboard compositions. He is from an old Danish musical family and was first interested in jazz. It is difficult to classify him with any "school" of composition but his works are distinguished by compact contrapuntalism and harmonic clarity. He is one of Europe's most individual talents and his contribution to 20th-century piano literature has been large. Bentzon has been active as music critic and has also appeared widely as virtuoso pianist. (WH) publishes all works unless otherwise indicated.

7 Small Piano Pieces Op. 3. Melodious, in a Hindemithian harmonic style.

Toccata Op. 10 (1941).

Passacaglia Op. 31 (1944). 19 p. Exceptional contemporary handling of a baroque form.

Partita Op. 38 (1945). Praeambulum, Allegro, Intermezzo I and II, Fanfare. A brilliant piece of pianistic writing requiring virtuoso technique. Ends FFFFF.

Koncert etude Op. 40 (1947).

Sonata No. 2 Op. 42 (1942). 24 p. Allegro; Adagio; Allegro. Bitonal writing in bravura Liszt tradition.

Sonata No. 3 Op. 44.

Sonata No. 4 Op. 57. 23 minutes.

Sonata No. 5 Op. 77 (1951). 20 minutes.

Sonata No. 7 Op. 121. 15 minutes.

Dance Pieces Op. 45. 1. Valse subtile, 2. Polonaise, 3. Danza burlesca. Published separately. No. 1 is full of clever metrical fluctuations. No. 2 uses Polonaise rhythm only at selected places. No. 3 is written in bravura style, octaves everywhere.

15 Two-Part Inventions Op. 159 (JWC). These pieces are colored with so much chromaticism that key feeling is often lost, although each piece has the key listed. Sometimes more than 2 parts. The ones in G and B♭ are outstanding.

3 Concert etudes Op. 48 (1950). Published separately.

Woodcuts Op. 65 (1951). 11 pieces of varying difficulty.

Kalejdoskop (Kaleidoscope) Op. 86 (1954). Tendency toward expressionism and atonality.

Das Temperierte Klavier Op. 157. 24 Preludes and Fugues that proceed upward chromatically from C, major then minor. Some fugues are very short (No. 9 E is 5½ bars long) and some are loosely constructed. No dynamics, slurs or touch indications are given. The harmonic relationships are especially interesting.

2 Frederiksberg Suites Op. 173, 174. ". . . and the wind came over from Brønshoj, crept past Godthabsvej Station and spread itself over the low terrain." This is the introduction to these 2 suites. Suite I: Praeludium, A, C, Sarabande, Passepied, M I and II, Capriccio. Suite II: Praeludium, A, C, Sarabande, B, Gavotte, G. No dynamic or metronome indications present. Varied moods. D.

ALBAN BERG (1885-1935) Austria

Sonata Op. 1 (UE 1908).
This work dates from Berg's student days while he was still studying with Schönberg. It is a one-movement SA design, highly chromatic, thick-textured and demands advanced pianism. All of its ideas grow from the opening measures.

GUNNAR BERG (1909-) Denmark, born France

Berg devotes all his time to composition and does not teach or hold any official position. He worked with Honegger and remained in France until 1957, when he returned to Denmark.

Gaffkys (SPDM).

Small Piano Pieces in Modern Music Series (WH).

ARTHUR BERGER (1912-) USA

"Clarity, refinement, perfect timing and impeccably clean workmanship are the keynotes to Berger's style," wrote Alfred Frankenstein in the June 6, 1948 *San Francisco Chronicle.*

Two Episodes (LG 1933). Contrasting, atonal. M-D.

Three Bagatelles (EBM 1946). Risoluto con moto, Poco andante, Allegro brillante. Dry sonorities, rhythmic punctuation, moderate length. M-D.

Suite for Piano (ACA 1946). Capriccio, Intermezzo, Rondo.

Rondo available through (Mer). Flowing, expressive writing requiring careful tonal balance.

Rondo F (Mer 1946). Jaunty rhythms, clever melodic treatment. M-D.

Fantasy (ACA). Moderato opening, flowing scherzo, short meno mosso leads to a quick close. M-D.

Partita (ACA 1947). 5 short movements: Intonazione, Aria, Capriccio, Intermezzo, Serenade. Stravinsky-oriented. M-D.

JEAN BERGER (1909-) USA, born Germany

Presently teaching at Temple-Buell College, Denver, Colorado.

Fandango Brazileiro (EBM 1942). Contains a biographical sketch of the composer.

Sonatina (TP 1952). 12 p. Allegro; Andante; Molto vivo. Shows a high order of craftsmanship. Style is post-Debussy.

ERIK BERGMAN (1911-) Finland

Bergman is an exponent of serial technique, one of the few Finnish composers who has adopted this style of writing to any degree.

Intervalles Op. 34 (Westerlund 1964). 24 p.
Each of the 7 pieces exploits a different interval: 2nds, 3rds, 4ths, 5ths, 6ths, 7ths, unison and octaves. Variety of style and mood. M-D.

WILLIAM BERGSMA (1921-) USA

Bergsma's style "tends towards a dissonant, angular counterpoint and has an intense lyric quality that finds expression sometimes in poetry, sometimes in petulance. The harmonic idiom is dissonant in a neutral rather than a personal way." GD, 1, 643.

Three Fantasies (Hargail 1943). Agitated opening, bass pedal tones. Relaxed melody over pizzicato basses. Energetic rondo in perpetual motion. M-D.

Tangents (CF 1950). Two books. Bergsma says "Although the pieces can be played separately, *Tangents* is planned as a contrasting set and specifically for the second half of a program." Book I: Prologue, Prophecies, De Rerum Natura; Book II: Masques, Pieces for Nickie, Epilogue. Both books display an unusual mixture of styles, pianistic figuration, strongly contrasted moods. 33 minutes. M-D to D.

LUCIANO BERIO (1925-) Italy

Berio studied with Giorgio Ghedini and Luigi Dallapiccola. He helped establish the Studio di Fonologia di Musicale of the Italian Radiotelevision in Milan and became its director. His interest in electronic music has broadened tremendously in the last few years and he has incorporated serial principles in composing electronic music. He is one of Italy's leading composers.

Cinque Variazioni per Pianoforte (SZ 1953). Dedicated to Dallapiccola. The composer's excellent serial craft shows through in all these variations. Variations 3 and 5 have codas, variation 3 also has a cadenza. An exciting vitality is evidenced in this work. It is full of interesting sonorities and written in a style that shows some influence of Stravinsky. Dynamic range: PPPPP to FFF. Revised version (1966): see especially the last variation.

Rounds for Harpsichord (UE 1966). 5 p.
Square notes are sharp, round ones natural. All note heads are black and the performer is to hold each note unless otherwise marked, or impossible. Form is A B A (upsidedown) C A (faster). Difficult notational system. This and other works show Berio's concern for developing a new notational system influenced by electronic music.

Sequenza IV (UE 1967). 7 p.
Lyric, colorful and grateful to performer. This work is a series of constantly changing chords (continual variation). Much use is made of the sustaining pedal. The score is a reproduction of the manuscript but fairly easy to read.

See: Mario Bartolotto, "The New Music in Italy," MQ, 51, January 1965, 61-77.

LENNOX BERKELEY (1903-   ) Great Britain

Berkeley studied with Nadia Boulanger in Paris. His style incorporates thin textures, delicate instrumentation and a lyric emphasis found all too seldom in many 20th-century works.

5 Short Pieces Op. 4 (JWC 1937). All are easily accessible. Nos. 1 and 5 have rhythmic problems.

Polka Op. 5 (JWC).

3 Pieces (Augener 1937). Etude, Berceuse, Capriccio.

Sonata A Op. 20 (JWC). 25 minutes. Dedicated to Clifford Curzon.

Moderato: lyric first subject contrasted with a kind of 2-part invention for second subject. Development employs bravura writing.

Presto: a scherzo that fits the fingers well.

Adagio: easy to play — miniature character piece.

Allegro (Rondo): Slow introduction before main theme. The eighth-note in the Allegro is twice as fast as in the Introduction.

3 Impromptus (W. Rogers 1937). Short contrasted works. Makes a convincing suite.

6 Preludes Op. 23 (JWC 1948).

3 Mazurkas Op. 32/1 (JWC 1951). 8½ minutes. Short, effective, MC.

Scherzo Op. 32/2 (JWC 1951). Rapid repeated single and double notes. D.

4 Concert Studies (Schott 1940).

Improvisation on a Theme of Manuel de Falla (JWC 1960). 3 p. Short character piece, fast mid-section, quiet ending.

MIGUEL BERNAL JIMÉNEZ (1910-1956) Mexico

Bernal Jiménez studied in Rome from 1928 to 1933. He was very active in the musical life of Mexico and published studies of Mexican music in Colonial times.

Antigua Valladolid (The Ancient City) (PIC). A pleasant suite for an intermediate student. Toccatina for RH alone, Double Minuet, Gavotte, Pleasantry.

Cartels (Pastels) (Southern 1957). 20 p.
8 pieces that employ Mexican folk rhythms and tunes. See especially Danza Maya, and Sandunga.

LORD GERALD TYRWHITT BERNERS (1883-1950)
Great Britain

Trois Petites Marches Funèbres (JWC). Satirical, effective, not difficult.
Pour un Homme d'Etat: slow and pompous.
Pour un Canari: clever, whimsical.
Pour une Tante à Héritage: Allegro giocoso.

Trois Fragments psychologiques (JWC). Three representations of psychological states of mind: Hate; Laughter; Sighing.

Poissons d'or (JWC). Difficult impressionistic study.

LEONARD BERNSTEIN (1918-) USA

Seven Anniversaries (Witmark 1944). For Aaron Copland (quiet), For my sister Shirley (light), In Memoriam: Alfred Eisner (elegiac), For Paul Bowles (ground bass followed by 4 variations and coda), In Memoriam: Natalie Koussevitsky (slow elegy), For Serge Koussevitsky (declamatory), For William Schuman (energetic). Int. to M-D.

Four Anniversaries (GS 1948). For Felicia Montealegre (lyric), For Johnny Mehegan (jazzy scherzo), For David Diamond (flowing), For Helen Coates (boisterous). M-D.

Five Anniversaries (GS 1964). For Elizabeth Rudolf, For Lukas Foss, For Elizabeth Ehrman, For Sandy Gillhorn, For Susanna Kyle. M-D.

FRANZ BERWALD (1796-1868) Sweden

Berwald was a violinist but devoted much of his life to composition. He spent time in Berlin, Vienna and Paris but was not recognized during his day. Today he is considered Sweden's most important nineteenth-century composer.

Complete Edition of his works (Br). Piano Works, Vol. 16.

See: Robert Layton, *Franz Berwald.* London: A. Blond, 1959.
List of Works: pp. 175-184.
Bibliography: pp. 185-187.
Discography: pp. 188-189.

BRUNO BETTINELLI (1913-) Italy

Bettinelli studied in Milan and Siena. In 1941 he became Professor of Harmony at the Milan Conservatory and music critic for the Milan paper "Italia." He has edited works of classic Italian masters. His style is mainly linear and dominated by a strong rhythmic pulse.

Tre Ricercari e Toccata (SZ 1948). 21 p. 11 minutes.
Ricercare is not used in the strict sense of the word. Toccata requires agile fingers. A well-made group that could also be played separately.

Fantasia (Ric 1955). 20 p. 12 minutes.
Preambolo, Ritmico, Notturno, Intermezzo, Fugato.

Improviso (A. Drago 1946). 20 p.

Piccoli Pezzi per Pianoforte (A. Drago). Vol. I (Studies).

Sonatina (A. Drago 1940). 15 p.

Suite C (A. Drago 1945).
Preludio, Sarabande, Minuetto, Siciliana, Giga. M-D.

LORNE M. BETTS (1918-) Canada

Betts studied composition with John Weinzweig, Ernst Krenek, Alan Rawsthorne and Roy Harris. He is Principal of the Hamilton, Ontario, Conservatory of Music.

Suite for Piano (CMC 1950).
4 movements. The third movement (Nocturne) is contained in the collection *14 Piano Pieces by Canadian Composers* (F. Harris).

Sonata for Piano (CMC 1950). 11 minutes.

Miniature Suite (CMC 1948). 5 minutes.

PHILIP BEZANSON (1916-) USA

Sonata (ACA).
A large three-movement work in neoclassic style. The slow movement is especially attractive: variations over an ostinato bass. Last movement (Toccata) is demanding with full chords in wide skips. D.

Piano Sonatina (ACA).
A well constructed one-movement work with plenty of pianistic problems. Accidentals are numerous, thin textures prevalent and change of mood corresponds to tempo changes. M-D.

HENK BIJVANCK (1909-) The Netherlands

Sonatine (Donemus 1952).

Sonate (Donemus 1958).

Pianosolo (Donemus 1962).

Sonate No. 2 (Donemus 1962).

Sonate No. 3 (Donemus 1964).

Sonate No. 4 (Donemus 1964).

GORDON BINKERD (1916-) USA

Binkerd studied composition with Bernard Rogers and Walter Piston. His music is often contrapuntal but great care is taken with vertical sonorities. Texture is frequently thick but a lyric impulse is usually present.

Sonata (Bo&H 1968). 51 p. 22 minutes. Composed in 1955.
First movement is in modified SA design.
Second movement demonstrates great power coupled with grand sonorities.
Third movement is influenced by jazz (Scherzo).
Fourth movement concludes dramatically.

Fine craftsmanship with well developed ideas permeates this formidable work.

Entertainments (Bo&H).
7 pieces opening with Brief Encounter and closing with Graceful Exit. No. 6 needs a sensitive rubato. Fun-to-play contemporary music. Int.

Concert Set (Bo&H).
4 short pieces that make for an unusual and successful group. Witch Doctor, Legend, Etude, Mice. M-D.

The Young Pianist (Bo&H).
10 short pieces bristling with contemporary ideas.

Piano Miscellany (Bo&H).
5 short works: Lake Lonely, Rough and Tumble, Something Serious, For the Union Dead, Country Dance.

HARRISON BIRTWISTLE (1934-) Great Britain

Birtwistle, along with Alexander Goehr and Peter Maxwell Davies, "constitute the 'Manchester Group,' linked initially by their being students in Manchester at the same time and forming in 1953, with the pianist John Ogdon, an actual Group that brought its music to London in 1956; re-linked subsequently (after each had pursued a rather different path) in their organizing a Summer School at Wardour Castle, Dorset, in 1964." Andrew Porter, MQ, 51, January 1965, 16.

Précis for Piano Solo (UE 1962).
5 short sections mirror each other. Open textures, delicate sonorities. D.

MARCEL BITSCH (1921-) France

Hommage à Domenico Scarlatti (Leduc 1967). 13 p. 7½ minutes.
3 one-movement Sonatinas for harpsichord or piano. More effective on the harpsichord. Excellent craftsmanship.

Sonatine (Leduc 1960). 8 minutes. 15 p.
Ravel influence. Well-written and difficult.

12 Easy Pieces (Marvelous Dreams) (Leduc).
Short, above-the-average pedagogy material.

GEORGES BIZET (1838-1875) France

Variations Chromatiques Op. 3 (Choudens 1868). Theme is chromatic scale over a pedal, 14 variations and a coda. This was revised by Felix Weingartner in a later edition (Choudens c 1933).

Trois Esquisses Musicales (Heugel 1905). Freely transcribed by I. Philipp. Light, airy.

6 Chants du Rhin (Heugel). Nos. 1 and 6 (Augener). Mendelssohn and Schumann influence.

Bilder vom Rhein; 6 Lieder ohne Wörte (CFP 1920). 36 p. German edition of the above.
Morgenstimmung
Fröhliche Fahrt
Träumerei: contained in *Album of French Composers* (EBM).
Die Zigeunerin
Nachklänge
Heimfahrt

NILS BJÖRKANDER (1893-) Sweden

Björkander established a music school in Stockholm in 1917 and became a well-known teacher as well as a composer of popular piano pieces.

3 Pianostychen Op. 1 (1934 NMS). 9 p.
Preludium, Capriccio, Humoresk. Written in a post-Brahms idiom.

Glimtar (AL).
Each is 2 pages long, published separately and written in same idiom and difficulty as Grieg *Lyric Pieces.* Excellent pedagogic material. Pastoral (1938), Danslek (1938), Visa i Folkton (1949), Ganglat (1949).

Fyra Skargardsskisser (NMS).

Sonatine Op. 20 (NMS 1950). Mature pianism required.
Allegro moderato e cantabile: angular melody, big closing, difficult; Andantino con grazia (Serenata Carezzante): melodic emphasis, romantic harmony; Vivace ma marcando (Rondo rustico): toccata-like.

BORIS BLACHER (1903-) Germany

Blacher is one of Germany's leading composers and teachers. He has taught at the Hochschule für Musik in West Berlin since 1948 and has been head of that institution since 1953. Major influences in his music have been Schönberg and the rhythmic innovations of Stravinsky. Jazz influence has also found its way into some of Blacher's compositions. His use of serial technique is very personal and his usage differs considerably from Boulez and Stockhausen. He has developed a system of variable meters, a technique which governed most of his compositions written during the 1950's and 1960's.

Zwei Sonatinen Op. 14 (Bo&Bo 1955).
In both of these sonatinas the main interest lies in the asymmetrical rhythms. M-D.

Trois Pièces pour Piano Op. 18 (UE 1943).
No. 2 displays jazz harmonies and rhythms.

Ornamente Op. 37 (Bo&Bo 1950).
7 pieces, each built on a tone-row, but not applied to pitch. Each measure is in a different meter (variable meters), thin textures, short.

Sonate für Klavier Op. 39 (Bo&Bo 1951).
2 sections: Allegro ma non troppo leads to somber Andante; inversion of the Andante leads to light Vivace. Ostinati beautifully worked out in the variable meter technique.

4 Studies (Bo&Bo 1964-67). For harpsichord.

EASLEY BLACKWOOD (1933-) USA

Blackwood studied composition with Messiaen, Hindemith and Nadia Boulanger. He writes astringent dissonances that penetrate essentially simple diatonic textures.

Three Short Fantasies Op. 16 (GS 1965). Serial, metric changes, wide skips, unusual sonorities. D.

ALBERTO BLANCAFORT (1929-) Spain

Blancafort studied with Nadia Boulanger for six years. He is one of the best-trained of the younger Spanish composers having also studied with Joaquin Rodrigo for one year upon his return to Spain.

Sonata para Piano (UME 1960). D.
Allegro vivace: mainly lyric with much 16th-note accompaniment. Some flexible metric changes.
Lento: A B A, song-like.
Prestissimo: very scalar, punctuated chords, exciting.

EMILE R. BLANCHET (1877-1943) Switzerland

Blanchet studied with Busoni at Weimar. For many years he taught at Lausanne and Paris. He wrote a great deal of piano music, much of it very interesting.

Première ballade Op. 29 (Composers Music Corp. 1920).

Deuxième ballade Op. 30 (Composers Music Corp. 1921).

Troisème ballade Op. 32 (Composers Music Corp. 1922).

Préludes Op. 10 (Foetisch Frères 1909).

Turquie: trois morceaux de piano Op. 18 (Rózsavölgyi 1913). Caiques; Eloub; Au jardin du vieux serail.

Variations sur un thème de Mendelssohn Op. 22 (Ric 1917).

64 Preludes Op. 41 (ESC 1926). Preface and explanatory notes in French, German and English. Fourth Book is devoted to the LH.

Neuf études de concert Op. 19 (Ric 1916).

10 Nouvelles Etudes (Henn 1920). Polyphonic and polyrhythmic problems.

Sérénade Grotesque Op. 25/3 (Foetisch).

Technique moderne du piano (Senart 1935). Preface by Robert Casadesus.

Etudes de Concert Op. 55 (ESC)

ALLAN BLANK (1925-   ) USA

Blank received degrees at New York University and the University of Minnesota. He teaches at Herbert H. Lehman College.

Music for Piano (ACA 1962).
Unusual meters, athletic textures and melodic notes used harmonically add up to some interesting sonorities. M-D.

4 Easy Pieces (ACA)
Overture (In the Style of a Fanfare)
Play
Song
Dance
About same difficulty as Vol. II of *Mikrokosmos*. Some notes can be left out if hand is too small. Appealing set.

6 Miniatures and a Fantasia (ACA 1967).
Varied moods in these mildly contemporary pieces. No. 4 (Anapests) and No. 6 (Dactyls) have more interest. The Fantasia is 4p. and exploits broad gestures. Some clusters are also called for. M-D.

Expansions and Contractions (ACA 1966). 6p. As the title would suggest, much emphasis on contrary-motion writing. Chromatic coloring, extremes in range, fluctuating tempi. D.

2 Pieces (ACA 1966). 5p. No titles, only metronome markings. No. 1 exploits interval of fourth. No. 2 uses imitation in a short-long rhythmic scheme. M-D.

4 Pieces (ACA 1965). 5p.
No. 1: tonal, melodic line against syncopated accompaniment.
No. 2: a staccato study, exploits minor seconds.
No. 3: phrases in 4 plus 3 arrangement.
No. 4: equality of hands in this little syncopation study.

A Short Invention (ACA 1965). 2p.
Thin textures punctuated with thicker ones. D.

Rotation: A Study for Piano (ACA 1959-60).
Rhythmic divisions are difficult. Requires large span, broad dynamic range. Effective sonorities. Technical and musical problems abound.

JOSEF BLATT (1906-) USA, born Austria

Blatt studied theory and composition with Joseph Marx in Vienna. He is presently teaching at the University of Michigan.

Sonata (AMC 1923).
A one-movement work in ABA form using tempo and mood changes for contrast. Impressionistic idiom and many 19th-century pianistic techniques are used. M-D.

ARTHUR BLISS (1891-) Great Britain

Bliss, Musical Director of the BBC from 1941 to 1944, was knighted in 1950 and became Master of the Queen's Music in 1953. He writes in a neoclassic style and leans toward English Romanticism.

Masks (Curwen 1925). 24p. 4 pieces that exploit the full range of the piano. 35 minutes.

2 Interludes (JWC 1925). 10p.

Study (Curwen).

Toccata (Curwen 1926). Effective concert piece.

Suite (Curwen 1926). 31p.
Overture, Polonaise, Elegy, Finale. Clever but involved writing. M-D.

Sonata (OUP).

Sonata (Nov 1953). 21 minutes.
3 movements (FSF), difficult but rather tame. The first movement (Moderato marcato) is the most coherent. Slow movement is chaconne-like.

Miniature Scherzo (Nov 1969).
Composed for the 125th year of "The Musical Times", 1969 and founded on a phrase from the Mendelssohn *Violin Concerto,* 1844. In e, chromatic, toccata-like, octaves, PP ending. M-D.

AUGUSTYN BLOCH (1929-   ) Poland

Wariacje ni fortepian (Variations for Piano) (PWM 1962). 13p. 10 minutes. Romantic theme with 7 variations that differ widely in tempi, meter and dynamics. Final variation is the most contemporary-sounding. M-D.

ERNEST BLOCH (1880-1959) USA, born Switzerland

Bloch's piano music is largely impressionistic. The damper pedal is used profusely to connect rich sonorities. Modal usage and rhapsodic character are present in many of his works. An Ernest Bloch Society was formed in 1967 with the address 220 S.W. Alder Street, Portland, Oregon 97204.

Ex-Voto (BB 1914). Short, expressive, easy. 2p.

Danse Sacrée (BB 1914).

Four Circus Pieces (BB).

Poems of the Sea (GS 1922). Descriptive cycle: Waves: modal and uses ostinato; Chanty: short, folkloric; At Sea: undulating figuration, hornpipe-like melody. M-D.

Enfantines (GS 1923) (CF). Ten pieces for young people. Int.

Nirvana (GS 1923). Short, colorful, mystic poem. Ostinato harmonies, unusual timbres. Int.

In the Night (GS 1923). An atmospheric "love-poem." M-D.

Five Sketches in Sepia (GS 1925). Impressionistic, each piece short, sensitive sonorities. Prélude, Fumées sur la ville, Lucioles, Incertitude, Epilogue. The final piece quotes from the others. Int. to M-D.

Sonata (Carisch 1935). A cyclic work in three large connected movements. Maestoso ed energico; Pastorale; Moderato alla Marcia. Requires stamina, power and drive, advanced pianism. Bloch's most important work for piano. D.

Visions et Prophéties (GS 1940). Five short rhapsodic pieces that are intense and achieve a telling effect. M-D.

KARL-BIRGER BLOMDAHL (1916-1968) Sweden

Blomdahl was probably the most internationally known Swedish composer of his generation. He helped propel the image of Scandinavian musical life firmly into the 20th century. Besides his work as a composer, his work as teacher and as Director of Music in the Swedish Radio and Television was unique. His style is characterized by a rhythmic vitality, architectonic forms, and great use of the principle of cumulative effect.

4 Polyphonic Pieces (NMS 1945).
Oriented toward Hindemith.

2 Smastycken für Piano (NMS 1946).

JOHN BLOW (1648-1708) Great Britain

Blow was probably the most important contemporary of Purcell. His style is simple and direct.

Six Suites (H. Ferguson-S&B 1965) Excellent edition.

Contemporaries of Purcell (Fuller-Maitland-JWC 1921) Two volumes, one and two of this series. Vol. I: 4 suites and miscellaneous pieces; *Suite I*: A, C, M. *Suite II*: A, Ayre, S. *Suite III*: Andante, C. *Suite IV*: Ayre, C I and II. Same keys throughout the entire Suite. Vol. II: other miscellaneous pieces, a Fugue, Prelude, Ayre, Theatre Tune, Ground, and The Hay's a Ground.

12 Compositions for the Harpsichord or Virginal (E. Pauer-K). These are transcribed for the piano and were realized in the taste of Pauer's day but are over-edited by today's accepted standards. No sources are listed. Probably some of these works are doubtful.

The Second Part of Musick's Handmaid (T. Dart-S&B) revised and corrected by H. Purcell. 35 easy keyboard pieces, mostly by J. Blow and H. Purcell. First published in 1689, re-issued in 1705. Vary in length from 2 lines to 2 pages; mainly dances with much ornamentation.

Gavot in Gamut. Short, brisk, two voices. *Musick's Handmaid* Pt. II; *Contemporaries of Purcell,* Vol. I.

Ground in g. Variations on a 4-bar harmonic structure. Vol. II *Contemporaries of Purcell.*

ALEXANDRE-PIERRE-FRANÇOIS BÖELY (1785-1858) France

Boëly was one of the first French organists to play and appreciate J. S. Bach. He had some influence on Franck and wrote etudes, sonatas, and short pieces for the piano.

41 Pieces (Senart 1915). Revised and annotated by M. Brenet.

Many of Boëly's piano works are published by (Sal).

See album: *L'Ecole Française de Piano* (1784-1845) (M. Cauchie-l'OL 1957).

GEORG BÖHM (1661-1733) Germany

Complete Piano and Organ Works in 2 volumes (G. Wolgast-Br&H). Volume I: 5 Preludes and Fugues, Capriccio D, 11 Suites in c, D, d, d, E♭, E♭, F, f, f, G, a, M in G and Partita on the air "Jesu du bist allzu schöne."
Volume II: organ compositions.

ADRIEN BOIELDIEU (1775-1834) France

Best known for his operas, Boieldieu was professor of piano at the Paris Conservatory and later professor of composition at the same institution.

Sonates pour le piano-forte (Société Française de Musicologie, 1944), Vols. 11 and 12. Edited for the first time with an historical introduction by George Favre. 6 sonatas, 2 in Volume 11 and 4 in Volume 12. Vol. I: 2nd Sonata Op. 1 (1795) and 1st Sonate Op. 2 (1795?). Vol. II: 3rd Sonate Op. 2, 2 Sonatas Op. 4, and Grande Sonate Op. 6. Written in the "Grand Style", long, dramatic gestures, some melodic beauty, pianistic. M-D to D.

JOSEPH BODIN DE BOISMORTIER (ca. 1682-1765) France

Quatre Suites de Pièces de Clavecin Op. 59 (1736) (E. Jacobi-Leuckhart c. 1960).
These suites contain 18 short movements, each descriptive of feminine characters. Every one sounds well on the piano and only one calls for two keyboards. Editor has done an excellent job. Important collection of unusual repertoire that also contains three pages of facsimile and a Table of Ornaments.

CHARLES BORDES (1863-1909) France

A pupil of Franck, Bordes was one of the founders, with d'Indy and Guilmant, of the Schola Cantorum. His reputation rests mainly on his musicological studies. He collected and published old church music and Basque folktunes.

Caprice à cinq temps (Edition Musicales de la Schola Cantorum). Changing meters, a small "tour de force."

Quatre fantasies rhythmiques (Heugel 1889). Interesting rhythmic and metric subdivisions. Significant writing for 1883-1901, when these pieces were composed.

JOHANNA BORDEWIJK-ROEPMAN (1892-) The Netherlands

Johanna Bordewijk-Roepman is the wife of the Dutch novelist F. Bordewijk. She was self-taught. Her works are highly influenced by Impressionism.

Drie dansen (Alsbach).

Sonate (Alsbach 1943). 11 minutes.

Impromptu (Donemus 1961). 13 minutes.

Debout, éveille-toi (Donemus 1953).

ALEXANDER BORODIN (1833-1887) Russia

Three Pieces (USSR) Intermezzo, Reverie, Nocturne.

Au Couvent (GS)

Scherzo A♭ (IMC) (Br&H). Effective virtuoso piece.

Mazurka C (Augener)

Petite Suite (CFP) (EBM) (Augener) (Leduc).
In the Monastery, Intermezzo, 2 Mazurkas, Rêverie, Sérénade, Nocturne.

ALEXANDER BOSCOVICH (1907-1964) Israel, born Transylvania

Boscovich was one of the first Israeli composers to explore the idioms of Oriental music and apply them to his work. In later years he abandoned this for greater emphasis on serial techniques. He taught for many years at the Rubin Academy of Music in Tel Aviv.

Semitic Suite (Israeli Music Publications).
Folkloristic pieces. Dance-like Allegretto; songful Andantino; lively, syncopated Folk Dance; recitative-like Andantino; quiet Pastorale; concluding vigorous Dance. Entire suite has a bare, non-romantic quality, modelled after folk idioms of the Near East. Other version for four hands at one and two pianos, orchestral version also. M-D.

Golden Chain (IMI).

ARTURO BOSMANS (1908-) Brazil, born Belgium

Sonatina Lusitana (ECIC c. 1947). On Portuguese folk tunes.
Allegro vivace: popular treatment of 2 tunes, interludes; Cantiga do Cêgo: Ballad of the Blind, quartal harmony over pedal point, open sonorities; Allegro non troppo: cheerful, rhythmic, fast double notes, animated closing. M-D.

Sonata en Colores (ECIC 1944). Rojo: spirited broken-chord figuration, etude style; Gris: melody in parallel fourths, quiet; Verde: rhythmic, some linear writing, impressionistic parallel chords. M-D.

ENRICO BOSSI (1861-1925) Italy

Bossi is best known as a composer of organ works. He was director of some of the most important music schools in Italy, including St. Cecilia in Rome from 1916 to 1923.

Kinderalbum (Hug). 6 easy pieces.

Sechs Kinderstücke Op. 133 (CFP).

Das Jugendalbum Op. 122 (Schott). The best of these three collections.

WILL GAY BOTTJE (1925-) USA

Bottje is Director of the Electronic Music Laboratory at the University of Illinois.

Sonata No. 1 (AMC 1958)
A 3-movement work (moderate FSF) in neoclassical style. Tonal writing with much dissonance. Lines move according to their own melodic function. The slow movement is built on an ostinato. Third movement bristles with octaves. Brilliant and effective piano writing. D.

CARLOS BOTTO (1923-) Chile

Botto studied composition with Dominigo Santa Cruz, Juan Orrego Salas in Chile and with Luigi Dallapiccola in New York. He is director and teacher of harmony and music history at the National Conservatory of Music of the University of Chile in Santiago.

Tres Piezas Intimas Op. 13 (IEM 1952-59).

Sonatina Op. 9 (IEM 1958).

Tres Caprichos Op. 10 (IEM 1959). Tonal but freely chromatic. Int. to M-D.

PIERRE BOULEZ (1925-) France

Boulez studied with Olivier Messiaen and René Leibowitz. "Leibowitz's teaching upheld a strict usage of Schönberg's 12-tone technique, and herein Boulez found an ideal means for utilizing to their utmost the rhythmic concepts expounded by Messiaen. Boulez proceeded to apply the principles of the Schönberg technique to effect a serial ordering of rhythmic design and then extended the application to all elements of musical expression . . . . Boulez emerged as the international leader in extending the basic concepts of serial composition by his total organization of musical elements. He incorporated new techniques into his serial style, such as improvisational and chance elements, and has also experimented with a new notational system." BBD, 50-1.

Première Sonate (Amphion Editions Musicales 1946). 2 movements. Lent; Assez large. 12-tone, many tempo changes, difficult for ear to comprehend, wide leaps, Messiaen influence especially noticeable in rhythmic practice. D.

Deuxième Sonate (Heugel 1948). 48p. 32 minutes. 4 movements: Extrèmement rapide; Lent; Modéré; Presque vif, Vif. Serialized "closed" structure, spasmodic outbursts, also shows influence of some of the rhythmic organizations of Messiaen. Complex and very difficult. For a thorough discussion of this work see: André Hodeir, *Since Debussy: A View of Contemporary Music*. New York: Grove Press, 1961, 129-133.

Troisième Sonate (UE c. 1961). Begun in 1957 and still not complete. Movements so far are: Texte, Parenthèse, Commentaire, Glose, Commentaire. One may begin with any movement and continue in a variety of orders. Serialized "open" structure, quasi-extempore freedom, intricate dynamics, pedaling, rhythms and touch. Sonorities vary from expressive refinement to violent outbursts. Virtuoso pianism required and even this may not overcome the lack of discernible continuity.

See: Pierre Boulez, *Notes of an Apprenticeship*. New York: Knopf, 1968. These are early critical writings of Boulez. *Boulez on Music*. Cambridge: Harvard University Press, 1971. A highly technical, abstract, philosophic treatise on basic problems in contemporary composition.

JOSSE BOUTMY (1697-1779) Flemish, Belgium

Werken voor klavecimbel. Vol. 5 of *Monumenta Musicae Belgicae* with a short biography by Susanne Clercx. *Troisième Livre de Pièces de clavecin* contains 6 suites, optional dance movements with colorful titles, (La Martiale, Fanfarinette, La Brillante, L'Obstinée, 1st and 2nd Tambourine etc.) as well as the standard suite movements, A, C, S, G. More than interesting writing.

YORK BOWEN (1884-1961) Great Britain

Bowen was trained at the Royal Academy of Music. He was a fine pianist and wrote a great deal for the piano. His pedagogical editions are highly regarded in Great Britain.

24 Preludes Op. 102 (JWC 1950). 4 books.
In all major and minor keys. Rachmaninoff influence. These works are highly pianistic and contain some impressive sonorities.

Barcarolle (OUP).

3 Novelettes (OUP).

Second Suite (Nov 1910). 24p.

Curiosity Suite. Op. 40 (J. Williams).

Sonata f Op. 72 (Swan 1923). 34p.
3 movements FSF plus introduction to first movement. Solid musical writing in a post-Brahms idiom.

Short Sonata (Swan 1922).

Nocturne Op. 78 (OUP).

Sonatina C Op. 144 (JWC 1954). 16p. Colorful work.

4 Bagatelles Op. 147 (JWC 1956). Ideas not too interesting but pianistic and fun to play.

PAUL BOWLES (1910-   ) USA

Bowles lived in Spain, Morocco, Central and South America, and Mexico for a number of years. These experiences have added a unique quality to his music.

El Indio (Mer). Employs Mexican Indian material. An arrangement from Bowles ballet *Pastorelas*. Int.

El Benjuco (Mer). Same inspiration as above, based on a popular song. Int.

Huapango No. 1 and 2 (Axelrod 1937). Short, changing meters, Mexican dance style. Int.

Sayula (Hargail 1946). Inspired by dance hall. M-D.

Six Preludes (Mer 1933-1944). Short, mainly lyric, popular style. Int.

Two Portraits (Axelrod). Short, Int.

Sonatina (EV 1947). Allegro ritmico; Andante cantabile; Allegro. Less use of exotic elements. Int.

Carretera de Estepona (EBM). Rhythmic, octaves, syncopation. M-D.

Folk Preludes (TP). Six easy, charming settings.

ATTILA BOZAY (1939-) Hungary

Studied with Ferenc Farkas at the Academy of Music, Budapest. He works at the Hungarian Radio System.

Bagatelle Op. 4 (EMB 1961). 3 movements. 11p. 7 minutes. M-D.
Andantino tranquillo: preference for seconds, grace notes, chromaticism.
Sostenuto: long effective pedal usage.
Agitato, fugato: rhythmic, driving non-strict fugue.

Medailles (Bo&H). 36 varied short pieces; the performer selects to make his own suite. Excellent introduction to 20th-century techniques. Easy to M-D.

SUSAN BRADSHAW (1931-) Great Britain

Bradshaw was educated at the Royal Academy of Music and had further study with Boulez, Max Deutsch and Matyas Seiber.

8 Hungarian Melodies (JWC 1961). 11p.
Comparable to Book V of *Mikrokosmos,* these pieces have a flair for rhythm and harmony. Not as easy as they seem to be.

JOHANNES BRAHMS (1833-1897) Germany

A severe critic of all his compositions, Brahms left us little that is not of fine quality for the piano. (CFP) and (K) have the complete piano works available in volumes edited by Emil Sauer. A more reliable edition is the one published by (GS) in 3 volumes and edited by Eusebius Mandyczewski. Mandyczewski was one of the two original editors of the 1926-27 complete edition of the *Gesellschaft der Musikfreunde* in Vienna. In that series the piano works were contained in Volumes 13, 14, and 15. Another reprint of this series was made available in 1949 by Edwards Music Reprints. (K) miniature study scores has 2 volumes that include Op. 24, 35, 56b, 4, 10 in Vol. No. 725 and Op. 76, 79, 116, 117, 118, 119 in Vol. No. 726. (Br&H) also have the complete works in 3 volumes: Vol. I: Op. 1, 2, 5, 9, 21, 24, 35; Vol. II: Op. 4, 10, 39, 39 (simplified by Brahms), 76, 79, 116-119; Vol. III: works without opus number. (IMC) also publishes the complete piano works in 3 volumes with a fine text and printing. (Augener) has a reliable text and publishes the complete piano works edited by Mann.

Three Sonatas (Mandyczewski-Dover) (Whiting-GS).

Sonata C Op. 1 (1853) (Br&H). Allegro; Andante (Nach einem altdeutschen Minnelied); Scherzo: Allegro molto e con fuoco; Finale: Allegro con fuoco.

Sonata f♯ Op. 2 (1853) (Br&H) (Mayer-Mahr-Schott). Allegro non troppo ma energico; Andante con espressione; Scherzo: Allegro; Finale: Introduzione — Allegro non troppo e rubato.

Sonata f Op. 5 (1854) (Cortot-EC) (Steuermann-UE) (Klasen-UE) (Ric) (Bauer-GS) (Br&H) (WH). Allegro maestoso; Andante espressivo; Scherzo: Allegro energico; Intermezzo: Andante molto; Finale: Allegro moderato ma rubato.

Scherzo e♭ Op. 4 (1854) (Klasen-UE) (Br&H) (Deis-GS). Rasch und feurig.

Four Ballades Op. 10 (1856) (Steuermann-UE) (Mayer-Mahr-Schott) (Ric) (Alnaes-WH) (GS) (Augener). No. 1 Andante (inspired by the Scottish ballad "Edward"); No. 2 Andante; No. 3 Intermezzo: Allegro; No. 4 Andante con moto.

Sixteen Waltzes Op. 39 (Georgii-Henle) (Sauer-UE) (Draths-Schott) (Br&H) (K) (Alnaes-WH) (IMC) (Ric) (Augener) (Whiting-GS). Brahms made a simplified version of these (Georgii-Henle).

Variations. Six sets of variations including:

Variations on a theme by Schumann Op. 9 (1854) (Br&H) (Ric). The theme is one of Schumann's *Bunte Blätter* Op. 99 followed by 16 variations.

Variations on an original theme Op. 21/1 (1861). (Br&H) (Ric) (Augener). A beautiful theme followed by 11 numbered variations.

Variations on a Hungarian song Op. 21/2 (1861). (Br&H) (Ric) (Augener). 13 short variations and a four-page Finale.

Variations and Fugue on a theme by Händel Op. 24 (1862). (Cortot-Curci) (Br&H) Ric) (WH) (GS). 25 variations plus the fugue. One of the greatest sets of variations for piano.

Variations on a theme by Paganini Op. 35 Books I and II (1866). (Cortot-Curci) (K), (Foldes-CF) with preparatory exercises; (Br&H) (Hughes-GS) (IMC). Each book contains 14 variations on the theme. A possibility is a selection from both books rather than one complete book or both books complete.

Complete Sonatas and Variations (Mandyczewski-Dover).

Later short pieces:

Complete Shorter Works (Mandyczewski-Dover).

8 Piano Pieces Op. 76 (1879). (Georgii-Henle) (Br&H) (Mayer-Mahr-Schott) (IMC) (Ric first 4) (WH first 4). No. 1, Capriccio f♯, No. 2 Capriccio b, No. 3 Intermezzo A♭, No. 4 Intermezzo B♭, No. 5 Capriccio c♯, No. 6 Intermezzo A, No. 7 Intermezzo a, No. 8 Capriccio C.

2 Rhapsodies Op. 79 (1880). (Georgii-Henle) (Klasen-UE) (Br&H) (Alnaes-WH) (Ric) (Augener) (Heinrichshofen) (Mayer-Mahr-Schott, separately). No. 1 b, No. 2 g.

Fantasies Op. 116 (1892). (Georgii-Henle) (Steuermann-UE) (Alnaes-WH in 2 vols) (Sauer-CFP). No. 1 Capriccio d, No. 2 Intermezzo a, No. 3 Capriccio g, No. 4 Intermezzo E, No. 5 Intermezzo e, No. 6 Intermezzo E, No. 7 Capriccio d.

3 Intermezzi Op. 117 (1892). (Georgii-Henle) (Steuermann-UE) (K) (Schott) (Ric) (WH) (IMC) (Augener). No. 1, E♭, No. 2 b♭, No. 3 c♯.

6 Piano Pieces Op. 118 (1893). (Georgii-Henle) (Steuermann-UE) (K) (Schott) (WH) (IMC) (Augener) (Sauer-CFP) (Ric, Schott, No. 3). No. 1 Intermezzo a, No. 2 Intermezzo A, No. 3 Ballade g, No. 4 Intermezzo f, No. 5 Romanze F, No. 6 Intermezzo e♭.

4 Piano Pieces Op. 119 (1893). (Georgii-Henle) (Steuermann-UE) (K) (Schott) (Br&H) (WH) (IMC) (Ric No. 4). No. 1 Intermezzo b, No. 2 Intermezzo e, No. 3 Intermezzo C, No. 4 Rhapsody E♭.

5 Studies (Ric). No. 1 Etude after Chopin (1869); No. 2 Rondo after Weber (1869); No. 3 Presto after J. S. Bach, first arrangement (1879); No. 4 Presto after J. S. Bach, second arrangement (1879); No. 5 Chaconne after J. S. Bach, for left hand (1879).

Gavotte after Glück (1871). (CFP) (Ric) (Schott).

2 Sarabandes and 2 Gigues (CFP). *2 Sarabandes* (Schott).

51 Exercises (1893). (GS) (K) (Br&H) (Ric, in 2 books) (IMC).

Collections:

Sonatas, Scherzo and Ballades (Georgii-Henle) includes Op. 1, 2, 5, 4, 10. Based on composer's copies.

Piano Pieces (Georgii-Henle) includes Op. 76, 79, 116, 117, 118 and 119.

Hungarian Dances 1-10 (Georgii-Henle) (Schütt-Schott).

20 Favorite Pieces (GS) (Augener). Andante from Op. 1, Op. 10/3, Op. 39/2-15, Op. 76/2-4, 6, Op. 116/5, Op. 117/1,

Op. 118/2-3, 5-6, Op. 119/1, 3-4, Gavotte after Glück, Hungarian Dances Nos. 3, 16.

Complete Transcriptions, Cadenzas and Exercises (Mandyczewski-Dover).

Pezzi Scelti (A. Cortot-EC).
6 pieces with elucidating remarks in French, Italian and English. Capriccio b Op. 76/2, Intermezzo A Op. 118/2, Ballad g Op. 118/3, Intermezzo e♭ Op. 118/6, Intermezzo C Op. 119/3, Rhapsody E♭ Op. 119/4. Exceptional edition.

Brahms Album (EMB c. 1966). Fine edition, clear printing. Waltz Op. 39/15; 2 Rhapsodies Op. 79; Fantasies Op. 116/1, 3, 4, 5, 6, 7; 3 Intermezzi Op. 117; Romance Op. 118/5; Hungarian Dances No. 5, 6; Rhapsody Op. 119/4.

See: Edwin Evans, *Handbook to the Pianoforte Works of J. Brahms.* London: Reeves, 1936.

Evlyn Howard-Jones, "Brahms in his Pianoforte Music," PRMA, 37, 1910-11.

Frank E. Kirby, "Brahms and the Piano Sonata" in *Paul A. Pisk: Essays in His Honor.* Austin: University of Texas Press, 1967, 163-80.

Colin Mason, "Brahms' Piano Sonatas," MR, 5, May 1944, 112-18.

William Murdoch, *Brahms.* London: Rich and Cowan, 1933. Contains an analytical study of the complete piano works.

HENRY BRANT (1913-) USA, born Canada

An avowed experimenter, Brant has said concerning his own works: "No two of my works have any surface resemblance in technique and style." His interest in Ives is not reflected in any of the following works.

8 Pieces (ACA 1929). 8 minutes.

4 Short Nature Pieces (MCA 1942).
Sand, Stars, Sun, Sky. Colorful, short (one page each), MC.

Confusion in the Salon (ACA).

2 Sarabandes (NME 1931).

FRANÇOIS BRASSARD (1908-) Canada

Les Noisettes (BMI Canada).

Oratoire à la Croisée des Chemins (BMI Canada).
Both are from the suite "Orleanaises." Two picturesque lyric pieces in postromantic style. M-D.

PIERRE DE BREVILLE (1861-1949) France

Breville was a pupil of both Dubois and Franck. He composed in a very refined style. All the pieces listed below are interesting and well worth examining.

Fantasie: Introduction, Fugue et Finale (Lerolle 1888). Franckian influence. Well planned for the piano.

Stamboul (Lerolle 1894-5).
Four movements, each depicting a section of Istanbul. An extra movement was added in 1913.

Impromptu et Chorale (Editions Musicales de la Schola Cantorum 1905).

Sonata d♭ (Lerolle 1923) 28p.
A fresh and spontaneous sounding one-movement work displaying fine lyric cantabile writing.

Sept Esquisses (Lerolle 1925).

FRANK BRIDGE (1879-1941) Great Britain

Bridge wrote a large number of works for piano. Most are short and are effectively conceived for the instrument.

Three Sketches (GS). April, Rosemary, Valse Capricieuse. Contrasting romantic moods.

Capriccio f♯ (Augener). Clever and brilliant writing. Good facility required.

Three Poems (Augener). Solitude, Ecstasy, Sunset. Impressionistic, varied moods.

The Hour Glass (Augener). 3 pieces. Dusk: delicate and legato; The Dew Fairy: rapid pianissimo figuration; The Midnight Tide: thick textures.

In Autumn (Augener). 2 pieces. Retrospect: austere chromatic writing; Through the Eaves: short, exploits upper register, twittering figuration in RH.

Sonata (Augener 1925). 46p. 28 minutes.
Three movements of serious, dissonant writing. One of the most ambitious British piano compositions of its period. Advanced pianism required.

ALLEN BRINGS (1934-) USA

Variations on an American Folk Theme (AMC 1954).
An unpretentious work employing a clever rhythmic and melodic theme. Needs well-rounded pianistic equipment. Would make a suitable substitute for the overworked Barber *Excursions.*

Sonata (AMC 1961).
A large-scale work in four movements. Demanding both technically and musically. Well-organized but many thorny passages must be patiently analyzed.

BENJAMIN BRITTEN (1913-) Great Britain

The most popular composer in Great Britain today, Britten has not seen fit to add much to the solo piano repertoire. Possessed of a remarkable melodic gift, his style is characterized by thin textures which add clarity and zest to his writing.

Holiday Diary (Bo&H 1934).
Suite in 4 movements.
Early Morning Bathe: fast 16th-note figuration.
Sailing: flexible melody, lively middle section.
Fun-Fair: brilliant bravura rondo, sharply accented rhythms, chords, octaves.

Night: melody unwinds surrounded by widely-spaced tranquil accompaniment.

Night Piece (Bo&H). Composed for the Leeds International Piano Competition, 1963.
Lento tranquillo: a Nocturne in B♭, with changing meters, orchestrally conceived. Requires fine control and balance. Middle section is reminiscent of "Night's Music" from Bartók *Out of Doors Suite.*

Walztes [sic] Op. 3 (Faber 1970). Composed 1923-5. Five pieces, tonal, eclectic, first four have contrasting Trios, No. 5 is a theme with four variations and a coda. Int.

NATANAEL BROMAN (1887-1966) Sweden

Pianist and composer who has written symphonic poems and chamber music as well as piano pieces.

Courtoisie (ms). Available from Eriks Musikhandel.

Rokoko (NMS).

EARLE BROWN (1926-) USA

Brown studied mathematics and engineering at Northwestern University but eventually turned to music. He has been associated with John Cage and David Tudor on *Project for Music and Magnetic Tape.* He is currently serving as artistic director for the *Contemporary Sound Series* of Time Records. Brown is very interested in aleatory techniques and the relationship of sound, space and time.

3 Pieces for Piano (Schott 1951). Serial, 2 rows in double counterpoint.

Perspectives for Piano (Schott 1952). Chromatic, free 12-tone writing.

Folio and Four Systems (AMP 1952-54). Graphic notation, open form. 6 movements as follows:
Oct. 1952
Nov. 1952 (Synergy)

Dec. 1952
MM 87 and MM 135
Music for Trio for 5 Dancers
1953

Four More (AMP 1956). For one or more pianos.

More Systems (AMP 1957). For one or more pianos.

Nine Rarebits for 1 or 2 Harpsichords (UE 1965).

See: BBD, 57-59.

Gilbert Chase, *American Composers on American Music*. Baton Rouge: Louisiana State University Press, 1966.

HOWARD BRUBECK (1916-) USA

A graduate of San Francisco State College, Brubeck also studied with Darius Milhaud at Mills College. He has made some unusual experiments combining elements of classical music and jazz.

5 Short Pieces for Ginger (Der).

3 Pieces for Chidren (Der).

3 Sketches (Der).

MAX BRUCH (1838-1920) Germany

Bruch worked in classic forms using a romantic harmonic language but he also favored folk material and employed Scottish themes in a violin fantasy, a Jewish lament in his *Kol Nidrei,* etc.

6 Klavierstücke Op. 12 (Br&H).
1. B♭ 2. g 3. Impromptu G 4. d 5. Walzer F♯ 6. E

Schwedische Tänze Op. 63 (Simrock).
Book I: 1-7 (1892).
Book II: 8-15 (1892).

THEO BRUINS (1929-) The Netherlands

Sei studi (Donemus 1963). 11 minutes. Serial.

Sonata (Donemus 1957).

JOHN BULL (1562-1628) Great Britain

Immense finger dexterity is required for some of this master's works. As Thurston Dart says in the preface to the *Musica Britannica* edition, "the music itself is extravagant and artificial, in the best sense of those words." These two volumes reveal Bull as a versatile composer, gentle as well as flamboyant. Some remarkable music here.

Keyboard Music, Musica Britannica Volumes XIV (J. Steele, F. Cameron) and XIX (T. Dart-S&B 1963). Vol. XIV contains 61 works and Vol. XIX contains 82 works.

Ten Pieces (Steele, Cameron-S&B). Reprint from *Musica Britannica* with a short discussion of the music by T. Dart, including critical commentary and calendar of Bull's life.

Selected Works of John Bull (M. H. Glyn-S&B) Four volumes. 60 works in the following arrangement: I. Dances and Fancy Pieces. II. Folksong Variations. III. Pavans and Galliards. IV. Plainsong and other Fantasies.

Harpsichord Pieces from Dr. John Bull's Flemish Tabulatura (H. F. Redlich-NV c. 1958). Pavane, Gagliarda, Courante Alarme, Corante The Princess, and Het Jewel.
These pieces all date from Bull's stay at Antwerp and are contained in a Tabulatura of 1629. In this Tabulatura a clear distinction is made between organ style and harpsichord style. These pieces are definitely written for the harpsichord.

Parthenia (K. Stone-BB 1951) (T. Dart-S&B 1960) contains 7 pieces by Bull.

Popular Pieces (Augener) (K). Pavans and Gagliards, Preludium, The King's Hunting Jigg, Les Bouffons, Courante Jewel. Practical edition.

Dr. Bull's My Self FVB, II, 116. Short, dotted rhythms.

Walsingham FVB, I, 1. Set of 30 variations on old tune "As I went to Walsingham." Amazing piece. Sums up idiomatic keyboard advances made by English virginalists.

See: G. W. Whittaker, "Byrd and Bull's Walsingham Variations," MR, III, 1942.

The King's Hunt FVB, II, 116. Vivid sounds of a hunt are reproduced by trills, syncopations and repeated notes. Excellent program music, brilliant figuration.

In Nomine FVB II, 34. An "In Nomine" is a fantasy built on prolonged notes of a plainsong melody. The plainsong serves as a skeleton around which the melody and harmony revolve. This remarkable piece has 11 quarter notes to the bar and produces an asymmetrical effect. Suspensions are plentiful.

See: John Henry van der Meer, "The Keyboard Works in the Vienna Bull Manuscript," Tijdschrift voor Muziekwetenschap, 18/2, 1957, 72-105.

Wilfrid Mellers, "John Bull and English Keyboard Music," MQ, 40, 1954, 364-83, 548-71.

RICHARD BUNGER (1942-) USA

Bunger has degrees from Oberlin College and the University of Illinois. He is an outstanding pianist and has given many premiere performances of contemporary and *avant-garde* piano works. He teaches at California State College, Dominguez Hills, California.

Hommage for Pianoforte. Commissioned by the North Carolina MTA and the MTNA, 1967. Available on loan, MTNA.
All 5 pieces are short. M-D. Designed for advanced high school student as an initial exploration of 20th-century idioms.

1. J. C. (John Cage). Directions are given to prepare the piano with a bamboo slit and penny, etc. Contains some fascinating sonorities.
2. A. S. (Arnold Schönberg). Serial writing. Pointillistic technique.
3. V. H. (Vladimir Horowitz). Indicated "Faster than possible"! 2 bars long, requires about 4 seconds. Double glissandi up and down in white and black keys.
4. C. I. (Charles Ives). A reharmonized version of "America."
5. S. R. (Sergei Rachmaninoff). Pianistically in the Rachmaninoff tradition but definitely more contemporary both melodically and harmonically.

Suite for Piano (1963). Available from composer. Prelude, Canon, Ostinato, Arioso, G. Conservative contemporary writing, except for G not technically demanding. G emphasizes full resources of keyboard.

Pianography (Fantasy on a theme by Fibonacci) Available from composer.
"Utilizes contact mike, tape loop, a chord-playing bar, soft mallets, hand-damped notes, several preparations and, as an option, a ring modulator. The central section makes deliberate references to past piano literature within a clearly sectionalized progression of aurally-diverse fantasy scenes." Letter from composer, June 1, 1971.

WILLI BURKHARD (1900-1955) Switzerland

Burkhard wrote in a highly individual, contrapuntal, Baroque style.

Sonate Op. 66 (UE 1945). 3 movements, FSF. 14 minutes. All 3 movements oriented toward Hindemith. Large span required in the second movement.

Christmas Sonatina Op. 71/1 (Br 1947). 6p. 3 movements FSF. Based on carols that are well camouflaged. Not easy.

Acht leichte Klavierstücke (Br 1948).
Short character pieces.

6 Preludes Op. 99 (Br 1956).
Short, varied, idiomatic.

Was die Hirten Alles erlebten (Br.)
6 Christmas carols simply arranged in a little "notebook" format.

EDWARD BURY (1919-) Poland

Bury studied at the Warsaw Conservatoire with Z. Drzewiecki, K. Sikorski and W. Bierdiajew. From 1945 to 1954 he was professor at the State College of Music in Cracow.

Variations and Fugue Op. 35 (PWM). Lengthy.
Contains a theme, 14 variations and fugue. Highly chromatic,

canonic, dramatic in style. Karol Szymanowski seems to have been the inspiration for this work. Great contrast in individual variations. D.

GEOFFREY BUSH (1920-) Great Britain

Bush studied at Lancing College and Oxford University and was coached in composition by John Ireland.

Sonatina (Elkin 1965).

Three Dance Variations (Elkin 1957). Theme, Sicilian, March, Saraband.

Nocturne and Toccata (Augener).

Four Pieces for Piano (Augener 1950). 6½ minutes.

Suite D (Augener 1951). 1. Marcia 2. Ostinato 3. Presto 4. Siciliana 5. Rondo 6. Marcia.

FERRUCCIO BUSONI (1866-1924) Germany, born Italy

One of the greatest and most creative pianists of all times, Busoni was constantly torn between composing and performing. Born in Italy but educated in Germany, he was always pulled between these two traditions. Belonging to neither, he, in many ways, belonged to both. A new evaluation of his work is taking place and it is the belief of this writer that Busoni will fare much better now than he has during the second third of this century. For a complete listing of Busoni's works see: E. J. Dent, *Ferruccio Busoni, A Biography*. London: Oxford University Press, 1933.

Sonatina No. 1 (1910) (Zimmermann). Perhaps the easiest of the 6.

Sonatina No. 2 (1912) (Br&H). Two movements. Demanding.

Sonatina No. 3 ('ad usum infantis') (1916) (Br&H).

Sonatina No. 4 (In diem Nativitatis Christi MCMXVII) (1917) (Br&H).

Sonatina No. 5 (after J. S. Bach) (1919) (Br&H). A free transcription of J. S. Bach's "little" Fantasia and Fugue d, S 905.

Sonatina No. 6 (1920) (Br&H). Fantasy on themes from Bizet's *Carmen.* In the tradition of the Liszt fantasies.

Nuit de Noël (1909) (Durand). Impressionistic.

Indianisches Tagebuch Op. 47 (1915) (Br&H). This "Indian Diary" consists of short works based on American Indian themes.

The New Busoni (F. P. Goebels-Br&H). A selection from the 5-volume *Klavierübungen* (1918-21) expanded to 10 volumes in 1925. Part I: Scales, changing fingers, arpeggios etc. Part II: Exercises and studies in the style of Bach, Mozart, Beethoven, Chopin and Cramer. Goebels quotes several of Busoni's remarks on technique that are still valid.

24 Preludes Op. 37 (Tagliapietra-Ric). 2 volumes.

Prélude et Etude en Arpèges (Heugel). Busoni's last piano work. Written for Isidore Phillip's *School of Arpeggio Playing.* A complex study in whirlwind arpeggios.

7 Elegies (1908) (Br&H).

Nach der Wendung. Recueillement.
All' Italia. In modo napolitano.
Meine Seele bangt und hofft zu dir. Choralvorspiel.
Turandots Frauengemach. Intermezzo: A fantasy on "Greensleeves."
Die Nächtlichen. Walzer.
Erscheinung. Notturno.
Berceuse. This was published separately and later added to the Elegies.

Sechs kurze Stücke zur Pflege des polyphonen Spiels (Br&H).

8 Etüden von Cramer (Br&H).

Fantasia contrapuntistica (Br&H). One of Busoni's major works, scholarly, and baroque-inspired. Several musical forms are combined that require virtuosity and concentration of a high degree. There are four versions. 1st version: with an appendix showing an earlier sketch of part of the 4th fugue (p. 37). 2nd version: this is described as a definitive edition. The earlier sketch of part of the 4th fugue appears in the main text and an introduction which is essentially the *Third Elegy* prefaces this version. 3rd version: this is a simplified version, published as a chorale prelude and fugue on a Bach fragment. A 4th version is arranged for 2 pianos. All four versions are available through Br&H. This work represents a sunmming up of Busoni's interest in Bach.

Transcriptions of works by J. S. Bach:

Prelude and Fugue D, S 532 (Br&H).

Toccata and Fugue d, S 565 (Br&H) (GS).

Toccata, Adagio and Fugue C, S 564 (Br&H) (GS).

Chorale Preludes:

Wachet auf S 645 (Br&H).

Num komm' der Heiden Heiland S 659 (Br&H).

Ich ruf' zu dir S 639 (Br&H).

Nun freut euch, lieben Christen S 737 (Br&H).

Chaconne for violin S 1004 (Br&H) (GS) (Siloti-CF).

See: Larry Sitsky, "The six sonatinas for piano of Ferruccio Busoni," Studies in Music, 2, 1968, 66-85.

SYLVANO BUSSOTTI (1931-) Italy

Bussotti makes radical use of the resources of the piano.

5 Pieces for David Tudor (UE 1959). 3 sections, each about 30, 15 and 45 seconds. The score is a maze of marks! Aleatory technique is used for the pianist to realize his impressions of three abstract paintings. One piece is to be played with the fingertips on the surface of the keys without depressing them. Strings are to be grabbed inside, the lid slammed, the piano case struck, and gloves are requested for one particularly violent portion. The pianist is asked to be a co-composer. One of John Cage's comments is pertinent here: "the composer resembles a camera who allows someone else to take the picture."

Pour Clavier (Moeck 1961). Aleatory.

PIETER BUSTIJN (16 ? -1729) The Netherlands

Drie Suites voor Clavecimbel (Alan Curtis-Vereniging voor Nederlandse Muziekgeschiedenis, 1964). Introduction in English. 3 suites in g, a, and A. The two suites in minor appear to have the most interest. 6 movements in the a suite and 5 movements in the g. These three suites are from Bustijn's nine suites.

DIETRICH BUXTEHUDE (1637-1707) Germany, born Denmark

Although known primarily as a composer for organ, Buxtehude did leave 21 suites for clavier and a few sets of variations. (WH) publishes an urtext edition edited by Emilius Bangert that contains 19 suites, 6 sets of variations and 3 anonymous pieces. This same edition is reprinted by (K). Suites 1-5 C, 6-8 d, 9 D, 10-12 e, 13 F, 14-16 g, 17 G, 18 a, 19 A. (CFP) publishes 4 suites for clavichord or lute, 2 not contained in the Bangert edition. The suites are short and normally in the order of A, C, S, G. A suite on the Choral "Auf meinen lieben Gott" is available through (Hug), edited by Herrmann, and is also contained in Georgii *400 Years of European Keyboard Music*. It contains an A with Double, S, C and G. Each movement is actually a variation on the chorale.

WILLIAM BYRD (1543-1623) Great Britain

Byrd, the greatest of the Virginal composers, tried his hand at all kinds of composition and was remarkably successful. Simple dance-tunes and complex contrapuntal pieces point up the extremes in his compositional style. This "Father of Musicke" had more influence on the development of English music than any other composer.

The Collected Works of William Byrd (E. H. Fellowes-S&B 1937-1950) Volumes 18-20, *Keyboard Works* (1950). Vol. 18 contains Preludes, Fancies, Voluntaries, Dance Measures, Almans, Corantos, Jigs, Lavoltas and The Battell, a suite of 14 pieces. Vol. 19 contains 40 Pavans and Galliards. Vol. 20 contains Airs and Variations, Grounds, Fantasies on Plainsong, 2 adaptations.

Keyboard Music I, Musica Britannica Volume XXVII (A. Brown-S&B 1969). Volume XXVIII (1971) *Keyboard Music II.* The most trustworthy text that takes into account all the known sources. Complete in 2 volumes.

15 Pieces (T. Dart-S&B 1956) Newly transcribed and selected from the FVB and *Parthenia.*

45 Pieces for Keyboard Instruments (S. D. Tuttle-1'OL). Scholarly edition.

Parthenia (K. Stone-BB 1951) (T. Dart-S&B 1960). Contains 8 pieces by Byrd.

14 Pieces for Keyed Instruments (Fuller-Maitland, B. Squire-S&B).

My Ladye Nevells Booke (H. Andrews-J. Curwen). A scholarly edition of 42 pieces by Byrd dating from 1591. Critical commentary, notes, sources, beautiful example of what a scholarly performing edition should be. Re-issued by (BB), (Dover). See: E. H. Fellowes, "My Ladye Nevells Book," ML, 30, 1949, 1-7.

Dances Grave and Gay (M. H. Glyn-Winthrop Rogers Edition). Contains Pavans and Gagliardas, The Earle of Salisbury, Gigg, La Volta, Coranto C, Martin Said to His Man, The Queen's Almand, Medley, Irish Marche, La Volta (Morley). Suggested dynamics and phrasings, not fingered.

Popular Pieces (Augener) (K). Preludes, Pavans, Gagliardas, Sellenger's Round, The Carman's Whistle. Practical edition.

The Bells. FVB, I, 274. Picturesque variations employing a ground-bass.

Walsingham Variations, My Ladye Nevells Booke, 173; FVB, I, 267. Based on the tune "Have With Yow to Walsingame."

The Carman's Whistle. Eight variations on a popular song. Followed by a conclusion in which a new subject is treated. FVB, I, 214; (Augener) other reprints.

Victoria, The Carman's Whistle, Pavana: *Mr. W. Petre* are found in Volume II of *Le Trésor des Pianistes.*

See: Robert L. Adams, "The Development of a Keyboard Idiom in England During the English Renaissance," unpub. diss., University of Washington, 1960.

Hilda Andrews, "Elizabethan Keyboard Music," MQ, 16, 1930, 59-71.

E. H. Fellowes, "My Ladye Nevells Book," ML, 30, 1949, 1-7.

Stephen D. Tuttle, "William Byrd: A Study of English Keyboard Music to 1623," unpub. diss., Harvard University, 1941.

Gilles W. Whittaker, "Byrd's and Bull's 'Walsingham Variations'," MR, 3, 1942, 270-9.

C

ROBERTO CAAMAÑO (1923-   ) Argentina

Caamaño teaches courses in instrumentation, orchestration, and advanced piano at the National Conservatory in Buenos Aires. He is also director of arts of the Colón Theatre in Buenos Aires.

6 Preludes Op. 6 (Barry & Cia 1948). 12 minutes.
2 Volumes: I-IV, V-VI.
Require large span and facility, MC.

Variaciones Gregorianas para Piano Op. 15 (Ric 1953).
Theme and 6 variations. Last variation leads to a Toccata with much rhythmic emphasis. Effective close. M-D.

JUAN CABANILLES (1644-1712) Portugal
Cabanilles occupies a place as one of the great masters of the Baroque era in Portugal.

Complete Edition (H. Anglès-Biblioteca Central, Sección de música, 1927, 1933, 1936, 1956). *Musici organici* (in progress) in vols. 4, 8, 13, 17. Vol. 4 contains *16 Tientos*. Scholarly edition. All mss (7) variants have been carefully noted.

See: Mary J. Corry, "The Keyboard Music of Juan Cabanilles: A Stylistic Analysis of the Published Works," unpub. diss., Stanford University, 1966.

ANTONIO DE CABEZÓN (1510-1566) Spain

Obras de música para tecla arpa y vihuela. (Revised and edited by M. S. Kastner-Schott 1951). Contains 8 compositions from this collection of 1578. A cross-section of Cabezón's art in capsule form.

4 Tientos für Orgel, Kleinorgel, Harmonium oder Klavier (M. Drischer-C. L. Schultheiss Musikverlag 1953). Built on 3 or 4 themes.

The complete *Obras de música* is found in volumes 3, 4, 7, and 8 of *Hispaniae Schola Musica Sacra* (Felipe Pedrell-J. B. Pujol, c. 1895-98).

See: John Hughes, "The tientos, fugas, and diferencias in the *Obras de música para tecla, arpa y vihuela* of Antonio de Cabezón," unpub. diss., Florida State University, 1961.

Charles G. Jacobs, "The Performance Practice of Spanish Renaissance Keyboard Music," unpub. diss., New York University, 1962.

JOHN CAGE (1912-) USA

Oriental philosophy exerted a major influence on Cage. A period of activity related to the "prepared piano" occupied him for some time. During the last few years his interest in the aleatoric or "random" element has been supreme. Cage has exerted a remarkable influence on many of today's young composers.

Amores (Henmar Press 1943). 4 works. The first and last are for prepared piano and require 9 screws, 8 bolts, 2 nuts and 3 strips of rubber, acting as mutes. The second piece is for 3 beaters on 3 tom-toms apiece. In the third piece the same players change to woodblocks. Studied unpretentiousness!

Winter Music (Henmar Press 1957). Consists of 20 unnumbered pages with detailed instructions that are somewhat confusing.

Music of Changes (CFP 1951). Vols. 1-4. 43 minutes. Involved notation that perhaps only the composer and David Tudor, the dedicatee, understand. Cage says: "it will be found in many places that the notation is irrational; in such instances the performer is to employ his own discretion."

Sonatas and Interludes (NME). For prepared piano. Includes a kit to prepare piano, 45 tones are prepared. Sonatas are one page in length. 4 Sonatas. First Interlude 3 pages long. 4 more Sonatas. Second Interlude 3 pages long. Third Interlude is one page long. 4 more Sonatas. Fourth Interlude. 4 more Sonatas. Many moods, characterizations.

The Seasons (Henmar 1947). Ballet in one act, piano transcription by Cage. Preludes are separate pieces and are short and contain fascinating sonorities. Winter, Spring, Summer, Fall.

A Metamorphosis (Henmar Press 1938). 5 pieces in various moods

Music for Piano 4-19 (Henmar Press). Directions: "these pieces may be played as separate pieces or continuously as 1 piece or!!" 16 pages, some pages have only one note per page.

A Room (CFP). 2 minutes.

Ophelia (CFP 1946). 5 minutes.

Dream (CFP 1948). 5 minutes.

In a Landscape (CFP 1948). 8 minutes.

Suite for Toy Piano (CFP 1948). 8 minutes.

For M. C. and D. T. (CFP 1952). 2 minutes.

7 Haiku (CFP 1952). 2 minutes.

Music for Piano 2 (CFP 1953). 4 minutes.

Music for Amplified Toy Pianos (CFP 1960). Part to be prepared from score by performer for any number of toy pianos.

Bacchanale (CFP 1938). 6 minutes. For prepared piano.

Meditation (CFP 1943). 3 minutes. For prepared piano.

Music for Marcel Duchamp (CFP 1947). 5 minutes. For prepared piano.

A Valentine out of Season (CFP 1944). For prepared piano.

See: *The Complete Works of John Cage* (CFP). A detailed catalogue containing illustrations and an interview with the composer.

Silence—Lectures and Writings by John Cage. Middletown, Conn.: Wesleyan University Press, 1961.

A Year from Monday. New Lectures and Writings by John Cage. Middletown, Conn.: Wesleyan University Press, 1967.

JAMES CALLIHOU (? -1941) Canada

Suite Canadiènne (Archambault 1955).

Rigaudon: in Ravel idiom similar to the *Tombeau de Couperin.* theme and variation pattern.

Chanson: charming but contains a tricky mid-section.

Gigue: clever adaptation of a familiar tune.

CONSTANTINE CALLINICOS (1913-) USA

2 Greek Dances (MCA). Published separately. Laludi; Nerantzula. Both are based on Greek folksongs and follow a free theme and variation pattern.

Nani-nani; berçeuse grecque (CF 1951).

CHARLES CAMILLERI (1931-) Great Britain, born Malta

3 Popular Maltese Dances (Curwen).

Carnival Dance, The Danse and the Kiss, Dance of Youth. All three are based on the Maltese national dance tune known as "Il Maltija." Simple, diatonic. Int.

Trois Pièces pour Piano Op. 7 (Fairfield c. 1947).

Prelude, Toccata, Scherzo.

Sonata No. 2 Op. 15 (Fairfield c. 1969).

3 movements of compelling writing, especially the second movement, Funèbre.

Sonatina (Nov).

Country Dance (JWC).

Nocturne (JWC).

Little African Suite (Nov). See "Discovery Series." Based on genuine African tunes and rhythms. Slow movements are easier than the fast ones. Int. to M-D.

HECTOR CAMPOS-PARSI (1922-) Puerto Rico

Campos-Parsi is a technical consultant to the Escuelas Libres de Musica in Puerto Rico, and a member of the Music Advisory Council of the Institute of Puerto Rican Culture He studied at the New England Conservatory and in Paris with Nadia Boulanger.

Sonata G (PAU 1952-53). This work was selected to be performed at the First Festival of Latin American Music at Caracas, in 1954. It is a three-movement tonal work in neoclassic style.
Calmo: Allegro
Mesto: grave e sostenuto
Vivo

CORNELIUS CARDEW (1936-) Great Britain

February Pieces (CFP). *Avant-Garde.* Cardew says: "Either play each or any of the 'February Pieces' separately — start with any section and play round the piece, joining the end to the beginning (In III read each section normally — forwards — but reverse the order of the sections — i.e. turn over pages backward and join the beginning to the end)" (Preface). His system for notating decaying sound is most unusual.

Octet "61" for Jasper Johns (CFP). "Not necessarily for piano."

Piano Sonata No. 2 (Selbstverlag des Komponisten 1956).

3 Winter Potatoes (UE 1966). Prepared piano is called for in Nos. 1 and 2. No. 2 is of cyclic construction and any barline may be used as the starting point. Other "interpretation" directions are given.

CLÁUDIO CARNEYRO (1895-1963) Portugal

Carneyro's style is a combination of classicism, folklore, and contemporary techniques.

Arpa-Eólea (Sassetti c. 1959).
Harp-like study in fast-changing chromatic harmony.

Raiana (Sassetti 1938). 6 p.
Dance with unusual rhythmic interest.

Poemas em Prosa Op. 27 No. 1-3 (1933) (Sassetti). Published separately.
3 extended works using sonorous writing. No. 2 shows French influence.

Fábulas (Sassetti).
Charming, intermediate in difficulty.

Paciências de Ana-Maria (Sassetti c. 1960). Piano Pieces for Children.
Nursery Tale
Blind Man Bluff (3 flats, B, A and G!)
Music-Box
Transfer-Picture: most difficult.

JOHN ALDEN CARPENTER (1876-1951) USA

Impromptu: July 1913 (GS). An excellent example of American impressionism. M-D.

Danza (GS). Energetic staccato, irregular meters, strong accents. M-D.

Little Dancer (GS). Quick, staccato. Int.

Little Indian (GS). Lento, melodic, serious. Int.

Polonaise Américaine (GS). Not easy, moderate length.

Diversions (GS). Five varied individual pieces, informal moods. M-D.

Sonata g. This manuscript is located at the Library of Congress. On the cover: "Graduation Exercises, Music Department, Harvard College, 1897." Sensitive writing, in a post-Brahms idom, effective.

See: Thomas Pierson, "The Life and Music of John Alden Carpenter," unpub. diss., Eastman School of Music, 1952.

BENJAMIN CARR (1768-1831) USA, born Great Britain

Carr was one of the most important early American composers. He had a varied musical career in Colonial America and played a major role in the development of music culture in Philadelphia.

Federal Overture (1974) (Musical Americana). A beautiful edition of this historic work edited by Irving Lowens. The pieces are a potpourri of 8 different tunes of Revolutionary times, including the earliest printing of "Yankee Doodle". Written in the style of the period, crude at some points, but delightful to play and hear. Excellent contribution to early musical Americana. Int. to M-D.

MANUEL CARRA (1931-) Spain

Cuatro piezas breves (UME 1960). Brilliant, pianistic, cohesive.

Prestissimo: Webern style.

Presto; based on a palindromic figure dynamically, rhythmically, and texturally.

Lento; strict canon.

Prestissimo: exciting perpetual-motion idea.

ANTONIO CARREIRA (1520?-1597) Portugal

Drei Fantasien für orgel, clavichord (M. S. Kastner-Harmonia Vitgave). Kastner surmises the mss originated about 1586 in a Monastery of Santa Cruz at Coimbra. It is one of the two most important Portuguese keyboard collections of the period. A preface in both Dutch and English includes a brief biographical discussion of Carreira's life and comments related to the performance and structure of the works.

ELLIOTT CARTER (1908-) USA

Carter, a ranking composer of distinction, has written little for the piano, but has given us one of the most important piano sonatas written by an American.

Sonata (Mer 1945). A large-scale work in two long movements. Maestoso introductory section alternates with fast sections, changing meters. Another flowing legato section also fits into this movement. A sonorous Andante misterioso leads to a fugal Allegro giusto that is capped with a large climax. Quiet ending. Colorful use of harmonics. Virtuoso pianism and musicianship required.

ELEAZOR DE CARVALHO (1912-) Brazil

Carvalho came to the United States in 1946 and was conductor of the St. Louis Symphony for a number of years.

Brazilian Dancing Tune (Ric).
Uses extreme registers of keyboard. Vigorous, very rhythmic. M-D.

ROBERT CASADESUS (1899-) France

All of Casadesus's writing is pianistic and exploits the piano's possibilities to their ultimate potential.

24 Préludes (ESC 1924). In 4 volumes. Dedicated to Ravel whose influence is apparent. Various moods, excellent concert and advanced teaching material.

8 Etudes (GS 1941). Problems in thirds, octaves, resonance, fourths and fifths, two against three, left hand, chords, lightness of touch. Facile dexterity required.

Toccata (Durand 1950). Double notes, octaves, requires bravura technique.

Sonata No. 1 Op. 14 (Sal 1947). 3 movements, FSF, many ideas, MC.

Sonata No. 2 Op. 31 (Durand 1953). Dedicated to Grant Johannesen. A large 3-movement work. The second movement, Adagietto grazioso, is especially beautiful.

Sonata No. 3 Op. 44 (Durand 1948). 3 movements. The third movement, Rondo giocoso, is a wild "romp."

Sonata No. 4 Op. 56 (Durand 1957). Published together with *Sonata* No. 3. A 4-movement work with the first movement, Allegro impetuoso, dramatic, driving and especially difficult.

Variations d'après "Hommage à Debussy" de Manuel de Falla Op. 47 (Ric 1960). An exciting set of variations fully exploiting the sonorities of the piano.

6 Enfantines Op. 48 (Durand 1955). Charming, short. Pedagogic material.

ALFREDO CASELLA (1883-1947) Italy

Casella constantly experimented with new styles and techniques throughout his life. He began as a romanticist, then tried impressionism and polytonal writing in various combinations and, at the end of his life, became interested in twelve-tone techniques. Perhaps he was more at home in a neoclassic style which he adopted for many of his works. He was an ardent champion of contemporary music.

Essential to a thorough understanding of his music is his book *Music in My Time,* translated by Spencer Norton, Norman, Okla.: University of Oklahoma Press, 1955.

Toccata Op. 6 (Ric 1904). Broken chords, octaves, long. D.

Sarabande Op. 10 (Sal 1908). Chromatic figuration, lyric, sonorous, long.

A la Manière de . . . Op. 17 (Sal). Short works "in the style of . . ." Delightful fun.

Vol. I:	R. Wagner	Prelude to a "3rd Act."
	G. Fauré	Romance sans Paroles. Lyric.
	J. Brahms	Intermezzo.
	C. Debussy	Entr'acte pour un drame en préparation.
	R. Strauss	Symphonia molestica, a symphonic transcription.
	C. Franck	Aria.
Vol. II:	V. d'Indy	Prélude à l'après-midi d'un Ascète.
	M. Ravel	Almanzor ou le mariage d'Adélaïde.

2 pieces in imitation of Borodin and Chabrier composed and contributed by Maurice Ravel.

Deux Contrastes Op. 31 (JWC 1916-18). Grazioso, Hommage à Chopin. Distorted treatment of Prelude A, Op. 28/7. Anti-Grazioso, grotesque dance, short.

A notte alta (Ric 1917). Impressionist, poetic, big climax, quiet close. One of his most important pieces.

Inezie Op. 32 (JWC 1918). Preludio, Serenata, Berceuse. Short, simple, contrasted.

Barcarola Op. 15 (Ric 1910).

11 Pièces Enfantines Op. 35 (UE 1920). Prélude, Waltz, Canon, Bolero, Hommage à Clementi, Siciliana, Giga, Minuetto, Carillon, Berceuse and Galop. MC. Excellent pedagogic material.

Due Ricercari sul nome di B.A.C.H. Op. 52 (Ric 1932).
Funèbre: 3 and 4 voices, intense, short, effective.
Ostinato: more difficult, marchlike, percussive.

Sinfonia, Arioso and Toccata Op. 59 (Carisch 1936). Dramatic Sinfonia, large gestures. Sensitive Arioso supported by varying textures. Virtuoso Toccata with pesante and festoso ending. Advanced pianism required.

Nove Pezzi Op. 24 (Ric 1919). 9 pieces in contrasting moods: barbaric, burlesque, elegiac, exotic, funereal, in "nenia" style, minuet, tango, in rustic vein. Large span required. Difficult.

Sonatina Op. 28 (Ric 1916).
Allegro con spirito
Minuetto
Finale
Long, difficult, interesting sonorities.

Variations sur une Chaconne (Sal 1920).

6 Studies Op. 70 (Curci 1944).

MARIO CASTELNUOVO-TEDESCO (1895-1968) Italy

Important influences on Castelnuovo-Tedesco's music were his native city (Florence), Shakespeare, his own Jewish heritage and the Bible. He is essentially a neoromanticist and his piano works display a style spread over the entire keyboard. The piano compositions tend to be technically difficult.

English Suite (Mills 1962). Preludio, quasi un improvisazione; Andante; Giga.

Il Raggio verde (Forlivesi 1916). Long, fast figuration. D.

I Naviganti (Forlivesi 1919). Romantic poem that works to large climax.

Cipressi (Forlivesi 1920). Broad gestures, undulating motion, sonorous.

Alt Wein (Forlivesi 1923). A Viennese rhapsody, clever, appealing.

Piedigrotta (Ric 1924). A difficult Neopolitan rhapsody.

Tre Corali su Melodie ebraiche (UE 1926). Three lengthy pieces on Hebrew melodies. D.

Candide (MCA 1944). Six musical illustrations for the Voltaire novel. Programmatic suite.

Sonata (UE 1928). 44 p.

Six Canons Op. 142 (MCA). Clear and incisive writing.

Ricercare sul nome di Luigi Dallapiccola (Forlivesi 1958).

Evangelion; the story of Jesus, narrated to the children in 28 little piano pieces (Forlivesi 1959). 4 volumes. Certain portions of scripture are suggested for each piece. M-D.

Sonatina Zoologica Op. 187 (Ric 1961). 4 movements, based on characteristics of small winged and creeping animals. Excellent recital material. M-D.

JACQUES CASTÉRÈDE (1926-   ) France

Quatre Etudes (Sal 1958). 23 p.
Brilliant virtuoso writing.

Variations (Sal 1959). 15 p.

Diagrammes (Sal 1953). 24 p.
Prelude: Vivo, ma non troppo. Fleeting, murmuring, perpetual motion.
Nocturne: Lento. Built around perfect and diminished fifths.
Toccata: Vivo. Ravel influence.

Sonate (Editions Rideau Rouge c. 1969). One large-scale movement, mixture of styles, impressionism, expressionism, cluster-like chords, freely chromatic, big climax, quiet ending. D.

NICCOLO CASTIGLIONI (1932-) Italy

Castiglioni is a fine pianist. He studied composition with Boris Blacher and Giorgio Ghedini.

Inizio di movimento (SZ 1958). 8 p. 3 minutes.
The unusual compositional vocabulary in this work is a synthesis of the styles of Cage, Debussy, Messiaen and Webern.

Cangianti (SZ 1959). 31 p. 10 minutes.
Performance directions present. Pointillistic writing. Organization is difficult for ear to comprehend. Unusual sonorities. Title means "changes," and 3 rows are announced at the same time.

Quattro Canti per Pianoforte (SZ 1954).

RICARDO CASTILLO (1894-1967) Guatemala

Castillo left his native Guatemala when he was fourteen years old to study in Paris. He stayed there for ten years studying violin and theory. Most of the piano works have an impressionist quality.

L'eau qui court (Hamelle 1919). 3 minutes.

Poème Pastorale (Hamelle 1919). 12 minutes.

Berceuse (Hamelle 1919). 4 minutes.

Suite D (PAU 1938). 4 short movements, contrasting moods. Clear textures neatly handled. Biographical sketch included. M-D.

Huit Préludes (Henri Elkan 1950). Short, delicate. M-D.

ALEXIS DE CASTILLON (1838-1875) France

Castillon worked with Franck and was a gifted composer with high ideals.

Suite pour le piano Op. 5 (G. Hartmann).

Second Suite Op. 10 (Heugel).

8 Fugues dans le Style Libre Op. 2 (G. Hartmann). 28 p. Many moods in this set. Fine pianism required.

24 Pensées Fugitives (Heugel 1900). All published separately. An interesting collection of turn-of-the-century character pieces. See especially: No. 4 Carillon, No. 2 Toccata, and No. 15 Feux Follets.

JOSÉ MARÍA CASTRO (1892-1964) Argentina

Sonata de Primavera (Southern 1939). Serious. Allegro moderato: smooth, easy-going, rich sonorities; Andante: flowing eighths contrasted with dotted rhythms, bitonal atmospheric coda; Allegro: bright, toccata-like, alternating hands. D.

Ten Short Pieces (Barry c. 1955). Estudio, La fuente, Canción de cuña, Canción triste, Danza, Circo, Marcha fúnebre á la tristeza criolla, Vals de la calle, Moto perpetuo, Campanas. Contemporary techniques including plenty of dissonance. Int. Four of these are contained in the collection *Latin-American Art Music for the Piano* (GS).

Pequeña Marcha (Southern). Short, staccato, 2 voices, for children. Easy.

Vals Miniatura (Southern). Pungent dissonances, 2 voices, for children. Easy.

Sonata (Grupo Renovacion, 1931). On the quiet and flowing side. Allegro moderato; Arietta con Variazioni (6); Finale. Clear textures throughout. M-D.

JUAN JOSÉ CASTRO (1895-1968) Argentina

The three Castro brothers are highly respected musicians within, as well as without, their native Argentina.

Toccata (EAM 1940). Conventional harmonic idiom, approximate difficulty of Ravel or Prokofieff toccatas. D.

Casi Polka (EAM 1946). Grotesque, polytonal, for children. Int.

Corales Criollos No. 1 (Southern 1948). 17 p. Chorale and 8 variations. Colorful figuration, large span required. M-D.

Five Tangos (Southern 1941). 18 p. Tango rhythm exploited in 5 different moods. M-D.

Bear Dance (CF). Modal, vague tonality. Int.

Playful Lamb (CF). Legato staccato contrast, irregular phrasing. Int.

Sonatina Española (UE 1956). 29 p. 14 minutes. First movement uses 12-tone technique; second movement is sensitive and lyric while the concluding movement is built on Carl Maria von Weber's *Perpetual Motion* C in RH while LH continues with a spirited Scherzo F♯. Effective. D.

WASHINGTON CASTRO (1909-) Argentina

Castro studied composition in his own country and violoncello both in Argentina and in France. He is conductor of the Symphony Orchestra of the Province of Santa Fé, Argentina and is on the faculty of the School of Music of the Universidad del Litoral.

Four Pieces on Children's Themes (EAM 1942). M-D.
Juegos: Jugglers. Clever, brilliant, varied rhythms.
Haciendo Nonito: A lullaby, three against two.
Era un pajorita . . . : Facile technique required.
Rondo: Energetic, clarity needed.

Three Intermezzi (EAM 1947). Andante serio, Allegretto placido, Molto appassionato.
Interesting sonorities, well-developed ideas, contrasting moods. M-D.

Cinco Preludios (Ric Americana 1954). Andante grave, Allegro scherzando, Andante dramatico, Appassionato, Allegro giubiloso. 10 minutes. M-D.

NORMAN CAZDEN (1914-) USA

Sonatina Op. 7 (NME 1935). 3 movements requiring a large span. Dissonant and difficult.

6 Demonstrations Op. 6 (ACA).

8 Preludes Op. 11 (Bo&H 1937). Originally part of the series "Music for Study," intended as a comprehensive course of piano study. All are short and mainly in two voices. No. 6 is a "Sonatina." Sophisticated and clever.

5 American Dances Op. 14 (AMC 1941). "Moneymusic I 7 II", "Running Set", "Cowboy Song", "Society Blues." Clear textures and sounds. Written for the New Dance Group.

7 Compositions Op. 21 (ACA 1933-39).

6 Children's Pieces Op. 22. Nos. 1 and 2 only (Meridian 1939) 3-6 (ACA).

Variations Op. 26 (Mer 1940). Separate variations not clearly defined. Builds to climax and subsides. Pedal-point technique effectively used.

Passacaglia Op. 46 (AMC 1944).

Music for Study: 21 Evolutions for Piano Op. 4 (Arrow 1933-36). 21 short melodies intended to provide an elementary foundation for musical and pianistic study. Most are in two voices.

Sonata Op. 53/2 (LG 1950).

EMMANUEL CHABRIER (1841-1894) France

Chabrier, an amateur composer, wrote music that has a certain uninhibited quality and is easily accessible. All his compositions are vigorous, unpretentious, expressive and pianistic.

Pièces pittoresques (1880) (B. Webster-IMC) (Enoch). Paysage, Mélancolie, Tourbillon, Sous bois, Mauresque, Idylle, Dance villageoise, Improvisation, Menuet pompeux, Scherzo-valse. (EBM) has the Scherzo-valse separately, and (IMC) publishes Idyll separately.

Habanera (BMC) (IMC).

Bourée fantasque (1891) (EBM) (Enoch). Athletic pianism required. Brilliant.

España (1883) (Enoch). Originally a piano solo, this work is better known in the ballet arrangement. A *Waltz* from España (Schott) is available separately.

Impromptu C (Enoch) (1860). A glimpse of things to come, stylistically speaking.

Ronde Champêtre (Enoch). Spirited rustic piece. M-D.

Capriccio (Costallat).

Joyeuse Marche (1889-90) (Enoch).

JULIUS CHAJES (1910-) USA, born Poland

Chajes came to the United States in 1937.

6 Palestinian Melodies (Independent 1943). 11 p. 5½ minutes.

3 Mazurkas (Transcontinental 1955). 5 p.

Sonata d (Transcontinental 1959). 35 p. 15 minutes.
A three-movement work filled with parallelism, many metric changes and a variety of rhythms. A three-voice fugue is contained in the final movement. Not especially pianistic yet a brilliant-sounding work in the hands of an advanced pianist.

JACQUES CHAMPION DE CHAMBONNIÈRES (c. 1602-1672) France

Deux livres de clavecin (T. Dart-l'OL). Earliest printed sources and manuscripts were consulted. Contains 11 ordres (60 pieces), dedication, original preface and table of ornaments. Any variants from the manuscripts are shown above or below the staves.

Complete Keyboard Works (P. Brunold, A. Tessier-Senart).

Complete Keyboard Works (BB). Facsimile of 1670 Paris Edition. Uses soprano and baritone clefs.

Antologia di musica antica e moderna per il pianoforte (G. Tagliapietra-Ric 1931-2). Volume VII includes 6 suites.

Art of the Suite (Y. Pessl-EBM).

Le Trésor des Pianistes (A.&L. Farrenc-Leduc) Vol. II contains two books of keyboard pieces.

See: Robert Lee Neill, "Seventeenth-Century French Clavier Style as Found in the *Pièces de Clavecin* of Jacques Champion de Chambonnières," unpub. diss., University of Colorado, 1965.

A thorough study of all available information about Chambonnières which draws some conclusions that define his contribution to the development of keyboard music. It also contains an English translation of a four-section treatise concerning the life of Chambonnières by Henri Quittard, a noted French scholar.

CÉCILE CHAMINADE (1857-1944) France

(GS) has a good selection of pieces published separately including: Autumn Op. 35/2, Spinning-wheel Op. 35/3, The Fauns Op. 60, Scarf Dance. 2 volumes of *Selected Compositions* (GS) with a portrait and biographical sketch includes: Vol. I: Sérénade; Minuetto; Air de ballet; Pas des amphores; Callirhoe; Lolita; Scarf dance; Pièce romantique; Gavotte. Vol. II: Pierrette; La lisonjera; La morena; Les sylvans; Arabesque; Valse caprice; Dance pastorale; Arlequine.

Enoch publishes most of the other works including a *Sonata* Op. 21 (1895) that is Chaminade's finest attempt at serious writing.

Children's Album (Enoch c. 1934). Vol. I Op. 123: Twelve very easy pieces. Vol. II Op. 126: Twelve easy pieces. Some of her most appealing writing.

CLAUDE CHAMPAGNE (1891-1965) Canada

Champagne studied at the Paris Conservatoire for eight years and held important posts in several schools in Montreal.

Quadrilha Brasileira (BMI Canada 1942).
Based on a theme from Marajo Island—exciting rhythms, frequent use of sevenths.

Prélude et Filigrane Op. 5 (BMI Canada). 3 minutes.
2 short romantically-influenced miniatures.

Petit Canon (G. V. Thompson).

Petit Scherzo (G. V. Thompson).

THEODORE CHANLER (1902-1961) USA

A Child in The House (Mer). 11 charming and witty pieces, a contemporary *Scenes from Childhood.* Int.

Three Short Pieces (Arrow). Andante sciolto; Andante con moto; Allegramente. Short, lyric, expressive, tonal. M-D.

Toccata (Mer 1939). Two voices in perpetual motion (à la Paradisi *Toccata*). Square-dance mood, traditional style. M-D.

Pas de Trois (AMC). Originally for piano and two dancers, but the piano part alone is effective. Two contrasting, sophisticated movements. The second is more difficult. M-D.

JACQUES CHARPENTIER (1933-   ) France

72 Etudes Karnatiques (Leduc 1960). In twelve cycles. Strong oriental influence.

Toccata (Leduc 1961). 11 p.

Allegro de Concert (Leduc 1965). 9 p. 6½ minutes.

ERNEST CHAUSSON (1855-1899) France

Although he studied with Franck and Massenet, Chausson's style does show individuality. There is some refined and sensitive, if not always pianistic, writing in the two works listed.

Paysage Op. 38 (Lerolle 1895).

Quelques Danses Op. 26 (Lerolle 1896). 20 p.

1. Dédicace et Sarabande. Franckian influence.
2. Pavane.
3. Forlane. The last two are more individual.

CARLOS CHÁVEZ (1899-   ) Mexico

The style exhibited in the piano works of Chávez is characterized by lean biting dissonances, complex rhythms, motivic fragmentation, and concentrated forms. His music is steeped in the native Indian tunes of Mexico. It demands more than an initial hearing to be appreciated.

Sonata No. 2 Op. 21 (Bo&Bo 1920). Allegro doloroso; Andante; Molto inquieto. Large-scale work employing much bravura writing. 27 minutes.

Sonatina (Arrow 1924). Moderato; Andantino; Allegretto; Vivo; Lento. 5 minutes. Modal, dissonant, three and four voices. Requires fine tonal balance and careful attention to sonorities. M-D.

Sonata No. 3 (NME 1928). 13 minutes. Moderato; Un poco mosso; Lentamente; Claro y conciso. Changing meters, cross-rhythms, percussive, biting harmonies, mainly on white keys, open textures. D.

Seven Pieces for Piano (NME). Poligonos (1925) powerful, sonorous; Solo (1926) short, diatonic melody, dissonant counterpoint; 36 (1925) percussive, perpetual motion, bravura writing; Blues (1928) 2 voices, wide intervals, little blues syncopation; Fox (1928) syncopated, wide skips, percussive; Paisaje (1930) short, melodic; Unidad (1930) longest of the set, bravura writing, repeated notes, cross-rhythms, mature pianism required. Int. to D.

Ten Preludes (GS 1937). Modal, varied moods, some dissonance, cross-rhythms, highly usable. Int. to M-D.

Estudio (*Homenaje à Chopin*) (Southern 1949-50). Nocturne-like, flowing lines, dissonant, dramatic closing. M-D.

Invención (Bo&H 1960). A large-scale work in linear style, contrasted moods, various techniques, dramatic closing. D.

Sonata No. 6 (Belwin-Mills 1965). 28 minutes, three movements, "classical" style. First movement A♭; second movement, Andantino D♭; third movement, Theme and 12 Variations, theme is folklike. D.

LUIGI CHERUBINI (1760-1842) Italy

Sei Sonate per Cembalo (T. Alati-Carisch c. 1958). 6 sonatas in F, C, B♭, G, D, E♭. Composed around 1780, all are two-movement works and all second movements are rondos. The first movements have the most interest, generally speaking, and are in SA design. Classic style, Alberti bass, ornamented melodic lines, standard tonal treatment in formal structure. Int. to M-D.

THOMAS CHILCOT (? -1766) Great Britain

English organist and composer. Wrote two sets of harpsichord concerti and other works.

Two Suites for Harpsichord (Pennsylvania State University Press, c. 1969). A number of printing errors are present in this otherwise fine edition.
Suite I: Overture, Aria I, Siciliano, C, Jigge, M.
Suite II: Allemanda and Presto, Aria, Jigge, M.

FRÉDÉRIC CHOPIN (1810-1849) Poland

A thorough knowledge of the piano works of this great Polish-French genius is a "sine qua non" for all pianists and piano teachers. His remarkable and highly original writing have made a unique contribution to the literature of the piano.

EDITIONS:

No "ultimate" in editions of his works has yet appeared although the Chopin Institute edition, that began to appear in 1949 and is now complete, has brought us closer to this ideal, based, as it is, on the autographs and original editions, with critical commentary. I. Paderewski is listed as editor but most of the work has been followed through by Ludwik Bronarski and Josef Turczynski. Reproductions of portraits and manuscripts are also included. The main objection to this edition is the fact that clear distinction between editorial and composer indications is not always possible. The content and organization of this edition is as follows: Volume I. Preludes; II. Etudes; III. Ballades; IV. Impromptus; V. Scherzos; VI. Sonatas; VII. Nocturnes; VIII. Polonaises; IX. Waltzes; X. Mazurkas; XI. Fantasia, Berceuse, Barcarolle; XII. Rondos; XIII. Concert allegro, Variations; XIV. Concertos (two pianos); XV. Works for piano and orchestra (two pianos); XVI. Chamber Music; XVII, Songs; XVIII. Minor works: Bolero, Tarantelle, March Funèbre Op. 72/2 (two versions), Trois Ecossaises Op. 72/3; XIX. Concerto No. 1 (Orchestra score); XX. Concerto No. 2 (Orchestra score); XXI. Works for piano and orchestra (orchestra score), Variations on "La ci darem" Op. 2, Fantasia Op. 13, Krakowiak Op. 14, Andante Spianato and Grande Polonaise Brillante Op. 22. Another volume, *Selected Easy Pieces, An Introduction to Chopin* (including Preludes Op. 28/2, 4, 6-8, 15, 20; Mazurkas Op. 17/4, Op. 24/1, Op. 33/3, Op. 67/2; Polonaises g, B♭ Op. posth.; Nocturnes Op. 9/2, Op. 37/1, Op. 72/1; Waltzes Op. 34/2, Op. 64/1-2, Op. 69/1-2 is also available in this edition. (EBM) is the American agent for this edition. Facsimiles of the following are also available: Ballades A♭, f; Krakowiak-Grand Rondeau de Concert; 24 Preludes; Scherzo E; Fantasie f.

Other complete editions include: (Br&H) reprinted by (K) with an editorial board consisting of W. Bargiel, J. Brahms, A. Franchomme, F. Liszt, C. Reinecke, E. Rudorff. This is considered the first critical edition and was published in 14 volumes, 1878-1880. A Revisionsbericht in 3 parts and a Supplement in 3 parts came out in the period 1878-1902. Vol. 1. Ballades; 2. Etudes; 3. Mazurkas; 4. Nocturnes; 5. Polonaises; 6. Preludes; 7. Rondos and Scherzos; 8. Sonatas; 9. Waltzes; 10. Miscellaneous Works; 11. Trios and Duos; 12. Orchestral Works (Op. 2, 11, 13, 14, 21, 22); 13. Nachlass: 35 Pianofortewerke; 14. Lieder und Gesänge.

(Oxford University Press) edition edited by E. Ganche (1932). This edition is interesting and should be compared with other editions but a lack of authoritative scholarship and careless proofreading mar its effectiveness. Vol. 1. Preludes, Etudes, Valses, Nocturnes, Polonaises; Vol. 2. Ballades, Impromptus, Scherzos, Rondos, Fantasie, Berceuse, Barcarolle, Bolero, Tarantelle, Allegro de Concert, Variations, Marche Funèbre, Ecossaises, Sonatas; Vol. 3. Mazurkas, "La Ci Darem" variations, Fantasie, Krakowiak, Grande Polonaise, Concertos, Rondo (2 pianos). Available in separate volumes.

(Augener) edition edited by C. Klindworth and revised by X. Scharwenka. A careful edition but full of editorial interpretations. Vol. 1. Waltzes, Mazurkas, Polonaises, Nocturnes; Vol. 2. Ballades, Impromptus, Fantasie, Rondos, Scherzos, Etudes, Preludes; Vol. 3. Sonatas, Variations Brillantes, Bolero, Tarantelle, Allegro de Concert, Berceuse, Barcarolle, Marche Funèbre, Ecossaises and works for piano and orchestra. Available separately.

(CFP) edition edited by H. Scholtz (1949) is excellent for its fingering. Vol. 1. Waltzes, Mazurkas, Polonaises, Nocturnes; Vol. 2. Ballades, Impromptus, Scherzos, Fantasie, Etudes, Preludes, Rondos; Vol. 3. Sonatas, Berceuse, Barcarolle, Bolero, Tarantelle, Allegro de Concert, Variations Brillantes, Variations sur un Air Allemand, Marche Funèbre, Ecossaises and works for piano and orchestra. These are also available in 12 separate volumes.

Other editions worthy of consideration include: (Br&H) I. Friedman (1913), (Debussy-Durand), (Merrick-Nov); (Mikuli-GS) with historical and analytical comments by James Huneker, in 15 volumes. Some textual errors are present in Mikuli. (Henle) has outstanding editions of the Preludes, Etudes, Walzes and Nocturnes with editors H. Keller, E. Zimmermann and Hans-Martin Theopold. The etudes include, in addition to Op. 10 and 25, the 3 etudes without opus number, f, A♭, and D♭. At this writing (1970) a full Chopin catalog by the Polish Chopin authority, Krystyna Koblyanska and a complete edition of the piano works is in preparation at (Henle).

(Cortot-Sal) edition presents exercises to help solve problems and is a fine practical edition.

(R. Pugno UE) has available Waltzes, Mazurkas, Polonaises, Nocturnes, Ballades and Impromptus, Etudes and Preludes.

(Joseffy-GS) Ballades, Barcarolle, Berceuse, Variations on "La Ci Darem", Op. 2, Grande fantasie sur thèmes polonais, Krakowiak, Grand polonaise brillante preceded by Andante Spianato, Fantasie, Impromptus, Mazurkas, Nocturnes, Preludes, Rondos, Scherzi, Tarantelle, Waltzes.

(WH) has Etudes (H. Knudson), Mazurkas (Mikuli), Polonaises (H. Knudsen), Waltzes (Uxtext) and numerous single pieces.

Other editions of merit:

Preludes: (W. A. Palmer-Alfred). Includes also Op. 45 and the A♭ posthumous (1918) preludes. Scholarly introduction; based on the 1839 autograph; all editorial suggestions in lighter print.

(Casella Heugel); (Brugnoli, Montani-Ric), also separately No. 15 and 24; (Y. Bowen-British and Continental).

12 Etudes Op. 10 (1828-32), *12 Etudes* Op. 25 (1832-36) (Brugnoli, Montani-Ric) (Schmitz-CF) (Sternberg-CF); (Sauer-Schott) Op. 10/3, 12; (Brugnoli, Montani-Ric) Op. 10/3, 5, 12, Op. 25/1-2, 9, 11. PWM has a facsimile of Op. 10/12.

Nocturnes: (Casella-Heugel) (Pinter-CF) (Bowen-Br&H); (de-Pachmann-Augener) has Op. 27/1-2, 37/1, 55/1. Posthumous Nocturne c♯ (IMC) (Henle) (Mertke-K); c Posthumous (Werner-Elkin).

The following chart is offered to help clarify some of the confusion relating to the *Nocturnes*.

No.	Opus No.	Key	Brown Index*	Chronological Order	Date of Composition	Publication Date
1	9/1	b♭	54	3	1830-31	1833
2	9/2	E♭	54	4	1830-31	1833
3	9/3	B	54	5	1830-31	1833
4	15/1	F	55	6	1830-31	1833-34
5	15/2	F♯	55	7	1830-31	1833-34
6	15/3	g	79	8	1833	1833-34
7	27/1	c♯	91	9	1835	1836
8	27/2	D♭	96	10	1835	1836
9	32/1	B	106	11	1836-37	1837
10	32/2	A♭	106	12	1836-37	1837
11	37/1	g	119	14	1838	1840
12	37/2	G	127	15	1839	1840
13	48/1	c	142	16	1841	1841-42
14	48/2	f♯	142	17	1841	1841-42
15	55/1	f	152	18	1843	1844
16	55/2	E♭	152	19	1843	1844
17	62/1	B	161	20	1846	1846
18	62/2	E	161	21	1846	1846
19	72/1	e	19	1	1827	1855
20		c♯	49	2	1830	1875
21		c	108	13	1837	1938

*Maurice J. E. Brown, *Chopin: An Index of His Works in Chronological Order*. New York: St. Martin's Press, 1960.

4 Ballades: (Bowen-Br&H); (Sauer-Schott) 1-3; (Brugnoli, Montani-Ric) 1-4 and separately; (WH) 2, 4; (MacFarren-Ashdown) 4.

4 Scherzi: (Sauer-Schott) (Bowen-Br&H) 1, 2; (WH) 2; (Biehl-Bosworth) (Köhler-Litolff) (Brugnoli, Montani-Ric); and (Brugnoli, Montani-Ric) separately 1, 2.

3 Impromptus: (Brugnoli, Montani-Ric) (Biehl-Bosworth); (Sauer-Schott) (Dunhill-Lengnick) No. 1 A♭ Op. 29; Fantasie-Impromptu c♯ Op. 66 (Rubinstein-GS) is a manuscript edition from the collection of Artur Rubinstein. Contains a detailed preface by Rubinstein, a facsimile of the autograph, fingering and performance suggestions by Rubinstein. (Brugnoli, Montani-Ric) also publishes Op. 66 separately.

Polonaises: (Zimmerman-Henle) (Biehl-Bosworth) (Brugnoli, Montani-Ric) (Mertke-K); (Sauer-Schott) Op. 26/1, 40/1, 53; (Brugnoli, Montani-Ric) Op. 22, 40/2, 44; (Dob) Op. 40/1, 53; (WH) Op. 26/1, 40/1, 53. (de Pachmann-Augener) Op. 53.

Waltzes: (Casella-Heugel) (Bowen-Br&H) (Mertke-K) (Brugnoli, Montani-Ric) (ABRSM, annotated by Thomas Fielding) (CF). (Sauer-Schott) Op. 18, 34/1-2, 64/1-2, 69/1-2, 70/1-3, e Posthumous; (Brugnoli, Montani-Ric) Op. 34/3, 42, 64/3; (Reinecke-Br&H) (MacFarren-Ashdown) Op. 42; (Speidel-Cotta) Op. 64; (Samuel-Paxton) (Dunhill-Lengnick) Op. 64/1; also transcribed by L. Godowsky (CF) and (de Pachmann-Augener) Op. 34/1, 64/2.

Mazurkas: (Friedman-CF) (Köhler-Litolff) (Reinecke-Br&H) (Riss - Arbeau-Orphee); (Sauer-Schott) Op. 7/1-2; (Brugnoli, Montani-Ric) Op. 17/2, 24/1, 33/1, 67/4, 68/2.

Sonatas: (Sauer-Schott) Op. 4, 35, 58. (PWM) has a facsimile of the original autograph. (Brugnoli, Montani-Ric) all 3 and No. 2 Op. 35, separately. (G. Agosti-Curci), Op. 35. Agosti's edition contains analytical and interpretative notes in English, French and Italian.

See: Rudolf Klein, "Chopins Sonatentechnik," Osterreichische

Musikzeitschrift XXII/7, July 1967, 389-99. Presents an interesting theory that all three sonatas reveal thematic similarities between movements and within movements consciously created by Chopin.

SEPARATE WORKS:

Fantasie f Op. 49 (Brugnoli, Montani-Ric) (Sauer-Schott).

Barcarolle Op. 60 (Brugnoli, Montani-Ric) (Sauer-Schott) (K); Facsimile (PWM).

Berceuse Op. 57 (Brugnoli, Montani-Ric) (Sauer-Schott) (Halle-Forsyth) (Dunhill-Lengnick).

Bolero Op. 19 (Brugnoli-Ric) (K).

Rondos Op. 1, 5, 16 (Pugno-UE) (Biehl-Bosworth) (Scholtz-CFP) (K).

3 Ecossaises Op. 72 (Sauer-Schott) (GS) (WH); (Brugnoli, Montani-Ric) No. 3.

Souvenir de Paganini (Werner-Elkin).

Contradanse (1827) (Werner-Curwen).

Song and 2 Bourrées (A. Orga-Schott).

Two Forgotten Pieces (A. Koszewski-PWM). Waltz E♭, Posthumous (1840): 1 page, includes copy of autograph. Waltz a, Posthumous: 2 pages, includes copy of autograph.

The Last Mazurka (J. Ekier-PWM). Reconstructed from the autograph. Includes autograph sketch. 4 pages. Vintage Chopin.

Prelude A♭ (c. 1918) (Merrick-Nov) (Henn).

Valse a (Werner-Curwen).

Tarantella Op. 43 (Brugnoli, Montani-Ric).

COLLECTIONS:

Piano Pieces (Scholtz, Pozniak-CFP). Op. 12 *Variations brillantes* B♭ on "Je vends des scapulaires;" Op. 19 *Bolero;* Op. 43

Tarantelle; Op. 46 *Allegro de Concert;* Op. 57 *Berceuse;* Op. 60 *Barcarolle;* Op. 72/2 *Funeral March*, Op. 72/3-5 *3 Ecossaises;* Op. Posthumous *Variations on a German Air.*

Introduction to Chopin (A. Mirovitch-GS 1959) Two Volumes. Graded works ranging from the Prelude c, Op. 28/20 to the Ballade g, Op. 23. Main emphasis is geared to the "use of the pedal". Helpful prefatory remarks on each piece.

Chopin Album (Friedman-Br&H) Two volumes.

I. Ballade A♭; Berceuse; Etudes Op. 25/1, 7; Fantasie-Impromptu; Mazurkas Op. 24/3, 33/3-4, 7/1, 56/1; Nocturnes Op. 15/2, 32/1, 37/1, 27/2.

II. Polonaises A, c♯; Preludes D♭, A; Scherzo b; Funeral March from Op. 35; Waltzes Op. 34/2, 70/2, 42, 70/1, e Posthumous.

The Easiest Original Chopin Pieces for the Piano (Rowley-Hin). Preludes A, e, b, c, D♭; Mazurkas Op. 63/2, 68/3, 7/2; Nocturne Op. 15/3; Waltz a.

Chopin Album (Scholz-CFP) 32 Pieces.
Waltzes Op. 18, 34/1-2, 42, 64/1-2, e; Mazurkas Op. 7/1-2, 33/1, 3-4; Polonaises c♯, A; Etudes Op. 25/1, 7, 9; Scherzo b; Prelude D♭; Fantasie-Impromptu; Berceuse; Funeral March from Op. 35.

Chopin Album (Sauer-Schott) Two volumes.

I. Waltzes Op. 34/2, 64/1-2; Mazurkas Op. 7/1, 17/1, 24/3; Nocturnes Op. 9/2, 15/2, 31/1, 37/2; Polonaises c♯, A; Preludes e, b, A, D♭, c; Funeral March Op. 35; Impromptu A♭; Berceuse; Ballade g; Fantasie-Impromptu.

II. Waltzes Op. 18, 34/1, 69/1; Mazurkas Op. 7/2, 33/3-4; Nocturnes Op. 27/2, 37/1, 55/1; Etude Op. 10/5; Scherzo b; Ballade A♭; Ecossaises.

Chopin Pastels (H. Kreutzer-BMC 1962).
Eight original pieces including Mazurka B♭ (1832); Valse A♭ (Posthumous); Contredanse G (1827?) originally G♭; Contabile B♭ (1834); Album Leaf E (1843); Largo E♭. Admirable collection, clear editing with measure numbers.

Album 28 Original Piano Works (WH).
Preludes C, e, A, c, b, D♭; 3 Ecossaises; Mazurkas Op. 7/1, 67/3, 33/2; Polonaises A, c♯; Nocturnes Op. 9/2, 32/3, 15/2; Fantasie-Impromptu; Waltzes Op. 34/2, 64/1-2; Berceuse; Etudes Op. 25/1-2; 10/3, 12; Scherzo b; Ballade g.

13 Transcriptions of Chopin's Minute Waltz, Op. 64/1 (MTP).
Arrangements by Joseffy, Rosenthal, I. Philipp, Max Reger, Giuseppe Ferrata, Michael Zadora, M. Moszkowski, A. Michalowski, Joe Furst, Kaikhosru Shapurji Sorabji. Appendix contains information about the different manuscripts and first editions. Virtuoso transcriptions, lavish edition.

Pezzi sconosciuti (Montani-Ric 1959).
13 of these 15 unknown pieces are contained in the Paderewski edition distributed among 5 different volumes. Mazurka D, Waltz a, Souvenir de Paganini (a set of variations in the style of Paganini based on "Carnival of Venice" melody), Polonaises and other works. Aimed at the pianist in early to intermediate status. Clean edition with some new repertoire from this composer.

Antologia di 21 Pezzi (Brugnoli, Montani-Ric).
Contains mainly familiar works: Preludes Op. 28/4, 6-7, 15, 20, 22; Mazurkas Op. 33/1, 68/2-3, 7/1-2; Waltzes Op. 34/2, 64/1-2, 69/1-2; Nocturnes Op. 9/1-2; Fantasia Impromptu Op. 66; Polonaise 40/1; and the rarely-found Nocturne c♯ Op. Posthumous.

Chopin Collection (W. Newman-SB).
14 selected Mazurkas, Nocturnes, Preludes and Waltzes from among the easier pieces. Excellent edition; not an "urtext" as Newman explains but an "authentic" one. Fine preface with explanation of ornaments, pedaling, fingering and phrasing.

See: Gerald Abraham, *Chopin's Musical Style*. London: Oxford University Press, 1939. Reprint, Oxford, 1960.

Edward Blickstein, "The Lost Art of Chopin Interpretation", International Piano Library, 1, Fall-Winter 1967, 2-10.

Alfred Cortot, *In Search of Chopin*. New York: P. Nevill, 1951.

J. P. Dunn, *Ornamentation in the Works of Chopin.* London: Novello, 1921. Reprint, New York: Da Capo Press, 1970.

Thomas Higgins, "Chopin Interpretation: A Study of Directions in Selected Autographs and Other Sources," unpub. diss., University of Iowa, 1966.

Jan Holcman, "The Labyrinth of Chopin Ornamentation," JR, 5, Spring 1958, 23-41.

Frank Merrick, "Some Editions of Chopin," MT, 97, November 1956, 575-7.

Felix Salzer, "Chopin's Nocturne in C♯ Minor, Op. 27, No. 1," The Music Forum, 2, 1970, 283-297.

Bruce Simonds, "Chopin's Use of the Term 'Con Anima'," MTNA Proceedings, 1948, 151-57.

WEN-CHUNG CHOU (1923-   ) China, came to USA in 1946

His early works were based on Chinese traditional music and folk songs but his later works used these only as "point of departure." Characteristic of his style are delicate coloring and weaving of unique textures.

The Willows are New (CFP 1957). 7 p. 6 minutes.
A broad range of color and delicacy evokes the oriental spirit. The half step is greatly exploited. Thin textured lines are similar to the fine brush strokes of Chinese painting. Effective.

Yan Kuan (after Wang Wei) (ACA 1957).

DOMENICO CIMAROSA (1749-1801) Italy

32 Sonatas (Boghen-ESC 1925-26). Three volumes.
These one-movement works are thin-textured and homophonic. They employ scalar passages and broken-chord figurations in early classic style with an admixture of Domenico Scarlatti's temperament. A wealth of unusual and usable material is contained in these three volumes.

Same as above published by (B & VP). Vols. I and III edited by J. Ligteliyn and Vol. II edited by J. Ruperink.

JEREMIAH CLARKE (ca. 1673-1707) Great Britain

Contemporaries of Purcell (Fuller-Maitland-JWC) Volume V in this series.

Five suites: No. 1 G, No. 2 A, No. 3 b, No. 4 c and No. 5 D. (JWC) also publishes some single works.

See: Thomas F. Taylor, "The Life and Works of Jeremiah Clarke," unpub. diss., Northwestern University, 1967.

ALDO CLEMENTI (1925-) Italy

Clementi studied with Goffredo Petrassi and Bruno Maderna and has attended courses at Darmstadt. He works with serial technique in a free manner and has added innovations to this procedure.

Composizione No. 1 per Pianoforte (SZ 1957). Begins with an 18 note "row" and reduces it by one note on each repetition. D.

Intavolatura per Clavicembalo (SZ 1963). Built on 3 simultaneous rows, presented together.

MUZIO CLEMENTI (1752-1832) Italy

Newman ranks Clementi, along with Frescobaldi and Domenico Scarlotti, as one of the three greatest Italian innovators of the keyboard (SCE, 754). Clementi enjoyed a varied career as composer, pianist, music publisher, instrument builder, impressario, conductor and theorist. Composing sonatas for the piano occupied him over a fifty-six-year period (1765-1821) and yet no two authorities agree on the number of solo piano sonatas Clementi wrote. The complete edition, published by Breitkopf and Härtel between 1802 and 1819 contains 60, including the composition *La Chasse* (Vol. XI, No. 4) which is a sonata though not entitled as such. Other sonatas by Clementi were not included and some were included that were not by Clementi. *Groves Dictionary,* fifth edition, lists 68 sonatas. Newman states there are 79 (SCE, 739). He also gives a chart listing the original opus number and key, and in other columns the opus number used by *Grove* (or elsewhere) along with various other important information. Riccardo Allorto, in a recent work, gives one of the most thorough listings of the sonatas: *Le Sonate per pianoforte di Muzio Clementi, studio critico e catalogo tematico.* Florence: Olschki, 1959. Errors are contained in this study. James D. Kohn's dissertation *The Manuscript Piano Sonatas of Muzio Clementi at the Library of Congress: A Comparative Edition with Commentary,* University of Iowa, 1967, lists a table (pages 35-37) of all the known existing sonatas. Volume I of this dissertation contains commentary, and Volume II is an edition of five sonatas that Clementi later revised, based on holographs at the Library of Congress. The works are printed as they first appeared with the revised edition printed immediately beneath. This is a fascinating study of Op. 1a/1 F, 13/4 B♭, 13/5 F, 13/6 f and 2/2 C. Alan Walker Tyson has completed a *Thematic Catalogue of the Works of Muzio Clementi* (Tutzing: Hans Schneider, 1967). This provides a helpful guide to the identification and numbering of Clementi's compositions with essential information about textually significant editions. Autographs are more fully discussed in an appendix. Two other appendices describe the complete edition of Breitkopf and Härtel mentioned above, and the arrangements and adaptations made by Clementi of music by other composers.

EDITIONS OF THE SONATAS:

4 volumes (Ruthardt-CFP) containing 24 sonatas.
- Vol. I: Op. 2/1 C; 12/1 B♭; 26/2-3 f♯, D; 34/1 C; 36/1-2 A, F.
- Vol. II: Op. 36/3 C; 40/1-3 G, b, D; 47/2 B♭.
- Vol. III: Op. 12/4 E♭; 24/2 F; 25/2 G; 39/2-3 G, D; 50/3 g.
- Vol. IV: Op. 12/2 E♭; 7/3 g; 24/3 E♭; 25/1 C; 26/1 A; 39/1 C.

2 volumes (Cesi-Ric) containing 12 sonatas.
- Vol. I: Op. 25/2 G; 26/3 D; 34/1 C; 36/1 A; 39/2 G; 47/2 B♭.
- Vol. II: Op. 2/1 C; 12/4 E♭; 26/1 A; 26/2 f♯; 40/2 b, 40/3 d.

3 Volumes (Piccioli-Curci) containing 18 sonatas. This edition is not faithful to original text, but Piccioli does explain his editorial procedure in the preface.

Vol. I: Op. 25/2 G; 26/3 D; 34/1 C; 36/1 A; 39/2 G; 47/2 B♭.

Vol. II: Op. 2/1 C; 12/4 E♭; 26/1 f♯; 40/2-3 b, D.

Vol. III: Op. 7/3 g; 24/1-3 E♭, F, E♭; 35/1 F; 50/3 g.

2 volumes (GS) containing 12 sonatas. (K) publishes the same as Volume I.

Vol. I: Op. 2/1 C; 12/1 B♭; 26/2-3 f♯, D; 34/1 C; 36/1 A; 36/2 F.

Vol. II: Op. 33/3 C; 40/1-3 G, b, d; 41/2 B♭.

(Heugel) 8 sonatas.

Op. 10/3 B♭; 30/1 g; 33/3 A; 40/1-3 G, b, D; 50/1, 3 A, g.

Separate Sonatas:

2/1 C (WH); 7/3 g (K&S) (K); 9/3 E♭ (Schott); 10/3 B♭ (K&S); 12/4 E♭ (WH); 14/1 B♭ (K&S) (ECS); 20 E♭ (WH); 26/2 f♯ (Ric) (K); 26/3 D (Ric); 34/2 g (Schott); 29/1 C (K&S); 34/2 g (Schott); 36/3 (Cranz); 39/2 G in *Collected Piano Sonatas by Classical Composers* (Henle) Vol. I; 39/3 D in *Collected Piano Sonatas by Classical Composers* (Henle) Vol. II; 40/1 G (Cranz); 40/2 b (K&S); 40/3 d (Cranz); 47/2 b (Cranz) *Capriccio in forma di Sonata;* 47/2 C (Schott); 50/3 g "Didone abbandonata" (Henle) (Ric).

Sonatinas:

6 Sonatinas Op. 36 (Palmer-Alfred). Based on an 1803 edition published by Clementi's own publishing company. A table of ornaments from Clementi's *Introduction to the Art of Playing the Pianoforte* is also included. Careful scholarship but the 1803 edition was not the first edition of these works. This was published in 1797 by Longmans and Broderip. Other editions are available through (K) (GS) (CFP) (Br&H) (Ric) (WH) (Schott) (CF).

12 Sonatinas Op. 36, 37, 38. (K) (GS) (CFP) (Br&H) (Ric) (Durand) (Augener) (CF).

Gradus ad Parnassum (Ric) (Augener) Three volumes.

(Durand) (GS) (Ric) (Schott) (CFP) (WH) have selections from this collection.

This work, finished in 1817, is much more than a collection of exercises. It was Clementi's manifesto and contains some fine fugues and canons, sonata movements, an extended "Scena Patetica" and many other fascinating pieces. The *Gradus* is unique and covers almost every aspect of piano technique. Do not judge it by the 29 selections, from the original 100, edited by Carl Tausig about 1865. This edition does much injustice to the original work.

COLLECTIONS:

Clementi—Rediscovered Masterworks (Mirovitch-EBM) Three volumes.

Vol. I: Arietta; Allegretto; Rondo; Waltzes Op. 38/1-2; Montferrine (country dance of solo type) Nos. 2-3, 5-9.

Vol. II: Sonatas 7/3 g (1782); 26/2 f♯ (1788); Rondo 34/1 g (c. 1788). 7/3 has Adagio movement from 14/1 substituted. Original slow movement of 7/3 is contained in appendix.

Vol. III: Sonatas 22/3 C (1787); 5/3 E♭ (1780); 14/3 (1784).

Le Trésor des Pianistes: Vol. XVI: 3 Sonatas Op. 2; 2 Sonatas Op. 7; 3 Sonatas Op. 8; 4 Sonatas and a Toccata from Op. 9, 10, 14.

See: Sister Alice E. Tighe, "Muzio Clementi and His Sonatas Surviving as Solo Piano Works," unpub. diss., University of Michigan, 1964. Part II of this study is an analytical study of fifty-three of Clementi's sonatas which have survived as solo piano works.

A. DeWayne Wee, "The Fugues and Canons of Clementi's *Gradus ad Parnassum*," unpub. DM paper, Indiana University, 1968.

LOUIS-NICHOLAS CLÉRAMBAULT (1676-1749) France

Pièces de Clavecin (1704) (P. Brunold-l'OL 1938) Revised by Thurston Dart in 1964. 2 suites of 14 pieces. One of the suites is in c and contains a Prelude, A, C, S, and G.

HALFDAN CLEVE (1879-1951) Norway

All of his writing was in a postromantic idiom. Cleve knew the instrument well and wrote for it in a virtuoso way. Effective, sincere, if somewhat dated writing.

Sieben Klavierstücke Op. 1 (Br&H 1902).
Prelude, Impromptu, Scherzo, Dreaming, Impatience, Pastorale, Improvisation.

Drei Klavierstücke Op. 2 (Br&H).
Fantastic Pieces, Capriccio, Perpetuum Mobile.

Vier Klavierstücke Op. 4 (Br&H).
Ballad, Norwegian Fantastic Piece, Etude, Waltz.

Etude für Pianoforte Op. 5 (Br&H 1904). 11 p. Dedicated to Busoni.

Fünf Klavierstücke Op. 7 (Br&H).
Storm, Elegy, Romance, Legende, Scherzo.

Ballade für Pianoforte e♭ Op. 8 (Br&H 1905). 18 p.

Scherzo Op. 23/2 (NMO).

2 Piano Pieces Op. 24/2 (NMO).
Preludium, Nocturne.

4 Piano Pieces Op. 25 (NMO).
Preludium, Vaarstemming, Mazurka, Valse.

MANUEL RODRIGUES COELHO (ca. 1583-ca. 1625 or after) Portugal

Flores de Musica pera o Instrumento de Tecla & Harpa (A Musical Garland for Keyboard Instruments and Harp) *Portugaliae Musica,* Series A, Volumes I and II (M. S. Kastner-Fundacão Calouste Gulbenkian c. 1959, 1961).

Vol. I contains the tentos and Susanas grosadas and 4 elaborations of di Lasso's famous 'Susanne un jour'.
Vol. II contains the versos. In addition there is a preface, in Portuguese and English, facsimiles, editorial notes, etc. Coelho's book was first published in Lisbon (1620) by the Flemish printer Craesbeeck. In all probability it was the first book of keyboard music published in Portugal, comparable to the English *Parthenia.*
This work is a fine contribution to our understanding of 16th and 17th-century keyboard music.

4 Susanas (Kastner-Schott). These are secular variations.

5 Tentos from *Flores de Musica* (Kastner-Schott).

See: Santiago Kastner, "Parallels and Discrepancies between English and Spanish Keyboard Music of the 16th- and 17th-Centuries," Annuario Musical, 7, 1952, 77-115.

RUY COELHO (1891-   ) Portugal

Coelho has written in many forms but is best known for his operas and ballets.

6 Promenades Enfantines (Leduc). 3 books.
Descriptive pieces of visits to different places near Paris. No. 3 is bitonal, while the rest are MC.

Sonatina (Senart). 10 minutes. Impressionist, effective writing.
Allegro
Expressivo
Allegro vivo

Suite Portuguesa No. 1 (Sassetti).
Dança Portuguesa
Fado
Chula

SAMUEL COLERIDGE-TAYLOR (1875-1912) Great Britain

A British composer of African descent, Coleridge-Taylor was trained at the Royal Academy of Music as a violinist. The folk element is predominant in his writing and many of his works were very popular during the first part of this century. (Augener) publishes many of his keyboard works.

Valse de la Reine (Willis).
Graceful salon writing.

African Suite Op. 35 (Augener). Four movements.

18 Negro Melodies Op. 59 (Rogers). 3 volumes.

YANNIS CONSTANTINIDIS (1913-) Greece

Greek Miniatures (Rongwen 1957). 3 volumes.
Varied moods, eastern flavor, folk-song element present. Easy to M-D. An interesting rhythmic vocabulary.

ARNOLD COOKE (1906-) Great Britain

Cooke studied at Cambridge University and with Hindemith in Berlin. He is presently teaching at Trinity College in London.

Suite C (OUP 1943). 10 p.
Capriccio
Sarabande
Finale: Allegro con spiritoso.
Neoclassic style with fresh sonorities.

Scherzo (Nov).

PAUL COOPER (1926-) USA

Composer-in-Residence and Professor of Composition and Theory of the College-Conservatory of the University of Cincinnati.

Partimento (JWC 1967). 10 minutes.
Changing meters, sections are to be freely improvised, harmonies exploited by use of silent clusters. Significant, difficult writing.

Cycles (JWC 1969). 12 minutes. Commissioned by the Kansas Music Teachers Association.
12 short pieces that exploit clusters, free rhythmic interpretation, strings dampened by LH, aleatoric writing, unusual notation, fascinating sonorities. Advanced pianism required. Numerous footnotes provided.

DAVID COPE (1941-) USA

Cope received his musical training at Arizona State University and the University of Southern California. He founded Composers' Autograph Publications and is a member of the theory-composition faculty of the Cleveland Institute of Music.

Sonata No. 1 (CAP 1969). 9½ minutes.
3 movements, no titles. Changing meters, good octave technique required, full chords.

Sonata No. 2 (CAP 1969). 3 movements.

Sonata No. 3 (CAP 1969). 3 movements.

Sonata No. 4 (CAP 1969). 9 minutes. 3 movements.

Three 2-Part Inventions (CAP 1969). 4 p.

Iceberg Meadow for unprepared piano (CAP 1969). 8½ minutes.
For partially prepared piano, strings struck and stroked within the instrument.

All these works show a keen ear for sonorities, and require mature pianism.

See: David Cope, *New Directions in Music*. Dubuque: W. C. Brown Co., 1971.

AARON COPLAND (1900-) USA

Copland's contribution to piano literature has not been large but nevertheless important. His style has gradually and naturally evolved from the early French-inspired *Scherzo Humoristique* to the twelve-tone *Piano Fantasy*. Copland has not forgotten the young piano student and has contributed solid works for this age group.

Scherzo Humoristique (The Cat and the Mouse) (Durand 1920).
Descriptive pianistic frolic.

Passacaglia (Senart 1922). 8-bar theme, varied treatment, big climax, exciting. In the French tradition. M-D.

Variations (Bo&H 1930). Theme, 20 variations, coda. Severe dissonantal treatment in a tentative serial style. A landmark in American repertoire. D.

2 Children's Pieces (CF 1936). *Sunday Afternoon Music* and *The Young Pioneers.*

Sonata (Bo&H 1939-41).
Molto moderato: freely developed SA, exploits interval of third.
Vivace: spasmodic, irregular meters.
Andante sostenuto: folk-like theme over pedal point. Quiet closing. D.

4 Piano Blues (Bo&H c. 1948). M-D pieces in jazz idiom. Freely Poetic (1947), Soft and Languid (1943), Muted and Sensuous (1948), With Bounce (1926).

Piano Fantasy (Bo&H 1955-57). Free serial technique.
A strong ten-note idea dominates much of this work. His most extended work for piano, massive, large-scale. D.

Down a Country Lane (Bo&H). Expressive pastorale style. Int.

4 Dance Episodes from Rodeo (Bo&H). Arranged by Copland. Buckaroo Holiday, Corral Nocturne, Ranch House Party, Saturday Night Waltz, Hoe-Down. Complex rhythms. M-D.

See: Arthur Berger, "Aaron Copland's Piano Fantasy," JR, 5, Winter, 1957-58, 13-27.

John Kirkpatrick, "Aaron Copland's Piano Sonata," MM, 19, May-June 1942, 246-50.

ROQUE CORDERO (1917-) Panama

Cordero was Director and professor at the National Music Institute of Panama for a number of years before coming to the United States. He served as Associate Director of the Latin American Music Center at Indiana University for some time.

Sonatina Ritmica (PIC). 16 p.
An exciting, short three-movement work. Written while Cordero was studying with Ernst Krenek in 1943. Tonal but moments of tonal ambiguity add to its interest. Influences of

Panamanian dances are felt in rhythmic treatment, 12-tone experimentation in occasional short passages.

First movement exhibits a furious intensity, changing meters and percussive effects.

Hands are crossed throughout the second movement with the RH singing the melody in the bass.

Third movement is driving and fits the hand well. Brilliant, effective writing.

Sonata Breve (PIC).

Short, connecting three movements. Exciting introduction, more relaxed first movement, flexible second movement, dramatic concluding movement exploiting the complete keyboard. Dissonant contemporary style, effective. D.

ANGELO CORRADINI (1914-) Italy

Corradini writes in an accessible neoclassic style.

5 Pezzi Brevi (Ric 1960). 11 p. Preludio, Studio sugli accordi, Toccatina, Recitativo, Danza.

5 separate works in impressionist style. Effective separately or as a group. Very pianistic. M-D.

Preludio e Toccata (Ric 1964). M-D.

A romantic Preludio that is coupled with a Toccata, repeated single notes and chords, slow mid-section, returns to opening idea, slow FF closing.

Suite (Ric 1967). 13 p. Preludio, Danza, Spiritual, Toccata: ostinato.

Excellent recital material. The Toccata has three contrasting moods that all fit well together. M-D.

9 Improvisazioni (Ric 1970). Short character pieces, varied moods, impressionist. M-D.

MICHEL CORRETTE (1709-1795) France

Organist at the Jesuit College in Paris (1738) and later to the Duc d'Angoulême, Corrette wrote masses, motets, instrumental pieces and several methods, including *Le Maître de Clavecin* (1753) (BB) Facsimile edition.

BENJAMIN COSYN (early 17th century) Great Britain

Cosyn was a "famous composer of lessons for the harpsichord, and probably an excellent performer on that instrument, . . . there are many of his lessons extant that seem in no respect inferior to those of Bull" (John Hawkins, *A General History of the Science and Practice of Music.* New ed., London: Novello, 1875, II, 522).

25 Pieces for Keyed Instruments from Benjamin Cosyn's Virginal Book (Fuller-Maitland, B. Squire-JWC). Works by Bull, Byrd, Gibbons as well as Cosyn and others. This work contains 98 pieces in all and dates from ca. 1600-10.

8 Dances from Benjamin Cosyn's Second Virginal Book (F. Cameron-Schott). Delightful, appealing music.

JEAN COULTHARD (1908-) Canada

Coulthard received her musical training at the Royal Conservatory in Toronto and at the Royal College of Music in London with Ralph Vaughan Williams. Her later studies were under Arthur Benjamin and Bernard Wagenaar.

Aegean Sketches (BMI Canada).
3 fine impressionist pieces. The Valley of the Butterflies: interesting figuration. Wine Dark Sea: a singing barcarolle with colorful use of the trill. Legend (The Palace of Knossos): resonant chords move to large climax. Large span required.

4 Etudes (BMI Canada 1945). Published separately.
Well written and not overly difficult. See especially No. 3 Toccata.

3 Preludes (BMI Canada). Published separately.
1. Leggiero 2. Torment 3. Quest. Short character pieces with well defined ideas.

Sonata (BMI Canada 1948).
A fine printed photostat of the manuscript. 3 movements FSF, of well-organized and contrasted ideas. Some ninths, carefully marked scores, tonally oriented although no key signatures present.

Requiem Piece for Piano (CMC 1968).

4 Piano Pieces (BMI Canada). Int.

White Caps (BMI Canada). Toccata-like, MC, small hands could manage it well, much variety in its five pages. Int.

FRANÇOIS COUPERIN (1668-1733) France

27 Ordres (suites), over 220 pieces, comprise the four books of *Pièces de Clavecin.* These pieces show Couperin as a most original and versatile composer. A gesture toward almost every emotion is seen in these works. Untold pleasures by this supreme master lie on every page. Couperin was very careful to notate precisely what he intended. He was always concerned that players would not perform his music as he wished. His treatise, *L'Art de toucher le Clavecin* is indispensible to a better understanding of his style. A table of ornaments is also contained in this treatise.

Complete Works (P. Brunold-l'OL 1932) 12 volumes. A beautiful library edition.

Vol. I contains *L'Art de toucher le Clavecin* and Vols. II-V the *Pièces de Clavecin.* A Tercentenary Edition (1969) of this complete edition is being brought out with Thurston Dart as the editor. The 1932 edition has been checked and corrected from original copies of Couperin's harpsichord works.

Pièces de Clavecin (Brahms, Chrysander-Augener). 4 volumes. I. (1713) Ordres 1-5. II. (1717) Ordres 6-12. III (1722) Ordres 13-19. IV. (1730) Ordres 20-27. Fine edition.

Pièces de Clavecin (L. Diemer-Durand). 4 volumes. Added dynamics and realized ornaments.

Pièces de Clavecin (K. Gilbert-Heugel). 4 volumes. Editor's notes in French, German and English.

Pièces de Clavecin (BB). A facsimile of the 1713, -17, -22, -30 editions.

Les Clavecinistes Français (L. Diémer-Durand) Vol. III. Contains 4 ordres.

Pièces de Clavecin (Bouvet-ESC). 2 volumes.

Pièces de Clavecin (K). 2 volumes containing ordres I and IV in Vol. I and Ordres V and VI in Vol. II.

The Music of Couperin (JWC). Keyboard, vocal, organ and instrumental music.

The Graded Couperin (M. Motchane-F. Colombo). 29 selected short pieces graded from easiest to more difficult. Also lists a summary of Couperin's rules of interpretation.

L'Art de toucher le Clavecin (Br&H 1933). Original French with German and English translations in parallel columns. A more recent translation by Dorothy Packard is available in the April 1968 *Clavier,* Vol. 7, pp. 20-25. Eight Preludes and an Allemande illustrating this important treatise are published by (JWC), overly edited by J. A. Fuller-Maitland.

Pièces de clavecin (J. Gat-EMB 1969). Vol. I: contains the first five Ordres in a fine, clean edition. Editorial additions easily identified, table of ornaments and realization included, measure numbers included. Vol. II: Ordres 6-12.

Selected Pieces (PWM). Varied selection from the Ordres. Includes Couperin's original ornaments together with detailed instructions for their execution. Fingering also included.

Selected Harpsichord Music (S. Marlowe-GS). Scholarly-performance oriented edition. A thorough introduction covers the areas of Couperin's keyboard instruments, Rondeau form, ornamentation and signs, tempo, rhythmic alterations, glossary of tempo markings and comments on the pieces. An appendix suggests ways to vary the ornamentation of the rondeau sections slightly. Contains 41 pieces from the 4 Books of Harpsichord Pieces. Beautiful edition.

See: Thurston Dart, "On Couperin's Harpsichord Music," MT, 110, June 1969, 590-4.

Winfrid Mellers, "Couperin on The Harpsichord," MT, 109, November 1968, 1010.
François Couperin and the French Classical Tradition. London: Dobson, 1950. Reprint, New York: Dover, 1966. "The Clavecin Works of François Couperin," ML, 7, 1946, 233-48.

LOUIS COUPERIN (ca. 1626-1661) France

Uncle of François, Louis wrote unbarred preludes, numerous dance movements, passacailles, chaconnes, a fantasie and a tombeau, all contained in the Brunold edition listed below.

Complete Keyboard Works (P. Brunold-l'OL).

Pièces de Clavecin (P. Brunold, T. Dart-l'OL 1959). Same as the above with added ornaments by Thurston Dart.

Pièces de Clavecin (Bouvet-ESC). Two Volumes.

Pièces de Clavecin (Alan Curtis-Heugel). Based on a recently discovered manuscript which brings to light not only new pieces, but also specific works known up till now in a different form. One hundred pieces, arranged in fifteen suites by editor. Preface in French, English and German, table of ornaments.

HENRY COWELL (1897-1965) USA

Henry Cowell is, as William Schuman states, "a founding father of 20th-century American music." (BMI Brochure) Cowell's music covers an enormous range, both in technique and expression. He has tended to disregard musical "trends" and fashions and has gone his own way. Cowell's clusters are well-known to most pianists today and his technique of manipulating the strings directly has become standard fare with many contemporary composers. Most of the piano music has as its basis folk materials, either American or Celtic. Cowell recorded 20 of his works written between 1911 and 1930 on Folkways disc FG 3349.

Piano Works (AMP). 9 pieces, written over a forty-year span, include a wide range of techniques and expressions. 5 of the pieces use clusters. Playing instructions, and a note on the music and its composer, are written by Oliver Daniel. The Tides of Manaunaun, Exultation, The Banshee, The Aeolian Harp, Fabric, Episode, 2-Part Invention, Tiger, Advertisement. Int. to M-D.

Dynamic Motion (AMP). Short and wide clusters, vigorous rhythmic treatment. M-D.

Amerind Suite (SP). Based on American Indian music. Int. to M-D.

Set of Four (AMP 1960). For harpsichord.

The Harp of Life (AMP). Forearm clusters both arms, triadic harmonization, harmonic effects, large climax. M-D.

Hilarious Curtain Opener and Ritournelle (NME, Oct. 1945). Taken from incidental music for a Jean Cocteau play. The Ritournelle is an example of elastic form, a kind of prescribed "aleatory" music where the length can be varied by omitting certain portions. M-D.

The Snows of Fuji-Yama (AMP 1927). Atmospheric, built on pentatonic scale. Int.

The Irishman Dances (CF 1936). Easy.

The Irish Minstrel Sings (CF 1936). Easy.

Two Woofs (NME, Oct. 1947). Short, bitonal writing. M-D.

Sway Dance (TP). Easy.

Bounce Dance (Merion). Easy.

Six Ings (AMP c. 1950). Composed early in Cowell's career, these pieces all need a well-developed pianism. Bitonal, dissonant. M-D.

Anger Dance (AMP). Int.

The Lilt of the Reel (AMP). Int.

Sinister Resonance (AMP). M-D.

What's This (AMP). M-D.

See: Carol Jennifer Henry, "The Piano Music of Henry Cowell," unpub. thesis, Indiana University, 1967.

JOHANN BAPTIST CRAMER (1771-1858) Germany

A pupil of Clementi, Cramer had a successful career touring as a virtuoso. Beethoven met Cramer in a competition and was quoted by Ries as saying that "Cramer was the only pianist of his time.

'All the rest count for nothing.'" (Harold Schonberg, *The Great Pianists*. New York: Simon & Schuster, 1963), p. 60. Cramer was one of the first pianists to feature works by other composers on his recitals. His own compositions are characterized by solid musical taste.

La Parodie Sonate Op. 43 (Schott c. 1913). Two movements. The first movement is strongest.

Les Menus Plaisirs (K&S). Divertimento in two movements: Allegro con brio serves as an introduction, then follows Rondo: Allegretto moderato. Facile writing. 15 p.

Sonata G Op. 11/3 (Ric).

Scherzo E♭ (Curwen).

Mazurka alla Rondo (Ric).

Sans Fracas: Notturno Op. 109 (Ric).

Cramer-Beethoven Studies (Shedlock-Augener). An edition of 21 of the Cramer etudes with annotations of Beethoven made by Anton Schindler. Newman suggests these etudes were perhaps to be used in Beethoven's projected "Klavierschule" (SCE, 517). The New York Public Library has a copy of this Shedlock edition of 1893.

60 Selected Studies (Bülow-UE) (Ric). 4 volumes published as one.

84 Studies (Schott Frères) 4 volumes. (Moszkowski-Heugel) in 2 volumes.

63 Studies from Op. 100 (Augener).

50 and 84 Studies from Op. 100 (GS). 2 volumes.

See: J. B. Brocklehurst, "The Studies of J. B. Cramer and his Predecessors," ML, 39, July 1958, 256-61.

PAUL CRESTON (1906-   ) USA

Five Dances Op. 1 (SP) (1932). Varied, tonal, MC, well-defined ideas. No. 5 (Tarantella) is longest and most attractive of the set. Int. to M-D.

Seven Theses Op. 3 (Templeton 1933). Complex contrapuntal pieces with changing meters, thick textures. D.

Five Dances Op. 7 (Templeton). Varied moods and techniques. Int. to M-D.

Sonata Op. 9 (Templeton 1936). 4 movements, dissonant, lively rhythmic usage, pianistic, strong closing. D.

Five 2-Part Inventions Op. 14 (GS 1937). Contrapuntal, dissonant, moderate length. M-D.

Prelude and Dance Op. 29/1 (Mer c. 1942). Moderate length and M-D.

Prelude and Dance Op. 29/2 (Templeton). Moderate length and M-D. Prelude: meditative; Dance: with passion.

Five Little Dances Op. 24 (GS 1940). Short, varied moods, attractive. Int.

Six Preludes Op. 38 (MCA). Various metric and rhythmic problems. Facility required. M-D.

Metamorphoses (Belwin-Mills). 20 pieces based on a fertile tone-row. Large design requiring mature pianism. D.

Narratives No. 1, 2 and 3 (Belwin-Mills).

Rumba Tarantella (Belwin-Mills 1964). Int.

Pony Rondo (Belwin-Mills 1964). Tonal, chromatic, clever rhythmic treatment. Int.

Virtuoso Technique (GS).

Rhythmicon (F. Colombo). "A practical dictionary of rhythms, its main purpose is to present a clear concept of meters and rhythms through explanatory notes, practice drills and short pieces leading to mastery of execution." Four volumes, elementary to lower intermediate (composer's grading).

BAINBRIDGE CRIST (1883-1969) USA

Crist received his training at George Washington University. Since 1927 he lived at Cape Cod, teaching and composing.

Fantasie D (OUP).

Chinese Sketches (CF 1927).

Nocturne (CF 1925).

WILLIAM CROFT (1678-1727) Great Britain

His suite movements are in French style, especially the ornamentation.

Contemporaries of Purcell (Fuller-Maitland-JWC). Two volumes, III and IV in this series. Six suites in each volume. Most of the suites contain 3 and 4 movements. Suite No. 1 c has an A, S, C, and Aire. Suite No. 3 c has a Ground, A and C. Suite No. 7 has only a Ground and Minuet.

GEORGE CRUMB (1929-) USA

Crumb studied with Ross Lee Finney at the University of Michigan. Since 1965 he has been teaching at the University of Pennsylvania.

5 Piano Pieces (CFP c. 1973).
Plucked strings, harmonics, stopped strings, fascinating sonorities. D.

IVO CRUZ (1901-) Portugal, born Brazil

Cruz studied in Lisbon and Munich, working in Musicology as well as applied music. In 1938 he became director of the Lisbon Conservatory and has been a guiding light in the musical activity of that city.

Hommages (Sassetti c. 1958).

1. *A Strauss:* to Richard Strauss. Reminiscences of *Til Eulenspiegel, Rosenkavalier* permeate this graceful piece. M-D.
2. *A Manuel de Falla.* Guitar-like effects interspersed with melodic writing. Big chordal climax, much use of trill, ends PP.

3. *A Oscar da Silva.* Takes as its inspiration "Coquetterie" from da Silva's *Images,* Op. 6. Bravura writing, glissandi, brilliant closing section.

Aguarelas (Sassetti). Water Colors, 4 pieces.

1. Dancam Moiras Encantadas (c. 1947). 5 p. Dance rhythms, changing meters, big climax, ends PP. Arpeggi, seconds and big chords exploited.
2. Caem Miosotis (c. 1949). 8 p. Syncopation, mid-section uses a chordal melody over arpeggi bass. PPP ending.
3. Canto de Luar (c. 1947). 4 p. Easiest of the group. Accompanied melody.
4. Palacio em Ruinas (c. 1949). 8 p. Best in the set. Octaves, full range of keyboard used. A rubato Andantino grazioso section provides contrast with outer sections. Virtuoso writing.

CÉSAR CUI (1855-1918) Russia

Least typically Russian of the group of Five, Cui wrote a number of piano works mainly in salon style.

Three pieces (MCA). Moderato-Andante-Moderato.

Four Spanish Marionettes (Nov).

A Argenteau Op. 40 (Bessel). 9 pièces caracteristiques.

2 Bluettes Op. 29 (Bessel).

2 Impromptus Op. 30 (Nov). A, D.

2 Mazurkas Op. 70 (Jurgenson). A♭, A.

3 Mazurkas Op. 79 (Jurgenson). A, b, C.

12 Miniatures Op. 20 (Nov).

6 Miniatures Op. 39 (Bessel).

4 Morceaux Op. 22 (Bessel).

5 Morceaux Op. 83 (Jurgenson).

5 Morceaux Op. 95 (Belaieff).

3 Mouvements de Danse Op. 94 (Belaieff).

Polonaise F Op. 30/1 (Nov).

24 Preludes Op. 64 (Jurgenson).

Theme and Variations Op. 61 (Jurgenson).

3 Waltzes Op. 31 (Bessel). A, e, E; No. 2 (Augener).

Dix-huit miniatures (Leduc).

5 Pieces Op. 52 (Bosworth).

Album of Piano Works by Cesar Cui (B. Tours-Nov).
Op. 20/1-12, Op. 21/3-4, Op. 22/1-4, Op. 30/1, Op. 31/2, Op. 35/1-2, Op. 39/1-6, Op. 40/2, 4.
All small pieces, miniatures, two movements from a suite, Polonaise, Waltz, Impromptus, etc.

RICHARD CUMMING (1928-   ) USA, born Shanghai, China

Cumming came to the USA in 1941. His composition study was with Ernest Bloch, Roger Sessions and Arnold Schönberg.

Sonata (JWC 1951). 30 p. 18 minutes. 4 movements. Dedicated to Rudolf Firkusny.
Allegro deciso; Scherzo: perpetual motion; Andante: modal, harmonic treatment of a 12-tone row; Passacaglia: Allegro molto moderato. Passacaglia motive serves as the backbone for complete sonata. 15 variations, closes with same idea sonata opened. Strong thematic usage, utilizes entire keyboard. M-D to D.

ARTHUR CUSTER (1923-   ) USA

Custer is a graduate of the Universities of Connecticut, Redlands and Iowa. His composition teachers were Paul Pisk, Philip Bezanson and Nadia Boulanger. Custer's music is largely serially oriented.

4 Etudes (Pioneer Editions 1964). 8 minutes. For Ruth Slenczynska.

1. Deliberately, but Freely: blurred quality desired, many seconds. A mid-section asks for a melody to be improvised using only pitches within indicated compass, accompanied by clusters. Plucked strings used at conclusion. Some half-pedaling indicated.
2. Scherzoso: large skips, FFF, trill in L.H. over 5 bars and more seconds. Vigorous writing.
3. Grave: interesting trill and arpeggio study.
4. Spiritoso: syncopated, motoric and percussive.

4 Ideas (Gen). Clusters, aleatory usage, but basically neoromantic. Contrasted works. M-D.

Rhapsodicality Brown (Gen). Popular styles, jazz, improvisation. M-D.

CARL CZERNY (1791-1857) Austria

Czerny's greatest contribution to music may have been through his training of such students as Liszt and Leschetizky. He was a prolific composer and wrote approximately 1,000 printed compositions, some with 50 or more parts. His scholastic studies of Op. 299, 300, 335, 355, 399, 400, and 500 published under the title *Complete Theoretical and Practical Pianoforte School* are the best in this category.

Variations on a theme by Rode Op. 33 "La Ricordanza" (IMC). 5 variations, 3 with florid figuration.

Valses di Bravura Op. 35 (UE) in Album *Viennese Masters for Piano Solo*. M-D.

Sonate d'étude Op. 268 (CFP No. 3239). Technical problems of every sort, flamboyant dexterity required.

6 Easy Sonatinas Op. 163 (Cranz).

Toccata Op. 92 (CFP) (GS). Right hand double-note figuration.

Capriccio (Arno Volk Verlag) see *Anthology of Music* volume on *Improvisation,* 155-57; Op. 200.

SCHOLASTIC STUDIES:

The School of Velocity Op. 299 (Vogrich-GS) (UE) (CFP) (Ric). 40 studies.

Czerny at Its Best (Podolsky-Belwin-Mills). A selection of 19 studies from Op. 299.

School for the Left Hand Op. 399 (Buonamici-Ric) (CFP).

The Art of Finger Dexterity Op. 740 (Buonamici-Ric) (Artia).

Czerny at Its Best (Podolsky-Belwin-Mills). A selection of 19 studies from Op. 740.

100 Recreations (Rauch-UE).

First Beginning—100 Easy Pieces (Rauch-UE).

Op. 777, 24 Studies (Artia).

Op. 821, 160 Exercises (Artia).

Op. 849 Etudes de Mecanisme (Artia).

D

FRANCOIS DAGINCOURT (1684-1758) France

Dagincourt studied with Le Bègue in Paris and later became a disciple of François Couperin. Couperin exerted a great influence on him evidenced by all the works in the following fine edition.

Pièces de clavecin (H. Ferguson-Heugel). 43 short pieces, highly ornamented.

INGOLF DAHL (1912-1970) USA, born Germany, came to USA in 1935

Sonata Seria (TP 1955). Weighty material, ideas convincingly handled, free dissonant counterpoint. D.

First, Second, Third March (TP). Published separately. Interesting form. *Third March* has an indefinite tonal center. M-D.

Fanfares. See Anthologies and Collections, U.S.A., *New Music for the Piano* (LG).

LUIGI DALLAPICCOLA (1904-   ) Italy

Dallapiccola was trained at the Cherubini Conservatory in Florence, Italy. He joined the faculty of that school in 1934 and has also taught since then at Queens College in New York and at Tanglewood.

Sonatina Canonica on Paganini Caprices (SZ). 9½ minutes. Four movements in a "tour de force" of contemporary canonic writing. Highly effective work. M-D to D.

Quaderno Musicale Di Annalibera (SZ 1953). 14 minutes. Eleven pieces based on a lyrically conceived row. The intervallic structure of the row permits the interlacing of impressionistic sounds with free or strict contrapuntal devices. One of the finest serial works for piano.

See: Ann P. Basart, "The Twelve-Tone Compositions of Luigi Dallapiccola," unpub. thesis, University of California, 1960.

Hans Nathan, "The Twelve-Tone Compositions of Luigi Dallapiccola," MQ, 44, July 1958, 289-310.

JEAN-MICHEL DAMASE (1928-) France

Sonata Op. 24 (Sal 1943). 28 p.

Passacaille pour Clavecin (EMT 1958).
Large span required. Tonal, effective handling of Passacaglia idea. M-D.

Intermezzo Op. 44 (EMT 1959). Toccata-like. Many fourths in fast sixteenth-note patterns. Big climax then quiet close. Advanced pianism required.

JEAN FRANÇOIS DANDRIEU (1682-1738) France

Music for Harpsichord (J. White-Br). Contains three suites: Nos. 1 and 4 from the *Pièces de Clavecin* of 1728, and No. 6 from Dandrieu's last volume of 1734.

Les Clavecinistes Français (L. Diémer-Durand) Vol. II. Over-edited.

RAM DA-OZ (1929-) Israel, born Germany

Da-Oz studied composition with Hajos in Haifa and also studied at the Rubin Academy of Music in Tel Aviv.

Capriccio (IMI).
Large-scale bravura piece written in an eclectic style. Stormy, with relief offered by middle-section slow variations. D.

Prologue, Variations and Epilogue (IMI 1966).
Prize winner in the Israel Music Institute's competition for a

piano piece in 1966. Large-scale work demanding musicianship and bravura. Both Prologue and Epilogue are variations on the theme of the middle movement. D.

LOUIS CLAUDE DAQUIN (1694-1772) France

Pièces de Clavecin (1735) (P. Brunold-Senart). These are also available in (BB) *Monuments of Music,* First Series.

See: Kathleen Dale, "The Keyboard Music of Daquin," MMR, August 1946.

ALEXANDER SERGEYEVICH DARGOMIZHSKY (1813-1869) Russia

Collected piano works (M. Pekeleese-USSR 1954). Almost all are in the salon style of the period and contain such titles as: Valse mélancholique, Cosaque, Variations sur l'air russe "People all blame me", Le rêve de la Esmeralda, Nouvelles mazurkas, Polka, Scherzo, Song without words, etc.

VOLFGANGS DARZINS (1906-) Latvia, now living in USA

The music of Darzins is unique and difficult to describe. Influences of Eastern and Western Europe are present as well as a special evocative, imaginative character. He writes well for the piano. The music is worth investigating.

Sonata No. 1 F (Dow). 16 p. Allegro agitato; Comodo; Allegro con spirito.

Sonata No. 2 (Dow 1955). 21 p. 13 minutes. Lento molto — Calmo; Intermezzo; Finale.

Sonatina G (Dow).

Triade de Preludes (Dow 1957). 13 p.

Trittico Barbaro (Dow 1958). 19 p.

Suite No. 7 (Dow 1961). 7 p. Con moto; Andante; Allegro risoluto.

Suite No. 8 (Dow 1961). 7 p. Published with *Suite* No. 7. Preludes: Prelude, Interlude, Postlude.

Latvian Folksongs (A. Kalnajs).
Two volumes bound as one. Accessible, appealing, fresh sounds. Range from easy to M-D.

GYULA DAVID (1913-) Hungary

Gyula was a pupil of Kodály and is presently Professor at the Budapest Academy of Music.

Szonata Zongorara (EMB 1957).
The dimensions of this sonata are more like a sonatina. Influence of Ravel shows in the melodic spontaneity. Expert craft and expressiveness are apparent throughout.

PETER MAXWELL DAVIES (1934-) Great Britain

5 Pieces for Piano Op. 2 (Schott 1955-56).
The influence of Webern is seen in both texture and technique while the musical character and quality show more Schönbergian influence. Nos. 1 and 4 are the easiest. Communicative works.

5 Little Pieces (Bo&H 1960-64).
Stylistically these pieces are close to Webern but they do recall Schönberg Op. 19 *Little Pieces*. Sparse textures but diverting. Plenty of vitality in these serially conceived works. Nos. 1 and 2 cover one page while Nos. 3, 4 and 5 cover two pages together.

See: Robert Henderson, "Peter Maxwell Davies," MT, 102, October 1961, 624-26.

EMIL DEBUSMAN (1921-) USA

Sonata No. 1 Op. 17 (AME 1958). 16 p.
A short three-movement work. The first movement is no more difficult than Clementi Sonatinas. Second and third movements require larger span, up to 11ths. Idiomatic and a very exciting final movement. Good RH octave technique and a crisp touch are required.

CLAUDE DEBUSSY (1862-1918) France

Claude Debussy, a seminal figure in 20th-century music, developed a keyboard style characterized by parallel chordal treatment, layers of refined sound, unresolved harmonies, unusual pedal effects, free modulatory procedures and full exploitation of the piano's resources. (Durand and Co.) and (Fromont) were the original publishers of Debussy's piano music but other publishers are now available. These editions should be compared with (Durand) for possible mistakes. A helpful corrective in this area is the article by Arthur B. Wenk, "Checklist of Errors in Debussy's Piano Music," PQ, 68, Summer 1969, 18-21. (GS) contains English translations of Debussy's indications. (CFP) has English titles but retains the French directions. (IMC) (K) and (UE) in cooperation with (B&VP) have a number of works available.

EARLY WORKS:

Danse bohémienne (Schott). Syncopated, mid-section more melodic and in parallel major.

Arabesque E (GS) (CFP) (IMC) (Bo&H) all published with *Arabesque* G. Legato triplets in RH plus flowing melodic lines.

Arabesque G (GS) (CFP) (IMC) (Bo&H). Persistent figuration, staccato touch.

Nocturne D♭ (1890) (Philipp-ESC), (CF) in collection *Modern Piano Music of Debussy and Ravel.* A B A design.

Rêverie (1890) (Jobert) (GS) (CF). Melody requires a cantabile legato.

Danse (Tarantelle Styrienne) (1890) (Jobert) (K). Contrasted meters of 3/4 and 6/8, interesting voice leading. One of Debussy's most brilliant early works.

Valse Romantique (1890) (Jobert). Experimental, influence of Chopin.

Ballade (1890) (Jobert) (B&VP). Chromatic, experimental, repetitious melody.

Mazurka f♯ (1890) (Jobert) (B&VP). Reflects influence of Madame Mauté de Fleurville, Debussy's piano teacher who was a pupil of Chopin.

Suite Bergamasque (1890) (Jobert) (CFP) (GS) (IMC) (EBM) (SP). A dance suite built on the heritage of the clavecinistes.
Prélude: brilliant, bravura-like, glissandi, whole-tone scales
Menuet: contrast of phrasing, staccato chords.
Clair de lune: (Jobert) (IMC) (GS) (K) (CFP). Flowing melodic passage work, legato thirds.
Passepied: busy non-legato accompaniment, modal, constant motion.

TRANSITIONAL WORKS:

Suite pour le piano (1901) (Jobert) (GS) (IMS) (K) (B&VP). A well-balanced work.
Prélude (Jobert): brilliant, bravura-like, glissandi, whole-tone scales and harmonies, stunning cadenza.
Sarabande: parallel solemn chordal treatment, sensitive rhythmic control needed.
Toccata: neoclassic, perpetual motion, exacting throughout.

D'un cahier d'esquisses (From a Sketchbook) (1903) (JWC) (Schott-Brussels). Sketch for *La Mer,* not intended as a piece. Mixture of styles.

Masques (1904) (K). Similar to vivacious treatment of material in *Danse,* but longer.

L'Isle joyeuse (1904) (K) (IMC) (B&VP). Orchestrally conceived, great animation, unrelenting rhythmic drive, dazzling coda, complex SA design.

MATURE WORKS:

Estampes (1903) (IMC) (B&VP) (K). Title refers to images printed from engraved copper or wood plates. (Durand) has published each movement separately.
Pagodes: pentatonic scale, atmospheric pedal effects, light clear touch.
Soirée dans Grenade: one of Debussy's three "Spanish" pieces for piano. Fast, soft staccato chords require great control.

A habanera rhythm permeates the whole piece. Five short ideas are used, punctuated by guitar-like interruptions.

Jardins sous la pluie (GS) (CFP): fast sixteenth-note figuration, stamina required to maintain excitement, broad tonal and dynamic range, simultaneous multiple melodic levels.

Images (1905) (IMC) (B&VP) (K). Underlying these pieces is the technique of free variation.

(Durand) has each movement separately.

Reflets dans l'eau (GS) (CF): careful timing required, delicate touch and sweeping figuration, demands complete facility.

Hommage à Rameau: noble lyric expressive quality reminiscent of the *Suite Bergamasque* and the Sarabande from *Pour le Piano*. Steady rhythm necessary.

Mouvement: vigorous ceaseless motion in triplet-sixteenth notes.

Images (1907). This set is generally more difficult than the 1905 set and comes off better in a small hall. Three staves are used to more clearly indicate layers of sound.

Cloches à travers les feuilles: transparent textures, chime effects, whole tone usage, atmospheric sonorities.

Et la lune descend sur le temple qui fut: sensitive pedal technique required.

Poissons d'or: fast delicate pianissimo passages are the most demanding. (Durand) has these three movements separately.

Children's Corner (1908) (CFP) (Paxton). Composed for Debussy's daughter, Chouchou, when she was five years old. Similar inspiration produced Schumann's *Kinderscenen* and Fauré's *Dolly Suite*. Each movement is available from (Durand).

Doctor Gradus ad Parnassum (CFP): characterization of a youngster's technical practice session. Fast harmonic rhythm requires clear chordal outlines.

Jimbo's Lullaby: limited dynamic range, varied touches and proper relation of the two tempi are necessary.

Serenade for the Doll: follow carefully Debussy's pedal indications. Legato and staccato contrast.

The Snow is Dancing: the most difficult of the set. Subtle,

delicate atmospheric painting. Distinguish between dots and dashes over notes.

The Little Shepherd: quiet, expressive, simple.

Golliwog's Cake Walk (CFP) (B&VP): a jazzy conclusion spiced with syncopated harmony, accents, dynamic contrasts, and a short, witty reference to Wagner's prelude to *Tristan und Isolde*.

Hommage à Haydn (1909). Originally written for a collection published by the Sociéte Internationale de Musique in honor of the centenary of Haydn's death. 6 pieces were contributed by Debussy, Dukas, Hahn, d'Indy, Ravel and Widor. Debussy's piece is built on a distillation of letters in Haydn's name, BADDG. This motif undergoes many transformations.

La plus que Lente (1910). This charming waltz needs a subtle rubato carefully indicated by Debussy.

Préludes — Book I (1910) (CFP).

Each of the 24 musical paintings in Books I and II has its own unifying mood or character, closely relating the musical materials to the poetic intent suggested by the titles.

Danseuses de Delphes (Delphic Dancers): simultaneous lines must be characterized individually. Steady, flowing rhythm.

Voiles (Sails): careful legato for whole-tone double thirds and sensitive tonal balance is required.

Le vent dans la plaine (Wind in the Plain): a six-note pianissimo figure needs firm technical command.

Les sons et les parfums tournent dans l'air du soir (Sounds and Scents Mingle in the Evening Air): imaginative tonal balance is a requisite. Not technically difficult.

Les collines d'Anacapri (The Hills of Anacapri): brilliant writing that leans considerably on a tarantella rhythm. Some folklike material employed in a brightly colored palette.

Des pas sur la neige (Footsteps in the Snow): a simple yet expressive and sustained legato is required throughout.

Ce qu'a vu le vent d'Ouest (What the West Wind Saw): technically, this is the most demanding work in Book I. Sonorous chords, broken octaves, fast tremolos and alternating passage work create strenuous problems.

La fille aux cheveux de lin (The Girl with Flaxen Hair): requires careful legato and flexible phrasing.

La sérénade interrompue (The Interrupted Serenade): calls for a light staccato in a guitar-like character plus sudden dynamic contrasts.

La Cathédral engloutie (The Submerged Cathedral): needs precise pedaling, tempo continuity, wide tonal range.

La danse de Puck (Puck's Dance): capricious rhythms, delicate touch, rather difficult.

Minstrels: Debussy asks for the interpretation to be "nerveux et avec humour."
Contrasting moods and a precise clarity make this music-hall piece one of the most attractive.

Préludes — Book II (1913) (CFP).

Brouillards (Mists): atmospheric figuration accompanies a vague melodic line. Exquisite control required.

Feuilles mortes (Dead Leaves): new use is made of the theme from *Les sons et les parfums.* Sustained legato at opening and not too fast. Even tonal balance needed in chords.

La Puerta del Vino (Gateway of the Alhambra Palace): marked "in the motion of a habanera." Observe dynamics carefully. Broad spectrum of tone.

Les fées sont d'exquises danseuses (The Fairies are Exquisite Dancers): delicate touch, great clarity desired. Use una corda pedal at the beginning.

Bruyères (Heaths): easier than most of the preludes, a flexible and smooth legato are necessary.

General Lavine—Eccentric: sharp rhythms, contrasting dynamic extremes. In same vein as *Minstrels.*

La terrasse des audiences du clair de lune (The Terrace for Moonlight Audiences): a phrase from "Au Claire de la Lune" forms the main motive of this imaginative work. Subtle mood changes must be underlined.

Ondine: expressive, scherzo-like changes of mood. D.

Hommage à S. Pickwick, Esq., P.P.M.P.C.: grotesque caricature of two main ideas. Quotes a part of the British national anthem and alludes to Sam Weller's whistling.

Canope: atmospheric, somber, technically easy.

Tierces alternées (Alternating Thirds): rapid alternation of hands, one more static than the other. Make contrasts with dynamic, not tempo. Foreshadows the later Etudes.

Feux d'artifice (Fireworks): notice the "moderately animated" tempo indication. A reference to "La Marseillaise" brings this festive piece to conclusion. Most difficult piece in both books.

See: Irwin Freundlich, "Random Thoughts on the Preludes of Claude Debussy," Otto Deri Memorial Issue, Current Musicology, 13, 1972.

12 Etudes (1915) (B&VP).

These last piano works deal with the most varied technical and musical problems. Contrasting moods vary from the most tender to the most ferocious. Debussy gives the performer many interpretative directions, verbally as well as graphically. He himself said concerning these pieces: "I must confess that I am glad to have successfully completed a work which, I may say without vanity will occupy a special place of its own. Apart from the question of technique, these 'Etudes' will be a useful warning to pianists not to take up the musical profession unless they have remarkable hands." (Léon Vallas, *Claude Debussy: His Life and Works*. Translated by Maire and Grace O'Brien. London: Oxford University Press, 1933, p. 259).

pour les "cinq doigts" d'après Monsieur Czerny (5-Finger Exercise): a take-off on Czerny's style. A five-finger exercise is transformed into a gigue. Differing scales are juxtaposed. Mainly on white keys.

pour les Tierces (Study in Thirds): problems of double thirds. Complements the prelude *Les tierces alternées*. Frequent modulation, wide dynamic range, basically moderato and lyric.

pour les Quartes (Study in Fourths): double fourths, sharp mood contrasts, calls for a flexible legato.

pour les Sixtes (Study in Sixths): very different from Chopin's treatment of this interval (Op. 25/8). Sostenuto pedal necessary for pedal points.

pour les Octaves (Study in Octaves): this brilliant piece employs effective syncopation, chromatic and whole-tone usage.

pour les huit doigts (Study for Eight Fingers): Debussy suggests this piece be played without thumbs, but careful use of the thumb can facilitate the performance. Rapid scale figuration, flexible meters and subtle phrasing are present in abundance.

pour les Degrés chromatiques (Study in Chromatic Steps): a chromatic perpetual motion with a diatonic melody. Chromatic scales in thirds.

pour les Agréments (Study in Ornaments): barcarolle-like with many embellishments in the melody. A great variety of note values are contained in this piece. See that their proper relationships are maintained.

pour les Notes répétées (Study in Repeated Notes): this virtuoso toccata recalls the earlier piece *Masques*. Restrained use of the pedal is essential for clarity.

pour les Sonorités opposées (Study in Opposed Sonorities): exploits contrasts of touches, dynamics, accents, etc.

pour les Arpèges composés (For Composite Arpeggios): delicate arpeggi study based on Lisztian technique. Musical pianism at its best.

pour les Accords (For Chords): a taxing piece that requires a well-developed topographical sense. Vigorous rhythmic activity. Serves as a fine conclusion to the set.

COLLECTIONS:

Album de six morceaux choisis (Durand). Arabesque E, En bateau (Petite suite), Menuet, Serenade for the Doll, La Fille aux cheveux de lin, La plus que lente.

Selected Works (GS).

Modern Piano Music of Debussy and Ravel (CF). D'un Cahier d'Esquisses, Nocturne, Rêverie, Dance and 4 works by Ravel.

Album (K). Clair de lune, Arabesques E, g, Soirée en Grenade, Jardins sous la pluie, Reflets dans l'eau, Prélude (*Pour le piano*), L'isle joyeuse, Danse.

Album of Claude Debussy Masterpieces (EBM).
Clair de lune, Ballade, D'un cahier d'esquisses, Fêtes (*Three Nocturnes*), Marionettes, Mazurka, Nuages (*Three Nocturnes*), Prélude (*Afternoon of a Faun*), Rêverie.

See: Alfred Cortot, *French Piano Music.* London: Oxford University Press, 1932.
Studies in Musical Interpretation. New York: Harrap, 1937.

Maurice Dumesnil, "Debussy's Influence on Piano Writing and Playing," MTNA Proceedings, 1945, 39-42.

Guido Maria Gatti, "The Piano Music of Claude Debussy," MQ, 7, 1921, 418-60.

Virginia Raad, "Musical Quotations in Claude Debussy," AMT, 18, January 1968, 22-23, 34.

Charles Rosen, "When Ravel Ends and Debussy Begins," HF, 9/5, May 1959, 42-4, 117-21.

E. Robert Schmitz, "Piano Music of Debussy and Ravel," MTNA Proceedings, 1949, 231-35.
The Piano Works of Claude Debussy. New York: Duell, Sloan and Pearce, 1950. Reprint, New York: Dover, 1966.

Dieter Schnebel, "Brouillards—Tendencies in Debussy," Die Reihe 6 (1964), 33-9.

Herbert D. Seldin, "An Analytical Study of the Debussy *Preludes* for piano," unpub. diss., Columbia University, 1965.

Arthur B. Wenk, "Checklist of Errors in Debussy's Piano Music," PQ, 68, 1969, 18-21.

ABEL DECAUX (1869-1941) France

Decaux was organist at the Basilique du Sacré-Coeur in Paris from 1903. He taught at the Eastman School of Music for several years.

Four Clairs de Lune (L. Philippo).
1. Minuit Passée (1901).

2. La Ruelle (1903).
3. Le Cimetière (1903).
4. La Mer (1907).

No. 4 is the least venturesome but the most pianistic. "These represent the earliest examples of serial composition." (Norman Demuth, *French Piano Music*. London: Museum Press, 1959, 63).

HELMUT DEGEN (1911-) Germany

Degen has written in many forms. He became a professor at the Hochschulinstitut für Musik in Trossingen in 1954.

3 Sonatinen (Süddeutscher Musikverlag 1944).
All are three-movement works and provide excellent teaching material. They would be a good introduction to easy contemporary sounds. Written in a contrapuntal and neoclassic style.

Sonate No. 1 (Br&H 1942-47). 3 movements. 15 p.

Sonate No. 2 (Br&H 1945). 3 movements. 20 p.

Sonate No. 3 (Br&H 1944). 3 movements. 27 p.

Sonate No. 4 (Br&H 1945). 3 movements. 27 p.

Kleine Klavierstücke für Kinder (Süddeutscher Musikverlag). Delightful pedagogic material.

Suite (Süddeutscher Musikverlag 1936-38). Hindemith influence.

Spielmusik für Klavier (Süddeutscher Musikverlag 1940-41).

30 Konzertetüden (Schott 1948). 3 books.

Capriccio scherzando (Schott). Not easy.

TON DE KRUYF (1937-) The Netherlands

De Kruyf has used serial techniques in his writing since 1958.

Sgrafitti per Pianoforte (Donemus 1960).
Free use of the row is made so more or less than 12 tones may be used. The title of the work comes from the Italian meaning to steal, or pilfer. Hence the relationship to the row usage. D.

MAURICE DELA (1919-) Canada

Dela received his musical education at the Montreal Conservatory. Later he studied composition with Claude Champagne.

La Vieille Capitale (BMI Canada 1953). Three romantic paintings.
Prélude
Chanson
Divertissment

Deux Impromptus (BMI Canada 1956). Romantic, chromatic harmony.
I. Moderato e molto espressivo
II. Allegro

REINBERT DE LEEUW (1938-) The Netherlands

De Leeuw studied composition with Kees van Baaren. He teaches theory and composition at the Royal Conservatory in the Hague.

Music for Piano I (Donemus 1964). 12 structures, free in order except that the player must begin with I and end with XII. Spatial notation, aleatory, unusual sonorities. D.

Music for Piano II (Donemus 1966). Score is a graphic reproduction of the movements to be made on the keyboard, in and under the piano. Explanation of symbols, objects required to realize piece. D.

TON DE LEEUW (1926-) The Netherlands

De Leeuw worked with Henk Badings, Olivier Messiaen and Thomas de Hartmann. Many contemporary techniques are exhibited in his writing.

Men Go Their Ways (Donemus 1964). 14 minutes.
Five interpretations of the Japanese haiku. Traditional and proportional notation used. Constantly changing permutations of the original rhythmic ideas characterize this work. Detailed instructions describe the proportional notation.

Drie Afrikaanse etudes (Donemus 1954). 7 minutes. Highly rhythmic.

Sonatine (Donemus 1949). 7 minutes.

FREDERICK DELIUS (1862-1934) Great Britain

3 Preludes (OUP).
Impressionistic, lyrical, and colorful patterns in symmetrical phrasing. Much use of arpeggi.

5 Piano Pieces (Bo&H).
Mazurka and Waltz for a Little Girl, Waltz, Waltz, Lullaby for a Modern Baby, Toccata.

Dance for Harpsichord (Bo&H 1922).

AZZOLINO BERNARDINO DELLA CIAJA (1671-1755) Italy

Experimenter in technical features unusual for his time; large skips, elaborate ornamentation, false relations and dissonantal treatment.

Six Sonatas Op. 4 (1727). Three of these are available. (Buonamici-Bratti c. 1912).
Each sonata includes a toccata, a canzone, and two short loosely connected sections called "tempi". Unusual style in the toccatas.

Sonata G (B. Bartók-CF). A transcription by Bartók of one of the above sonatas. Consists of a toccata, canzone, primo tempo, secondo tempo. A quiet ending is preceded by a perpetual motion. Also an edition by Buonamici for Edizioni R. Maurri of Florence.

Three Sonatas (Bratti & Co.) contain some unusual stylistic features.

Toccata. In *Antichi Maestri Italiani* (Boghen-Ric).

NORMAN DELLO JOIO (1913-) USA

Paul Hindemith, jazz, the dance, and Roman Catholic liturgical chant have been the major influences in the development of Dello Joio's style. It emphasizes strong melodic usage, a vigorous rhythmic practice and great communicative power. None of the piano works are overly demanding yet some movements call for a much-above-average technique and fine musical equipment. For a more thorough discussion of the piano works see M. Hinson's article

"The Solo Piano Music of Norman Dello Joio," AMT, 19, January 1970, 34, 48.

Prelude: To a Young Musician (GS 1944). Sensitive melodic line over flexible accompaniment.

Prelude: To a Young Dancer (GS 1945). Works to large climax then ends PP. M-D.

Suite (GS 1940). 4 movements. 11 p. Int. except for a more difficult last movement.

Nocturne E (CF 1946). 4-part writing, contrasting mid-section with melodic emphasis.

Nocturne f♯ (CF 1946). Calm opening, more exuberant mid-section, large span required.

On Stage (GS 1946). Suite arranged by composer from ballet of same name. Much rhythmic emphasis.

Sonata No. 1 (Hargail 1943). Three movements: Chorale Prelude; Canon; Capriccio. Final movement (with double notes and fast octaves) presents most problems.

Sonata No. 2 (GS) 1943). Three movements: Presto martellato; Adagio; Vivace spiritoso. Each movement has a big climax and requires fast octaves and chords. More difficult than No. 1.

Sonata No. 3 (CF 1948). Four movements: 5 variations and coda on a Gregorian chant; Presto e leggiero is a short scherzo with jazz influence; Adagio extends the mood of the opening theme in melodic fashion; Allegro vivo e ritmico is full of compelling rhythms, and melodic invention. M-D.

Capriccio (EBM 1969). "On the interval of a second." 12 p. Written for the Third Van Cliburn International Piano Competition, 1969. A virtuoso show-piece that exploits the interval of a second both harmonically and melodically. D.

Suite for the Young (EBM). 10 pedagogy pieces.

Lyric Pieces for the Young (EBM 1971). 6 pieces. Int.

See: Edward Downes, "The Music of Norman Dello Joio," MQ, 48, April 1962, 149-72.

CLAUDE DELVINCOURT (1888-1954) France

After World War II Delvincourt was Director of the Paris Conservatoire. He was a very versatile and individual composer.

Boccacerie (Leduc 1926). 37 p. Five pieces.
Each piece is dedicated to a different pianist. No. 5 (Buffalmacco), one of the most accessible, is dedicated to Beveridge Webster. Varying moods, long, neoclassic, full of rhythmic accentuations.

Croquembouches (Leduc 1931). 33 p. Twelve pieces.
Each piece is published separately. Traditional and MC harmonic language.

Heures juveniles (Leduc 1931). 29 p. Twelve pieces.

Cinq Pièces pour le Piano (Leduc 1926). 25 p.
Prélude
Danse pour rire
Tempo di Minuetto
Berceuse
Danse hollandaise
Mildly impressionistic. Contains some glittering pianistic writing.

SUZANNE DEMARQUEZ (1899-) France

Demarquez's compositions "are remarkable for their distinctive, crisp and somewhat acidulated charm." GD, 2, 663.

Deuxième Sonatine (Sal 1960). 20 p.
Romantico
Intermezzo (effective ostinato use).
Toccata
Similar in difficulty to Ravel *Sonatine* but individual in style.

LUIS DE PABLO (1930-) Spain

De Pablo has written in a serial style from his earliest works.

Sonata para Piano Op. 3 (UME 1960). Considered to be the first serial work written in Spain. Thin textures, silence used effectively, original rhythmic treatment, closely akin to late Webern in style.

Libro para le Pianista Op. 11 (Tonas Verlag 1964).
Partially serial, partially aleatory. De Pablo intends adding to this three-sectioned work.

AUGUSTE DESCARRIES (1896-) Canada

Toccata (BMI Canada 1953).
Chromatic, ninths, numerous skips. Material is well developed. D.

R. NATHANIEL DETT (1882-1943) USA

Eight Bible Vignettes (Belwin-Mills). Descriptive, romantic style, program notes. M-D.

In the Bottoms (SB). Suite containing the popular *Juba Dance*. Int.

ANTON DIABELLI (1781-1858) Austria

11 Sonatinas (CFP) (Ric) (Heugel).
Op. 151 G, C, F, C.
Op. 168 F, G, C, B♭, D, G, a.

Variations on a theme of Diabelli (W. Newman-SB). 16 variations by as many composers, all contemporaries of Diabelli, including Schubert, Liszt, etc. 50 were originally asked for and were supplied! Originally published in 1824, all 50!

DAVID DIAMOND (1915-) USA

A romantic element, vitality and a personal lyric quality, are present in Diamond's writing. He teaches at Manhattan School of Music in New York City.

Sonatina (Mer 1947). 3 short movements. Largo assai; Allegretto; Allegro vivace.

8 Piano Pieces (GS). Illustrates familiar nursery rhymes. Easy.

The Tomb of Melville (MCA 1949). Extended development, intense, sonorous.

Sonata (Southern 1947). 66 p. 3 movements. 30 minutes. Advanced pianism required throughout. Constant modulation and meter changes. Near end of first movement a fugue appears, then a vigorous coda. The last movement is interrupted by a double fugue and proceeds to an exciting coda.

Then and Now (Southern 1962). 11 sophisticated pieces for the young pianist, preferably one who has had some experience with contemporary sounds.

A Private World (Southern). 13 pieces for young pianists.

Alone at the Piano (Southern). Book 1: 11 pieces. Book 2: 10 pieces. Book 3: 13 pieces. These 3 books are all subtitled "Pieces for Beginners" but the material ranges from elementary to Int. and all are very contemporary sounding.

Gambit (Southern 1967). Dedicated to Rudolf Serkin. Changing meters and tempi, broad climax in low register, quiet atmospheric ending. M-D.

HILDA DIANDA (1925-   ) Argentina

Dianda studied in her native country as well as in Europe. Composition teachers included Hermann Scherchen and Gian Francesco Malipiero.

Tres Sonatas (Ric 1956).

Armonica 2 p. Melodica 2 p. Ritmica 4 p.

Each is short, in the same vein as the Scarlatti Sonata. Large span required, big octave technique necessary, some rhythmic problems.

MARCEL DICK (1898-   ) USA, born Hungary

A member of the Schönberg circle, at present living in Cleveland and teaching at the Cleveland Institute of Music.

Suite (CAP 1959). 29 p.

7 movements, neoclassic style containing numerous pianistic

problems, not the least being full, quick-changing chords in different registers.

EDWARD DIEMENTE (1923-) USA

Clavier Sonata (Greenwood Press 1966). 14 p.
An attractive, short, three-movement work employing imitation and clear tonal centers, in neoclassic style.

Sarcasms (AMC 1947).
Short, bright, percussive, somewhat in style of Prokofieff.

JOHN DIERCKS (1927-) USA

Diercks received his doctoral training at the Eastman School of Music. He is head of the music department at Hollins College, Virginia.

Theme and Variations (CAP 1948). 18 p.
Theme and 7 variations. Each variation well-developed. Exploits coloristic and textural capabilities of the instrument. Each variation a kind of character piece, yet relating closely to theme either in melodic outline, choice of harmony, and/or musical design. Final variation is free (in rondo form), conforming to classic practice. M-D.

CHARLES DIEUPART (? -1740) France

Six Suites pour Clavecin (P. Brunold-l'OL c. 1934). A, D, b, e, F, f. All suites contain an A, C, S, and G with optional dances M, Gavotte, Passepied. Each suite contains 7 movements. A corrected issue of this edition with Thurston Dart as editor came out in 1969 (l'OL).

The Art of the Suite (Y. Pessl-EBM) contains Suite f (copied by J. S. Bach in his own hand): Ouverture, A, C, S, Gavott, M and G.

GIROLAMO DIRUTA (ca. 1550- ?) Italy

Il Transilvano: I, 1593; II, 1609 (Forni).
A reprint of the well-known treatise on organ-playing contain-

ing toccatas and ricercari by Diruta, Banchieri, Quagliati, Bell'haver, Fattorini, Mortaro, Romanini and others.

See: Carl Krebs, "Girolamo Diruta's Transilvano: ein Beitrag zur Geschichte des Orgel-und Klavierspiels im 16. Jahrhundert," Vierteljahrschrift für Musikwissenschaft," 8, 1892, 307-88. This fine study reprints a canzone by Mortaro and four compositions by Diruta, 379-88.

A ricercare and two toccatas are found in Vol. III of Torchi's *L'Arte Musicale in Italia* (Ric).

HUGO DISTLER (1908-1942) Germany

Distler was one of Germany's most important twentieth-century composers of church music.

Elf kleine Klavierstücke für die Jugend Op. 15B (Br).
Eleven short pieces in neobaroque style. Not easy.

KARL DITTERS VON DITTERSDORF (1739-1799) Austria

20 Englische Tänze (K. Herrmann-Schott).

Sonata No. 2, A (W. Newman-UNC) in *13 Keyboard Sonatas of the 18th and 19th Centuries.*

CHARLES DODGE (1942-) USA

Sonata for Piano (ACA 1962).
A thorny serial work in 4 movements. Pointillistic writing. D.

ERNST VON DOHNÁNYI (1877-1960) Hungary

Dohnányi was first known due to his international success as a virtuoso of the highest order. Most of his music is in the Brahms tradition but stamped with an individual quality.

4 Clavierstücke Op. 2 (Dob 1905). Scherzo c♯ (EBM), Intermezzo a, Intermezzo f, Capriccio b (EBM).

Passacaglia Op. 6 (Dob).

4 Rhapsodies Op. 11 (Dob) (UE) (K) (EBM). No. 1 g 2. f♯ 3. C 4. e♭. Nos. 2, 3 (Willis).

Winterreigen Op. 13 (Dob) (GS) (EBM). This set of 10 Bagatelles covers a wide variety of difficulty and mood. Widmung (EBM), Marsh der lüstigen Brüder, An Ada, Freund Victors Mazurka, Sphärenmusik, Valse aimable, Um Mitternacht, Tolle Gesellschaft, Postludium (EBM).

Variations and Fugue on a Theme from E. G. Op. 4 (UE). Extensive work in 19th-century idiom.

Humoresken (in form of a suite) Op. 17 (UE). March, Toccata, Pavane with Variations, Pastorale, Introduction and Fugue.

3 Clavierstücke Op. 23 (Simrock). Aria, Valse impromptu, Capriccio a.

Suite in the Olden Style Op. 24 (Lengnick). Prelude, A, C, S, M, G.

6 Concert Studies Op. 28 (EMB) 2 volumes; (Bo&H) 1 volume; No. 6 (EBM) (BMC). a, D♭, e♭, b♭, E, f.

Variations on a Hungarian Folk Song Op. 29 (EMB).

Ruralia Hungarica Op. 32a (EMB). Folklike material is used in these 7 pieces.

Fugue (AMP 1913). For left hand, or both hands.

6 Piano Pieces Op. 41 (Lengnick 1947). Impromptu, Scherzino, Canzonetta, Cascades, Ländler, Cloches.

Pastorale (Ungarisches Weihnachtslied) (EMB).

3 Singular Pieces Op. 44 (AMP). Burletta, Nocturne—Cats on the Roof, Perpetuum mobile.

12 Short Studies for the Advanced Pianist (AMP 1951). Each study is devoted to a different pianistic problem. Some of the finest writing from Dohnányi's last years.

Gavotte and Musette (Dob 1905).

3 Concert Transcriptions on themes of Schubert, J. Strauss and Delibes (Rózsavölgyi).

Selected Piano Compositions (Kultura). Six Concert Etudes Op. 28, Variations on a Hungarian Folk Song Op. 29, Ruralia

Hungarica, Pastorale on a Hungarian Christmas Song. M-D to D.

Album of Dohnányi Masterpieces (EBM).
A Dedication Op. 13/1, A Joyous Party Op. 13/8, Capriccio b Op. 2/4, Intermezzo a Op. 2/2, Postludium Op. 13/10, three Rhapsodies Op. 11/2, 3, 4, Scherzo c♯ Op. 2/1.

See: Marion Ursula Rueth, "The Tallahassee Years of Ernst von Dohnányi," unpub. thesis, Florida State University, 1962. Concentrates on the years 1949-60 and contains an abbreviated catalogue of works.

SAMUEL DOLIN (1917-) Canada

Little Toccata (BMI Canada). Fast staccato repeated notes. Int.

*Sonatin*a (BMI Canada 1960).
Resembles easier Prokofieff with some legato melodic writing. Int.

ANTHONY DONATO (1909-) USA

Recreations (PIC 1953). Five teaching pieces. MC.
The Surfboard, The Motorboat, A Whim, Table Tennis, The Squirrel Cage. Int.

FRANCO DONATONI (1927-) Italy

Donatoni teaches at the Milan Conservatory. He has experimented in combining serial and aleatory techniques.

Composizione (Schott 1955). The row is used both harmonically and melodically. Pointillistic writing. Strict control combined with great variety of freedom in these 4 movements.

Tre Improvisazioni per Pianoforte (Schott 1957).

Doubles: Essercizi per Clavicembalo (SZ 1961). Special notation system used. 3-note sections of the row keep recurring. Complex.

Babi per Clavicembalo (SZ 1964). Graphic notation. This work is a revision of *Doubles*. A wooden prongs apparatus attached to the piano is necessary for performance.

RICHARD DONOVAN (1891-) USA

Donovan studied at Yale University, the Institute of Musical Art and later with Widor in Paris. He taught at the Yale University School of Music for a number of years.

Adventure (Merion 1956).

Suite for Piano (NME 1932).
Prelude, Hornpipe, Air, Jig.
Effective writing. The phrasing in the Hornpipe is deceptively difficult.

Suite No. 2 (ACA 1953). 11½ minutes.
Invention, Intermezzo, Elegy, Toccata.
In neoclassic style. Most problems are found in the tender Elegy and jazz-colored Toccata.

JAROSLAV DOUBRAVA (1909-1960) Czechoslovakia

Sonata pro Klavir (Artia 1948-49).
Allegro molto; Andante mesto; Allegro molto ed impeto. Bravura writing, biting dissonance, representative of mid-20th-century Czech piano writing.

SABIN V. DRAGOI (1894-) Rumania

Little Suite of Rumanian Folk Dances (Simrock).
Dedicated to memory of Béla Bartók. 7 short pieces, Bartók influence. Varied moods.

Miniatures (Artia 1956).
8 short pieces, a present day Rumanian "Album for the "Young."

EMILIO ANTONIA DUBLANC (1911-) Argentina

Since 1940 Dublanc has taught at the Institute of Advanced Musical Studies of Sante Fe, Argentina. He has served as director of this institution since 1964.

Nativa Op. 14/1 (LOT).

2 Preludios y Fugas Op. 27 (UNL).
Mi major
Fa sistenida menor

PIERRE MAX DUBOIS (1930-) France

Toccata (Leduc 1956). 12 p.

Trois Pièces pour Clavecin ou Piano (Leduc 1960). 8 p.
1. Hommage à Scarlatti. 2. Bransle de Touraine. 3. Tempo di gavotta.

10 Etudes de Concert (Leduc 1960). 2 volumes. Effective.

Esquisses (Leduc 1961). 22 p. Moderately easy 10 pieces.

Hommage à Poulenc (Leduc 1963). 4 p.

Arlequin et Pantalon (Leduc 1964). 11 p. 6 minutes.
Arlequin: Pastorale, impressionistic harmonies, fluctuating tempi.
Pantalon: Toccata-like, presto leggiero, glissandi, effective program closer.

Partita pour Clavecin (or Piano) (ESC 1963). 14 p. Neoclassic idioms. Prélude, Pavane, Toccata.

Les Fous de Bassan (Leduc). Improvisatory beginning and closing with a "Scherzo" mid-section.

Au Pays Tourangeau, Suite pour Piano (Sal 1948). 15 p.
Ouverture, Sarabande, Improvisation, Intermède, Berceuse, Rondo. Full chords, large span required, facile writing. Impressionistic devices used throughout.

Fantaisie de Concert (Leduc) 1961). 16 p.

THEODORE DUBOIS (1837-1924) France

Chaconne (Heugel).

Douze Petites Pièces (Heugel).

6 Poèmes Virgiliens (Heugel 1890).
Tityre, Galatea, Daphnis, Les Abeilles, Le Léthé (constant motion throughout), Diana (Tempo di Minuetto).

MARVIN DUCHOW (1914-   ) Canada

Passacaglia (BMI Canada 1961).
A 12-note subject makes artistic and varied rounds before the final statement resolves into a PP ending. M-D.

PAUL DUKAS (1865-1935) France

Sonata e♭ (Durand 1899-1900). 55 p. 65 minutes. Modérément vite; Calme — un peu lent — très soutenu; Vivement, avec légèreté; Très lent — Animé, mais sans hâte et bien scandé. Four movements of imposing dimensions. Inspired by Beethoven, it employs a Franckian keyboard technique with sensitive taste and elegant style.

Variations, Interlude et Finale sur un thème de Rameau (Durand 1901-2). 27 p.
Eleven variations, improvisatory interlude, animated finale.

Prélude élégiaque sur le nom de Haydn (Durand 1910).

La plainte, au loin du Faune (Durand 1921). In *Le Tombeau de Claude Debussy.* Plaintive melody over pedal tones and sustained harmonies. An elegy using the opening theme of *Prelude à l'après-midi d'un Faune,* in memory of Debussy.

VERNON DUKE (Vladimir Dukelsky) (1903-1969) USA, born Russia

Sonata (Souvenir de Venise) (BB 1955). For piano or harpsichord. One movement in unusual form, SFS. Large span necessary.

Parisian Suite (BB 1956). 10 pieces.

Sonata E♭ (Bo&H). Written under his original name of Dukelsky.

3 Caprices (CF). Dukelsky.

Surrealist Suite (MCA). Dukelsky. 9 pieces.

HENRI DUMONT (1610-1684) France

L'Oeuvre pour Clavecin (Editions Musicales de la Schola Cantorum c. 1956).
17 works including 11 A's and a C. Influence of the French lutenists appears, the "style brisé" or broken (arpeggio) playing.

JACQUES DUPHLY (1715-1789) France

Duphly made his living by giving lessons and concerts on the harpsichord, without holding an official position. This is the first modern edition of his music. Much charm and spirit are to be found in these works.

Pièces pour Clavecin (F. Petit-Heugel). These 4 books were published between 1744 and 1768, and present a fascinating kaleidoscope of brilliant keyboard writing. They also throw some interesting light on the period during which the piano began to supersede the harpsichord. Some dance titles are used (A, C) but generally descriptive titles are employed. Book I: 15 pieces, Book II: 14 pieces, Book III: 11 pieces (including an extended chaconne), Book IV: 6 pieces. There is also a biographical introduction on the composer with an indication of historic and musical sources.

See: Ray Davis Byham, "The Clavecin Works of Jacques Duphly," unpub. diss., University of Washington (in progress).

MARCEL DUPRÉ (1886-1971) France

One of France's most renowned organists.

4 Pièces Op. 19 (Leduc 1923). Dedicated to Clara Haskil.
Etude e♭.
Cortège et litanie: Later arranged for organ. Effective on piano.
Chanson: Romantic harmonic and melodic treatment.
Air de ballet: Brilliant closing.
This group could be divided and numbers played separately.

6 Préludes Op. 12 (Leduc).

Variations in c♯ Op. 22 (Leduc 1924). 22 p.
Theme, 19 variations and Final. Most variations are short, with many devices used: 4ths, octaves, perpetual motion, chromatic harmony. Well-suited for the piano even though written by an organist.

FRANCESCO DURANTE (1684-1755) Italy

Durante achieved a fine reputation during his lifetime. Expert craftsmanship plus a combination of old and new make Durante an above-average composer.

Sonate per Cembalo divise in Studii e Divertimenti (1732) (Paumgartner-Br c. 1949). Six Studii and six Divertimenti paired together, Studii in duple and Divertimenti in triple meter. The Studii are more polyphonic and the Divertimenti more homophonic. Scarlatti influence.

4 Toccatas (I Classici della musica italiana) Vol. 11. See Anthologies and collections, Italian. Some are reprinted in (K) *Old Masters of the 16th, 17th and 18th Centuries;* TPA Vol. 18; and *Le Trésor des Pianistes* Vol. 9. Nos. 1, 2, and 3 are perpetual motion pieces and 4 is a calm allegretto; all are one-movement.

LOUIS DUREY (1888-) France

Première Sonatine C (Heugel). Modérément animé; Lent; Très animé. Not easy.

Dix Inxentions (Heugel). Graceful two-voice writing, mixture of homophonic and contrapuntal textures.

Romance Sans Paroles (ESC).

Nocturne e♭ (JWC 1932).

Nocturne D♭ (JWC).

ZSOLT DURKO (1934-) Hungary

Durko is a graduate of the Budapest Academy of Music. He studied composition with Ferenc Farkas, then worked two years with Goffredo Petrassi.

Psicogramma (Kultura). 15 p. 9½ minutes.

This work balances two elements — one static and expressive, the other dynamic. The work is in 9 sections: Prologo, Double Psicogramma I, Motto, Psicogramma II, Canone all prima (Logicogramma), Anti-Evidenze, Un enfant terrible, Psicogramma III, and Epilogo. A shattering climax is reached in "Un enfant terrible," with a five-octave tritone glissando. Ostentatious sonorities plus some string strumming help dramatize states of mind, as the title suggests. Durko is ecletic, yet resourceful and convincing in his melodic treatment. His is an intense musical feeling.

FRANTISEK XAVER DUŠEK (DUSSEK, DUSCHEK, ETC). (1731-1799) Bohemia

Dušek was not related to J. L. Dussek. He was a pupil of Wagenseil and taught Kozeluch. Dušek left a set of eight sonatas, more sonatina-like in proportion, all in three movements, FSF. Written in the "galant" style of the period, they show some similarities to Mozart.

Eight Sonatas (*Aria*). These are Volume 8 of MAB.

Four separate sonata-movements (more technically involved than the 8 Sonatas) are found in volumes 14 and 17 of the same series.

JOHANN LADISLAV DUSSEK (1760-1812) Bohemia

Dussek was the first pianist to sit with his right side to the audience. He was also one of the first to indicate pedal instructions in his own compositions. Newman discusses the sonatas (SSB, 658-75) and gives a concordance of 42 sonatas (664-5), a very helpful aid since much confusion exists concerning opus numbers. A valuable dissertation that contains, among other information, an extended thematic catalog of approximately 300 works by Dussek has recently appeared (Howard Allen Crowe, "A Biography and Thematic Catalog of the Works of Dussek (1760-1812)," unpub. diss., University of Southern California, 1964). Dussek is one of the first composers to truly exploit the piano. In some ways (harmony and tonality) he anticipates later romantic traits.

MAB (Racek, Sykora-Artia) has 29 sonatas available in Vols. 46, 53, 59, 63.

MAB Vol. 46: *Sonatas* 1-7: Op. 9/1-3, 10/1-3, 18/2. Appeared in Paris before 1769. 10/2 g (K&S) in Organum, Series 5, No. 4.

MAB Vol. 53: *Sonatas* 8-16: Op. 23, 25/2, 31/2, 35/1-3, 39/1-3. Written between 1790 and 1800 in England. 35/3 c, is sometimes suggested as having influenced Beethoven's Op. 13 in the same key (K&S, Organum, Series 5, No. 22). 23 B♭ (Thumer-Augener).

MAB Vol. 59: *Sonatas* 17-23: Op. 43, 44, 45/1-3, 47/1-2. (K&S) (Artia) have Op. 44 *The Farewell,* dating from 1800. Op. 45/1 (K&S) (Br).

MAB Vol. 63: *Sonatas* 24-29: Op. 61, 69/3, 70, 75, 77. Op. 61, f♯, "Elégie harmonique sur la mort du Prince Louis Ferdinand" (CFP).

6 Sonatinas for Harp MAB Vol. 22. Preface in English. Well suited to the piano.

6 Sonatinas Op. 20 (CFP) (Ric) (GS) (Augener) (Heugel).

12 Melodic Etudes Op. 16 MAB Vol. 21.

Les Adieux. Rondo B♭ (Schott) (Heinrichshofen).

La Chasse (GS). Excellent study in staccato.

Les Adieux and Consolation Op. 62 (Artia).

8 Pieces (CFP). La Chasse, Consolation, Les Adieux, L'Amusoire, 3 Preludes, Partant pour la Syrie, Alla tedesca, La matinée.

Rondo on "Oh dear what can the matter be?" (Werner-Francis, Day and Hunter 1958).

In *Le Trésor des Pianistes:* 3 Grandes Sonates Op. 35; Sonata Op. 64.

HENRI DUTILLEUX (1916-   ) France

Sonata (Durand 1949). 3 movements, 22 minutes. 55 p. Neo-classic in style. Allegro con moto: SA design, placid beginning. Slow movement is lied-like. Finale is a chorale with 4 variations. Many added notes. This work has become something of a classic in France. It was one of the required pieces at the Montreal Competition in 1960.

ANTONÍN DVOŘÁK (1841-1904) Czechoslovakia

Dvořák's music has a natural freshness supported by fine craftsmanship and an engaging spontaneity. Smetana, Czech folksong and Brahms were the main influences on his music. Most of Dvořák's piano compositions are character pieces with a pronounced nationalistic element. The piano works are found in the complete edition, Series V, Volume IV, published by Artia.

Works without opus numbers are numbered according to : Jarmil Burghaser, *Antonín Dvořák: Thematic Catalogue, Bibliography, Survey of Life and Work* (in Czech, German, and English). Prague: Artia, 1960.

Album Leaves B. 109 (1880) (Hudební Matice). Nos. 2 and 3 Souvenirs, No. 4 Impromptu G.

Berceuse G, B. 188/1 (1894) (Artia).

Capriccio g, B. 188/2 (1894) (Artia).

Dumka (Elegy) Op. 35 (1876) (Artia). Sudden mood changes characterize the Dumka.

Dumka and Furiant Op. 12 (1884?) (Artia) (Augener).

4 Eclogues Op. 56, B. 103 (1880) (Hudební Matice).

8 Humoreskes Op. 101 (1894) (Bo&H) (Lengnick) in 2 books.

Impromptu d, B. 129 (1883) (Simrock).

6 Mazurkas Op. 56, B. 111 (1880) (Artia) (Bo&Bo).

2 Minuets Op. 28 (1876) (Artia). A♭, F.

6 Piano Pieces Op. 52 (1880) (Artia).
Impromptu g, Intermezzo c, Gigue B♭, Eclogue g, Allegro molto g, Tempo di Marcia E♭. Nos. 1, 2 (UE).

13 Poetic Tone Pictures Op. 85 (1889) (Artia) (Simrock) (Ric); (GS) Nos. 3, 4, 9, 13. No. 1. Twilight Way 2. Toying 3. In the Old Castle 4. Spring Song 5. Peasant's Ballad 6. Sorrowful Reverie 7. Goblin's Dance 8. A Dance (Furiant) 9. Serenade C 10. Bachanale 11. Tittle-tattle 12. At the Hero's Grave 13. On the Holy Mount. Programmatic writing.

12 Silhouettes Op. 8 (1879) (Bo&H) (Br).

Suite A (American Suite) Op. 98 (1894) (Artia).
Moderato; Molto vivace; Allegretto; Andante; Allegro.

Tänze (Artia). Polka E♭, 10 Menuette, Schottische Tänze.

Theme and Variations Op. 36 (1876) (Artia).

8 Waltzes Op. 54 (1879-80) (Artia) (Simrock); (Mitteldeutscher Verlag) Nos. 1, 2,; (Ric) No. 1.

Two Little Pearls (Laska Artia).

24 Selected Piano Pieces (CFP) in 1 volume. 5 Humoresques from Op. 101; 4 Mazurkas Op. 56; 3 Waltzes Op. 54; Sousedska from Two Pearls; Andante from Op. 98; Impromptu No. 1; 2 Silhouettes from Op. 8; 2 Poetic Mood-Pictures from Op. 85; Eclogues Nos. 1, 4; Album Leaves Nos. 2, 3; Dumka Op. 12.

E

ANTON FRANZ JOSEF EBERL (1765-1807) Austria

Sonatine Op. 6 (1796) in *The Solo Sonata* (Giegling-Arno Volk). (See Anthologies and Collections, General). 3 movements: Allegro; Andante; Rondo. Strict sonata form in Mozart style.

Sonata c (Geiringer-UE). Allegro only.

12 Variations Op. 5 on "Zu Steffen sprach im Träume" (Augener). Formerly ascribed to Mozart K. Anhang 288.

12 Variations Op. 6 on "Freundin sanfter Herzenstriebe" (Augener). Formerly ascribed to Mozart K. Anhang 287.

Grand Sonata Caractéristique f Op. 12 (CFP c. 1815).

Sources disagree as to which work is Op. 6.

See: A Duane White, "The Piano Works of Anton Eberl (1765-1807)," unpub. diss., University of Wisconsin. In progress.

JOHAN ERNST EBERLIN (1702-1762) Germany

6 Preludes and Fugues are in *Trésor des Pianistes* Vol. 12.

See: *Klaviermusik des 17. und 18. Jahrhunderts* (K. Herrmann-Hug) Vol. III. See Anthologies and Collections, General.

JOHANN GOTTFRIED ECKARD (1735-1809) Germany

Mozart apparently admired Eckard's writing for he used a movement from one of Eckard's sonatas in the third (K. 40) of the four composite keyboard concertos of 1767.

Oeuvres Complètes pour le Clavecin ou le Pianoforte (E. Reeser-Edition Heuwekemeijer 1956).

With an introduction by Eduard Reeser, annotated by Johan Ligtelijn. 94 pages.
Contains: Six sonatas pour le clavecin ou le pianoforte, IIème Oeuvre. — Menuet d'Exaudet, avec des variations, pour le clavecin. These were the first sonatas composed in Paris specifically for the pianoforte and date from 1763.

See: Paul Badura-Skoda; M&M, 17, February 1969, 70.

S. C. ECKHARDT-GRAMATTÉ (1902-) Canada, born Russia

Sophie Carmen Eckhardt-Gramatté attended the Paris Conservatory where she was a student of Bronislaw Hubermann, among others. She studied composition with Max Trapp in Berlin. In 1954 she established her residence in Winnipeg, Canada.

Klavierstück (Sonata No. 5) (International Gesellschaft für neue Musik 1950). 15 minutes.
A three-movement work in thick polyphonic texture. The second movement uses harmonics, the final movement octave glissandi.

Suite for Piano No. 1 (Sonata C) (Simrock 1923).
Allegro moderato; Andante; Allegro.

YITZCHAK EDEL (1896-) Israel, born Poland
Edel was on the teaching faculty of the Lewinsky Seminar for Music Teachers in Tel Aviv for thirty-six years. He has been active in the Israel Composer's League and has also written extensively on musical subjects.

Capriccio (IMI 1946).
Vigorous large-scale piece requiring vigor and strong articulation. In mixolydian mode. Rondo-sonata form.

Triptyque (IMI 1963).
Invention (Sostenuto) Quiet: brief theme with variations.
Scherzino (Fresco) Dry: staccato, double counterpoint at various intervals.
Toccata (Presto): Driving rondo.

Israeli Dance (Publications of the Cultural Department of the General Labor Federation in Israel).
Large-scale concert piece, quartal harmonies, oriental in flavor. Requires bravura and strong rhythmic sense. D.

HELMUT EDER (1916-) Austria

Sonata No. 1 (Br&H 1950).
3 movements of solid linear writing. The final movement, Marschmässig, is the most accessible.

Sonatina Op. 13 (Dob 1960).
3 movements in neoclassic style. The second movement, Lento con espressione, is more difficult than it appears. Changing meter in final movement, Allegro scherzando, has an engaging lilt.

Mouvements Op. 44 (Dob).

CHRISTOPHER EDMUNDS (1899-) Great Britain

Sonata b (Lengnick).
First movement is a romantic rhapsody in b. An elegiac second movement is in e. The last movement is a dashing Allegro scherzando in a! Fervent writing. M-D.

Suite G (Hin 1960).

3 Pieces Op. 31 (J. Williams).
September, A Northern Legend, Green Magic.

FLORIN EFTIMESCU (-) Rumania

Sonata, Pentru Pian (Editura Muzicala 1964). 23 p.
Allegro moderato; Andante con moto; Allegretto.
Virtuoso writing, much chromaticism but generally tonal in conception. Interesting harmonic vocabulary.

KLAUS EGGE (1906-) Norway

Egge's style is polyphonic, dissonant and is stamped with a vigorous rhythmic technique.

2 Klaverstykker Op. 1 (NMO).
Valse Dolce, Arkvarell.

Draumkvede Sonate Op. 4 (EMH 1942). Based on Draumkvede tunes, this four-movement well-contrasted work is of M-D.

Fantasie I Halling Op. 12 A (EMH). Based on a familiar Norwegian folkdance tune. A richly intertwined contrapuntal movement is developed from this tune.

Fantasie I Springar Op. 12B (Lyche). Spring Rhythm.

Fantasie I Gangar Op. 12C (Norwegian Information Service).

Gukkoslatten (Lyche 1944). Goathorn-Dance.

Sonata No. 2 (Patética) Op. 27 (Lyche 1956).
A large, impassioned work in 3 movements, FSF, with a Grave stentato introduction. Extensive use of sevenths and ninths. Extreme dynamic contrasts. Freely tonal.

WERNER EGK (1901-) Germany

Sonata (Schott 1947). Written in a diatonic style with fresh coloration.
Andante; Allegro molto; Andante; Allegro molto.

GOTTFRIED VON EINEM (1918-) Austria, born Switzerland

Vier Klavierstücke Op. 3 (UE 1943). 11 p.
4 short character pieces, stimulating, rhythmically interesting. No. 4 is most appealing.

Two Sonatinas Op. 7 (UE 1947). 20 p. Written in neoclassic style.
No. 1: Molto allegro; Moderato.
No. 2: Allegro; Adagio; Molto allegro.

Two Capriccios for Harpsichord Op. 36 (Bo&H 1969) Neoclassic style. M-D.
Adagio: tonal, recitative-like, trills, LH skips.
Allegro moderato: arpeggiated chords, thin textures, changing meters, linear, some perpetual motion.

HANNS EISLER (1898-1962) Germany

Variations (Br&H 1940).

Petites morceaux pour les enfants (Heugel). 2 volumes. Outstanding.
I. 18 pieces 1 page each.
II. 7 pieces, more difficult.

Sonata Op. 1 (UE 1924). 3 movements. Schönberg and Berg influence. Advanced pianism required throughout.
Allegro; Intermezzo; Finale.

Klavierstücke Op. 3 (UE 1926).
4 pieces in atonal style, many tempi changes. D.

HALIM EL-DABH (1921-) Egypt

Mekta in The Art of Kita (CFP 1959). (Microcosm in The Art of Macrocosm). Books I, II, III. Fascinating. Many repetitions of simple material, melodic and rhythmic variations.

Soufiane (CFP). 4 minutes.

Arabyiat No. 7, 13, 15 (1955); *Drum-Takseem* (1951); *Felucca* (1953); *Barbeuse Shadia* (1955); *Barbeuse Amira* (1959); *Sonata Tahmeel* No. 1 and 2. All are available from (ACA). They lean heavily on national folksong and dance.

EDWARD ELGAR (1857-1934) Great Britain

3 Dances from the Bavarian Highlands Op. 27 (J. Williams). The Dance, Lullaby, The Marksman.

Sonatina (K. Prowse 1931).

The Wand of Youth Op. 1a (Suite I), Op. 1b (Suite II) (Nov).

Concert Allegro Op. 41 (Nov c. 1969) 10 minutes.
A recently brought-to-light piece Elgar wrote at the request of English pianist Fanny Davies in 1901-2.

BENTSION ELIEZER (-) Bulgaria

Sonata for Piano (Edition d'Etat, Science et Arts, 1956). 24 p. 4 movements, tonal. Many octaves, chromatics used for coloring, wide dynamic range. Pianistically effective, large-scale final movement.

ROBERT ELLIOT (1932-) Great Britain

Sonatina Op. 2 (Augener 1957).
3 movements, well organized, contemporary, M-D.

3 Lyric Pieces (HWG 1957).

JÓSEF ELSNER (1769-1854) Poland, born Germany
Teacher of Chopin.

Sonata No. 2, D (1805) (PWM c. 1964). 2 movements.
Allegro; Andantino—Allegro—Andantino—Allegro.
Average writing for the period. The Andantino section (d) is most interesting.
Edition contains biographical notes in English and Polish.

HERBERT ELWELL (1898-) USA

Plaint (TP). Easy, interesting modulation.

Busy Day (TP). Modal. M-D.

Procession (TP). No key signature. M-D.

Sonata (OUP). Allegro; Andante espressivo; Allegro con brio. Requires good cantabile, tonal balance, octave facility especially in last movement. M-D.

MAURICE EMMANUEL (1862-1938) France

Première Sonatine Bourguignonne (Heugel 1893). 13 p. Delightful writing based on Burgundian folk dances. D.
Allegro con spirito
Branle à la manière de Bourgogne
Andante semplice (ostinato)
Ronde à la manière Morvandelle

Deuxième Sonatine (Pastorale) (Heugel 1897).
La Caille; Le Rossignol; Le Coucou.

Troisième Sonatine (Heugel 1920). Impressionistic.

Sonatina IV sur des modes hindous (Durand 1920). 19 p.
Colorful, 3 movements, not easy.

Sonatina V alla francese (Lemoine 1926). 15 p.
Ouverture (in the French Style, SFS), C, S, Gavotte, Pavane et Gaillarde, G. Attractive, impressionistic.

Sonatina VI A (Lemoine 1926). 10 p.

GEORGES ENESCO (1881-1955) Rumania

Suite in Ancient Style Op. 3 (Enoch c. 1898). 16 p.
Prelude, Fugue, Adagio, Finale.

Suite pour Piano Op. 10 (Editura de Stat Pentru Literatură Si Artă c. 1956). 34 p.
4 movements of virtuoso writing. Toccata, S, Pavane, B.

Prelude and Fugue C (Editura Muzicala a Uniunii compozitoritor din F. P. R. c. 1965). 10 p.

Sonata f♯ Op. 24/1 (Editions d'Etat pour la Litterature et l'Art, c. 1956). Composed in 1924, this large three-movement work requires advanced pianism. A difficult piece to hold together. Allegro molto moderato e grave; Presto vivace; Andante molto expressivo.

Sonata No. 3 D, Op. 24/3 (Sal 1933-35).
A poetic, lengthy work permeated with Rumanian elements. Changing tempi, textures. This edition is a reproduction of the composer's autograph. D.
Vivace con brio; Andantino cantabile; Allegro con spirito.

Prélude et Fugue No. 3 D (Sal 1903).
The three-voice fugue uses short trills, and is heavy with notes.

See: Leontina Coban, *Specificul naţional în creaţia pianistică a lui George Enescu (National Elements in the Piano Compositions of George Enescu). National si universal în muzică (The National and Universal in Music)* Bucharest: Conservatorul de Musica "Ciprian Porumbescu", 1967. In Rumanian: summaries in French, English, German and Russian. Coban's article is an analysis of the piano works of Enescu that reveals (1) an expressively modal melody reflecting the composer's preference for the intervals of a 2nd, 3rd, and 4th, which clings to one, two, or three notes and combines delicate ornamentation with folk chromaticism, (2) a parlando rhythmic style made up of formulas and the asymmetrical arrangement of bars of different meters, (3) discrete but complex polyphony, and (4) a fluid, gliding harmony.

HEIMO ERBSE (1924-) Germany

Erbse studied with Boris Blacher. His works show a lusty vitality.

Sonata Op. 6 (Bo&Bo 1953).
Allegro moderato: tricky rhythms and figuration.
Vivace: biting dissonances, Tarantella, fast triplets. D.

CEZMI ERINC (-) Turkey

4 Turkish Piano Pieces Op. 9 (UE 1935).
Efe Türküsü (Chant d'Efé)
Ninni (Berceuse)
Sari Kiz (Chant de la blonde)
Oyun (Caprice)
Short, folklike. No. 2 contains an ad lib violin part. Interesting flavor.

JOSEF ERIKSSON (1872-1957) Sweden

Sonatine d Op. 22 (WH c. 1916). 18 p.
Allegro; Adagio; Menuetto; Finale: Allegro molto.
Romantic vocabulary with some obvious harmonic treatment. M-D.

Sonat G Op. 23 (NMS).

Sechs kleine Klavierstücke Op. 19 (NMS).

LUIS A. ESCOBAR (1925-) Colombia

Escobar was a pupil of Nicolas Nabokov at the Peabody Institute in Baltimore. He also took courses in composition at Columbia University in New York and completed his musical studies with Boris Blacher in Berlin. He teaches at the National Conservatory in Bogota.

Sonatine No. 2 (PAU 1952). 14 p.
3 movements, written in an easy, gay, accessible contemporary idiom. Hemiola rhythms prevalent.
Contains a biographical sketch of the composer.

OSCAR ESPLÁ (1886-) Spain

Esplá's style is a combination of romantic and German scholasticism.

Tres Movimientos (UME 1930).

Evocations Espagnoles (UME 1936).

Sonata Española Op. 53 (UME 1944). Written in homage to Chopin. Andante romantico; Mazurka sopra un tema popolare; Allegro brioso.

Lirica Española Op. 54 (UME c. 1952).
Book I: Esquisses Levantines
Book II: Tonadas antiguas (Airs anciens)
Book III:
Book IV:
Book V: Suite caracteristica (c. 1954). Habanera; Ronda Serrana; Sonnatina Playera. Spanish temperament permeates these 3 works.

Romanza Antigue (ESC c. 1929). 4 p.

Scherzo (UME c. 1929). 11 p.

ALVIN ETLER (1913-) USA

Etler studied composition with Arthur Shepherd and Paul Hindemith. He is Professor of Composition at Smith College.

Sonatina (A. Broude 1955).

ROBERT EVETT (1922-   ) USA

Sonata No. 2 (PAU 1952-53). 18 minutes.
In 3 sections: Allegretto alla breve; Vivace; Chorale en Rondeau (Adagio). Strong neoclassic style, solid writing throughout, harsh sonorities. M-D.

Sonata No. 3 (ACA 1954). 20 minutes.
Allegro; Adagio; Allegro.

Sonata No. 4 (ACA 1956). 22 minutes.
Allegro; Vivace; Adagio; Presto.

F

FRANCISCO NICOLA FAGO (1676-1745) Italy

Toccata for harpsichord (CFP).

RICHARD FAITH (1926-   ) USA

Faith received his musical training at the Chicago Musical College, Indiana University, and in Rome, Italy, as the recipient of a Fullbright scholarship in piano and composition. He teaches at the University of Arizona, Tucson.

Finger Paintings (SP 1968).
12 imaginative miniatures employing many resources of the instrument. Both hands receive equal importance. MC. Moderately easy.

5 Preludes and Nocturne (SP 1969).
Tonal, contemporary treatment, varied moods. Ideas evolve naturally. Moderately difficult. The Nocturne is a slowly flowing lyrical work with a faster mid-section. Chromatic.

Sonata No. 1 (SP 1970). 17 p.
Allegro grazioso: unison writing, much chromaticism, B♭.
Allegro: repeated notes (chords), imitation, scherzo effect, centers around C.
Lento and Mesto: romantic harmonies, F.
Allegro Maestoso: rhythmic motives carefully developed, B♭.

The Dark Riders (Toccata) (SP 1970). 7p.
Brief introduction leads directly to perpetual motion open fifths in LH, single note in RH. Punctuated with longer note values and rhythmic drive. Long pedal effects. M-D.

Travels (SP 1970). 7 pieces. 15 p. The Highlander, Chant, Limerick, Provence, Genie, Express, Caravan. Varied, short, coloristic, Int.

Four Cameos (SP 1971). 11 p. Waltz, Toccatina, Lullaby, Rondina. MC, Int.

Three Sonatinas (GS 1971). Each is in three short movements, MC, appealing. Easy to Int.

MANUEL DE FALLA (1876-1946) Spain

Homenaje (JWC). "For the death of Debussy," a guitar piece arranged by De Falla. Rhythmic treatment punctuated with staccato figuration. Based on motive from Debussy's "Soirée dans Grenade."

Pièces espagnoles (Durand 1908).
Aragonesa: exciting Spanish rhythms.
Cubana: cross-rhythms and interesting melodic treatment.
Montañesa: folksong influence.
Andalusa: staccato dance rhythms.

Fantasia Baetica (JWC 1919).
Most demanding of De Falla's solo piano works. Rhythmic repetitions, brilliant and effective keyboard writing, simple harmonic treatment, difficult.

7 Canciones Populares Españolas (ESC). Effective piano transcriptions by E. Halffter.

FERENC FARKAS (1905-) Hungary

Farkas' "harmonic language is firmly based on diatonicism, with a purposefully enlarged vocabulary; his rhythmic patterns, though sometimes seemingly intricate, are always logically balanced; his principal strength lies in his melodic invention, which is completely uninhibited and immediately comprehensible. Permeated with Latin clarity on the one hand and Hungarian flavour on the other, his music is eminently enjoyable." GD, 3, 26.

3 Burlesques (Artia 1949).

3 Initials (Kultura).

Kit Akvarell Zongorara (EMB 1955).
Geburtstagsgrüss: 3 p. Slow, declamatory, chromatic.
Aprilwind: 7 p. Fast, polytonal, scalar over open fifths.

5 Hungarian Danses (ZV c. 1952). Transcribed by F. Farkas. Unusual group, less modal than Bartók's *Hungarian Dances.* Int.

Ballade (Belwin-Mills 1955). 12 p.

Correspondences (Belwin-Mills 1957). 16 p. 8 pieces.

5 Easy Piano Pieces (EMB c. 1958).

GILES FARNABY (ca. 1560-ca. 1620) Great Britain

Although untrained, Farnaby, nevertheless, was an instinctive musician whose spontaneous simplicity lends a freshness to his compositions.

Keyboard Music of Giles and Richard Farnaby, Musica Britannica XXIV (R. Marlow-S&B). Contains 53 works by Giles Farnaby, 4 works by Richard and a doubtful Coranto by Giles (?)

Selected Works (M. H. Glyn-S&B) 25 works in 2 volumes. I. Selected Pieces. II. Folksong Variations.

17 Pieces selected from the Fitzwilliam Virginal Book (T. Dart-S&B).

Tower Hill in collection *Keyboard Music of the Baroque and Rococo* Vol. I.

Masque. FVB, II, 264. Grave and severe feeling of the pavan, minor mode, virtuosity out of place.

Woodycock Variations. FVB, II, 138. Six variations based on a popular Elizabethan dance tune. First part of variation five, with its rapid and animated thirds in the middle range of the keyboard, is charming and unique in the literature of this period. The second part of this variation, with the subject brought out in augmentation on counterpoint in triplets requires a virtuoso technique if the tempo is maintained.

His Humor. FVB, II, 262. 4 episodes, A B C D.

See: Richard Marlow, "The Keyboard Music of Giles Farnaby," PRMA, 92, 1965-6, 107-120.

ARTHUR FARWELL (1872-1952) USA

A great champion of American music, Farwell was at his best in working with American Indian material.

The Domain of Hurakon (Wa-Wan 1902). 13 p.
A large work based on three Indian melodies of widely divergent origin. Our word "hurricane" comes from the Indian Word "Hurakon." Well worth reviving.

Navajo War Dance No. 2 (Mer). Ostinato figures, bravura octaves and chords.

Pawnee Horses (GS).
Short Omaha melody treated in a galloping figuration.

Sourwood Mountain (GS). In *51 Piano Pieces from the Modern Repertoire*.
A "Rip-snorting development of a good old American tune." Virtuoso treatment.

GABRIEL FAURÉ (1845-1924) France

Melodic spontaneity, rhythmic subtlety, harmonic reticence and restraint are characteristic of Fauré, one of the finest and creative French composers. Many of his piano works have a seeming similarity, but closer examination and greater familarity reveal a striking originality. His nocturnes, preludes, barcarolles and impromptus were inspired by Chopin but Fauré's individual and instinctive pianism make him once of the great 19th-century composers for the piano. The piano works demand musicianship and pianistic maturity.

Ballade Op. 19 (1881) (Hamelle). Original solo piano version of the *Ballade* for Piano and Orchestra.

13 Barcarolles. (IMC) publishes 6, (K) publishes 6, 13 complete.
1. Op. 26 a 2. Op. 41 G 3. Op. 42 G♭ 4. Op. 44 A♭

5. Op. 66 f♯ 6. Op. 70 E♭ (Hamelle 1-6); 7. Op. 90 d 8. Op. 96 D♭ 9. Op. 101 a (Heugel 7-9); 10. Op. 104/2 a 11. Op. 105 g 12. Op. 106 E♭ 13. Op. 116 C (Durand 10-13).

Berceuse Op. 56/1 (GS) (Hamelle).

Impromptus (IMC) (K) and (Hamelle) have Nos. 1, 2, and 3; (BMC) No. 1; (Heugel) Nos. 4 & 5.
No. 1, Op. 25 E♭ 2. Op. 31 f 3. Op. 34 A♭ 4. Op. 91 D♭ 5. Op. 102 f♯.

Mazurka Op. 32 B♭ (Hamelle).

13 Nocturnes (IMC) publishes 8.
No. 1 Op. 33/1 e♭ 2. Op. 33/2 B 3. Op. 33/3 A♭ 4. Op. 36 E♭ 5. Op. 37 B♭ 6. Op. 63 D♭ 7. Op. 74 c♯ 8. Op. 84/8 D♭ (Hamelle 1-8); 9. Op. 97 b 10. Op. 99 e (Heugel 9-10); 11. Op. 104/1 f♯ 12. Op. 107 e 13. Op. 119 b (Durand 11-13).

8 Pièces Brèves Op. 84 (IMC) (K) (Hamelle).
Capriccio, Fantaisie, Fugue, Adagietto, Improvisation, Fugue, Allégresse, Nocturne.

9 Préludes Op. 103 (Heugel) separately, and in a collection. 1. D♭ 2. c♯ 3. g 4. F 5. d 6. e♭ 7. A 8. c 9. e. See especially numbers 2, 3, 6, 8.

3 Romance sans Paroles Op. 17 (K) (Hamelle).
A♭, a, A♭.

Theme and Variations Op. 73 (IMC) (K) (Hamelle). A beautifully polished set considered a classic by the French, exemplifying all of Fauré's subtlety, grace and reticence to the nth degree.

3 Valse-Caprices (Hamelle). Op. 30 A, Op. 59 G♭, and Op. 62 A♭.

Collection (Heugel). Contains Barcarolles, Op. 90, 96 and 101; Impromptus, Op. 91 and 102; Nocturnes, Op. 97 and 99.

See: Tombeau, Hommage section in Anthologies and Collections. *Hommage musical à Gabriel Fauré.*

SAMUEL FEINBERG (1890-) USSR

Feinberg's early works are based on a style similar to Scriabin. The later works become more diatonic. He has concentrated on the piano sonata.

Sonata No. 2 Op. 2 (MCA 1916). One-movement work, Scriabinesque, dramatic, D.

Fantasy E♭ Op. 5 (MCA 1917). Not easy, one movement, dramatic.

Fantasy e Op. 9 (MCA 1919). Somber, melancholy.

Suite Op. 11 (MCA). 4 short lyric pieces.

Sonata No. 5 a Op. 10 (MCA 1921). One movement, complex.

Sonata No. 6 b Op. 13 (UE 1923). One movement, many tempi changes, thick textures, involved.

Sonata No. 9 (MCA). One movement, lyric, sonorous ending.

Sonata No. 11 Op. 40 (USSR).

MORTON FELDMAN (1926-) USA

John Gruen in Vogue, December 1968 said: "Feldman's music has always dealt with actual sound, produced by actual instruments, but the sounds he produced were always exceedingly quiet . . . His is a vocabulary that may be linked to Impressionist painting without subject matter. Only the hazy, diffused light may be equated to the imperceptible aural language of Feldman's music. It is a music of deep intimacy. One must really listen to a Feldman work, or it might easily slip by without being heard at all." Feldman is a disciple of John Cage.

Illusions for Piano (NME 1950). 4 pieces, all short with tempo marks for titles. 12-tone technique. Very Fast, Slow and Tranquil, Very Fast, Very Fast. Changing meters, extreme dynamic range (FFF to PPPPP), advanced pianism required. Fascinating timbres.

Intermission V (CFP).

Intersection II, III (CFP). Graphs.

Piano Pieces (CFP 1952, 1955, 1956a,b, 1963).

3 Pieces (CFP).

Vertical Thoughts IV (CFP).

Last Pieces (CFP 1959). 4 short pieces with directions such as "Slow. Soft." "Durations are free for each hand." Only pitch notated.

Extensions III (CFP).

HOWARD FERGUSON (1908-) Great Britain

Sonata f Op. 8 (Bo&H). Advanced pianism required.
Lento: declamatory.
Allegro inquieto: restless undercurrent.
Poco adagio: florid.
Allegro non troppo: scampering, opening Introduction returns.

5 Bagatelles Op. 9 (Bo&H).
A cycle of varied sketches built on themes by the composer's friends.

ARMANDO JOSÉ FERNANDES (1906-) Portugal

Fernandes worked with Nadia Boulanger and Roger-Ducasse in Paris. His style leans towards neoclassicism.

5 Preludios Op. 1 (Sassetti).

Sonatina (Sassetti 1941). 9 p.
Allegretto grazioso: dance-like.
Tempo di Folia: leads to an Andante expressivo that requires span of a ninth.
Allegro non troppo: fugal.

Scherzino (Sassetti c. 1960). 6 p.
Chromatic, arpeggi, broad dynamic range, Moderato mid-section, effective. M-D.

OSCAR LORENZO FERNANDEZ (1897-1948) Brazil

Fernandez is not afraid to write an old fashioned melody and use characteristic South American rhythms.

First Brazilian Suite (PIC). 5½ minutes. Each movement published separately.
Old Song, Sweet Cradle Song, Serenade. Folk-like, lyric, romantic harmony.

Second Brazilian Suite (PIC 1938). 7½ minutes. Each piece published separately.
Prelude, Song, Dance. Based on original themes.

Third Brazilian Suite (PIC 1938). Each piece published separately.
Song: rich harmonization, fine climax.
Serenade: constant RH double notes. Effective, difficult.
Negro Dance: a "tour de force" in rhythm and dynamic control. Large span required, full dynamic range.

Nocturne (PIC).

Tres Estudos em Forma de Sonatina (Ric 1929). 10 minutes.

Sonata Breve (PIC 1947). 12 minutes.
Energico
Largo e Pesante
Impetuoso: RH mainly has seventh chords.
An effective, forceful work requiring facile technique.

Suite das 5 Notas (PIC 1942). 8 minutes. 8 short movements. Easy.

Dolls (PIC 1945). 5 separately published pieces. Int. Spanish Ballerina, Portuguese Shepherdess, Italian Peasant Girl, Russian Girl Woodcutter, Chocolate Cake Girl Vendor.

Children's Visions (PIC 1942). 3 separately published pieces. Int. Little Cortège, Nocturnal Round, Mysterious Dance.

Yaya, The Doll (PIC 1946). 3 pieces. Int.
Dancing Yaya, Dreaming Yaya, Jumping Yaya.

JACOPO G. FERRARI (1763-1842) Italy

3 Sonatas (L. Podolsky-SB c. 1952). Interesting pieces in classic style.

I. Allegro; Larghetto; Anglaise.
II. Spiritoso; Andante con expressione; Rondo-Allegretto.
III. Allegro; Thema con variazioni.

PIERRE-OCTAVE FERROUD (1900-1936) France

Au parc Monceau (Rouart, Lerolle 1921). 18 p.
1. Chat jouant avec des moineaux 2. Sur le banc 3. Nonchalante 4. Bambins.

Prélude et Forlane (Durand c. 1924). 9 p.
Ravel influence obvious in this charming set.

Types (Rouart, Lerolle 1922-24).
Some brilliant pianistic writing, especially in the third movement.

Fables (Durand 1931). 28 p.

Sonatine C (Durand 1928). 21 p.

Trois études pour le piano (Schneider 1932).

PETER FEUCHTWANGER (1934-) Germany

Settled in Israel, now living in London. All Feuchtwanger's work is inspired and influenced by Oriental folk and art music, in which he has done intensive research and about which he has lectured extensively in Europe and the U.S.A. He studied composition with Lennox Berkeley and Dr. Hans Heimler.

Study No. 1 in the Eastern Idiom Op. 3 (Augener 1960). 8 p. 4 minutes.
Rooted in the folklore of Macedonia and Bosnia; both regions were strongly under oriental influence. Key signatures are present, modal scales, changing and complex meters, sectional, fast repeated notes.

Study No. 2 in an Eastern Idiom Op. 4 (Augener 1966). 12 p. 5 minutes.

Contains an explanation of the melodic and rhythmic Maqamat, the basis of the piece. In 4 sections, should sound like an improvisation. Fascinating sonorities. D.

Study No. 3 in an Eastern Idiom Op. 5 (Augener 1966). 5 p. 4½ minutes.
Based on the Ahir-Bhirav Raga. Only effective if given a superb performance. D.

Variations on an Eastern Folk Tune (ms 1957). 2 books.
Book I: 25 p. 9 difficult variations.
Book II: 26 p. 9 difficult variations.
Beautiful manuscript, esoteric style, beautiful handling of sonorities. Very difficult but worth the effort to perfect this work. Score available from the composer:
17 Rutland Mews South
Knightsbridge
London S.W. 7, England.

GEORGE FIALA (1921-) Canada

Fiala is considered one of Canada's leading composers.

Sonatina Op. 1 (BMI Canada 1960).
A clever 3-movement work in neoclassical style. The third movement, Tarantella, is much more difficult than the other two movements.

Dix Postludes (Waterloo 1968).
All are short, one page each, tonal and MC sounding. No. 6, A la Shostakovitch, is particularly evocative of that composer's style.

Trois Bagatelles Op. 6. (G. V. Thompson 1968).

Australian Suite (BMI Canada). Birds and Beasts like the Emu, Kookaburra, Lyre Bird, Kangaroo, Platypus and Koala occupy this imaginative set. Int.

Miniature Suite (BMI Canada). Four Pieces: Overture, Almost a Waltz, Ancient Story, Spinning Wheel. Clear forms, some dissonance, flowing, pianistic. Easy.

ZDENKO FIBICH (1850-1900) Czechoslovakia

Fibich's use of dynamics was one of the most interesting facets of his style. He preferred the softer levels, PP-PPP etc.

Sonatina d (Urbanek c. 1947). In Dvořák style. Int.

Detem (Vera Koubkova-Artia c. 1960). A collection of 11 solo pieces and 5 duets. Excellent, interesting pedagogic material, all colorful.

Scherzo I and II Op. 4 (Hudebni c. 1953).
I. e II. E♭. Both are delightful, somewhat in Mendelssohn style, pianistic, Int.

Poem (Artia).

Nálady, dojmy a upomínky (Urbanek). Published separately: Op. 41 ("Moods, Impressions and Recollections.") 4 volumes of 46 pieces (1891-94). Op. 44 ("Novella") 4 volumes of 33 pieces (1895). Op. 47, 10 volumes of 148 different pieces ranging in difficulty from easy to M-D (1895-97). Op. 57, 2 volumes of 17 pieces (after 1897). A wonderful range of delightful sounds is contained in these collections. Traditional piano techniques involved.

JACOBO FICHER (1896-) Argentina, born USSR

Ficher came to Argentina in 1917 and has assumed a leading role in the Argentine musical scene since that time. He writes in a traditional style although exceptions do occur.

5 Preludes Op. 4 (Ric 1924).

5 Canciones Sin Palabras Op. 1 (Ric). 5 Songs Without Words. Lyrical, expressive.

Tres Preludios Op. 23 (Grupo Renovacion, Buenos Aires 1934). 15 p.

6 Animal Fables Op. 38 (Axelrod 1942). Short descriptive barnyard pieces including an arrogant rooster, a humble hen, a pussy cat, a nanny goat, two sparrows and some bears. M-D. last 3 most difficult.

Sonata Op. 44 (CF). Lento-Allegro; Andantino; Allegro molto.

Sonata No. 4 Op. 72 (Ric 1950). In one movement with numerous meter, texture and tempi changes. Large span required.

3 Pieces for Children (EAM). El Desfile, Polka, and Cancion triste. Easy.

6 Fables (Southern 1962). Attractive, descriptive works.

Tres Danzas (Southern). Written in popular Argentine style, colored by polytonal treatment. M-D.
En Estilo de Zamba
En Estilo de Vidalita
En Estilo de Gato: most difficult.

JOHN FIELD (1782-1837) Ireland

The Irish-born pianist John Field dedicated his opus 1 (3 piano sonatas) to his famous teacher, Muzio Clementi. But the nocturne, not the sonatas, established Field's reputation as a composer. These nocturnes were written between 1814 and 1835 and make a fine introduction to the Chopin nocturnes. Liszt edited Field's nocturnes and wrote a highly appreciative foreward that was published in 1859. Both the GS and Augener editions still retain this preface.

18 Nocturnes (Liszt-GS) (Augener) (CFP) (Ric); 9 Nocturnes (K). No. 1 E♭ 2. c 3. A♭ 4. A 5. B♭ 6. F 7. C (Rêverie-Nocturne) 8. A 9. E♭ 10. e 11. E♭ 12. G 13. d (Song without words) 14. C 15. C 16. F 17. E (Grande Pastorale) 18. E (Nocturne charactéristique "Noontide"). No. 12 G in Anthology *Romanticism in Music,* 85-6.

3 Sonatas Op. 1 (1801) (Augener).
No. 1 E♭ No. 2 A No. 3 c.

A *Sonata* B appeared in 1814, (Br&H) but is no longer available on the market.

Rondo E♭ (GS).

Cavatina; "Reviens, reviens" (K. Long-OUP).

Bear Dance (Waldwick). Doubtful authenticity but attractive teaching piece, 2 p.

See: The International Piano Library Bulletin, Volume 2, (Special Issue) September 1968, is devoted entirely to Field. Contains: David Doscher, "John Field, The Pianoforte's First Modern Composer," "Life of John Field," "The Nocturne," "4 Unpublished Manuscripts," "Ferruccio Busoni on John Field." Franz Liszt on John Field, Robert Schumann on John Field, "A Field Discography."

Hibberd T. Davies, "The Slow Movements in the Sonatas of John Field," MR, 22, 1961, 89-93.

IRVING FINE (1914-1962) USA

Lullaby for a Baba Panda (TP). Vague key-center. Easy.

Victory March of the Elephants (TP). Modal. Easy.

Homage to Mozart (Bo&H 1957). M-D.

Music for Piano (MCA 1947). Four movements, oriented toward Stravinsky. Prelude, Waltz-Gavotte, Variations, Interlude-Finale. M-D.

VIVIAN FINE (1913-) USA

Fine, a former student of Roger Sessions, is presently on the faculty at Bennington College in Vermont.

Suite E♭ (ACA) 1940). Prelude (lyric), S (stately), Gavotte (delicate), Air (hushed), G (short, lively).

Variations (ACA 1952). Large-scale work. 20 minutes. D.

Sinfonia and Fugato (LG 1952). 6 minutes. M-D.

ROSS LEE FINNEY (1906-) USA

Finney, who is composer-in-residence at the University of Michigan, studied with Alban Berg and Nadia Boulanger. His earlier works had their roots in our American heritage but during the 1950's Finney's tonal language became more chromatic and dissonant. More recently serial technique has interested him. His five piano sonatas and smaller sets of pieces are a notable contribution to American piano literature.

Sonata No. 1 d (NME, Oct. 1937). Adagio Cantabile, Allegro; Aria; Toccata. Composed in 1933, this sonata shows great clarity both in texture and form. Obvious in the entire work is the composer's preference for unison and octave writing. The Toccata is in a perpetual motion style but interrupted by a short lyric section. M-D.

Fantasy (Bo&H 1939). This is, in reality, the second sonata and although written in a number of sections it gives the impression of a large three-movement work. Numerous homophonic textures are present, including arpeggi figuration, agitated unison-writing, syncopated chords, singing melodic lines supported by broken figuration. Fast repeated notes characterize the toccata-like finale with harmonics required in the final bars. D.

Sonata No. 3 E (Valley Music Press 1942). Allegro giusto; Lento; Prestissimo. A rhythmic motive in tonic-dominant relationship generates the first movement. Scale passages are used extensively, especially in the coda. Contrasted melodics in chorale style make up the second movement. Fast repeated-note motive in 7/8 generates the final movement and brings it to a stunning climax. D.

Sonata No. 4 E (Mer 1945). Hymn, Invention, Nocturne, Toccata, Hymn. Subtitled "Christmastime 1945," this is one of the few pieces that came into existence during the second world war. Varied pianistic treatment in this compact piece: chorale-like writing, imitation, double-note passage work, octave playing. D.

Nostalgic Waltzes (Mer 1947). Five waltzes: Chattery, Intimate, Capricious, Conversational, Boisterous. Although inspired by Chopin Mazurkas they also provide a clever commentary on the romantic waltz. Picturesque directions are used as well as change of mode, ostinato and some brilliant passagework. A delightful and rewarding set. M-D.

Inventions (CFP 1971). A collection of 24 pieces where "the name of the pieces rarely gives any clue as to the game that is being played with the notes." Most of the pieces involve the chromatic scale. A few use 12-tone techniques. These works wear well with both children and adults. Int.

Sonata No. 5 (CFP 1961). Entitled "Sonata quasi una Fantasia," this is Finney's major piano contribution in serial technique. Even so, tonality is never abandoned and a tremendous gamut of sounds, register, and dynamics are exposed. Virile and dramatic writing in all three movements. The most involved of the sonatas. D.

Games (CFP 1969). Finney declared that the object of this collection "is to introduce children to the entire sonority and articulation of the piano and to the types of notation that contemporary composers use." These 32 short pieces assume "that the child can reach the two extremes of the piano keyboard, and that he can reach the pedal." Improvisation is encouraged, unconventional notation. Easy to Int.

See: Maurice Hinson, "The Solo Keyboard Works of Ross Lee Finney," AMT, 20, June-July 1971, 16-18, 40.

JOSEPH-HECTOR FIOCCO (1703-1741) Flemish, Belgium

Pièces légères pour clavecin (Schott Frères). Easy to Int.

Werken voor Clavecimbel (ca. 1730) (BB) Facsimile edition.

Werken voor Clavecimbel (J. Watelet-De Ring). Vol. III in *Monumenta Musicae Belgicae*.
Contains 2 suites. Suite I: L'Angloise, L'Armonieuse, La Plaintive, La Villageoise, Les Promenades, L'Inconstante, L'Italienne, La Françoise, Adagio, Andante, Vivace.
Suite II: Allemande, La Légère, G, S, L'Inquiète, Gavotte, M, Les Sauterelles, L'Agitée, Les Zéphirs, La Musette, La Fringante. François Couperin appears to be the main inspiration for the format of these suites. Excellent craftsmanship.

EDWIN FISCHER (1886-1960) Switzerland

Sonatine C (Ries & Erler 1958). 9 p. Three movements. Classic style, efficient fingering, clever, attractive. Int.

JOHANN KASPAR FERDINAND FISCHER (1665-1746)
Germany

Fischer was one of the important predecessors of J. S. Bach. His music shows French influence and his interest in the suite must be noted. His *Complete Works for Keyboard* (clavier and organ) was published in 1901 by Br&H and was reprinted in 1965 by BB. Selections of his works can be found in *Old Masters* (Niemann-K), *The Art of the Suite* (Y. Pessl-EBM) and *Selected Keyboard Pieces* (Döflein-Schott) including Partitas in D, C and Preludes and Fugues. Also see collection: *Teachers of J. S. Bach* (Herrmann-Hug).

Musicalisches Blumen-Büschlein (1698). Selections: (L. J. Beer-HV). 8 suites, each preceded by a Prelude (among the earliest to do so), including A, C, S, Gavotte, M, Gigues, Ballet, Canaries, Passepied, Passacaille, B, Branle, Amener, Chaconne, Plainte.

Notenbüchlein (Notebook) (F. Ludwig-Schott). Includes 17 short pieces, among them Menuetts, Bourrées, Gavottes, Gigue, Marche, Sarabande.

Musikalischer Parnassus (1738) (Schott). 9 suites, each named after one of the Muses. Opening movements are titled Praeludium, Overture, Tastada, Toccata, Toccatina, Harpeggio. Usual dance movements plus Ballet anglois, Air anglois and Rigaudon.

Ariadne Musica (1702) (Schott) (D. Townsend-Sam Fox). A collection of 20 short preludes and fugues in as many different keys, a forerunner of the *Well-Tempered Clavier*. Also includes 5 short ricercari for different festivals of the church year, based on chorales.

Musikalischer Blumenstrauss (1733) (Schott). This "musical nosegay" contains 8 small suites, each containing a prelude, 8 fugues and a finale. Fischer included a table of ornaments in this collection. Intended for the organ.

See: George C. Mulacek, "The Musicalisches Blumen-Büschlein of Johann Kaspar Ferdinand Fischer," unpub. diss., University of Colorado, 1965. Excellent for historical and stylistic information pertaining to the music; also presents opinions on various aspects of performance practice. Offers the keyboard suites (1698) in a modern version.

JERZY FITELBERG (1903-1951) Poland

Sonate No. 1 (ESC).
Free tonal writing, one movement, toccata-like. Staccato repeated chords, fast broken octaves and sevenths require an advanced technique.

NICOLAS FLAGELLO (1928-) USA

Piano Sonata (Gen 1962). 38 p.
Andante con moto e rubato.
Rubato quasi recitativo: flexible tempo, large gestures.
Allegro Vivace quanto possibile: perpetual motion, advanced pianism required.

Episodes (BMC).
March, Lullaby, Pulcinella.

Prelude, Ostinato and Fugue (BMC).
Organ-like Prelude over pedal points. Homophonic textures appear in the Fugue. Brilliant figuration.

3 Dances (BMC 1945).
Abstract Dance: motoric rhythms.
Ceremonial Dance: melodic.
Tarantella: lively. Ostinato figures.

Petite Pastels (Gen).
7 drawings for young pianists.

WILLIAM FLANAGAN (1926-1969) USA

Sonata for Piano (PIC 1950). 12 p. 12 minutes. 3 movements. The first 2 movements are linked "attacca." Open harmonic texture; varying moods with abrupt dynamic and metric changes. Fluctuating tonal centers. Technical and interpretative problems.

Passacaglia (ACA 1947). 7 minutes.

ROBERT FLEMING (1921-) Canada

Fleming studied composition with Herbert Howells and Healey Willan. He is a staff composer and music Director of the National Film Board of Canada.

Sonatina (OUP 1941). 4 minutes. 2 movements.
The first movement makes much use of chordal triplets, chromaticism for coloration, and a free lyricism. Second movement exploits constant eighth-note figuration within clearly-flowing harmonies. Pleasant writing.

MARIUS FLOTHUIS (1914-) The Netherlands

Since 1955 Flothuis has been Artistic Director of the Concertgebouw Orchestra in Amsterdam. His music is very poetic and highly expressive with a tendency toward a romantic lyricism.

Suite Op. 4 (Donemus 1938). 8 minutes.

Zes Moments Musicales Op. 31 (Donemus 1947). 6 Easy Pieces.

Variations Op. 12 (B&VP 1941). 6 minutes.

CARLISLE FLOYD (1926-) USA

Teaches at Florida State University in Tallahassee, Florida.

Sonata (Bo&H 1958). Three movements, tonal, clever pianistic figuration with contrapuntal texture, brilliant closing. Large-scale. Demands virtuosity. D.

Episodes (Bo&H). Two volumes. 15 pieces, short and interesting. Int.

RICHARD FLURY (1896-1968) Switzerland

Sonata d Op. 7 (Hug).

Klavier Album (Hug). Contains 34 Miniaturen, 100 p. 16 Preludes, 54 p. 12 Kleine Stücke, 22 p.
A great variety of moods and difficulties are contained in these 176 pages of challenging writing.

ANDOR FOLDES (1913-) USA, born Hungary

Foldes has a number of pedagogic pieces published by Century Music Publishing Co.

Prelude (CF).

2 Miniatures (CF).
No. 1: folksong-like, thin textures, bitonal.
No. 2: more melodic.
Both require good finger technique. Accidentals are plentiful.

Twin Finger's Dance (EV).

Four Short Pieces (EV). Bear Dance, Hommage à Robert Schumann, Simple Story, Toy Soldiers' Parade. Int.

JOHANN NIKOLAUS FORKEL (1749-1818) Germany

Sonata d (H. Albrecht-K&S) Organum, Series V, No. 17.

Sonata D (H. Albrecht-K&S) Organum, Series V, No. 11.
Foreword in German, suggested tempo indications.
Allegretto
Andantino sustenuto
Tempo di Gavotta.

ANTOINE FORQUERAY (1671-1745) France

Pièces de clavecin (Colin Tilney-Heugel).

One of a family of musicians, Antoine Forqueray was violist to Louis XIV. These are his viol pieces, skillfully transcribed for the harpsichord by his son Jean-Baptiste (1699-1782), who has added to the edition three pieces of his own. Twenty-two pieces arranged in five suites, preface and performance suggestions in French, English and German, colorful titles.

JOHN VÄINÖ FORSMAN (1924-) Denmark, born Finland

Sonata No. 1 Op. 3 (WH 1950). 16 p.
Adagio espressivo
Presto scherzando (with a Trio: Andante cantabile)
Allegro con fuoco

Forsman mentions the lack of phrasing in this sonata. He contends that its absence gives the performer more freedom to decide his own.

Sonata No. 2 Op. 8 (Augener 1953). 15 p.
The same motive is exploited in all four movements. Tightly-knit organization resourcefully exploits the central motive.

Sonata variato No. 3 Op. 11 (Br 1955). 23 p.

Sonata No. 4 Op. 12 (Br 1955).

Sonatine Op. 2/1 (WH 1946).

Sonatine Op. 2/2 (WH 1947). 11 p.

5 Improvisations Op. 6/3 (WH 1950).
This suite for piano is reminiscent of Poulenc's *Mouvements Perpetuels*.

Piano Ideas Op. 4 (WH c. 1949). 9 p. (Suite No. 1).
Preludio, Scherzo, Intermezzo, Polka, Humoresque, Andantino, Burlesca, Impressionisme, Pastorale, Fantasia. Neoclassic style. A usable grouping might be: Intermezzo, Scherzo, Impressionisme, Humoresque.

Snefnug-Suite miniature pour les enfants (WH).

WOLFGANG FORTNER (1907-   ) Germany

Fortner studied at the Leipzig Conservatory from 1927 to 1931. He is well known as a teacher and conductor in addition to his work as a composer. Fortner is presently Director of Music at the Akademie der Künste in Berlin.

Sonatina (Schott 1934).

Kammer-musik (Schott 1944). 6 movements in neoclassic style.

Sieben Elegien für Klavier (Schott 1950). 12-tone. All 7 pieces are based on the same row.

Epigramme (Schott 1964). Mature serial writing utilizing severe contrapuntal techniques.

LUKAS FOSS (1922-) USA, born Germany, came to USA 1937

Four 2-Part Inventions (CF 1938). To be performed as a group. Lengthy. M-D.

Grotesque Dance (CF 1938). Virtuoso pianism. D.

Fantasy-Rondo (GS 1944). Lengthy, changing meters, cross rhythms, broken-chord treatment. M-D.

Scherzo Ricercato (CF 1953). M-D.

Prelude D (Hargail 1947).

WOLFGANG FRAENKEL (1897-) Austria

Variations and Fantasies on a Theme by Schönberg Op. 19/3 (UE 1954). 23 p. 15 minutes.
10 variations and 3 fantasies. First fantasie is a fugue while the last one is a passacaglia. Chomatic, involved. D.

ANTONIO FRAGOSO (1897-1918) Portugal

Composicies para Piano (Valentin de Carvalho). Vol. 1, 27 p. Contains: Petite Suite: Preludio, Berceuse, Dance. 7 Preludios. Some of the most interesting "period" piano music written in Portugal.

JEAN FRANCAIX (1912-) France

Françaix received a thorough musical training from Nadia Boulanger. He limits himself to a small harmonic vocabulary. His shorter works are his most effective.

Cinq Portraits de Jeunes Filles (Schott 1936). 9 minutes.

Eloge de la Danse (6 Epigrams of Paul Valéry) (Schott 1947).

Danse des Trois Arlequins (EMT 1959). Salon style, chromatic, effective.

L'Insectarium (Schott 1957). A suite of 6 sketches for harpsichord including the centipede, ladybug, ants, etc.

Sonata (Schott 1960). 4 movements: Prélude; Elégie; Scherzo; Toccata.
More like a suite than a sonata, abounds in dance-like rhythms.

Cinq Bis (Schott) (Five Encores). Requires advanced pianism.
To Entice the Audience
For Romantic Ladies
In Case of Success
In Case of Triumph
In Case of Delirium

Six Grandes Marches dans le Style du Ier Empire (EMT 1956).
Marche Française, Marche Autrichienne, Marche Polonaise, Marche du Sacre, Marche Russe, March Européenne.
Witty, elegant, suite-like.

Scherzo (Schott 1932). Short, delightful, delicate.

5 Etudes (Sal).

Polymélodie preparatoire (Sal).

Si Versailles m'etait contre (Editions Ray Ventura 1954). (Suite pour piano).
Henry IV, Louis XIII, Monsieur de Montespan, La Voisin, Le Grand Trianon, Jeune fille, Ronde Louis XV (for 4 hands), Napoléon, Les Cent Marches.
Technically easier and shorter than most of the other works.

CÉSAR FRANCK (1822-1890) France

Although he began his career as a concert pianist writing piano works of a showy nature, Franck soon turned to the organ and to composing for other instruments. Nearly 40 years passed before he wrote the few great piano works that still remain in the repertoire.

7 Traditional French Noëls (Werner-Curwen). Easy pedagogical pieces.

18 Short Pieces (CFP). An excellent introduction to Franck's piano style. Numbers 1 and 10 are more suited to the piano.
Int.

Grand Caprice No. 1 Op. 5 (Lemoine). One of the early virtuoso works, bravura chord playing, cadenza, fast octaves, cantabile melody, brilliant closing. D.

Prélude, Chorale et Fugue (1884) (Cortot-Curci) (CFP) (K) (Litolff). 3 connected movements requiring superb legato. The fugue, especially, needs a well-developed sense of voice delineation. D.

Prélude, Aria et Finale (1886-87) (Cortot-Curci) (Bauer-BMC) (Hamelle). Solid musicianship and fluent octave technique required. M-D.

Prélude, Fuge et Variation Op. 18 (Durand). Harold Bauer effectively transcribed this piece for piano. Easier than the immediately preceding two works. M-D.

46 Short Pieces for Piano (D. Agay-TP). Some charming unknown miniatures. Int.

TP has the pieces for solo piano in one volume edited by Vincent d'Indy.

JOHAN FRANCO (1908-) USA

3 Temple Dances (ACA 1948). 9 minutes.

1. Allegro con spirito: pentatonic influence, imitation, bitonal, thin textures.
2. Andante: chorale-like, preference for major sevenths. Colorful. Careful legato needed.
3. Allegretto molto gracioso: Rondo, terse dissonance, most dance-like of group. Imitation, interesting chord progressions, abundance of accidentals present.

Partita No. 6 (ACA 1952). 4 movements.
"Blues" influence, contrasted movements, inspiration not consistent throughout, added-note technique used. First and last movements most effective.

3 Piano Sketches (TP 1954). Church Bells, Playing Tag, Barcarolle. Short pedagogic works.

Toccata (OD) Short. Repeated accented notes.

ISADORE FREED (1900-1960) USA

Sonorités Rhythmiques (Sal 1931). Six studies. Rhythmic problems, contrasting sonorities, chromatic. M-D.

Une Fête fantasque (Sal). Colorful, impressionistic. M-D.

Five Pieces (ESC 1928-1930). Sophisticated writing, Moderately long, varied. M-D.

Sonata (ESC 1933). Allegro non troppo e ardente (irregular meters); Andante sostenuto (open harmonies, big climax); Allegro e ben ritmato (shifting accents, repeated notes, octaves, quiet closing). D.

Pastorales (ESC). 8 small pieces for young people. Mild modern flavor. Int.

Intrada and Fugue (Axelrod). Sonorous opening, sensitive 3-voiced fugue, flowing. M-D.

Sonata No. 1 (Southern 1954). 3 short movements, pleasant. M-D.

Toccatina (TP). Modal, harmonic fluctuation. Int.

Waltz on the White Keys (TP). Easy.

Inca War Song (TP). Easy.

Sonatina No. 1 (Southern 1954). Three movements, dissonant, 12-tone. Int. to M-D.

FREDERICO DE FREITAS (1902-) Portugal

The music of Freitas shows a combination of various styles and influences such as Romantic, Impressionistic and Contemporary.

10 Bagatelas (Gulbenkian Foundation). Photograph of autograph. Short, varied, mixture of styles.

O livro do Maria Frederica (Sassetti 1960).
A contemporary Portuguese "Album for the Young", variety of difficulty. 36 short pieces that explore contemporary idioms. Folk element present. Most pieces are a page in length.

Ciranda (Schott 1944). 11 p.
Extended rhapsodic poem. Varied moods and textures, large gestures.

Six Morceaux (WH 1950). 19 p.
Varied collection of teaching pieces, intermediate level, superbly contrasted. No. 6 "The Dance of the Gypsy Girl" is the most difficult. Portuguese folk elements shine through these more than interesting works.

Ingenuidades (Sassetti c. 1960).
A berceuse, arpeggio accompanimental figuration, chromatic. Voicing of line is a problem. M-D.

LUIS de FREITAS BRANCO (1890-1955) Portugal

Freitas Branco had a major influence on Portuguese music during his life. He was long associated with the National Conservatory in Lisbon.

15 Prelúdios (Sassetti c. 1961).
Varied moods and difficulty, beautifully laid out for the piano, impressionistic. Int. to M-D.

Sonatina (Sassetti). 5 p.
Allegro moderato
Andante
Rondo: Allegretto
Charming intermediate writing in a mild neoclassic style. Rondo presents the most problems. Would make an excellent program "opener."

Duas Dances (Sassetti).

Capriccietto (Sassetti).

Luar (Sassetti).

Mirages (Sassetti).

Rêverie (Sassetti).

GIROLAMO FRESCOBALDI (1583-1643) Italy

Frescobaldi was the dominant figure in Italian keyboard music of the early 17th century and one of the boldest innovators in the history of keyboard music in general. A mixture of scholar and artist pervades his highly individual style. His keyboard works are mainly of three types: fugal pieces, toccatas, and variations. The fugal pieces are the ricercari and canzonas, capriccios, and versets. The toccatas, sectional and frequently virtuoso-like, have a pulsing restlessness about them due, in part, to the unstable harmonic relationships that characterize this pre-tonal music. Frescobaldi's Preface to the 1614 edition of the toccatas contains some remarkable and necessary instructions for performance.

Complete Keyboard Works (P. Pidoux-Br) Five Volumes. I. Fantasie 1608, Canzoni alla Francese 1645. II. Capricci, Ricercari and Canzoni alla Francese 1626. III. Toccate, Partite, Balletti, Ciaconne e Passacaglie 1626. IV. Toccata Partite, etc. 1637. V. *Fiori Musicali* 1635.

Three Volumes of Keyboard Works (F. Germani-De Santis). I. 12 Toccatas from the first book of toccatas, 1614-16. II. 11 Toccatas from the second book of toccatas, 1627. III. *Fiori Musicali* includes toccatas, kyrie, canzoni, capricci, ricercari in open score using the C clefs.

Fiori Musicali (CFP).

25 Canzoni, Correnti and Balletti, 5 Partite, 16 Ricercari, Sette Toccate, Nove Toccate. Each is a separate volume edited by F. Boghen and published by Ric. Heavily edited. The Partitas are sets of variations, some quite long. Cuts may be made as sanctioned by Frescobaldi in the Preface of 1614. A wealth of beautiful and unusual music awaits the inquiring student and performer.

15 Capricci (F. Boghen-Senart).

Other reprints are contained in *L'Arte Musicale in Italia,* III; TPA, IV and V; *Trésor des Pianistes,* II.

9 Toccatas. Monumenti di Musica Italiana (Mischiati, Scarpat, Tagliavini-Br&H). Series I, Volume II (S. D. Libera 1962).

See: James F. Monroe, "Italian Keyboard Music in the Interim Between Frescobaldi and Pasquini," unpub. diss., University of North Carolina, 1959.

PETER RACINE FRICKER (1920-) Great Britain

Fricker studied at the Royal College of Music and later with Mátyás Sieber for 2 years. Serial composition and jazz have both influenced his writing. He is presently on the music faculty at the University of California at Santa Barbara.

4 Impromptus Op. 17 (Schott 1950-52).
Original pianistic writing. Effective as a group or performed individually. D.

Suite for Harpsichord (Schott 1956).
Toccata, Waltz and Variation, Alla Marcia, Arietta, Fugue.

12 Studies Op. 38 (Schott 1962) . 23 minutes.
Each study concentrates on some device: mirror-chords, Toccata (minor seconds and fourths), cantabile for LH, octaves, etc. These are studies in piano textures. Free serialism.

Variations for Piano Op. 31 (Schott). 12-tone but the basic row is never stated in full. Rhapsodic tonal sections effected by chordal treatment and rhythmic patterns.

14 Aubades (Schott 1963).
These brief works are a fine introduction to contemporary piano music. They explore a variety of techniques and textures. M-D.

4 Sonnets (Schott 1956). 12-tone. Each Sonnet is based on one of the forms of the row.

Episodes I Op. 51 (Schott 1968).

GÉZA FRID (1904-) The Netherlands

Dimensies (Donemus).

Douze caricatures musicales Op. 8 (Donemus 1930). 25 minutes.

Trois morceaux pour piano Op. 17 (B&VP 1936). 13 minutes.

JOHANN JAKOB FROBERGER (1616-1667) Germany

Froberger combined the warm harmony of his teacher Frescobaldi with French style and German melodic treatment. Probably best known as the composer who solidified the suite arrangement of dances as A, C, S, G, although the G was not always last in this organization. The emotional range of his music is great. Both Händel and Bach greatly respected Froberger.

Complete Keyboard Works Vols. VIII, XIII, and XXI of DTOe, 1901—reprinted, Graz, 1960. Contains 25 toccatas, 8 fantasias, 6 canzoni, 18 capricci, 15 ricercari and 30 suites.

6 Suites for Piano (W. Frickert-Bosworth).

Selected Keyboard Works (CFP).

Zwölf Phantasien und vier Stücke (G. Walter-Hug).

Selected Pieces (Schott).

See Anthologies and Collections: *Le Trésor des Pianistes*, Vol. III; *Klaviermusik des 17. und 18. Jahrhunderts*, Vol. I; *Old Masters; Keyboard Music of the Baroque and Rococo* (Georgii), Vol. I.

See: Avo Somer, "The Keyboard Music of Johann Jakob Froberger," unpub. diss., University of Michigan, 1963.

GERHARD FROMMEL (1906-) Germany

Sonata No. 1 F (Schott 1955). 19 p. Unusual work, fantasy-like quality, engaging for performer and audience. M-D.
Allegro: exploits triplet figuration.
Andante cantabile: ostinato-like.
Allegro (quasi una grotesca): dramatic gestures add to a rousing climax.

Sonata f♯ Op. 6 (Süddeutscher Musikverlag 1942). Postromantic harmonies, linear. M-D.

Sonata No. 4 Op. 21 (Süddeutscher Musikverlag c. 1949). M-D.

GUNNAR DE FRUMERIE (1908-) Sweden

Frumerie studied in Paris with Cortot. His works have a Gallic flavor.

Circulus Quintus Op. 62 (GM). 24 piano pieces.

Sonatina No. 2 (GM 1950). 3 movements. 9½ minutes. Thin textures. Second movement is a theme with 4 variations.

Piano Suite No. 2 (NMS 1936). Toccata, M, S, Rigaudon.

Piano Suite No. 3 (NMS 1948). Introduction, Fuga, S, Gavotte, Musette, Tarantella.

Chaconne (WH 1932). Theme and 8 variations. Abrupt ending. Reissued in 1968.

SANDRO FUGA (1906-) Italy

Sonata (Ric 1957). Large-scale 4-movement work. Advanced pianism required.

Variazioni Gioconde (Ric 1957). Theme and 12 well-developed variations. Audience appeal here.

Toccata (Ric 1935).

Sonatina (Ric 1936). 18 p. Allegro vivo, Sarabanda, Fughetta. MC, tonal.

Divertimento (Ric 1950).

Tre Preludi per pianoforte (Curci 1963).

Danza Selvaggia (Ric 1934).

Canzoni per la Gioventu (SZ 1953-55). 2 volumes.

Serenata (SZ 1940).

ANIS FULEIHAN (1900-1970) USA, born Cyprus, came to USA 1915

Cypriana (Southern). Six colorful pieces exploiting melodic and harmonic resources from the island of Cyprus. The Girl from

Paphos (staccato dance alternating with a florid song accompanied with guitar-like effects), Syrtós (rhythmic dance), Kyrenía (slow melody accompanied with broken-chord figures), Serenade (habanera or tango style), Café Dancer (like a jota in fast 3/8, drum and guitar effects). M-D.

Sonatina No. 1 (MCA 1949). Three movements using open sonorities, modal scales, march in 5/4, folk melody. M-D.

Sonatina No. 2 (MCA 1946). Three short movements: melody surrounded by flowing figuration; slow movement features 2 voices; energetic finale, quasi-fugal. M-D.

Sonata No. 1 (PIC 1940). Two extended movements: Allegro con brio e energico; Molto moderato. The second movement is a lengthy theme with variations. Mature pianism required. D.

Sonata No. 2 (Southern 1953). Three movements: Allegro: driving first theme contrasted with lyric second theme; Moderato: parallel chords; Allegro marciale: martellato theme, brilliant cadenza, pianistic throughout. D.

From the Aegean (Southern 1950). Four short dances with biting dissonances and shifting pulses: 1. Serenade 2. Tango 3. Sicilienne 4. Greek Dance. M-D.

Harvest Chant (PIC). Short, simple tune accompanied by bell-like harmonies. Int.

Fifteen Short Pieces (CF). Each is 1 or 2 pages long, varied problems in linear writing, changing meters, octaves, double notes, etc. Int.

Five Tributes (PIC 1951). Prelude, M, Gavotte, Sicilienne, Capriccio. M-D.

Sonata No. 4 (PIC 1951). Large three-movement work: Allegro moderato; Andantino mesto leads directly to a contrapuntal Intermezzo; Allegro molto, ritmico (à la grecque): a driving syncopated finale. D.

Around the Clock (Southern 1964). 12 Preludes for young pianists, short. Int.

Sonata No. 9 (Southern). Four movements, MC. M-D.

Sonata No. 11 (Bo&H c. 1970). Allegro giusto; Allegro, molto ritmico; Andantino; Allegro frenetico, e molto ritmico. Varied figuration, freely chromatic, quartal writing used in second movement, driving rhythmic closing movement, octaves. M-D.

Sonata No. 12 (Bo&H c. 1969). Allegro molto vivace; Andantino con moto; Presto. Thin textures, homophonic first movement. Large span required for lyric and expressive Andantino con moto. Cadenza-like closing ends a driving Presto. M-D.

Sonata No. 14 (Bo&H 1968). Allegro vivace; Tempo giusto, misurato, molto ritmico; Allegretto grazioso; Allegro vivace. Numerous tempo changes within the movements are skillfully carried out. Bravura sections, brilliant conclusion. M-D.

Five Very Short Pieces for Talented Young Bipeds (PIC). Int.

Ionian Pentagon (Bo&H c. 1970). 5 pieces: Allegretto, Moderato, Molto vivace, Largamente, Allegro grazioso. Mainly thin textures, varied moods, tonal. Int.

JOHANN JOSEPH FUX (1660-1741) Germany

Capriccio and Fugue K.V. 404 (I. Ahlgrimm-Dob). Excellent edition, fine preface. Editorial comment clearly distinguished from composer's markings. There are short movements after the fugue.

12 Minuets (Schenk-OBV).

3 Pieces (Schenk-OBV). Ciacona, Harpeggio e Fuga, Aria passegiata.

Sonata No. 4. See collection: *Viennese Masters from the Baroque, Classical and Biedermeier Periods.*

See: Ludwig von Köchel, *J. J. Fux.* Vienna, 1872, with thematic catalogue of all his works.

G

JENÖ GAÁL (1906-   ) Hungary

Gaál studied composition with Zoltán Kodály and completed his degree at the Franz Liszt Academy of Music in Budapest.

Piano Sonata (ZV c. 1958).

3 movements, FSF. A short-long rhythmic idea is exploited in the first two movements. The third movement utilizes nineteenth-century pianistic techniques, such as arpeggio accompaniment to chordal melodies, etc. Dramatic work. M-D.

Sonata No. 2 (EMB).

ANDREA GABRIELI (ca. 1510-1586) Italy

Gabrieli's main contribution to keyboard music was a more idiomatic style free of vocal traits.

Complete Keyboard Works (P. Pidoux-Br) In five volumes.

I: Intonazioni.
II-III: Ricercari, 1595, 1596.
IV: Canzoni and Ricercari ariosi.
V: Canzoni alla Francese.

The intonazioni are liturgical preludes, usually from 12 to 16 bars, that begin chordally and gradually introduce passage-work in faster motion. The 17 ricercari contained in the two books are monothematic (5) and polythematic (12).

Other reprints are found in TPA, I.

NIELS W. GADE (1817-1890) Denmark

Strongly influenced by Mendelssohn and Schumann, Gade retained a distinct Scandinavian character, especially in his early works.

3 Character Pieces Op. 18 (WH).

Aquarellen (Water Colors) Op. 19 (1850) (GS) (CFP) (WH) (K&S). 10 pieces, his most familiar set. A second set of 5 pieces Op. 57 appeared in 1881 (WH).

Arabeske Op. 27 (Augener).

Folkdanses Op. 31 (1855) (WH).

Idyller Op. 34 (1857) (WH). 4 pieces.

4 Fantastic Pieces Op. 41 (1862) (WH) (Augener).

The Children's Christmas Eve Op. 36 (GS) (WH). 6 elementary pieces.

Sonata Op. 28 (Br&H).

Scandinavian Folksongs (WH).

HANS GÁL (1890-) Great Britain, born Austria

Sonate Op. 28 (Simrock 1927).
A large 4-movement work with the second movement, Quasi menuetto, cast in an unusual form. Captivating. M-D.

24 Preludes (UE 1965).
In all the major and minor keys, romantic style. Each piece has at least one characteristic idea. Int. to M-D.

2 Sonatinas Op. 58 Nos. 1 and 2 (Augener (1953).

Drei Skizzen Op. 7 (UE 1921).
Short character pieces in Brahms idiom. Int.

Suite Op. 24 (Simrock).
Präludium, Menuett, Capriccio, Sarabande funèbre, Gigue.

3 Small Pieces Op. 64/1, 2, 3 (Augener).

3 Preludes Op. 65 (Augener 1956).

BLAS GALINDO-DIMAS (1910-) Mexico

Galindo-Dimas studied with Chavez, Rolón, Huizar and Copland.

Cinco Preludios (Ediciones Mexicanas 1945). M-D.

Siete Piezas (Ediciones Mexicanas 1952).
Both sets contain subtle influences of Indian folkmusic cast in a modal and linear idiom. Int. to M-D.

RAYMOND GALLOIS-MONTBRUN (1918-) France

Gallois-Montbrun is Director of the Paris Conservatoire.

Trois Pièces pour Piano (Leduc 1944).
Prélude, Menuet, Danse. Neoclassic style. Menuet is in 5/4 meter. M-D.

Mélodies et Proverbes (Leduc).

NOËL GALLON (1891-1966) France

Gallon studied piano with I. Philipp and Risler. He won the Prix de Rome in 1910 and since 1920 has taught solfège, counterpoint and fugue at the Paris Conservatory.

Sonatine (Leduc c. 1931). 20 p.
A charming work, Fauré influence. M-D.

Ker an Diskouiz (Lemoine c. 1928).
6 pieces. See especially No. 5 Escargots et Papillins.

Pour un arbre de noël (Deiss c. 1932). 28 p. A suite.

Sonate brève f# pour Clavecin ou Piano (M. Combre 1960). 16 p.

Tout en Canon (Durand).
30 musical canons in all major and minor keys.

BALDASSARE GALUPPI (1706-1785) Italy

The Venetian composer Galuppi, although primarily known for his "opere buffe", left approximately 90 keyboard sonatas. Some are in 2 and 3 movements, while a very few are in 1, 4 and 5 movements. Motivic development and 'galant' melodic treatment characterize these works.

12 Sonatas (Bongiovanni).

6 Sonatas (Benvenuti-Bongiovanni).

6 Sonatas (E. Woodcock-Galliard c. 1963). Contains excellent notes on interpretation and intelligent editing.

4 Sonate (Piccioli-SZ c. 1952).

Sonata G (M. Maffioletti-Carisch).

See also *TPA, XII.*

Sonata D, *Pièces de Clavecin des 17me et 18 me siècles* (B. Selva-Senart).

Sonata A, *Cembalisti Italiani del Settecento* (Benvenuti-Ric).

Sonatas A♭, D *Italian Sonatas of the 18th Century* (de Paoli-JWC).

Passatempo al Cembalo-Sonate (Franco Piva-Institute per la collaborazione Culturale, Venice c. 1964). Vol. VI of the *Cembalo collana di musiche veneziane, Inedite o Rare* (TP). Six multi-movement sonatas dating from 1781 (?), late works. These sonatas differ in many ways from his other keyboard works, suggesting a probable later date of composition. They are cast in sonata design, employing binary forms within a three-part thematic tonal organization. Sonata No. 1 in 3 movements, the others in 2. Lyric melodic treatment, sequential passage-work and brusque cadences are abundant. Discrepancies between the holograph manuscript and this edition are not always explained.

Sonate per il Cembalo, Transcribed and revised by Hedda Illy, Vol. 1-15 *Sonate* (De Santis).

Sonata D (Georgii-Arno Volk). Vol. III of *Keyboard Music of the Baroque and Rococo.* 4 movements: Adagio, Allegro, Staccato, Giga.

RUDOLPH GANZ (1877-1972) USA, born Switzerland

Ganz, distinguished pianist and pedagogue, has been President-Emeritus of Chicago Musical College since 1954.

Peasant Danse Op. 24/3 (EBM 1912). Humorous. Int.

Scherzino Op. 29/2 (CF). Short and brilliant. M-D.

Idée Mélancolique, Idée Rhythmique Op. 30 (Art Publication Society of St. Louis 1932). Well-written, pianistic. D.

Little Sphinx, Little Elf Op. 31 (Remick 1934). Ganz says: "the Sphinx is for good players, the Elf for better ones."

Animal Pictures (CF c. 1932). 20 pieces for children.

Symphonic Variations on a Theme by Brahms Op. 21 (CF). D.

4 Compositions for Piano Op. 27 (CF c. 1909).

1. After moonlight
2. Louis XV
3. On the Lake
4. Hoffmannesque

Exercises for Piano—Contemporary and Special (SB). Int. to D. "It is to train student's ears as well as their hands for the new sounds in the 20th-Century music that I have devised this book."

ALEJANDRO GARCÍA-CATURLA (1906-1940) Cuba

García-Caturla's music blends Afro-Hispanic tunes and rhythms in a unique style.

Comparsa (NME 1930). Negro dance, bravura writing, rich sonorities, syncopated rhythm, ostinato basses. D.

Sonata Corta (NME 1927). One short movement, 2-part linear writing, allegro con brio. M-D.

Berceuse Campesina (CF 1939). Short, folk lullaby. Int.

Son f (CF 1939).

Preludio Corta No. 1 (NME 1927). To the memory of Erik Satie, simple melody, open textures, unbarred. Int.

ROBERTO GARCÍA-MORILLO (1911-   ) Argentina

García-Morillo's style is characterized by stringent harmonies, forceful rhythmic treatment and primitive qualities. He teaches at the National Conservatory of Music in Buenos Aires.

Tres Piezas Op. 2 (Ric 1933). Excellent recital group, requires large span. M-D.

Cortejo Barbaro: tumultuous, energetic, drum-like bass built on ostinato, sonorous.

Poema: chromatic introduction, lyric, long pedal points, improvisatory.

Danza de los animales al salir del Arca de Noe: "Homage to Stravinsky," driving, grotesque.

Conjuros Op. 3 Incantations. (Southern 1934). Suite, primitive, atmospheric. M-D.

Tchaka: stark opening, builds to large climax over ostinato basses.

El Genio de las Aguas: primitive melodies, gruff bass treatment, contrasted second half.

Schango, el Genio del Trueno: animated, driving, incisive.

El Primogénito del Cielo y de la Tierra: descending chromatic fourths under quiet trills, leads to a marcha funebre with ostinato bass, dissonant accented melody.

Sonata del Sur Op. 4 (EAM 1935). Danza, Marcha funebre; Scherzo; Danza, Himno, Coda. Much rhythmic drive throughout entire piece. M-D.

Sonata No. 2 (Ric 1935, revised 1959). 10 minutes. Prológo (Patético, Marziale, Arioso); Scherzo; Epílogo (Patético, Marziale, Arioso).

Danza de Harrild Op. 9 (Ric 1941). 3 minutes.

Variaciones Op. 10 (Ric 1942). Six variations on four three-bar phrases, parallel seventh chords. Astringent, bare, fine craft, climax, finale. M-D.

Variaciones Op. 13 (ECIC 1944). Five minutes. Seventeen variations on a three-measure theme. Stark sonorities, major seventh and minor ninth featured, reminiscent of the variations of Aaron Copland, to whom these variations are dedicated. D.

Sonata No. 3 Op. 14 (Ric 1944-45). 10 minutes. Allegro; Lento; Allegro.

Cuentos para Niños Traviesos (Ric 1953). Second series. 12 minutes. Caperucita Rosa; Amazonas; Gladiadores. Int.

Variaciones Apolíneas Op. 25 (Ric 1958-59). 13½ minutes.

Sonata No. 4 Op. 26 (Ric 1959). 12 minutes.
Allegro: brisk 7/8 with lyric second theme.
Lento: mildly dissonant.
Toccata: 8/8 (3, 3, 2), brilliant, lyric second theme of first movement returns treated differently, tumultuous conclusion. D.

JANINA GARŚCIA (-) Poland

2 Sonatiny for fortepiano Op. 4/1, 2 (PWP 1947). Interesting writing. Also contains a Polish Folksong Op. 26/9, harmonized. Fun to play. Int.

STEPHANOS GASULEAS (1931-) Greece

11 Aphorisms (UE 1961) 8 p.
Volume I in a series edited by Hanns Jelinek called *Libelli Dodecaphonic* whose aim is to introduce "the New World of Music" to those with limited pianistic techniques. The preface states that all of these pieces are by Mr. Gasuelas' pupils. The pieces are 2 or 3 lines long and introduce a variety of contemporary techniques. Int. to M-D.

WALTHER GEISER (1897-) Switzerland

Geiser's music shows strong neoclassic tendencies. He studied at the Berlin Academy of Arts in the master class of Busoni, who greatly influenced his style.

Suite Op. 41 (Br 1952).
5 formal structures in contrapuntal technique. D.

Sonatine (Vogel).

Aria and Impromptu Op. 4 (Hug).

ARTHUR GELBRUN (1913-) Israel, born Poland

Gelbrun studied with Molinari and Casella at the Accademia Santa Cecilia in Rome and with Scherchen and Burkhardt in Switzerland after graduating from the Warsaw Conservatory in violin and orchestra conducting. He teaches conducting and composition at the Rubin Academy of Music in Tel Aviv.

Four Preludes (IMI 1959). Constructed on a 12-tone row. M-D. Quiet lyric Molto Lento, toccata-like Vivace assai, impressionistic Languido, thoughtful Tranquillo.

HARALD GENZMER (1909-) Germany

"Genzmer's style combines the contrapuntal writing of Hindemith's middle period with a certain amount of expressive colouring." GD, 3, 596.

Studies (CFP). Vol. I: 11 pieces. Vol. II: 10 pieces. Complex but grateful to the pianist. Vol. II more difficult.

Sonata No. 2 (Schott 1942). 4 movements. Neoclassic style. Final fugue works to great climax. D.

10 Preludes (CFP).

Sonatinas Nos. 1 and 3 (Schott). Reminiscent of Hindemith. M-D.

Capriccio (Second Sonatina) (Schott 1954). A concise 4-movement work, well proportioned, careful attention to details. M-D.

ROBERTO GERHARD (1897-1970) Spain, lived in Great Britain since 1939

Gerhard studied piano with Granados and composition with Pedrell and Schönberg. He is skillful at mixing styles but twelve-tone technique has great appeal to him.

3 Impromptus (K. Prowse 1950).

EDWIN GERSCHEFSKI (1909-) USA

Gerschefski is chairman of the Music Department at the University of Georgia.

3 Dances for Piano Op. 11 (ACA). D. Lento: Complex chromatic writing, difficult notation.

American Tarantella: Presto preciso, rhythmic drive, many sequences.
Andantino gracieusement: Highly chromatic rondo.

6 Waltzes Op. 19 (ACA 1961).
Varied moods and tempi, much chromaticism, one key signature used for entire set. M-D.

Sonata Op 22 (CFE 1963). 4 movements.
Thin textures, unison writing between hands in first and last movement, angular melodic construction, preference for major sevenths, imitation (Menuetto), chromatics in abundance (last movement). Some awkward spots. D.

GEORGE GERSHWIN (1898-1937) USA

Preludes (New World Music). Three short pieces using jazz as their inspiration. M-D.
Allegro ben ritmato e deciso: mainly rhythmic, syncopated rhythms, bravura playing.
Andante con moto e poco rubato: lyric blues with ostinato-like accompaniment.
Allegro ben ritmato e deciso: craggy rhythms, syncopated, brilliant closing for the group.

GEORGIO FEDERICO GHEDINI (1892-1965) Italy

Since 1936 Ghedini developed a personal style, transparent, sometimes leaning towards twelve-tone technique, but always clear in texture.

Puerilia (Ric c. 1961). 9 p. Originally composed 1922.
4 clever short pieces on 5 notes. Mixture of influences.
La formica; Il gatto; Il cucu; Il gallo.

Capriccio-Ricercare (SZ 1944).

Divertimento contrappuntistico (Ric).

MATTHIAS VAN DEN GHEYN (1721-1785) Flemish, Belgium

"As a composer van den Gheyn is of the Handelian school; his works are written in the idiom of his contemporaries and resemble the music of Arne." GD, 3, 624.

Collection d'oeuvres composées par d'anciens et de célèbres Clavecinistes Flamands (van Elewyck-Schott Frères).
Contains 6 *Divertimenti* (about 1760) and 6 *Suites*, Op. 3.

Sonata f: in collection *L'Arte Antica e Moderna* (Ric). Vol. III.

LUIS GIANNEO (1897-) Argentina

Gianneo's piano pieces are written in a fluent and graceful style. He is professor of harmony and composition at the La Plata Conservatory.

Cuatro Composiciones (Ric Americana 1916-17). 13 minutes. Vieja cancíon; Berceuse; Arabesca; En bateau. A fresh folk-like spirit permeates all 4 pieces. Int. to M-D.

Bailecito (Ric Americana 1931). 4 minutes.

Sonatina (Southern 1938). An extended work, charming, gentle. Allegro: running sixteenths; Tempo di Minuetto: quartal harmonies; Allegro vivo: dancelike rondo, florid passage work, staccato texture. M-D.

Three Argentine Dances (Southern 1939). Gato, Tango, Chacarera. FSF, tonal, attractive harmonies and syncopated rhythms. Int.

Música para Niños (Southern 1941). Ten delightful pieces, many styles, some are based on Southern American tunes and rhythms. Int.

Cinco pequeñas Piezas (ESC 1938). Five short pieces: Coquetry, Cradle Song, March, Waltz, Perpetual Motion. Int.

Sonata b♭ (CF 1943). 20 minutes. Allegro: cross-rhythms, some bitonal usage, running 6/8; Romanza: a simple Andante accompanied melody, florid da capo, short; Allegro molto: a brilliant 6/8 movement, some dissonance, dramatic closing. M-D.

Villancico (EAM 1946). Melancholy 3/4, sensitive use of chromaticism. Int.

Caminito de Belén (EAM 1946). Marchlike, simple staccato clusters. Int.

Sonata No. 3 (Ric Americana 1957). 18 minutes. Allegro impetuoso; Adagio sostenuto; Allegro deciso.

Cinco Bagatelas (Ric Americana 1958). 10 minutes.

VITTORIO GIANNINI (1903-1966) USA

"Giannini . . . showed in his many compositions a superlative craftsmanship that always served to communicate a warmth of feeling far from academic . . ." MTC, 436-7.

Prelude and Fughetta (TP). Modal, interesting modulations, pedal point, contrapuntal neoclassic style. Prelude, crisp toccata style, 2-voice fughetta. M-D.

Variations on a Cantus Firmus (EV). Moderato Var. 1-10, Aria Var. 11-12, Toccata Var. 13-22, Interlude Var. 23-24.
Large work, varied pianistic demands, requiring some virtuoso playing. Can be played in groups or as a whole. Published in four parts. D.

Sonata (Ric c. 1966). Three movements, 24 p.
The first movement is a vigorous and exciting allegro, the second movement a lovely slow song, the last movement is fast with ostinato bass figures, a good LH octave technique is necessary. Pianistic. D.

WALTER GIANNINI (1917-   ) USA

Sonatina (AME 1958).
Cantabile: flowing melody.
Chorale: many accidentals, sophisticated writing.
Dance Finale: gigue-like, thin textures, effective, MC. M-D.

Modal Variations (AME 1951).
Theme and 7 variations based on first 6 tones of the mixolydian mode beginning on E♭. Unusual sonorities. Variation 3 calls for a fine legato octave technique. M-D.

ORLANDO GIBBONS (1583-1625) Great Britain

In addition to the 6 pieces in *Parthenia,* there are some forty surviving manuscripts containing keyboard works of Gibbons. The keyboard music, with the exception of the variations and dance-tunes, is reserved and austere. Although Gibbons was one of the finest performers of his day, virtuosity plays a relatively small role in these works.

Keyboard Music, Musica Britannica XX (G. Hendrie-S&B c. 1962). 45 works, 5 doubtful and incipits of 9 spurious works.

Complete Keyboard Works (M. H. Glyn-S&B) Five volumes containing 52 works. I: Masks and Dances. II: Variations. III: Pavans and Galliards. IV and V: Fancies.

A Collection of 8 Keyboard Pieces selected from Volume XX of *Musica Britannica* (G. Hendrie-S&B).

A Selection of Short Dances (S&B).

The King's Juell. An Allmaine consisting of variations on a double theme. In *Complete Keyboard Works* Vol. II & *Benjamin Cosyn's Virginal Book* (J&WC).

Fancy A re. Fugal, sustained, noble. *Complete Keyboard Works* Vol. IV.

The Woods so Wilde. Gibbon's most extended set of variations developed differently from Byrd's, on the same tune. FVB, I, 144. Incomplete in this volume. No. 29 in *Complete Keyboard Music.*

See: Gerald Hendrie, "An Edition and Critical Study of the Keyboard music of Orlando Gibbons," unpub. diss., Cambridge (Selwyn) University, 1961-2.
"The Keyboard Music of Orlando Gibbons (1583-1625)," PRMA, 89, 1962-3, 1-15.

MIRIAM GIDEON (1906-   ) USA

Every note is meaningful in Miriam Gideon's music, a music which has both style and polish. She studied with Roger Sessions and has been on the faculties of Jewish Theological Seminary, Manhattan School of Music and College of the City of New York.

6 Cuckoos in Quest of a Composer (ACA). 15 minutes.
Il Cuculo Nel Rinascimento: 3-voice ricercar, short (17 bars).
Kleines Praeludium in Barockstil: delightful two-voice writing.
Klassische Sonatina auf ein berühmtes Motiv: an extended first movement, difficulty of Clementi Op. 36 *Sonatinas*. Second movement is a theme and 4 contrasted variations. Third movement is a Rondo.
Le Coucou Au Dix-Neuvième Siècle: Prélude sentimental, chromatic harmony.
Impression D'un Coucou: more difficult than other movements.
The Bird: contemporary idioms.
A clever suite tracing the development of musical composition from the Renaissance to the present using the "Cucu" theme in various guises. Int. to M-D.

Piano Suite No. 3 (LG 1951). Five brief atonal movements. M-D. In collection *New Music for the Piano*.

Canzona (NME, Jan. 1947). One movement, two-voice texture, wide skips, crisp touch, energetic, atonal. M-D.

Of Shadows Numberless (Composer's Facsimile Edition—ACA 1966). Suite for piano based on Keat's "Ode to a Nightingale" 5 movements each headed by a short quotation from the poem. 12 minutes. M-D.

WALTER GIESEKING (1895-1956) Germany

Drei tanz-improvisationen (A. Fürstner c. 1926). 11 p.

GILARDO GILARDI (1889-1963) Argentina

la Serie Argentina (Ric 1931).
Noviando, La Firmeza, Chacarera.

Cantares de mi Cantar (Ric 1939).
Endecha, Trova, Elegia, Rondel.

Cuatro Preludios Unitonales (Ric 1950).
Impresionista, Clasico, Romantico, Danzante.

ANTHONY GILBERT (1934-) Great Britain

Sonata Op. 1 (Schott). 3 movements. 19 p.
Post-Webern style, many subtle effects; staccato bass notes half caught by the pedal, harmonics, sensitive use of sostenuto pedal, etc. First movement, SA design. Second movement, a sensitive cantilena; third movement, a Scherzo with two trios. Percussive treatment is highly effective. D.

ALBERTO GINASTERA (1916-) Argentina

Ginastera was trained in his native country and has developed a personal style that combines certain nationalistic traits with advanced contemporary techniques. His contribution to piano literature, while not large, is significant.

Danzas Argentinas (Durand 1937). A suite of three dances. Danzas del viejo boyero: polytonal with RH on white keys, LH on black keys; Danza de la moza donosa: swinging motion, attractive; Danza del gaucho matrero: energetic, driving motion. M-D.

Tres Piezas (Ric Americana 1940). Cuyana: flowing, lyric, melodic; Norteña: involved rhythms, atmospheric; Criolla: driving, propulsive. M-D.

Malambo (Ric Americana 1940). Driving rhythmic dance in 6/8, ostinato, dissonant. M-D.

Twelve American Preludes (CF 1944). Int. to D.

Vol. I: For Accents: bitonal, broken chords, arpeggi.
Sadness: melodic, single accompanying voice.
Creole Dance: rhythmic, dissonant, violent.
Vidala: melodic, flowing dissonance in 3/8.
In the First Pentatonic Minor Mode: 2-part counterpoint, Andante, in 7/8.
Tribute to Roberto García Morillo: presto alternating hands, sixteenth notes.

Vol. II: Octaves: skips, etude style.
Tribute to J. J. Castro: short, melodic, tango tempo.
Tribute to Aaron Copland: bravura playing required.

Pastorale: lento soprano melody, alto ostinato, open texture in bass.

Tribute to Heitor Villa-Lobos: wild, unison writing, skips, syncopated.

In the First Pentatonic Major Mode: pedal point under bell sonorities, FFFF ending.

Suite de danzas criollas (Barry 1946). A set of five varied dances in Creole style. 12 p.

Clusters are called for in No. 2, span of ninth required, unusual rhythmic treatment. M-D.

Rondo on Argentine Children's Folk Tunes (Bo&H 1947). 4 p. Delightful reharmonizations, clever rhythmic treatment, gliscando, crashing close. Int.

Sonata (Barry 1952). Four movements written in the post-romantic, dramatic tradition although some thematic treatment stems from nationalistic sources. Allegro marcato: changing meters, contrasted textures, great excitement; Presto misterioso: double octaves spread 3 octaves apart proceed in a breathless 3/8; Adagio molto appassionato: rhapsodic, three sections; Ruvido ed ostinato: toccata-like, percussive, hemiola usage brilliantly executed. D.

Milonga (Ric 1948). Slow, 2-page dance, some tricky rhythmic problems. Int.

LODOVICO GIUSTINI (18th cen., Flourished 1736) Italy

Sonate da cimbalo di piano e forte (Florence, 1732), facsimile, with preface by Rosamond E. M. Harding. (Cambridge University Press, c. 1933).

Contains 12 sonatas: eight in 4 movements and four in 5 movements. Some movements have dance titles, others have only tempo indications. This is the first known published music that specified the use of the pianoforte. Contains bibliographical notes. Int. to M-D.

LOUIS CHRISTIAN AUGUST GLASS (1864-1936) Denmark

Fantasi for Klavier Op. 35 (SPDM 1919). 16 p.

Klaverstykker Op. 66 (K&S 1931). 11 p.
Pastorale
Nocturne
Ecossaise

Landlige billeder Op. 48 (WH c. 1915). (Pictures from the Country). 17 p. 6 pieces.

Sonata A♭ Op. 25 (Br&H c. 1898). 31 p.

Aquareller Op. 58 (WH).

Impromptu and Capriccio Op. 52 (WH).

ALEXANDER GLAZUNOV (1865-1936) USSR

Glazunov, a pupil of Rimsky-Korsakov and later greatly influenced by Liszt, Wagner and Brahms, was more successful with smaller forms than with the sonata. He was a master craftsman whose music sometimes lacks direction, even though beautiful melodies and original harmonic treatment abound at every turn.

Complete Piano Works (USSR) 1 volume, (1955). This volume includes all of the following works except the sonatas and sonatinas (other editions available as indicated):

Suite on the theme "S-a-s-c-h-a" Op. 2 (1882-83). 32 p. Sascha was a derivative of his own name Alexander. Consists of an introduction, prelude, scherzo, nocturne and valse.

2 Pieces Op. 22. Barcarolle D♭. Novelette D.

Waltzes on the theme "S-a-b-e-la" Op. 23.

Prelude and 2 Mazurkas Op. 25 (1888). Prelude D, Mazurkas A, D♭.

3 Concert Studies Op. 31 (1889). No. 3 is the best known. Also available separately (Belaieff). No. 1 has 16th-note repetition from beginning to end in 3rds, 4ths, 5ths, and single line. M-D.

Nocturne D♭ Op. 37. Rich harmonies, interesting inner voices, influenced by Liszt.

3 Miniatures Op. 42 (1893), Pastorale D, Polka B♭, Valse D. No. 3 (Belaieff).

3 Morceaux Op. 49 (1893). Prelude, Caprice-Impromptu, Gavotte. No. 3 (Belaieff).

2 Impromptus Op. 54 (1896). D♭, A♭.

Prelude and Fugue d Op. 62 (1899). 10 minutes. Chromatic, dramatic.

Theme and 15 Variations f♯ Op. 72 (1900). Imitation of styles of various composers. Also available (IMC) (Belaieff).

Grand Valse de Concert E♭ Op. 41 (Belaieff).

Prelude and Fugue e (GS). Impressive Prelude, complex Fugue.

First Sonata b♭ Op. 74 (1901) (Belaieff) (USSR). See: SSB, 714-15. 3 movements. 39 p.

Second Sonata E Op. 75 (1901) (Belaieff) 39 p. A large 3-movement work. First movement is SA design with an interesting development section, leads to a second movement Scherzo in ABA design. Finale employs thick chordal structures throughout until fugue begins 6 pages before end. Brilliant close.

Sonata G (Easy Sonata) (1880-82) (Sorokin-USSR).

Sonatina a (1880-82) (Sorokin-USSR).

REINHOLD GLIÈRE (1875-1956) Russia

Most of these pieces require well-developed finger dexterity.

5 Esquisses Op. 17 (Jurgenson). B♭, e♭, A, C, F♯.

2 Esquisses Op. 40 (USSR). D♭, c♯.

3 Morceaux Op. 19 (Jurgenson). Mazurka a, Intermezzo B, Mazurka b.

3 Morceaux Op. 21 (Jurgenson). Tristesse, Joie, Chagrin.

6 Morceaux Op. 26 (Jurgenson). Préludes B♭, E♭, b, Chanson simple, Mazurka c♯, Feuille d'album. Chanson simple (JWC).

25 Preludes Op. 30 (Jurgenson).

3 Mazurkas (CF).

12 Student Pieces Op. 31 (Mirovitch-MCA) (CFP).

Album of 21 Pieces (USSR).

MICHAEL GLINKA (1804-1857) Russia

Complete piano works in volume 6 of *Complete Edition* (N. Zagornie-USSR 1958).

Variations on an original theme F (1824). Cadenza-like introduction, theme and 4 variations.

Variations on a theme from Mozart's Don Giovanni E♭. For harp or piano, 2 versions 1854 and 1856. Theme and 5 variations.

Variations on Benedetta siá la madre E (1826). Theme and 6 variations. Variation 6 is fantasy-like, in Tempo di polacca a capriccio, and extended. A second set is entitled *Romance Variations*.

Variations on a Russian Air, Mid Gentle Dales (1826; written down 1854). Theme and 5 variations.

Variations on a theme from Cherubini's opera Faniska (1827). 4 variations and a Brilliante Finale.

Nocturne E♭ for piano or harp (1828). ABA and extended coda.

7 Mazurkas.

4 New Contredanses with a Finale.

Variations on a theme from Donizetti's Anna Bolena (1831). Theme and 4 variations. Variation 3 is in 2 parts: Un poco piu vivo, and Andante.

5 Nouvelles Quadrilles Françaises.

Variations on 2 themes from the ballet Chao-Kang (1831). Theme and 4 variations.

Rondino brillante on a theme from Bellini's I Montecchi ed i Capuleti. In Mendelssohnian style, brilliant, glittering, showy.

Boléro, based on song "O my Wonderful Maiden" (1840).

Tarantella (1843) on the Russian theme *"In the Field There Stood a Birch Tree."*

Prayer Without Words (1847).

Child's Polka (1854).

BENJAMIN GODARD (1849-1895) France

Au Matin Op. 83 (Cranz) (GS).

Etude A♭ Op. 82 (Cranz). C (Prélude) Op. 149/1 (Simrock).

Chopin (GS). A graceful Waltz.

Second Mazurka B♭ Op. 54 (WH) (GS). *Fourth Mazurka* Op. 103/4 (GS).

Nocturnes F Op. 68 and D♭, Op. 139 (Durand).

Sonata Fantastique Op. 63 (ca. 1880) (Hamelle). More like a four-movement suite with programmatic titles for each movement. Highly polished, salon style, facile.

18 Selected Pieces with portrait and biographical sketch (GS). 2 volumes. Vol. I: Gavotte Op. 16, 1st Valse, 1st Mazurka, Les hirondelles, Pan, En valsant, Novellozza, Chopin, Le cavalier fantastique, Alfred de Musset.
Vol. II: 2nd Mazurka, 2nd Valse, Au matin, Valse chromatique, Venitiènne, Française, Guirlandes, 4th Mazurka.

Waltz No. 2 Op. 56 (Schott).

LEOPOLD GODOWSKY (1870-1938) Poland

Godowsky is considered by many authorities to have possessed one of the most perfect pianistic mechanisms of all times. His piano compositions are unique in many ways and their contrapuntal complexities and elaborate detail make many of them very difficult.

53 Studies based on Chopin Etudes (CFP) 5 volumes. These pieces push piano technique beyond the frontiers established by Liszt. Godowsky explained his transcriptions of these

Etudes as follows: "The fifty-three studies based upon twenty-six Etudes of Chopin have manifold purposes. Their aim is to develop the mechanical, technical and musical possibilities of pianoforte playing, to expand the peculiarly adapted nature of the instrument to polyphonic, polyrhythmic and polydynamic work, and to widen the range of possibilities in tone colouring. The unusual mental and physical demands made upon the performer by the above mentioned work, must invariably lead to a much higher proficiency in the command of the instrument, while the composer for the piano will find a number of suggestions regarding the treatment of the instrument, and its musical utterance in general. Special attention must be drawn to the fact, that owing to innumerable contrapuntal devices, which frequently compass almost the whole range of the keyboard, the fingering and pedalling are often of a revolutionary character, particularly in the twenty-two studies for the left hand alone. The preparatory exercises included in a number of the studies will be found helpful in developing a mechanical mastery over the pianoforte by applying them to the original Chopin studies as well as to the above mentioned versions. The fifty-three studies are to be considered in an equal degree suitable for concert purposes and private study." Harold Schonberg, in his book *The Great Pianists* says: (p. 323) "And despite the enormous difficulties, the *Paraphrases* (Studies) were not intended to be played as bravura stunts. Godowsky had musical aims in mind . . . they . . . represent a philosophy where the piano itself was the be-all and the end-all, less a musical instrument than a way of life, and the paraphrases end up not music for the sake of music but music for the sake of the piano."

Sonata e (1911) (Schlesinger). 5 movements, 58 pages, great range of emotional and technical difficulties. For a thorough discussion see: SSB, 419-20.

Triakontameron (GS). 6 volumes. 30 pieces in triple time. Not overly difficult.

ıonoramas (1925) (CF). 12 pieces of descriptive Javanese music. 4 books. D.

Moto Perpetuo (Durand).

Polonaise C (Durand).

Passacaglia b (CF). A huge work on the bass theme from the opening of Schubert's *Unfinished Symphony.*

Numerous transcriptions published by (Cranz) (Schott) (CF). (Southern) has three concert paraphrases on themes of Johann Strauss: Fledermaus; Wine, Women and Song; Artists' Life. Published separately.

See: L. S. Saxe, "The Published Music of Leopold Godowsky," Notes, 14, March 1957, 165ff.

ROGER GOEB (1914-) USA

Goeb studied with Nadia Boulanger and Otto Luening. He received advanced degrees from New York University and the University of Iowa. Luening has observed that "Goeb has developed in recent years a melodic-rhythmic line which brings a lyric expressiveness to some of his most complex pages. In his harmonic practice, Goeb projects contrasting sounds in such a way and with such rhythm that the listener is able to absorb even new and daring material without too much difficulty. This approach to harmony can also give a new sound to more familiar chordal material."

Dance Suite (ACA). 14 minutes.

Martial: steady march in fourths and fifths, crisp staccato required.

Largo: built on an ostinato-like bass in octaves, many accidentals.

Grazioso: flexible ostinato-like figure, needs steady rhythmic drive.

Blues: "slow and swinging" mood, boogie bass in mid-section. Reminiscent of Second Gershwin *Prelude.*

Animato: lively rhythmic melodic line throughout, scale passages, shifts from 3/8 to 2/8. Strong energetic ending. M-D.

Fuga Contraria (ACA 1950). Five 12-tone fugues, problems in clarity of texture. D.

Fantasia (ACA 1950). Broad-scale work, dissonant and percussive. D.

ALEXANDER GOEHR (1932-   ) Great Britain, born Germany

Goehr studied with Olivier Messiaen at the Paris Conservatory. He uses dissonance to a high degree and his rhythmic procedure is complex. Serial writing appeals to Goehr and all of the piano works listed below employ this technique.

Sonata Op. 2 (Schott 1951-2). 12 minutes (In memory of Serge Prokofieff.) A 3-sectioned one-movement dodecaphonic work employing clusters at climaxes, octave doubling and ostinati. D.

Capriccio Op. 6 (Schott 1958). 5 minutes. Complex rhythmic subleties produce sensitive expressive nuances. D.

Three Pieces for Piano Op. 18 (Schott 1965). 10 minutes. Cantus firmus techniques used in all 3. No. 3 is a set of variations. Colorful writing. No. 1 was published in M&M, 18, October 1969, 40-1.

RICHARD FRANKO GOLDMAN (1910-   ) USA

Goldman, a musician who has been conductor, critic, teacher and writer, is presently President of both Peabody Conservatory of Music and Peabody Institute of the City of Baltimore.

Nine Bagatelles (Axelrod). Small pieces for children illustrated by Alexandra Rienzi. Easy.

Sonatina (Mer 1942). Three contrasted movements. Energetic opening movement with a contrasting lyric theme; rich harmonies are present in the slow movement; fast finale in 5/8 with hornpipe qualities. Large span plus rhythmic agility required. M-D.

Etude on the White Keys (Mer). Double notes, chords, irregular rhythms, brilliant. M-D.

Aubades (Mer). Four short pieces: 1 and 3 are melodic, 2 and 4 contain running figuration. M-D.

EUGENE GOOSSENS (1893-1962) Great Britain

Concert Study Op. 10 (JWC). Broken chords, staccato sixteenths both hands. D.

Kaleidoscope Op. 18 (JWC). 12 short pieces, chromatic harmony. Int.

Four Conceits Op. 20 (JWC 1917). Short, M-D. First three pieces grotesque in character.
Gargoyle; Dance Memories; Marionette Show; Walking Tune: chordal treatment.

Nature Poems Op. 25 (JWC 1919). Lengthy works, chordal treatment, chromatic harmony. M-D.
Awakening; Pastoral; Bacchanal.

Homage to Debussy Op. 29 (JWC).

Two Studies Op. 38 (JWC).
Folk Tune: quiet harmonization, chromatic harmony.
Scherzo: lively, lyric mid-section.

Ships: 3 Preludes (Curwen). Character sketches, M-D.
The Tug; The Tramp; The Liner.

HÉCTOR MELO GORIGOYTIA (1899-) Chile

Gorigoytia teaches at the University of Chile. He founded the Society of Chilean Composers, the National Association of Composers and other groups.

Manchas de Color (Southern).
3 short pieces in dissonant idiom. M-D.
Prelude: large chords.
Spring: melodic.
This Age a King: shifting chords.

LOUIS MOREAU GOTTSCHALK (1829-1869) USA

Gottschalk was one of the most flamboyant figures in nineteenth-century American music. He was the first American to rank with the greatest European virtuosi of his time. His piano compositions, over 100, require a solid technique. Many demand virtuosity of the highest degree and all are well laid out for the piano. Gottschalk drew on Afro-American and Creole sources for much of his inspiration.

The Piano Works of Louis Moreau Gottschalk with a biographical essay by Robert Offergeld (1969) (Arno Press), 5 volumes, 112 pieces, 1,520 pp.

Piano Music of Louis M. Gottschalk (J. Behrend-TP 1956). Brief notes and biography. Bamboula Op. 2, Le Bananier, The Banjo Op. 15, Berceuse Op. 47, The Last Hope Op. 16, L'Union Op. 48, Pasquinade Op. 59, Ricordati Op. 26.

A Compendium of Piano Music compiled and edited by Eugene List (CF 1971). Seven pieces: The Banjo; La Savane, Souvenir de Porto Rico; Danza Op. 33; Ojos Criollos Op. 37; Minuet a Seville Op. 30; La Mancenillier Op. 11.

Gottschalk Album (Augener).
Danse Ossianique, The Banjo Op. 15, Pasquinade.

Orfa Grande Polka (TP). Introduction, polka, marziale section; all sparkle and dash.

Souvenir de Porto Rico (Mer). Introduction, theme and refrain, continuous variations.

Ojos Criollos (Paxton). A Cuban dance.

Le Poète Mourant (Paxton). One of Gottschalk's most popular works.

See: Robert Offergeld, *The Centennial Catalogue of the Published and Unpublished Compositions of Louis Moreau Gottschalk.* New York: Stereo Review, 1970.

John G. Doyle, "The Piano Music of Louis Moreau Gottschalk (1829-1869)," unpub. diss., New York University, 1960.

Louis M. Gottschalk, *Notes of a Pianist.* New York: Knopf, 1964. Edited by Jeanne Behrend.

MORTON GOULD (1913-   ) USA

Gould's versatility is not too well-known. His identification with popular music is balanced by more serious works of a vigorous nature.

Americana (CF). Five mood sketches, clever, attractive, folk inspired. Corn-cob: barn dance; Indian nocturne; Hillbilly; Night song; Music hall. Int. to M-D.

Prologue—1945 (Belwin-Mills). A celebration piece in honor of the founding of the United Nations. Chordal, dissonant, sonorous. M-D.

Boogie-Woogie Etude (Belwin-Mills). Brilliant, energetic, percussive ostinato. Requires endurance and drive. D.

Sonatina (Belwin-Mills 1939). Moderately fast-spirited: driving, energetic, non-legato eighths in alla breve; Spiritual: flowing melody, homophonic accompaniment; Minuet: crisp, caricature-like; Finale: fast driving, satirical, requires strong fingers. M-D.

Dance Gallery (Chappell 1952). Six movements. M-D.

At The Piano (Chappell). Two books, 8 and 9 pedagogic pieces. Easy.

Ten for Deborah (Chappell). Ten short pieces, MC, varied keys and meters. Int.

Pavane (Belwin-Mills).

CHARLES GOUNOD (1818-1893) France

Six Morceaux Faciles (Leduc c. 1907).
L'Angelus, Invocation, Les Pifferari. Also (Augener), Prélude, Serenade, Musette.

Suite Concertante (G. Pierné-Leduc).

Romances sans Paroles (Augener).

1. La pervenche (1861)
2. Le ruisseau (1861)

3. Le Soir (1865) also (Paxton).
4. Le Calm (1865) also (Reid).

Valse Caractéristique (Augener).

GUILLERMO GRAETZER (1914-) Argentina, born Austria

Graetzer has lived in Buenos Aires since 1939. He has been very active in the musical life of Argentina and is professor at the National University of La Plata and the National School of Dance.

Tres Toccatas (ECIC 1937-8). Lengthy works employing a contemporary harmonic and pianistic vocabulary. Allegro: syncopated rhythms, fast unison writing, dramatic closing; Con brio: alternating hands, double-note octaves, quick chordal passages, rhetorical section, dramatic closing; Allegro ma non troppo: lyric, but drives to enormous closing. D.

Five Bagatelles (EAM 1943-1946). Short, unmetered, varied, all atonal except No. 5, interesting sonorities. M-D.

Sonatina (Ric Americana 1945). 12 minutes. Allegro Moderato; Andante; Allegro non troppo.

Rondo para niños (EAM 1947). Mainly two voices, light allegretto, swinging, free C tonality, for children. Int.

PERCY GRAINGER (1882-1961) Australia, came to USA in 1914

The Music of Percy Grainger (GS). 15 pieces that provide contrast in style. A broad sampling of his piano compositions. Int. to M-D.

The Young Pianists's Grainger (R. Stevenson-Schott c. 1967). Some of the pieces are by Grainger, others are settings by Grainger of folksongs and pieces by Bach, and Dowland. Notes on the music, as well as some photographs of Grainger throughout his career, add to the interest of this collection. Contains: Country Gardens, Shepherd's Hey, Molly on the Shore, Mock Morris, Beautiful Fresh Flower, Australian Up-Country Song, Irish Tune from Country Derry, Walking, Hill-Song, To a Nordic Princess, One More Day, My John, Spoon River,

Blithe Bells, Over the Hills and Far Away, Now, O Now, I Need Must Part. A charming and interesting collection. Easy to Int.

Ländliche Gärten (Schott). M-D.

Paraphrase on Tschaikowsky's Blumen-Walzer (Schott). M-D.

HAROLD GRAMATGES (1918-) Cuba

Dos Danzas Cubanas (PIC 1953). M-D.
Montuna: fast 2/4 syncopation, rhythmic, ends quietly on dominant.
Sonera: more rhythmic drive, brilliant close.

Tres Preludios para Piano (PAU). 29 p. 16 minutes.

Suite Cubana (Ric 1958). 7 p.

ENRIQUE GRANADOS (1867-1916) Spain

A fine pianist and teacher, Granados composed numerous works for his favorite instrument. The earlier works (many are picture-post cards in sound) show influences of Chopin, Grieg and Liszt and are built on a traditional pianism. The two books of *Goyescas* (1911), inspired by the painter Goya, reveal a highly developed and exuberant piano style. These piano tone poems are extended and show a facile improvisator rather than a master craftsman.

Allegro de concierto (GS) (UME).

12 Spanish Dances (4 books) (GS) (K) (EBM) (UME) (IMC). Moderately easy and immediately accessible. Minuet G; Oriental c; Zarabanda D; Villanesca G; Andaluza, Playera e; Jota-Rondalla Aragonesa D; Valenciana G; Asturiana C; Majurca B♭; Danza triste G; Zambra g; Arabesca a.

Bocetos (UME). A collection of 4 easy pieces.
Desperta del Cazador, El Hada y el Niño, Vals muy lento, La Campana de la Tarde.

Goyescas (1911) (IMC) (Sal) (UME). 6 works constituting the composer's most grandiose piano style. Approximately 53 minutes are required to perform this entire masterpiece. Los

Requiebros (Flattery): double-note technique required. Coloquio en la Reja (Love Duet): complex melodic line. El Fandango de Candil: double-note technique required. Quejas ó la Maja y el Ruiseñor (Laments, or the Lady and the Nightingale): romantic rhapsody. (GS) publishes this piece with a translation of the first stanza of the verses sung to this music in the opera *Goyescas*. Helps increase the understanding of this lovely extemporization. El Amor y a Muerte (Love and Death): difficult interpretative problems. Epilogo (Serenade of the Spectre): this "dance of death" contains the Dies Irae in the middle section, staccato fabric.
See: Charles Wilson, "The Two Versions of *Goyescas*," MMR, 81, October 1951, 203-7.

6 Estudios Espressivos (UME). Int.
Tema con variaciones y final; Allegro moderato; El caminante; Pastorale; La última pavana; María.

6 Pieces on Spanish Folk Songs (UME). Published separately.
Añoranza; Ecos de la Parrando; Vascongada; Marcha Oriental; Zambra; Zapateado.

7 Valses Poéticos with Prelude and Postlude (UME).

2 Impromptus (UME). a, G.

PARKS GRANT (1910-) USA

Sonata No. 2 Op. 45 (ACA 1953). About 17 minutes. M-D.
Molto moderato e tranquillo: cross rhythms, tertial writing, begins quietly.
Lento quasi andante: chorale-like, needs fine legato.
Allegro assai e giocoso: gigue-like perpetual motion idea works to climax.

The World of Muse Op. 55/2 (ACA 1965). 4½ minutes. M-D.
Wistful short mood-piece, bitonal, chromatic. Not technically difficult but requires a sensitive pianist to probe past the notes.

CARL HEINRICH GRAUN (ca. 1701-1759) Germany

Sonata d, Vol. 1 *German Keyboard Music of the 17th and 18th Centuries* (H. Fischer, F. Oberdoerffer-Vieweg).

Concerto F, Vol. 9 *German Keyboard Music of the 17th and 18th Centuries* (H. Fischer, F. Oberdoerffer-Vieweg).

Gigue b♭, *Old Masters* (K). Fine recital opener.

JOHANN CHRISTOPH GRAUPNER (1683-1760) Germany

8 Partitas (L. Hoffmann-Erbrecht-Br&H). This is Graupner's only extant set of two known sets of partitas. Unusual movements found in dance suites of the period with the exception of an occasional rigaudon or chaconne in place of the G. Numerous optional dances.

Klavierfrüchte (W. Frickert-Litolff). A collection of dances and pieces including an Entrée C, Polonaise F, M I&II A, B in e, Le Sommeille, Aria con variazioni c, Chaconne e, and Suite C in 13 movements, from the larger work *Monatliche Klavierfrüchte*, 1722.

GIOVANNI BATTISTA GRAZIOLI (ca. 1746-1820) Italy

Graceful melodic writing, standardized organization, Alberti bass, chromatic appoggiaturas and feminine cadences add interest to these works.

Dodici Sonate per Cembalo (R. Gerlin-Fondazione Eugenio Bravi 1941-43). Vol. XII of *I Classici Musicali Italiani.* No. 11 G is available from Litolff edited by Kohler. All 12 of these sonatas are in 3 movements, FSF.

Sonata G. *Alte Meister* (Pauer-Br&H). Vol. IV has a reprint of the second movement, Adagio. (L. Podolsky-CF).

RAY GREEN (1908-) USA

Green studied with Ernest Bloch and has been very active in supporting American music through his American Music Editions.

Sonate Brevis (AME).

Tempo giusto, Andante con moto, Adagio cantabile, Allegro vivo, Maestoso.

The style resembles serial writing. This is a revision of *Sonatina* published in "New Music", April 1934. M-D.

12 Inventions (AME 1955). Key-scheme is based on a circle of fourths, C F Bb, etc. Can be performed as a group or separately. Variety of moods, idioms and techniques, emphasis on linear writing. Int. to M-D.

Quartet: 4 Preludes (AME c. 1964).
Short colorful tone pictures in contemporary sonorities. Large span (ninth) required.

Short Sonata C (AME 1965). Three effective movements.
Contemporary "Alberti Bass" with freely moving melodic line. M-D.

Pieces for Children (AME). Four pieces "to introduce contemporary music materials to children—and to adults who hear or play them." Thoroughly attractive writing. Int.

Festival Fugues (An American Toccata) (Arrow).
Prelude Promenade, Holiday Fugue, Fugal Song, Prelude Pastoral, Jubilant Fugue. American folk elements present. M-D.

MAURICE GREENE (1695-1755) Great Britain

A Selection of Harpsichord Music by Maurice Green (Paterson's Publications, Ltd. 1935) Two Volumes. Contains single pieces Andante f, Molto Allegro F, Air with Variations, Aire G, Allegro D, Presto F, Jig, etc. Some charming, unfamiliar music. Easy to Int.

3 Suites (P. Williams-J. Williams)
Int. to M-D.

5 Pieces from Harpsichord Works (P. Williams-Bosworth).
Contains Prelude F, Gigue F, Minuet D, Scherzando F, Courante D. Added fingering, ornamentation adequately realized. M-D.

ALEXANDER GRETCHANINOFF (1864-1956) Russia

Schott publishes a wide variety of Gretchaninoff's piano works including:

Sonata g Op. 129 (1931).

Sonatina G Op. 110/1.

Sonatina F Op. 110/2.

A Child's Day Op. 109. 10 short pieces.

Dew Drops Op. 127a. 9 Pieces.

Glass Beads Op. 123. 12 easy pieces. Also (Agay-MCA).

Grandfather's Book Op. 119. 17 easy pieces.

In the Meadows Op. 99. 10 pieces for young people.

Sonata No. 2 Op. 174 (Axelrod c. 1947). Two movements. Second movement a set of variations. Romantic harmonies and techniques. M-D.

Aquarelles Op. 146 (Augener) 5 pieces.

4 Pieces for Children Op. 170 (Hargail).

12 Little Sketches for Children Op. 182 (IMC).

Pastels: 5 Miniatures Op. 3 (1894) (Belaieff). M-D.

By the Fireside Op. 183 (1952) (Bo&H). 10 pieces.

Pervenches Op. 158 (Belaieff). 8 miniatures.

Children's Album (Agay-MCA).

EDVARD GRIEG (1843-1907) Norway

Nationalistic elements play a large part in the piano works of Grieg, especially the smaller character pieces, Grieg's finest contribution to the piano repertoire.

Complete Piano Works (CFP) 3 volumes.
- I: Lyric Pieces, all 10 books; also available separately in 13 volumes.
- II: Op. 1, 3, 6, 19, 24, 28, 29, 41, 52, 73.
- III: Op. 17, 34, 35, 37, 40, 46, 50, 56, 63, 66, 53, 55.

Lyric Pieces 13 volumes (CFP).
Book I: Op. 12 (Ric) (CF) (WH) (K).
Arietta, Waltz, Watchman's Song, Fairy Dance, Popular Melody, Norwegian Melody, Album Leaf, National Song.

Book II: Op. 38 (K).
Cradle Song, Folksong, Melodie, Halling, Springdance, Elegie, Waltz, Canon.
Book III: Op. 43 (K).
Butterfly, Lonely Wanderer, In the Native Country, Little Bird, Erotik, To the Spring.
Book IV: Op. 47.
Valse-Impromptu, Album Leaf, Melodie, Halling, Melancholy, Springdance, Elegie.
Book V: Op. 54.
Bells, March of the Dwarfs, Norwegian Peasant March, Notturno, Scherzo, Shepherd Boy.
Book VI: Op. 57, 2 volumes.
Vanished Days, Gade, Illusion, Secrecy, She dances, Home-Sickness.
Book VII: Op. 62, 2 volumes.
Sylph, Gratitude, French Serenade, Brooklet, Phantom, Homeward.
Book VIII: Op. 65, 2 volumes.
From Years of Youth, Peasant's Song, Melancholy, Salon, In Ballad Vein, Wedding-Day at Troldhaugen.
Book IX: Op. 68.
Sailor's Song, Grandmother's Minuet, At thy Feet, Evening in the Mountains, At the Cradle, Valse mélancolique.
Book X: Op. 71.
Once upon a Time, Summer Evening, Puck, Peace of the Woods, Halling, Gone, Remembrances.

Other smaller sets include:

3 Poetic Tone-Pictures Op. 3 (1863) (CFP) (WH).

4 Humoresques Op. 6 (1865) (CFP). These are in effect "Norwegian Dances".

Norwegian Dances and Songs Op. 17 (1870) (CFP). Also contained in *Norwegian Notebook* (CFP), 16 pieces from Op. 17 and 66: excellent introduction to Grieg for intermediate student.

3 Norwegian Sketches Op. 19 (1872) (CFP) (WH).

4 Album Leaves Op. 28 (1864) (CFP) (WH). Folk dances.

Improvisations on 2 Norwegian Folk Songs Op. 29 (1878) (CFP).

Norwegian Folk Tunes Op. 66 (1896) (CFP).

Slätter Op. 72 (1902) (CFP). Norwegian peasant dances.
See: John Horton, "Grieg's 'Slätter' for piano," ML, 26/4, 1945, 229-35.

Larger Works:

Sonata e Op. 7 (1865) (CFP) (Schott) (Br&H) (CF) (GS). 4 movements. See: SSB, 612-15.

Ballad g Op. 24 (1875) (CFP). Based on a Norwegian folksong, 14 variations.

Holberg Suite Op. 40 (1884) (CFP). Neoclassical work in 5 movements: Prelude, S, Air, Gavotte, Rigaudon.

Radio City Album of Selected Compositions for Piano by Grieg. Two Volumes (EBM).
21 and 20 compositions respectively. A wide selection containing some of Grieg's own transcriptions of his songs.

CHARLES TOMLINSON GRIFFES (1884-1920) USA

Love of oriental subjects and a preoccupation with impressionist techniques were the major influences on Griffes' music. His stature continues to grow. His *Piano Sonata* was one of the most important works in that genre to appear in America during the first quarter of this century.

Three Tone Poems Op. 5 (GS). Impressionistic. M-D.
The Lake at Evening, Night Winds, The Vale of Dreams.

Fantasy Pieces Op. 6 (GS). M-D to D.
Barcarolle: delicate, atmospheric; Nocturne: sensitive, poetic; Scherzo: bravura writing.

Four Roman Sketches Op. 7 (GS). Impressionistic, subtle, atmospheric, imaginative. M-D to D.
The White Peacock (1915): best-known of the set. Legato chords, running arpeggi.

Nightfall (1916).
The Fountain of the Acqua Paola (1916).
Clouds (1916).

Three Preludes (CFP c. 1967). Recently discovered works. Different mood in each piece. No titles, tempo marks, dynamics. Enigmatic. M-D.

Sonata (GS 1917-18).
Feroce-Allegro con Moto: driving 12/8, varied textures.
Molto tranquillo: more melodically oriented.
Allegro vivace: energetic 6/8, dramatic presto close.
Advanced pianism required.

See: Donna Kay Anderson, "The Works of Charles Tomlinson Griffes: A Descriptive Catalogue," unpub. diss., Indiana University, 1966.

COR DE GROOT (1914-) The Netherlands

De Groot is best known as a pianist. He has concertized throughout the world and has recorded extensively. His piano works require much facility.

Apparition (Donemus 1960).

Etude (B&VP).

Galop (Alsbach 1954). 2 minutes.

Oud-Hollandse suite (Donemus 1950). 20 minutes.

Sonatine (Albersen 1940).

WILHELM GROSZ (1894-1939) Austria

Symphonische Variationen über ein Eigenes Thema Op. 9 (UE 1921). Theme and 15 variations in a post-romantic idiom. Thick textures, chromatic writing. Big technique is required. D.

Kleine Sonate Op. 16 (UE 1923). 21 p.

Tanzsuite (UE 1922). 17 p.
Menuett, Gavotte und Musette, Walzer, Polka. M-D.

Sonate Op. 21 (UE 1927). 24 p. D.
Allegretto: numerous tempo changes—cheerful.
Andantino con grazia (Siziliana).
Allegro molto: biting dissonances, triplet accompaniment.

GABRIEL GROVLEZ (1879-1944) France

7 Fancies (Augener 1915). See especially Nos. 1, 2, and 5.

A Child's Garden (JWC). 6 short imaginative pieces.

Sarabande (Durand 1921). Chordal, chromatic, stately.

L'Almanach aux Images (Augener). 8 pieces with accompanying poems.

Improvisations on London (Augener). Interesting writing. M-D.

RUDOLPH GRUEN (1900-) USA

Sonata Op. 29 (GS 1941). 3 movements.
Based on artificial scale, mainly pentatonic: D, F, G♭, C plus 2 auxiliary tones E♭ and B, polytonal or atonal in effect. Traditional forms: first movement SA, second movement song form, third movement rondo, perpetual motion idea. D.

Classical Variations on an Original Theme Op. 51 (ACA).
17 variations, differing styles and textures: Sicilienne, minuet, canon, ostinato, etc. Virtuoso writing with some exciting moments. D.

GOTTFRIED GRÜNEWALD (1673-1739) Germany

2 Partitas (H. Ruf-Ric) G, A. These two works are from five Partitas, the only extant works of Grünewald.

JEAN-JACQUES GRÜNEWALD (1911-) France

Suite de danses (Sal 1948). Spirit of clavecin dances permeates this set. M-D.

Fantasmagorie (Sal).

La mélodie interieure (Leduc).

Prélude (Leduc).

Partita (Rideau Rouge). Written as "pièce imposée" for the 1971 Marguérite Long Piano Competition in Paris. D.

ALFRED GRÜNFELD (1852-1924) Austria

Good craftsmanship and pianistic understanding are evident in these works. None are overly difficult (M-D).

Barcarolle Op. 61 (Dob).

Strauss' Kaiserwalzer Op. 62 (Dob).

Ungarische Tänze Op. 64 (Dob).

Phantasie nach Schubert Op. 65 (Dob).

CAMARGO GUARNIERI (1907-) Brazil

Guarnieri's style is characterized by subtle nationalistic influences coupled with a complete command of the general technical resources of composition. An elastic counterpoint permeates many of his more extended compositions. His piano works vary from simple lyric pieces like *Maria Lucia,* to pianistic virtuosity of the highest order, as found in *Danza Selvagem* or the *Toccata.*

Dansa Brasileira (AMP 1928). Samba rhythms, repeated octaves, popular flavor, rich sonorities. M-D.

Primeira Sonatina (Ric Americana 1928). Molengamente; Ponteado e bem dengoso; bem depressa.

Chôro torturado (AMP 1930). Agitated, chromatic, chords, octaves, cross-rhythms, mature pianism required, displays numerous moods. D.

Ponteios (Ric). Five volumes. I: 1-10 (1931-1935); II: 11-20 (1947-1949); III: 21-30 (1954-55); IV: 31-40 (1956-57); V: 41-50 (1958-59). These 5 volumes of *Preludes* are all musical, well-written and have a special appeal. Int. to D.

Dansa Selvagem (Ric 1931). A savage jungle dance, drumbeats imitative with open fifths and seventh-chords, bravura style. D.

Little Horse with the Broken Leg (AMP 1932). Limping figuration, syncopated, 3-voice texture, mid-section. Int.

Lundú (Ric 1930). Brazilian song-dance, fast, rhythmic, 4 against 3, exotic. M-D.

Toccata (AMP 1935). Chromatic, double-note technique. D.

Sonatina No. 3 (AMP 1937). Written in G clef only. Allegro: eighth-note motion, 3 voices; grazioso, melody over broken chord figuration in the Con tenerezza; Two-Part Fugue: rhythmic, moving sixteenth notes, forte conclusion. M-D.

Maria Lucia (Music Press 1944). Short, calm lyric piece, smoothly flowing eighth notes.

Dansa Negra (Ric) (AMP) (1946). Mournful, intense, blues element, resonant mid-section. M-D.

Improviso (Ric 1948).

Ficarós Sosinha (Music Press 1939). Based on a Brazilian children's game, short, graceful, peaceful. Easy.

Valsa No. 6 (Ric 1949).

5 Estudios (Ric 1949-50, 1954).

Suite Mirim (Ric 1953). Ponteando; Tanguinho; Modinha; Cirandinha.

Valsa No. 7 (Ric 1954).

Valsa No. 8 (Ric 1954).

Valsa No. 9 (Ric 1957).

5 Peças Infantis (Ric 1935). Estudando piano; Criança triste; Valsinha manhosa; A criança adormece; Polka. Int.

Sonatina No. 5 (Ric 1962). Three movements, modal, thin textures, syncopation.

CARLOS GUASTAVINO (1914-) Argentina

Tres Sonatinas (Ric 1949). Three one-movement works. Published together, based on Argentine rhythms. M-D.
Movimiento; Retama; Danza.

Diez Preludios (Ric 1952).
Short pieces based on themes of popular Argentine children's songs. Int. to M-D.

La Siesta (Ric 1942). Suite of three pieces.
El Patio; El Sauce; Gorriones.

Suite Argentina (Ric 1952). 12 minutes.

Sonata (Ric 1947). 16 minutes. Solid craftsmanship, interesting sonorities. D.
Allegretto Intimo
Scherzo. Molto vivace
Recitativo-Lento
Fuga y Final: based on a Riojana popular melody.

Diez Cantilenas Argentinas (Ric 1956-58). 45 minutes.

Tres Romances Nuevos (Ric 1954-55). 18 minutes. La niña del Río Dulce; El chico que vino del sur; Chaco.

ELISABETH JACQUET DE LA GUERRE (1669-1729) France

Pièces de Clavecin (1707) (P. Brunold, T. Dart-l'OL 1956). Contains twelve dances, all of individual interest.

See: Edith Borroff, *An Introduction to Elisabeth Jacquet de la Guerre,* Brooklyn: Institute of Mediaeval Music, 1966.

PIETRO ALESSANDRO GUGLIELMI (1728-1804) Italy

See: SCE, 726-27

Sonata (Carisch).

Sonata No. 6 E♭ (M. Maffioletti-Carisch? 1929).

Sonata No. 3 of Op. 3 See: David Stone, "The Italian Sonata for Harpsichord and Pianoforte in the Eighteenth Century (1730-1790)," III, unpub. diss., Harvard University, 1952.

ALEXANDRE GUILMANT (1837-1911) France

6 Little Pieces for the Pianoforte (OD). Written for Guilmant's little daughter Cécile. Int.
Alla Siciliana; Chanson d'enfant; Fughetta; Petite March; Scherzettino; Tarantella.

GENE GUTCHE (1907-) USA, born Germany

Gutche received degrees from the University of Minnesota and the State University of Iowa. He has referred to his work as "a blending of the most modern language and technique with a genuinely classical feeling for structure."

Sonata No. 6 (Highgate).
A one-movement work, complex harmonic idiom, unusual notation, a few tone clusters. D.

Fugue for Piano (ACA). 12 minutes.

Piana Sonata Op. 6/3 (Galaxy). 12 minutes.

Piano Sonata Op. 32/1 (Highgate). 11 minutes. 24 p. Repeated notes, numerous meter changes. D.

Piano Sonata Op. 32/2. (Highgate c. 1973). 18 minutes. 23 p.

Theme and Variations (ACA). 27 minutes.

Utilitarian Fugue for Piano (ACA). 5 minutes.

H

ALOIS HÁBA (1893-) Czechoslovakia

Around 1920 Hába evolved a system of quarter-tone and sixth-tone music based on equal temperament. He had microtonic instruments constructed including a quarter-tone piano and has written a number of treatises about his experiments.

Variations on a Canon of Schumann Op. 1B (UE 1923).

2 Morceaux Op. 2 (UE 1920)
Scherzo; Intermezzo.

Sonata d Op.3 (UE 1919). 28 p.
Thick chromatic idiom in all 3 movements, contains some lovely moments. D.

6 Pieces Op. 6 (Hudebni Matice 1920).

Suite No. 3 Op. 16 (UE 1925). For quarter-tone piano.

Fantasia No. 2 Op. 19 (UE 1925). For quarter-tone piano.

Tango (UE).

YOSHIO HACHIMURA (–) Japan

Improvisation pour piano (Ongaku no Toma Sha, Tokyo 1964). No. 29 in *Contemporary Japanese Music Series.*

REYNALDO HAHN (1875-1947) France

Chanson de Midi (Heugel).

Sonatina C (Heugel 1907). 19 p.

Thème Varié (Durand 1910). Hommage à J. Haydn.

Valse No. 3 A♭ (Ninette) (Heugel 1898).

Soleil d'Automne (Heugel 1912). 3 p.

Le Bouquet de Pensées (Heugel 1912). 1 p.

La Danse de l'Amour et de l'Ennui (Heugel 1912). 3 p.

Premières Valses (10) (Heugel 1898).

Le Rossignol Eperdu (Heugel c. 1912). A series containing 53 pieces by Hahn. Series I: 30 pieces; Series II: Orient: 6 pieces; Series III: Carnet de Voyage: 9 pieces; Series IV: Versailles: 8 pieces.

Deux Etudes (Heugel c. 1927).
1. A♭: 16th-note accompaniment over melody in LH.
2. d: triplet study.

ALEXEI HAIEFF (1914-) USA, born Siberia, Russia

"Haieff's music is neoclassic in the best sense of that 'school'. It moves with clean crispness and a boundless vitality and natural attractiveness." GD, 4, 17.

Five Pieces (Bo&H 1946). 15 minutes. Allegro, Andantino, Vivace scherzando, Lento molto, Allegro molto. Ranges from M-D imitative counterpoint to bravura writing in the final piece.

Sonata (EMM 1948). 3 movements.

Four Juke Box Pieces (Bo&H 1952). Waltz (you can whistle an ad lib cornet obbligato), March (with 2/4 and 3/8 juxaposed), Nocturne, Polka. Humorous. M-D.

11 Bagatelles (EMM 1950). Short, exploit contemporary idioms. M-D.

Gifts and Semblances (Bo&H 1954). 4 pieces.

Sonata (Chappell 1956). 3 movements. A large MC work with

more interpretative problems than technical, tonal ambiguity, large skips in melody, contrasting textures. M-D.

Sonata No. 2 (PAU 1955). 4 movements. Transparent textures. Effective bitonal final movement. M-D.

Notes of Thanks (Chappell 1961). 6 short pieces, jazz influence. Numerous pianistic problems present, especially wide skips. M-D.

Saint's Wheel (Chappell 1960). Variations on a circle of fifths. In reality, a fine contemporary chaconne. Looks more difficult than it is but requires sensitive voicing of lines. Contemporary sounds, trill plays an important part, LH skips, all require mature musicianship.

MIHÁLY HAJDU (1909-) Hungary

Hajdu teaches at the Budapest Conservatory. He studied with Zoltán Kodály and is one of the few contemporary Hungarian composers not noticeably influenced by Bartók.

5 Piano Pieces (EMB). Each piece is well-developed. M-D.
Prelude, Meditation, Scherzo, Improvisation, Toccata.

Sonatina (EMB 1962). 3 movements.
Unique personal style.

KNUT HÅKANSON (1887-1929) Sweden

Håkanson wrote in a romantic, folk-inspired idiom.

Fran Kullaberg Suite Op. 14 (ms). Available from Eriks Musikhandel.

Swedish Suite in Contrapuntal Style Op. 18 (NMS).

Tio variationer och fuga over en evensk folkvisa Op. 37 (MK).

Tolv sma svenska inventioner (NMS).

CRISTOBAL HALFFTER (1930-) Spain

A nephew of the composers Ernesto and Rudolfo Halffter, Cristobal Halffter studied under Conrado del Campo and Alexandre

Tansman. "His earlier compositions are in an atonal style, marked by the influence of Bartók and Stravinsky. He has employed serial techniques since the mid-1950's." BBD, 82.

Sonata para Piano (UME 1951). One movement.
Neoclassic style, influenced by Bartók and Stravinsky. M-D.

Introducción, Fuga y Final Op. 15 (UME 1957).
Carefully worked out serial technique. Thin textures contrasted with thicker octave doublings. Registers are widely separated. 12-tone. D.

ERNESTO HALFFTER (1905-) Spain

Halffter studied with de Falla and was strongly influenced by the critic Adolfo Salazar and the composer Oscar Esplá. He has championed modern music in his role as conductor in Spain and in South America.

Pregón. Cuba (ESC). Effective salon piece.

Dance of the Shepherdess (ESC 1927). Broken chords, sixteenth-note motion. Fine encore.

Sérénade à Dulcinée (ESC 1951). Spanish coloration.

Habanera (ESC 1950).

Sonata D (ESC 1926-32). One movement.
French and Spanish influence. Tertial harmonies, fugal section, full sonorities. M-D.

March Joyeuse (ESC).

Dance of the Gypsy (ESC). Double thirds, exotic. D.

RODOLFO HALFFTER (1900-) Mexico, born Spain

Halffter, brother of Ernesto, emigrated to Mexico in 1939 and teaches at the Conservatorio Nacional de Musica in Mexico City. His musical style "is characterized by a great economy of material. His harmonic idiom is basically tonal, with occasional excursions into bitonality. His contrapuntal lines are sharply defined: his rhythms are often asymmetrical, necessitating frequent changes of time-signature." GD, 4, 22.

Sonata No. 1 Op. 16 (EMM 1948) (UME 1963). 18 minutes. Three movements. M-D. Tonal, added-note technique used in third movement Allegro con spirito, which is light hearted and dancelike.

Sonata No. 2 Op. 20 (PIC 1951). 33 p. Four movements. M-D. Thin textures, pianistic, musical. Final movement, a rondo, has a dancelike quality.

Once Bagatelles Op. 19 (UME 1947). 26 p. M-D.
Lively rhythms, canonic imitation, colorful effects characterize these 11 short pieces.

Homenaje a Antonio Machado (UME 1944). 22 p.
Fascinating four-movement suite.

Tres Hoias de Album Op. 22 (UME 1964). Three well-constructed works.
Somber moving elegy; Scherzo and Trio; Clever amusing march.

Danza de Avila (CF 1936).

HALLGRIMUR HELGASON (1914-) Iceland

Sonata No. 1 (Musica Islandica). M-D.
A three-movement work, romantic style. First movement, a theme and 11 variations. Second movement, an Adagio with a dancelike mid-section. Third movement, jig-like, then interrupted by an Intermezzo, followed by a brilliant conclusion. A few native folk tunes creep in briefly.

HILDING HALLNÄS (1903-) Sweden

"In his early works Hallnäs used rich harmonies and melodies for expressive purposes." GD, 4, 26. Since the mid-1950's he has used twelve-tone technique in a personal manner.

Fem impressioner (ms).

Kort svit (1955) (ms).

Pas de deux, liten danssvit (ms).

Sonat (1936) (ms). All (ms) are available from Eriks Musikhandel.

Triptyk (GM).

BENGT HAMBRAEUS (1928-) Sweden

Hambraeus represents the avant-garde movement in Sweden. He has been influenced by musicological studies, mainly of medieval and non-European music, by his work as an organist (he was the first organist in Sweden to play Messiaen) and by participation in the Darmstadt Festival. He was the first Swedish musician to compose electronic works.

Cercles (NMS 1955).

Toccata Op. 7/1 (ms). Available from Eriks Musikhandel.

IAIN HAMILTON (1922-) Scotland

Hamilton is a member of the music faculty at Duke University in Durham, North Carolina. "Even though Hamilton has employed serial techniques increasingly, he has not abandoned tonality. Rather, he shows a masterful control over varied stylistic features in which he effectively imposes a serial form as in *Nocturnes with Cadenzas*. He has been able to avoid suggestions of an overtly synthetical style." BBD, 83.

Sonata Op. 13 (Schott 1951). Three movements. Rhythmic exuberance, percussive chordal usage, Bartók influence. D.

Three Pieces for Piano Op. 30 (Schott 1955). Tonal, exhibits fine usage of 12-tone technique. D.

Nocturnes with Cadenzas (Schott 1963). A cycle of pieces, impressionistic yet firmly controlled by an underlying serial technique. D.

GEORGE FREDERIC HANDEL (1685-1759) Germany

Although Handel wrote other keyboard music, his suites are the most important contribution to this medium. The eight suites of

1720 are remarkable works, no two being similar. The second set, published in 1733, does not have the variety and uniqueness of the 1720 set. These suites reach back to the Italian chamber sonata from which Handel took over a number of forms. Along with the standard dances, A, C, S, G, and others, we find movements titled Andante, Allegro, Largo, etc.

Hallischer Händel-Ausgabe (Br) Series IV. Vol. 1 (Steglich c. 1955) 1720 set of suites; Vol. 5 (Northway c. 1971) 7 suites, 2 chaconnes; Vol. 6 (Best c. 1971) shorter pieces. Scholarly. Vol. 17 forthcoming.

(Serauky-CFP) urtext has the *Keyboard Works* in 5 volumes, with 16 suites in the first 3 volumes.

(Ruthardt-CFP) publish *Suite* IX g separately. This edition contains a photographic reproduction of Händel's Rucker Harpsichord. Over-edited.

(G. Ropartz-Durand) also publish the complete *Keyboard Works* in 4 volumes, 16 suites in 2 volumes. Sal has the first 8 suites. Augener and K publish 16 suites in 2 volumes. Movements of the suites are listed below numbered according to Serauky-CFP. Suite No. 1 A: Prelude, A, C, G. No. 2 F: Adagio, Allegro, Adagio, Fuga. No. 3 d: Prelude, fuga, A, C, Air (with variations), Presto. No. 4 e: Fuga, A, C, S, G. No. 5 E: Prelude, A, C, Air con variazioni (Harmonious Blacksmith). No. 6 f♯: Prelude, Largo, Fuga, G. No. 7 g: Ouverture, Andante, Allegro, S, G, Passacaglia. No. 8 f: A, C, G. No. 9 g: A, C, G. No. 10 d: A, Allegro, Air, G. No. 11 d: A, S, C, G. No. 12 e: A, S, G. No. 13 B♭: A, C, S, G. No. 14 G: A, Allegro, C, Air, M, Gavotte with variations. No. 15 d: A, C, S, G. No. 16 g: A, C, S, G.

Other works:

(Ruthardt-CFP) 4 volumes including the 16 suites, Leçons, 7 pieces, 6 Grande Fugues, 2 Chaconnes, and Fughettas.

Ausgewählte Klavierwerke (Döflein-Schott) contains 11 works: C, Aria, Allegro, Ouverture, Praeludium, Suite d, A, Fuga, Sonata. This collection is intended as an introduction to Handel's style and the many forms of composition characteristic of his time.

Pieces for Harpsichord (F. Brodszky-ZV c. 1964). A fascinating collection, contains 5 works published for the first time. Included is a three-movement solo concerto F with a virtuoso Allegro opening movement, an Adagio and a Tempo di Menuet; Prelude, Introduzione e Capriccio; Badinage; Prelude e capriccio; Allemande e canzona.

Zwölf Phantasien und vier Stücke (G. Walter-Hug).

Chaconne G with 21 variations (Georgii-Schott) (Koschinsky NV) (A. Winding-WH).

Chaconne F (Georgii-Schott).

6 Fughettas (CFP) (Schott) (Ric).

Gavotte with variations (Sal) (Durand).

Passacaglia g (Ric) (Durand).

Collections of easier works:

76 Pieces (Fuller-Maitland, Squire-Schott). Small pieces of many moods. Excellent for use in the early grades of piano study.

20 Little Dances (Frey-Schott).

Little Piano Book (K. Herrmann-Schott). 17 smaller pieces.

Easier Pieces (Rowley-Hin). 14 pieces including Sonatina B♭.

14 Easy Original Pieces (O. Beringer-Augener), arranged in progressive order.

The Young Pianist's Handel (M. Aldridge-OUP c. 1969) Book I, 21 pieces, well-edited, excellent preface, mainly unknown works.

See: Gerald Abraham, "Handel's Clavier Music," ML, 16/4, 1935, 278-85.
Editor, *Handel. A Symposium.* London: OUP 1954.

Terence Best, "Handel's Keyboard Music," MT, 112, September 1971, 845-8.

O. E. Deutsch, *Handel. A Documentary Biography*. London: Black, 1955.

Paul H. Lang, *George Frederic Handel*. New York: Norton, 1966.

Thurston Dart, "Handel and the Continuo," MT, 106, May 1965, 348-50.

Phyllis K. Rueb, "Handel's Keyboard Suites: A Comparison with those of J. S. Bach," AMT, 20, April-May 1971, 33-6.

HOWARD HANSON (1896-) USA

Hanson's music is romantic in style with marked influences of Edward MacDowell and Carl Nielsen.

The Eccentric Clock (CF).

Dance of the Warriors (CF).

Enchantment (CF).

The Bell (CF). All four of these pieces are contained in the *Masters of Our Day* series. Each has its individual mood and quality. Easy to Int.

Clog Dance Op. 13 (CF). From *Scandinavian Suite*. 6/8, quintal harmony, rhythmic bounce. Int.

Three Miniatures (CF). Reminiscence, Lullaby, Longing. More advanced than the above-listed pieces, requires more than average sensitivity. M-D.

ALGOT HAQUINIUS (1886-) Sweden

Haquinius studied with Moszkowski in Paris and with Ignaz Friedman in Berlin.

Preludier (Foreningen Svenska Tonsattare, Stockholm).

Svensk dans Nos. 1, 2, and 3 (NMS). Published separately.

DONALD HARRIS (1931-) USA

Harris studied composition with Ross Lee Finney at the University of Michigan. While a resident of Paris, he served as Music

Consultant to the United States Information Service where he lectured and produced festivals and concerts of American music. Harris is on the administrative staff at the New England Conservatory.

Sonata (Jobert). 13 minutes. Four movements. Numerous meter changes, 12-tone techniques. The last movement, a theme and set of variations, shows a fine grasp of variation technique. Pianistic, unusual sonorities. D.

ROY HARRIS (1898-) USA

Sonata Op. 1 (AMP 1928).
Prelude: majestic, chordal, varied rhythmic treatment.
Andante Ostinato: slow, homophonic.
Scherzo: jazz influence, partly contrapuntal, mainly two voices, leads through a cadenza to a closing.
Coda: recalls grandeur of opening movement. D.

Little Suite for Piano (GS 1938). Bells, Sad News, Children at Play, Slumber. Short pieces, sonority, rhythmic problems, quartal harmony, changing meters. M-D.

American Ballads (CF 1946). Five settings of American folk tunes; Kirby says they "are American equivalents of Bartók's folk-song arrangements." SHKY, 455. Varied pianistic treatment, mainly homophonic. Int. to M-D.
See: Maurice Hinson, "An American Tune for Today's Student," Clavier, 10, September 1971, 24-7. Discusses No. 1 *Streets of Laredo,* in this set.

Suite for Piano (Mills 1944). Three movements: Occupation: driving octaves, changing meters, sonorous; Contemplation: varied textures support folklike tunes, slow; Recreation: sprite-ly 6/8 motion, energetic. M-D.

Toccata (CF 1949). Improvisatory, sustained chordal textures, two-voice fugato, cadenza finale, open sonorities, melody in octaves or double octaves.

LOU HARRISON (1917-) USA

"Lou Harrison is one of the most unclassifiable of the younger American composers. He chooses musical 'systems' as other composers will select styles or idioms. He will write an atonal piece, a neoclassical piece, a strict medieval-modal poyphonic piece, or a piece based on Hindu or Balinese rhythm and polyrhythm constructions, according to his mood or the occasion for which he writes." GD, 4, 116.

Suite for Piano (CFP 1943). 20½ minutes, 5 pieces, serial writing. D.
Prelude, Aria, Conductus, Interlude, Rondo.
Conductus presents the row beginning each time with the next note in all 4 arrangements or 48 short variations. Advanced pianism required.

Praises for Michael the Archangel (ACA). 4 minutes.

Three Piano Sonatas (ACA).

Little Suite (Meridian). 2 minutes.

Prelude and Sarabande (NME).

Six Sonatas (NME, Oct. 1943). For cembalo or pianoforte. All in one movement, thin textures, chamber style, modest dimensions. M-D.

TIBOR HARSÁNYI (1898-1954) Hungary

Harsányi lived in Paris from 1925 until his death. His style is characterized by lightness of touch and clarity.

Cinq Préludes brefs (ESC).

Suite (Sal 1930). 12 p. Prélude, Romance, Intermezzo, Nocturne. See especially Nocturne.

Suite brève (Sal). 5 pieces.

4 Pieces (Sal). Prélude, Serenade, Air, Dance.

12 Easy Pieces (Sal).

Petite Suite pour Enfants (Sal).

Rhapsody (Sal).

Rhythmes (Sal). 5 Inventions.

Sonata (UE 1926). 4 movements. Changing meters, thick chromaticism. 17 p.

3 Lyric Pieces (JWC 1944).

5 Etudes Rhythmiques (JWC 1933).

Trois Pièces de Danse (Heugel 1928). Mouvement de Tango (clusters, bitonality), Mouvement de Boston, Mouvement de Fox trot.

Pastorales (ESC 1934). Prélude, Elegy, Musette, Danse. See especially Danse.

La Semaine (Heugel 1924). 20 p. 7 pieces, one for each day of the week. Impressionistic.

Deux Burlesques (Heugel 1927). No. 1, scalar, broad gestures, dramatic. No. 2, Bartók influence, varied meters.

Six pièces courtes (Heugel).

Bagatelles (Leduc 1929). 5 pieces. See especially No. 5.

Baby Dancing (Sal 1930). In Jazz style.

Trois Impromptus (Heugel 1948-52). Mouvement (toccata-like), Flânerie (Burlesque), Nocturne (chordal and chromatic).

See: J. S. Weissman, "Tibor Harsányi: a General Survey," Chesterian, 27, July 1952, 14-17.

WALTER S. HARTLEY (1927-   ) USA

Hartley is a product of the Eastman School of Music having received all three degrees there. He teaches at State University College, Fredonia, New York.

Sonata No. 2 (Tenuto 1968). 11 minutes.
Manuscript beautifully reproduced. A two-movement work, changing tempi in the second movement. Fast, large leaps, big chords, tremolandos, dramatic. Effective writing, requires fine pianistic equipment. D.

PETER EMIL HARTMANN (1805-1900) Denmark

Hartmann "was a prolific composer who ranks with Gade, his son-in-law, as a leader of the Danish romantic school." GD, 4, 124.

Fantasi Op. 7 (WH).

Sonatine Op. 48 (WH). Three movements, charming nineteenth-century traditional writing. M-D.

6 Characteristic Pieces Op. 50 (WH 1912).

Sonata No. 2 Op. 80 (WH). 29 p. Four movements, nineteenth century bravura writing. D.

THOMAS DE HARTMANN (1885-1956) France, born Russia

Hartmann studied composition with Arensky and Taneyev at the Moscow Conservatory and piano with Annette Essipov. He was a versatile composer with strong leanings toward nationalism.

Sonata No. 1 Op. 67 (Beliaeff 1943).

Sonata No. 2 Op. 82 (Beliaeff 1956).
A three-movement work, eclectic in style. Bitonal writing and parallel harmonies are integrated into a picturesque work. D.

Three Pieces Op. 74 (Beliaeff).

JOHANN ADOLF HASSE (1699-1783) Germany

Two Sonatas B♭ and d (H. Ruf-Ric). The d sonata is Op. 7. Also available (Kohler-Litolff). See Collections: *Classic Sonatas for Piano* (Podolsky), and *Sonatas of the Pre-Classic Period* (M. Frey). *Sonata F* (Englander-K&S). *Sonata Eb* (R. Steglich-Wolfenbuttel: Verlag für musikalische Kultur und Wissenschaft c. 1936). Attractive, excellent for teaching and/or performance. Int. See SBE, 278-9 for a discussion of the sonatas.

JOHANN WILHELM HÄSSLER (1746-1822) Germany

Hässler's earlier keyboard style shows a preference for the clavichord idiom but his later works make use of the colors and techniques of the pianoforte. He was active in Moscow for many years, writing numerous easy, short works for a large amateur public.

3 Easy Sonatas C, e♭, c (Glöder-Nag).

6 Easy Sonatas (1780) (Döflein-CFP). All are three-movement works except the last sonata which has two movements. Pianistic, expressive. Fine preparatory works to Haydn and Mozart. Helpful preface.

2 Easy Sonatas F, a (Hoffmann-Erbrecht-K&S). Organum, Series V, 26.

2 Easy Sonatas E♭, F (K&S). Organum, Series V, 28.

2 Easy Sonatas C, B, (K&S). Organum, Series V, 30.

24 Studies in Waltz Form (Schott). Fine pieces through all keys, very pianistic. Int.

Der Tonkreis (Schott). Pieces in all keys arranged in order of difficulty. Easy to Int.

See: Helen S. Walker, "Johann Wilhelm Hässler (1747-1822); Eighteenth-century Solo Keyboard Literature for Amateurs," unpub. thesis, Smith College, 1968.

ROMAN HAUBENSTOCK-RAMATI (1919-) Poland, now living in Vienna

After traditional training in theory, composition and musicology, Haubenstock-Ramati embraced avant-garde techniques including *musique concrète*. He is music adviser to Universal Edition in Vienna.

Decisions (UE 1960).
May be played right side up or upside down by 1 or 2 pianists. Can be taped and subjected to electronic distortions. Interpretation of the graphics is left to the performer. Can be played any number of times (aleatory). D.

5 Klavierstücke (UE 1966).
Wide intervals and skips interspersed with tone clusters. The

second piece is the same as No. 5 but rearranged. Unusual notation and instructions for performance. D.

CHARLES HAUBIEL (1892-) USA

Portraits (Composer's Press 1941-1944). Three large works: Capriccio, Idyll, Scherzo. Varied contemporary pianistic techniques, rewarding. D.

Ariel (EBM). Filigree accompaniment to melody, use of triplets, romantic sonorities. M-D.

Solari (Composer's Press). Three works: Dawn Mist, Toccata, The Plane Beyond. Postromantic idiom. D.

Classical Suite (Composer's Press).

Elves Spinning (Composer's Press). Light scherzo, requiring facile touch. M-D.

HERBERT HAUFRECHT (1909-) USA

Haufrecht studied with Herbert Elwell, Quincy Porter and Rubin Goldmark.

Five Etudes in Blue (AMP 1956). Unpretentious, fun to play. Toccata, Quasi Ostinato, Dialogue, Nocturne, Capriccio. M-D.

Three Nocturnes (AMP 1957). 8 minutes. M-D.

Sicilian Suite (ACA 1944). Preludio: etude figuration; Siciliana: graceful siciliano rhythms contrasted with changing meters; Tarantella: brilliant, short. (EBM) also has the Tarantella. M-D.

Sonata (ACA 1956). Fine craft in all four movements. M-D.

Passacaglia and Fugue (ACA 1947). Large work, 16 variations, advanced pianism required. D.

Toccata on Familiar Tunes (Schroeder & Gunther c. 1969). Folk-like, bitonal, good octave technique required. M-D.

GERHARDUS HAVINGHA (1696-1753) The Netherlands

Werken voor Clavecimbel. Monumenta Musicae Belgicae, Vol. 7, 1951. Contains 8 suites (1722) and Havingha's own table of ornamentation. The suites contain Overtures, some in French style. These movements are always the most involved and longest. There are also Allemandas, Correntes, Sarabandas, and Gigas, some optional dances, Marsch, Air met d'Agréments, M, Entrée, Fantasia. Some unusual keys: one suite b♭, another A♯. Very original writing.
Short biography by Suzanne Clercx included.

MITSUAKI HAYAMA (1932-) Japan

Piano Sonata (Ongaku-no-Tomo-Sha 1963). 32 p. 3 movements. From *Contemporary Japanese Music Series* No. 10.
Allegro assai
Lento: ostinato bass treatment
Allegro molto
Serially organized, no meter signatures, pianistic. Technique is handled in an interesting way. The composer has had western training. Advanced pianism required.

JOSEPH HAYDN (1732-1809) Austria

It is no exaggeration to say that Haydn is a relatively unknown composer, not only to pianists but to the musical world at large. So very few of his sonatas are played and studied and then often with condescension, since he has been labelled (in the public mind) as "precursor to Mozart". May it be pointed out that at least twenty of his numerous keyboard sonatas are eminently worthy of study and performance and merit the serious attention of pianists. As a matter of fact, the difficulties are not only as great but sometimes greater than those encountered in the Mozart sonatas, especially from a musical angle.

It should be noted that the definitive numbering of Haydn's works follows the catalogue of Anthony van Hoboken (H or Hob), who was to Haydn as Köchel was to Mozart: *Joseph Haydn: Thematisch-bibliographisches Werkverzeichnis* Vol. I: Instrumentalwerke. Mainz: Schott, 1957.

The main editions of the sonatas are:

Vienna Urtext Edition in 3 Vols. (Christa Landon-UE). The most up-to-date edition based on the most authentic, scholarly sources and an eminently musical approach (fingered by Oswald Jonas). Pushes the number of known Haydn sonatas to sixty-two (seven lost). Important prefatory material discussing performance, ornamentation and related matters.

Lea Pocket Scores in 4 Vols. A reprint of the original Collected Edition by Karl Päsler, (Br&H 1918). Fifty-two sonatas.

Sonatas in 4 Vols. (Marticnsscn-CFP). Thc most accessible edition but contains editorial additions by the editor. 43 Sonatas. A fifth volume contains 6 Divertimenti.

Sonatas in 4 Vols. (Zilcher-Br&H). Indications from Haydn's time in heavy type, additions of the editor in light type. 42 Sonatas.

Selected Sonatas in 2 Vols. (Feder-Henle). 21 Sonatas. The first two in E♭ published for the first time after manuscripts in the Mährisch Landesmuseum in Brünn. Careful urtext edition. Preface discusses performance and sources.

Five Sonatas (Arthur Loesser-Music Press). Interesting choice, painstakingly edited.

Selected Sonatas in 2 Vols. (Lajos Hernadi-EMB). A superb student edition meticulously fingered and discreetly edited by a leading professor at the Liszt Academy in Budapest. Available through Bo&H.

Eight Selected Sonatas (ABRSC).

Separate Sonatas:

Henle has a facsimile of the autograph of Sonata A, H 26 with notes in German by Jens Peter Larsen. A fine edition of Sonata E♭, H 52 is (Badura Skoda-Dob). The following separate sonatas edited by Franzpeter Goebels are available from Schott: A♭ H 46, C H 15, C H 35, c H 20, c♯ H 36, D H 19, D H 37, E H 34, E♭ H 49, E♭ H 52, F H 23, G H 27.

HAYDN'S KEYBOARD SONATAS

As Numbered in Hoboken and Seven Editions

VIENNA URTEXT EDITION (H. C. Robbins Landon and Christa Landon)	Vol. 1—Nos. 1-35 Vol. 2—Nos. 36-52 Vol. 3—Nos. 53-62
PETERS EDITION (Martienssen)	Vol. 1—Nos. 1-11 Vol. 2—Nos. 12-23 Vol. 3—Nos. 24-33 Vol. 4—Nos. 34-43 Divertimenti Nos. 1-6
COLLECTED EDITION (Päsler) LEA POCKET SCORES	Vol. 1—Nos. 1-18 Vol. 2—Nos. 19-28 Vol. 3—Nos. 29-41 Vol. 4—Nos. 42-52
BREITKOPF EDITION (Zilcher)	Vol. 1—Nos. 1-11 Vol. 2—Nos. 12-22 Vol. 3—Nos. 23-32 Vol. 4—Nos. 33-42
HENLE EDITION (Feder)	Vol. 1—Nos. 1-12 Vol. 2—Nos. 13-21
KALMUS EDITION	Vol. 1—Nos. 1-20 Vol. 2—Nos. 21-34
SCHIRMER EDITION	Vol. 1—Nos. 1-10 Vol. 2—Nos. 11-20

V. Urtext	Hoboken XVI & Päsler	Peters	Breitkopf	Kalmus	Schirmer	Henle
1	8	D4 (9) (D=Divertimento)				
2	7	D5 (8)				
3	9	D6 (10)	42			
4						
5	11	11 (12)	31			

(Haydn's Keyboard Sonatas as Numbered in Seven Editions, cont.)

V. Urtext	Hoboken XVI & Päsler	Peters	Breitkopf	Kalmus	Schirmer	Henle
6	10	43				
7						
8	5	23	41			
9	4	D3				
10	1	D1				
11	2	22	40			
12	12	29	28		26	
13	6	37	36		31	
14	3	D2				
15	13	18	18	17	17	
16	14	15	15	14	14	
17						17
18						18
19						
20	20	19	19	18	18	20
21						
22						
23						23
24						
25						
26						
27						27
28					23	
29	45	26	25			
30	19	9	9	9	9	30
31	46	8	8	8	8	
32	44	4	4	4	4	32
33	20	25	24		22	
34	33	20	20	19	19	34
35	43	41	11			35
36	21	16	16	15	15	36
37	22	40	39		34	37
38	23	21	21	20	20	
39	24	22	32			
40	25	32				40
41	26	33				41

(Haydn's Keyboard Sonatas as Numbered in Seven Editions, cont.)

V. Urtext	Hoboken XVI & Päsler	Peters	Breitkopf	Kalmus	Schirmer	Henle
42	27	12	12	11	11	42
43	28	13	13	12	12	
44	29	14	14	13	13	44
45	30	36	35		30	
46	31	30	29		27	46
47	32	39	38		33	
48	35	5	5	5	5	48
49	36	6	6	6	6	49
50	37	7	7	7	7	50
51	38	35	34		28	51
52	39	17	17	16	16	52
53	34	2	2	2	2	
54	40	26	10	10	10	
55	41	27	26		24	
56	42	28	27		25	
57	47	34	33		28	
58	48	24	23		21	
59	49	3	3	3	3	
60	50	42	22			
61	51	38	37		32	
62	52	1	1	1	1	

Miscellaneous works:

Among Haydn's miscellaneous works the two most outstanding are the extraordinary *Fantasia C* (Georgii-Henle) and the much-loved *Variations* f (Georgii-Henle). *Capriccio* G (Riemann-Augener) is also of interest but somewhat diffuse. (K) has a volume of miscellaneous works but the most authoritative collection is *Klavierstücke* (Gerlach-Henle) which contains:

Capriccio G, (H XVII: 1), Variations E♭, (H XVII: 3), Variations A, (H XVII: 2), Variations C, (H XVII: 5), Fantasia C, (H XVII: 4), Variations f, (H XVII: 6), Variations D, (H XVII: 7), Adagio f, (H XVII: 9).

32 Pieces for Clock (Schmid-Nag) contains some easy and charming pieces. See also *Album of Easy Pieces* (Schott), *Easy Dances*

(Fries-Giesbert-Schott), *Ochsen-Menuett* (Voss-Schott), and *Rondo all' Ongarese* (Lechner-Schott).

See: Harold Lee Andrews, "Tonality and Structure in the First Movements of Haydn's Solo Keyboard Sonatas," unpub. diss., University of North Carolina, 1967.

Alan R. Aulabaugh, "An Analytical Study of Performance Problems in the Keyboard Sonatas of F. J. Haydn," unpub. diss., State University of Iowa, 1958.

Edward J. Dent, "Haydn's Pianoforte Works," MMR, 62, 1932, 1-4.

William J. Mitchell, "The Haydn Sonatas," PQ, 7, 1954, 13-17.

Philip Radcliffe, "The Piano Sonatas of Joseph Haydn," MR, 7, 1946, 136-48.

T. E. Willett, "A Study of Haydn's Piano Sonatas," unpub. thesis, University of Illinois, 1946.

MICHAEL HAYDN (1737-1806) Austria

Sechs Menuette für Klavier (NV). Written in Salzburg in 1784. Easy to Int.

BERNHARD HEIDEN (1910-   ) USA, born Germany, came to USA 1935

Heiden worked with Paul Hindemith for five years. His works are characterized by skill and melodic fluency.

Sonata No. 2 (AMP 1952). 16½ minutes. D.
Four movements, difficult, tonal, well-contrasted themes. Neoclassic orientation, many meter changes.

WALTER HELFER (1896-1959) USA

Helfer studied with William Mason in Boston and later with Respighi in Rome.

Elegiac Sonata (UE 1935).
Tonal, brilliant writing in third movement. Slow movement is a flowing Andante. M-D.

DANIEL HELLDÉN (1917-   ) Sweden

Sonatina Rapsodica (GM 1957). 16 p.
4 movements, frequently changing meters and key signatures. Bitonal. Exploits full range of the keyboard. M-D.

STEPHEN HELLER (1813-1888) born Hungary, lived mostly in France

Although old-fashioned by today's standards, Heller's works include plenty of fine pedagogical material readily available.

The Art of Phrasing Op. 16 (GS). 26 melodious studies in 2 books.

25 Studies Op. 45 (GS) (Augener) (CFP). Famous *L'avalanche* is number 2 in this set.

30 Studies Op. 46 (GS) (Ashdown) (CFP).

25 Studies Op. 47 (GS) (Ric) (CFP) (Augener).

Flower and Thorn Pieces Op. 82 (GS) (K). 18 characteristic pieces.

24 Preludes Op. 81 (GS) (Augener).

32 Preludes Op. 119 (GS).

Sonatina Op. 146 (Ric).

40 Compositions (Ashdown) from Op. 45, 46, 47, 73, 80, 81, 138, etc.

56 Studies and Pieces (A. Alexander-Mills). 2 volumes.
Contains some of his best works.

Album of 10 pieces (CFP) from Op. 33, 77, 78, 80, 81, 85, 86, 119.

50 Selected Studies (GS) from Op. 45, 46, 47.

See: Ronald E. Booth, Jr., "The Life and Music of Stephen Heller," unpub. diss., University of Iowa, 1967.

EVERETT HELM (1913-) USA

Helm worked in composition with Walter Piston, Francesco Malipiero, Ralph Vaughan Williams, Darius Milhaud, and in musicology with Hugo Leichtentritt and Alfred Einstein. His style blends linear clarity with dissonant counterpoint and lively rhythmic treatment.

Sonata Brevis (Hargail 1945).
Easily moving: flowing chromatic lines over ostinato-like bass.
Slow and Contemplative: flexible, colorful melodic writing.
Vigorous: driving idea, slower mid-section that recalls main idea of first movement. Presto coda, M-D.

Brasiliana Suite (CF).
I Would Flee Thee: slow, colorful, melody based on folksong.
Pardon Emilia: slow, melodic.
Toccata Brasileira: driving, syncopated, requires good octaves.
In the AMC library there is a fourth movement entitled "Vernca, meuanjo." Shorter than the other movements, only 2 pages. Attractive. M-D.

Dance Suite (AMC). 7 pieces for piano.
Each piece approximately 2 pages long. Range in difficulty from No. 1 to No. 7. No. 4, most sophisticated of the set. Variety of moods, idioms and techniques. Clever writing. Int. to M-D.

New Horizons (GS c. 1964).
Twelve pieces intended to help the piano student bridge the gap between traditional and contemporary music. Notes on each piece explain the technique of modern composition employed. Also contains an excellent introduction to the styles and practice of contemporary music, within the scope of well trained high school students.

CHARLES-JOSEPH VAN HELMONT (1715-1790) Flemish (Belgium)

Werken voor orgel en/of voor Clavicimbel. Monumenta Musicae Belgicae, Vol. 6 (1948) with a short biography by Suzanne Clercx.

Contains *Pièces de Clavecin* and his own table of ornaments, similar to F. Couperin's. Suite I: La Françoise (rondeau), La Moderne, La Caille, Le Barc, La Boulonnoise. Helmont was a great admirer of the French style. Doubles are written for some of the movements. 4 fugues are also included from his *6 Fugues.*

ROBERT HELPS (1928-) USA

Helps studied piano with Abby Whiteside and composition with Roger Sessions. He is currently teaching at the New England Conservatory.

Portrait (CFP). 6½ minutes. A M-D lyric mood picture. Broken octave technique, PPPP closing.

3 Etudes (CFP). For virtuoso pianists. Preference for seconds, fourths, fifths, sevenths, and ninths. No. 2 contains interesting pedal effects. No. 3 is a "program" closer.

3 Recollections (CFP 1968). 15 minutes. Difficult character pieces. Bloch influence.
In Memoriam, Interlude, Epilogue.
Interlude No. 2 is especially colorful.

Image. See Anthologies and Collections, USA, *New Music for the Piano* (LG).

WALTER HENDL (1917-) USA

Prelude to "Dark of The Moon" (Hargail 1945).
Piano reduction of the score for the play *Dark of the Moon.* A short slow introduction, followed by exciting driving rhythmic figuration with frequent meter changes. Mild dissonances, bitonal, unison writing, fast octaves, tenths. M-D.

HANS HENKEMANS (1913-) The Netherlands

Henkemans studied with Willem Pijper, and has won international fame as a pianist mainly through his interpretation of Mozart and Debussy. A fondness for Debussy is seen in his compositions.

Etude No. 1 (B&VP 1937). 3 minutes.

Etude No. 2 (Donemus 1937).

Sonate (Donemus 1958). 11 minutes. 21 p.
Allegro molto moderato: undulating, triplet figuration, PP closing leads directly to Molto adagio: light broken chords used in a brush-stroke technique, leads directly to Allegro ma non troppo: motivic development, driving, tumultuous closing. D.

RICHARD HENSEL (1926-) USA

Hensel received his training at the American Conservatory of Music and the University of Illinois. He studied composition with Leo Sowerby, Goffredo Petrassi, Milton Babbitt, Burrill Phillips and Gordon Binkerd. He teaches at Eastern Kentucky State University in Richmond, Kentucky.

Sonata No. 1 (CAP 1967). 17 p.
First movement: theme, episode one.
Second movement: theme, episode two.
Third movement: theme, episode three.
Same theme generates the entire work. Strong linear conception, thin textures, harmonic ninths, MC. M-D.

ADOLF HENSELT (1814-1889) Germany

One of the great pianists of the nineteenth century, Henselt composed mainly "studies" for his instrument. These still have value, especially in his approach to "stretches" and wide extensions of the hand.

12 Etudes Op. 2 (GS). No. 6, *Si oiseau j'etais* most popular of this set. Available separately from (Augener) (Schott) (Paxton).

Pieces from Op. 5, 13, 15, and 25 (Augener).

Piano Concerto f Op. 16 (Musical Scope Publishers). Original solo version by the composer.

HANS WERNER HENZE (1926-) Germany

Henze studied with Wolfgang Fortner and René Leibowitz. His works display a variety of forms, as well as atonality, polytonality and tonality.

Variationen für Klavier Op. 13. (Schott 1949). 9 p.
Strict 12-tone style based on Schönberg technique. D.

Sonata for Piano (Schott 1959). 24 p.
Rows are used constantly, freely producing continuous changes in pitch and dynamics. Pointillistic writing, rhythmic complexities. D.

Six Absences pour le Clavecin (Schott 1961).
Better suited to the harpsichord yet can be played effectively on the piano. Atonal. D.

EDUARDO HERNANDEZ-MONCADA (1899-) Mexico

Costeña (Southern 1962).
Cross-rhythms, bitonal writing, interesting sonorities. M-D.

Cinco Piezas Bailables (Southern).
Colorful contemporary idiom, dance forms. M-D.

MANUEL HERRARTE (1924-) Guatemala

Herrarte studied composition in Guatemala City with Ricardo Castillo and at the Eastman School of Music with Howard Hanson and Bernard Rogers. He is an excellent pianist and has appeared in recitals throughout the United States.

6 Sketches (EV c. 1953).
Valsante, Melancolico, Vivo, Simple, Sombrio, Festivo. M-D.

3 Dances (PAU 1957).
Allegro; Andantino; Presto. Latin-American rhythms. Sound easier than they are. Int. to M-D.

JOHANN WILHELM HERTEL (1727-1789) Germany

Sonata d Op. 1 (H. Erdmann-Br). Vol. 49 of *Hortus Musicus*.
Three movements. An attractive work. Slow movement contains some lovely passages, as expressive and surprising as almost anything found in his contemporary C. P. E. Bach.

HENRI HERZ (1803-1888) Germany

Regarded by Schumann as the model of musical philistinism. SHKY, 271.

24 Exercises and Preludes Op. 21 (CFP) in all major and minor keys.

Scales and Exercises (Gammes-CFP) (GS) (UE).

Methode Complète de Piano Op. 100 (Ric).

Collection of Exercises and Scales (Tagliapietra-Ric).

1,000 Exercises (Ric).

Variations élégantes sur une Styrienne de Weber Op. 120 (WH).

Le perpetuel mouvement Op. 91/3 (WH).

Variations on Rossini's "Non più mesta" from La Cenerentola (Music Treasure Publications). Foreward by Earl Wild. Originally published in 1831, contrasting keys, meters, tempi, cliches, brilliant, effective. M-D.

JACQUES HÉTU (1938-) Canada

Petite Suite Op. 7 (CMC 1962).
6 movements use much disjunct motion. Broad dynamic range, extremes of keyboard exploited. D.

Variations pour Piano (Berandol c. 1970).
12-tone writing, ebullient, brilliant. D.

JOHANN ADAM HILLER (1728-1804) Germany

Leichte Tanzstücke (K. Herrmann-Sikorski).

PAUL HINDEMITH (1895-1963) Germany

One of the major composers of our century whose enormous output has contributed to the repertoire of every instrument. Hindemith approached composition through linear writing and his expanded tonal concept is unique. For a thorough understanding of his ideas on this subject *The Craft of Musical Composition* (AMP) should be consulted. (Schott) publishes all the piano works.

Tanzstücke Op. 19 (1928). Eight dance pieces, all requiring vigorous octave and chord playing. The last five are grouped under the heading *Pantomine*. An effective collection. M-D to D.

Suite "1922" Op. 26. Five movements: Marsch, Schimmy, Nachtstück, Boston, Ragtime. Old dances of the suite are replaced by parodies of early 20th-century dance styles. Concerning the Ragtime Hindemith says "Forget everything you have learned in your piano lessons. Don't worry whether you must play D sharp with the fourth or the sixth finger. Play this piece wildly but in strict rhythm, like a machine. Use the piano as an interesting kind of percussion instrument and treat it accordingly." The lyric Nachtstück is effective performed separately. Subtle rubato is called for in the Boston. M-D to D.

Sonata No. 1 (1936). Inspired by Friedrich Hölderlin's poem *Der Main,* this large-scale work is in 5 movements and requires textural clarity and solid chord playing. D.

Sonata No. 2 (1936). Smaller in dimensions than the other sonatas, this graceful piece has 3 movements: the first in SA design, the second a bright Scherzo, while the finale is a rondo with a short, slow introduction. M-D.

Sonata No. 3 (1936). 4 movements make up this large-scale work that closes with a powerful double fugue. Sonorous passages add to the excitement of the close. Mature pianism required. D.

Ubung in drei Stücken Op. 37 Part 1 (1925). Exercise in 3 parts, reveals aggressive writing throughout. No. 1: energetic 2-part writing, changing meters, colorful jazzy mid-section. No. 2: calm melody with involved figuration proceeds to prestissimo close over ostinato bass. No. 3: rhythmic problems permeate this brilliant rondo.

Reihe Kleine Stücke Op. 37 Part 2 (1927). 13 fairly complex short pieces. Varied moods and titles. M-D.

Kleine Klaviermusik (1929). 12 five-tone pieces, various moods, severe polyphonic writing. Int.

Wir bauen eine Stadt (1931). 6 pieces from the cantata *Let's Build a City*. Int.

Ludus Tonalis (1942). *Studies in Counterpoint Tonal Organization and Piano Playing*. "Twelve Fugues, in as many keys, connected by Interludes in free lyric and dance forms, old and new, and framed by a Prelude and Postlude that have more in common than meets the casual ear." This contemporary *Well-Tempered Clavier* is a cyclical whole arranged in a key sequence based on Hindemith's ranking of tonalities as given in his *Craft of Musical Composition*. The Fugues (all in 3 and 4 voices), as well as the Interludes exhibit a great variety of moods and difficulty. Int. to D.

See: Jane Carlson, "Hindemith's *Ludus Tonalis,* A Personal Experience," PQ, 65, Fall 1968, 17-21. A descriptive survey of the entire work from a pianist's point of view.

Hans Tischler, "Remarks on Hindemith's Contrapuntal Technique. Based on his *Ludus Tonalis* of 1942," In *Essays in Musicology —A Birthday Offering for Willi Apel*. Bloomington: University of Indiana, 1968, 175-84.
"Hindemith's *Ludus Tonalis* and Bach's *WTC*—A Comparison," MR, 20, 1959, 217-27.

Peter Evans, "Hindemith's Keyboard Music," MT, 97, November 1956, 572-5.

ALUN HODDINOTT (1929-   ) Wales

Second Nocturne Op. 16/1 (Nov). Impressionistic, quasi-atonal style. Wide dynamic range, no key signatures. Requires a good sense of rubato. M-D.

Sonata Op. 17 (OUP 1959). 17 minutes. 44 p.
Some serial technique present but tonal centers are easily recognizable. Rhythmic vitality, much dissonance, linear textures. Advanced pianism required. Andante, Allegro, Adagio, Allegro assai.

Sonata No. 2 Op. 27 (Nov 1960). 20 p.
First movement all craft and little inspiration. Second movement lyric and poetic. Third movement full of rhythmic drive. D.

Sonatina for Clavichord or Piano Op. 18 (S&B). 11 p.
4 short movements. M-D.

Sonata No. 3 Op. 40 (Nov 1966). 14 p. 10 minutes.
No. 2 in "Virtuoso," a modern piano series published by Novello. Adagio: expressive, free, declamatory. Allegro: energetic and driving. (See Anthologies and Collections: General: Contemporary.

Sonata No. 4 Op. 49 (OUP 1968). 21 p.
In 5 concise movements: Toccata 1, Toccata 2, Aria, Notturno, Toccata 3. Largely atonal, except the 6-line Notturno which is impressionistic. Much use of pedal, powerfully written work. D.

Sonata No. 5 (OUP 1968). 28 p. 14-15 minutes.
Begins with a cadenza, developed, and moves to two contrasting Aria movements, ends with a Toccata, a mirror canon. Unusual form, freely tonal. D.

E. T. A. HOFFMANN (1776-1822) Germany

Hoffmann wrote six piano sonatas. Four were published in 1922 by Kistner and Siegel, edited by Becking: No. 1 f, No. 2 F, No. 3 f, No. 4 c♯. No. 4 is contained in the collection *Thirteen Keyboard Sonatas of the 18th and 19th Centuries* (W. S. Newman-UNC).

Sonata A (F. Schnapp-Br). Composed 1804-1805.
Andante; Minuets (2); Allegro assai: a bright rondo. Most interesting of the movements.
Not technically difficult. Serves as good introduction to nineteenth-century piano literature, although not as interesting as some of the later sonatas.

Sonata c♯ (1805). From *Anthology of Music,* Vol. 21, *Romanticism in Music,* 71-2.
Scherzo: Five-note main theme dominates entire movement.

LEE HOIBY (1926-   ) USA

Hoiby teaches at the University of Wisconsin.

Toccata Op. 1 (GS 1953). A concert study.

5 Preludes Op. 7 (GS 1955). 22 p. Unpretentious, delightful to play. More difficult than they at first appear. M-D.

Capriccio on 5 Notes Op. 23 (Bo&H 1962). Commissioned for the first Van Cliburn International Piano Competition, 1962. Advanced harmonic idiom, designed to show off many sides of the pianist's technical and musical abilities. A mixture of styles, broad dynamic range, restless rhythmic motion, breathless coda. D.

HEINZ HOLLIGER (1939-   ) Switzerland

Elis (Schott 1961). Three nocturnes in the Webern tradition. D.

VAGN HOLMBOE (1909-   ) Denmark, born Africa

Holmboe's music is strongly influenced by Carl Nielsen and Béla Bartók. He leans toward linear textures. He is Denmark's leading symphonist (nine symphonies), and is Professor at the Royal Danish Music Conservatory in Copenhagen.

Suono da bardo Op. 49 (Viking 1949). A symphonic suite, employs unusual development technique. Nielsen's influence is especially seen in this work. D.
Toccata, Interlude, Fantasia, Metamorfosi, Finale, Postludio.

Rumainsk Suite Op. 12/1 (Viking). Holmboe's wife is a Rumanian pianist with whom he explored folk music in many remote villages of Rumania. This suite dates from that period. M-D.

GUSTAV HOLST (1874-1934) Great Britain

Nocturne (Faber c. 1965). Colorful writing, impressionistic, contrasting quiet and lively moods. Int.

Jig (Curwen). Animated, rhythmic, cross rhythms. M-D.

Toccata (Curwen). On the tune "Newburn lads." More contemporary than above-listed works.

SIMEON ten HOLT (1923-) The Netherlands

ten Holt studied theory and piano with Jacob van Domselaer. He lived for some years in France where he attended the Ecole Normale in Paris.

Sekwensen for 1 or 2 pianos (Donemus 1965). Six pieces, *avant-garde,* directions in Dutch and French.

Sonata (diagonal) (Donemus 1959). D.
Agitato; Allegretto scorrendo; Adagio lamentoso; Allegro vivace. Freely chromatic, some bitonal writing, changing meters, broad dynamic range, octave facility required.

20 Epigrams (Donemus 1959).

Cyclus to Lunacy (Donemus 1961).

RUDOLPH HOLZMANN (1910-) Peru, born Germany

Holzmann moved to Lima, Peru in 1938. He studied composition with Vladimir Vogel and Karol Rathaus in Europe and spent the year 1957-58 at the University of Texas. He is professor of orchestral conducting at the National Conservatory of Music in Lima.

Cuarta Pequeña Suite (ECIC 1942). Based on Peruvian folk materials. Preludio Pastorale: peaceful, melodic; Bailan las Muchachas: little girl's dance, staccato, syncopated; Melodía triste: melancholy moderato; Fanfarria Campestre: a Country Fanfare, horn calls; Interludio Evocativo: atmospheric, nocturne-like; Danza Final: Octaves, fast double notes, energetic 3/8, most difficult of set. Int. to M-D.

Niñerías (Editorial Tritono). Six short movements.
Preludio para Tota; Una mano postinada; Val del Do con su Dominante; La Fuga del La perseguido por el Fa; Mi amigo el Pedal; La bella Marinera.

3 Remembranzas (Editorial Tritono 1949).
Muy tranquilo; Caprichoso; Solemne.

ARTHUR HONEGGER (1892-1955) Switzerland, born France

More at home in the larger than smaller forms, Honegger did not pour his finest efforts into his piano works. Nevertheless, his compositions show a certain substance that many of his contemporaries lacked.

Trois Pièces (Sal 1915-19). Prélude: intense, large climax; Hommage à Ravel: flowing, lyric; Danse: repeated intervals, brilliant, driving. M-D.

Toccata et Variations (Sal 1916). 17 minutes. Contrasted sections in the Toccata, facile. Variation theme is choral-like, double notes, serious, more involved than Toccata. M-D.

Sept Pièces Brèves (ESC 1919-20). Souplement, Vif, Très lent, Legèrement, Lent, Rhythmique, Violent. Short, contrasted moods and techniques. M-D.

Le Cahier Romand (Sal 1921-23). 5 sensitive pieces, mainly lyric except No. 4. M-D.

Hommage à Albert Roussel (Sal 1928). Short, chordal, syncopated melody. Int.

Prélude, Arioso et Fughetta sur le nom de BACH (Sal 1932). 4½ minutes. Broken-chord pattern in Prelude; Arioso is improvisatory with an ostinato bass; 3-voice fugue. M-D.

Souvenir de Chopin (Choudens 1947). Int.

Deux Esquisses (Durand 1943). No. 1, rhapsodic in character; No. 2, wistful. M-D.

La Neige sur Rome (Sal).

JAMES HOOK (1746-1827) Great Britain

Guida di Musica London c. 1785, Part I, Op. 37 (BB) Facsimile edition. "Being a complete book of instructions for beginners on the harpsichord or piano forte . . . to which is added 24 progressive lessons." Part II, 1794, "consisting of several hundred examples of fingering . . . and 6 exercises . . . to which is added, a short . . . method of learning thoro bass . . . Op. 75."

The Precepter London c. 1785, "for piano-forte, the organ or harpsichord to which is added 2 celebrated lessons by James Hook." (BB) Facsimile edition.

ANTHONY HOPKINS (1921-) Great Britain

5 Short Preludes in the form of Variations on 3 Notes (JWC 1948). 15 p.

Sonata No. 1 d (JWC 1944-45). 25 p.

Toccata (JWC c. 1953). 7 p.

Tango from "The Skin of Our Teeth" (JWC).

Sonata No. 3 c♯ (JWC 1948). 24 p. 14 minutes. D.
Allegro vigoroso: SA, well-contrasted material, clearly defined sections, many dynamic changes.
Largo: harmonic opening leads to contrapuntal section. Slow fugato leads to rhythmic Allegro giusto. Coda requires utmost rhythmic precision.

ALAN HOVHANESS (1911-) USA

The Orient has had a profound effect on this American-born composer yet his music is based on classical forms. Strict discipline, great freedom, consonance and dissonance, tonality and atonality, while seeming to be opposites are all woven into Hovhaness' style. A more complete discussion of the solo works is found in an article by Maurice Hinson: "The Piano Works of Alan Hovhaness", AMT, 16, January 1967, 22-24, 44. All the works listed below are published by (CFP) unless otherwise identified.

Toccata and Fugue Op. 6.

3 Preludes and Fugues Op. 10.

Sonata Ricercare Op. 12. 3 movements of imitative writing.

Fantasy Op. 16. Various objects are to be employed to contact the strings.

Mystic Flute Op. 22. Easy.

2 Ghazals Op. 36/1, 2.

Mazert Nman Rehani Op. 38. Imitates ancient Oriental instruments.

Artinis Op. 39.

Moonlight Night Op. 52a (Merion).

Slumber Song, Siris' Dance Op. 52/2, 3 (MCA). Easy.

12 Armenian Folk Songs Op. 43. Excellent intermediate material.

Invocation to Vahakn Op. 54/1.

Vanadour Op. 55/1.

Farewell to the Mountains Op. 55/2.

Achtamar Op. 64/1 (PIC).

Fantasy on an Ossetin Tune Op. 85/6 (PIC).

Jhala Op. 103 (PIC). Virtuoso writing.

Suite Op. 96. 5 movements: Prelude, Fugue, Dance, Aria, Madrigal.

Orbit No. 2 Op. 102/2 (PIC). Calls for timpanum stick to play bass strings.

Allegro on a Pakistan Lute Tune Op. 104/6 (LG). In collection *New Music for the Piano.*

Pastoral No. 1 Op. 3/2 (PIC). Marimba and timpanum stick required for glissandi.

Hymn to a Celestial Musician Op. 3/3 (PIC). Soft plectrum required for circular glissandi.

Haiku Op. 113/1, 2, 3. 1 minute each.

Sonatina Op. 120. 3 movements. Expressive.

Macedonian Mountain Dance Op. 144b/1.

Mountain Dance Op. 144b/2.

Sonata Op. 145. 3 movements. 11 minutes.

Do You Remember the Last Silence? Op. 152. Thin melody accompanied by thick harmonies. Effective contemporary character piece.

The Lake of Van Sonata Op. 175. 3 movements.

Bardo Sonata Op. 192. 3 movements. Interesting use of harmonics.

Madras Sonata Op. 176. 3 movements. 10 minutes. A 3-voice fugue concludes this work.

Shalimar Op. 177. Suite in 8 movements. 11 minutes. D.

Poseidon Sonata Op. 191. 2 movements. 10 minutes. Span of ninth required.

Bare November Day Op. 210. For clavichord, piano, organ, or harpsichord. 3 movements.

Dark River and Distant Bell Op. 212. For harpsichord but can be played on piano, organ, or clavichord. 4 movements.

Lullaby (EBM). In album *American Composers of Today.* Easy.

Mountain Idylls (AMP). 3 pieces: Moon Lullaby, Moon Dance, Mountain Lullaby. Pedal studies. Int.

EGIL HOVLAND (1924-) Norway

Hovland is an organist in Fredrikstad, Norway. He studied composition with Holmboe, Copland and Dallapiccola.

Scherzo and Rondino Op. 29 (Lyche).
Clever pedagogical material, bitonal. M-D.

HERBERT HOWELLS (1892-) Great Britain

"The music of Howells, without being consciously 'national', is unmistakably English in character." GD, 4, 389. He made an attempt to revive the use of the clavichord in his two sets of pieces including the instrument's name.

Suite: Sarum Sketches Op. 6 (OUP 1917). 7 pieces.

Snapshots Op. 30 (1916-18 Swan).

Little Book of 6 Dances (OUP).

Lambert's Clavichord Op. 41 (OUP). 12 pieces. Sophisticated writing. Character pieces named after friends including: Lambert's fireside, Fellowe's delight, Hughe's ballet, Wortham's grounde, Sargent's fantastic sprite, Foss' dump, My Lord Sandwich's dreame, Samuel's air, De la Mare's pavane, Sir Hugh's galliard, H. H. his fancy, Sir Richard's toy. Int. to M-D.

Howells' Clavichord (Nov 1961). 2 books, 10 pieces each. More character pieces used to pay tribute to 20 of Howells' musical friends. Uses old forms and titles, MC. M-D.

ALEXANDRU HRISANIDE (1936-) Rumania

Sonata No. 1 (Editura Muzicala 1955-64). 51 p.
Flames, Duality, Study No. 4.

Can be played in its entirety, or in parts. Movements can be re-arranged. *Avant-garde* notation, unusual directions are used such as "estatico," "Olimpico," "durabile Ped." "III Steinway"" (referring to the sostenuto pedal). Highly organized and controlled. Advanced pianism required.

MARK HUGHES (1934-) USA

Hughes had some private composition lessons with Ingolf Dahl, Nadia Boulanger and Roy Harris. He also worked with Will Gay Bottje at the University of Illinois.

Reflection and Dance for Piano. Commissioned by the Virginia MTA and the MTNA, 1968. (Available on loan from MTNA). Reflection refers to the subdued mood and also to the contrapuntal devices of simultaneous inversion or "mirroring" which occurs intermittently between various melodic lines. Plucked strings are called for.

Dance is bright and pungent and has a variety of asymmetric rhythms. It is cast in free rondo form. The entire work is based on melodic principles found in an 8-tone scale with the resultant harmonies being predominantly bitonal. Many sevenths and ninths. M-D.

JOHANN NEPOMUK HUMMEL (1778-1837) Hungary

During his life Hummel was considered by many as the greatest pianist in Europe and an outstanding composer. He was also a fine improviser.

Bagatelles Op. 107 (Waldwick). 2 vols. Scherzo, Rondoletto Russe, "La Contemplazione" una piccola fantasia, Rondo, Variazioni (4), Rondo all' ongarese. M-D.

16 Characteristic Pieces (Augener).

Rondo E♭ Op. 11 (GS) (CFP). *Rondo* Op. 122 (Carisch). *Rondo* C (CF).

Fantasie Op. 18 (Hamelle).

Scherzo (Willis). Fine encore or recital piece.

Selected Sonatas (Heugel). Op. 13 E♭, Op. 20 f, Op. 106 D *Sonata brillante.*

6 Easy Pieces (WH).

Variations on a Theme from Armide (CF).

Variations on a Gavotte by Gluck Op. 57 (CF) (K&S).

18 Grandes Etudes Op. 125 (Leduc).

Romance G (Durand).

Album of 37 Pieces (WH).

24 Preludes (Marmontel-Heugel). Some are very short, only 3 or 4 bars.

Theme and Variations (Dunhill, Anglo-French).

Collection (CFP). Contains 24 Preludes Op. 67, Sonatas f Op. 20, E♭ Op. 13, Rondo Op. 11, and Fantasie Op. 18, Polacca "La bella capricciosa."

See: Frederick F. Broer, "The Solo Piano Sonatas of Johann Nepomuk Hummel," unpub. thesis, Indiana University, 1967.

Richard Davis, "The Music of J. N. Hummel, Its Derivation and Development," MR, 26, 1965, 169-91.

CONRAD F. HURLEBUSCH (1696-1765) Germany

Keyboard Sonatas (A. Jambor-EV c. 1963) in two volumes, six sonatas in each. From the Preface: ". . . his style of writing was so progressive that it may have aroused controversial reactions among his contemporaries. He was searching for new harmonies, strange modulations, lyricism and pathos, and application of German, French and Italian musical styles. His courageous experimentation put him far ahead of his time." Worthy music, moments of inspiration, use of numerous dance movements (M, Gavotta, G) lend it a suite character. Editorial policy not always clear. Int. to M-D.

KAREL HUSA (1921-) Czechoslovakia, came to USA in 1954

After leaving Prague in 1946 Husa studied composition with Honegger and Nadia Boulanger. He writes in an advanced contemporary style but with a strong lyric emphasis. Husa teaches composition, orchestration and conducting at Cornell University.

Elegy (Leduc).

Sonata Op. 11 (Schott 1949). 23 minutes.
Three movements including a "misterioso" introduction, leads to an Allegro moderato. A powerful structure, full of expressive dissonance, requires advanced pianism.

ELEK HUZELLA (1915-) Hungary

Huzella studied composition with Albert Siklós at the Academy of Music, Budapest. He wrote a doctoral dissertation on Debussy. Since 1949 he has been professor at the Béla Bartók Conservatory.

Cambiate per pianoforte (Bo&H c. 1968). 6 p. Short suite. M-D.
Invocazione: legato seconds, thirds and fourths, chromatic, contrary and parallel motion.
Esclamazione: quartal broken chords, some triadic sonorities.
Nenia (canone enigmatico): rubato, large span required, both musical and technical problems.

I

JACQUES IBERT (1890-1962) France

Histoires (Leduc). 10 descriptive attractive pieces. Varied moods, techniques. Int. to M-D.
La Meneuse de tortues d'Od, Le petit âne blanc, La vieux mendiant, A Giddy Girl, Dans la maison triste, Le palais abandonné, Baja la mesa, La Cage de cristal, La Marchande d'eau fraîche, Le Cortège de Balkis.

Petite Suite en Quinze Images (Foetisch 1943). 15 colorful sketches. Int. Prélude, Ronde, Le gai vigneron, Berceuse aux étoiles, Le cavalier sans-souci, Parade, La promenade en traineau, Romance, Quadrille, Sérénade sur l'eau, La machine à coudre, L'adieu, Les crocus, Premier bal, Danse de cocher.

Les Rencontres (Leduc). A small suite in the form of a ballet, 5 movements. Delightful writing, some difficult figuration. Les bouquetières, Les créoles, Les mignardes, Les bergères, Les bavards.

Toccata sur le nom d'Albert Roussel (UMP 1929).

Le vent dans les ruines (Leduc).

Scherzetto (Leduc).

Matin sur l'eau (Leduc).

Féerique (Leduc).

Valse from ballet "L'eventail de Jeanne" (Heugel 1927). Good octave technique required.

Divertissement (EV).

TOSHI ICHIYANAGI (1933-   ) Japan

Ichiyanagi studied composition with Chieko Hara and Tomijiro Ikenouchi in Japan and with Aaron Copland, Lukas Foss, and John Cage in the United States. His compositions have been performed at various contemporary concerts in Japan and North America.

Music for Piano Nos. 2, 3, 6, 7 (CFP). Four separately published works.
Avant-garde notation, aleatory writing, detailed directions. D.

ANDREW IMBRIE (1921-   ) USA

Sonata (SP 1947). Serious compact work requiring advanced pianism.
Allegro nervoso: linear, driving, dramatic.
Adagio quasi elegiaco: impassioned, dynamic central climax.
Presto con brio: percussive, dissonant, dramatic closing.

VINCENT d'INDY (1851-1931) France

3 French Folk Dances (OUP). Easy.

Tableaux de Voyage Op. 33 (1888). (Leduc). 13 descriptive Travel Pictures, uneven in quality but worth playing. Written to commemorate d'Indy's travels in the Black Forest and along the banks of the Rhine. Excellent substitute for Schumann *Forest Scenes* and Mendelssohn *Songs Without Words.*

Thème varié, Fugue et Chanson Op. 85 (1925) (Sal). Exceptional set of variations.

Nocturne Op. 26 (Hamelle).

Promenade Op. 27 (1888) (Hamelle).

Schumanniana. Trois chants sans paroles pour piano Op. 30 (1888) (Hamelle).

Six Paraphrases sur des chansons enfantines de France Op. 95 (1928) (Heugel).

Mountain Poems Op. 15 (Hamelle).

24 Pièces (for children of all ages) Op. 74 (Rouant). 3 books.

Contes de fées Op. 86 (1926) (Rouart). A suite of 5 Fairy Tales.

Sonata e/E Op. 63 (1907) (Durand). 3 movements, cyclic construction, D. See: SSB, 536-37.

Petite Sonata dans la forme Classique Op. 9 (1880) (Hamelle). 4 movements, academic. M-D.

Menuet sur le nom d'Haydn Op. 65 (1909) (Durand).

Fantasia on an old French air Op. 99 (1930) (Heugel). Introduction, 6 variations, finale.

Helvetia: Trois Valses Op. 17 (1882) (Hamelle). Aarau, Schïnznach, Laufenburg.

Quatre Pièces Op. 16 (1882) (Hamelle). Serenade, Choral grave, Scherzetto, Agitato: Etude.

MANUEL INFANTE (1883-1958) Spain

Gitanerias (Sal 1923). Varied moods in virtuoso Spanish dance style. Exciting close.

Sevillana (Sal 1922). A fantasy of impressions of the Fête at Seville. Traditional harmonic treatment, virtuoso writing. D.

El Vito (Sal). Six variations on a popular theme in virtuoso style. A brilliant "Danse Andalouse" closes the work.

Guadalquivir (Leduc).

Pochades Andalouses (Gregh).
Canto flamenco, Danse gitane, Aniers sur la route de Séville, Tientos.

DÉSIRÉE-ÉMILE INGHELBRECHT (1880-1965) France

La Nursery (Sal). Six volumes, six pieces in each, of French nursery tunes, clear textures. Also available in four-hand version for teacher and student. Int. to M-D.

Trois Poèmes Dansées (UE).
Rêve, La danse pour les oiseaux, L'album aux portraits.

Paysages (Rouart, Lerolle). Five impressionistic pieces.

Suite Petite-Russiènne (ESC).
Five pieces based on popular tunes.

Six Danses Suédoises (Sal).

Pastourelles (Durand c. 1949). Seven pieces.
Nazareth, Le départ pour Bethléem, Prière de Marie, Danse des bergers, Berceuse du boeuf et de l'âne, La Marche à l'Etoile, Les bergers à la crèche. M-D.

Deux Esquisses (Senart).

JOHN IRELAND (1879-1962) Great Britain

Most of Ireland's piano works have a mildly-contemporary sound, are well written for the instrument and have unusually relevant and interesting titles.

Decorations (Augener). Three pieces. M-D to D.
The Island Spell, Moon-glade, The Scarlet Ceremonies.

Four Preludes (Bo&H).
The Undertone, Obsession, The Holy Boy, Fire of Spring. M-D to D.

Ballade of London Nights (Bo&H). Large three-part design gossamer quality. D.

London Pieces (Augener). Chelsea Reach, Ragamuffin, Soho Forenoons. D.

Equinox (Augener). Continuous motion etude. D.

Green Ways (Bo&H). The Cherry Tree, Cypress, The Palm and May. M-D.

A Sea Idyll (JWC). M-D.

Sonata e (1918-20) (Augener). Three contrasting movements requiring complete pianism.

Sonatina (1928) (OUP). Three movements. Well worth the effort. M-D.

Rhapsody (Bo&H). D.

CHARLES IVES (1874-1954) USA

Posterity continues to brighten Ives' position not only in American music but in 20th-century music in general. He is the first authentic American composer of the 20th century. His piano music is exceedingly complex and although it has not yet been printed in its entirety, all that is available, and more, has been recorded by Alan Mandel in a three-volume set for Desto. Ives' *Essays Before a Sonata and Other Writings,* edited by Howard Boatwright, New York: W. W. Norton, 1961, reveals his intellect and imagination on a variety of subjects and should be read by anyone who contemplates exploring this highly problematic music.

First Piano Sonata (PIC 1902-10). 50 p. 5 movements. 42 minutes. Intricate and complex patterns, hymn tunes, polyrhythms, polytonality, ragtime, are all present in a work of depth and grandeur. This landmark of American piano literature has more cohesion than the *"Concord" Sonata.* Virtuoso writing. Movements are: 1. Adagio con moto, 2. Allegro moderato—"In the Inn", 3. Largo, 4. No tempo indication, 5. Andante maestoso.

Second Piano Sonata "Concord, Mass., 1840-1860" (Arrow 1909-1915). 68 p.
4 movements: Emerson, Hawthorne, The Alcotts, Thoreau. ". . . a group of four pieces called a sonata for want of a more exact name. The whole is an attempt to present one person's impression of the spirit of transcendentalism that is associated in the minds of many with Concord, Mass. of over a half century ago . . . impressionistic pictures of Emerson and Thoreau, a sketch of the Alcotts, and a scherzo supposed to reflect a lighter quality which is found in the fantastic side of Hawthorne." (Ives' note on the work). Virtuoso musicianship and technique required throughout.

Three-Page Sonata (Mer 1905). The original manuscript was 3 pages in length. Makes fun of traditional sonata design. Difficult polyrhythms.

The Anti-Abolitionist Riots in Boston in the 1850's (Mer 1908). Short Adagio maestoso with no bar lines. Thick textures, FFF climax, quiet closing.

Some Southpaw Pitching (Mer 1908). Melodic line coupled with harmonies in RH, chromatic treatment of LH figuration.

3 Protests (NME 1910?). Tiny sketches, enigmatic writing.

22 (NME 1912). Page number in Ives's music notebook on which this piece was written.

See: Conrad Brueder, "The Studies of Charles Ives," unpub. DM paper, Indiana University, 1968.

JEAN EICHELBERGER IVEY (1923-) USA

Ivey is a composer, pianist, and electronic music specialist. She is presently Director of the Electronic Music Laboratory at the Peabody Conservatory of Music and has given piano recitals in this country and Europe.

Theme and Variations (AMC 1952).
A single short subject and 26 variations that fall into 3 groups: lyrical, humorous, and dramatic. Thoroughly contemporary in idiom, makes full use of the instrument's technical possibilities.

Prelude and Passacaglia (AMC 1955).
The Prelude is a burst of fireworks which suggests motives that are to be developed in the Passacaglia. The Passacaglia subject uses all 12 tones although no attempt is made to treat the work in dodecaphonic style. Continuous variations tend to group themselves into an overall rondo form, ABACA.

Sonata (AMC). 4 movements. Well-organized, neoclassic in form and style. Coloristic potentialities of the piano are carefully explored. Demands complete pianistic equipment.

Sleepy Time and *Water Wheel* (Lee Roberts). 2 easy works on black keys.

Pentatonic Sketches (McLaughlin & Reilly). 5 pieces, easy, attractive.

Magic Circles (SB). In *Contemporary Collection No. 2* (SB).

J

WOLFGANG JACOBI (1894-   ) Germany

Sonata No. 2 (Leuckhart 1936). 15 p. 12 minutes. 3 movements.

Sonata No. 3 (Leuckhart, 1939). 20 p. 3 movements.
Both sonatas are written in a neoclassic style.

Suite in the Ancient Style, Op. 10 (R&E). 7 movements.

Sonatina for Harpsichord (Kahnt). M-D.

RHENÉ JACQUE (–   ) Canada

This is the pen name of Soeur Jacque-René who teaches at the Ecole Vincent d'Indy in Outrement, Quebec.

Suite pour Piano Op. 11 (BMI Canada 1961). Int.
5 short contrasted movements, neoclassic in style. The last movement, G, is colorfully written.

Deuxième Suite (BMI Canada 1964). M-D.
Prélude: light, airy, graceful.
Impressions: introspective.
Toccate: brilliant, fits fingers well, requires a good octave technique.

LEOŠ JANÁČEK (1854-1928) Czechoslovakia

Janáček studied his native Moravian folk music, a study that conditioned the character of all his thematic invention. His music skillfully integrates folk materials into valid artistic entities.

'Sonata der Strasse: I-X. 1905' (Artia). 2 movements. 10 minutes.
Inspired by the death of a worker in a demonstration. 1. The presentiment. 2. The death.

Music for Indian Club Swinging (Artia).

Theme and Variations (Zdenka's Variations) (Artia 1880). 14 p.

The Overgrown Path (Artia). 53 p. Book 1: 10 pieces, 22 minutes. Book 2: 5 pieces, 8 minutes. In nineteenth-century character-piece tradition. Int. to M-D.

6 Lachian Dances (Artia).

Pilky (Artia). One of the *Folk Dances of Moravia.*

In the Mist (Hudební Matice c. 1938). 21 p. 4 pieces. 14 minutes.

Folk Dances of Moravia (Artia). 2 books.

Music for Gymnastic Exercises (Artia 1950).

PHILIPP JARNACH (1892-) France, active in Germany

5 Feuilles d'Album (Durand 1914).

4 Humoresques (Durand 1914).

Sonatina Op. 18 (Schott 1925). Chromatic, changing textures, intense. M-D.
Allegretto vivace, Concitato, Sostenuto assai quasi largo e con summa espressione.

Drei Klavierstücke (Schott). 3 difficult dance works.
Ballabile, Sarabande, Burlesca.

Kleine Klavierstücke (Schott). 10 short pieces, mainly 2- and 3-part writing. Not easy.

Das Amrumer Tagebuch Op. 30 (Schott 1947). 3 pieces.
Hymnus: chordal; Elegie: imposing mid-section; Sturmreigen: quiet closing.

Sonata No. 2 (Schott 1952). 28 p. 3 movements, impeccable craftsmanship.

Fantasia (Schott).

HANNS JELINEK (1901-) Austria

Jelinek studied with Schönberg and Berg and is one of the main supporters of strict adherence to the Schönberg technique. Since his opus 13, all works have been written in the 12-tone idom. He has written a text on the subject of strict dodecaphony.

Sonatine Op. 9/4 (UE 1951). 9 minutes. 4 movements.
Second movement, Menuett is the easiest and most accessible of this well-written work. M-D.

Vier Strukturen Op. 20 (Moseler 1953).

Zwölftonwerk (12-Tone Music) Op. 15 (UE 1949-51). 5 volumes.
Musical examples to the above-mentioned text.

1. 4 Two-part Inventions: uses the row in different treatment, retrograde, inversion, etc.
2. 6 Short Character-Sketches.
3. 3 Dances: Walzer, Sarabande, March.
4. 4 Toccatas: solenne, burlesca, funèbre, frizzante.
5. Suite: contains 9 movements.

All the pieces are short, some require only 30 seconds to perform. A clever and fascinating introduction to serial technique.

Zwölftonfibel Op. 21 (Moseler 1953, 1954, 1955). 12 volumes bound in 6 volumes. A "Twelve-tone Primer."
12 times 12 easy to intermediate studies and pieces.
I/II Preliminary Studies
III/IV Elementary Studies
V/VI Easy 2-Voice Studies
VII/VIII Little Concert Pieces
IX/X Intermediate Studies
XI/XII Recital Pieces

SÁNDOR JEMNITZ (1899-1963) Hungary

Jemnitz studied with Max Reger, Karl Straube and Arnold Schönberg. Complex contrapuntal textures are found in much of his writing.

Dance-Sonata Op. 23 (UE 1927).

Sonata III Op. 26 (UE 1929).

Recueil Op. 39 (Rózsavölgyi 1938-1945). Six pieces. M-D.

Sonata No. 5 Op. 64 (EMB 1961). D.
Allegretto poco sostenuto: folk influence, much repetition of opening rhythmic and melodic idea.
Agitato: 2-voice texture in tenths, mid-section more chordal.
Andantino sereno: serious quality, syncopation, tempo changes, ends quietly.

DONALD JENNI (1937-) USA

Jenni studied at The Juilliard School.

10 Laconic Variations (ACA 1952).
Short, terse, pianistic, pleasant. M-D.

Sonatine (BMI 1954).
Won the BMI Young Composers Radio Award in 1952. Short, appealing, MC. M-D.

ADOLF JENSEN (1837-1879) Germany

Scenes of Travel Op. 17 (Ric) (CFP). The Mill Op. 17/3 (Ric) (GS).

25 Studies Op. 32 (Tagliapietra-Ric) (GS) (CFP). 3 vols.

20 Lieder und Tänze Op. 33 (WH) (Augener). Short and easy.

Innerer Stimmen Op. 2 (Augener). 5 character pieces.

Berceuse (Moszkowski-Heugel).

JÖRGEN JERSILD (1913-) Denmark

Jersild studied with Albert Roussel. He is mainly interested in teaching and has published some useful textbooks.

Trois Pièces en Concert (WH 1945). Influenced by Couperin and Rameau.
Tambourin: dramatic gestures; Romanesque with 10 variations; Farandole: brilliant closing.

CARLOS JIMÉNEZ-MABARAK (1916-) Mexico

Jiménez-Mabarak teaches at the National Conservatory of Music in Mexico City. He studied in Santiago, Chile, Brussels and with René Leibowitz in Paris, France.

Allegro Romantico (EB 1935). 3 minutes.

Danza Española No. 1 (Schott, Brussels 1936).

Danza Española No. 2 (EB 1936).

Sonata del Majo Enamorado (EB).

KAREL JIRÁK (1891-) Czechoslovakia

Jirák teaches at Roosevelt University in Chicago.

Little Piano Suite Op. 12 (Artia 1916). 5 movements, varied moods.

Suite in Ancient Style Op. 21 (Artia 1920).

At the Crossroad Op. 24 (UE 1924). 6 short polytonal pieces. M-D.

Sonata Op. 30 (UE 1924). 32 p. 3 movements in a dissonant style.

Sonata No. 2 Op. 64 (Panton, Prague-Bratislava 1950). 17 minutes. Notes in English concerning Jirák and his work.
Allegro appassionato: 2 themes, movement dominated by second theme, parallel seventh-chords, heroic in character.
Tempo di marcia funèbre: similar (heroic idea) in opening movement.
Allegro risoluto: passionate, energetic, 3 themes. After development section all 3 themes are recapitulated and climaxed by an exciting coda. D.

GRANT JOHANNESEN (1921-) USA

Improvisation on a Mormon Hymn (OUP).
Hymn "Come, Come, Ye Saints." Quiet reflective melody with sonorous harmonies. Large chords require good handspan. M-D.

HENRIK FILIP JOHNSEN (1717-1779) Sweden

Sonata pour le Clavecin a (Hans Eppstein-NMS).
Allegro assai; Adagio; Poco Presto. Interesting work in early classic style.

HUNTER JOHNSON (1906-) USA

Johnson teaches at the University of Texas.

Sonata (Mer 1933-34). Revised in 1936 and 1947-48, large-scale cyclic three-movement work requires advanced pianism. Johnson says of the work: ". . . my spirit was teeming defiantly with America . . . It is an intensive expression of the South . . . the nostalgia, dark brooding, frenzied gaiety, high rhetoric and brutal realism are all intermingled." The movements: Allegro molto e dinamico; Andante cantabile; Allegro giusto. Varied textures and sonorities, changing meters, driving rhythms, conclusion refers to earlier used thematics from previous movements. D.

See: Joseph Bloch, "Some American Piano Sonatas," JR, 3, Fall, 1956, 9-14.

LOCKREM JOHNSON (1924-) USA

Chaconne Op. 29 (Mer 1948). 6 minutes.
Lyric idea serves as subject that is worked through numerous guises to an exciting climax before a quiet close. Legato, finger substitution and quick pedaling required. M-D.

Fifth Sonata Op. 34 (CFE 1949). 7 minutes. 1 movement. Subtitled "Sonata Della Comedia ironica Della Vita," dramatic, bold gestures, harmonics, chromatic. Large dynamic range: PP-FFFFFF. D.

Ricercare Op. 36 (CFE 1950).
Introduction, 3 fugues: No. 1 is in one voice, No. 2, two voices and No. 3, three voices. Contrasted moods. D.

Vacation Waltzes Op. 41 (CFE 1953). 7½ minutes.

Sonata No. 6 Op. 43 (CFE 1954). 15½ minutes.

Two Sonatinas (Puget Music Publications).
No. 2 is more difficult than No. 1. Three movements each. MC. Int.

ROBERT SHERLAW JOHNSON (1932-) Great Britain

Educated at King's College in the University of Durham, the Royal Academy of Music and in Paris where he studied piano with Jacques Fevrier and composition with Nadia Boulanger, Johnson has established a considerable reputation as a concert pianist specializing in performance of piano music by major 20th-century composers. He has taught at Leeds University and is now Lecturer in Music at Oxford University.

Sonata No. 1 (OUP 1963).
Advanced modern idiom, single multi-sectioned work, influence of Messiaen, strong rhythmic writing, clearly defined themes, concludes with an imposing coda. D.

Sonata No. 2 (OUP 1967). In 3 short movements with cyclic overtones. New notation symbols used, formidable. Comments on preparation, interpretation and blank staves. Strummed strings in the second and third movements provide an orchestral palette. Supple handling of serial technique. D.

7 Short Piano Pieces (OUP 1968-9).
Imaginative mixture of traditional and *avant-garde* techniques. Prelude, Catena, Chameleon (the possibilities can be greatly extended by the uses of any kind of stick or a wire brush), Phoenix, Acanthus, Bleak Ecstasies, Epilogue, Chameleon 2. Detailed explanation of the signs. D.

See: Meirion Bowen, "Robert Sherlaw Johnson," M&M, 19, June 1971, 34-36.

ANDRÉ JOLIVET (1905-) France

Jolivet is one of the strongest creative forces in French contemporary music.

Suite Mana (Costallat 1935). 6 pieces with rhythmic complexities developed from a linear treatment. Strongly percussive. D.

Cinq Danses Rituelles (Durand 1947). Colorful, dynamic and exotic set.
Danse initiatique: decorated melodic line, imposing climax, quiet close.
Danse du Héros: bold, furious, percussive.
Danse nuptiale: arched climax, flexible, quiet close.
Danse funèraire: processional, intense.
Danse du rapt: drumlike basses, rumbling effects, quick passages.

3 Temps: No. 1 (Sal 1931).

Etude sur des modes antiques (Durand 1947). 4 p.

Prélude (ESC 1938).

Chanson Naïve (Billaudot). Int.

Sonata No. 1 (UE 1945). 3 movements. 22 minutes. Strong modal language with free polytonal writing. Advanced pianism required.

Sonata No. 2 (Heugel 1957). 33 p. 3 movements. Complete and partial tone-rows. Asymmetrical rhythms add to the excitement. D.

CHARLES JONES (1910-   ) USA, born Canada

Jones has been on the composition faculty at Aspen Institute in Colorado for many years.

3 Pieces (Arrow 1943). M-D.
Fanfare: covers entire range of keyboard, rhythmic punctuation, lively. 5 p.
Song: expressive, lyrical. 3 p.
Finale: rhythmic, driving, trills. 7 p.

Sonata (AMC).

DANIEL JONES (1912-   ) Wales

Bagatelles for Piano (University of Wales Press). Three books. Brahms and Chopin influence.

Book I (1943-45).
Book II (1948-53). Most interesting of the set.
Book III (1955).

JOSEPH JONGEN (1873-1953) Belgium

Jongen was greatly influenced by César Franck and the impressionists. He uses a most refined and elegant melodic language.

Sérénade Op. 19 (Sal).

Deux Pièces Op. 33 (Durand).

Deux Rondes Wallonnes (Durand).

Sonatine (JWC).

Sept Esquisses (Rouart 1911). Rhapsody, Polichinelle, Berceuse pour un coeur lassé, Pochade, Rythmes de danse, Fantasque, Mascarade.

Crépuscule au lac Ogwen Op. 52 (JWC c. 1917). 9 p.

Suite en Forme de Sonata Op. 60 (JWC 1918). 43 p.

Petite Suite pour Piano (L'Art Belge 1924). 5 movements: Petite Marche Militaire, Conte plaisant, Nostalgie, Valse gracieuse, Tambourin. All require technical facility.

13 Préludes Op. 69 (Schott 1930). 2 volumes. Many moods and pianistic effects in this unusual collection.

First Ballade Op. 105 (CeBeDeM).

MIHAIL JORA (1891-) Rumania

Sonata Op. 21 (Editura de Stat Pentru Literatura si Arta 1942). 27 p. 3 movements, FSF, some chromaticism, mainly tonal. M-D.

Joujoux pour ma Dame Op. 7 (UE c. 1925). 5 pieces.

Marche Juive Op. 8 (UE).

ROLAND JORDAN (-) USA

Four — A Set of Small Pieces for Piano. Commissioned by the

Delaware MTA and the MTNA, 1965. (Available on loan from MTNA). Style of Webern, pointillistic writing, almost every note artticulated with a dynamic mark. Requires first-rate pianism.

1. Eighth note equals 208.
2. Quarter note equals 76.
3. Quarter note equals 48. Creates a hypnotic effect.
4. Quarter note equals 76. Longest of the set, ABA design.

ERIK JORGENSEN (1912-) Denmark

Variazioni per Pianoforte (SPDM 1966). 11 minutes.

WILFRED JOSEPHS (1927-) Great Britain

Second Piano Sonata Op. 40 (Weinberger 1965). 22 p. 14 minutes. 8 sections played as one movement. Trills and tremolos, exploits minor ninths and major sevenths. Well-integrated writing, shows excellent command of keyboard resources. D.

14 Studies (OUP 1969). 2 books.
Influenced by Debussy *Etudes*: seconds, thirds, octaves, ninths, etc. Numerous kinds of piano technique called for, written in an advanced pianistic idiom. No. 3, A Spectral Waltz, Nos. 5 and 7 are especially attractive. M-D.

WERNER JOSTEN (1885-1963) USA, born Germany

Piano Sonata (AME 1937). 3 movements.
Extensive thematic development. Large span required, MC, preference for seconds. M-D.

JOHN JOUBERT (1927-) Union of South Africa

Dance Suite Op. 21 (Nov 1958).
5 short studies contrasted in style juxtaposing regular and irregular rhythms. No. 5 is especially dramatic and closes with a powerful climax. M-D.

Sonata Op. 24 (Nov 1959). One movement. 20 p.
A long tarantella appears between the exposition and recapitulation but first and second exposition subjects are in usual

key-relationships. Changing meters and tonalities, well-timed large gestures. Good rotational technique will help. D.

See: Peter Dickinson, "John Joubert Today," MT, 112, January 1971, 20-22.

K

DMITRI KABALEVSKY (1904-   ) USSR

Kabalevsky's writing is designed for immediate utility and popular consumption. His music for young people is unusually appealing.

Four Preludes Op. 5 (MCA 1927-28). Short, lyric, varied moods.

Sonata No. 1 Op. 6 (MCA) (K). Three contrasting movements, postromantic style, brilliant close. M-D.

Sonatina C Op. 13/1 (MCA) (K) (GS) (IMC). Three movements. Cheerful, bright, outside movements brilliant.

Sonatina G Op. 13/2 (MCA) (K). Attractive, more serious, longer than No. 1.

Four Little Pieces Op. 14 (MCA). Charming pedagogic works.

Fifteen Children's Pieces Op. 27 Book I (MCA) (IMC) (K). Easy teaching pieces.

Ten Children's Pieces Op. 27 Book II (MCA). Many are available separately (MCA).

Seventeen Selected Children's Pieces from Op. 27 (CFP).

Twenty-four Preludes Op. 38 (1947) (MCA) (CFP) (IMC) (K). Many pianistic styles. Easy to M-D.

Twenty-four Little Pieces Op. 39 (MCA) (CFP) (IMC) (GS). Easy teaching pieces.

Variations Op. 40/1-2 (MCA) (IMC). Two easy sets. Set I: 12 variations, Set II: 5 variations.

Sonata No. 2 e♭. Op. 45 (MCA) (CFP) (IMC) (GS) (K).

Three large contrasted movements. Most difficult of the three sonatas.

Sonata No. 3 F Op. 46 (MCA) (CFP) (GS) (K) (IMC). Three movements, shorter and more accessible than No. 2. Middle movement is the weakest.

Five Easy Sets of Variations Op. 51 (MCA). Based on Russian, Slovakian and Ukrainian folksongs. All attractive.

Rondo a Op. 59 (MCA) (CFP) (IMC). Much dissonance and rhythmic drive, in 3/8 time, slow mid-section. Part of the required repertoire in the 1958 International Piano Competition in Moscow.

Four Rondos Op. 60 (1959) (MCA) (IMC). March: dotted rhythms, sixths; Dance: needs light touch; Song: singing tone required; Toccata: staccato study. M-D.

Six Preludes and Fugues Op. 61 (MCA) (IMC). Neobaroque orientation. Contains two 2-voice fugues, three 3-voice fugues, and one 4-voice fugue. M-D to D.

Spring Games and Dances Op. 81 (1965) (MCA). Free form suite in playful, dance-like character. M-D.

Variations on an American Folksong (1966) (MCA). Theme and six variations. Int.

See: Cortlandt M. Koots, "Kabalevsky for the Piano," AMT, 20, April-May 1971, 26, 46.

PÁL KADOSA (1903-   ) Hungary

Kadosa is a disciple of Béla Bartók. His music is characterized by harsh dissonances, pounding rhythms and instrumental melodic practice. He is head of the Piano Department at the Liszt Academy in Budapest.

Sonatina Op. 11b (ZV 1927). First movement, Con Fiducia needs steady rhythmic drive and much intensity. Last movement, Triste (1 page) is slow, sad but equally intense. Broad dynamic range, PPP-FFF, large span required.

Epigramme Op. 8 (Bo&H). 8 short pieces.

Sonata II Op. 9 (ZV c. 1965). 15 p. 4 short movements. M-D.

Sonata III Op. 13 (ZV). 7 p.

Sonata IV Op. 54 (ZV). 26 p. A powerful four-movement work, fine craft. Requires excellent pianistic facility. Dissonant. D.

6 Kleine Präludien Op. 35a (UE).

Rhapsodie Op. 28a (UE 1937). Driving rhythms in style of Bartók's *Allegro Barbaro.*

Hommage to Bartók Op. 38b (Bo&H).

55 Small Piano Pieces (EMB). A miniature *Mikrokosmos,* not so modal or dissonant. Appealing.

6 Little Etudes from 55 Little Piano Pieces (EMB).

7 Bagatelles (EMB). Short, in folk style. Some fast octaves, large span needed for No. 6.

Kaleidoscope (Bo&H).

Al Fresco Op. 11a (Bo&H). Based on folksongs collected by Bartók and Kodály. Rhythmic vitality, requires good octave technique. M-D.

Suite No. 2, Op. 1/2 (EMB).

4 Capriccios Op. 57 (Bo&H). Bartók influence present.

3 Tristia Op. 38b (EMB).

Pen and Ink Sketches Op. 38e (EMB).

5 Sketches Op. 18b (EMB).

Capriccio Op. 23h (EMB).

ERICH ITOR KAHN (1905-1956) Germany

Ciaccona dei tempi di guerra Op. 10 (Bomart 1943). 25 minutes. This Chaconne "in time of war" is a large-scale work in non-strict serial technique. The straight row is presented be-between the fantasie-like Introduction and the beginning of the

Ciaccona proper. 40 variations of ingenious invention follow. Very pianistic but will challenge the finest performers. See Russell Smith's discussion of this work in his article, "Erich Itor Kahn," ACA Bulletin, 9/2, 1960, 8-9.

3 Bagatelles (CFE 1938). 11 minutes.
12-tone materials not used strictly. Stunning sonorities, pianistic. No. 1 dates from 1935-36. Interpretative problems in all three require a sensitive pianist. D.

Huit Inventions Op. 7 (ACA 1937).
No. III, Sur un thème de Brahms, and VI, Hommage à Ravel, are the most attractive. Mature pianism required.

6 Small Bagatelles (ACA 1938). 5 minutes.

Short Piano Pieces Op. 12 (Bomart 1951). 2½ minutes.

FRIEDRICH KALKBRENNER (1785-1849) Germany

Etudes Op. 43 (Litolff). Book 2.

Fantasia E♭ (Ashdown & Parry).

30 Selected Etudes from Op. 20, 108, 126, 143 (Vaillant-Heugel).

JOSEPH KAMINSKI (1903-) Israel, born Russia

Triptyque (MCA).

Suite for Piano (Edition Negen 1952).

SIGFRIED KARG-ELERT (1877-1933) Germany

Reisebilder Op. 7 (C. Simon 1911). 27 p. A suite of 8 pieces.

Partita in geschlossener Folge Op. 13 (CFP 1927). 31 p.

Mosaik: 29 Studies (WH).

Aphorismen Op. 51 (C. Simon c. 1908). A cycle of 17 sketches.

Heidebilder Op. 127 (Simrock). 10 short impressions.

3 Sonatinen Op. 67 (C. Simon).
Sonatine facile, Sonatine mignonne, Sonatine exotique.

Exotische Rhapsodie Op. 118 (Simrock).

Dekameron Suite Op. 69 (Hug).

Poetic Bagatelles Op. 77 (C. Simon). 10 pieces.

Sonata No. 3 Op. 105 (Patetica) (Simrock).

MAURICE KARKOFF (1927-) Sweden

Karkoff has studied with Karl-Birger Blomdahl, Erland V. Koch, Luigi Dallapiccola, André Jolivet, Nadia Boulanger and György Ligeti.

Miniature Suite Op. 39 (GM 1960). 7 p. Pleasant contemporary sounds. M-D.
4 pieces: Preludietto doloroso, Intermezzo 1 and 2, Toccatino.

Oriental Pictures Op. 66 (GM).

Capriccio on Football (GM 1960). Pointillistic writing. M-D.

Partita Piccola Op. 32 (Föreningen Svenska Tonsättares Manuskriptserie 1958). Complex rhythmic usage.
Pezzo drammatico, Meditazione, Toccatina.

Femton latta pianostycken (GM).

Sex sma pianostycken (GM).

PÁL KÁROLYI (1934-) Hungary

Toccata Furiosa (EMB c. 1969). 12 p.
Avant-garde notation, clusters, string glissandi, sometimes with fingernail or with a stick, palm tremolo, plucked strings, etc. Barbaric handling of the keyboard, dies away to PP ending. D.

UDO KASEMETS (1919-) Canada, born Estonia

Kasemets studied at the State Conservatory, Tallinn, Estonia, in Stuttgart and Darmstadt, Germany. He taught at the Hamilton Conservatory of Music after coming to Canada in 1951. He is music critic for the Toronto Daily Star.

Sonata Op. 24/1 (CMC 1951).
Theme and 6 Variations
Minuet
Elegy
Tempo of A Waltz
Many chromatics, variety of styles. Elegy is the most appealing. M-D.

6 Preludes Op. 30 (CMC 1952). "Meditations to 12-tone serial, rhythmical and metrical questions." Short, dodecaphonic pieces with interesting sonorities. M-D.

LUCRECIA R. KASILAG (1915-) Philippines

Kasilag studied at Philippine Women's University and the Eastman School of Music. She is Dean of the College of Music and Fine Arts at The Philippine Women's University in Manila. Works listed without publishers are available from the composer.

Theme and Variations based on a Filipino Folk Tune "Walay Angay" (PIC 1950).
Simple theme followed by 11 variations and Finale. Nineteenth-century pianistic devices, closely related key signatures. Balance between harmonic and melodic variations. M-D.

April Morning (1941).

Passacaglia (1950).

Burlesque (1957).

Elegy (1960).

Sonata Orientale (1961).

Derivation III: Hendai-Hogaku (for prepared piano 1966).

Derivation IV: Orientalia (for prepared piano 1969).

ULYSSES KAY (1917-) USA

8 Inventions (ACA 1946). Variety of idioms, styles and moods.

4 Inventions (MCA 1964).
4 of the above: 1. Transfer of line between hands is difficult.
2. Bouncy 5/8.
3. Melodic, large span required for tenths.
4. More like a true invention-imitation.

10 Short Essays (MCA 1939).
1 or 2 pages each. Varied tempo and meter changes. Contrapuntal devices used.

Sonata (ACA 1941).

LEIF KAYSER (1919-) Denmark

6 Short Improvisations Op. 1 (SM).

4 Piano Pieces Op. 4 (SM).

Pièce Symphonique pour piano Op. 9 (SM).

ISFRID KAYSER (1712-1771) Germany

Suite pour piano (Hin). Prelude, C, M and Trio, Passepied and Trio, Adagio, G. Passepied is written in 5/8 meter! This work is actually *Partita* No. 1, for harpsichord, from *Concors Digitorum Discordia,* a set of 4 Partitas, published in Augsburg in 1746.
See: C. L. Cudsworth, "Ye Olde Spuriosity Shoppe," Notes, 12, September 1955, 538.

MILKO KELEMEN (1924-) Yugoslavia

Kelemen "represents the most 'radical' trends of younger Yugoslav composers . . . the fact that his music has a special quality is attributable, . . . to his inherited Croation feeling for traditional melody." Some of his later works combine . . . "pointillistic technique with somewhat more conventional expressionist procedures." Everett Helm, MQ, 51, January 1965, 221.

Piano Sonata (H. Litolff 1954). Three movements: Allegro veemente: flexible meters, staccato punctuation, thin texture; Andante sostenuto: three-part form, varied textures, extreme ranges; Presto: toccata-like, good octave and scale technique required. Strong influence of Yugoslav folk music. M-D.

Dessins Commentés (CFP 1964). Seven pieces, *Avant-garde* notation, clusters, glissandi on strings, extreme sonorities. D.

The Donkey Walks Along the Beach (CFP 1961). 9 pieces. Picturesque titles, contemporary sonorities, sophisticated writing. Int.

JOHANN PETER KELLNER (1705-1772) Germany

Ausgewählte Klavierstücke (C. Schroeder-CFP). Praeludium F, Suite d, Ouverture G, Concerto pastorale F (programmatic).

BRYAN KELLY (1934-) Great Britain

Kelly teaches at the Royal College of Music, where he also studied.

Sonata for Piano (Nov).

Nocturne and Toccata (Arcadia).

RUDOLF KELTERBORN (1931-) Switzerland

Monosonata (Br). D.

HARALD KEMPE (1900-) Sweden

Fyra pianostycken (NMS)

WILHELM KEMPFF (1895-) Germany

Sonata Op. 47 (Sal 1959). 16 p.
Praeambulum, Scherzo, Introduction and Toccata.
Skillful pianistic writing, traditional harmonic vocabulary, weighty musical ideas, a convincing work. D.

Zwei lyrische suiten für klavier (Simrock 1923).
Op. 17 No. 1 E♭
Op. 17 No. 2 A♭

TALIVALDIS KENINS (1919-) Canada, born Latvia

Kenins studied at the Paris Conservatory and worked with Tony Aubin and Olivier Messiaen. Coming to Canada in 1951, he has been a lecturer on the Faculty of Music, Royal Conservatory of Music of Toronto, since 1952.

Sonata (F. Harris 1961).

Three-movement work, Adagio introduction to first movement. Harmonic treatment merges postromantic and contemporary idioms. Well-organized, fine craftsmanship.

Diversities (Leeds Canada 1968).

12 studies in contemporary styles for young pianists. Int.

LOUIS KENTNER (1905-) Great Britain

Sonatina No. 1 F (OUP 1939).

Sonatina No. 2 C (OUP 1939).

Sonatina No. 3 G (OUP 1939).

JOHANN KASPAR KERLL (1627-1693) Germany

Selected Keyboard Works DDT, II No. 2. 8 Toccatas, 6 Canzonas, Capriccio Cucu, Battaglia, Ciaconna, Passacaglia, Ricercare in Cylindrum phonotacticum transferenda, Der steyrische Hirt.

Ciacona (Haselböck-Dob).

Passacaglia (Haselböck-Dob).

See: Charles David Harris, "Keyboard Music in Vienna during the Reign of Leopold I, 1640-1705," unpub. diss., University of Michigan, 1967.

HARRISON KERR (1897-) USA

Piano Sonata No. 2 (Arrow 1943). 13 minutes.

A one-movement work, tempo changes correspond with formal structure. Driving, biting dissonance, well-written for piano. Ostinato, broad dynamic range, rhythmic element has most interest. M-D.

Preludes for Piano (BMI 1943). 9 minutes.

OTTO KETTING (1935-   ) The Netherlands

Son of the composer Piet Ketting, Otto Ketting studied at The Hague Conservatory and in Munich. Since 1957 he has developed a style closely related to the work of Webern.

Komposition mit zwölf Tönen (Donemus 1957). D.
7 short pieces in serial style. Repeated rhythmic pattern is employed. Ketting was one of the first to experiment in the Netherlands with parameters other than pitch.

ARAM KHATCHATURIAN (1903-   ) USSR

Nationalistic elements play a large part in the music of this Soviet-Armenian composer.

Two Characteristic Pieces (MCA 1942, 1947).
A Glimpse of the Ballet; Fughetta. Two-part counterpoint.

Two Pieces (MCA) (CFP) (K).
Valse Caprice, rubato; Danse, strongly rhythmic. This work could give the overworked *Toccata* a rest.

Poem (1927) (MCA) (K).
Long Allegro ma non troppo has a Scriabinesque flavor, exploits changing textures and unusual colors. M-D.

Adventures of Ivan (MCA). 8 varied pieces for students.

Children's Album (CFP) two volumes. Int.

Sonatina (MCA 1959) (CFP) (K). Three movements, MC writing. Broken octaves are plentiful in the first movement, a rubato-like waltz serves as a middle movement and the final movement is a toccata that is impressionistic in style. Int. to M-D.

Sonata (MCA 1961) (CFP) (K).
Three movements, colorful, material is overworked, especially in the final movement. M-D.

Toccata (MCA) (CFP) (K). Driving rhythm, brilliant, contrasting colorful mid-section. M-D.

YRJÖ KILPINEN (1892-1959) Finland

Kilpinen was a traditionalist in his writing and drew on folk song for inspiration. He was considered the leading songwriter of modern Finland and wrote over 600 songs.

Pastoral Suite Op. 82 (Br&H).

Totentanz Suite Op. 84 (Br&H).

Sonata Op. 85 (Br&H 1943). 12 p. 3 movements, FSF. Postromantic idiom.

Sonata No. 6 Op. 89 (Br&H).

LEON KIRCHNER (1919-) USA

Kirchner's style is characterized by strong dissonance, driving rhythms, rhapsodic, quasi-improvisational qualities and a personal lyricism.

Sonata (Bomart 1948). Lento—poco a poco doppio movimento serves as an introduction and moves to a vigorous, rhythmic propulsive allegro which connects with an Adagio, a highly atmospheric movement. The final movement, an Allegro Barbaro, uses violent rhythmic patterns in a unique manner plus material from the opening movement. The whole work pulsates with rubato. Exceedingly demanding. D.

Little Suite (Mer 1950). Prelude, Song, Toccata, Fantasy, Epilogue.
Brief sketches of approximately one page each. Intense, flexible, resilient, serious. M-D.

See: Robert C. Ehle, "Romanticism in the *Avant-Garde*: Leon Kirchner's Piano Sonata," AMT, 19, April-May 1970, 30 32, 45.

JOHANN ERASMUS KINDERMANN (1616-1665) Germany

Tanzstücke für Klavier (R. Baum-Br 1950). 14 short dances including Ballets, A, C, S, and a Fuga.

JOHANN PHILIPP KIRNBERGER (1721-1783) Germany

Clavierübungen (Berlin 1762). Available in BB *Monuments of Music Series.*

Kirnberger Collection (O. Jonas-SB). Characteristic dances of the period in different keys. Not overly edited.

Tanzstücke (K. Herrmann-Schott). Collection of 22 dance pieces.

See Collections: *Le Trésor des Pianistes* Vol. 14; and *Old Masters of the 16th, 17th and 18th Centuries* (Niemann-K).

GISELHER KLEBE (1925-) Germany

Klebe studied at the Berlin Conservatory where Josef Rufer and Boris Blacher were among his teachers. Hindemith, jazz, Mahler and Stravinsky influenced his early works. Twelve-tone technique was incorporated into his style during the 1950's.

Wiegenlieder für Christinchen: Neun Stücke für Klavier Op. 13 (Bo&Bo). Dedicated to Boris Blacher, makes use of his variable meter system. Rows are also used.

Vier Inventionen Op. 26 (Bo&Bo 1957).

Drei Romanzen Op. 43 (Bo&Bo 1964). Influence of Berg, Schönberg and Webern, mastery of free serial techniques. D.

MARCELO KOC (1918-) Argentina, born USSR

Koc has resided in Buenos Aires since 1938 as teacher and composer. He has written extensively for the piano. All of his works are available through Editorial Argentina de Musica (EAM).

Variaciones para piano (1949).

Tres Preludios (1951).

Sonata (1953).

Musica para Piano (1960).

Variantes y Transparencias (1967).

ERLAND VON KOCH (1910-) Sweden

Koch has been Professor of Harmony at the Royal Music Conservatory in Stockholm since 1953.

Sonatina No. 1 Op. 41 (NMS 1950). 15 p. Oriented toward Hindemith.

Intermezzi Concertanti No. 1-3 (NMS 1963). 5 minutes each. Caprice, Pastorale, Haxpolska.

Rhythmic Bagatelles (GM 1957).

Elegisches Thema mit Variationen Op. 17 (NMS 1938).

Varianti Virtuosi 1965 (Nov). 9 minutes. From "Virtuoso" series, edited by John Ogdon. Theme and 16 variations. Ogdon says in the notes: "The last 4 variants produce an escalation of virtuosity. Bartókian dance rhythms, broken octaves, a decorated chorale, double octaves, compound arpeggi and broken chord sequences vindicate the work's title and provide the most testing technical demands in it." See Anthologies and Collections General: Contemporary.

Nordiska Impromptus 1-5 (NMS).
Issued in the composer's manuscript. Short, varied and well-conceived for the instrument. Would be most effective if played as a complete set.

Tanzstück (NMS).

Caprice (NMS 1955).

ZOLTÁN KODÁLY (1882-1967) Hungary

Nine Piano Pieces Op. 3 (Agay-MCA) (Ku) (K).
Varied moods and musical ideas, impressonistic influence, improvisatory style, supple rhythmic treatment, a thoroughly fine set. See especially Nos. 4, 5, 7, 8, 9. The (MCA) edition contains a Valsette, in salon style, not up to the other pieces.

Twenty-four Little Canons on the Black Keys (Bo&H).
The first 16 pieces are small studies in rhythms and syllables only, without complete staves. They can be sung as well as played.

Seven Piano Pieces Op. 11 (UE 1910-1918). *Zongoramuzsika.* Folk-inspired, impressionistic influence. See especially No. 1. Lento, 3. Il pleut dans mon coeur comme il pleut sur la ville, and 5. Tranquillo.

Méditation sur un motif de Claude Debussy (UE 1907). Impressionistic, improvisational, resonant, serious. M-D.

Gyermektáncok (Bo&H 1945).
12 children's dances on the black keys, based on Hungarian folk tunes. About same difficulty as Bartók *For Children.*

Dances of Marosszek (UE 1930). Based on peasant tunes. Requires complete pianism.

CHARLES KOECHLIN (1867-1951) France

Koechlin's keyboard style combined a love of folk song, nursery rhyme, medieval music, free rhythms and modal usage. Sometimes the writing may seem involved but the sonority always seems the "correct" thing at that moment. Koechlin experimented with many of the "isms" and "alities" in the early part of this century. A great deal of charming music is listed below.

L'Anciènne Maison de Campagne Op. 124 (l'OL 1932-3). Suite of 12 pieces, 40 p. Bar lines usually indicate phrase endings. Thin textures. Nos. 6, 8 and 10 are especially recommended.

Douze Esquisses Op. 41 (Sal). 2 series, 12 pieces in each of these varied "Songs without Words."

Douze Pastorales (Senart).

12 Petite Pièces Faciles (Heugel 1946). Delightful pedagogic material. Easy.

Douze Petites Pièces Op. 41 (Sal). Programmatic miniatures.

12 Préludes Op. 209 (Sal).

Cinq Sonatines Op. 59 (Sal). 3-and 4-movement works written for his children. Nursery rhymes and folk songs are suggested. Arranged in progressive order of difficulty.

Nouvelles Sonatines Op. 87 (Sal 1926). 4 pieces, each in 4 movements. Progressively more difficult.

Paysages et Marines Op. 63 (Sal 1918). 2 collections, 6 pieces each. Lyric landscape and marine sketches. M-D.

See: Frank Cooper, "Sleeping Beauty: The Pianistic Legacy of Charles Koechlin," Clavier, 8, December 1969, 18-20.

HANS JOACHIM KOELLREUTTER (1915-) Germany

Koellreutter left Germany in 1938, moved to Brazil and taught at Rio de Janeiro and São Paulo. He is considered the father of Brazilian atonalism. He is now serving as director of the German-Indian Institute in New Delhi.

Musica 1941 (ECIC 1942).
3 pieces in 12-tone idiom. Tranquillo, Muy expressivo, Muy ritmado y destacado. M-D.

Tres Bagatelles (Musica Viva, Rio de Janeiro).

JÓSEF KOFFLER (1896-1943) Poland

Koffler was the only Polish composer to adopt serial techniques before World War II.

Sonatine Op. 12 (UE). Highly chromatic, dissonant. Neither serial nor tonal.

15 Variations Op. 9 (Senart). 12-tone technique.

Musique de Ballet Op. 7 (Sal).

Musique quasi una sonata Op. 8 (Sal).

Variations on a Waltz of Johann Strauss Op. 23 (UE 1936).

KARL KOHN (1926-) USA, born Austria

5 Pieces for Piano (CF 1965).
Contrasted pianistic ideas in a strong contemporary idiom. Short, freely atonal. Flexible rhythmic handling, no meter indications in Nos. 2, 3, 4, or 5. Demanding musically. D.

5 Bagatelles (CF 1961).

Rhapsody (CF 1960). 5 p. Varied tempi and contemporary textures. D.

ELLIS B. KOHS (1916-   ) USA

Kohs has been teaching at the University of Southern California since 1950. He employs both tonal and atonal methods in his writing.

Toccata (Mer 1949). Free use of the row, extended work employing canon, chorale, chordal sections, cadenzas, recitative, free passages. Form inspired by baroque models. D.

Variations (Mer 1946). A basic set of 4 chords serve as the inspiration for this work. No break between variations, free use of the row technique. M-D.

Scherzo (TP).

Variations on "L'Homme Armé" (Mer 1946-47). 18 variations built on this famous Renaissance song. Advanced pianism required.

Forlane (TP 1947).

Sonata No. 2 (Cameo 1962). Third part of a larger work entitled *Studies in Variation*. From the composer's notes: "Movements I-II and III-IV are thematically related, in pairs. There is a limited use of serial procedures throughout, not without some tonal orientation however, with transposition (modulation), based on the row, occurring only in the finale. In addition to R, Я, ꓤ, ᴚ, an odd-even series (1-3-5-7-9-11 — 2-4-6-8-10-12) is employed. Several levels of variation: 1. Serial procedures. 2. Inter-movement thematic connections. 3. Each composition a variant of the others. 4. The row as a basis for modulatory scheme (in IV). 5. Character variation in the manner of a dialog (in III). 6. Formal theme and variation structure (in IV). — may be observed. All four works of 'Studies in Variation' are laid out simultaneously on each page thereby facilitating the comparison and analysis." A major work showing great craft and outstanding inspiration. D.

ERNST KÖLZ (1929-) Austria

Sonate (UE 1951). Reproduced from the autograph.
3 short movements using quartal and quintal harmony. One of the easier contemporary sonatas examined. Thin textures. M-D.

Partita (Dob). 5 p. For harpsichord or piano.

Emotion (UE 1955).

6 Bagatellen (Dob 1950).

3 Tanzstücke (Dob 1959).

HERMAN D. KOPPEL (1908-) Denmark

Early in his career Koppel was interested in jazz. He follows the Carl Nielsen tradition and writes mainly in larger forms.

10 Pieces Op. 20 (SM).

Suite for Klaver Op. 21 (SPDM) (K&S 1935).

FELIX KÖRLING (1864-1937) Sweden

I sommartider (AL).

Reflexer (AL).

PETER JONA KORN (1922-) Germany

Korn's style of composition "is that of pragmatic romanticism marked by polycentric tonality in the framework of strong rhythmic counterpoint." *Baker's Biographical Dictionary,* 1965 Supplement, 70.

3 Piano Pieces (AMC 1945). Highly chromatic.

1. Rubato, rhythmic problems, voice-leading difficult to follow.
2. Lento cantabile: chromatic motives well-developed.
3. Rondo: more contrapuntal, disjunct motion. Cantus firmus originally 3/4 returns 3/2.

Sonata No. 1 Op. 25 (Bo&H 1957). 3 movements. D.
Chromatic, preference for harmonic sevenths, persistent driving of the pulse in outside movements. Pedal points, ostinati stabilize tonalities.

Eight Bagatelles Op. 11 (Bo&H 1961).
Not trifles but a difficult set with various moods and pianistic idioms.

EGON KORNAUTH (1891-1959) Austria

Fünf Klavierstücke Op. 2 (UE). Salon style.

Kleine Suite Op. 29 (Dob). Notturno, Walzer, Finale.

Vier Klavierstücke Op. 32 (Dob). See especially No. 4 Rondo-Burleske.

Praeludium und Passacaglia Op. 43 (Dob 1949). D.

Fünf Klavierstücke Op. 44 (Dob 1951).

GREGORY W. KOSTECK (1937-) USA

Kosteck studied piano with György Sandor and is composer-in-residence at East Carolina College.

Second Sonata for Piano (B&VP 1963). 3 movements.
Dedicated to Sandor. 9 minutes.
Scintillating: toccatalike, equal interest between the hands.
Sustained: contemporary lyric writing.
Driving: opens with a pointillistic statement of the row, followed by lyric section with ostinato accompaniment. Ends with brilliant octave passages. D.

ERIC W. KORNGOLD (1897-1957) Austria

7 Märchenbilder Op. 3 (Schott). *Fairy Tales.* Written and published when Korngold was 11 years old.

Sonata d (UE 1910).

Sonata No. 2 E Op. 2 (Schott 1911). 36 p.
A large four-movement work in postromantic idiom. Richard

Strauss' influence obvious yet Korgold was only 14 years old when he wrote it. D.

Sonata No. 3 C Op. 25 (Schott 1931).
A large four-movement work, anchored in postromantic techniques and sonorities. More developed than Op. 2.
Allegro molto e deciso: dramatic opening leads to a cantabile section, gradually returns to the opening idea. Broad sweeping close.
Andante religioso: lyric idea broadly developed.
Tempo di Menuetto molto comodo: full chords and romantic harmonies.
Rondo: Allegro giocoso: energetic theme treated to a variety of situations.

BORIS KOUTZEN (1901-1966) USA, born Russia

Koutzen's style is almost exclusively polyphonic. He came to the USA in 1923.

Sonatina (Gen 1931). 12 minutes. Three movements in one. M-D.
Vivo: marcato, chromatic, rhythmic punctuation.
Andante pensieroso: quiet opening leads to energetic climax, calm closing.
Allegro vivo: bitonal contrasted moods, extensive coda.

Eidolons (Gen 1953). 13 minutes. One-movement poem for piano, varied moods, tempi and textures, repeated notes, grandiose climax, quiet close, neoclassic style. M-D.

HANS KOX (1930-   ) The Netherlands

Kox's music displays a measured balance between harmonic, melodic and rhythmic elements. A variety of techniques are used in his writing. He studied with Henk Badings.

Twee Klavierstukken (Donemus 1954). 7 minutes.

Sonata No. 1 (Donemus 1954). 12 minutes.

Sonata No. 2 (Donemus 1955). 11 minutes.

Barcarolle (Donemus 1960).

Drie Etudes (Donemus 1961).

LEOPOLD ANTON KOŽELUCH (1747-1818) Bohemia (Czechoslovakia)

This Bohemian composer, who wrote in almost all media, left over 100 solo piano sonatas.

5 Sonatas (Dana Setkova-Artia). No. 1 c Op. 2/3; No. 2 g Op. 15/1; No. 3 d Op. 20/3; No. 4 E♭ Op. 26/3; No. 5 f Op. 38/3. Clean edition.

Sonata E♭ Op. 51/2 (K&S) Organum, Series V, No. 5.

Sonata d Op. 51/3 (K&S) Organum, Series V, No. 23. 29 p. 3 movements. M-D.
Largo: expressive, reminiscent of Beethoven. Cadence on dominant leads to Allegro Molto e agitato: based on eighth-note figuration as found in Beethoven Op. 31/2. Interesting key relationships, foreign keys. Rondo: charming.

JOHANN LUDWIG KREBS (1713-1780) Germany

Klavierübung (Soldan-CFP). 12 Preludes and Chorales.

Partitas No. 2 B♭, No. 6 E♭. See collection *Alte Meister* Vol. II (Pauer-Br&H).

Suite b (L. Hoffmann-Erbrecht-K&S). No. 34 Series V, Organum. A, C, S, Passepied, Air, M, G.

Suite c (K&S). No. 32 Series V, Organum. A, C, S, Rondeaux, M, G.

3 Fugues (W. Frickert-Ric c. 1958). F, G and C.

See: Jean Horstman, "The Instrumental Music of J. L. Krebs," unpub. diss., Boston University, 1969. Discusses all the organ and clavier works as well as the other instrumental music.

JULIAN KREIN (1913-) USSR

Eight Pieces Op. 9 (UE).

Four Piano Pieces Op. 14 (UE).

Rhapsody Op. 17 (UE).

Six Pieces Op. 40 (MCA). French influence, poetic, free style. M-D.

Ballade (USSR).

Forest Paths (USSR). Eight Pieces.

Ten Pieces (USSR).

Ten Preludes on Folk Themes (USSR). Lengthy, based on Uzbek folk material.

Pièce à la Memoire de Paul Dukas (Supplément de la Revue Musicale May-June 1936). See *Le Tombeau de Paul Dukas* in Anthologies: Tombeau.

ERNST KRENEK (1900-) Austria

Krenek's compositional career has been many-faceted. Op. 6-17 display an atonal style. Op. 17-66 were written during a time of great experimentation when Krenek used ideas of jazz, Bartók, Hindemith, and others. The first 12-tone piano work was the *Zwölf Variationen* Op. 79. Most of his works have since followed this style of writing but other experimentation has taken place, especially in electronic music. Krenek has exerted influence on many younger composers through his teaching and writing.

Toccata and Chaconne Op. 13 (UE). Extended Toccata, Chaconne based on the choral "Ja, Ich glaub an Jesum Christum." Difficult, contrapuntal, atonal.

Little Suite Op. 13A (UE). A supplement to Op. 13 *Toccata and Chaconne*. 6 small movements thematically related. Not as difficult as Op. 13.

Dance Study Op. 1B (UE).

2 Suites Op. 26 (UE 1924). 10 minutes each. 5 short movements in each suite. D.

5 Piano Pieces Op. 39 (UE 1925). 10 minutes. Short, mildly dissonant mood pieces.

Sonata No. 1 Op. 2 E♭ (UE 1921). 30 p. 3 movements of intellectual, contrapuntal writing.

Sonata No. 2 Op. 59 (UE 1928). 3 movements. 20 minutes. Freely tonal, chordal, exhilarating. Allegretto, Alla marcia, energico, Allegro giocoso.

12 Short Piano Pieces Written in the Twelve-Tone Technique Op. 83 (GS 1938).
Excellent introduction to 12-tone writing. All pieces written on same row. Explanation contained. M-D.

Sonata No. 3 Op. 92/4 (AMP 1943). 12-tone, M-D, tonal.
Allegretto piacevole: lyrical.
Theme, Canons and Variations: varying moods, textures.
Scherzo: alternating moods and idioms.
Adagio: thick textures build to climax, end PPPP.

Sonata No. 4 (Bomart 1948). 12-tone but the row in its basic form seldom appears. D.
Sostenuto—Allegro ma non troppo—Allegro assai: restless, introspective.
Andante sostenuto, con passione: alternating contrasting sonorities.
Rondo — vivace: Scherzando opening, wild rhythmic section, rolling ostinato figures.
Tempo di minuetto, molto lento: 10-bar theme, variations, quiet close.

8 Piano Pieces (Mer 1946). 12-tone works accompanied by the composer's analysis and interpretative suggestions. M-D.
Etude, Invention, Scherzo, Toccata, Nocturne, Waltz, Air, Rondo.

20 Miniatures (WH 1954). Strict 12-tone writing, some pleasant sounds. M-D.

George Washington Variations Op. 120 (Southern 1950). 11 minutes. The main theme, Washington's Grand March and the closing Martial Cotillon are from the 18th century. 6 elaborate and contrasted variations including an Elegy, Canon and a Sarabande. Fine amusement! M-D.

Echoes from Austria (Rongwen 1958). 12 minutes.
7 pieces based on folk song, revealing yet another facet of Krenek. The last one is the most difficult. M-D.

Sechs Vermessene Op. 168 (Br 1958) . 12 minutes. Vermessene is the German word for "completely measured." Directions describe the system of 5 layers set up in which the first has density, 1 tone at a time, the next has 2 tones together, the third 3, etc. D.

GEORG ADAM KRESS (1744-1788) Germany

Klavierübungen des frankischen Dorfshulmeisters Georg Adam Kress (S. Kress-Schott).
An 18th-century notebook of dances and pieces. Int.

JOHANN KRIEGER (1652-1735) Germany

Ausgewählte Klavierwerke aus den *Sechs musikalischen Partien 1697* und der *Anmuthigen Clavier-Ubung 1699* (Kreutz-Br). 18 pieces including Partita G, easy dance pieces, Praeludium F, Phantasien d, C, Fuge d, Praeludium g, Ricercar a.

See collection *Klaviermeister des Barock* (G. Ochs-Mitteldeutscher Verlag).

TON DE KRUYF, See: DE KRUYF, TON

GAIL KUBIK (1914-) USA

Celebrations and Epilogue (Southern 1938-1950). Ten short pieces, fresh rhythms, varied moods, clear sonorities, clever titles such as: Birthday Piece, Wedded Bliss (parody on traditional wedding march), A Gay Time, etc. See especially Movies, Saturday Night. Int. to M-D.

Sonatina (Mer 1941). Four short movements: Moderately fast; Lively; Very slowly; Toccata. Changing meters, repeated percussive notes, canonic writing, flowing melodies. M-D.

Dance Soliloquy (Mer 1942). Homophonic style, 3-part form, ostinato under melody, clever rhythmic usage. Int.

Sonata (Southern 1947). Four-movement work based on American idioms. D.
Moderately fast, gracefully
Gaily
Slowly, expressively
Fairly fast: hard, bright, mechanical

Whistling Tune (TP). Changing meters, crisp rhythms, polytonal. Int.

Quiet Time (TP). Int.

JOHANN KUHNAU (1660-1722) Germany

Bach's predecessor in Leipzig at the Thomas Kirche occupies a special place in the history of keyboard music. His B♭ sonata in the appendix to his partitas (Neuer Clavier-Ubung Part II, 1692) is one of the earliest examples of the use of the term "Sonata." His complete keyboard works are contained in DDT, Vol. 4, first series, as follows:

Neue Clavier-Ubung Part I (1689) 7 suites (Partitas) in C, D, E, F, G, A, B♭.

Neue Clavier-Ubung Part II (1692) 7 suites in c, d, e, f, g, a, b, plus the Sonata B♭.

Frische Clavier-Früchte (1696) 7 sonatas in g, D, F, c, e, B♭, a.

Musicalische Vorstellung einiger Biblischer Historien in 6 *Sonaten* (1700). These sonatas, Kuhnau's most effective for keyboard, are programmatic works based on scenes from the Old Testament. They employ many forms from the dance to the chorale prelude. Available in an urtext edition by Kurt Stone for (BB). Included in English translation is Kuhnau's own essay to the "Gentle Reader." Each is published separately by (CFP).

Sonata I C: *The Battle between David and Goliath.* (K).

Sonata II g: *Saul Cured through Music by David.* Daring chromaticism.

Sonata III G: *Jacob's Wedding.*

Sonata IV c: *The Mortally Ill and Then Restored Hezekiah.*

Sonata V F: *Gideon, Saviour of Israel.*

Sonata VI E♭: *Jacob's Death and Burial.*

Other Collections: *4 Selected Keyboard Works* (K. Schubert-Schott) Partitas IV and III, F and e, *Biblical Sonatas* I and IV.

Easy Suite Movements (Frickert-Leuckhart). 24 pieces.

MEYER KUPFERMAN (1926-) USA

Little Sonata (BMC 1947). 10 minutes. 3 movements. Short, MC, fun to play, especially the final movement.

Recitative (BMC 1947). Highly chromatic.

Partita: Praeludium, Ariso and Toccata (BMC 1949). 29 p. 14 minutes. Both outer movements require virtuoso techniques. Expressive writing in Arioso. Powerful closing to Toccata.

Variations (BMC). Set of serial variations, economical writing.

Sonata on Jazz Elements (Gen 1958). 13 minutes. Imaginative writing, avoidance of clichés. D.

Pieces for Piano (Gen 1968).

Short Suite (Gen).

ROBERT KURKA (1921-1957) USA

Kurka's style changed from a complex, intricate approach *(For the Piano)* to a more direct, clear style based on his growing preoccupation with folkmusic.

For the Piano (Mer 1949). Lengthy, improvisational, no bar lines, numerous ideas, requires mature pianism. D.

Sonata Op. 20 (Chappell 1954). Three fresh-sounding movements based on American folk materials, open fifths, percussive chords. Final movement requires some bravura playing. M-D.

Notes from Nature (Weintraub). Twelve pedagogical works published two together in six pairs.

Sonatina Op. 6 (Weintraub). Excellent intermediate material, appealing writing.

Sonatina for Young Persons Op. 40 (Weintraub). Int.

GYÖRGY KURTAG (1926-   ) Hungary

One of Hungary's significant post-Bartókian composers.

8 Piano Pieces Op. 3 (EMB). D.
Short pieces with complex problems. In the last piece, forearm clusters are called for in one hand while the other has to play pianissimo glissandi. Firm mastery and control of style. Worth exploring. Non-Bartókian in idiom.

L

WIKTOR LABUŃSKI (1895-) Poland, came to USA in 1928

Labuński has been associated with the Kansas City Conservatory of Music for many years.

4 Variations on a Theme by Paganini (CF). Traditional harmonic language. M-D.

STEFANIA LACHOWSKA (1898-1966) Poland

Lachowska was both a composer and teacher. She studied music in Prague, at the Conservatoire in Lwow and then in Warsaw, among others with Karol Szymanowski.

6 Preludes (Ars Polona 1956-60). Inventive, pianistic, concert level.

EZRA LADERMAN (1924-) USA

Laderman studied composition with Stefan Wolpe, Otto Luening and Douglas Moore.

Sonata No. 1 (OUP c. 1967). 25 p. 13 minutes.
4 movements, neoclassical in style, based on a three-note motif. Effective. M-D.

Sonata No. 2 (OUP c. 1966). 44 p. 22 minutes.
A large four-movement work, neoromantic in style. The second movement, Romanza, shows Scriabin influence, effective large gestures. MC harmonic writing throughout. D.

CONSTANT LAMBERT (1905-1951) Great Britain

Sonata (OUP 1928-29). Three movements, based on jazz rhythms. D.

Elegy (OUP 1938). Short, energetic, improvisational Lento, molto rubato. M-D.

Alla Marcia (OUP 1933).

JOHN LA MONTAINE (1920-) USA

La Montaine writes in a postromantic style influenced by the French school.

Toccata Op. 1 (BB 1957). Short, brilliant, effective. M-D.

Sonata Op. 3 (Eastman School of Music Publications 1950). 20 p. D. Three movements.

12 Relationships for Piano Op. 10 (CF). A set of canons, each at a different interval. Int. to M-D.

6 Dance Preludes Op. 18 (BB). 10 minutes. Well-conceived set, appropriate titles. Effective as complete set or selected movements. M-D.
Preamble, Aria, Burlesque, For Those Who Mourn, Intermezzo, For Those Who Dance.

Fuguing Set Op. 14 (CF c. 1965). 12½ minutes. 7 pieces. 3 fugues, separated by Prologue, Pastorale, Cadenza and Epilogue, each complete in itself. A miniature *"Ludus Tonalis."* Advanced writing, large span required, long pedals. D.

A Summer's Day Op. 32A (GS). 5 minutes.

A Child's Picture Book (BB). 5 imaginative pieces. Int.

Copycats (SB). Canons for young pianists.

Sparklers (SB). Single teaching piece.

WALTER LANG (1896-1966) Switzerland

Lang studied with Emil Jacques-Dalcroze and later taught at the Institut Jacques-Dalcroze. "His style is determined mainly by rhythmic vitality and impressionist tone-colour." GD, 5, 46.

7 Pieces Op. 13 (R&E).

Bulgaria Op. 16 (R&E). A small suite of 10 movements.

Sonata Op. 66 (Hug 1956). 16 p. Clear textures, well-developed ideas. M-D. Vivace, Andante, Presto: changing meters.

Sonata Op. 70 (UE 1958). 23 p. 13 minutes.
Tumultuoso; allegro molto
Lento
Allegro energico
Thematic construction clearly delineated, fits fingers well, written in neoclassic style. D.

Capriccio Op. 36 (Hug).

LARS-ERIK LARSSON (1908-) Sweden

Larsson's style during the 1930's displayed clear classicistic features but more recently he has digressed into Nordic late romanticism, classicism and twelve-tone technique.

6 Croquises Op. 38 (GM 1948). 1. Capriccioso 2. Grazioso 3. Semplice 4. Scherzando 5. Espressivo 6. Ritmico. Hindemith influence.

Sonatine B Op. 16 (UE 1936). 4 movements. 20 p. Widespread broken chords. Second movement, Intermezzo is romantic. Warm, lyric writing, effective. M-D.

Sonatine Op. 39/2 (GM 1948). 3 movements. 10 minutes. Mainly homophonic writing. MC.

12 Little Piano Pieces Op. 47 (GM). 12-tone technique.

Miniaturer (NMS).

T. LATOUR (1776-1837) France

Quatre Sonates pour le Pianoforte (Edition Heuwekemeijer). In c, G, C, F. Interesting works worth investigating. Would be fine substitutes for some of the overused sonatinas of Kuhlau, Clementi, etc. Each work is short and in three movements. Alberti bass is employed to a large degree.

CHRISTIAN I. LATROBE (1757-1836) Great Britain

Latrobe was a Moravian clergyman and amateur musician. The influence of Joseph Haydn on the three sonatas listed below is the result of his friendship with the composer. Sensitive embellishments and keen development procedures contribute toward the imaginative qualities of these three works.

Three Sonatas for the Pianoforte Op. 3 (Charles E. Stevens-Bo&H c. 1970). M-D. See SCE, 765-7.
Sonata I: Allegro, Lento, Menuetto, Finale: Presto.
Sonata II: Allegro, Lento: an interesting Vivace mid-section provides contrast, Allegro molto.
Sonata III: Adagio molto; Andante, pastorale serves as a poignant introduction to the Allegro.

FELICE LATTUADA (1882-1962) Italy

6 Preludi (SZ). 2 volumes.
Titles such as Elegia, L'allegra fucina, Primavera, etc. Romantic descriptive writing. Requires above-average technique.

CARLOS LAVÍN (1883-) Chile

Lavín is equally known as a musicologist. He was director of the Folklore Archive of the University of Chile for a number of years.

Suite Andine (ESC 1926).
3 pieces that depict scenes from the Andes mountains. Mood pieces.

Dos trozos para piano (Ediciones "Los Diez", Santiago de Chile 1926).
Mañana de sol, Crepusculo.

Mythes Araucans (ECS 1926).
El Traucao, El Huallipen, El Guirivilo, El Lampalagua.

BILLY JIM LAYTON (1924-) USA

Layton completed his musical studies at the New England Conservatory, Yale and Harvard Universities. He teaches at Harvard University.

Three Etudes Op. 5 (GS). D.
Serial technique brilliantly handled. A strong musical personality. Virtuosic approach needed. D.

ERNESTO LECUONA (1896-1963) Cuba

Suite Espagnole (EBM).
6 pieces all using Spanish rhythms, melodies. Int.

Danzas Afro-Cubanas (EBM).
6 pieces with pianistic color and varied rhythmic background. Int. to M-D.

Danzas Cubanas (EBM).
6 pieces published together. All demand above-average technique.

19th-Century Cuban Dances (EBM).
A suite of 10 works, based on 19th-century dance tunes. Most are 2 pages in length.

Malagueña (EBM).

NOEL LEE (1924-) USA, born China

Sonatine (OUP 1959). 5½ minutes.
Allegretto, Song, Rondo: Presto.
Neoclassic style, impressionist influences especially in Song (molto lento ed espressivo). M-D.

BENJAMIN LEES (1925-) USA, born China

Lees grew up in the USA and completed his studies at the University of Southern California. In 1954 he went to Europe and spent eight years there. Since returning to this country he has continued to compose and has taught at Peabody Conservatory and Queens College.

Fantasia (Bo&H 1953). 6 minutes.

Kaleidoscopes (Bo&H 1959). 10 short pieces.

Sonata Breve (Bo&H 1955). 3 movements in one. 11 minutes.
Triadic harmony, smooth pianistic chromatic figuration. D.

Toccata (Templeton). Biting dissonance, triplets, chromatic, bravura writing.

6 Ornamental Etudes (Bo&H 1957). 15 minutes.
Displays an incisive and robust style with a preference for ostinato, ornamental quality in melodic line. Tonal, variety of moods. M-D.

3 Preludes (Bo&H 1962). Finely organized ideas, contrasted. Tonal, sensitive. M-D.

Sonata No. 4 (Bo&H 1964). 3 movements. 22 minutes.
Dedicated to Gary Graffman. 50 p.
Bravura keyboard style designed to show off virtuoso skills. Themes worked out thoroughly. Advanced pianism required.

REINBERT DE LEEUW See: DE LEEUW, REINBERT

TON DE LEEUW See: DE LEEUW, TON

RENÉ LEIBOWITZ (1913-) France, born Poland

Leibowitz studied with Schönberg and Webern from 1930 to 1933. His style reflects his dedication to the twelve-tone technique. "Leibowitz is a fanatical disciple of Schönberg, and his activities have done a great deal for the cause of twelve-note music in France and other countries." GD, 5, 117.

Quatre Pièces pour Piano Op. 8 (UE 1943).
Highly organized serial writing, exploits full range of the keyboard. Thick textures, complex rhythmic treatment. Advanced pianism required.

KENNETH LEIGHTON (1929-) Great Britain

Leighton was educated at Queen's College, Oxford, and studied composition in Rome with Goffredo Petrassi.

Sonata No. 1 (Lengnick 1950). 35 p. 4 movements.
Clever enharmonic modulations, vivid sense of color. Freely chromatic. M-D.

Sonata No. 2 Op. 17 (Lengnick 1954).

Sonatinas Nos. 1 and 2 (Lengnick).
Witty, appealing, moderately easy, MC. Excellent pedagogic material.

5 Studies Op. 22 (Nov 1956).
Brilliant writing, demands advanced pianism.

Fantasia contrappuntistica Op. 24 (Ric 1958). "Homage to Bach." 20 p. Toccata, Chorale, Fugue I and II. Four movements are linked together by a motive heard in opening section. Intervals of perfect and augmented fourths determine the melodic structure throughout and form the basis of the two fugues. D.

Variations Op. 30 (Nov 1958).
Nine variations, serial, grateful writing, concludes with a fugue. Part of the series "Virtuoso", edited by John Ogdon, who also wrote two pages of detailed commentary. D. See Anthologies and Collections General: Contemporary.

8 Pieces for Angela Op. 47 (Nov). Int.

Fantasy on Two Themes Op. 51 (Nov).

GUILLAUME LEKEU (1870-1894) Belgium

Lekeu studied with both Franck and d'Indy in Paris.

Sonate g (Lerolle 1891). Five movements. 19 p. More like a suite than a sonata. Fugal writing is supremely beautiful. Wagnerian harmonies. D.

See: O. G. Sonneck, "Guillaume Lekeu (1870-1894)," MQ, 5, January 1919, 109-47. Article also printed in *Miscellaneous Studies in the History of Music*. New York: Macmillan, 1921, 190-240.

ALFONSO LENG (1884-) Chile

Sonata (PAU 1951). 17 p. M-D.
Allegro con brio: militant.
Andante: most expressive.

Allegretto: animated, energetic.
Contemporary sounds throughout, well-written. Large span required. One of the finest works in Chilean piano literature.

4 Doloras (Instituto de Extension Musicale).

4 Preludes (Facultad de Bellas Artes de la Univ. de Chile).

LEONARDO LEO (1694-1744) Italy

Although mainly known for his sacred music and comic operas, Leo did write *13 Toccate per cembalo.* Some of these have been published as sonatas but Leo did not use this term.

Six Toccatas for Cembalo (M. Maffioletta-Carisch).
Close to Scarlatti sonatas in style but easier. Fingered, editorial dynamic suggestions. Some errors in printing.

See: Anthologies and Collections, General, *Early Classics for the Piano* (Mirovitch-GS) and Italian, *Clavicembalisti Italiani* (Montani-Ric).

JOHN LESSARD (1920-   ) USA

Lessard studied composition with Nadia Boulanger and is a disciple of Igor Stravinsky. A French neoclassicism permeates much of his writing.

4 Preludes (ACA 1954). Contrasted ideas. Effective ostinato in No. 3. M-D.

Perpetual Motion (Gen). Dissonant study in toccata style. M-D.

Toccata (Gen c. 1959). 20 p. 4 movements. Moderato; Adagio; Allegro vivace; Adagio-Presto. D.
For harpsichord or piano, more effective on harpsichord. Dramatic, tonal, MC.

Little Concert Suite (Gen c. 1964). Prelude, Dance, Lullaby, March, Pastoral, Procession. Short, tonal, thin textures, contrasted movements and thematics. Int.

Mask (TP 1947). 6 p. Brisk, dissonant, dancelike, octaves and skips. M-D.

JEAN YVES DANIEL LESUR (1908-   ) France

Lesur was a pupil of Charles Tournemire and a member of the group "Le Jeune France." ". . . in all he appears as a musician of refined sensibility whose art is distinguished by its lyrical and poetic qualities." GD, 5, 149.

Suite Française (Amphion 1934-5). 3 movements: Divertissement, Menuet, Catilène et ronde pastorale. Pleasant, colorful writing, reflects influence of old French dance movements. M-D.

Les Carillons (Sal 1930). Experimentation in sonorities. M-D.

Pavane (Durand 1938).

Trois Etudes (Durand). 1. Hands crossing study 2. Sonorities study. 3 Tremolando study. M-D.

Pastorale variée (Durand 1947). Eight variations on a whimsical theme. Final variation contains some choice writing. M-D.

2 Noëls (Amphion).

Nocturne (Rongwen 1952). Romantic sounds.

Ballade (Durand 1950).

Le Bal (EMT 1954). 18 minutes. A suite in seven movements: Préambule, Moment Musical, Valse, Mirages, Les Frénétiques, Idylle, Epilogue. Lyric and poetic qualities, sweeping gestures. Pianistic requirements vary, movements 1, 5, and 7 are most demanding.

ALFONSO LETELIER (1912-   ) Chile

Letelier is Dean of the Conservatory, University of Chile in Santiago.

Variaciones en Fa (Bo&H 1948). D.
A romantic theme followed by 10 variations and a Finale. Imaginative writing. Variation form seems to be especially appealing to Chilean composers. Domingo Santa Cruz, Gustavo Becerra and Orrego-Salas are cases in point.

ERNST LÉVY (1895-   ) USA, born Switzerland, came to USA in 1941

Since coming to this country Lévy has taught at the New England Conservatory of Music, Bennington College and Brooklyn College.

5 Pieces (AMP 1945).
Fine craftsmanship, tonal, neoclassic. Changing meters. No. 5 is a robust fugue, effective ending. M-D.

7 Piano Pieces (Bo&H 1954).
Linear writing, irregular meters, quartal and quintal harmonies, conventional forms. M-D.

BERNHARD LEWKOVITCH (1927-   ) Denmark

Lewkovitch's writing displays great delicacy, refinement, depth of feeling and architectural strength.

Sonata No. 1 (WH).

Sonata Op. 2 (WH 1949). 3 movements. M-D.

Sonata No. 3 Op. 4 (WH 1950). 19 p. 1 movement, strong polychordal approach. D.

Sonata No. 4 Op. 5 (WH 1954). 3 movements. M-D.

Dance Suite Op. 16 (WH 1956). 15 p. 6 movements: Introduction, Dance song about a bird's wedding, Quiet melody in the field, Gopak, Cradle-song, Singing game.

Dance Suite No. 2 Op. 17 (WH 1960). Originally for orchestra, arranged by composer for piano. Both suites are MC, M-D. Influenced by N. V. Bentzon and Prokofieff.

Sonatine (WH 1947). 7 p.

SALVADOR LEY (1907-   ) Guatemala, now living USA

Danza Exotica (PIC 1959). 6 minutes. Concert piece written in a virtuoso style, energetic drive.

Danza Fantastica (EBM 1950). 3 minutes.

ANATOL LIADOFF (LIADOV) 1855-1914) Russia

This composer's works range from single pedagogic pieces to extended compositions.

Collected works for Piano (USSR).

Ballade Op. 21 (Belaieff).

Berceuse Op. 24/2 (Belaieff).

Une tabatière à musique, Valse badinage Op. 32. (Belaieff) (GS). The popular "Musical Snuff-box."

Variations sur un thème de Glinka Op. 35 (Belaieff).

Etude Op. 37 (Belaieff). Five sixteenths in RH against two eighths in LH. Inner melody. M-D.

Variations sur un thème populaire polonais Op. 51 (Belaieff).

4 Russian Folk Songs (Siloti-MCA).

4 Arabesques (Leduc).

Album pour piano (Belaieff). Works from Op. 23, Op. 30-32, Op. 38-40, Op. 44 (Barcarolle), Op. 46/3, Op. 48, Op. 53/1, Op. 57/2, Op. 64/1, 2.

SERGEI LIAPUNOFF (1859-1924) Russia

Liapunoff's style combines elements of folk music with the more traditional European training he experienced in his early studies. He was also trained as a concert pianist and came under the influence of Liszt, to whom he dedicated his *Studies* Op. 11. This influence is reflected in most of his piano works.

Selected Works Vol. I and II (USSR).

Etudes d'exécution transcendante Op. 11 in 4 volumes (CFP).

I. Berceuse, Ronde des fantômes, Carillon.
II. Terek, Nuit d'été, Tempête.
III. Idylle, Chant épique, Harpes éoliennes.
IV. Lesghinka (available separately EBM), Rondes des sylphes, Elégie en mémoire de Franz Liszt.

Sonata f Op. 27 (Zimmermann) (USSR). See SSB, 729-31.

Sonatine D♭ Op. 65 (1917) (USSR). Steeped in Russian folk music.

Fêtes de noël Op. 41 (USSR). Folk oriented.

Variations on a Russian Theme Op. 49 (Zimmermann) (Nov).

Toccata and Fugue (USSR).

Rêverie du soir Op. 3 (Zimmermann).

Barcarolle Op. 46 (Zimmermann).

Six Morceaux faciles Op. 59 (Zimmermann).

See: Richard Davis, "Sergei Liapunoff (1859-1924): The Piano Works: A Short Appreciation," MR, 21, August 1960, 186-206. Contains a complete list of his piano works, with publishers.

INGVAR LIDHOLM (1921-) Sweden

Medieval music has been a major inspiration to Lidholm. He was the first of his generation to use the twelve-tone technique.

Sonata a (GM 1947).

Tio miniatyrer (GM).

Ur Pa Konungens Slott (NMS 1946).
Konungen, Pagernas marsch, Prinsessan, Visa och dansscen.

Klavierstück (NMS 1949).

JOSÉ LIDÓN (1746-1827) Spain

Sonata para Clave o para Organo con trumpet real (S. Kastner-Schott).

ROLF LIEBERMANN (1910-) Switzerland

Liebermann employs a variety of styles; tonal, polytonal and atonal. He has been Director of the Hamburg Staatsoper and presently Director of the Paris Opera.

Sonata (UE 1951). 19 p. 12 minutes. Four movements, serial technique. This sonata was part of an opera *Leonora* (1940-45); it was played in act one, scene one, where a piano recital takes place. Both works (the opera and sonata) share some of the same material.

INGEMAR LILJEFORS (1906-) Sweden

Liljefors uses Swedish folk music in his compositions. He teaches at the College of Music in Stockholm and has written, among other things, a textbook on harmony.

Andante och Scherzo (NMS).

Fem studier (ms).

Fyra impromptus (ms).

Sonat (ms).

Sonatin Op. 23 (ms).

Sonatin (1954) (ms).

Svit (ms). All (ms) are available from Eriks Musikhandel.

BO LINDE (1933-1970) Sweden

Linde's style shows the influence of his teacher Lars-Erik Larsson, and Prokofieff. A warm, lyrical strain is also noticeable in his writing.

Preludio e capriccio Op. 11 (ms).

Sex karaktarsstycken Op. 4 (ms).

Sex stycken Op. 24 (ms).

Sonatin Op. 15/1 (ms). All (ms) items are available from Eriks Musikhandel.

DINU LIPATTI (1917-1950) Rumania

Sonatine (Sal 1947). For LH alone. Three movements in a clear neoclassic style. M-D.

Nocturne f♯ (Sal c. 1961). 3 p. Tonal, chromatic mid-section builds to climax, span of 10th required. M-D.

MARIJAN LIPOVSEK (1919-   ) Yugoslavia

Sonata za Klavir (Savez Kompozitora Jugoslavije Drustvo Slovenskih Skladateljev 1955). 34 p. Melodically oriented, full of chromatic coloration and bombast. Poor printing. M-D. Allegro appassionata, Adagio, Agitato.

FRANZ LISZT (1811-1886) Hungary

The piano works of Franz Liszt are an essential ingredient of the pianist's repertoire. The complete gamut of pianistic resources is encountered in his works. A re-evaluation of Liszt's contribution is presently going on and his star appears to be in the ascendency. We now realize that his later works contain the seeds of impressionism and that these pieces have exerted a major influence on such twentieth-century composers as Debussy and Bartók. The American Liszt Society, formed in 1966, has helped stimulate interest in this great romantic personality. (Dr. David Kushner, Chairman, Board of Directors, ALS, c/o Music Department, University of Florida, Gainesville, Florida 32601).

EDITIONS:
Gregg Press has reprinted the Collected Works, Leipzig 1901-36, 34 volumes bound as 33. The editors of this edition include Busoni, Bartók, Raabe and da Motta. The final volume of this reprint incorporates a specially revised version by Humphrey Searle of his catalogue of Liszt's compositions and literary publications. The series and volume numbers of the solo piano works of this edition are listed below:

Etudes I (II/1)

Etudes II (II/2)

Etudes III (II/3)

Album d'un voyageur (II/4)

Du temps de pèlerinage (II/5)

Années de pèlerinage (II/6)

Miscellaneous piano works I (II/7)

Miscellaneous piano works II (II/8)

Miscellaneous piano works III (II/9)

Miscellaneous piano works IV (II/10)

Hungarian Rhapsodies (II/12)

Bärenreiter and EMB are publishing a *New Edition of the Complete Works of Franz Liszt* (available through Belwin-Mills). The solo piano works are found in Series I (Works for Piano Two Hands, 18 volumes) and Series II (Transcriptions and Arrangements of Original and Other Works for Piano Two Hands, ca. 6 volumes). Announced as edited by Zoltan Gardonyi and Istvan Szelenyi are the first nine volumes of Series I:

Volume I: *Transcendental Etudes* (c. 1970).

Volume II: *Etudes* (c. 1971).

Volume III-IV: *Hungarian Rhapsodies.*

Volumes V-VI: *Miscellaneous Piano Works.*

Volume VII: Années de Pèlerinage. Première année; Suisse.

Volume VIII: Années de Pèlerinage. Deuxième année; Italie.

Volume IX: Années de Pèlerinage. Troisième annés.

The most extensive accessible performing edition of the piano works is: *Piano Works* 12 vols. (Sauer-CFP).

I: *Hungarian Rhapsodies* Nos. 1-8

II: *Hungarian Rhapsodies* Nos. 9-15 and *Spanish Rhapsody*

III: *12 Etudes d'exécution transcendante*

IV: *6 Paganini Etudes, 3 Concert Etudes, Waldesrauschen, Gnomenreigen.*

V: *Original Compositions,* Volume 1: 2 Polonaises, 2 Ballades, Mephisto Waltz I, Valse-Impromptu, Première Valse oubliée, Grand Galop chromatique, Consolations, 2 Légendes.

VI: *Original Compositions,* Volume 2: 3 Liebesträume; Harmonies poétiques (Bénédiction de Dieu dans la solitude, Funérailles, Cantique d'amour); Berceuse; Années de Pèlerinage (première année): Au Lac de Wallenstadt, Au bord d'une source; (seconde année):

Sonetto 47, 104, 123 del Petrarca, Venezia e Napoli: Gondoliera, Canzone, Tarantella; Sonata b.

VII: 13 *Transcriptions from Wagner Operas:* Rienzi, Tannhäuser (2), Lohengrin (4), Der Fliegende Holländer (2), Tristan und Isolde, Meistersinger, Ring des Nibelungen, Parsifal.

VIII: 9 *Transcriptions from various Operas:* Auber: La Muette de Portici; Bellini: Norma; Donizetti: Lucia di Lammermoor; Gounod: Faust; Mendelssohn: Midsummer Night's Dream; Mozart: Don Giovanni; Rossini: Stabat Mater; Verdi: Rigoletto, Trovatore.

IX: *Song Transcriptions of Schubert* (19 Lieder), Schumann (2 Lieder), Beethoven (3 Lieder), Chopin, Lassen, Liszt, Mendelssohn.

X: *Transcriptions:* Soirées de Vienne (Schubert); 6 Preludes and Fugues for organ (Bach); Variations on "Weinen, Klagen" (Bach); Fantasy and Fugue g for organ (Bach); La Regatta veneziana; La Danza (Rossini).

XI: *Concerti* and other *Works with Orchestra*

XII: *Supplement:* 2 Original works; 6 Transcriptions. Scherzo and March; Fantasy and Fugue on BACH; Wagner, Tannhäuser-Ouverture; Mayerbeer, Prophet; Liszt, Faust-Symphonie; Schubert, 3 Marches.

(GS) has most of the works in editions by Joseffy, Gallico, Hughes, Friedheim, Busoni, Deis, Pauer, Fraemcke, etc. The (Br&H) edition, well-edited by Busoni is no longer immediately available. (Dannreuther-Augener) has *Concert Etudes, Paganini Etudes* and the *12 Transcendental Etudes.* (Ric) has a large selection including all 20 *Rhapsodies* (19 Hungarian and one Spanish) and the 12 volumes of the *Technical* Exercises (Winterberger). (Johnson-Hin) *Christmas Tree* in 2 volumes; 5 Pieces from *Christmas Tree* (C. Clifton-Mer): Nos. 1, 3, 6, 10, and 8 of the original 12 pieces.

Works published separately:

12 Etudes d'exécution transcendante (Br, EMB c. 1970) joint publishers: critical, scholarly edition; (Sauer-CFP) (Br&H) (Cortot-Sal) (Durand) (K). (Br, EMB) have Nos. 4, 5, 8,

10, 11 available separately. First version of these works is available (Robert Howat-Hin). *Mazeppa, Eroica* (Ric), *Chasse-neige* (Br&H), *Paysage* (Br&H).

See: Joseph Banowetz, "Liszt Etudes d'exécution transcendante," AMT, 20, January 1971, 18-19, 38.

Paganini Etudes (Cortot-Sal) (Busoni-Br&H) (Brugnoli-Ric) (K) (Durand) (Augener) (GS). *La Campanella* (Br&H) (Schott) (Ric) (WH) (K). *La Chasse* (1st and 2nd versions) (Ric).

3 Concert Etudes (Cortot-Sal) (Ric); with *Leggierezza* and *Sospiro* (Augener) (Durand) (Schott) (WH) (Dob) (K).

Walderauschen, Gnomenreigen (Schott) (Ric) (Augener) (Cortot-Sal) (Durand) (CFP).

Hungarian Rhapsodies (Ric) in 2 vols. including Nos. 16-19 and *Spanish Rhapsody;* (Durand) 5 vols.; (Sauer-CFP) in 2 vols. through No. 15 plus *Spanish Rhapsody;* (d'Albert-Br&H) No. 1, 2, 5, 6, 14, 15; (Spanuth & Orth-OD) Nos. 2, 6, 8, 9. 10, 11, 12, 13, 14, 15; (Cortot-Sal) Nos. 2, 6, 9, 10, 11, 12, 13; (Piccioli-Curci) Nos. 2, 6, 9, 12, 13, 14, 15, 19 and *Spanish Rhapsody;* (CFP) (WH) No. 2; see especially the cadenza to this by Rachmaninoff (Mer).

Sonata b (Sauer-CFP) (Ric) (Cortot-Sal) (Durand) (Augener) (GS) (K) (EMB).

Balladen No. 1 (Ric) (Schott); No. 2 (Cortot-Sal).

St. François d'Assise. La prédication aux oiseaux and *St. François de Paule marchant sur les flots:* (K) (Ric) (Cortot-Sal) (UE) (Augener); No. 1 (Durand) (Heugel).

Années de Pèlerinage:

Première année: Suisse (1835-1851) (CFP) (GS).

Chapelle de Guillaume Tell, Au lac de Wallenstadt, Pastorale, Au bord d'une source, Orage, Vallée d'Obermann, Eglogue, Le mal du pays, Les Cloches de Genève.

Separately: Eglogue, Guillaume Tell, Cloches de Genève, Au bord d'une source (Ric); Au bord d'une source (K) (Schott) (GS).

Deuxième année: Italie (1838-1849) (CFP) (GS).

Sposalizio, Il pensieroso, Canzonetta del Salvator Rosa, Sonnetto 47 del Petrarca, Sonnetto 104 del Petrarca, Sonnetto 123 del Petrarca, Après une lecture de Dante, fantasia quasi una sonata; *Supplement* (1839) Venezia e Napoli: Gondoliera, Canzone, Tarantella. Venezia e Napoli: separately (Ric) (Schott).

Separately: 3 Sonetti del Petrarca (Ric), No. 104 (Schott) (GS), No. 123 (Augener) (GS); Sposalizio (Augener) (GS); Il pensieroso (Augener); Canzonetta del Salvator Rosa (Augener); Après une lecture de Dante (Cortot-Sal); Venezia e Napoli (Ric) (Schott), Gondoliera and Tarantella only (Cortot-Sal).

Troisième année (1867-1877)

Angelus! Prière aux anges gardiens, Aux cyprès de la villa d'Este-Thrénodie I, Aux cyprès de la villa d'Este-Thrénodie II, Les jeux d'eau à la villa d'Este, Sunt lacrymae rerum—En mode hongrois, Marche funèbre. En memoire de Maximilien I, Sursum corda. See collection: *The Final Years.*

Only Les jeux d'eau à la Villa d'Este is presently available separately: (K) (Ric) (GS) (Schott).

6 Consolations (Schott) (UE) (Augener) (K) (GS) (CFP) (Cortot-Sal) (Durand); (Ric) 1-3 separately.

3 Liebesträume (CFP) (WH) (GS) (Ric); No. 3 separately (Schott); each one separately (UE) (K).

2 Polonaises (Ric) (Durand) (Sal) (Augener); (Schott) No. 2.

Mephisto Waltz I (Schott) (Ric) (Cortot-Sal) (Durand) (GS) (Augener) (K).

Mephisto Waltz II (Parsons-Fürstner).

Mephisto Waltzes III and IV (Liszt Society Publications, Schott). Vols. I and II.

Valse-Impromptu (CFP) (Schott) (Durand).

Valse oubliées (Schott). *Second Valse oubliée* (Durand). No. 1 (Philipp-Heugel); Nos. 1, 2, 3 (Bo&Bo).

Valse oubliées Nos. 2 and 3 (Liszt Society Publications, Schott). Vol. IV. No. 4 (TP).

Romance Oubliée (Musica Obscura).

Harmonies poétiques et religieuses (1845-1852) (K).
Invocation; Ave Maria; Bénédiction de Dieu dans la solitude; Pensées des morts; Pater noster; Hymne de l'enfant à son réveil; Funérailles; Miserere (d'après Palestrina); Andante lagrimoso; Cantique d'amour.

Separate: Bénédiction de Dieu dans la solitude (Cortot-Sal) (Augener). Funérailles (Ric) (Schott) (Cortot-Sal). Cantique d'amour (GS).

Allegro di Bravura Op. 4 (Waldwick).

Three Late Works (R. C. Lee-Br) (1879). Toccata, Carrousel de Mme. Pelet-Narbonne, Sospiri.

Variations on Weinen, Klagen (after J. S. Bach)(Cortot-Sal).

Fantasie and Fugue on B A C H (Cortot-Sal).

Portraits of Hungarian Heros (EMB). 7 pieces portraying Hungarian heros, written in 1885. 3 or 4 pages each, M-D.

Organ Transcriptions:

6 organ preludes and fugues of Bach (1842-1850). S. 543-548 (CFP). In a, C, c, C, e, b (Ric) (GS).

Fantasia and Fugue g (S. 542) (Ric) (GS).

Song Transcriptions:

See Vol. IX (CFP) for *34 Song Transcriptions.* (GS) has two books of *24 Song Transcriptions.*

Opera Transcriptions:

3 volumes of Operatic Transcriptions (USSR). Vol. I all-Wagner (15 works). Vol. II transcriptions on operas by Bellini, Berlioz, Glinka. Vol. III on works by Beethoven, Auber, Meyerbeer, Donizetti, Bellini, Glinka.

Separately: Rossini *La Regata Veneziana* (Ric) (Schott) (HV). *La Danza* (Ric). *Rigoletto-Paraphrase* (Schott) (Ric) (HV). *Don-Juan Paraphrase* (Br&H) (Cortot-Sal).

Other Transcriptions: *Soirées de Vienne* on Schubert Waltzes (GS) (CFP) (WH) (Durand) (K) (Augener). *Soirées italiennes* on motifs of Mercadante (Durand).

Technical Studies (J. Esteban-Alfred c. 1971). Contains twelve books (86 exercises) in one volume, excellent preface.

Collections:

The Final Years (J. Prostakoff-GS). These piano works of the late period include music written after 1861 when Liszt had retired from his duties at Weimar. Many of these works have only been available in the complete edition (Liszt-Stiftung, Leipzig, 1908-33, or its reprint by the Gregg Press, 1966). Includes: Nuages gris (1885-6), Richard Wagner-Venezia (1883), Unstern! (1885-6), La Lugubre gondola I and II (1882), 5 Hungarian Folksongs (ca. 1873), 2 Historical Hungarian Portraits (1870), Czárdás macabre (1881-2) Czárdás obstinée (1884), 4th Mephisto Waltz (1885), Wiegenlied (1881), Abschied (1885), 4 little piano pieces (1865-76), 3 pieces from third part (Book III) of *Années de Pèlerinage:* Sunt lachrymae rerum, Aux cyprès de la villa d'Este, Sursum Corda (1872 and 1877), and the 2nd and 3rd Valse Oubliées (1882-3). Practical, discreetly edited.

Liszt Society Publications (Schott) Volumes I, II and IV are available through (K).

Vol. I: *Late Piano Works.* Csárdás Macabre; En Rêve; Nuages gris; La lugubre gondola I and II; Richard Wagner-Venezia; 4 Kleine Klavierstücke; 3rd Mephisto Waltz; Trauervorspiel and March; Unstern!

Vol. II: *Early and Late Piano Works.* Am Grabe Richard Wagner, piano or string-quartet and harp; Apparitions Nos. 1 and 2; Harmonies poétiques et religieuses, first version: Lyon; 4th Méphisto Waltz; Reminiscences de Boccanegra.

Vol. III: *Hungarian and Late Piano Works.* Csárdás obstiné:

Elegy Nos. 1 and 2; Funeral music to Mosonyi's death: 5 Hungarian folksongs; 2 Pieces in Hungarian Style (1828); Schlaflos, Frage und Antwort; To the memory of Petöfi.

Vol. IV: *Dances.* Valse mélancolique (1839-40); Valses oubliées Nos. 2 and 3 (1884); Valse de concert; Galop a.

Vol. V: Mazurka brillante (1856); Mephisto-Polka (1883); all the other works have some connection with the Swiss volume of the *Années de Pèlerinage.* Fleurs mélodiques des Alpes nos. 3 and 2 were rewritten as nos. 3 and 8 respectively of the *Années.* The Swiss melodies of the Romantic Fantasy (Le mal du Pays and Ranz des vaches) were both used in the later collection. Also included are early versions of Vallée d'Obermann and Cloches de Genève. Interesting comparisons.

Liszt Album (Compiled, edited and fingered by Percival Garratt-Hin 1953).

Feuille d'Album: This work later (1st version 1840, 2nd 1851) became the Valse mélancolique.

Chanson d'Arcadelt—Ave Maria: A transcription of an Arcadelt 3-voice chanson.

Kleine Klavierstücke: Moderato A♭, composed in 1865. Appassionato, no date known.

Valse: First appeared under the title Albumblatt in Walzerform, 1842.

En Mode Russe: This Russian melody is No. 22 of 24 pieces called *Bunte Reihe* for violin and piano, composed by Ferdinand David, famous violinist (1810-73).

Csárdás: A Hungarian dance.

Ave Maria.

Liszt Album I (K). Sonata b, Méphisto Waltz No. 4, 6 Consolations, 3 Concert Etudes, La Campanella.

Liszt Album II (K). 3 Liebesträume, Nuages Gris, La Gondola Lugubre I, II, Hungarian Rhapsody II, Easy Valse Mélancolique, Waldesrauschen, Les Jeux d'eaux à la Villa d'Este, St. Francis Walking on the Water.

Liszt Album (EMB c. 1966). Valse Impromptu (1850), Valse Oubliée No. 1 (1880), Consolations 3 & 4, Rhapsodie Hongroise No. 2 (1847) (transcribed Fr. Bendel), La Regatta Veneziana (1837), La Pastorella Dell'Alpi (1837), Chant Polonais (1860), Soirées de Vienne No. 6 (1852).

In Various Moods (Kreutzer-BMC). Eight original works including: Valse (1842), Album Leaf (ca. 1840), Nocturne (1883), Csárdás (1884), Hungarian Folksong Nos. 1, 2, 5, (1875), Grey Clouds (1881). Technically, some of the easiest Liszt.

Album (Augener). Au bord d'une source, Consolation No. 1, Liebesträum No. 3, Il pensieroso, Sposalizio.

Five Liszt Discoveries (Werner-Curwen). Ländler A♭, Wiegenlied, Ave Maria, Tyrolian Melody, La cloche sonne.

Collection of Piano Works (Z. Gardonya and I. Szelenyi-EMB). Fifteen separate pieces covering 50 years of Liszt's career. Some familiar, some less well-known.

Fourteen Pieces for the Piano (F. Dillon-EBM). Excellent collection of easier works. 4 small Pieces (1865, 1873), Etude d (1827), Consolation E (1850), Pater Noster (1846), Nocturne (1885-6), 3 Hungarian Folksongs I, II, IV, Gloomy Clouds (1881), Sancta Dorothea (1877), Dirge (The Funeral Gondola) (1882). "Each selection has the property of evoking in the performer the capacity to convey emotional shapes and patterns stimulated by the Master's conceptual pictures." Additional pedaling indicated by editor in dotted lines.

Liszt Klavierstücke (Hinze-Reinhold-CFP #4667). 12 easy to M-D works including: Vier kleine Klavierstücke (1865), No. 8 from The Christmas Tree (1875), En Rêve (1885), No. 8 from Années de Pèlerinage, first year (1835-36), No. 7 from Années de Pèlerinage first year, No. 2 from Anées de Pèlerinage second year (1838-39), No. 3 from Années de Pèlerinage second year (1849), Präludium on "Weinen, Klagen, Sorgen, Zagen" (1859), 5 Hungarian Folksongs (1873), Puszta-Wehmut (around 1885), Hungarian Rhapsody No. 3 (1853), Csárdás macabre (1881-82). Reliable edition.

See: Barbara Allen Crockett, "Liszt's Opera Transcriptions for Piano," unpub. diss., University of Illinois, 1968.

T. P. Currier, "Difficulties Overcome—Liszt's Etudes," Musician, 16, December, 1911, 810.

Phillip Friedheim, "The Piano Transcriptions of Liszt," Studies in Romanticism, 1, 1962, 82-96.

William M. Goode, "The Late Piano Works of Franz Liszt and Their Influence on some Aspects of Modern Piano Composition," unpub. diss., Indiana University, 1965. Covers primarily the period from 1865 to Liszt's death in 1886.

Eva Mary Grew, "Liszt's Dante Sonata," Chesterian, 21, 1940, 33-40.

Humphrey Searle, *The Music of Liszt.* London: Williams and Norgate, 1954.

Bence Szabolcsi, *The Twilight of Ferenc Liszt.* Budapest: Publishing House of the Hungarian Academy of Sciences, 1959. Discusses the later phases of Liszt's compositional career. Includes complete musical examples of six of the late works.

Alan Walker, Editor, *Franz Liszt The Man and His Music.* New York: Taplinger, 1970.

NORMAN LLOYD (1919-) USA

Five Pieces for Dance (Orchesis Publications 1935-1939). Puritan Hymn, Blues, Piping Tune, Dance Hall Study, Theme and (5) Variations. Variety of styles, pulse and beat of the dance central in its orientation. Easiest is Puritan Hymn, most difficult is Theme and Variations.

Three Scenes from Memory (EV 1963). Winter Landscape, Sad Carrousel, City Street. Each 2 p. long. Fresh, original recital material in contemporary idiom. M-D.

Episodes (EV 1964). 5 pieces, jazz influence, improvisatory style, varied moods. M-D.

Sonata (Mer c. 1964). 31 p. 4 movements.
Bitonal, polytonal writing, contrasted and developed ideas. Brilliant finale. D.

MATTHEW LOCKE (ca. 1630-1677) Great Britain

Melothesia (1673) (BB) Monuments of Music Literature Series. This treatise on music contains many compositions listed below. Emphasis on basso continuo realization.

Keyboard Suites from Melothesia (1673) (A. Kooiker-PSM 1968). Five suites and eleven other short pieces, 34 pieces altogether (46 pages), many with charm and interest, especially the jigs and hornpipes. Eight composers represented.

Seven Pieces from Melothesia (1673) (Hin).
Gordon Phillips, the editor, deals with ornamentation, registration, and performance in a scholarly introduction. Urtext.

Suites (S&B).

See: Anthony Kooiker, "Locke's 'Melothesia': Its Place in the History of Keyboard Music in Restoration England," unpub. diss., University of Rochester, Eastman School of Music, 1962.

JEAN-BAPTISTE LOEILLET (1680-1730) Belgium

Much of Loeillet's music was erroneously ascribed to J. B. Lully and published under his name.

Werken voor Clavicembel (J. Watelet-De Ring 1932) (BB). In *Monumenta Musicae Belgicae,* Vol. I contains:

Lessons for the Harpsichord or Spinet. 3 suites e, D, g.
Suite No. 1: A, Aire, C, M, and Jigg. Suite2: A, C, Gavot, S, and Minuet Rondo. Suite 3 contains Aire, Hornpipe and Cibel.

Also contains: *Suites of Lessons.* 6 suites in g, A, c, D, F, and E♭. Each suite contains an A, C, S, Aria, M and Giga. Reprints of numerous movements from these suites are available from (Durand) (GS) (UE) (Br&H) (Elkin) (Augener) and (TP).

See: Brian Priestman, "Catalogue thématique des oeuvres de Jean-Baptiste, John et Jacques Loeillet," Revue Belge de Musicologie, 6, October-December 1952, 219-74.
"The Keyboard Works of J. B. Loeillet," MR, 16, May 1955, 89-95.

GEORG SIMON LÖHLEIN (1725-1781) Germany

Tänze und Stücke (K. Herrmann-Sikorski).

ROBART LOMBARDO (1932-) USA

Lombardo studied composition with Arnold Franchetti, Philip Bezanson and Boris Blacher. He is composer-in-residence at the Chicago Musical College of Roosevelt University.

Laude, Fuga e Cavatina (CFP 1955). M-D.
Laude: expressive, exploits open fifths.
Fuga: energetic, many harmonic seconds and sevenths.
Cavatina: short, melodic but contains some intense moments.

HARVEY W. LOOMIS (1865-1930) USA

The works of Loomis should be restudied and resurrected. He was a composer of excellent craft and exquisite originality. The music, published by the Wa-Wan Press, is now available again in the Arno Series of American Music, Arno Press.

Intermezzo from The Tragedy of Death (Wa-Wan Press, Vol. 1 No. 4, 1902).

Lyrics of the Red-Man (Wa-Wan Press, Vol. 3 No. 3, 1903-4).
Book 1: Music of the Calumet, A Song of Sorrow, Around the Wigwam, The Silent Conquerer, Warrior's Dance.
Book 2: Prayer to Wakonda, On the War Path, Ripe Corn Dance, Evening at the Lodge, The Chattering Squaw, Scalp Dance, The Thunder God and the Rainbow, The Warrior's Last Word.

NIKOLAI LOPATNIKOFF (1903-) USA, born Russia, came to USA in 1939

Sonatine Op. 7 (Edition Russe 1926). Allegro energico (Toccata): fugal, martellato touch, double notes, octaves, quartal harmony, brilliant climax; Andante: unmetered, expressive melodic writing, accompaniment relies on quartal outlines, builds to climax, subsides to quiet close; Allegro molto vivace: fugal texture, similar to opening movement. A strong work with some bravura writing. M-D.

Five Contrasts Op. 16 (Schott 1930). Five moods: impassioned, tender, agitated, expressive, energetic. Linear, dissonant, bravura writing. M-D.

Dialogues Op. 18 (Schott 1932). Moderato, Allegro molto, Vivace, Grave, Epilog. Two-part writing, linear, complex. M-D.

Variations Op. 22 (Schott 1933). Six variations, modal, short note values on strong beats, quartal and quintal harmony, highly contrasted. M-D.

Sonata E Op. 29 (AMP 1943). Allegro risoluto: toccata-like rhythm with cross accents; Andantino: elegiac, folklike melodies; Allegro molto vivace: vigorous rhythmic treatment, contrapuntal richness, bravura writing. D.

Dance Piece for Piano (TP 1955). Changing meters, bitonal midsection. Int.

Intervals Op. 37 (MCA 1957). Seven studies based on intervals of the second, third, fourth, fifth, sixth, seventh and octave, Contemporary techniques handled with much imagination. M-D.

FERNANDO LOPES-GRAÇA (1906-) Portugal

Lopes-Graça is one of Portugal's most frequently performed composers. He is also active as lecturer, musicologist, teacher, writer and arranger of Portuguese folk songs. All (ms) items available through the Gulbenkian Foundation, Lisbon.

Nove dancas breves (ms 1938-48 Rev. 1964).

Onze glosas (ms 1950).

24 Preludios (ms 1950-55).

Sonata No. 3 (Prelio do circula de Cultura Musical 1952).

Viagens na minha terra (ms). Short pieces based on Portuguese folk melodies.

Melodias rusticas Portuguese (ms). Book 1 (1956) Book 2 (1957).

Cinco Nocturnos (ms) 1957.

Sonata No. 4 (ms 1961).

Album for the Young Pianist (Nov). 21 short pieces.
Vol. I in series *Discovery.* Many seconds and asymmetrical rhythms are used in this collection. See especially No. 13 Alla Bartók with a folklike melody set to an interesting accompaniment, and No. 16, Song Without Words. Portuguese folk elements subtly permeate these pieces.

CARLOS LÓPEZ-BUCHARDO (1881-1948) Argentina

López-Buchardo studied composition with Albert Roussel in Paris. In 1924 he founded the National Conservatory of Music and Theatrical Arts in Buenos Aires, which is now named in his honor.

Bailecito (Ric 1936).

Campera (Ric 1936).

Nocturno (Ric 1944).

Vidala (Ric 1944).

Sonatina (Ric 1944).

Danzon (Ric 1944).

VINCENT LÜBECK (1654-1740) Germany

Clavierübung 1728 (H. Trede-CFP). Prelude and Fugue a, Suite g, A, C, S, G, Chaconne on "Lobt Gott ihr Christen allzugleich." The Chaconne is also available (R. Steglich-Nag).

THEODORE LUCAS (1941-) USA

Lucas studied composition with David Ward-Steinman at San Diego State College and with Nadia Boulanger in Paris. He received his doctorate in composition from the University of Illinois.

Aberrations No. VII (CAP 1967).
Aleatory, "time blocks", extensive directions, clusters. Unusual notation. Piece concluded by pianist sitting on the keyboard. Experiment in free or implicit notation.

Sonette (CAP 1968). 3 movements. 11 p. 6½ minutes. M-D.

OTTO LUENING (1900-) USA

Luening's early works made use of polytonal, atonal and near-serial techniques while much of his latest writing involves the tape recorder. He has taught many of our younger American composers.

8 Preludes (NME). Short polytonal pieces, eclectic in mood and style. Span of ninth required. M-D.

2 Inventions (Mer 1943). M-D.

1. Imitation, scale work, choralelike melody brought in near closing.
2. Four variations on a ground bass, each variation treated differently, variation 4 adds a hymnlike tune, FF ending, well constructed.

Gay Picture (Merion).

Andante (Highgate).

2 Bagatelles (Highgate).

Dance Sonata for Piano (Highgate).

8 Piano Pieces (Highgate).

Music for Piano (A Contrapuntal Study) (CFE).

Phantasy (CFE) (Highgate).

6 Preludes (Highgate).

6 Short and Easy Pieces (Highgate).

First Short Sonata (CFE) (Highgate).

Second Short Sonata (Highgate). 3 movements FSF. Concise movements, clear neoclassic style. More musical problems than technical. M-D.

Third Short Sonata (Highgate).

Fourth Short Sonata (Highgate).

Sonata for Piano (Highgate).

5 Intermezzi (Highgate).

RAY LUKE (1928-) USA

Luke received degrees in theory and composition from Texas Christian University and Eastman School of Music.

5 Miniatures for Piano. Commissioned by the Oklahoma MTA and MTNA, 1964. M-D. (Available on loan from MTNA).

1. Declamation: large octave gestures, mid-section drops back, builds to a dramatic close.
2. Fugue: in a, 3 voices, much rhythmic drive; last 12 bars use pedal point.
3. Waltz: whimsical, uses 4/4 and 2/4 to break up triple meter. Much chromaticism.
4. Lament: built on rhythmic idea "short-long," quartal harmony.
5. Toccata: a driving work in 8/16, thin sonorities, requires close working together of hands.

DAVID LUMSDAINE (1931-) Australia, living in Great Britain

Lumsdaine studied with Matyas Seiber and Lennox Berkeley. In 1970 he was appointed Lecturer in Music at Durham University.

Kelly Ground (UE 1966). *Avant-garde* work in three cycles. Detailed notation and explanations.

Cycle 1: 5 strophes in contrasting phrasing, texture and rhythm, clusters.
Cycle 2: short, exploits intervals of fourth and fifth.
Cycle 3: built on intervals exploited in cycle 2 but varied rhythmic patterns permeate harmonic structure.

LENNART LUNDBERG (1863-1931) Sweden

5 Marinen (AL).

Mazurka Op. 45 (NMS).

Sonat Op. 33 (MK).

Tekniska studier (NMS).

JACOB WILHELM LUSTIG (1706-1796) Germany

Sonata A (F. Krakamp-NV). More characteristic of a suite than a sonata. Contains a Prelude, A, C, S, G. Cheerful, full of original ideas, decorative flourishes, passing notes, trills, cadenzas (in the S). Editorial markings clearly distinguished from composer's.

WITOLD LUTOSLAWSKI (1913-) Poland

Popular Melodies of Poland (PWM 1949). 12 easy pieces based on Polish folk tunes.

Bucolica. 5 Stücke (PWM c. 1957). Short, freely chromatic, linear, M-D.

ELIZABETH LUTYENS (1906-) Great Britain

All the pieces, except *The Check Book* are based on serial technique. Lutyens, along with Humphrey Searle, introduced 12-tone writing to Great Britain about 1939.

Piano e Forte Op. 43 (Belwin-Mills). A Fantasialike dramatic study in dynamics. Finale is rondolike.

Five Intermezzi Op. 9 (Lengnick 1942).

Three Improvisations (Lengnick 1948). 1. Adumbration 2. Obfuscation 3. Peroration.

Five Bagatelles Op. 49 (Schott 1962).

The Check Book (Augener 1938). 12 children's pieces.

DONALD LYBBERT (1923-) USA

Lybbert studied composition with Elliott Carter, Otto Luening and Nadia Boulanger. He is head of the Department of Music of Hunter College, New York City.

Sonata Brevis (CFP 1962). 20 p. 9 minutes.
A one-movement serial work, changing duple and triple rhythmic patterns, powerful. D.

M

EDWARD MacDOWELL (1861-1908) USA

Considered by many as America's first truly professional composer, MacDowell was at his best composing miniatures for the piano. He left a large legacy of romantic character-pieces. Many are no longer available.

Forgotten Fairy Tales Op. 4 (1897). No. 1 Sung Outside the Prince's Door (Elkin).

Six Fancies Op. 7 (1897). No. 2 To a Humming Bird (Elkin).

First Modern Suite Op. 10 (1883). Eight movements of which only the Prelude and Intermezzo are available (AMP).

Second Modern Suite Op. 14 (1883) (Taubmann-Br&H). Praeludium, Fugato, Rhapsody, Scherzino, March, Fantastic Dance.

Two Fantastic Pieces Op. 17 (1884). No. 2 Witches Dance (TP) (K).

Six Poems after Heine Op. 31 (1887). No. 2 Scotch Poem (GS).

Four Little Poems Op. 32 (1888) (AMP) (K) (GS). The Eagle, The Brook, Moonshine, Winter.

Etude de Concert F♯ Op. 36 (1889) (Elkin).

Twelve Studies Op. 39 (1890) (BMC) (K) (Elkin). Hunting Song, Alla tarantella, Romance, Arabesque, In the Forest, Dance of the Gnomes, Idyl, Shadow Dance (Separately IMC), Intermezzo, Melody, Scherzino, Hungarian (Separately IMC).

Twelve Virtuoso Studies Op. 46 (1894) (AMP) (K). Novelette, Moto perpetuo, Wild Chase, Improvisation, Elfin Dance, Valse triste, Burleske, Bluette, Träumerei, March Wind, Impromptu, Polonaise. Nos. 5 and 8 separately (Br&H).

Ten Woodland Sketches Op. 51 (1896) (GS) (BMC) (EBM) (Schott) (Elkin) (IMC) (K). To a Wild Rose, Will-o'-the-Wisp, At an Old Trysting Place, In Autumn, From an Indian Lodge, To a Water-Lily, From Uncle Remus, A Deserted Farm, By a Meadow Brook, Told at Sunset.

Eight Sea Pieces Op. 55 (1898) (GS) (K) (Elkin). To the Sea, From a Wandering Iceberg, A.D. 1620, Starlight, Song, From the Depths, Nautilus, In Mid-Ocean.

Six Fireside Tales Op. 61 (1902). No. 2 Of Br'er Rabbit (Elkin).

Ten New England Idylls Op. 62 (1902) (GS) (K) (Schott). An Old Garden, Midsummer, Midwinter, With Sweet Lavender, In Deep Woods (Separately, Elkin), Indian Idyl, To an Old White Pine, From Puritan Days, From a Log Cabin, The Joy of Autumn (Separately Elkin), Nos. 5 and 10 (Separately Elkin).

Four Sonatas: Sonata Tragica Op. 45 (1893) g (GS).
Sonata Eroica Op. 50 (1895) g (Br&H) (K) (GS).
Norse Sonata Op. 57 (1900) d (K).
Keltic Sonata Op. 59 (1901) e (K) (Elkin).

For a discussion of the sonatas see SSB, 760-67. All four sonatas require advanced pianism.

16 Selected Pieces (W. Weismann-CFP). Contains works from Op. 37, Op. 51, Op. 55, Op. 61, Op. 62, with a preface in English and German.

Music by MacDowell (G. Anson-Schroeder & Gunther).

Book 1: The Eagle Op. 32/1, From a Log Cabin Op. 62/9, From a Wandering Iceberg Op. 55/2, From Uncle Remus Op. 51/7, Humoreske Op. 24/1, Hungarian Op. 39/12, March Wind Op. 46/10, Novellette Op. 46/1, Of Br'er Rabbit Op. 61/2, Rigaudon Op. 49/2, Scotch Poem Op. 31/2, To an Old White Pine Op. 62/7, To the Moonlight Op. 28/3.

Book 2: Alla Tarantella Op. 39/2, From an Indian Lodge

Op. 51/5, Improvisation Op. 46/4, In the Woods Op. 28/1, Moonshine Op. 32/3, Song Op. 55/5, Soubrette Op. 38/2, Starlight Op. 55/4, Sung Outside the Prince's Door Op. 4/1, Tin Soldier's Love Op. 7/1, To a Water Lily Op. 51/6, To a Wild Rose Op. 51/1, Villain Op. 38/6, The Witch Op. 38/4.

See: Nancy Eagle, "The Pianoforte Sonatas of Edward A. MacDowell, a Style-Critical Study," unpub. M. A. thesis, University of North Carolina at Chapel Hill, 1952.

David Kaiserman, "Edward MacDowell—The Keltic and Eroica Piano Sonatas," MJ, 24, February 1966, 51, 76f.

Marian MacDowell, *Random Notes on Edward MacDowell and His Music*. Boston: A. P. Schmidt, 1950. Helpful as an aid to interpreting his piano works.

NIKITA MAGALOFF (1912-) Switzerland, born Russia

Magaloff, distinguished faculty member at the Geneva Conservatory, is internationally known as pianist and pedagogue.

Toccata Op. 6 (Edition Russe de Musique 1933).
A virtuoso work by a virtuoso pianist emphasizing melodic fourths, fifths, glissandi, brilliant octave passages. Dedicated to Vladimir Horowitz.

MARIE-VERA MAIXANDEAU (1929-) France

Sonate No. 2 (ESC 1965). 18 p.
Allegro assai, Intermezzo, Toccata.
Well-written, requires large span, incisive sonorities. M-D.

PAUL DE MALEINGREAU (1887-1956) Belgium

Les Angélus Du Printemps: Suite Op. 17 (JWC 1919). 19 p.
Picturesque writing, programmatic, impressionistic. M-D.

Nocturnes Op. 8 (Lauweryns).

Prélude, Chorale et Fugue Op. 7 (JWC 1915). Franck influence. M-D.

Suite Op. 9 (JWC 1920). 36 p. Toccate-Ouverture, A, S, G. M-D.

Suite enfantine (Sal).

WILHELM MALER (1902-) Germany

"Maler was strongly influenced by neobaroque tendencies and by Hindemith's linear polyphony." GD, 5, 531.

Sechs Sonaten: A, B, C, D, e, F (Süddeutscher Musikverlag c. 1952).
D: 20 p. Allegro Concertante; Intermezzo über ein Praeludium von J. S. Bach; Allegro non troppo (Doppel-Fuge).
F: 19 p. *Sonatine,* tonal with chromatic flavor. Last movement has much bounce.

Der Mayer: Suite für Klavier (H. Gerig c. 1947). 10 p. Theme, A, C, Air, Gavotte. MC, neoclassic in style.

Der Jahreskreis (Schott). Inventions based on German folk song. Int.

Drei kleine Klavierstücke über alte Weihnachtslieder (Schott 1938). Int.

GIAN FRANCESCO MALIPIERO (1882-) Italy

Impressionist techniques are used extensively in Malipiero's writing. Many of his piano works are descriptive.

Poemetti Lunari (Sal 1909-10). Seven pieces. See No. IV, Presto scherzando and No. VII, lengthy, agitated grotesque.

Preludi Autunnali (Sal 1914). Four pieces, varied and impressionistic.
Lento, ma carrezzevole: chromatic, flowing nocturne.
Ritenuto, ma spigliato: horn calls, varied figuration, atmospheric, short.
Lento, triste: solemn ostinato dirge.
Veloce: bright, thin textured scherzo.

Barlumi (JWC 1917). Five pieces, one of his most successful sets.
Non lento troppo: atmospheric.
Lento: somber, widely separated sonorities in parallel motion.
Vivace: contrasting sonorities, double notes, effective ending.
Lento, misterioso: broken chord sonorities.
Molto vivace: vigorous dance with fast repeated chords.

Maschere che passano (JWC 1918). Five fantasylike sketches. D.

Hommage à Claude Debussy (JWC 1920). Short, parallel harmonies, quiet ending. M-D.

La Siesta (ESC 1920). Four delicate sketches, much parallel usage, improvisational.

Tre Omaggi (JWC 1920). A un papagallo, a un elefante, a un idiota. Clever, amusing caricatures. M-D.

Cavalcate (Sal 1921). Three modes of four-legged locomotion.
Somaro: Recalcitrant donkey: Chords, octaves, broken rhythms, humorous.
Camello: Swaying camel: A lyric Lento, flowing figuration.
Destriero: Fiery steed: Rhythmic emphasis, fast detached chords, climatic.

Il Tarlo (Sal 1922). Four short pieces, impressionistic.

Pasqua di Risurrezione (Sal 1924). Extended, atmospheric, varied pianistic techniques. D.

3 Preludi a una Fuga (UE 1926).
Three connected contrasted preludes lead to a legato three-voice fugue, sonorous ending.

Hortus Conclusus (Ric 1946). Eight sketches in contrasting styles: Prelude, Lento, Allegro, Andante, Tranquillo, Lentamente, Allegro moderato, extended finale, variationlike, in eight short sections.

Cinque Studi per Domani (UE 1954).
Some imitation, transparent textures, three against four. D.

Variazione (JWC 1960). Variations on Pantomine from *El Amor brujo* by Manuel de Falla.

RICCARDO MALIPIERO (1914-) Italy

Inventions (SZ 1949).
Nine pieces in serial technique intended as an introduction to this system. One-, two-, and three-voiced works. M-D.

Piccola Musica (SZ 1941).

Costellazioni (SZ 1965). 22 p. 12 minutes.
Extensive directions, pointillistic, flexible chord technique necessary. D.

JOSÉ MALSIO (1924-) Peru

Prelude and Toccata (PAU 1952). 8 p. M-D.
Prelude: in three sections: Recitativo, Arioso, Tempo Primo. Dissonant linear texture.
Toccata: built on a one-bar ostinato.

LUIGI MANENTI (1899-) Italy

Toccata (Ric).
Tightly organized, driving, neoclassic style. D.

Lai (Ric 1956). 4 p. Sonorous, dirgelike, bitonal. M-D.

HENNING MANKELL (1868-1930) Sweden

Mankell wrote mainly for the piano. "His style was not typically Swedish and his compositions were considered very original and much in advance of their time. His use of form was influenced by Chopin's, his harmonic colouring by Liszt, Grieg and Sjögren, and he also had affinities with the French impressionists. His music is predominantly homophonic, the melodic and harmonic elements being closely integrated." GD, 5, 551.

Ballade pour piano (Br&H 1911). 15 p.

2me Ballade (Br&H 1911). 17 p.

Andante med variationer Op. 57 (MK).

Barcaroll Op. 60/1 (MK).

Improvisation Op. 70/2 (NMS).

Impromptu Op. 50/2 (NMS).

Miniatyrer Op. 52 (NMS). Four pieces.

Nocturnes Op. 25/1, 3 (NMS).

BENEDETTO MARCELLO (1686-1739) Italy

According to Newman, SBE, 176, Marcello may have left as many as twenty keyboard sonatas. Two-part textures, harmonic interest and balanced phrase structure are characteristic of his music.

Sonates pour clavecin (L. Bianconi & L. Sgrizzi-Heugel).

Sonatas d, g (Malipiero-Notari).

Sonata g (G. Tagliapietra-Zanibon). 4 movements including some brilliant figuration.

Sonata B *Alte Meister* (Pauer-Br&H) Vol. V: Bartók has transcribed this work (CF); (M. Maffioletti-Carisch). Three movements, straightforward, processionallike closing.

Toccata c (Eposito-OD) *Early Italian Piano Music*. (I. Philipp-IMC) *Italian Masters*. Effective study in repeated double notes.

Concerto d (CFP). Contained in a volume of J. S. Bach Concerto transcriptions. Transcribed by Bach from a work originally writen for oboe in c.

See: W. S. Newman, "The Keyboard Sonatas of Benedetto Marcello," AM, 29, January-March 1957, 28-41.

LOUIS MARCHAND (1669-1732) France

Pièces de Clavecin (T. Dart-l'OL 1960).

Two suites: I in d: A, C I and II, S, G, Chaconne, Gavotte en Rondeau; II in g: Prelude, A, C, S, Gavotte, Menuet en Rondeau. Contains a table of ornaments. Performer is to make his own selection of movements.

See: Geoffrey B. Sharp, "Louis Marchand, 1669-1732. A Forgotten Virtuoso," MT, 110, November 1969, 1134-37.

ANDRÉ F. MARESCOTTI (1902-   ) Switzerland

Suite en sol (Jobert c. 1929). 17 p. Prélude, S, M, G. Captures the spirit of the baroque suite with vigorous, rhythmic, colorful writing. D.

2me Suite (Jobert c. 1933). 21 p.
Prélude, S, Gavotte, G.

3me Suite (Jobert 1946). 23 p.
Prélude, Aria, Toccate.

Croquis (Jobert 1946). Free "Sketches" in an unencumbered style. Blue Girls, Rêverie, Fidelia (Bourrée).

Fantasque (Jobert). Required piece at the Geneva International Competition, 1939.

FRANCO MARGOLA (1908-   ) Italy

Sei sonatine facili (EC 1955). 8 p.

Tarantella-Rondo (Carisch 1933).

Leggenda (Carisch 1958).

Berceuse (SZ 1957).

Piccolo Rapsodia d'Autunno (Carisch 1941).

Sonatas 1, 2, 4, (Ric 1956).

4 Sonatinas (Ric).

Sonata No. 3 (Ric 1957). 16 p. Allegro; Adagio; Movimento finale.
Pandiatonic, thin textures, dancelike, on the scale of a sonatina. Neoclassic style. M-D.

IGOR MARKÉVITCH (1912-   ) France, born Russia

Markévitch's style is basically tonal but laced with dissonant counterpoint.

Stefan le Poète: Impression of Youth (SZ 1941).
A 7-piece cycle, romantic titles, lyric style, requires fine legato. Int. to M-D.

Variations and Fugue on a Theme by Handel (SZ 1942). D.
Theme is from the *Harmonious Blacksmith,* entire work requires advanced pianism.

Noces (Senart).
Préambule; A l'église; Réjouissances.

JOAQUIN MARROQUIN (-) Guatemala

Chapiniana (PIC 1964). 19 p. Suite of 5 pieces. M-D.
Titles refer to certain areas of the country, individual pieces relate to its moods and activities.
Pastorale: somber flutes; Burlesque: brusque humor; Nocturne: mysterious; Ronda: wistful; Fiesta: bright and colorful closing.

HENRI MARTELLI (1895-) France, born Corsica

Cinq danses Op. 47 (ESC 1941). 23 p. Rhythmic vigor, chromatic, spontaneous, dry style. M-D.
Danse d'Introduction, Rondino, Tempo di Walzer, Passacaille, Saltarelle.

Première petite Suite (ESC c. 1935). 9 p.

Deuxieme petite suite Op. 38/2 (ESC c. 1946). 10 p. 4 contransting movements, MC, traditional.

Suite Op. 46 (ESC 1939). 22 p.

Sonatine (ESC 1934).

IB MARTENS (1918-) Denmark

Huits petits instructives morceaux (WH 1947). Eight well-written pieces for younger students. MC.

Deux morceaux (WH). Allegro giocoso, Caprice.

Passata (WH).

Suite populaire (WH).

FRANK MARTIN (1890-   ) Switzerland

Eight Preludes for Piano (UE 1948). 20 minutes. D.
Free chromatic style. Unusual, personal, highly successful handling of serial technique. One of the major contributions to the 20th-century piano literature. Martin combines French clarity with German harmonic idioms.

PADRE GIAMBATTISTA MARTINI (1706-1784) Italy

Famous throughout Europe, this composer and teacher of J. C. Bach and Mozart, among others, was highly respected by the musical world of his day. His sonatas were indicated for organ or harpsichord. Strong craft but the inspiration is less than impressive. The sonatas range from two to five movements and include dance movements.

12 Sonatas Op. 2 (1742) *I Classici della Musica Italiana,* XVIII. Two sonatas in TPA, XII. *Le Trésor des Pianistes,* IX.

Sonate d'Intravolatura per l'Organo e l'Cembalo (BB). Facsimile of the 1742 Dutch edition. Contains 12 sonatas. Dance pieces and free movements form the basis of these works.

6 Sonatas (1747) (Hoffman-Erbrecht-Br&H) (K).

Prelude and Fugue e (Esposito-OD) *Early Italian Music.*

Sonata E (de Paoli-JWC) *Italian Sonatas of the 18th Century.*

See: Howard Brofsky, "The Instrumental Music of Padre Martini," unpub. diss., New York University, 1963.

DONALD MARTINO (1931-   ) USA

Martino studied composition with Ernst Bacon, Milton Babbitt, Roger Sessions and Luigi Dallapiccola. He is Head of the Composition Department at the New England Conservatory.

Fantasy (Ione 1958). "The first derived set is a combination of the original series and its inversion. Each new prime is successively combined with its inversion or retrograde inversion." BBD, 125. D.

Pianississimo (A Sonata for the Piano) (ECS 1970). 436 bars. Detailed performance directions including a location off the piano for the score when playing the work. Highly organized writing (pitch, rhythm, dynamics) that requires the most advanced pianism. Contains some almost unbelievable sonorities.

Seven Piano Pieces (ECS).

JEAN MARTINON (1910-) France

Epilogue d'un conte d'amour Op. 35/1 (Costallat c. 1948). 6 p. A berceuse, many meter changes, added-note technique, impressionist. M-D.

Introduction et Toccata Op. 48 (Costallat c. 1948). Biting dissonance, changing meters in Toccata, aggressive. D.

Sonatine No. 3 Op. 22 (Costallat 1945). 14 p. Three tightly-knit movements. M-D.

BOHUSLAV MARTINŮ (1890-1959) Czechoslovakia, came to USA in 1941

Czech folksong, French clarity and exactness, are all fused in the music of Martinů.

Eight Preludes (Leduc 1930). Neoclassically oriented; in the form of Blues, Scherzo, Andante, Danse, Capriccio, Largo, Etude and Foxtrot. M-D.

Borová: Seven Czech Dances (Leduc 1931). M-D.

Film en Miniature (*Hudebni Matice* 1925). Amusing, sophisticated writing. Six pieces: Tango, Scherzo, Berceuse, Valse, Chanson, Carillon. Int. to M-D.

Marionettes (Artia 1925). Three books. Graceful dance movements. Int.

Three Czech Dances (ESC 1929). Okračak, Dupák, Polka. Virtuoso writing including octaves, double notes, highly rhythmic. D.

Esquisses de Dances (Schott 1933). Five spirited dances, irregular meters. M-D.

Les Ritournelles (Schott 1933). Six varied etudelike pieces, very pianistic. M-D.

Etudes and Polkas (Bo&H 1946). Three books. 16 pieces, each Etude alternates with a Polka. Stamina is required for the Etudes while the Polkas demand a flexible rhythm, sensitivity and eloquent tonal balance. M-D to D.

Fables (Artia 1947). Not the most interesting Martinů. Five pieces: On the Farm, The Poor Rabbit, The Monkeys, The Chicken, The Angry Bear. Int. to M-D.

Les Bouquinistes du Quai Malaquais (Heugel 1954). Light lullaby, a kind of street song. Int.

Spring in the Garden (Artia 1948). Four easy children's pieces. Int.

Two Dances (Artia 1950). Valse, Polka. In the style of Ravel's *Valses Nobles*. M-D.

Fenêtre sur le Jardin (Leduc 1957). Four pieces: No. 1 is easiest (Int), the others are M-D.

Sonata No. 1 (ESC 1958). 19 minutes. Three movements, FSF. Bitonal, numerous figures, often developed from each other. D.

Fantaisie et Toccata (AMP 1940). Large-scale, bravura work, variety of textures exploited. Mature pianism required.

The Fifth Day of the Fifth Moon (Heugel 1951). Metrically free, impressionistic. M-D.

Bagatelle (ESC .

Le Train Hanté (ESC).

Trois Esquisses (ESC). 6 minutes.

Barcarolle (ESC). 1½ minutes.

Sonata for Harpsichord (ESC c. 1964). Two movements, mainly homophonic writing. M-D.

See: B. J. Large, "Bohuslav Martinů: an analysis and appraisal," unpub. diss., University of London (External), 1964.

GIUSEPPE MARTUCCI (1856-1909) Italy

Martucci was a pioneer in restoring instrumental music to a place of prominence in nineteenth-century operatic Italy. He was oriented toward German music, especially to Schumann, Brahms, and Wagner. Fine craftsmanship is always in evidence. (Ric) publishes all the works listed below, including a volume of *Selected Compositions* and *20 Little Pieces*. His collected piano works fill almost 6 volumes.

Tarantella Op. 44/6.

Barcarolle Op. 20.

Fantasia Op. 61.

Variations Op. 58.

Caprice Op. 3.

Scherzo Op. 53/2. Scarlatti-like.

Nocturne f♯ Op. 70/2. Brahms influence.

DANIEL GREGORY MASON (1873-1953) USA

Country Pictures Op. 9 (Br&H). Book I: Cloud Pageant, Chimney Swallow. Book II: At Sunset. The Quiet Hour, The Whippoorwill, Night Wind. Descriptive works in Brahms and MacDowell tradition. Numbers two and six demand facile technique. M-D.

Three Preludes (EBM 1943). M-D.
Con fantasia, quasi improvvisata: nocturnelike.
Tristamente, ma con moto: melodic line transferred between voices. Semplice: one page long, span of ninth required.

Color Contrasts. See Anthologies and Collections: USA, *U.S.A.*, II(MCA).

JULES MASSENET (1842-1912) France

Papillons Noirs (Heugel 1907). Lyric, salontype pieces.

Papillons Blancs (Heugel 1907). More difficult and more interesting.

Deux Impromptus (Heugel). Eau dormante, Eau courante. M-D.

Valse Très Lente (Heugel).

WILLIAM MATHIAS (1934-) Great Britain

Mathias was born in Wales and studied at the Royal Academy of Music in London.

Toccata alla Danza (OUP 1961). 3 minutes.
Pianistic, brilliant, punctuated driving rhythms, changing meters add a flexible rhythmic punch. Span of tenth required. M-D.

Sonata Op. 25 (OUP 1963). 30 p. 18 minutes. 3 movements. A large-scale work, free tonalities, bravura writing. Well-contrasted ideas, interesting pedal notation. D.

RODOLPHE MATHIEU (1896-) Canada

Sonata No. 1 (CMC).
A large-scale one-movement work in postromantic style. D.

JOHANN MATTHESON (1681-1764) Germany

Pièces de Clavecin (1714) are available in a facsimile edition from (BB). 2 volumes: Ouvertures, Preludes, Fugues, Allemandes, Courantes, Sarabandes, Gigues and Aires.

Die wohlklingende Fingersprache (1735) (Hoffmann-Erbrecht-Br&H). 13 fugues and A, C, G, and Seriosita. The fugues are mainly in 2 and 3 voices.

WILLIAM MAYER (1925-) USA

Sonata (CF 1961). 30 p. 18 minutes. 3 movements. 12-tone idiom. Second movement has plucked string effects. Interlude appears between second and third movements. Quintal and major-seventh harmonies, staccato chords, bravura writing. D.

ROBERT McBRIDE (1911-) USA

McBride studied at the University of Arizona with Otto Luening. He is presently teaching at his Alma Mater.

Dance Suite (ACA). 16 min.

Harpsipatrick Serenade (ACA). For harpsichord.

Patriharpsic Serenade (ACA). For harpsichord.

School Bus (TP). Pedagogic.

Tall-in-the-Saddle (TP) Pedagogic.

18 Piano Pieces For Children (ACA). 12 minutes.

JOHN McCABE (1938-) Great Britain

Variations Op. 22 (Nov). 10 minutes.
Unusual theme suggests an Indian Raga. 18 short variations build in a peculiar, steady and exciting manner. Exotic music, demands advanced pianism. In "Virtuoso" Series. See Anthologies and Collections, General: Contemporary.

5 Bagatelles (Elkin).
Short examples written to demonstrate certain aspects of serial writing: Capriccio, Aria, Elegia, Toccata, Nocturne. D.

3 Impromptus (OUP 1963).
Three short terse pieces, MC. Nos. 1 and 3 are highly rhythmic, No. 2 is a Siciliano lento malinconico. Written for John Ogdon. An orchestral imagination will aid the performer. M-D.

Fantasy on a Theme of Liszt (Nov 1969).
This one-movement form is in a neo-Lisztian idiom but stamped with McCabe's personal style.

Capriccio (Nov 1969).
Study No. 1. Clusters, harmonics, hammered octaves, printed on three staves. D.

GEORGE FREDERICK McKAY (1899-) USA

Dance Suite No. 2 (NME 1938). Five movement work, MC.
Insouciant Proclamation: march-like, sardonic.
Naive Pastorale: wistful, plastic.
Athletic Poem: martelé, enérgico.

Calisthenics à la Hollywood: jazz elements.
A Giddy Pace: gay, folkish, thin textures.

Caricature Dance Suite Op. 4 (Schott 1930).
Snickertyship, Jabbertyflip, Swaggerhop, Burlesque March.

7 Outdoor Pieces (TP).

Vistas (Sam Fox).

Prairie Horizon (R. B. Brown).

Explorations (JF). Vols. I and II.

COLIN McPHEE (1901-1964) USA

Invention (NME).

Kinesis (NME).

NICHOLAS MEDTNER (1880-1951) Russia

Medtner has enlarged the piano repertoire considerably. 14 sonatas, some of imposing dimensions, 33 Fairy (Folk) Tales, 41 character pieces (Mood Pictures, Improvisations, Arabesques, Dithyrambs, Novels, Lyric Fragments, Hymns, Romantic Sketches, Elegies, etc.), 3 volumes of *Forgotten Melodies,* and a set of variations make up the bulk of his solo piano writing. His music is based on classic foundations, with a special fondness for complex rhythmic procedure. A vivid imagination shows through in all his work. All of the piano pieces require a well-developed pianism. Many can only be classified as difficult. A Medtner Society was formed in London in 1948 mainly to issue recordings of the composer playing his own works.

The complete piano works are published in 4 volumes (USSR). (Zimmermann) also has a good selection of the piano works. (USSR) 4 volumes: I. Op. 1-14, II. Op. 17-31, III. Op. 34-47, IV. Op. 48-59.

Piano sonatas: See SSB, 721-27 for thorough discussion.

Sonata f Op. 5 (1904). 44 p.
Allegro, f. Intermezzo, c. Largo, E♭. Allegro risoluto, f.

Sonata-Triad Op. 11 (1907) (Frey-Simrock).
No. 1 Allegro non troppo, A♭, 14 p.
No. 2. Andante molto espressivo, d, 9 p. *Sonata elegie.*
No. 3. Allegro moderato, con passione innocente, C, 11 p.
Each movement is in SA design. Can be played as 3 separate pieces or together as one work.

Sonata g Op. 22 (1911). 28 p.
Tenebroso, sempre affrettando: Allegro assai.
Interludium: Andante lugubre (leads to) Allegro assai.
Written as a two-movement work but sounds like three with contrasting sections in a bravura-contrapuntal style. Fine motivic treatment, unusual rhythms. Excellent recital piece.
See: Harold Truscott, "Medtner's Sonata in G minor, Opus 22," MR, May 1961, 112-23.

March Sonata (Fairy Tale Sonata) Op. 25/1 c (1912) 20 p.
Allegro abbandonamente, c. Andantino con moto, E♭; cadenza leads to Allegro con spirito, c; in 5/2, 3/2.

Sonata e Op. 25/2 (1913). 60 p.
Introduzione: Andante con moto. Allegro. Tranquillo. Giocondamente. Stentato. Largamente. Allegro. Allegro molto sfrenatamente, Presto. Tenebroso tranquillo. Meno mosso, con meditazione. Concentrado, ma sempre con moto. These are some of the tempo-character directions used in this one-movement, diffuse work.

Sonata-Ballade f♯ Op. 27 (1913). 41 p.
Allegretto, F♯-f♯; large coda. Introduzione: Finale. Cyclic in form and more lyric than Op. 22.

Sonata a Op. 30 (1914). 27 p.
Allegro risoluto. Many tempo-character directions.

Sonata a Op. 38/1 (1918). 21 p. "Reminiscenza."

Sonata c Op. 39/5 (1920?). 20 p. "Tragica."

Sonata b♭ Op. 53/1 (1930). 48 p. "Romantica". Cyclic, cross-rhythms, complex harmonies and polyphonic textures.

Sonata f Op. 53/2 (1931-32 ?). 37 p. "Orageuse" or "Minacciosa".

Sonata G Op. 56 (1937?). 20 p. "Idylle; Pastorale".

Smaller forms:

8 Mood Pictures Op. 1 (1902) . 30 p.
Varied moods—all require facile technique.

3 Improvisations Op. 2 (1902). 26 p. D.

4 Pieces Op. 4 (1903). 20 p. Etude g♯, Caprice, Moment Musical, Prelude E♭.

3 Arabesques Op. 7 (1905). 18 p. An Idyll, Tragedy-fragment A, Tragedy-fragment g.

2 Fairy Tales Op. 8 (1905). 16 p.

3 Fairy Tales Op. 9 (1906). 14 p.

3 Dithyrambs Op. 10 (1906). 21 p.

2 Fairy Tales Op. 14 (1908).

3 Novels Op. 17 (1909).

2 Fairy Tales Op. 20 (1910).

4 Lyric Fragments Op. 23 (1912).

4 Fairy Tales Op. 26 (1913).

3 Pieces Op. 31 (1913).

3 Pieces Op. 31 (1915). Improvisation, Funeral March, Fairy Tale.

4 Fairy Tales Op. 34 (1916).

Forgotten Melodies Op. 38 (1919) (Zimmermann). Vol. 1: Sonata reminiscenza, Danza graziosa, Danza festiva, Canzone fluviale, Danza rustica, Canzone serenata, Danza silvestra.

Forgotten Melodies Op. 39 (1920) Vol. II: Lyric Tunes. Mediatazione, Romanza, Primavera, Canzone mattinata, Sonata tragica.

Forgotten Melodies Op. 40 (1920) Vol. III: Danza col canto, Danza sinfonica, Danza fiorata, Danza giubilosa, Danza ondulata, Danza ditirambica.

3 Fairy Tales Op. 42 (1922). No. 1. (Zimmermann).

Improvisation Op. 47 (1926) (Zimmermann).

2 Fairy Tales Op. 48 (1927). No. 2. (Zimmermann).

3 Hymns in Praise of Toil Op. 49 (1928). Before work, At the Anvil, After Work.

6 Fairy Tales Op. 51 (1929) (Zimmermann).

Romantic Sketches Op. 54 (1933) 4 Books. (Zimmermann).

Theme and Variations Op. 55/1 (1934).

Two Elegies Op. 59a (1945) (Zimmermann).

Album of Selected Pieces (IMC).
4 Fairy Tales, Etude, Mood Picture, Idyll, Novellette, Dithyramb.

See: Nicolas Medtner, *The Muse and the Fashion; being a defence of the foundations of the art of music;* tr. with some annotations by Alfred J. Swan. Haverford, Pa., Haverford College Bookstore, 1951. Available through CFP.

Richard Holt (ed.), *Nicholas Medtner (1879-1951): A Tribute to his Art and Personality.* London: Dennis Dobson, 1955. A memorial volume of 38 articles on Medtner.

Richard Holt, *Medtner and His Music, a Tribute to a Great Russian Personality,* ed. by Fred Smith. London: Rimington, Van Wyck, 1947.

ETIÈNNE HENRI MÉHUL (1763-1817) France

Sonata A Op. 1/3 (Podolsky-CF) and *Alte Meister* Vol. I (Pauer-Br&H).
Allegro, Minuet and Trio, Rondo.

Sonata Op. 2/3 *Keyboard Music of the Baroque and Rococo* (Georgii-Arno Volk) Vol. 3 contains Minuet A, second movement only.

WILFRID MELLERS (1914-) Great Britain

Natalis Invicti Solis (Nov 1968).
This is the sixth work in "Virtuoso Series of Modern Music", edited by John Ogdon. Reflects Mellers' interest in primeval rites and necromancy. Plucked strings, harmonics occasionally called for. Unusual. D. See Anthologies and Collections, General: Contemporary.

Canticle of the Waters: variations.
Earth Rounds: requires electronic amplification, a rondo.
Canticle of the Moon: static, derived from a single chord.
Sun Rounds: interesting rondo technique.

FELIX MENDELSSOHN-BARTHOLDY (1809-1847) Germany

One of the finest pianists of his time, Mendelssohn also had a remarkable memory and was probably one of the greatest of all improvisers. Synonymous with his style are well-thought-out ideas, smoothly-flowing melodies, symmetrical designs, a highly individual scherzo style and a complete familiarity with the piano. A sameness of harmonic idiom is sometimes brought about by his fondness for diminished and dominant sevenths. Opus numbers after 72 are assigned posthumously and are often incorrect chronologically.

Complete Piano Works in 5 volumes (T. Kullak-CFP) I: Songs Without Words. II: Op. 5, 7, 14, 16, 33, 72. III: Op. 28, 35, 54, 82, 83, 104 (Book 2), Scherzo b, Etude f, Scherzo and Capriccio f♯. IV: Concerti, Capriccio Brilliant Op. 22, Rondo Brilliant Op. 29, Serenade and Allegro Op. 43. V: Op. 6, 15, 104 (Book 1), 105, 106, 117, 118, 119, Prelude and Fugue e, Gondellied A, 2 Piano Pieces B♭, g.

Complete Piano Works in 3 volumes (K) I: Op. 5, 7, 14, 16, 33, 72, Andante Cantabile. II: Op. 28, 35, 54, 82, 104 (3 Etudes), Etude f, Scherzo b, Scherzo à Capriccio f♯. III: Op. 6, 15, 104 (3 Preludes), 105, 106, 117, 118, 119, Prelude and Fugue e, Barcarole A, 2 Piano Pieces B♭, g.
Separately: Songs Without Words; Children's Pieces Op. 72; Variations Sérieuses Op. 54.

Complete Piano Works in 9 volumes (Ravel-Durand).

Complete Piano Works in 5 volumes (Falkenberg, Pierné-Heugel).

Complete Piano Works in 5 volumes (Thumer, Pauer, Taylor-Augener).

3 volumes of *Selected Compositions* (Romaniello-Ric). I: 48 Songs Without Words. II: Op. 72, Gondellied A, 2 Piano Pieces B♭, g, Op. 117, 118, 119, 16, 15, 5, 14. III: Op. 28, 33, 7.

Miscellaneous Compositions (Kullak-GS). Op. 5, 7, 14, 16, 33, 72, Andante cantabile e presto agitato (no opus number).

Separately:

Songs Without Words (CFP) (GS) (Friedman-WH) (K) (Ric) (CF) (Novello). A suggested graded order of difficulty of a few selections from this popular collection: Op. 19/6, 30/3, 19/4, 30/6, 19/2, 102/3, 38/2, 19/1, 67/5, 38/4, 53/2, 19/3, 30/1, 67/3, 102/2, 5, 38/3, 67/4, 62/5, 19/5. (Werner-Curwen) publish a 49th *Song Without Words* F.

Capriccio f♯ Op. 5 (Ric) (Augener). Long, wide spectrum of technical requirements.

7 Characteristic Pieces Op. 7 (Augener). See especially Nos. 2, 4, and 7.

Andante and Rondo Capriccioso Op. 14 (CFP) (Schott) (Ric) (WH) (GS) (Durand) (Augener) (Nov). Still a fine work and one of Mendelssohn's most representative contributions.

3 Fantasies Op. 16 (WH) (Augener). a, e (deservedly the most popular), E.

Fantasia f♯ Op. 28 (Ric) (GS) (Augener). Also known as *Sonate écossaise* (1833).
See: SSB, 301. Deserves more playing, a major work.

3 Caprices Op. 33 (Augener). a, E, b♭. a and b♭ have slow introductions, mid-sections are prestos.

6 Preludes and Fugues Op. 35 (Scharwenka-IMC) (Augener). e, D, b, A♭, f, B♭. (GS) has No. 1, the most frequently played of the set. Prelude has melodic line moving through arpeggio figuration while fugue concludes on the chorale "Ein' feste Burg."

Andante cantabile and Presto agitato (1838) B. No opus number. Lyric Andante followed by a SA Presto. Effective passage-work.

Variations Sérieuses Op. 54 (1841) (Bramley-Schott) (CFP) (GS) (Ric) (Durand) (K).
17 variations continuous in effect, ingeniously treated and probably Mendelssohn's finest piano work.

Variations E♭ Op. 82 (1841). (GS) has this, Op. 54 and 83 in one collection. Smaller in dimension than Op. 54 but similar figurations throughout.

Variations B♭ Op. 83 (1841). Five variations with long finale.

6 Children's Pieces Op. 72 (CFP) (K) (Durand) (GS) (Augener). G, E♭, G, D, g, F. Composed in London and known as "Christmas Pieces."

3 Etudes Op. 104a (GS) (WH). b♭, F, a. Facile, perpetual motion studies with No. 1 dividing melody between hands. Ingenious, charming.

3 Preludes Op. 104b (Romaniello-Ric). B♭, b, D. Single studies.

Sonata E Op. 6 (1826) (Augener). See: SSB, 299-300. Four movements to be played without a break.
Allegretto con expressione: In SA design. Recalls Beethoven Op. 101.
Tempo di menuetto: minuet tempo plus scherzo.
Adagio e senza tempo: recitative, lengthy, free transition.
Molto allegro e vivace: main theme of first movement re-quoted.

Sonata g Op. 105 (1821) (Augener). Earliest published work. Allegro: chromaticism recalls Mozart; Adagio: improvisatory; Presto: SA design.

Sonata B♭ Op. 106 (1827) (Augener).
Allegro vivace: opening modelled after Beethoven Op. 106.
Scherzo:
Andante quasi allegretto followed by Allegro molto bridge.
Allegro moderato: scherzo theme returns at Allegro non troppo.

Scherzo b. No opus number. Staccato study.

Scherzo à Capriccio f♯ (Ric). No opus number. Binary design. Pianistic demands vary from light staccato to demanding octaves.

3 Posthumous Pieces (E. Walker-Nov). "Im Kahn," Song Without Words d, Canon f♯.

Mendelssohn Album (EMB c. 1964).
Songs Without Words Op. 19/6,3, Op. 30/6, Op. 67/34, Op. 62/3, 6; Kriegsmarsch Op. 61; Hochzeitsmarsch Op. 61; Auf Flügeln des Gesanges Op. 34/2 (arr. F. Liszt); Fantasies Op. 16/1, 2, 3; Rondo capriccioso Op. 14; Skizze from Zwei Klavierstücke Op. post.; Scherzo Capriccioso f♯ Op. post. Performing edition, tastefully edited.

See: Hans and Louise Tischler, "Mendelssohn's Songs Without Words," MQ, 33, January 1947, 1-16.

Eric Werner, *Mendelssohn: A New Image of the Composer and His Age,* translated from the German by Dika Newlin. New York: Macmillan, 1963.

JAIME MENDOZO-NAVA (1925-   ) Bolivia

Three Bolivian Dances (Rongwen 1956).
Lively, full sonorities, based on native dance rhythms. M-D.

Gitana (BB 1957).
Mixed meters, much glitter. M-D.

MISHA MENGELBERG (1935-   ) The Netherlands

Mengelberg studied composition with Kees van Baaren. He has been involved with jazz since 1960.

3 Pianopieces and Pianopiece No. 4 (Donemus 1966). Nos. 1-3 are short, conventional notation, varied tempi and mood. No. 4, *avant-garde,* cluster technique emphasized.

PETER MENNIN (1923-) USA

Mennin's music is characterized by propulsive rhythms, long flowing melodies, effective treatment of dissonance and linear writing of the highest order.

Five Piano Pieces (CF 1949). An eloquent and forceful work.
Prelude: short, transparent, perpetual motion.
Aria: tranquil adagio, sustained, sonorous.
Variation — Canzona: contrapuntal treatment of a rhythmic idea in 5/8.
Canto: cantabile style, flowing andante.
Toccata: energetic rhythms, strongly accented, perpetual motion, most difficult of set. D.

Sonata (CF c. 1967). A large-scale three-movement (32 p.) work. Opening movement characterized by frequent meter and tempi changes. Pedal point in the second movement adds tonal stability. Third movement uses changing meters. Brilliant closing. D.

GIAN CARLO MENOTTI (1911-) USA, born Italy

Poemetti (Ric). 12 pieces. Romantic, impressionist. Excellent teaching material. Int.

Ricercare and Toccata, on a theme from "The Old Maid and the Thief" (Ric 1953). Appealing melodic material, propulsive, "running" Toccata. D.

PAVLE MERKU (1927-) Italy

Merku "considers his adoption of the twelve-tone technique to have been a natural development, since his music had become so highly chromatic." BBD, 126.

Phyllobolia (SZ 1963) "consists of a set of short piano pieces, of which the first, third, and last, are serial. The last is a canon developed from the 4 basic forms of the row." BBD, 126.

TARQUINIO MERULA (ca. 1595-1665) Italy

Merula held appointments alternatively at Bergamo and Cremona, except in 1624 when he served as court organist at Warsaw. He also wrote motets and madrigals.

See: *Monumenti di Musica Italiana,* Series I, Volume I: Tarquino Merula. *Composizioni per organo e cembalo* (A. Curtis 1961).

CLAUDIO MERULO (1533-1604) Italy

Merulo was first-organist at St. Mark's. His ability as a fine performer was matched by his excellent compositional talent. Some of his compositions are among the first, if not the earliest, examples of their type.

Canzonas (Pidoux-Br).

Four Toccatas (G. S. Bedbrook-Schott). Contains much subtle and flexible passage work, often highly expressive. Merulo wrote two books of *Toccatas,* 1598 and 1604; both represent the pompous splendor of the late Renaissance.

OLIVIER MESSIAEN (1908-) France

Messiaen has continued to develop the whole line of French piano music from Debussy, beginning with the early *Préludes* and progressing to the unique *Catalogue d'oiseaux.* "His piano idiom has revived the grand piano style created by Beethoven in his late sonatas and further developed by Liszt and Ravel." André Hodeir, *Since Debussy.* New York: Grove Press, 1961, p. 113. His writing has developed into a complex style and is best understood and described in his own book *Technique of My Musical Language.* Paris: Leduc, 1944. All his music is greatly influenced by his beliefs as a Catholic mystic. The piano style is varied and contains emphasis on multiple modality, free use of dominant discords that often produce fresh sonorities, and use of the piano orchestrally. Bird calls and Hindu ragas have also influenced him. Messiaen's music is extremely colorful. The emphasis on sonority is striking and the musical gestures are generous and almost ritualistic in the obsessive use of characteristic rhythmic procedures. Most of the piano works require advanced pianism but a few of the earlier works like *Fantasie burlesque,* the *Pièce pour le tombeau de Paul Dukas,* the *Rondeau* and a few of the Préludes are less involved. Messiaen has also made a significant contribution through his influence on composers such as Boulez, Barraqué and Stockhausen, all of whom have studied with him.

Fantaisie Burlesque (Durand 1932). Free, jazzy, polytonal counterpoint, brilliant sonorities.

Rondeau (Leduc 1943).

Préludes (Durand 1930). 8 pieces. La Colombe: short, expressive. Chant d'Extase dans un Paysage triste: slow, somber. Instants Défunts: short, atmospheric. Le Nombre Léger: melodic line over light, rapid figuration. Les Sons Impalpables du Rêve: complex, lengthy. Cloches d'Angoisse et Larmes d'Adieu: slow, complex, lengthy. Plainte calme: short, melodic, wistful. Un Reflet dan le Vent: flowing, climactic, long.

Vingt Regards sur l'Enfant Jésus (Durand 1944). 1¾ hours. Messiaen lavishes his religious expression on the contemplations of the child Jesus by 20 different personages: the Father, the Virgin, the Star, etc. Leitmotifs represent the Cross and the heavenly arch, God, and the Star. Complex writing that requires virtuoso technique and musicianship. "More than in all my preceding works, I have sought a language of mystic love; at once varied, powerful, and tender, sometimes brutal, in a multi-colored ordering."

Quatre Etudes de Rhythme (Durand 1949). 17½ minutes.

Ile de Feu I

Ile de Feu II (Published separately). Rhythmic theories at work and best explained in *Traité du Rhythme* of Messiaen. *Mode de valeurs et d'intensité* (Durand 1949). (Published separately.) This was "the first musical work embodying the principle of the integral organization of the world of sound." This work "employs (1) A melodic mode of 36 sounds, all different, the same sounds never being repeated from one octave to another. (2) A mode of 24 'durations' or different rhythmic values. (3) A mode of 7 different intensities. (4)

A mode of 12 different keyboard attacks, these attacks being to the piano what the timbres of the different instruments are to the orchestra." Antoine Goléa, "French Music Since 1945," MQ, 51, January 1965, p. 25.

Neumes Rythmiques (Durand 1950). Complex rhythmic study with fixed resonances and intensities.

Cantéyodjaya (UE 1953). 11½ minutes. This large work repeats the opening phrase extensively. Ragas, retrograde inversion, a 6-voice canon, and fixed rhythms make this a most complex work. A hypnotic effect is created.

Catalogue d'oiseaux (Leduc 1956-58). Seven books. Large-scale pieces based on bird calls collected by Messiaen on travels throughout France. A list containing the names of the birds and a verbal description about each call is included. Fascinating sonorities requiring the most advanced pianism, the whole comprising a set of pieces unique and perhaps unprecedented in the history of music. I. Alpine Chough, Golden Oriole, Blue Rock Thrush. II. Blackeared Wheatear. III. Little Owl, Woodlark. IV. Reed Warbler. V. Short-toed Lark, Cetti's Warbler. VI. Rock Thrush. VII. Buzzard, Black Wheatear, Curlew.

JOSEPH MESSNER (1893-1969) Austria

Messner served as organist of the Salzburg Cathedral for many years. His music is written in a neoclassic style.

Phantasie und Fuge Op. 14 (Dob 1924). D.

Romanze Op. 15 (Dob).

ARTHUR MEULEMANS (1884-1966) Belgium

Sonatine No. 3 (CeBeDeM 1941). 16 p. 6 minutes, 4 movements. Impressionist influence although the composer's style is individual. M-D.

Reflesksen (Senart 1928). 16 p.

Sonatine (Senart 1927). 8 p.

NIKOLAI MIASKOVSKY (1881-1950) USSR

Miaskovsky was a prolific composer for the piano. He wrote nine sonatas and numerous separate pieces. His style was essentially romantic, and is marked by a somber element that permeates much of his music. The harmonic and melodic fourth plus imitative textures are common in his writing.

All the piano music is contained in Volume 10 of the *Complete edition* (USSR).

Sonata C No. 3 Op. 19 (USSR). A large one-movement sectionalized work. Entire range of keyboard is exploited, large span necessary. D.

Sonata c No. 4 Op. 27 (USSR). Three movements. Declamatory Allegro moderato; Variations on a theme quasi-sarabanda; toccata-like finale, many double notes. D.

Recollections Op. 29 (UE).

Two Sonatas Op. 64/1, 2 (USSR). No. 1 b, 2 A♭.

Sonata C Op. 82 (USSR).

Sonata d Op. 83 (USSR). Three movements, more traditional, easier than other sonatas. M-D.

Sonata F Op. 84 (USSR) (CFP).

PETER MIEG (1906-) Switzerland

Mieg studied with Frank Martin. Neoclassicism is the major influence found in his work.

Sonata D (Henn 1959). 13 p. Alla breve, Andantino, Vivace. Clear linear and rhythmic idiom. M-D.

FRANCISCO MIGNONE (1897-) Brazil

Portuguese, Indian and Negro elements are combined in Mignone's music. His piano style is romantic in conception and full of rich sonorities. Many other piano works are published by companies in Brazil.

Congada (Ric 1928). Brilliant Brazilian dance. M-D.

Lenda Brasileira (EBM 1923, 1928, 1930). Four dramatic ballades, rewarding to study and play.

1. Atmospheric, restful, sonorous climax, quiet closing. M-D.
2. Short, arpeggio figuration, subtle. M-D.
3. Recitative-like passages, sudden dynamic changes, ferocious. M-D.
4. Flowing, brilliant climax, peaceful closing. M-D.

Tango Brasileira (EBM). Double sixths present problems. M-D.

Four Sonatinas (Ric 1951). All are short, one or two movements, clever rhythmic treatment contrasted with varied moods. Int. to M-D.

Quasi Modinha (EBM 1940). Melodic, samba rhythms. Int.

Miudinho (EBM). Crisp, rhythmic. Int.

Crianças Brincando (EBM 1934). Brilliant, some dissonance, percussive, alternating hands. Int.

Six Preludes (Ric). Varied moods, mainly rhythmic. Int. to M-D.

Sonata No. 1 (Ric 1941). Three movements, strong melodic writing, bitonal sonorities but tonal. M-D.

See: Sister Marion Verhaalen, "Francisco Mignone: His Music for Piano," Inter-American Music Bulletin, No. 79, November 1970-February 1971, 1-36.

GEORGES MIGOT (1891-) France

Migot writes in a highly linear style.

4 Nocturnes (Leduc 1935). Interesting ideas, wandering, improvisatory style.

Le Zodiaque: 12 Etudes de Concert (Leduc 1933). His most solid contribution to piano literature. D.

Sonatine; sur les touches blanches pour les enfants et les musiciens (Leduc 1952).

Le calendrier du petit berger (Leduc c. 1934). 2 volumes. Int.

Préludes pour le piano en deux livres (Lemoine c. 1927).

Sonate-Polonia (Leduc 1939).

Trois Epigrammes (Senart).

Le petit fablier (Leduc 1930). 8 pieces of intermediate difficulty.

Prélude (Leduc).

La Fête de la Bergère (Senart 1924). 19 p.

Le tombeau de Dufault (Senart 1923). 3 pieces.

La Nimura: dance (Leduc 1935).

La Ségue: danse lente (Leduc).

MARCEL MIHALOVICI (1898-) France, born Rumania

Chanson, Pastorale and Danse Op. 32 (Sal). In popular Rumanian style. M-D.

Quatre Caprices (ESC 1928). Primitive rhythms exploited. M-D.

Cinq Bagatelles (ESC 1934). Varied moods and difficulty. No. 4, Toccata, is most effective.

Ricercari Op. 46 (Heugel 1941). 21 minutes. Free variations on an eight-bar passacaglia theme, variations grouped into eleven movements. Broad-scale, chromatic, sonorous, virtuoso technique necessary. D.

Quatre Pastorales Op. 62 (Heugel). Short, chromatic, colorful, No. 2 is toccata-like. M-D.

Trois Pièces Nocturnes Op. 63 (Heugel 1948-51). Impromptu, Rêve, Epilogue. Light, colorful sketches. M-D.

ANDRÁS MIHÁLY (1917-) Hungary

2 Pieces in Old Style (EMB 1961). M-D.
No. 1: fugal, requires large span.

No. 2: Presto, flowing 6/8 meter, thin-texture works up to thick-textured climax. Many accidentals but tonal. Essentially folk-derived.

Ciaconna (EMB).

DARIUS MILHAUD (1892-) France

Milhaud uses a variety of techniques, both old and new. Polytonality, contrapuntal textures, folksong and jazz are all utilized in generous measure. In addition, contrasting moods of tenderness and gaiety have been popular with this prolific composer. Much of the music is M-D, with the two sonatas being the main exceptions.

Suite en cinq parties (Durand 1913). One of Milhaud's most successful pieces. M-D. Lent, Vif et clair, Lourd et rhythmé, Lent et grave, Modéré—animé.

Sonata No. 1 (Sal 1916). Décidé, Pastoral, Rhythmé. Polytonal treatment, folklike melodies, exploits full use of keyboard. M-D.

Printemps (ESC 1915-1920). Two books. Three pieces in each, short, varied. Int.

Saudades do Brazil (ESC 1921). Two volumes. Int. to M-D.

I: Sorocaba, Botafogo, Leme, Copacabana, Ipanema, Gavea.

II: Corcovado, Tijuca, Paineras, Sumaré, Laranjeiras, Paysandu.

Dances in popular Brazilian style employing bitonality, tango and habanera rhythms, changing sonorities, varied figuration, each two pages in length. Titles are names of different sections in Rio de Janeiro.

Trois Rag-Caprices (UE 1922). Dated but clever rhythms in ragtime style. No. 2 is easiest.

L'Automme (Sal 1932). Septembre, Alfama, Adieu. The first two pieces are brisk, require good double-note, broken-chord and octave technique. Adieu is easier, somewhat contrapuntal, song-like.

Quatre Romances sans Paroles (Sal 1933). Short, lyric. Int.

L'Album de Madame Bovary (Enoch 1933). Seventeen short, sensitive pieces from the film *Madame Bovary.* Int.

Four Sketches (Mer 1941). Four pieces of M-D. Eglogue, Madrigal, Alameda, Sobre la Loma. Rhumba rhythm in Sobre la Loma.

The Household Muse (EV 1941). Three volumes. Fifteen short lyric sketches depicting activities such as Cooking, Laundry, The Son Who Paints, etc. Int.

Une Journée (Mer 1946). Five lyric miniatures. Int.
L'Aube, La Matinée, Midi, L'Après-Midi, Le Crépuscule.

L'Enfant Aime (MCA 1948). Five short children's pieces. Chromatic. Not easy.

Sonata No. 2 (Heugel 1949). Alerte; Léger; Doucement; Rapide. Transparent textures, linear movement, arid. M-D.

Le Candélabre à Sept Branches (Southern 1951). The Seven-Branched Candelabrum.
A suite of seven pieces based on the festivals that make up the Jewish Calendar: New Year, Day of Atonement, Feast of the Tabernacles, Resistance of the Maccabees, Feast of Esther, Passover, Feast of Weeks. Varied moods, styles and difficulty.

Accueil Amical. Pièces enfantines (Heugel 1943-1948). Seventeen short easy pieces. In the same tradition as *Album for the Young.*

Hymne de Glorification (ESC 1954). Polytonal, bright, pretentious. M-D.

Sonatine (EMT 1956). Décidé; Modéré; Alerte. More dissonance than in most of his other piano works. Each movement ends quietly. M-D.

The Joys of Life (Belwin-Mills). Six contrasting movements. M-D.

The Globetrotter Suite (Belwin-Mills).

CHARLES MILLS (1914-) USA

Mills studied composition with Aaron Copland, Roger Sessions and Roy Harris.

3 Bagatelles (ACA). 4 minutes.

30 Penitential Preludes (ACA).

Sonata No. 1 (ACA). 15 minutes. Toccata, Aria and Fugue. Clear form, clear textures. M-D.

Sonata No. 2 (ACA). 24 minutes. Three movements, well-contrasted. Much dissonance. D.

Sonatina No. 1 E (ACA). 7 minutes

Sonatinas Nos. 3, 4 (ACA).

Sonatine No. 6 F♯ (ACA 1958). 3 movements. Maestoso-Allegro, Adagietta, Vivace. 14 p. Strong, tonal, vigorous. M-D.

Sonatine No. 9 D (ACA 1945). M-D.
Allegretto grazioso: thin textures.
Andante sostenuto: clever rhythmic treatment.
Allegretto con moto: PP-FFFF.
Poco maestoso-vivace: toccatalike.

ALBERT MOESCHINGER (1897-) Switzerland

Strict polyphony, Reger, romantic and impressionist harmonic vocabulary have all exerted an influence on Moeschinger's style.

Toccata I Op. 30a (Br 1930).

Toccata II Op. 30b (Br 1930). Easiest of the three.

Toccata III Op. 72 (Br 1945).

Suite D 'un cahier valaisan Op. 63 (Br 1944). In style of Honegger and Poulenc.

Sonatine Op. 66 (Vogel). D.

Leichte Klavierstücke und Lieder (Krompholz). Easy.

ROBERT MOEVS (1920-   ) USA

Sonata (ESC 1950). D.
1. Preludio: toccatalike, modal.
2. Aria: modal, melancholy, homophonic.
3. Canone: tricky perpetual motion.
4. Rondo: many skips, striking climax.

Fantasia, sopra un motivo (ESC 1951).
Difficult 12-tone display piece.

FEDERICO MOMPOU (1893-   ) Spain

Mompou's miniature impressionist tone-poems are steeped in the folk music of his native Catalonia. Lack of bar lines, key signatures and cadences are characteristic of his style. His understatement recalls Satie.

Scènes d'Enfants (Sal 1915). Five short, colorful descriptive pieces. Int.

Suburbis (Sal 1916-17). Five picturesque suburban scenes. M-D.

Cancion y Danza 1-4 (UME); 5, 7 (EBM); 5-12 (Sal). In popular Spanish style. M-D.

Cantos Magicos (UME 1919). Five short varied works. Span of tenth required.

Impressions Intimes (UME 1911-1914). Nine short charming pieces. M-D.

Fêtes lointaines (Sal 1920). Six dancelike pieces. Int.

Trois Variations (ESC 1926). Les soldats, Courtoisie, Le crapaud. Mainly harmonized melodies. Int.

Dialogues (ESC 1926). Two declamatory, atmospheric pieces, widely spaced figuration. M-D.

Paysages (Sal). Two pieces: La fontaine et la cloche, Le lac. M-D.

Quatre Préludes (Heugel 1928). Short, varied moods, diatonic melodic writing, delicate, folklike melodies. Int.

Musica Callada (Sal 1959). Two volumes. Nine pieces, chromatic. Int.

Variations on a Theme by Chopin (Sal 1961). Twelve variations and a final Lento, based on Prelude A. Variation 3 is for LH alone. M-D.

Six Préludes (Sal 1962). No. 6 for LH alone. M-D.

Charmes (ESC c. 1925). Six small sketches, subtle, sensitive. Int.

MARIUS MONNIKENDAM (1896-) The Netherlands

Monnikendam studied in Paris with Vincent d'Indy.

Le Carillon de Cythère (Senart).

Six inventions à deux voix (Senart 1928).

XAVIER MONTSALVATGE (1912-) Spain

Tres Divertimentos (Southern). 3 Divertissements on Themes of Forgotten Composers. Bitonal. M-D.

1. Brisk: marchlike.
2. Tango: with a few unexpected twists.
3. Spanish rhythms: polychords, fast tempo.

DOUGLAS MOORE (1893-1969) USA

Suite for Piano (CF c. 1951).

Prelude: changing meters, bright tune supported by two voices, con brio.

Reel: complex 6/8, evolves into florid writing.

Dancing School: thin textures, bouncing rhythms, melody in unison octaves.

Barn Dance: involved, fun, skips, needs facility.

Air: clear sonorities, sustained melody.

Procession: marchlike allegro moderato requiring steady staccato octaves, good accentuation, energetic. M-D.

Museum Piece (Alexrod). Tonal, colorful, short. Int.

Three Pieces from *Masters of Our Day* series (CF).

Careful Etta: humorous minuet. Easy.

Fiddlin' Joe: captures spirit of an old New England folk dance. Easy.
Grievin' Annie: suggestive of an American folk-ballad. Easy.

Prelude (TP).

OSCAR MORAWETZ (1917-   ) Canada, born Czechoslovakia

Morawetz received his musical education in Prague, Vienna and Paris. At the Royal Conservatory in Toronto he worked under Alberto Guerrero and Leo Smit. He teaches at the Royal Conservatory in Toronto.

Fantasy, Elegy and Toccata (Leeds 1956).
A large, sonatalike tonal work, effective and colorful. Elegy is modal. Uses canon and chordal counterpoint. D.

10 Preludes (CMC 1964).
Large, contrasted pieces, each well-developed. Too long as a complete set but a selection could be effective. M-D to D.

Scherzo (Bo&H 1948).

Suite for Piano (Leeds, Canada 1968). D.
Prelude: dissonant, changing meters, bold gestures.
Nocturne: quiet opening, dramatic climax, PP closing, span of ninth required.
Dance: rhythmic drive, martellato, changing meters.

THOMAS MORLEY (1557-ca. 1603) Great Britain

Keyboard Works (T. Dart-S&B 1959) Two Volumes.
5 Pavans, 4 Galliards, an Alman, Fantasia, Nancy (a single piece), and a set of 7 variations on Goe From My Window. Excellent commentary, urtext.

FVB contains 9 compositions:
Alman: Bright, uneven strains make for freshness. II, 171.
Fantasia: An extended fugue. II, 57.
Goe From My Window: This same piece, with slight changes is attributed to John Munday. A set of variations on a popular tune. I, 42.

La Volta: Set by William Byrd. This piece is erroneously attributed to Morley. II, 188.
Nancie: Theme and 2 variations, the third variation greatly elaborated. I, 57.
Pavan on Dowland's *Lachrymae:* A serious, complex piece in 3 large sections. II, 173.
Galiarda: Follows the above Pavan, also in 3 large sections. More constant figurations. II, 177.
Pavana F: II, 209.
Galliarda F: II, 213.

HAROLD MORRIS (1890-1964) USA

Sonata No. 4 (Composers Press 1941). Four movements. Strong rhythms permeate the opening movement, followed by a short, comical staccato Scherzino, nocturne-like slow movement. Concludes with a brilliant, tarantella-like movement. M-D.

FINN MORTENSEN (1922-) Norway

Mortensen developed from a classical background and has moved to a uniquely personal serial style.

Sonatina Op. 1 (NMO). 8 minutes. 3 movements.
The last movement, a three-voice fugue, is more difficult than the first two movements.

Sonata Op. 7 (NMO). 9½ minutes. 2 movements.
The final movement is a difficult fugue.

Fantasy and Fugue Op. 13 (NMO). 9 minutes.
Resembles a two-movement sonata, serial. This work was performed at the International Society of Contemporary Music meeting in 1960.

IGNAZ MOSCHELES (1794-1870) Bohemia, Czechoslovakia

Collection complète des oeuvres composés pour le piano. (Société pour la publication de Musique Classique et Moderne).
Vol. 1. Ouvrages pour piano seul.
Vol. 2. Piano seul; Piano et violon.
Vol. 3. Musique à 4 mains.

Vol. 4. Septeur, sextuor, trio et divers.
Vol. 5. Musique pour piano seul.

Sonata mélancolique f♯ Op. 49 (Augener). See: Newman *Thirteen Keyboard Sonatas of the 18th and 19th Centuries*—UNC. See: SSB, 189-90.
One-movement work, eclectic style.

3 Concert Etudes Op. 51 (CFP). La Forza, La Legerezza, Il Capriccio. Virtuoso, bravura.

24 Studies for Perfection Op. 70 (Ric) (UE).

12 Characteristic Etudes Op. 95 (Ric) (Augener).

Canon à la Septieme (Musica Obscura).

MORITZ MOSZKOWSKI (1854-1925) Poland

Salon music of the excellent variety that Moszkowski composed can often be used to unravel thorny technical problems. This music is much more appealing than many etudes and technical studies. Lockwood says that "the player of Moszkowski's music needs well-developed fingers capable of executing spidery passage work and wide skips with delicacy and accuracy, without both of which qualities and pieces make little appeal." (Albert Lockwood, *Notes on the Literature of the Piano,* Da Capo reprint, 1968, p. 143.) (CFP) (Ric) and (Augener) publish many of his piano works.

Spanish Dances Op. 12 (CFP) (Ric). Originally written for piano duet but by "popular demand" arranged for piano solo by the composer. Exotic superficial picturesque quality.

Scherzino F Op. 18/2 (GS).

Mélodie Italienne Op. 38/4 (GS).

Etincelles Op. 36/6 (GS). Superb staccato study.

Jongleurin Op. 52/4 (CFP). Clever, descriptive.

20 Petites Etudes Op. 91 (Philipp-Leduc). Very musical short pieces, each one emphasizes one aspect of piano playing.

15 Etudes de Virtuosité Op. 72 ("per aspera") (Enoch) (GS). Nos. 6 and 12 are popular.

Caprice Espagnol Op. 37 (CFP) (Ric). Long, effective dance piece, study for fast repeated notes.

Guitarre Op. 45 (CFP) (Ric.)

3 Concert Studies Op. 24 (Ric). G♭, c♯, C.

Menuett Op. 77/10 (Schott) (Ric).

Etude de Legato Op. 81/3 (Schott).

School of Double Notes Op. 64 (Ric).

Three Pieces in Dance Forms Op. 17 (Musica Obscura). Polonaise D; Minuet G; Waltz A.

Radio City Album of Selected Piano Compositions of Moszkowski (EBM). Mazurkas Op. 10/3, Op. 38/3, Scherzino Op. 18/2, Etude Op. 18/3, Melodie Op. 18/1, Polonaise Op. 18/5, Etincelles (Sparks) Op. 36/6, Guitarre Op. 45/2, Serenata Op. 15/1, Valse Brillante A♭, Valse Mélancholique Op. 31/3, Air de Ballet Op. 36/5.

JOSÉ VIANNA DA MOTTA (1868-1948) Portugal

Da Motta studied with Liszt in Weimar and eventually became Director of the Lisbon Conservatory. During his life he was considered one of the leading musicians of Portugal.

Ballada Op. 16 (Sassetti c. 1957). Romantic, bravura writing. For many years a required piece in piano exams at the Lisbon Conservatory.

Serenata Op. 8 (Sassetti).

Tres Improvisos Op. 18 (Sassetti).

Barcarola Op. 17 (Moreira de Sá).

Chula Op. 9/2 (Araujo).

Rhapsodia Portuguesa No. 4 (Neuparth & Carneiro).

Scenas Portuguezas Op. 15 (Sassetti). 3 pieces.

Vito: Danca popular Op. 11 (Sassetti).

LEOPOLD MOZART (1719-1787) Germany

Notebook for Nannerl (H. Schulungler-Schott). 16 pieces including Menuets, Marches, Scherzo, Allegro, Andante.

Notebook for Wolfgang (H. Schulungler-Schott). 32 pieces, some by other composers.

See: Leopold Mozart, *A Treatise on the Fundamental Principles of Violin Playing.* Translated by Editha Knocker. London: Oxford University Press, 1951. This treatise is one of the great sources from which the spirit and technique of baroque music can be reconstructed.

WOLFGANG AMADEUS MOZART (1756-1791) Austria

EDITIONS OF THE SONATAS:

(Broder-TP) 18 sonatas in 1 volume: a comprehensive critical edition with a penetrating preface that describes ornamentation practice of the period.

(Lampe-Henle) 20 sonatas in 2 volumes: a comprehensive critical edition with suggestions for performance of ornaments, added fingering, careful distinction is made between the marks Mozart used for staccato indications.

(H. & R. Scholz-UE, Salzburg Mozarteum Edition). 18 sonatas in two volumes.

(Rudorff-Br&H) 20 sonatas, a critical edition published originally in 1895.

(K) a reprint of the (Rudorff-Br&H). 20 sonatas. Urtext available in two volumes. Each sonata is also available separately. This edition omits many footnotes from the Rudorff edition.

(Martienssen-CFP) 20 sonatas: a good practical edition.

(E. Fischer-Curci) a personal edition with text in French, English, Germany and Italian.

(F. Taylor-Augener) an "instructive" edition.

(Georgii-Schott) has 14 of the sonatas published separately. Indicated by each sonata discussed in the following text.

(Bischoff-WH).

(Bowen, Raymer-ABRSM). Two volumes, commentary. Each sonata available separately.

The Sonatas: Köchel's original numbers (and Einstein's revisions) are given. See: SCE, 482-89.

The first six sonatas were written 1775-76. The first five were composed in Salzburg and the sixth in Munich. Early sonatas are based on the graceful Italian Rococo style.

Sonata C K 279 (189d) (Georgii-Schott) (WH). Allegro; Andante; Allegro. Improvisatory first movement, expressive Andante, Haydn influence in third movement.

Sonata F K 280 (189e) (Georgii-Schott). Allegro assai; Adagio; Presto. Haydn influence especially in slow movement. Effective use of rests in last movement.

Sonata B♭ K 281 (189f) (WH). Allegro; Andante amoroso; Rondo: Allegro. First two movements Haydnlike. Rondo has unusual dynamic markings and some improvisational-like passages.

Sonata E♭ K 282 (189g) (Lampe-Henle) (Georgii-Schott). Adagio; Menuetto I and II; Allegro. Haydn influence, unusual form. Dynamic contrast in Minuets. Spirited finale.

Sonata G K 283 (189th) (Georgii-Schott) (Podolsky, Jonas-SB) (Ching-Prowse). Allegro; Andante; Presto.
J. C. Bach influence, graceful Allegro, flowing Andante, delightful final movement in SA design.

Sonata D K 284 (205b) Allegro; Rondeau en Polonaise; Andante; Theme and (12) Variations.
In 1777 Mozart said "this sonata sounds exquisite on Stein's pianoforte," Mozart's favorite pianoforte maker. (Letter from Mozart to his father, October 17-18, 1777 translated by Emily Anderson. *The Letters of Mozart & His Family,* II, London: Macmillan, 1938, 479-80). The Allegro is orchestral in style. More advanced virtuoso writing in the whole sonata. Rondeau en Polonaise, theme keeps returning in more elaborate textures each time. Final movement is probably Mozart's finest set of variations. Unusually effective. D.

The second group of sonatas dates from 1777-78 and was written in Mannheim and Paris. The LH participates more fully in these sonatas and the middle register of the keyboard is cultivated in a new way.

Sonata C K 309 (284b) (Georgii-Schott). Allegro con spirito; Andante un poco adagio; Rondo: Allegretto grazioso. One of the most effective of the sonatas. Watch the "FP" markings in the middle movement: this means only a small accent for expressive reasons.

Sonata a K 310 (300d) (Georgii-Schott). Allegro maestoso; Andante cantabile con espressione; Presto. The first sonata in minor. Tragic, pathetic in style, probably related to the fact that Mozart's mother died at this time.
Allegro is broad, majestic, marchlike. Care should be taken not to play the sixteenth notes in the second subject too fast. Single-note repetition in the slow movement shows the influence of Johann Schobert, an acquaintance of Mozart. Landowska thinks this movement "may be a minuet or a sarabande step." (*Landowska on Music*. Ed. by Denise Restout. New York: Stein and Day, 1964, 321.) Presto is an agitated rondo with tricky leaps and persistent breathless rhythmic pattern.

Sonata D K 311 (284c) (Georgii-Schott). Allegro con spirito; Andante con espressione; Rondo; Allegro. Mannheim influence is seen in the orchestral conception of this work. In the brilliant opening movement, themes return in reverse order in the recapitulation. The Andante con espressione reflects a childlike, innocent, simplicity. Many contrasts characterize the large brilliant Rondo movement.

Sonata C K 330 (300h) (Georgii-Schott). Allegro moderato; Andante cantabile; Allegretto. Smaller dimensions than the preceding three sonatas. First and last movements are in SA design. The slow movement is in minuet and trio form. The last four bars were added at a later time and are as elegant as anything Mozart ever wrote.

Sonata A K 331 (300i) (Schnabel-EBM) (Lampe-Henle) (Georgii-Schott) (Podolsky, Jonas-SB) (J. Ching-Prowse) (WH). Andante grazioso; Menuetto; Alla Turca: Allegretto.
Contains no movement in SA design. Careful attention to Mozart's articulation must be observed. Last movement must not go too fast or it loses its charm.

Sonata F K 332 (300k). Allegro; Adagio; Allegro assai. Change of mode plays a large part in the Allegro. Adagio contains lavish ornamentation, influenced by J. C. Bach. Final movement in SA design is brilliant, contrasts dramatic and lyric elements.

Sonata B♭ K 333 (315c). Allegro; Andante cantabile; Allegretto grazioso. Lyric quality throughout this sonata. Slow movement contains some bold harmonic usage. Cadenza in the last movement is a concerto characteristic. Wanda Landowska (BB) has written an effective cadenza for this movement.

Sonata c K 457 (Schnabel-EBM) (Georgii-Schott) (WH). Allegro (autograph) Molto Allegro (first edition); Adagio; Molto allegro (autograph) Allegro assai (first edition). This work and the Fantasia c, K 475 were dedicated to a pupil, Thérèse van Trattner. They were originally conceived as two separate works but Mozart let them be published together. Opening and closing movements are intense, dramatic and carry over some of the character from the Fantasia. The middle movement is one of Mozart's finest slow movements: elaborate, florid and highly expressive.

Sonata F K 533 and 494. Allegro (1788); Andante (1788); Rondo: Andante (1786). Mozart permitted these three movements to be published together. Virtuoso arpeggio-writing appears in the broad concertolike Allegro. Andante is profoundly emotional with unusual harmonic clashes. The Rondo may be performed separately.

Sonata C K 545 (Lampe-Henle) (Georgii-Schott) (Ching-Prowse) (WH). Allegro; Andante; Rondo: Allegretto.
This work was intended by Mozart for the instruction of beginners. It was not published during his lifetime.

Sonata F K 547a (Anh. 135, Anh. 138a) (Georgii-Schott). Allegro; Rondo: Allegretto; Thema: Allegretto.
First and last movements of this work come from a piano and violin sonata, K 547. The second movement is a transcription from K 545. It is likely that Mozart made the arrangements but we are not sure if he wanted them combined into a sonata. Einstein thinks he did.

Sonata B♭ K 570 (Georgii-Schott). Allegro; Adagio; Allegretto. Solo piano, and piano and violin versions exist. This is one of the most beauifully formed of all the sonatas. Contrapuntal interest is found throughout the complete work.

Sonata D K 576. Allegro; Adagio; Allegretto. Imitative treatment in the Allegro recalls J. S. Bach. The profound Adagio contains some written-out ornaments, unusual for Mozart. The Allegretto main theme, simple and usually piano, contrasts with forte virtuoso passages. This sonata presents the most technical problems of all the sonatas.

Viennese Sonatinas

These works were originally written for two clarinets and bassoon. Editions for piano are transcriptions unknown to Mozart. (Rowley-Hin) (IMC) (Prostakoff-GS) (Rehberg-Schott).

EDITIONS OF THE VARIATIONS:

(Zimmerman, Lampe-Henle). A comprehensive critical edition with sources identified and suggestions for interpreting ornaments. 15 sets, plus 3 sets in the Appendix including: a fragment consisting of a theme and 2 variations; Theme and 6 variations from the clarinet Quintet K 581 (K Anh. 137); 8 variations Come un agnello, K 460 (454a).

(K. v. Fischer-Br). The *Neue Mozart Ausgabe,* Series 9, Part 26. It contains 14 sets plus 4 fragments from incomplete sets.

(K) 17 sets.

(Bruell-IMC) 15 sets.

The early sets of variations mainly employ melodic embroidery. In a few later sets the melody is completely changed. The norm for Mozart is a slow variation (next to last) with the final variation in a fast tempo. Usually one variation is in a minor mode if the theme is in major.

8 Variations G on a Dutch Song K 24 (K Anh. 208) (1766) (Br). Baroque pattern employed: note values in each variation progress toward shorter durations. Lovely adagio.

7 Variations D on Willem van Nassau K 25 (1766) (Br). Theme is the old Netherlands national anthem. More contrast between variations seen in this set.

6 Variations G on "Mio caro Adone" from *La Fiera di Venezia* of Salieri, K 180 (173c) (1773). Theme is transformed rather than embellished.

12 Variations on a Minuet of J. C. Fischer K 179 (189a) (1774). Fischer was a famous oboist who, for a while, was at the Mannheim Court. Theme comes from the final movement of his oboe concerto. Some virtuoso writing.

12 Variations E♭ on the Air "Je suis Lindor" K 354 (299a) (1778). Theme comes from Count Almaviva's aria in the first act of Beaumarchais's *Le Barbier de Seville* by Nicholas Dezède (1745?-1792?). Each variation exploits a different figuration, melodic chromatic filler, broken octaves, cadenza passages.

12 Variations C on "Ah, vous dirai-je, Maman" K 265 (300e) (1778) Paris. (Zimmerman, Lampe-Henle) (Br) (GS) (Schott) (K) (IMC) (Durand). Pedagogic implication by use of scales, arpeggi, varying touches. One of the most charming sets.

12 Variations E♭ on "La belle Françoise" K 353 (300f) (1778) Paris. All variations begin and end in similar fashion except Nos. 1 and 9.

9 Variations C on "Lison Dormait" K 264 (315d) (1778) Paris. Theme comes from an air from opera *Julie* by Nicholas Dezède. Exploits trill (variation 4), broken octaves (variations 6 and 7), dramatic quality (variation 8), 2-octave glissando in sixths (variation 9).

8 Variations F on March from Grétry's opera *Les Mariages Samnites* K 352 (374c) (1781) Vienna.

6 Variations F on "Salve tu, Domine" from Paisiello's *I Filosofi Imaginarii* K 398 (416e) (1783) Vienna. Theme is in two sections. Last three variations are joined by cadenzas. An excellent program-opener.

10 Variations G on "Unser dummer Pöbel meint" from Gluck's opera *Pilger von Mekka* K 455 (1784) Vienna. (Br) (Zimmerman, Lampe-Henle) (Nag). Much humor in this set, one of the very finest. Trills, cadenza, wide keyboard range, many contrasts.

12 Variations B♭ on an Allegretto K 500 (1786) Vienna. Theme is possibly by Mozart. Influence of Clementi may be observed in new idiomatic technique, triplet figuration, chords in upper register, etc.

6 Variations F on an Allegretto K 54 (1788) Vienna. Third movement of violin sonata K 547 plus a new fourth variation arranged by Mozart for solo piano.

9 Variations D on a Minuet of Duport K 573 (1789) Potsdam. See: Eva and Paul Badura-Skoda *Interpreting Mozart on the Keyboard,* 133.

8 Variations F on "Ein Weib ist das herrlichste Ding K 613 (1791) Vienna. Theme from an operetta *Der dumme Gärtner oder Die zween Anton* by Benedict Schack and Franz Gerl.
See: Eva and Paul Badura-Skoda *Interpreting Mozart on the Keyboard,* 236-8.

8 Variations A on "Come un agnello" from Sarti's opera *Fra i due litiganti* K 460 (454a) (1784) Vienna. Brilliant passagework (variations 1 and 3), bass melody (variation 5), LH over RH (variation 6), cadenza (variation 7). Kurt von Fischer doubts the authenticity of this work .

EDITIONS OF THE MISCELLANEOUS WORKS:
(Wallner, Lampe-Henle) *Klavierstücke.* A comprehensive urtext edition containing works from the earliest period: Menuetts K 1, 2, Allegro K 3, Menuetts K 4, 5, Allegro K 9 (5a), Klavierstücke F, Menuetts K 61g II, 94 (73h). Mature works: Sonata movement g K 312, Fantasie C K 395 (300g), 8 Minuets K 315a (315g), Sonata movement B♭ K 400 (372a), Praeludium (Fantasie) and Fuge C K 394 (383a), Fantasie c K 396 (385f), Fantasie d K 397 (385g), March C K 408 (383e), part of a Suite C: Ouverture, A, C, K 399 (385i), March funèbre del Signor Maestro Contrapunto C K 453a, Rondo D K 485, Rondo a K 511, 6 Deutsche Tänze K 509, Adagio b K 540, Gigue K 574, Menuett D K 355 (594a), Andantino E♭ K 236 (588b). Appendix includes "The London Notebook" (1764-65). This con-

tains 38 short works (Minuettos, Sonata movements, Rondeaus, etc.), Sonata F K 547 (Anh. 135, Andante F for a Waltz in a monica.

(Soldan-CFP). *Piano Pieces.*

(CFP) also has a volume of *Selected Piano Pieces* including Fantasy and Fugue C K 394, Fantasies C, d K 396-7, Rondos D, F, a K 485, 494, 511, Andante F K 616, Suite C K 399, Adagio b K 540, Minuet D K 355, Gigue G K 574.

(H. and R. Scholz-Mozarteum Edition-UE) *Rondos and Fantasias.*

(K) *Miscellaneous Works.*

(Klee-GS) *12 Piano Pieces.* Adagio K 540, Allegro K 312, Fantasias d K 397 E♭ K 396, c K 475, Gigue K 574, Minuetto K 355, Ouverture, Suite K 399, Romanza K 205, Rondos D K 485, a K 511, F K 616.

20 Piano Compositions by Mozart (C. Reinecke-OD).

Mozart Album (M. Kiadas-EMB).
9 Variations on "Lison dormait" K 264, 12 variations on "Ah, vous dirai-je Maman" K 265, Fantasie c K 396, Fantasie d K 397, Rondo D K 485, Rondo a K 511, Adagio b K 540, 9 Variations on a Menuet of Duport K 573. Performing edition sensitively edited.

See: Eva and Paul Badura-Skoda, *Interpreting Mozart on the Keyboard.* Translated by Leo Black. London: Barrie and Rockliff, 1962.

A. Hyatt King, "Mozart's Piano Music," MR, 5, 1944, 163-91.

John Kirkpatrick, "Mozart's D minor Fantasy (K. 397, KE 385g)," Cornell University Music Review, 11, 1968, 15-17.

Wilton Mason, "Melodic Unity in Mozart's Piano Sonata, K. 332," MR, 22, February 1961, 28-33.

Hans Neumann, "The Two Versions of Mozart's Rondo K. 494," The Music Forum, 1, 1967, 1-34.

J. F. Porte, "Mozart's Pianoforte Works," ML, 7/4, 1926, 374-7.

Thomas Richner, *Orientation for Interpreting Mozart's Piano Sonatas*. New York: Columbia Teacher's College Press, 1953.

Fritz Rothschild, "Mozart's Pianoforte Music—Some Aspects of Its Interpretation," The Score, 9, September 1954, 3-11.

Eileen Stainkamph, *The Form and Analysis of Mozart's Pianoforte Sonatas*. Melbourne: Allans Music (Australia), 1967, 35 p.

ROBERT MUCZYNSKI (1929-) USA

Muczynski received his formal training at DePaul University where he studied both piano and composition with Alexander Tcherepnin. He is currently on the music faculty of the University of Arizona.

6 Preludes Op. 6 (GS 1961). 15 p. MC, requires agility. M-D.

Suite Op. 13 (GS 1960). 9 minutes. 6 movements: Festival, Flight, Vision, Labyrinth, Phantom, Scherzo. Polytonal triads, all movements show fine craftsmanship and pianistic imagination. M-D.

Toccata Op. 15 (GS 1971). Chromatic, driving, hemiola, thin textures, dramatic gestures, imposing climax. M-D.

A Summer Journal Op. 19 (GS). 7 pieces, varied moods.

Fables Op. 21 (GS). 9 pieces in a fresh diatonic idiom.

Second Sonata Op. 22 (GS 1969). 33 p. A strong work.
Allegro: SA design.
Con moto, ma non tanto: lyrical, flows easily.
Molto andante: somber, climactic, dirgelike.
Allegro molto: monothematic.

Diversions Op. 23 (GS). 9 varied, short, chromatic pieces for students, MC. Int.

Sonatina F Op. 52 (AMP 1949). 3 cheerful movements, large LH span required. M-D.

GOTTLIEB MUFFAT (1690-1770) Germany

French influence predominates in Muffat's writing. Thin textures are especially prevalent in his keyboard suites.

Componimenti Musicali per il Cembalo (1735-39). Facsimile edition (BB), DTOe Vol. 7.
6 suites and a Chaconne G with 38 variations (uses the same bass that Bach used in the first 8 bars of the *Goldberg Variations*). Opening movements (Overture, Prelude and Fantasie) precede the usual suite movements (A C S G). Various optional dances are inserted before and sometimes after the Gigue, such as Air, M & Trio, Adagio, Finale, Rigaudon, Hornpipe, La Hardiesse, La Coquette, Menuet en Cornes de Chasse (Minuet in Imitation of Horns). Also contains a table of ornaments. Unusually fine suites. Suite II g, is contained in *The Art of the Suite* (Y. Pessl), *Partitas and Pieces* (Georgii-Schott), *Old Masters* (K).

12 Toccatas and 72 Versetl (ca. 1726) Facsiimile edition (BB), DTOe Vol. 58.
Each toccata is followed by 6 short fugues. Originally used for alternating with the choir during vesper services. Fine for teaching purposes, easy but substantial music.

PAUL MÜLLER (1898-) Switzerland

Müller teaches counterpoint at the Zürich Conservatory.

6 Klavierstücke Op. 10 (Hug). Linear, show a strong tie with the past but contain fresh and original ideas. M-D.

WALTER MÜLLER (1899-) Switzerland

Müller is Director of the Basel Musik-Akademie.

2 Sonatinas Op. 8 (Reinhardt Edition). M-D.

JOHN MUNDAY (1563?-1630) Great Britain

Five of his works are contained in the FVB:

Fantasia: An early example of program music: Faire Wether, Lightening, Thunder, Faire Wether, Thunder, etc. Ends in A Cleare Day. I, 23.

Fantasia: Contrapuntal, running passages. I, 19.

Goe From My Window: A set of variations on a popular tune. Changing figurations. I, 153.

Robin: Three sections, variation. Each section has shorter note values. I, 66.

Munday's Joy: Short three-section character piece with section three a variation of section two. II, 449.

MODEST MUSSORGSKY (1839-1881) Russia

Sämtliche Werke (Pavel Lamm-USSR 1928-34). Piano music contained in Volume VIII.

Pictures from an Exhibition (1874) (Lamm-IMC) (Thumer-Schott) (Casella-Ric) (Dallapiccola-Carisch) (CFP) (K) (Augener) (GS). 25 minutes. This unique cycle of 10 pieces is by far his most important work for piano. Musical representations of drawings and paintings by Victor Hartmann, a friend of the composer. The pieces are connected by a "Promenade" theme which also appears in some of the pieces, a fine unifying device. These highly original character pieces are not always the most pianistic but they represent the greatest masterpiece of piano writing to come from the nineteenth-century Russian national school. D.

9 Selected Pieces (Schott). Meditation, Nurse and I, A Tear, Child's Prank, Gopak, In the Village, The Seamstress, Intermezzo, First Punishment. M-D.

8 Selected Pieces (USSR).

2 Piano Pieces (CFP). Intermezzo, Child's Prank. M-D.

Gopak (Schott) (Augener).

JOHANN GOTTFRIED MÜTHEL (1728-1788) Germany

One of J. S. Bach's last pupils, Müthel was a fine keyboard performer who wrote in the expressive (empfindsam) style. His keyboard works show the direct influence of C. P. E. Bach.

Three Sonatas F, G, C (Hoffmann-Erbrecht-Br&H).

Sonata B♭ with 6 variations (Organum K&S). Each in three movements in the FSF order.

Sonata C (Organum-K&S).

2 Ariosi with 12 Variations (Hoffmann-Erbrecht-Br&H).

12 Menuette (Hinnenthal-Br.).

See: Robert G. Campbell, "Johann Gottfried Müthel, 1728- 1788." Vol. I: Life and Works. Vol. II: Music and Catalogue, unpub. diss., Indiana University, 1966.

JOSEF MYSLIVEČEK (1737-1781) Bohemia, Czechoslovakia

4 Rondos

2 Minuets

Sonata D. All are edited by Racek and published by Artia, Vol. 17, MAB.

See: SCE, 227-8.

N

YOSHINAO NAKADA (1923-   ) Japan

Japanese Festival (MCA). 17 pieces for students. Westernized sounds permeate this music. Easy to Int.

Sonata (Japanese Society of Rights of Authors & Composers 1956).

JOHANN GOTTLIEB NAUMANN (1741-1801) Germany

Three Sonatas (H. Eppstein-NMS) (WH). Short, two-movement works, attractive.

10 Stücke. No. 7 in series *Werke aus dem 18. Jahrhundert. Sammlung Sondheimer* (Edition Bernoulli).

Sonata No. 1. No. 17 in same series.

LUYS DE NARVÁEZ (16th century) Spain

El Delphin de Musica (1538) (E. M. Torner-Tracio).
Book I: 8 Fantasias
Book II: 6 Fantasias
Volume of lute music contains some of the earliest examples of variation form. Effective on piano.

A collection containing five extracts from *El Delphin de Musica* (Torner) is available through Centro di estudios historicos, Madrid, Spain.

JORGE ARANDIA NAVARRO (   ) Argentina

Sonata (EAM 1955). A three-sectioned work without break. Bravura virtuoso writing, exciting, style of the Ginastera *Sonata,* for which it would make a good substitute. D.

MANUEL BLASCO DE NEBRA (ca. 1750-1784) Spain

Six Sonatas for Harpsichord or Piano Op. 1 (Robert Parris-UME c. 1964).
The first edition of these sonatas appeared in Madrid in 1780 and seem to be the only extant work by this composer. They are musical and technically demanding. Introduction is excellent, mainly a discussion of the works since little is known about the composer.

Sonata I. See Collection: W. S. Newman: *Thirteen Keyboard Sonatas of the 18th and 19th Century*.

CHRISTIAN GOTTLOB NEEFE (1748-1798) Germany

Twelve Sonatas (1772) Vol. 10 of the *Denkmäler Rheinischer Musik* (Musikverlag Schwann 1961). In 2 volumes. A critical edition of these works, mostly in three movements, a few in two. Rewarding material, should be investigated.

CARL NIELSEN (1865-1931) Denmark

Nielsen was not a brilliant pianist but the piano obviously interested him since he wrote for the instrument throughout most of his creative life. His piano works have great original versatility and deserve more performance.

Five Pieces Op. 3 (WH). Folketona, Humoreske, Arabeske, Mignon, Alfedans. Int.

Symphonic Suite Op. 8 (WH 1894). 16 minutes. Intonation: Maestoso, Quasi allegretto; Andante; Finale: Allegro. Brahms influence, especially in the thick chordal passages. Fresh tonal and harmonic treatment. Sparkling finale very effective, themes of the first three movements are reviewed.

Humoreske-Bagatelles Op. 11 (WH). 6 pieces 13 p. Int.
Good Morning! Good Morning!, The Top, A Little Slow Waltz, The Jumping Jack, Doll's March, The Musical Clock.

Chaconne Op. 32 (WH 1916). 17 p. 10 minutes. D.
Grows from a stark theme and displays a tremendous range of invention.

Theme and Variations Op. 40 (WH 1916). 27 p.

Suite Op. 45 (CFP 1919). 22 minutes. 6 movements. D. Allegretto un pochettino; Poco moderato; Molto adagio e patetico; Allegretto innocente; Allegretto vivo; Allegro non troppo ma vigoroso. His greatest piano contribution. Nielsen's "progressive tonality" is at work here: the key of B♭ gradually supplants the opening key of f♯.

Music for Young and Old (SM 1930). Op. 53. 2 volumes. In five finger position but not easy.

Three Piano Pieces Op. 59 (CFP 1928). 11 minutes. 1. Impromptu: Allegro fluente: grotesque. 2. Molto adagio: mysterious. 3. Allegro non troppo: brilliant. These pieces show the most advanced aspects of his writing.

Klaveralbum (WH). 13 selected pieces.

TAGE NIELSEN (1929-) Denmark

Since 1963 Nielsen has been Director and Professor at the Music Conservatory of Aarhus.

To nocturner for klaver (SPDM 1960-61). 8 p.

SERGE NIGG (1924-) France

Nigg studied with both Messiaen and Leibowitz and has evolved a very complex musical idiom.

Deux Pièces for Piano Op. 5 (Le Chant du Monde 1946). 5 minutes. 12-tone writing with jazz rhythms appearing infrequently.

Lied Op. 8 (ms, Société des Auteurs, Compositeurs 1948). 15 p.

Deuxième Sonate pour Piano (Jobert 1965). 37 p.
Written especially for piano competition at the Paris Conservatory. Very difficult.
Tempo I-II-III-IV: virtuoso writing.
Theme and Variations: five very free variations on a row.
Allegro ruvido e marcato: idea of non-retrogradable rhythms exploited.

BO NILSSON 1937-   ) Sweden

Nilsson is a disciple of Karlheinz Stockhausen.

Quantitäten (UE).
A series of 12 phrases arranged on facing pages to be played in a set order. No tempo marks are given but tempo is determined by speed at which the smallest note values can be played. High pitches sound longer than low pitches. A dynamic scale of 20 steps from 1.0 to 10.5 for P and F is indicated. Nilsson suggests that at concerts the piano should be "equipped with one or more loudspeakers."

JOAQUÍN NIN (1879-1949) Spain

Nin's style is romantic and permeated with Spanish harmonic idioms, guitar and other coloristic effects.

Cadeña de Valses (ESC 1927). A chain of waltzes in Spanish dance style with musical commentary between the first six. An Invocation à la valse is followed by "Messages" to Schubert, Ravel, Chopin and concludes with a Spanish national dance, Homenaje à la Jota. M-D.

Message á Claude Debussy (ESC 1929). An extensive "symphonic sketch", moody Tempo di Habanera. M-D.

Trois Danses Espagnoles (ESC 1938). M-D.
Danza Murciana: 5½ minutes, 6/8 and 3/4 alternating rhythm, cadenzas.
Danza Andaluza: brilliant, fast rhythmic dance on El Vito. Repeated notes.
Secunda Danza Iberica: guitar effects, ornamental cadenzas.

Iberian Dance (ESC 1925). Lengthy, percussive Allegro vivace, sonorous Lento, recitatives, exciting ending. M-D.

Canto de cuña para los Huerfanos d'España (ESC 1928). Long, ornamental berceuse for the orphans of Spain.

Variations sur un thème frivole "1830" (ESC 1934), 17 p. M-D.

JOAQUÍN NIN-CULMELL (1908-) Cuba, born Germany

Nin-Culmell is the son of Joaquín Nin. He studied composition with Paul Dukas in Paris and with Manuel de Falla in Granada.

Sonata Brève (Rongwen 1934). 3 movements FSF. 7½ minutes. Short colorful work employing impressionist techniques, thin textures, span of tenth required. M-D.

Tonadas (Rongwen 1957-59). 4 volumes. Int.
22 short pieces, colorful, pianistic.

3 Impressions (Sal 1931). Habanera; Las mozas del cantaro; Un jardin de Tolède.

PER NÖRGAARD (1932-) Denmark

Nörgaard bases his work on short tonal motives treated in contrapuntal style. Motives undergo rhythmic displacement and several forms of contraction or expansion.

Sonata in One Movement Op. 6 (WH 1952 revised 1956). 13 minutes. Contemporary contrapuntal style, thematic material deftly manipulated. D.

Trifoglio Op. 7 (WH 1953). 15 minutes.

Preludio espansivo e Rondo Op. 9 (WH 1953). 10 minutes.

Sonata No. 2 Op. 20 (WH 1956). 3 movements. 25 minutes. Dynamic contemporary writing. D.

Five Fragments (WH 1961).

Sketches (WH).

Grooving (WH). 14 minutes. Variations, no time or key signatures. Unusual pedal effects.

Nine Piano Pieces Op. 25 (WH). Ostinato technique, principal theme varied in such a way that it logcally returns to its starting point. Contemporary treatment of isorhythmic technique. M-D.

IB NORHOLM (1923-) Denmark

Strofer og marker (Stanzas and Fields) Op. 33 (Engström & Södring). Two types of textures: pointillistic, conventional. Two contrasting cycles of six pieces make up the design.

GUSTAF NORDQVIST (1886-1949) Sweden

Lyriskt poem Om sommaren skona (NMS).

Poetiska tonbilder (AL).

Suite (AL).

Tre pianostycken (AL).

Tva preludier (NMS).

SPENCER NORTON (1909-) USA

Three Etudes for Piano. Commissioned by the Oklahoma MTA and the MTNA 1966. (Available on loan from MTNA).
1. Tempo di Sarabanda: legato study, accompanied melody, rhythmic problems with 5 against 6, 4 against 5, impressionistic. 3½ minutes. M-D.
2. Allegro giusto: rhythmic drive, excellent octave technique required, bristling. M-D.
3. Maestoso: rhapsodic, dramatic, broad rhythmic gestures, tonally centered, chromatic. Advanced pianism required.

VÍTĚZSLAV NOVÁK (1870-1949) Czechoslovakia

Novák used folk inspiration in classic forms, such as the variation, chaconne, and fugue.

Variations on a Theme of Schumann (Artia 1893). Based on Schumann's Op. 68/34. 19 minutes.

Bagatelles Op. 5 (Urbanek 1945). 4 pieces. 6½ minutes.

4 Barcarolles Op. 10 (Simrock 1896).

4 Eklogen Op. 11 (Artia).

3 Bohemian Dances Op. 15 (Simrock). Polka, Sousedká, Furiant.

Sonata Eroica Op. 24 (Artia). Romantic emotionalism, folksong influence. M-D.

Pan: Symphonic Poem Op. 43 (Artia 1963). 66 p.
Preface in English. 5 movements: Prolog, Berge, Meer, Wald, Weib. Monothematic, everything comes from single note motive. D.

Slowakische Suite Op. 32 (Artia). 5 movements: In the church, Amongst the children, In love, With the dancers, At night.

Youth: Suite Op. 55 (Hudebni Matice 1945). 2 books. Book 1: 12 pieces. Book 2: 9 pieces. Easy to Int.

6 Sonatinas Op. 54 (Artia). 3 in 2 books each. Int.-M-D.
1. C, Spring 2. A, A Child's Life 3. F, On Holiday 4. E, A Fairy Tale 5. F, The Brigands 6. G, Christmas.

LIONEL NOWAK (1911-) USA

Nowak has taught at Bennington College, Bennington, Vermont for many years. His music is serious, uncompromising and significant, displaying high craft and original ideas.

Soundscape One (ACA 1964).
Four well-contrasted sections, energetic conclusion. Pianistically conceived, full sonorities. First rate concert material.

Capriccio (ACA 1962). 6 p.
The first section to be played "hard and dry", granitic-like punched sounds. A lyric section leads to a toccata-like finale. M-D.

Fantasia (CFE 1954). Impressive, large-scale, imposing work demanding complete equipment. Worth exploring.

Four in a Row (CFE). Easy 12-tone pieces.

Nocturne and Toccata (CFE).

Sonatina (CFE).

Suite: For Days Remembered (CFE).

3 Bagatelles (CFE).

2 Phantasms (CFE).

6 Pieces for Young Musicians (CFE).

2 Problems for Piano (CFE). The pianist "finds" his own solutions.

Praeludim (CFE 1963). For Irwin Freundlich.

KNUT NYSTEDT (1915-) Norway

Sonatina Op. 35 (NMO 1955). Three movements. 11 p. MC, neoclassic. M-D.

O

LEV OBORIN (1907-   ) USSR

Oborin teaches piano at the Moscow Conservatory. He has had a fine career as a concert pianist and is a distinguished pedagogue.

Sonata e♭ Op. 3 (UE 1926-27). 47 p. 3 movements FSF. Large work in Prokofieff idiom. Virtuoso writing.

Quatre Morceaux Op. 2 (USSR).

ROBERT OBOUSSIER (1900-1957) Switzerland, born Belgium

From 1942 until his death, Oboussier was Director of the Zentralarchiv schweizerischer Tonkunst in Zürich.

25 Abbréviations (Henn 1932). Neoclassic, French and German influence. D.

Phantasie (Foetisch 1948). 12-tone influence. 3 sections are partly serialized. Bold gestures, much dissonance, wide dynamic scale. D.

JOHN OGDON (1937-   ) Great Britain

Ogdon is regarded as Britain's most outstanding pianist of his age group. Much of his composing has naturally been directed toward his chosen instrument. His style is eclectic and highly pianistic.

5 Preludes (Ascherberg). Pianistically expert ideas directly expressed.
Bagatelle, Pensée héroïque, Hommage, Pensée militaire, In modo napolitano. Final piece is a kind of modern tarantella.

Sonatina (Ascherberg 1965). 20 p. 4 movements. 10 minutes.

Freely moving tonalities, rhythmic problems, linear texture, M-D.

Theme and Variations (Ascherberg).
Liszt influence throughout this work. Complex theme followed by 10 variations, each complete in itself. Bravura style, rhythmic complexities.

Dance Suite (Ascherberg 1967). 20 p.
Prelude, Sarabande, Arabesque, Cortège, Finale. Arabesque is pianistically colorful. M-D.

HAJIME OKUMURA (1925-) Japan

Sonatine No. 4 (Ongaku-no-Toma Sha, Tokyo 1963).
This is no 14 in *Contemporary Japanese Music Series.*

Sonatine No. 3 (Ongaku-no-Toma Sha, Tokyo 1964).
No. 26 in *Contemporary Japanese Music Series.*

CARL ORFF (1895-) Germany

Klavier-Ubung (Schott). Easy children's pieces. MC.

BEN-ZION ORGAD (1926-) Israel, born Germany

After studies with Ben-Haim and Josef Tal in Israel, Orgad furthered his studies in the United States with Aaron Copland and Irving Fine. He is not only a graduate of the Academy of Music in Jerusalem but also received a degree in musicology from Brandeis University in 1961. He is Supervisor of Music Education in the Israel Ministry of Education and Culture.

Two Preludes in Impressionistic Mood (IMI 1960).
Short, sensitive. M-D. First performed by the American composer Harold Shapero at a symposium at Brandeis in 1960.

LEO ORNSTEIN (1895-) USA, born Russia

In his earlier years (1910-1935) Ornstein was considered something of an "enfant terrible" on the compositional scene.

Wild Men's Dance (Schott 1915). Dissonant, noisy, clusters.
Requires sustained percussive playing. M-D.

Impressions de la Tamise Op. 31/1 (Schott 1920).

Impressions de Notre Dame Op. 16 (Schott 1914).

Arabesques Op. 42 (AMP).

A la Mexicana Op 35 (AMP).

Scherzino Op. 5/2 (AMP).

Serenade Op. 5/1 (AMP).

A la Chinoise Op. 39 (AMP 1928). Clusters, polytonal, brilliant concert piece. D.

JUAN ORREGO-SALAS (1919-) Chile

Orrego-Salas teaches composition at Indiana University and is Director of the Latin-American Music Center located at the same school.

Suite No. 1 Op. 14 (Barry 1945). 12 p.
Preludio, Interludio, Fantasia, Interludio, Fuga.

Suite No. 2 Op. 32 (Bo&H 1951). "In the Baroque Style." 5 movements. Vigorous, arresting writing. Any movement could be played separately. M-D.

Variaciones y Fuga sobre el Tema de un Prégon Op. 18 (Hargail 1946). 8 variations and fugues on a street cry. Diatonic, parallel chords, modal repeated notes, bravura writing. Three-voice fugue. D.

Rustica Op. 35 (PAU 1952). Rustic dance, joyous, meter changes, rhythmic bounce.

Diez Piezas simples para niños Op. 31 (Barry 1951). 2 books. Easy to early intermediate.

LÉON ORTHEL (1905-) The Netherlands

Orthel is professor of piano at the Royal Conservatory in The Hague. He has also had a successful career as a concert pianist. His style is based on traditional tonal practice.

Préludes Op. 7 (Albersen 1925). Int.

10 Klavierstücke Op. 14 (Albersen). Children's pieces based on Dutch folksongs. Easy.

Epigrammen Op. 17 (Albersen 1938). M-D. 6 minutes.

Sonatine No. 3 Op. 28 (Alsbach).

Tre Pezzettini Op. 42 (Donemus 1958).

Cinq Etudes-Caprices (Donemus). M-D.

2 Hommages en Forme d'Etude (Donemus).

HANS OSIECK (1910-) The Netherlands

Osieck's "works are influenced largely by the folksongs of various countries and by what he heard and saw on his extensive travels." GD, 6, 457.

Sonatine No. 2 (Donemus 1956). 9 minutes.

Sonate (Donemus 1939). 17 minutes.

Berceuse antique (Albersen). 2 minutes. M-D.

HANS OTTE (1926-) Germany

Tropismen (UE). D.
Tiny motifs can be grouped in any (aleatoric) arrangement. Extension of Boulez and Stockhausen models.

HALL OVERTON (1920-) USA

Overton has had an impressive double career in jazz and concert music. He is "opposed to the practice of trying to make jazz 'respectable' through the unnatural imposition of classical forms of materials." (BMI brochure on the composer.) He teaches theory and composition at The Juilliard School.

Sonata (ACA 1952). One movement. 12 minutes.
An intricately interconnected form with much melodic beauty, rhythmic and mood variety. Quiet ending. D.

Polarities (LG 1959). 3 minutes. See Anthologies and Collections USA, *New Music for the Piano.*

HISATO OZAWA (1907-) Japan

Sonatine e (Ryunginsha). Three movements. Inspired by Ravel (*Jeux d'eau*). D.

P

LUIS DE PABLO See: DE PABLO, LUIS

JOHANN PACHELBEL (1653-1706) Germany

An important precursor of J. S. Bach, Pachelbel composed in all the usual genres of his day. His keyboard compositions may be found in DTB Vol. 2 and DTOe Vol. 17.

Hexachordum Apollinis (1699) (Moser, Fedtke-Br). Six arias with figural technique in d, e, F, g, a, f. This edition also contains an Ariette F and 2 Chaconnes C, D. The Ariette has 9 variations. The C Chaconne has 24 variations, D Chaconne has 12 variations. Introduction in English by Hans J. Moser.

7 Choralpartiten (Matthaei-Br) for klavier or organ.

7 Selected Pieces (Döflein-Schott). Phantasie D, Fuga a, Aria con variazioni g, Aria mit Variationen A (Fragment), Aria mit Variationen a, "Werde munter, mein Gemüte" from *Musikalischen Sterbensgedanken* (Musical Meditations on Death), Suite e.

Selected Keyboard Works (H. Schultz-CFP) 12 works including Suites, Choralthema D with 8 variations, Fantasia g, Prelude and Fugue f♯, Ciacona d, etc.

17 Suites (DTB Vol. 2). Short, in usual order of A, C, S, G with some optional dances.

Suiten für Cembalo (Moser, Fedtke-Br).

See: E. V. Nolte, "The Instrumental Works of Johann Pachelbel," unpub. diss., Northwestern University, 1954.

WILHELM HIERONYMUS PACHELBEL (1685-1764) Germany

Werke für Orgel und Clavier (Moser, Fedtke-Br). Clavier works include Preludes and Fugues D, C, Fantasia D.

IGNACE JAN PADEREWSKI (1860-1941) Poland

Melodie Op. 8/3 (GS).

Menuet Op. 14/1 (GS). Famous salon piece.

Caprice à la Scarlatti Op. 14/3 (Musica Obscura).

Chant d'amour Op. 10/2 (GS).

Nocturne B♭ Op. 16/4 (GS).

Légende A♭ Op 16/1 (GS). Attractive, requires octave technique.

Theme with variations A (GS) (Schott). Poetic, pianistic, M-D.

Introduction and Toccata Op. 6 (PWM 1934). 14 p. D.

Album de Mai: Scènes romantiques Op. 10 (Ashdown 1884). 5 pieces. M-D.

Cracoviènne fantastique Op. 14/6 (Ashdown). Facility and scale passages in thirds required.

Variations and Fugue on an Original Theme a Op. 11 (Ashdown). Variations are more effective than the fugue. M-D.

Homage to Paderewski (Bo&H). See: Collections and Anthologies, Tombeau or Hommage section.

See: A. M. Henderson, "Paderewski as Artist and Teacher," MT, 97, August 1956, 411-13.

GIUSEPPE ANTONIO PAGANELLI (1710-1765) Italy

Sei Sonate per Pianoforte (1757) (G. Tagliapietra-Ric 1936). First part of his *Divertissement du Beau Sexe; ou Six Sonatines pour le Clavecin.*

Sonata F (Pauer-Br&H). In collection *Old Masters,* 5.

JOHN KNOWLES PAINE (1839-1906) USA

Paine was one of our most important nineteenth-century native-born composers. All works listed below are located at the Library of Congress.

A Funeral March (Beer and Schirmer 1865). 4 p. In memory of A. Lincoln.

3 Piano Pieces Op. 41/1, 2, 3 (A. P. Schmidt 1884). 11 p. A Spring Idyl, Birthday Impromptu, Fuga Giocosa.

Nocturne Op. 45 (A. P. Schmidt 1889). 6 p. Paine often played this for friends.

Romance Op. 39 (OD 1883). 6 p. One of the most agreeable of his pieces.

In the Country Op. 26 (G. D. Russell 1875). 10 pieces. Kind of a *Forest Scenes!* (Schumann).
Woodnotes, Wayside Flowers, Under the Lindens, Shepherd's Lament, Village Dance, Rainey Day, Mill, Gipsies, Farewell, Welcome Home.

4 Characteristic Pieces Op. 25. 23 p.
Dance, Romance, Impromptu, Rondo giocoso.

Romance Op. 12 (A. P. Schmidt 1869). 6 p. Schumannesque.

A Christmas Gift (G. D. Russell 1864). For his sister.

GIOVANNI PAISIELLO (1740-1816) Italy

The sonatas listed below were probably written during 1776-84 when Paisiello was living in St. Petersburg, Russia.

Six Sonatas (C. Mola-Carisch). One-movement works in spirited rococo style. From his 19 sonatas. Not sonatas, even in the sense of the day, but closer to the rondo idea. No. 1 f, 2 E♭, 3 G, 4 D, 5 F, 6 E♭.

Largo F (Pauer-Augener).

Rondo E♭ (Pauer-Augener).

ROMAN PALESTER (1907-) Poland

"Palester belongs to the most advanced group of Polish modernists." GD, 6, 505

Preludes (Southern 1963). 26 p. 12 minutes.
Ten short works, tempi on slow side, introspective, highly chromatic, 12-tone, no meter or bar lines. A selection could be made but more rewardingly played as a whole. D.

ROBERT PALMER (1915-) USA

Palmer's style is based on melodic thematic material, asymmetric rhythmic patterns, and varied processes of motivic expansion. He teaches at Cornell University.

Three Preludes (PIC 1941).
Vivace con grazia: lyric emphasis, changing meters, ideas well-developed.
Molto tranquillo e cantabile: flowing, legato, in 17/16.
Molto pesante-Allegro con energia: dissonant, heavy, broken figuration in LH requires stamina. M-D.

Toccata Ostinato (EV 1945). Vigorous, percussive, brisk, ostinato bass, sturdy writing. Steady rhythmic drive required. M-D.

Three Epigrams (PIC 1960).
Allegretto grazioso: meter changes, contemporary sonorities.
Agitato ma leggiero: flexible meters, tricky tonal balance in a few passages.
Andante con moto: musically the most interesting. M-D.

Evening Music (TP). Expressive, lydian and mixolydian modes. M-D.

See: William Austin, "The Music of Robert Palmer," MQ, 42, January 1956, 35-50.

SELIM PALMGREN (1878-1951) Finland

May Night (BMC) (WH) (GS). Impressionistic.

6 Lyric Piano Pieces Op. 28 (WH) (BMC). Prelude, Skuggornas, Sada, Mor sjunger, Svanen, Ringdans. (WH) publishes these separately.

Finnish Rhythms Op. 31 (WH). 5 pieces ranging from easy to M-D. (BMC) publish No. 1 Karelian Dance.

Piano Sketches Op. 35 (WH). 4 pieces. (WH) publishes 1, 2, and 4. Humorous dance 1, Old Finnish cradle song, Humorous dance 2. M-D.

Northern Summer Op. 39 (WH). 5 pieces. (WH) publishes Nos. 1 and 4. Evening Piece, Little Ballade.

Pastorale in 3 Scenes Op. 50. Morgon, Afton (WH).

Light and Shade Op. 51 (WH). 6 piano pieces. Fosterlandshymn, Finnish Ballad, Twilight, Serenata, Elegi, Valse caprice. Published separately.

3 Piano Pieces Op. 54 (WH). Regndroppar, Valse mignonne, Mansken. Published separately.

6 morceaux Op. 67 (WH). Prélude, Ricordanza, En sjömannsvals, Humoristisk studie, Improvisation, Pa lagunen. Published separately. M-D.

3 morceaux Op. 74 (WH). Morceau Romantique, Morceau élégant, Morceau burlesque.

3 Fantasies Op. 83 (WH).

Finnish Folksongs (WH). 8 songs arranged for piano. Published separately. Also (Reid).

6 Selected Pieces (J. Garratt-JWC). Prelude-Caprice, Barcarolle, The Dragon Fly, Prelude-Nocturne, Refrain de Berceuse, En Route.

The Sea (BMC) (JWC). LH study. Int.

Berceuse (JWC).

The Dragon Fly (BMC). Light broken octaves. M-D.

En Route Op. 9 (EBM). Facile study for RH.

Aria c (BMC). Int.

Rococo (JWC).

ANDRZEJ PANUFNIK (1914-) Poland

Panufnik composes in an advanced musical style. He moved to England in 1953.

Suite A La Quinte (PWM 1949). 12 pieces in variation form. 20 minutes. D. Prelude c♯, Interlude f♯, Study b, Interlude e, Study a, Interlude d, Study g, Interlude c, Study f, Interlude b♭, Study e♭, Postlude a♭.

6 Miniature Studies (Bo&H 1955). 2 vols. A valuable contribution to modern piano technique. Vol. 1: One technical problem per study. No. 1, alternating chromatic and diatonic passagework; No. 2, three layers of simultaneous contrasting dynamics; No. 3, study in octaves and thirds; No. 4, melody in tenor and bass accompanied by seconds; No. 5, study in fifths and thirds; No. 6, contrasted sonorities.

6 Miniature Studies (Bo&H c. 1966). Vol. 2: Various problems in each piece. No. 7, rhythm study in 3/8 plus 2/8 plus 3/8; No. 8, expressive pedaling called for; No. 9, groups of five eighths, many ninths embedded into figuration; No. 10, study in tonal balance; No. 11, perpetual motion, tonal balance, melody in LH; No. 12, in time signature 1/2, crescendo from beginning to end, shifted accents. Fascinating textures. M-D.

MAGDELEINE PANZERA (1893-) France

Children's Piano Recital (EMT 1966). Books I and II. Book I: Five charming, well-written, MC sounding pieces. Berceuse, Siciliènne, Le petit ruisseau chante, Je suis punié, Pastorale. Book II: Promenons-nous, Habanera, Carillon, Mon beau jouet s'est brisé, Voici les vacances. Easy to Int.

JEAN PAPINEAU-COUTURE (1916-) Canada

Papineau-Couture received his musical education under Françoise d'Amour, Léo-Pol Morin, Gabriel Cusson and Nadia Boulanger. He is professor of Music at the University of Montreal and President of the Canadian League of Composers.

Mouvement Perpétuel (BMI Canada). Much LH passagework. M-D.

Suite (BMI Canada 1959). Four movements: Prelude and Bagatelle No. 1, Aria and Bagatelle No. 2. Aria requires sensitivity, Bagatelle No. 2 is whimsical. M-D.

Rondo (BMI Canada 1951). Toccatalike character, large span required, neoromantic style. D.

Etude B♭ (PIC 1959). Effective, difficult concert-etude.

YORAM PAPORISZ (1944-) Israel, born Poland

Discoveries (Southern). Three volumes, graded. Vol. I easiest, etc. Based on idioms from around the world: 5th-century Ambrosian hymn, Hindu ragas, Mozarabic cantillation, etc. Some of the finest pedagogic material encountered. Compares favorably with *Mikrokosmos* in scope and quality.

LÁJOS PAPP (1935-) Hungary

Papp received his musical education at the Academy of Music, Budapest and studied with Ferenc Szabo. He teaches at the Municipal Music School of Budapest.

Variazioni (Bo&H) 1968). 11 p.
Theme and 9 variations, final one a partial repeat of the theme. Large span required, chromatic harmony, preference for seconds and sevenths. Contemporary sounds, M-D.

6 Bagatelles (EMB). 15 p.

27 Small Piano Pieces (EMB). Problems on the elementary level. Short, musical, five-finger position.

3 Rondos (EMB c. 1967).

PIETRO DOMENICO PARADIES (PARADISI) (1707-1791) Italy

One of the strongest composers of this period, Paradies' sonatas were admired by Clementi, Cramer and Mozart. Each sonata, in two movements, demonstrates amazing variety in figural treatment, rhythmic vitality, unusual dissonances, idiomatic keyboard style, etc. According to Newman, "So much variety of style makes it necessary to place Paradies rather broadly in pre-Classic sonata history." SCE, 686-91. Masterly writing, deserves more performance.

12 Sonate di Gravicembalo 1754 (Ruf, Bemmann-Schott). Two vols.; *I Classici della Musica Italiana* Vol. XXII. Of special interest are: *Sonata* No. 1 G, also available (Br&H), *Sonata* No. 6 A, also available (CF), No. 10 D available (CF) and (Litolff). See TPA, XII, and *Le Trésor des Pianistes* XIV contains 10 sonatas. *Sonata* B♭ in *Italian Sonatas of the 18th Century* (de Paoli-JWC). *Toccata* A (Schott) and *Toccata* e (Vitali-Ric).

See: David Stone, "The Italian Sonata for Harpsichord and Piano in the 18th Century (1730-90)," 3 volumes, unpub. diss., Harvard University, 1952.

PAUL PARAY (1886-   ) France

Paray won the Prix de Rome in 1911. "His works are sincere, finely written, occasionally a little academic." GD, 6, 546.

Impression (Jobert 1912). 3 pieces. Nostalgie, Eclaircie, Primesaut.

Thème et Variations (Jobert 1913). 15 p.

Reflets romantiques (Jobert 1912).

Prélude (Jobert 1913).

D'une âme. (Jobert 1914). 9 pieces.

4 Compositions for Piano (BMC 1913). Romanza, Capriccio, Improvisata, Portraits d'enfants.

ROBERT PARRIS (1924-   ) USA

Parris studied at The Juilliard School, University of Pennsylvania, Columbia University and the Berkshire Music Center. In 1952 he did post-graduate work at the Ecole Normale de Musique in Paris. He teaches composition at George Washington University.

Variations (ACA 1958). 4 minutes.
Simple octave theme, each variation colorfully treated (including a fugato). Final statement dramatically conceived. D.

Six Little Studies in Contemporary Rhythmical Problems (ACA). 10 minutes.

CHARLES HUBERT HASTINGS PARRY (1848-1918) Great Britain

Shulbrede Tunes (Augener). 10 pieces, suggested by Parry's daughter's family.
Shulbrede, Elizabeth, Dolly 1, Bogies and sprites, Matthew, Prior's chamber by firelight, Children's pranks, Dolly 2, In the garden—With the dew on the grass, Father Playmate. Final piece is a passacaglia, more difficult. M-D except last piece.

Hands across the Centuries (Augener). A Suite inspired by the 18th-century.
Prelude, The Passionate Allemande, The Wistful Courante, Quasi Sarabande (very sensitive writing), Gavotte and Musette, Quasi Minuetto, The Whirling Jig. M-D.

OEDOEN PARTOS (1907-) Israel, born Hungary

Distinguished performer, composer, educator and recipient of many international prizes, Partos is an influential and respected member of the Israeli musical community. He is presently Director of the Rubin Academy of Music in Tel Aviv.

Prelude (IMI 1960).
Rhapsodic. Large musical gestures. Short. M-D.

Piece for Piano (IMI).

CLAUDE PASCAL (1921-) France

L'Album de Lisette et Poulot (Durand). Twelve exercise pieces exploiting different pianistic problems. Int.

La bal improvisé (Durand). Nine varied pieces. MC, M-D.

Le cahier du lecteur (Durand). Three volumes. Easy to M-D.
I: 24 varied pieces.
II: 12 pieces in canon form.
III: 18 varied pieces.

Portraits d'enfants (Durand). Twelve small sketches for young people. Easy to Int.

Toccata (Durand c. 1952). Short, M-D.

Suite (Durand). Five movements, neobaroque. D.

BERNARDO PASQUINI (1637-1710) Italy

Pasquini was one of the finest Italian keyboard composers of the second half of the 17th century. His music is vigorous and terse yet abounds in melodic grace. Pasquini wrote suites consisting of allemandes, courantes and gigues, using the term 'sonata'. In some ways he anticipated techniques of D. Scarlatti.

Collected works for Keyboard (M. B. Haynes—American Institute of Musicology) Part V of CEKM, see: Collections and Anthologies, General.

Sette Toccate per Organo e Cembalo (A. Esposito-Zanibon).

Sonata (Boghen-SZ).

Sonata d (Torchi-Ric).

Toccata sul Canto del Cucu in *I Clavicembalisti* (Rossi-Carisch 1946).

3 Arias (Rehberg-Schott).

Works in *L'Arte Musicale in Italia* III; TPA VIII; *Le Trésor des Pianistes* III; *Selection of Pieces composed for the Harpsichord* (Shedlock-Nov 1895). Still a fine source.

See: Maurice B. Haynes, "The Keyboard Works of Bernardo Pasquini (1637-1710)," Vols. I-V, unpub. diss., Indiana University, 1960. This study is in two parts. Part II presents transcriptions into modern notation of all the known and available keyboard compositions of Pasquini. This comprises Vols. II-V. Part I is a detailed study of the music contained in the transcriptions. Vols. II-V are available in five volumes through the American Institute of Musicology as Part Five of the *Corpus of Early Keyboard Music.*

JUAN CARLOS PAZ (1897-1972) Argentina

Paz was the first South American composer of renown to adopt 12-tone technique. He is highly respected in his native Argentina and is music critic for several Argentine magazines and periodicals.

Sonatina No. 3 Op. 25 (ECIC 1933).
3 movements, thin textures, severe writing. M-D.

Canciones y Baladas Op. 31. No. 1 (In *Musica Viva,* No. 10. Rio de Janeiro, 1941). No. 2 (GS) in album *Latin American Anthology of Music*. Short, 12-tone.

Diez Piezas Sobre una Serie dodecafónica Op. 30 (Editorial Politonía). Strict use of the row, but rather easy works.

En la Casta del Parana (CF). Seven colorful variations on a tango theme.

JOSÉ ENRIQUE PEDREIRA (1904-) Puerto Rico

Plénitude (Nocturne) (EBM). Smooth modulations.

Tus Cariccas (EBM). Popular dance style.

Vals en La Mayor (EBM). Appealing.

CARLOS PEDRELL (1878-1941) Uruguay

A Orillas del Duero (ESC 1922).
Colorful suite of 4 pieces depicting musical pictures "On the Outskirts of Duero." Good technique required. M-D.

MARTIN PEERSON (ca. 1572-1650) Great Britain

FVB contains the following 4 works: *Alman*: light, 2 beats per bar, varied texture. I, 359. *The Fall of the Leafe*: short, plaintive, two phrases. II, 423. *Piper's Paven*: slow, 3 sections, changing figuration. II, 238. *The Primrose*: short, dance tune, lively. II, 422.

FLOR PEETERS (1901-) Belgium

Peeters studied with Marcel Dupré and Charles Tournemire in Paris. He is director of the Antwerp Conservatory and tours extensively as a concert organist.

Sonatina Op. 46 G (Hin).

Sonatina Op. 45 (Cnudde 1941).

Toccata Op. 51a (CFP). Effective perpetual motion writing, hands close together. D.

10 Bagatelles Op. 88 (CFP 1958). Short MC, varied styles and moods. Int.

Sketches of Childhood Op. 27 (Cranz). Books 1 and 2.

BARBARA PENTLAND (1912-) Canada

Pentland's musical education included studies in Paris with Cécile Gauthiez, in New York at The Juilliard School with Bernard Wagenaar and Frederick Jacobi, and at the Berkshire Music Center with Aaron Copland. She is a faculty member in the Music Department at the University of British Columbia in Vancouver.

Studies in Line (BMI Canada 1941). 6 minutes.
"Four studies from single ideas developed in four short movements. Each is headed by a sketch rather than a title. The contours of each sketch are descriptive not only of the general contour of the following study but of the emotional effect as well." Clever writing. M-D.

Fantasy (BMI Canada 1962). 7 minutes.
Serial, harmonics, specific and unusual directions (white tone).

Dirge (BMI Canada 1948). Short, effective sonorities. M-D.

Toccata (BMI Canada 1957-58). 12-tone, brilliant. D.

Shadows (Waterloo).

CLERMONT PÉPIN (1926-) Canada

Pépin studied in Montreal, at the Curtis Institute in Philadelphia, and with Arthur Honegger, André Jolivet, and Olivier Messiaen in Paris.

Short Etudes 1, 2, 3 (Western Music).
Impressionistic, individual ideas well worked out. M-D.

Petite Suite (Harris 1953).

ERNST PEPPING (1901-) Germany

Pepping prefers Baroque forms and linear textures.

Sonate I (Schott 1937). 3 movements. 20 p. Second movement is especially delightful.

Sonate II (Schott 1937). 22 p.
Canzona con variazioni: expressive.
Rondo pastorale
Finale alla marcia: very rhythmic.

Sonate III D (Schott 1938). 31 p. Cheerful.

Sonata IV (Br 1948). 43 p. D. 24 minutes.

Sonatine (Schott c. 1931). 15 p. More difficult than it looks.

Tanzweisen und Rundgesang (Schott 1939). Dances and Rounds. Large work. 27 p. M-D.

3 Fugues on B A C H (Schott 1955).

Variationen (Br 1947). 2 volumes. Continuous variation treatment, fugue begins 5 pages before the end. D.

12 Phantasien (Br 1949). Pieces individually characterized, of moderate length.

Zuhause (Br 1949). 4 variations. M-D.

MARIO PERAGALLO (1910-) Italy

Fantasia (UE 1953).
Dissonant free counterpoint, pianistic. D.

Baletto (De Santis 1929).
Vivace, Andante "Minuetto", Vivace.

Composizione (De Santis 1927).

GIOVANNI BATTISTA PERGOLESI (1710-1736) Italy

Complete Edition (Amici della Musica da Camera, Rome). Vol. I contains 6 sonatas and 3 suites. Sonatas are short, one-movement, homophonic. Spurious works permeate this edition. See "Walker" (listed below).

Sonata D (G. Azzoni-Carisch).

Sonata prima G (Montani-Ric).

Sonata D (Fuller-Maitland-Schott).

See: C. L. Cudworth, "Notes on the Instrumental Works Attributed to Pergolesi," ML, 30, October 1949, 321-28.

Frank Walker, "Two Centuries of Pergolesi Forgeries and Misattributions," ML, 30, October 1949, 297-320.

GEORGE PERLE (1915-) USA

Perle studied at DePaul University, the American Conservatory of Music, and New York University. He also studied composition privately with Ernest Krenek. He teaches at Queens College in New York.

Sonata Op. 27 (ECIC 1950). 8 p. 2 movements. Serial writing. First movement requires large span and a fine octave technique. Dissonant, major sevenths and minor seconds. The second movement (only 1 page) is thorny and sonorous.

6 Preludes in album *New Music for the Piano* (LG 1958). Combination of atonal and 12-tone technique. M-D.

Short Sonata (TP 1964). 16 p. 3 movements, FSF. 8 minutes. A tightly knit work, extreme dynamic changes, flexible meters. Specific pedaling required in the impressionist second movement. Invigorating writing. D.

Interrupted Story (TP).

See: George Perle, *Serial Composition and Atonality.* 2nd ed. Berkeley: University of California Press, 1968.

Leo Kraft, "The Music of George Perle," MQ, 57, July 1971, 444-465.

VINCENT PERSICHETTI (1915-) USA

Persichetti is an outstanding pianist and knows how to write for the instrument. Much of his music, difficult as it sounds, is only moderately difficult because it "fits" the fingers. Occupied with the piano throughout his career, Persichetti has given us eleven solo piano sonatas and other smaller works. For a more detailed discussion of his solo piano works see the article by Maurice Hinson, "The Solo Piano Works of Vincent Persichetti", AMT, 15, April-May 1966, 38-39, 59. All works listed below are published by Elkan-Vogel unless otherwise indicated.

Serenade No. 2 Op. 2 (1929). 3 short movements: Tune, Strum, Pluck. Textural rather than melodic in emphasis, a characteristic that shows throughout almost all his music.

Poems Op. 4 and 5 (1939). 2 volumes. Titles come from twentieth-century poets. Wide range of technical and interpretative problems. Int. to M-D.

Variations for an Album Op. 32 (Mer 1947). Theme and 5 melodic variations in free style.

Serenade No. 7 Op 55 (1952). 6 short pieces "that are distillations of a musical expression that has undergone clarification to the point of great simplicity." (Letter to M. Hinson from Mrs. V. Persichetti.)

Parades Op. 57 (1952). 3 pieces: March, Canter, Pomp. Sprinkled with ostinati and simple polychordal combinations. Int.

Little Piano Book Op. 60 (1953). 14 short pieces displaying many characteristics of the composer in distilled form. A "classic" with many teachers. Easy to Int.

Sonatinas 1, 2, 3 (1950). Published separately: Op. 38, Op.45 most difficult, Op. 47.

Sonatinas 4, 5, 6 (1954). All 6 published in 1 volume. Op. 63, Op. 64, Op. 65.

Sonata No. 1 (1939). In preparation, to be published.

Sonata No. 2 Op. 6 (1939). In preparation, to be published.

Sonata No. 3 Op. 22 (1943). 3 movements: Declaration, Episode, Psalm. M-D.

Sonata No. 4 Op. 36 (1949). 3 movements. 17 minutes. Large span required. D.

Sonata No. 5 Op. 37 (1949). 3 movements: With motion, tenderly, Briskly. M-D.

Sonata No. 6 Op. 39 (1950). Large span required. Short final movement. M-D.

Sonata No. 7 Op. 40 (1950). 3 movements. 7 minutes. Large span required. Thin textures. M-D.

Sonata No. 8 Op. 41 (1950). 3 movements. 14 p. 9 minutes. More melodically conceived.

Sonata No. 9 Op. 58 (1952). 4 sections. 9 minutes. Moderato, Allegro agilite, Larghetto, Allegro risoluto. M-D.

Sonata No. 10 Op. 67 (1955). 22 minutes. 4 divisions. The largest of the solo piano works. Beautifully developed.

Sonata No. 11 Op. 101 (1965). 1 movement. 16 minutes. Risoluto, Articolato, Sostenuto, Leggiero. A new style for Persichetti. D.

GIOVANNI BATTISTA PESCETTI (ca. 1704-ca. 1766) Italy

Selected works found in *Clavecinistes Italiens* (Heugel).

Sonata c, *Cembalisti Italiani del Settecento* (Benvenuti-Ric). Three movements, FSF, lovely slow movement.

Allegretto C, Italian Harpsichord Compositions I (Vitali-Ric). Single sonata movement, Scarlatti style, perpetual motion.

Sonata g, TPA XII.

WILHELM PETERSON-BERGER (1867-1942) Sweden

Peterson-Berger's style is based mainly on folk song.

Earina (AL) 2 books.

Frösöblomster (AL). 3 volumes in 1. Named after Frösö, a beautiful area in Sweden where the composer lived most of his life. Bk. 1: 8 melodies, Bk. 2: 6 melodies, Bk. 3: Isommarhagen: humoresker och idyller.

Italiana Suite (AL).

Anakreontika Suite (ELK).

Svensk folkmusik, danser (AL).

GOFFREDO PETRASSI (1904-) Italy

Partita (De Santis 1927). Preludio, Aria, Gavotte, Giga.

Toccata (Ric 1933).
Diatonic harmonic and melodic idiom, linear excursions out of established tonality. Different from later works. Difficulty of Ravel *Sonatine.*

8 Inventions (SZ 1944). 20 minutes.
Varied moods and characterizations skillfully worked out in a very personal, contemporary style, unusual lyric quality. Not as difficult as his *Toccata.*

FELIX PETYREK (1892-1951) Austria

24 Ukrainische Volksweisen (UE 1920).
Polyphony is especially effective in Nos. 2, 3, and 10. Could be performed as a suite. M-D.

Chorale, Variations and Sonatina (UE 1924). Theme in Chorale. 6 variations, utilizing advanced pianistic devices follow. Sonatina attacca, theme still present. Variation 7 becomes the second movement of the Sonatina and concludes the work PPP. A successful, curious mixture of formal structures. D.

Sechs Griechische Rhapsodien (UE 1927). Each utilizes full chords, free dissonant treatment, syncopated rhythms, interesting sonorities. None are easy and all require fine pianistic background.

6 Grotesques (UE 1914-20). Picturesque titles such as Procession By Night, Excentric, The Official Reception, Night Adventure, etc. Colorful even though not so "unusual" sounding today. M-D.

Sonatine C (OBV 1947). 19 p.

Sonata (Dob 1944). 4 movements, effective. M-D.

CHRISTIAN PETZOLD (1677-1733) Germany

Suite de Clavecin B♭ (Br).
A, vivemente, C, G, M en rondeau.

HANS PFITZNER (1869-1949) Germany

Fünf Klavierstücke Op. 47 (Johann Oertel Verlag, 1941).
Entitled: Last effort, In High Spirits, Hieroglyphics, Anxious Restlessness, Melody. Late 19th-century-sounding character pieces involving considerable technical difficulties. Highly chromatic.

6 Studien Op. 51 (Oertel 1943) . No 6 is a trill study. Slightly more difficult than Op. 47.

ISIDOR PHILIPP (1863-1958) France, born Hungary

Philipp, eminent teacher and pianist of international renown, left a number of salon pieces of high quality in addition to his numerous etudes and finger exercises.

Trois pièces de concert (Heugel 1935).
Inquiétude, Quiétude, Etude.

Scènes d'enfants Op. 69 (Durand 1929). 2 volumes, 6 pieces in each volume.

Miniatures Op. 72 (Heugel). 12 Pièces faciles.

6 Pièces Fantaisistes (Heugel).

Nocturne Op. 90 (Heugel).

Impromptu Op. 100 (Heugel).

Troisème Barcarolle (Heugel).

2 Etudes de Concert (Heugel).

6 Danses et Airs Anciens (Heugel).

6 Valses capricieuses Op. 36 (Heugel).

12 Preludes in Double Notes Op. 85 (Sal). All are short but fairly demanding.

15 Etudes melodiques (Sal).

Etude de Concert (Durand 1948). 5 p. D.

Feux-follets Op. 24/3 (GS). Jack-o'-lanterns. Effective. M-D.

PETER PHILIPS (1550?-1628) Great Britain

Philips cannot be considered a truly English composer since he lived on the continent for most of his life. 19 keyboard pieces, the earliest dated 1580, appear in the FVB. These include arrangements of vocal pieces by Caccini, Lassus, Marenzio and Striggio. His keyboard music is contrapuntal in character.

Pavana Dolorosa. Tregian. Expressive, three sections, clash of accidentals. FVB, I, 321.

BURRILL PHILLIPS (1907-) USA

A Set of Three Informalities (GS 1945).
Blues: chordal accompaniment to melody.
Scherzo: short, fast, passages alternate between hands, parallel triads.
Sonatina: romantic melodic treatment, fast mid-section, most difficult of set. M-D.

Three Divertimenti (EV 1946). Fancy Dance, Homage to Monteverdi, Brag. Brief pieces that exploit single ideas. Int.

Toccata (EV 1946). A boogie-woogie bass ostinato supports two voices throughout, distribution between hands. M-D.

Five Various and Sundry (EV 1961). Short, varied character pieces, effective as a set or individually. Int.

The Chatterer (TP).

GIOVANNI PICCHI (ca. 1620) Italy

Tänze für Klaver (G. Wohlgemut-Mitteldeutscher Verlag). Dances in different styles: German Dance, Hungarian Dance, Gagliarda con variazioni, Corrente con variazioni, Hungarian Pavan, Dance in Polish style, etc. Modal harmonies add interest to this early example of dance forms. Also found in TPA, V.

GABRIEL PIERNÉ (1863-1937) France

15 Pièces Op. 3 (Leduc). M-D.

Etude de Concert Op. 13 (Leduc). 4 minutes. Tarantelle, souvenir de Naples. D.

6 Pièces Op. 14 (Leduc).

Sérénade à Columbine Op. 32 (Enoch).

Trois Pièces Formant Suite de Concert Op. 40 (Hamelle 1906).

1. Preludio e fughetta. D.
2. Nocturne en forme de valse. M-D.
3. Etude symphonique. D.

Passacaglia Op. 52 (Sal 1934). Etude de concert. D.

Viennoise (Sal). Suite.

Album pour mes petits amis Op. 14 (Leduc). 6 charming teaching pieces on level of Chopin Prelude A.

Rapsodie Basque (Enoch).

Variations c Op. 42 (Hamelle 1918). 36 p. Large work, bravura writing. Alfred Cortot considered this one of the most important works in twentieth-century French pianism.

Pastorale variée Op. 30 (Durand).

Scherzando de concert Op. 29 (Durand).

Sérénade à Izeyl (Durand).

PATRICK PIGGOTT (1915-) Wales

8 Preludes (University of Wales Press, 1963).
Studies in piano textures alternating between fast and slow movements (4 fast, 4 slow). Fluent sequential passages, well-projected moods, gratifying writing. M-D.

WILLEM PIJPER (1894-1947) The Netherlands

Pijper was a much respected composer, a craftsman of high quality

Drie aphorismen (Donemus 1916).

Three folk dances of the world (Donemus 1926).
De Boufon, Dutch children's dance, Scharmoes.

Sonatine No. 1 (Basart 1917).

Sonatine No. 2 (B&VP 1925).
One movement, short, changing meters, scherzo quality. M-D.

Sonatine No. 3 (B&VP 1925). Five minutes.
Impressionist and jazz influences, irregular meters, whimsical. M-D.

Sonata (Donemus 1930). Five minutes.
Allegro: short and rhythmic; Adagio molto: atmospheric and serious; Allegro volante: bright. M-D.

DANIEL PINKHAM (1923-) USA

Pinkham's music is always accessible technically. He constantly keeps the performer in mind in his writing.

Prelude (ACA 1946). Presto, changing meters, about 30 seconds long, ostinato effect. M-D.

A Song for the Bells (CFP 1962). 3 minutes. Written for carillon, freely-flowing, comes off surprisingly well on the piano especially when pedal is used liberally. No time signatures but many instructions for tempo changes are indicated. Atmospheric, impressionistic. M-D.

Partita for Harpsichord (CFP 1958). 24 minutes. Toccata, Andante and Fugue, 3 Inventions, Interlude and Rondo, Fantasia,

Scherzo and Trio, Envoi. An extended work: a series of movements, contrasting moods and technical devices. Superficial resemblance to a baroque partita but more like a sonata. Contemporary rhythmic and harmonic idioms. Movements may be played separately although intended to be performed as a continuous work. M-D.

GEORGE FREDERICK PINTO (1785-1806) Great Britain

Sonata e♭ Op. 3/1 (S&B c. 1963). 3 movements. 17 minutes. See: SSB, 567-9. Remarkable writing, especially for a 16 or 17 year old boy.

Complete Suites (S&B). 8 suites.

See: Nicholas Temperley, "George Frederick Pinto," MT, 106, April 1965, 265-70; with related correspondence on 446 and 523-24.

OCTAVIO PINTO (1890-1950) Brazil

Dança Negreira (GS 1945).
Constant sixteenth-note motion, energetic, syncopated. Requires rhythmic vitality. M-D.

Marcha do Pequeña Polegar (GS).
Crisp, short. Int.

Scenas Infantis (GS).
Five descriptive scenes for childhood. Int.

Festa de crianças (Children's Festival) (GS). Five easy, attractive children's pieces.

PAUL A. PISK (1893-) Austria, living in USA

Vier Klavierstücke Op. 3 (UE). 9 minutes. Short, freely-tonal.

Sechs Konzertstücke Op. 7 (UE 1922). 11 minutes. Atonal, chromatic, rhapsodic. D.

Speculum Suite Op. 17 (ACA). Toccata, Sarabande, Intermezzo, Menuet, March. Chromatic, tightly organized, turbulent. D.

5 Sketches Op. 39 (NME 1936). 9½ minutes. Short, contrasted, contemporary, brilliant close.

5 Piece Set (Mills) M-D.

Engine Room (MCA) A "Motor Study for Piano." Vigorous perpetual motion. M-D.

Dance from The Rio Grande Valley (LG 1957). Attractive.

Nocturnal Interlude (LG 1963). Well-written mood music.

Caribbeana (ACA). 3 p. 3 section work: bitonal, tango rhythm.

Sonatina E Op. 94 (CFE 1958). 6½ minutes. 3 movements FSF. Neoclassic, numerous chromatics, fluctuating tonalities, much imitation. M-D.

Sonatina (Death Valley) Op. 49 (Southern 1944). 3 movements.

WALTER PISTON (1894-) USA

Passacaglia (Mer 1943). Short, grows in intensity with each variation to sonorous climax, involved textures, excellent craftsmanship. M-D.

Improvisation (MCA). In *U.S.A. Vol. I* with works of other American composers. Short, lyric, quartal harmony, peaceful closing. Int.

GIOVANNI BENEDETTO PLATTI (ca. 1690-1763) Italy

G. B. Platti E La Sonata Moderna. Vol. II Istituzioni Dell' Arte Musicale Italiana (Nuova Serie) edited by Fausto Torrefranca (Ric 1963).
A scholarly work with 211 pages of introduction and all extant 18 sonatas for the cembalo (188 pages). A handsome work, with index, 413 pages.

12 Sonatas (Hoffmann-Erbrecht-Br&H). Two books.

HUBERT DU PLESSIS (1922-) Union of South Africa

Preludes Op. 18 (Galliard).
Seven pieces, linear writing in a romantic idiom. Imaginative pianism. M-D.

IGNAZ JOSEPH PLEYEL (1757-1831) Austria

See: SCE, 551.

Sonata g (Hin).

ALESSANDRO POGLIETTI (? -1683) Italy

Poglietti, an Italian, worked in Vienna and died there during the Turkish siege.

Harpsichord Music (W. E. Nettles-PSM 1966).
Suites a and C. Capricietto sopra il Cu Cu, Toccata del 7 tuono, Canzon Teutsch, Trommel, Canzon Francaix Trommel, Toccata fatta sopra L'Assedio. Descriptive works: bird calls, battle sounds, droning bagpipes, etc. Fascinating notes by the editor.

The *Capricietto* is found in W. Georgii's *Keyboard Music of The Baroque and Rococo I.*

Il Rossignolo (F. Goebels-Br). Set of variations.

Aria Allemagna con alcuni Variazoni (DTOe XXVII, 13-22). Written in 1677 as a birthday present for the Empress of Austria, Eleonora Maddalena Theresa. 20 variations, one for each year of her age, based on programmatic connotations such as Bohemian Bagpipe, Hungarian Fiddles, Bavarian Shawn, French Kiss-the-Hand, Juggler's Rope-dance, Old Hag's Procession, Dance of the Honor-guard, etc. Delightful picturesque music. Also found in *Alte Meister des Klavierspiels* (W. Niemann-CFP) Vol. I.

Suite F is contained in the anthology series *The Suite,* 113-17. Toccata, A, Double, C, S.

See: Friedrich W. Riedel, "Ein Skizzenbuch von Alessandro Poglietti," *Essays in musicology—A birthday offering for Willi Apel.* Bloomington, Ind.: School of Music, Indiana University, 1968, 145-52.

Charles David Harris, "Keyboard Music in Vienna during the Reign of Leopold I, 1658-1705," unpub. diss., University of Michigan, 1967.

MANUEL M. PONCE (1886-1948) Mexico

Gavota (PIC 1941). Refined, lyric dance. Int.

Elegia de la Ausencia (PIC 1959). Melody accompanied by rhythmic ostinato. M-D.

Preludio Tragica (PIC 1950). Expressive but full of fast repeated double notes. M-D.

Tema Mexicano Variado (PIC 1960). Sentimental theme, 4 variations, much use of shifting rhythms. M-D.

Sonata No. 2 (PIC c. 1968). 33 p. Two movements in romantic and impressionist idiom. Revised, fingered and edited by Carlos Vazquez. First movement has much rhythmic drive while the second movement, Allegro Scherzo contains a contrasting trio section. M-D.

Momento Doloroso (PIC c. 1960). Short, expressive. Int.

Quatro Danza Mexicanas (PIC 1941).

Estrellita (My Little Star) (CF) (PIC).

Twenty Easy Pieces for Piano (PIC). Based on folk tunes, many Indian. Charming and clever writing throughout. Easy to Int.

MARCEL POOT (1901-) Belgium

Poot's style is full of facile lyricism, naturalness and spontaneity. He is Director of the Royal Academy of Music in Brussels.

Sonatine D (Cnudde 1945).

Suite (UE 1943). 10½ minutes. 4 movements.
Preludio, Fughetta, Passacaglia, Toccata. Excellent for concert use.

Sonate C (ESC 1927). 3 movements.
The Andante has a Menuet as "B" section and returns to Andante. Much rhythmic vitality. M-D.

Etude (ESC 1951). Written for the Brussels competition. Technical and lyrical display.

Variationen (UE 1952). Finely contrasted moods.

Ballade (ESC 1958). MC, M-D.

In All Directions (UE). Collection of 5 teaching pieces, bright, witty, folk inspiration.

Burlesque (Cranz).

6 Petites Pièces (Cranz).

Gute Reise (UE). 10 easy pieces.

6 Petites Pièces Recreatives (ESC).

ENNIO PORRINO (1910-1959) Italy

Sonata drammatica Op. 35 (SZ 1949). 16 minutes.
A choreographic diversion, for speaking voice and piano, now available in a solo edition for piano. Introduction, a suite of 9 short dances portraying characteristic moods and rhythms of the people of 9 different parts of the world. Interesting series of contrasting tone-pictures. Considerable technique is required.

Preludio in modo religioso e ostinato (SZ 1947). 13 p.

QUINCY PORTER (1897-1966) USA

Sonata (CFP 1929-30). 3 movements. 15 minutes.
Outer movements are very rhythmic (syncopation and cross-accents) while the middle movement is more fantasia-like. MC, M-D.

6 Miniatures (BMC 1943). 12 minutes.

Day Dreams (TP 1957).

Lonesome (CF). 4 minutes.

See: Howard Boatwright, "Quincy Porter," American Composers Alliance Bulletin, 6, 1957, 2-5.

HANS POSER (1917-) Germany

Bagatellen Op. 1 (Sikorski 1947).

Sonata No. 1 Op. 7 (Sikorski 1953). 3 movements.
Free linear writing. Second movement contains a fugue. M-D.

Musik für Ursula Op. 10 (Sikorski 1950). 7 easy pieces in style of Gretchaninoff.

2 Sonatinas Op. 12/1, 2 (Sikorski 1950). In A, G, Int. No. 2 a little more difficult.

Musik für Klavier Op. 24 (Sikorski 1957). Pastorale-Recitative, Aria-Allegro rubato. 12-tone technique. M-D.

Sonatine No. 3 Op. 44/1 (Sikorski 1959). Linear. 8 p. Int.

Sonatine No. 4 Op. 44/2 (Sikorski 1959). 8 p. More difficult.

Alte Volkslieder (Sikorski). Easy settings.

FRANCIS POULENC (1899-1963) France

It is possible that Francis Poulenc's music will prove to be the most durable of all the group known as "Les Six." His music is characterized by unpretentiousness, wit, freshness and accessibility. It bespeaks the "music hall" and all that it implies. Poulenc's spontaneous melodic writing is one of his most unique and easily identifiable qualities.

Mouvements Perpétuels (JWC 1918 revised 1962). Three homophonic pieces.
Assez modéré: ostinato bass, sans nuances; Très modéré: casual mood; Alerte: bright, more energetic than the others. Int.

Suite C (JWC 1920). Three short movements, mainly diatonic, busy. Presto, Andante, Vif. M-D.

Five Impromptus (JWC 1920-21). Short parody pieces in varied moods. M-D.

Promenades (JWC 1921). The title explains the significance of the ten pieces. A pied, En auto, A cheval, En bateau, En avion, En voiture, En chemin de fer, A bicyclette, En diligence. M-D.

Pastourelle (Heugel). Transcription from the ballet *L'Eventail de Jeanne*. Enticing melody. Int.

Feuillets d'Album (Sal 1923). Ariette, Rêve, Gigue. Interesting part writing in the outside movements. Int.

Napoli (Sal 1925). One of Poulenc's best piano works. Barcarolle: lyric, mixed meters, unusual harmonies; Nocturne: short, rich harmonies, contrasting mid-section; Caprice Italien: brilliant Presto tarantella, cadenza, long. The last movement is considerably more difficult than the first two movements. M-D.

Trois Novelettes (JWC 1927-28). C, b, e. No. 3 published separately by (JWC). No. 1 is best known. No. 3 based on a theme by Manuel de Falla. M-D.

Trois Pièces (Heugel 1928). Pastorale, Toccata, Hymne. The Pastorale is most characteristic; Toccata is a brilliant perpetual motion; Hymne is chordal, ornamental melody, quiet close. M-D.

Huit Nocturnes (Heugel 1929-1938). C, A, F, c, d, G, B, E♭, coda to the cycle. Popular melodic style, rich harmonies, some of his most beautiful writing. See C, A, G, E♭ especially.

Hommage à Albert Roussel (Leduc 1929). Short, lyric, quiet ending. Int. to M-D.

Intermède d (Sal 1932). M-D.

Villageoises (Sal 1933). Five pieces for young people. Attractive melodic and harmonic writing. Int.

Presto B♭ (Sal 1934). Fresh, whimsical staccato etude. Excellent encore. Requires facility.

Suite Française (after Claude Gervaise) (Durand 1935). Seven sixteenth-century French dances freely arranged in Poulenc's harmonic and modal language. Diatonic. Int. to M-D.

Intermezzi (Sal 1934). C, D♭. No. 1, a delightful Presto con fuoco; No. 2, quiet. M-D.

Badinage (Sal 1934). A salon piece. M-D.

Improvisations (Sal). Book I: 6 pieces (1932), Book II: 6 pieces (1933-34, 1941). Nos. 13-14 (1958). No. 15, Hommage à Edith Piaf (1959). Nos. 1-10 are available separately. Informal, moderate length, varied moods. See especially Nos. 1,

3, 5-8, 10. Nos. 4 and 9 are brilliant and expressive. Nos. 13 and 14 go together well as a group. M-D.

Les Soirées de Nazelles (Durand 1930-1936). Most important solo piano work.
Préambule, Variations (8), Cadence, Finale. Poulenc said of this work: "The variations which form the center of this work were improvised at Nazelles during the course of long soirées in the country when the author played at 'Portraits' with friends grouped around the piano. We hope today that, presented between a Préambule and a Finale, they will evoke the memory of this game played in the setting of a Touraine salon, a window opening on to the night." Complete pianism required.

Mélancolie (ESC 1940). A romantic pastorale. M-D.

Intermezzo A♭ (ESC 1943). Fauré influence, melody supported by widely-spaced figuration. Romantic, salon style. M-D.

Thème Varié (ESC 1951). A banal theme with eleven well-crafted variations. M-D.

Bourrée au Pavillon d'Auvergne (Sal). In album *A l'Exposition* (Sal). Melody over drone bass, drum effects, short, attractive. Int.

Histoire de Babar (le petit éléphant) (JWC 1940). For narrator and piano. 22 minutes. Contains some of Poulenc's most charming piano writing. An English translation of the text is available through the publisher. Sections may be excerpted. M-D.

Humoresque (Sal 1935). M-D.

Caprice C (Sal). Based on the Finale of *Bal masqué,* a secular cantata. "Music Hall" style, contrasting habanera mid-section. Effective. M-D.

Album of Six Pieces (JWC). Revised and corrected by the composer. Mouvement perpétuel No. 1 (1918), Presto, from Suite in C (1920), Impromptu No. 3, Française (d'àpres C. Gervaise) (1939), Novelette No. 1 C (1927), à Pied (Promenade No. 1) (1921).

HENRI POUSSEUR (1929-   ) Belgium

Pousseur studied with Pierre Boulez and was the first Belgian composer to work with electronic music.

Exercices pour Piano: Variations I (SZ 1956).

Exercices pour Piano: Impromptu et Variations II (SZ 1955-56). Webern influence, with thicker textures. D.

Caractères I (UE 1961).
Unusual notation including inexact metric indications which are to represent values "felt as units, whose relations are of a qualitative nature." "This notation presupposes in the interpreter both an understanding of the 'semantic kernel' from which all structural principles are derived (i.e. integral aperiodicity) and a clear idea of what, as a means of fulfilling this demand, is in fact possible with our sensory apparatus." The performer can begin with any one of six pages. D.

Caractères II (UE). Three pieces. Nos. 1 and 3 have variable forms as found in *Caractéres* I. No. 2 (La Chevauchée fantastique) begins in an early classic style and progresses to twelve-tone technique. D.

MEL POWELL (1923-   ) USA

Powell was a jazz pianist in his teens and made a reputation playing in Benny Goodman's band. He later studied with Bernard Wagenaar, Joseph Schillinger, Ernst Toch, and Paul Hindemith and is presently associated with the California School of Allied Arts in Los Angeles.

Sonatina (Ric 1951).
- Vivace: free moving counterpoint, light, fleeting touch exploited.
- Chorale-Variations: mixed meters, chorale intricately woven into texture, big climax exploits melody.
- Largo assai-Allegro: brief introduction requiring large span leads to Allegro that uses repeated notes in percussive fashion. Animato ending. M-D.

Recitative and Toccata Percossa (Ric 1952). For harpsichord. Brilliant Scarlatti style clothed in twentieth-century idioms. M-D.

Etude (LG 1957). See Anthologies and Collections, USA, *New Music for the Piano.*

ANDRÉ PREVIN (1929-) USA

Impressions (MCA). 20 short pieces in a combination of styles. Pianistic. Int.

Birthday Party (Robbins 1949). A suite of eight short descriptive pieces, each employing at least one contemporary device of composition. Int.

SERGE PROKOFIEFF (1891-1953) USSR

Prokofieff's nine sonatas (now firmly established in the pianist's repertoire) and the approximately one hundred smaller pieces constitute a treasured contribution to twentieth-century piano literature. His percussive manner of treating the piano is uniquely blended with a lyric element frequently accompanied by strong dissonance. The pianistic demands vary, from the *Music for Children* Op. 65 to the highly motoric *Toccata* Op. 11 and the virtuosic *Sonatas* Nos. six, seven and eight. Biting percussive effects, physical endurance and a fine octave technique are requirements for many of Prokofieff's works.

Sonatas in one volume (Sandor-MCA) (Freundlich-Leeds) (IMC) (K). (MCA) and (K) have each available separately.

Sonata No. 1 Op. 1 f (1909) (CFP) (Simrock) (Rahter). One movement, romantic, enthusiastic. M-D.

Four Etudes Op. 2 (1909) (MCA) (IMC) (CFP) (K). d, e, c, c. Involved studies in double notes, octaves, running figuration, broken octaves. D.

Four Pieces Op. 3 (1907-1911) (GS) in collection *Selected works for the Piano,* (K) has two. Conte, Badinage, Marche, Fantôme. M-D.

Four Pieces Op. 4 (1910-11) (Bo&H) (MCA) (IMC) (K). Réminiscence: melody accompanied by chromatic harmony; Elan: short, energetic; Désespoir: chromatic ostinato: Suggestion diabolique: mocking, bravura, driving, most difficult of set. M-D.

Toccata Op. 11 (1912) (MCA) (IMC) (K). Motoric perpetual motion, skips, double notes, chromatic chords in contrary motion, virtuosic. D.

Ten Pieces Op. 12 (1913) (Freundlich-MCA) (CFP) (IMC) (K). Marche, Gavotte, Rigaudon, Mazurka, Caprice, Légende, Prélude, A, Scherzo humoristique, Scherzo. Neoclassic influence. M-D. Nos. 1, 2, 3, 7, 9, and 10 available separately (CFP).

Sonata No. 2 Op. 14 d (1912) (CFP) (Simrock). Lyric Allegro ma non troppo; Scherzo with motives crossing hands; melodic Andante; tarantella-like Vivace. M-D.

Sarcasms Op. 17 (1912-1913) (Freundlich-MCA) (EBM) (Simrock) (K). Five pieces, bitonal, brusque, percussive, much rhythmic motion. Tempestoso, Allegro rubato, Allegro precipitato, no title for No. 4, Precipitosissimo. D.

Visions fugitives Op. 22 (1915-1917) (Freundlich-MCA) (Bo&H) (Drzewiecki-EBM) (IMC) (K). Twenty short pieces, Prokofieff's "Preludes", lyric, varied moods and difficulty. M-D.

Sonata No. 3 Op. 28 a (1917) (IMC) (Simrock) (Bo&H). One movement, Allegro tempestoso, based on earlier sketches (1907), bravura, rhythmic drive, requires power and great energy. D.

Sonata No. 4 Op. 29 c (1917) (Bo&H). Three movements, based on earlier sketches (1908). Allegro molto sostenuto: Mainly lyric, pondorous; Andante assai: enticing melody with rich figurative accompaniment; Allegro con brio, ma non troppo: a facile rondo. D.

Tales of the Old Grandmother Op. 31 (1918) (MCA) (IMC) (K) (Bo&H). Four short, melodic pieces. Int.

Four Pieces Op. 32 (1918) (MCA) (IMC) (K). (Bo&H) have Nos. 3 and 4. Dance, Minuet, Gavotte, Waltz. Neoclassic influence. Gavotte is finest in the set. Int. to M-D.

Sonata No. 5 Op. 38 C (1925) (Bo&H). Three movements; Allegro tranquillo: forceful melodic writing, parallel harmonies; Andante: dancelike, mocking; Un poco allegretto: requires large span.

Divertissement Op. 43B (1925-26) (Bo&H) (MCA). Four pieces arranged by Prokofieff, from his other works. Divertissement (from *Trapèze*), Nocturne, Dance (*Trapèze*), Epilogue. M-D.

Things in Themselves Op. 45 (1928) (Bo&H). Two lengthy, somewhat involved pieces with strong lyric overtones. Allegro moderato, Moderato scherzando. M-D.

Six Transcriptions Op. 52 (1931) (Bo&H) (AMP). Both editions publish these separately. Intermezzo, Rondo, Etude, Scherzino, Andante, Scherzo. M-D to D, the Scherzo especially difficult.

Two Sonatinas Op. 54 e, G. (1931) (Bo&H) (K). Each in three movements, short but not easy. Diatonic, linear, sophisticated writing. M-D.

Three Pieces Op. 59 (1934) (Bo&H). Promenade, Paysage, Sonatine pastorale. Available separately. The one-movement Sonatine is somewhat easier than Op. 54. Int. to M-D.

Pensées Op. 62 (1933-34) (Bo&H). Adagio penseroso, Moderato: double melody two octaves apart, ornamental RH; Lento: chorale-like; Andante: longest of the set, melodic, chromatic. M-D.

Music for Children Op. 65 (1935) (Bo&H) (IMC) (GS). Twelve pieces involving a variety of problems. Provides an excellent introduction to the composer. Easy to Int.

Peter and the Wolf Op. 67 (1936). (MCA). Arranged by Prokofieff. M-D.

Ten Pieces Op. 75 (1937) (MCA) (CFP). From the ballet

Romeo and Juliet. Short sketches: Danse populaire, Scène, Menuet, Juliette jeune fille, Masques, Mercutio, etc. Effective as a group or separately. Int. to M-D.

Gavotte Op. 77 E♭ (1938) (K). From music to *Hamlet.* Forceful, effective. M-D.

Sonata No. 6 Op. 82 A (1939-40) (CFP) (Bo&H). Largest of the sonatas. Requires virtuoso equipment. Allegro moderato: biting, dissonant, driving, SA; Allegretto: March-like, staccato chords, lyric mid-section; Tempo di valzer lentissimo: long, slow, romantic waltz; Vivace: brilliant rondo, sparkling melodic treatment, sonorous climax. D.

Sonata No. 7 Op. 83 B♭ (1939-1942) (IMC) (CFP) (Bo&H) (K). Most popular of the sonatas. Allegro inquieto: bare, percussive; Andante caloroso: lush harmonic treatment; Precipitato: perpetual-motion toccata, one of the finest ever written. D.

Sonata No. 8 Op. 84 B♭ (1939-1944) (CFP) (Bo&H) (K). Most lyrical of the sonatas. Andante dolce: melodic but includes a powerful climax; Andante sognando: lyric intermezzo; Vivace: lengthy rondo leads to a highly spirited Allegro ben marcato. D.

Three Pieces Op. 95 (1942) (Bo&H). From ballet *Cinderella.* Intermezzo, Gavotte, Valse lente. M-D.

Sonata No. 9 Op. 103 C (1947) (CFP) (Bo&H) (K). A strange mixture of styles pervades this work. Four movements. Less difficult than *Sonatas* six and seven. D.

Selected Works for the Piano (Balogh-GS).
Contains Op. 2/3, 4; Op. 3/1, 2, 3, 4; Op. 4/4; Op. 11; Op. 12/1, 7; Gavotte from *Classical Symphony* Op. 25; March from *The Love of Three Oranges* Op. 33; Op. 45/1; Op. 52/6; Op. 54/2; Op. 59/3; Op. 62/1, 2, 3; Op. 77/4; Contradance from the film *Lermontov* Op. 96/2; Mephisto valse from film *Lermontov.*

See: Patricia Ashley, "Prokofieff's Piano Music: Line, Chord and

Key," unpub. diss., University of Rochester, Eastman School of Music, 1963.

Malcolm H. Brown, "Prokofieff's Eighth Piano Sonata," Tempo, 70, Autumn 1964, 9-15.

David L. Kinsky, "The Piano Sonatas of Serge Prokofieff; a Critical Study of the Elements of Their Style," unpub. diss., Teachers College of Columbia University, 1959.

Frank Merrick, "Prokofieff's Piano Sonatas," PRMA, 75, 1948-49, 13-21.

"Prokofieff's Piano Sonatas One to Five," MT, 86, January 1945, 9-11.

"Prokofieff's Sixth Piano Sonata," MT, 85, January 1944, 9-11.

Eric Roseberry, "Prokofieff's Piano Sonatas," M&M, 19, March 1971, 38-42.

HENRY PURCELL (ca. 1659-1695) Great Britain

French and Italian influences are evident in Purcell's keyboard works. He left eight suites and a few separate pieces, all thinly textured. 3 or 4 movements make up the suites and they usually begin with Preludes, followed by Almands, Corants, Sarabands, and sometimes a Hornpipe, a Minuet, etc.

6 Suites (G. M. Cooper-Nov) Vol. 7 in the Purcell Society Practical Edition. Suites in G, g, G, a, C, D.

8 Suites (H. Ferguson-S&B 1964). Superb edition.

Suites, Lessons and Pieces for the Harpsichord (W. Squire-JWC). Four Volumes. A reprint of the 1696 edition is available in (BB) *Monuments of Music* Series. The Squire edition has suites and smaller pieces in Vols. I-III; Vol. IV contains 12 lessons from *Musick's Handmaid* Part II.

Miscellaneous Keyboard Pieces (H. Ferguson-S&B 1964).

Prelude C and *A Ground in Gamut* in collection *Keyboard Music of the Baroque and Rococo,* Vol. I.

Stücke für Klavier oder Cembalo (Hillemann-Schott). Suites in C, F; Chaconne g; 15 pieces.

The Second Part of Musick's Handmaid (T. Dart-S&B) revised and corrected by H. Purcell. 35 easy keyboard pieces mostly by J. Blow and H. Purcell. First published 1689, re-issued in 1705, extensive notes printed in their entirety. Includes Purcell's setting of *Lilliburlero* and his *Sefauchi's Farewell.*

Easy Keyboard Pieces (CFP).

Selected Pieces (PWM). Varied selection, contains the composer's original ornaments with detailed instructions for their execution, plus suggested fingerings.

See: Thurston Dart, "Purcell's Harpsichord Music," MT, 100, June 1959, 324-5.

Gloria Rose, "Purcell, Michelangelo Rossi and J. S. Bach: Problems of Authorship," AM, 40, 1968, 203-19.

R

SERGEI RACHMANINOFF (1873-1943) Russia, came to USA in 1918

The piano music of Rachmaninoff is written in an eclectic individual style derived from Chopin, Liszt, Schumann and Brahms. Melodic writing is of the highest order and is supported by sonorous harmonies with florid decoration resulting in unusually effective music for the instrument. Many character-pieces are contained in his works.

Complete Piano Works (USSR).

5 Pieces Op. 3 (1892) (GS) published separately. Elégie (Belwin-Mills), Prelude c♯ (Schott) (IMC) (Bo&H) (WH), Mélodie, Polichinelle, Sérénade (Belwin-Mills). M-D.

7 Pieces Op. 10 (1894) (K). Nocturne (WH), Valse (Schott), Barcarole, Mélodie (GS), Humoreske (Belwin-Mills) (GS) (WH) (CF), Romance, Mazurka. M-D.

6 Moments musicaux Op. 16 (1896) (K) (IMC). b♭, e♭ (Belwin-Mills), b, e, D♭, C. See especially e and e♭. Brilliant salon pieces more difficult than Op. 5 and 10.

Variations on a Theme by Chopin Op. 22 (1903) (IMC). A long set based on Chopin's *Prelude* c Op. 28/20. D.

10 Preludes Op. 23 (1903-4) (Bo&H) (GS) (IMC) (EBM) (K). f♯, B♭, d, D, g (WH), E♭, c, A♭, e♭, G♭. M-D to D. Every one is a gem with B♭ and e♭ most difficult.

Sonata No. 1 d Op. 28 (1907) (Bo&H) (IMC). 33 minutes. Three movements, highly complex.

13 Preludes Op. 32 (1910) (Bo&H) (IMC) (EBM) (K). C, b♭, E, e, G, f, F, a, A, b, g♯, D♭. b is perhaps the finest of all 24 Preludes. Rachmaninoff patterned his key relationships after Chopin and wrote one Prelude in each major and minor key. The famous *Prelude* c♯, published separately, is No. 24.

6 Etudes-Tableaux Op. 33(1911)(MCA)(IMC)(Gutheil)(K). f, C, e♭, E♭, g, c♯. In the (Gutheil) and (MCA) editions 2 more, c, d, are included. They were discovered in Russia in 1947. Only published with Op. 39 (MCA). D.

Sonata No. 2 b♭ Op. 36 (Bo&H) (IMC). The composer originally wrote this work in 1913 but revised it in 1931, tightening the structure while simplifying some of the performance problems. Three movements, although at first hearing it gives the impression of one-movement work. As involved and difficult as the first sonata.

9 Etudes Tableaux Op. 39 (1916-17) (Bo&H) separately, (MCA) (IMC) (K). c, a, f♯, b, e♭, a, c, d, D. Only published with Op. 33 (MCA). D.

Variations on a Theme of Corelli Opus 42 (1932) (Belwin-Mills). Based on "La Folia" Op. 5/12, this set is in reality two series of variations, generally of parallel construction, separated by an "Intermezzo" and concluded by a Coda. Less complicated than Op. 22. D.

2 Fantasy-Pieces Op. Posthumous (Mirovitch-MCA).

Oriental Sketch (Belwin-Mills).

Album (Schott). 9 selected pieces including; from Op. 3: Elégie, Prelude c♯, Mélodie, Sérénade, Polichinelle; from Op. 10: Nocturne, Valse, Humoreske, Romance.

Album (GS). Barcarolle g, Elégie e♭, Mélodie E, Polichinelle, Prélude c♯, Prélude g, second piano concerto, third movement condensed and arranged by C. Deis, Sérénade b♭, Valse A.

Radio City Album of Selected Composition for Piano by Rachmaninoff (EBM).

Etude-Tableau f Op. 33/1, Moment Musical D♭ Op. 16/5, Polichinelle Op. 3/4, 3 Preludes Op. 3/2, 23/5, 32/5, Romance Op. 10/6, Valse Op. 10/2, and themes from Concerti No. 1 and 2. Practical collection.

See: Anthony J. La Magra, "A Source Book, for the Study of Rachmaninoff's Preludes," unpub. diss., Columbia University, 1966. Mainly devoted to individual structural analyses of the twenty-four *Preludes*: their musical content, performance requirements and Rachmaninoff's contributions as a composer.

JOACHIM RAFF (1822-1882) German, born Switzerland

Cavatina Op. 157/1 (Reid) (Paxton).

La Fileuse Op. 157/2 (GS) (Schott) (Reid). Facile melody, broken chord accompaniment.

Polka de la Reine: Caprice Op. 95 (Augener).

Romanzen in Etüdenform Op. 8 (Ashdown). 12 character pieces of M-D.

Suite e Op. 72 (Ashdown). Prelude and fugue only.

Suite g Op. 162 (Metzler). 4 movements. Elegie in Sonatenform, Volkslied mit Variationen, Ländler, Märschen.

Tarantella (Augener). From *Sonatina* a Op. 99. Effective, Int.

Fabliau Op. 75/2 (Schott).

Giga con Variazioni Op. 91 (Musica Obscura).

DIEUDONNÉ RAICK (1703-1764) Flemish, Belgium

Werken voor orgel en/of Clavecimbel. Monumenta Musicae Belgicae, Vol. 6 (1948) with a short biography by Suzanne Clercx. Six suites for clavecin with movements such as Andante, Minuet, Allegro, Gavotte, Gratioso, Cecilane, Capricio moderato, Gique. Some movements have a "double" written out with added ornamentation and differing treatment.

JEAN-PHILIPPE RAMEAU (1683-1764) France

Rameau left fifty-three pieces for keyboard that show dramatic sweep, boldness and an art more firmly rooted in the Baroque than his older contemporary François Couperin. Rameau's keyboard works have a more sustained quality and are more suited to the piano than Couperin's. The suite idea is present. He uses some or all of the four basic movements and adds other movements with illustrative titles.

Pièces de Clavecin (Jacobi-Br 1958).
Four books of pieces dating from: 1706, 10 pieces; 1724, 21 pieces; 1736, 16 pieces; and 1741, 5 arrangements from the *Pièces en Concert* and a single work (*La Dauphine*) from 1747. Also Rameau's treatise *On the Technique of the Fingers on the Harpsichord,* and a table of ornaments from the 1724 and 1731 editions of the *Pièces de Clavecin.* Expertly translated by the editor, Erwin R. Jacobi. Urtext edition.

Pièces de Clavecin (Saint-Saëns-Durand). Does not include the treatise mentioned above. (K) has these in miniature score as well as Lea Pocket Scores. *Nouvelles Suites de Pièces de Clavecin* ca. 1727 and *Pièces de Clavecin* 1731 are available in facsimile editions from (BB). Lea Pocket Scores reprints the Durand edition.

Popular pieces (Augener). Les Tendres Plaintes, Le Rappel des Oiseaux, La Poule, Les Niais de Sologne, Gavotte et Variations, L'Agaçante, Menuet et Trio G, 2 Gigues en Rondeaux from his operas.

Selected Pieces (PWM). Varied selection, includes the composer's original ornaments together with detailed instructions for their execution, and suggested fingering.

The Graded Rameau (M. Motchane, Belwin-Mills). 25 pieces, edited.

Collection *Keyboard Music of the Baroque and Rococo* Vol. II (Georgii-Arno Volk) contains Musette en Rondeau, Gavotte, 2 Menuette, La Poule, L'Egyptiènne and L'Enharmonique.

See: Kathleen Dale, "The Keyboard Music of Rameau," MMR, December 1947, January 1948.

Cuthbert Girdlestone, *Jean-Philippe Rameau His Life and Works.* London: Cassell & Co., 1957.

Zelik Klitenic, "The Clavecin Works of Jean-Philippe Rameau," unpub. diss., University of Pennsylvania, 1955.

PHILIP RAMEY (1939-) USA

Ramey studied composition with Alexander Tcherepnin at De Paul University and in France. He also worked with Jack Beeson at Columbia University.

Epigrams (Bo&H 1968).
Eleven short unrelated pieces showing various influences and pianistic effects of the twentieth century: from serialism to pointillism. Each has a distinctive mood: sarcastic, dreamlike, jaunty, etc. M-D.

SHULAMIT RAN (1947-) Israel

Miss Ran is a graduate of the Mannes School of Music where she studied composition with Norman Dello Joio.

Short Piano Pieces (IMI 1967). 7 pieces, 12 minutes. 15 p. M-D.
Crescendo, Semplice, Pesante, Staccato, Legato, Lugubre, Ritenuto.

Piano Sonata No. 2 (IMI 1967). 10 minutes. 21 p. M-D.
Moderato: thin textures, linear.
Lento: impressionistic, colorful pedal effects.
Vivo (Rondo): folk influence.

BERNARD RANDS (1935-) Great Britain

Rands studied with Roman Vlad, Luigi Dallapiccola, Reginald Smith Brindle and has been associated with Luciano Berio. Rands is presently at Princeton University.

Tre Espressioni (UE 1965).
Serial technique handled with much freedom. Aleatory writing, exploits pointillistic technique. Extensive directions are included.

TURE RANGSTRÖM (1884-1947) Sweden

"In his work Rangström was at first influenced by French 'impressionism', but later he developed a style essentially Swedish." GD, 7, 45.

Mälarlegender (AL). Three musical vignettes to Strindberg's "The City Journey." Lyric.

Improvisata (NMS).

Plaisirs d'Amour (WH).

Preludium I, II, III, IV (WH). Each published separately.

Sommarskyar (NMS).

Spelmansvar (NMS).

GYÖRGY RANKI (1907-) Hungary

Ránki worked with Kodály, then studied oriental folk music at the Paris Musée de l'Homme and in London.

Piano Sonata No. 2 (EMB c. 1964). 12 p. M-D.
Allegro Capriccioso: energetic theme exploited in opening and closing sections. Mid section is not development but a new rhythmic figure serves as the inspiration.
Largo espressivo: choral, intense, many seconds, fourths, fifths.
Allegretto "al" bulgarese: in Bulgarian dance style, accelarando to PP closing. Bold colors.

Scherzo (EMB).

GÜNTER RAPHAEL (1903-1960) Germany

Raphael writes in a neoclassic linear style. All the sonatas are of moderate difficulty.

Kleine Sonata e Op. 2 (Br&H 1922).

Sonate a Op. 38/1 (Br&H 1939). 3 movements. 17½ minutes. Chromatic.

Sonate E♭ Op. 38/2 (Br&H 1939). 3 movements. 17 minutes.

Sonatina seria Op. 51/1 (Süddeutscher Musikverlag 1944). 12 p. Some of his best writing.

Sonatina giocosa Op. 51/2 (Süddeutscher Musikverlag 1944). 7 p. Slightly more difficult than Op. 51/1.

6 Improvisations Op. 3 (Steingräber 1923).

Partita in 5 Parts Op. 18 (Br&H 1926).

Advents- und Weihnachslieder (Süddeutscher Musikverlag 1948). Int.

SAM RAPHLING (1910-) USA

American Album (Mer). 8 cleverly written portraits of Americana. MC. Redskin, Cowboy, Jitterbug, Square Dance, Introduction and Rag, etc.

Sonata No. 1 (Belwin-Mills 1961). 3 movements. Contemporary idiom. Clever rhythms, free tonality. Last movement is a perpetual motion, mixed meters. M-D.

Sonata No. 3 (Edition Musicus 1958). 3 movements. Quartal and quintal harmony. First movement chromatic, transfer of register. Second movement, expressive theme with interesting contour. Third movement is agitato, rhythmic, energetic, percussive chords. M-D.

Sonata No. 5 (Gen c. 1966). 24 p. 4 movements. D.
Slow Introduction to Agitato section. Many sequences.
Lively; alternating 4/8 and 3/8, slower mid-section, return to opening idea.
Moderately Slow; expressive harmonic and melodic writing.
Lively, maintains basic exciting tempo, chromatic.

24 Etudes (Gen c. 1965). 2 volumes, 12 in each volume. Contemporary techniques, wide skips, dissonant harmonic and melodic intervals, pedal and tone production problems. Some etudes are lyric. M-D to D.

7 Mobiles (Gen 1968). Chordal, trills, span of 10th required, varied moods. Int.

9 Encore Pieces (Belwin-Mills c. 1966). Int.

Sonatina No. 1 (TP).

Five Forcasts (MCA). Easy.

KAROL RATHAUS (1895-1954) Poland, came to USA in 1938

Sonata No. 1 Op. 2 c (UE 1920). A large four-movement work, bravura style, highly chromatic. D.

Sonata No. 2 Op. 8 (UE 1924).

Five Pieces Op. 9 (UE 1920). Linear, rhythmically strong, thick textures. M-D.

Six Little Pieces Op. 11 (UE 1926). Miniatures grotesques. M-D to D.

Sonata No. 3 Op. 20 (UE 1927). A work of much intensity and sweep, fine skill displayed. D.

Three Mazurkas Op. 24 (UE 1928). Follows the Chopin tradition. Flexible tempo in No. 2 especially effective. Szymanowski influence. M-D.

Ballade Op. 40 (Bomart 1936). Variations on a Hurdy-Gurdy Theme. M-D.

Mazurka (CF). Modal. Int.

Cross Talk (CF). Polytonal, humorous. Int.

Three Polish Dances Op. 47 (Bo&H 1942). Oberek, Kujawiak, Mazurka. Long dances, varied moods, demand mature pianism. D.

Four Studies after Domenico Scarlatti Op. 56 (TP 1945-6). Stinging dissonance, sharp rhythms, modern commentary on an 18th-century style. D.

Variations on a Theme of Georg Böhm (ACA).

See: Boris Schwarz, "Karol Rathaus," MQ, 41, October 1955, 481-95. A survey of his life and music.

VALENTIN RATHGEBER (1682-1750) Germany

Musikalischer Zeitvertreib auf dem Klavier (Steglich-Nag). Consists of nineteen pieces, nine Arien Pastorellen and other short pieces: Allegro, Langsamer, Kräftig, etc. The Arien Pastorellen are for Christmas time. The collection dates from 1743.

MATTI RAUTIO (1922-) Finland

Suita per piano (Westerlund 1951). Int. to M-D. Preludio: pays homage to Czerny. Intermezzo: dancelike. Ostinato ritmico: tricky rhythms. Intermezzo: quiet and mysterious. Toccata: driving, some melodic emphasis.

MAURICE RAVEL (1875-1937) France

The piano music of Ravel is characterized by precise attention to detail, sharp outlines, and clear forms. Ravel, a classicist with romantic leanings, extended the pianistic traditions of Franz Liszt. Ravel's influence on the piano writing of Claude Debussy was of major importance (*Jeux d'Eau,* 1901).

Menuet antique (1895) (Enoch) (IMC).
Charming foreshadowing of things to come. M-D.

Pavane pour une Infante défunte (1899) (ESC) (Schott) (GS).
Diatonic, a few wide-spread chords, requires steady tempo. Original edition listed quarter note at 54. Int. to M-D.

Jeux d'Eau (1901) (ESC) (Schott) (GS).
This early masterpiece lies under the fingers but demands much facility. D.

Sonatine f♯ (1905) (Durand) (EBM) (CF) (GS) (IMC).
Short, cyclic, three movements. Thin textures, exploitation of upper register, careful rubato necessary. Final movement requires facility. M-D to D.
Modéré, Mouvement de Menuet, Animé.

Miroirs (1905) (ESC) (EBM) (GS) (Schott) (K). M-D to D.
Noctuelles: flitting melodic lines, evasive, scurrying figuration.
Oiseaux tristes: melancholy lament, needs sensitive balance of tone.
Une barque sur l'océan: a consummate barcarolle, broad arpeggi, changing rhythms make continuity difficult.
Alborada del gracioso: Spanish guitar serenade, repeated notes, double glissandi, most difficult of the set. Compare with orchestral version.
La vallée des cloches: careful pedaling required for this atmospheric study in sonorities.

Gaspard de la Nuit (1908) (Durand).

Three poems for piano based on the prose poems of Louis Bertrand. This set is one of the peaks in 20th-century French piano music. Transcendentally difficult.

Ondine: opening accompanying figure must be pianissimo, flowing LH melody rhythmically free.

Le gibet: a dirge over a hypnotic pedal point, large span helpful, tonal balance is a problem.

Scarbo: diabolic scherzo, a major challenge to the pianist, great contrasts, sweeping gestures, most difficult of set.

See: Irwin Freundlich, "Maurice Ravel's Gaspard de la Nuit," PQ, Fall 53, 1965, 19-21.

Menuet sur le nom de Haydn (1909) (Durand).

Short, unpretentious. Written for the 100th anniversary of Haydn's death. M-D.

Valses nobles et sentimentales (1911) (Durand).

Eight connected pieces ranging from a forceful opening to a delicate closing that recapitulates the previous waltzes.

Prélude a (1913) (Durand).

Relaxed tempo, interesting inner voices. Int.

A la manière de Borodin, de Chabrier (1913) (Sal).

Written in imitation of the style of these composers. Available separately. M-D.

Le Tombeau de Couperin (1914-1917) (Durand).

Six pieces related to the clavecin suite of the eighteenth century. M-D to D.

Prélude: fast finger figuration, mordents, 6/8 meter.

Fugue: lyric, concentrated, rather static.

Forlane: modal, dotted 6/8 rhythm, skips in melody.

Rigaudon: vigorous, mostly diatonic, mid-section more chromatic.

Menuet: lyric, use of mordent prominent, modal, parallel chords in Musette (Trio).

Toccata: virtuoso piece, repeated notes, pentatonic theme, imposing climax.

Album (Durand).
Prélude a; Menuet sur le nom Haydn; Transcriptions: Les Entretiens de la Belle et de la Bête, Danse de Daphnis, Habanera; Menuet from the Sonatine.

Album of Maurice Ravel Masterpieces (EBM).
Miroirs, Jeux d'Eau, Pavane, Lento (excerpt from the string quartet).

See: Stelio Dubbiosi, "The Piano Music of Maurice Ravel: An Analysis of the Technical and Interpretative Problems Inherent in the Pianistic Style of Maurice Ravel," unpub. diss., New York University, 1967.

ALAN RAWSTHORNE (1905-1971) Great Britain

4 Bagatelles (OUP 1938). 6 minutes. Set of four short pieces. M-D.
Allegro: scherzando. Allegretto: siciliano. Presto non assai: sprint-like. Lento: serious.

Sonatina (OUP 1949). 11 minutes. 4 movements. M-D. Freely chromatic, first 3 movements on subdued side.
Allegro sostenuto e misterioso.
Lento ma con movimento: dramatic climax, quiet closing.
Allegretto con malinconia.
Allegro con brio: energetic, poco brusco, some alternating hands, broad gestures close movement.

4 Romantic Pieces (OUP 1953). 10 minutes.
Accessible textures and colorful harmony. "Romantic" refers more to style than to material.

Ballad (OUP c 1967). 16 p. 12 minutes.
Commissioned by Cardiff Festival of Twentieth-Century Music and first performed by John Ogdon in March 1967. Tightly constructed, mainly from two figures in the quiet introduction. Ternary form, contrasted sections. Virtuoso technique required, effective display piece.

GARDNER READ (1913-) USA

American Circle (SB). Short, varied settings of a folklike melody. Int.

Poem Op. 20 (JF 1945). Short, romantic. Int.

Intermezzo Op. 42a (SB 1959). Short, lyric, open fifths. Int.

Capriccio Op. 27/3. See Anthologies and Collections, USA, *U. S. A.*, II (MCA).

VLADIMIR REBIKOV (1866-1920) USSR

2 Volumes (USSR c. 1968). Preface in Russian. Contains wide sampling of his piano writing.

9 Silhouettes Op. 31 (IMC) (Simrock). Int.

Pictures for Children Op. 37 (IMC).

Album (Schott). 2 volumes.

Rêveries D'Autumne Op. 8 (Augener). 2 books, 8 pieces in each.

H. OWEN REED (1910-) USA

3 Nationalities (Belwin-Mills 1951). 4 p. Suite. Int.
El Muchacho: melodic, syncopated.
Le Sonneur: bitonal, harmonic vocabulary most interesting.
Mr. Jazz: most difficult.

MAX REGER (1873-1916) Germany

"The piano music of Reger is hardly known in the U.S.A. while it is enormously respected and played in his native Germany. "The pianism is demanding. Thick textures, leaps, intricate polyphony, wide dynamic range, bravura playing, delicate balance of the parts; in short, all the problems of first-class keyboard control are here present. The style is often crowded with details, the more extended works herculean in concept." MFTP, 157. The character-piece abounds in Reger's piano writing.

Complete Edition (Br&H 1954).
Six volumes of piano music: Piano solos in Vols. IX-XII; piano duets Vol. XIII; 2-piano music Vol. XIV.

7 Waltzes Op. 11 (1891) (Schott) (Augener). A, c♯, D, A♭, E, f♯, A. M-D.

Lose Blätter Op. 13 (1895) (Schott) (Augener). 14 sketches in salon style. See especially No. 2 Valsette A♭, No. 5 Petite caprice b♭, Danse des Paysans A. M-D.

Aus der Jugendzeit Op. 17 (1895) (Schott). 2 books of 7 pieces each from the original 20 pieces. In the tradition of Schumann's *Album for the Young*. See No. 6 Cheerfulness, No. 8 Anxious Question, No. 9 Almost Too Bold, No. 10 First Quarrel. Int.

Improvisationen Op. 18 (1895) (Schott) (Augener). 2 volumes, 4 pieces in each. See Nos. 2, 3, 4, 6 and 7. M-D.

5 Humoresken Op. 20 (1898) (UE). Some of the best pieces in the early works. No. 2 b (in Magyar style) and No. 6 Vivace assai g are outstanding.

6 Morceaux Op. 24 (1898) (CFP). Valse-impromptu, Menuet, Rèverie fantastique, Un moment musical, Chant de la nuit, Rhapsody e (in style of Brahms). Elegant writing. M-D to D.

Aquarellen Op. 25 (Augener). 5 small sketches. See No. 2 Humoreske and especially No. 3 Impromptu. M-D.

7 Fantasiestücke Op. 26 (CFP). See No. 4 Humoreske c, and No. 6 Impromptu b. M-D.

7 Charakterstücke Op. 32 (UE). Brahms influence. 1-4 Book 1, 5-7 Book 2. D.

Bunte Blätter Op. 36 (UE). 9 small pieces, M-D. 1-4 Book 1, 5-9 Book 2. See No. 6 Elegie, also No. 2 Albumblatt and No. 3 Capricietto e.

10 Little Instructional Pieces Op. 44 (UE). In progressive order: Albumblatt, Gigue, Scherzo, Burletta, Es war einmal, Moment musical, Capriccio No. 4, Fughette, Capriccio No. 10, Humoreske.

6 Intermezzi Op. 45 (UE). Title is misleading. Nos. 2, 4, and 6 are virtuoso pieces. D.

Silhouetten Op. 53 (UE). 7 pieces M-D to D. e, D, F♯, A C, E, B♭. No. 2 shows Brahms influence, No. 3 is reminiscent of Grieg. D.

10 Klavierstücke Op. 79a (Sikorski). Short and relatively uncomplicated for Reger. M-D. See Nos. 2, 3, 6, 7, 8.

Variationen und Fuge über ein Thema von J. S. Bach Op. 81 (1904) (Bo&Bo) (CFP). D. Probably Reger's masterpiece for piano. 14 variations and fugue on a theme from Cantata No. 128. Bravura writing of the highest order, involved and lengthy fugue, gigantic conclusion.

Aus meinem Tagebuch Op. 82 (Bo&Bo). 4 volumes. Vol. 1: 12 pieces, Vol. 2: 10 pieces, Vol. 3: 6 pieces, Vol. 4: 7 pieces. M-D. Contains some of Reger's most beautiful lyric writing. See: Vol. 1 No. 5 Gavotte; Vol. 2 No. 4 Andantino, No. 7 Larghetto, No. 8 Vivacissimo; Vol. 3 No. 4 Romanze, No. 2 Albumblatt, No. 6 Humoreske; Vol. 4 No. 5 Silhouette, No. 7 Humoreske. Volumes 3 and 4 are more difficult than 1 and 2. (CFP) has one volume with 10 selections.

4 Sonatinas Op. 89 (Bo&H). No. 1 e (1905) No. 2 D (1905) No. 3 F (1908) No. 4 a (1908). All are M-D, long, and in three movements, except for No. 2 which has four and is a little less involved.

6 Preludes and Fugues Op. 99 (Bo&Bo). 2 volumes comparable in difficulty to Bach's "WTC." M-D.

Episoden Op. 115 (Bo&Bo). 8 pieces for big and little people. Published in 1 or 2 books. In the same style as Op. 82. M-D.

Variationen und Fuge über ein Thema von Telemann Op. 134 (CFP). 32 minutes. Based on a theme from Telemann's "Hamburger Tafelkonfekt." As difficult as Op. 81 but more classic in structure and style.

Träume am Kamin (1916) Op. 143 (CFP). 12 short pieces. No. 12 *Studie* based on Chopin's *Berceuse*. M-D.

Blätter und Blüten (1898-1902) (Br&H). No opus number. 12 pieces, each with title. Int. to M-D.

6 Klavierstücke (1898) (Br&H). No opus number. No. 3, Abenddämmerung and No. 4, Albumblatt have the most interest. M-D.

ANTON REICHA (1770-1836) Bohemia

L'Art de varier Op. 57 (Artia). Contained in Vol. 50 MAB. A theme and 57 variations. M-D. Introductory notes by Jan Racek and Dana Setkova.

10 Fugen (Artia).
A, D (Cercle harmonique), g (On a theme of D. Scarlatti), C, f (On a theme of Haydn), Fuga-fantasia d (On a theme of Frescobaldi), c, G, a, C. M-D.

Sonata B♭ Op. 46/2 (Artia).
Rondo only.

JOHANN FRIEDRICH REICHARDT (1752-1814) Germany

Stücke für Klavier (A. Kuster-Verlag für Musikalische Kultur und Wissenschaft). Vol. I of *Musik in Goethes Haus*. Poco vivace e scherzando from Op. 2/1; Tempo di Minuetto Op. 2/3; Andante a mezza voce Op. 2/5; Andantino innocentemente Op. 3/3; Romanze Op. 3/6; Andantino a mezza voce Op. 3/1.

See: *Thirteen Keyboard Sonatas of the 18th and 19th Centuries* in Anthologies and Collections, General.

PAUL REIF (1910-   ) USA, born Czechoslovakia

7 Musical Moments (Gen). Provides an introduction to contemporary writing. Pensive, Impatient, Friendly, Fickle, Sleepy, Laughing, Heroic. Int.

ALEXANDER REINAGLE (1756-1809) USA, born Scotland

Reinagle's early years were spent in England and Scotland where he studied with Raynor Taylor. He met C.P.E. Bach during a visit to the continent. Reinagle came to Philadelphia in 1786 where he was a major influence in shaping the musical life of that city. He was probably the most important composer in America during the early life of our country. His contribution to the musical life of America was significant.

Sonata No. 1 D (McClenny, Hinson-Willis). In *Collection of Early American Keyboard Music*. 2 movements. Allegro con brio; Allegro. Written in Philadelphia, both movements are in abbreviated SA design, the first theme being omitted in the recapitulation. In classic style. M-D.

Sonata No. 2 E(JF). A shortened form is contained in the album *Early American Piano Music*. Bright, facile Allegro; long florid improvisatory Adagio; cheerful Rondo in style of Haydn.

Shorter pieces in collection *Early American Music* (McClenny, Hinson-Belwin-Mills).

See: Charles Allison Horton, "Serious Art and Concert Music for Piano in America in the 100 Years from Alexander Reinagle to Edward MacDowell," unpub. diss., University of North Carolina, 1965.

Anne McClenny, "Alexander Reinagle," AMT, 19, September-October 1969, 38, 50.

Ernst C. Krohn, "Alexander Reinagle as Sonatist," MQ, 18, 1932, 140-9.

CARL REINECKE (1824-1910) Germany

6 Liedersonatinen (Br&H). Easy teaching material.

Libro di musica per piccola gente (Carisch). 30 short pieces in style of Gurlitt. Easy.

Weihnachtssonatine (Hofmeister). Int.

3 Sonatinas Op. 98 (Hamelle). Graceful. Int.

Notenbuch für kleine Leute Op. 107 (K&S).

Serenaden für die Jugend Op. 183 (CFP).

FRANZ REIZENSTEIN (1911-1968) Great Britain, born Germany

Reizenstein studied piano with Leonid Kreutzer in Berlin and Solomon in England. He was a fine pianist and always had a dual interest in performance and composing.

Children's Pieces (Lengnick 1952). 7 pieces published separately.

Sonata B Op. 19 (Lengnick 1948). 47p. 26 minutes.

Legend Op. 24 (Lengnick 1952). 5 minutes.

Scherzo Fantastique Op. 26 (Lengnick 1952). 8 minutes. This work and the Op. 24 are grateful to play, full of sophisticated harmonies. Op. 26 is Chopinesque in design.

Suite (Rogers). 14 minutes. 7 movements.
Preludio, Aria, Burlesca, Siciliano. Marcia barbara, Lullaby, Tarantella.

Scherzo A (Lengnick). Lively recital repertoire.

12 Preludes and Fugues Op. 32 (Lengnick 1955). 2 books, 6 in each. 50 minutes. Linear, transparent textures. Regerian, Hindemithian style. In each pair the fugue subject is presented in the prelude, an interesting unifying device. D.

The Zodiac Op. 41 (Leeds). 12 pieces, available in 3 books or 1. A suite using names of Zodiac: Aries, Aquarius, etc. Various styles, fine recital material. Int.

Sonata No. 2 A♭ Op. 40 (Galliard 1966). 34p. 26 minutes. 3 movements. Dramatic, romantic writing. Many moods: somber, passionate, delicate, fiery. Virtuoso technique required. D.

Impromptu (Lengnick 1947).

Intermezzo Op. 17 (Lengnick). 4 minutes.

SÁNDOR RESCHOFSKY (1887-) Hungary

Eminent pianist, pedagogue and composer. Collaborated with Béla Bartók in writing a *Piano Method*.

Sonata No. 3 f (Kultura 1966). 14 p. 3 movements. Interesting tonal writing, well-developed material. M-D.

OTTORINO RESPIGHI (1879-1936) Italy

Notturno (GS) (Bongiovanni). Charming salon writing. M-D.

Etude A♭ (Bongiovanni). Interlocking hands and double note technique required. M-D.

Canon (Bongiovanni).

Minuetto (Bongiovanni).

Re Enzo (Bongiovanni). "Intermezzo."

Valse caressante (Bongiovanni).

3 Preludes on Gregorian Melodies (UE). More complex. No. 2 the most difficult. M-D.

Ancient Dances and Airs (Ric). Selections from symphonic suites.

RUDOLPH RETI (1885-1957) USA, born Yugoslavia

Terassen: drei Stücke Op. 2 (UE 1922). 14 p. D.
Ausdrucksvoll, bewegt: dissonant, sixteenth-note runs in sevenths.
Burleske: rhythmic, brusque.
Im charakter eines ruhigen Tanzes: syncopation, dramatic sweep (arpeggi, 64th-note scale passages), demanding.

Träume, Liebe, Tänze Op. 4 (UE 1923). D.
More extensive than Op. 2, many of same devices and techniques. Interesting sonorities.

The Magic Gate (BB 1957). 22 p. 15 minutes. 5 parts. Large work. Through a Glass Darkly, The Gate Opens, Of Demons and Angels, The Dead Mourn the Living, March and Transcendence. 12-tone technique, flowing counterpoint. D.

JULIUS REUBKE (1834-1858) Germany

Grosse Sonate b (G. Cotta'sche c. 1926). 55 p.
Large virtuoso work in the style of his teacher Franz Liszt. There is a copy in the New York Public Library. Similar in plan to Liszt's *Sonata* b. See: SSB, 406-8.

HERMANN REUTTER (1900-) Germany

Reutter writes in a neoclassic style and follows Hindemith in his treatment of musical materials.

Fantasia apocalyptica Op. 7 (Schott 1926). 23 p. D.
Two familiar chorales "A Mighty Fortress" and "O Sacred Head" form the basis of this work.

Variationen on "Komm süsser Tod" Op. 15 (Schott).

Die Passion in 9 Inventionen Op. 25 (Schott). Short descriptive pieces on Biblical scenes. No key signatures but all are tonal. Interpretative sensitivity required. D.

Kleine Klavierstücke Op. 28 (Schott 1928).

Tanz-Suite Op. 29 (Schott).
Ländler-Walzer aus der Ferne, Tarantella, Spanischer Tanz-Valse, Boston-Shimmy.

ROGER REYNOLDS (1934-) USA

Reynolds majored in engineering and then pursued his interest in music, obtaining a master's degree in music at the University of Michigan in 1961.

Epigram and Evolution (CFP 1959). 6½ minutes.
This work "develops a certain row in a strict and then in a free manner. A playful characteristic found throughout other scores appears in several sections." BBD, 145.

Fantasy for Pianist (CFP 1964). 17 minutes
"A more advanced work, based on premutation of a segmental row (hexachords or tetrachords). The serial concept is also extended to the time structure of all 4 movements. The method used to create this proportional time structure derives the rhythmic patterns from the row by numbering up by semitones from the lowest tone of a transposition." BBD, 145.

ALAN RICHARDSON (1904-) Scotland

Sonatine F Op. 27 (Weinberger 1960). 13 p. 3 movements, post-romantic in style. Fine for small hands. M-D.

Sonatina (Augener 1950). 10 minutes.

The Clydesdale Party (Augener). Scottish Dance.

Sonata Op. 26 (Augener). 33 p. 15½ minutes. 3 movements. Consonant, effective keyboard writing with driving rhythms. M-D.

Rhapsody (JWC 1959). 8 minutes. Effectively designed.

4 Romantic Studies Op. 25 (Augener). More emphasis on pedaling and phrasing than on facile fingers. M-D.

2 Nocturnes Op. 30 (Augener 1957). Bold, striking. M-D.

3 Pieces Op. 35 (JWC 1959). 6 minutes.
Tableau, Silver Night, Fantasy-Study. Imaginative, eminently playable. The Fantasy-Study, in constant motion, makes most demands.

Suite D Op. 38 (ABRSM 1956). Prelude, Gavotte, S,M,G.

ALAN RIDOUT (1934-) Great Britain

Dance Bagatelles (S&B). Three pieces.
Rhythmic studies. Moderate technical demands. Strong rhythmic sense required. Allegro molto: rondo. Andante: "blues" quality. Vivace: driving rhythm, percussive, most difficult.

Suite for Clavichord or Piano (S&B 1961). 16 p.

Sonatina (S&B 1968). M-D.
First movement: broad unison melodic writing. No key signature.
Second movement: 3/4 pulse with third beat shortened.
Third movement: 4/4 plus 3/4 syncopated dissonant treatment.

WALLINGFORD RIEGGER (1885-1961) USA

Blue Voyage Op. 6 (GS 1927). Impressionist, rhapsodic piece, after poem of Conrad Aiken.

4 Tone Pictures Op. 14 (CFP 1932). M-D.
Prelude: atmospheric, impressionistic.

Angles and Curves: bouncing rhythmic idea contrasted with melodic idea.
Wishful Thinking: two-bar ostinato supports melody.
Grotesque: rhythmic emphasis, tone clusters, pentatonic scale.

New Dance Op. 18 (AMP 1935). South American rhythms incorporated into brilliant bravura writing. A fine closing number. D.

New and Old Op. 38 (Bo&H 1944). 12 pieces illustrating contemporary compositional techniques. Analytical notes. M-D.

Toccata (Bo&H 1957). No. 12 of the above with a new brilliant closing.

Petite Etude Op. 62 (Merion 1956). Bitonal study. Int.

CARLOS RIESCO (1925-) Chile

Semblanzas Chileñas (Southern). "Chilean Sketches." 3 pieces published together. M-D.
Zamacueca: gay and rhythmic, many seconds.
Tonada: richly harmonized folksong.
Resbalosa: begins as a waltz then moves to a lively dance.

VITTORIO RIETI (1898-) Italy, born Egypt, resided in USA since 1950

Rieti embraced the neoclassic cause and has always remained faithful to it.

Poema Fiesolana (UE 1921). Large dramatic work requiring bravura technique.

Due Studi (UE 1923).

Sonatina (UE 1925). March, Theme and Variations, Finale: infused with lightness and vitality.

Suite (UE 1926). Clever, rewarding work.
Preludio, Valzer, Barcarola, Canzonetta, Rondo variato.

Sonata A♭ (Gen. 1938 c. 1966). MC, traditional tonal relationships, emphasis on melodic writing.

First movement: moderate tempo with modulatory excursions. Second movement: slow and expressive, frequent meter changes. Third movement: rondo, perpetual motion, clever rhythmic rumba idea near middle of movement.

Variations Académiques (F. Colombo 1950). Theme and 8 variations, a fugue and a chorale. Classical method combined with contemporary vitality and humorous character. Thunderous closing.

Sonata all'Antica for Harpsichord or Piano (BB 1957). 11 minutes. 3 movements. Well-defined ideas, excellent craftsmanship. Imitative counterpoint, repeated chords, brisk closing Rigaudon. Works well on either instrument.

Sonata (F. Colombo 1966). 24 p. 3 movements. MC, work is based on a 3-note motive heard at opening.

Medieval Variations (Gen). Theme, 7 variations, quick mood changes, catchy tunes, fine recital piece.

5 Contrasts (Gen 1967). Preludio, Variazioni, Bagatella, Elegia, Girandola. Short. Int. to M-D.

Allegro Danzante (Bo&H 1942).

3 Preludes (Sal).

Madrigal (Sal).

3 Marches for Animals (Bongiovanni).

KNUDAAGE RIISAGER (1897-) Denmark, born Russia

Riisager's style recalls that of Poulenc. Riisager is presently Director of the Royal Conservatory in Copenhagen.

Quatre Epigrammes Op. 11 (WH c. 1936). Lento, Burla, Andante, Capriccio. M-D.

Sonate Op. 22 (WH 1931). 23p. 14 minutes. 3 movements. D. Allegro intransigente, Andante reconciliante, Allegro scevro e molto ardito.

Sonatina (GM). 6 minutes.

Deux Morceaux (WH). Moderato, Vivace.

En glad trompet og andre Klavierstykker (WH). "A funny trumpet and other piano pieces." 6 innocent pieces. Int.

NICOLAS RIMSKY-KORSAKOV (1844-1908) Russia

Collected Edition (USSR). The piano works are in volume 49a. Contains:
3 Fughettas on Russian Themes g, d, g.
11 Fugues
3 Pieces Op. 15 (1875): Valse C♯, Romance A♭, Fugue c♯.
4 Pieces Op. 11 (1878): Impromptu, Novellette (Belaieff), Scherzino, Etude.
Prelude
Allegretto

Variations on B A C H Op. 10 (Rahter). His best work for piano. M-D.

JOHANN CHRISTOPH RITTER (ca. 1650-1725) Germany

Drei Sonate für Cembalo (E. R. Jacobi-Br).

JEAN RIVIER (1896-) France

Cinq mouvements brefs (Sal 1931). 9½ minutes. Prélude, Caprice, Berceuse, Ronde, Final. Amusing, light, witty. M-D.

Musiques pour piano (Sal 1937-38). 14½ minutes. Printemps, Jeux, Les bouffons, Tumultes. Fresh, brilliant, rumba rhythms, ostinati. M-D.

Pour des mains amies (EMT 1956). Suite of 5 movements. Nostalgie, Confidence, Danse triste, Crépuscule, Cabrioles. Dance qualities, MC, bright, last dance requires a big technique. D.

Torrents (EMT 1960). 4½ minutes. Dancelike, many fourths, full resources of keyboard explored. D.

Tornades (Sal 1952). Formidable octave technique required. D.

Nocturne sur le nom de Marguérite Long (Sal 1957).

Récréations (Sal 1962). Bitonal. Int.

MERVYN ROBERTS (1906-) Wales

Four Preludes (Nov c. 1949).

Sonatina (Nov c. 1949). 6 minutes.

Sonata (Nov c. 1951). 39 p. Three movements, romantic in character.

GEORGE ROCHBERG (1918-) USA

Rochberg is presently Chairman of the Department of Music at the University of Pennsylvania.

12 Bagatelles (TP 1952). 12-tone.

Sonata-Fantasia (TP 1958). 23 minutes. D. 3 movements separated by interludes, a Prologue and Epilogue, without a break. This work "is a very complex realization of the potential freedom in a single row. No single form is consistently employed and many kinds of manipulation appear. The harmonic structure of the work, especially with regard to the use of hexachords, is true to the theoretical principles on which Rochberg has written." BBD, 149. Ingenious piano writing.

Nach Bach (After Bach) Fantasy for Harpsichord or Piano (TP). D. A 20th-century commentary on Bach themes, especially the *Chromatic Fantasia* and the sixth *Partita*. Dreamlike, without barlines, improvisatory.

Bartókiana (TP 1959). 1½ minutes.

Arioso (TP 1959). 3 minutes.

ROCCO RODIO (153?-161?) Italy

Quinque Ricerate, Una Fantasia Per Organo, Clavicembalo, Clavicordo o Arpa. Revised and transcribed by M. S. Kastner (GZ). An extensive preface in English gives many details concerning the composer and the music. Fascinating pieces, colorful and delightful to play. The Fantasia has a particularly appealing south Italian rhythm.

JOAQUIN RODRIGO (1902-) Spain

Rodrigo is recognized as one of Spain's outstanding contemporary composers. Gilbert Chase, in his survey of Spanish music, credits Rodrigo with the most interesting work between Falla and Carlos Surinach.

Serenata Española (Sal 1931). 11 p.

Danzas de España (Sal 1936, 1941).

Bagatelle (Sal).

Suite pour Piano (Sal).

4 Estampas Andaluzas (UME).

Sonatas de Castilla (UME 1952).
Contains a Toccata "a modo de pregón" and 5 sonatas.

4 Pièces (ESC 1948). In the style of Granados. M-D.

Pastoral (UME).

Sonada de Adios (ESC). Open texture, mournful, requires fine tonal balance for rich sonorities. Int.

JEAN JULES ROGER-DUCASSE (1873-1954) France

Arabesques 1 and 2 (Durand). Published separately. D.

Barcarolles 1, 2, and 3 (Durand). Published separately. D.

Chant de l'aube (Durand). D.

Esquisses (Durand). D.

4 Etudes (Durand). D. Prélude C, Fugue C, Etude E, Etude e♭.

6 Préludes (Durand 1907). The first three are easiest, the others difficult.

Romance (Durand). D.

Variations on a Chorale (Durand 1915). Contrapuntal, classical tendencies. D.

Rythmes (Durand). D.

Exercises de Virtuosité (Durand 1910). After Czerny, Liszt, Chopin, Schumann, Balakirev, Tchaikowsky, Rubinstein, Fauré.

WILLIAM KEITH ROGERS (1921-) Canada

6 Short Preludes on a Tone Row (BMI Canada 1963). Mostly one page each. Original handling of serial technique. Int.

ERIC ROLLINSON (? -1963) Canada

3 Folk Songs (F. Harris 1955). Int.
Barbara Allen, Greensleeves, Sea-Shanty.
Short, clever realizations. The canon in Barbara Allen is most effective.

JOHAN HELMICH ROMAN (1694-1758) Sweden

See: Newman SBE, 349-50.

12 Suites (Patrik Vretblad-NMS) in 2 Vols.
Vol. I: Suites 1-6. Vol. II: Suites 7-12.

JOHANNES RÖNTGEN (1898-) The Netherlands

Muzikale Dias (Donemus). Musical Slides.
12 canons and 12 fughettas in all keys.

Sonatine (Alsbach 1953). 15 p. Three movements, MC. M-D.

NED ROREM (1923-) USA

Rorem is best known for his songs but he has written for different media in a personal style that recalls Poulenc and Satie.

Sonata No. 1 (CFP 1948). 3 movements. 20 p. D.

Sonata No. 2 (Noël Edition 1949-50). 4 movements. Melodic first and third movements, brilliant Scherzando and a flexible finale. D.

Sonata No. 3 (CFP 1954). 4 movements. 26 p. D.

3 Barcarolles (CFP 1949). Dedicated to Leon Fleischer. Pianistic, spontaneous writing. No. 3 is most extensive and most exciting. M-D.

A Quiet Afternoon (PIC 1949). 9 pieces. 10½ minutes. Varying moods in this contemporary "Scenes from Childhood." Good musicianship and technique required. Int.

Toccata (CFP 1948). "Clear, fast and hard." A tour de force with traditional modulation. Is also used as final movement of *Sonata* No. 1.

Burlesque (Hargail 1956).

Spiders (Bo&H 1968). For harpsichord. Flexible meters, opposing textures, effective trills and arpeggios, superimposed triads, toccatalike. Better on harpsichord. D.

THOMAS ROSEINGRAVE (1690-1766) Great Britain

The major influences on Roseingrave's compositions were the music of Palestrina and the harpsichord playing of Domenico Scarlatti. While visiting Italy he became a close friend of Scarlatti and later, when he had returned to London, edited a collection of Scarlatti's sonatas. Roseingrave developed a fine contrapuntal technique. His powers of improvisation were widely known.

Compositions for Organ and Harpsichord (D. Stevens-PSM 1964). Volume Two of the Penn. State Music series. Voluntary IV, Fugue X, Double Fugue V, Introduction to Scarlatti's "Lessons", First, Third, Sixth and Eighth Suites of Lessons. First Suite of Lessons E♭: Overture, A, C, Presto, and Chaconne; Third Suite d: A, C, S, G; Sixth Suite e: A, C, S, G, M; the Eighth Suite g: A, S, G.

Eight Suites of Lessons for the Harpsichord or Spinet (1728?) (BB) Facsimile edition.

HILDING ROSENBERG (1892-) Sweden

Rosenberg was influential in introducing new musical resources into Swedish musical life during the first quarter of this century. He was also very important as a teacher.

Sonata No. 1 (NMS).

Sonata No. 2 (NMS 1925).

Sonata No. 3 (NMS 1926). 18 minutes. M-D.
Andantino: no key signatures, centers around F♯, flowing theme, thin textures.
Lento: much doubling of part writing, many seconds, elegant.
Scherzo: many tempo changes, not true scherzo, Valse tempo used part time, variable tonal areas.
Finale: Allegro energico: sixteenth-note motion, thematic material resembles first movement, thin textures, PP ending.

Improvisationer (NMS 1939). 7 variations on opening marchlike ideas. Contemporary harmonic and melodic language, mood changes with each variation. Large span required. M-D.

Tema con Variazioni (NMS 1941). Large-scale work with 17 variations on theme in a. All types of pianistic treatment involved. D.

Polyfona, Föredragsstudier for Piano Op. 6 (NMS 1945).

Sonatin (GM 1949).

Suite (NMS). 19 p. Präludium, Arabesk, Impromptu, Pastoral, Burlesk.

MANUEL ROSENTHAL (1904-) France

Rosenthal writes in the tradition of Chabrier and Ravel and is a superbly refined craftsman.

Huit bagatelles (Senart c. 1924). Most are 2 p. long, clear, bright textures. Pastorale, Berceuse, Remember, Le joli jeu, Romance, Rag, Romance, Finale. M-D.

MORIZ ROSENTHAL (1862-1946) Poland

Papillons (Musica Obscura) (Fürstner). Staccato study employing alternating hands. M-D.

Variationen über ein eigenes Theme (Fürstner). Theme and 10 variations. D.

Carnaval de Vienne (CF). "On Themes of Strauss." M-D.

Study on Waltz Op. 64/1 of Chopin (Fritzsch). Also in *13 Transcriptions of Chopin's Minute Waltz.* See Chopin collections.

LORENZO DE ROSSI (1720-1794) Italy

"His music is light, fresh, skillful and convincing". SCE, 202.

Sei Sonate per Cembalo (R. Tenaglia-Ric). Edited and transcribed by Tenaglia, these sonatas are two-movement works on the slow-fast order written in early classic style.

MICHELANGELO ROSSI (ca. 1600-1674) Italy

Bold chromatic alterations, virtuoso scale passages, and polyphonic treatment account for the unusual expressiveness in these works. Toccata style continued from Frescobaldi. Some of his works are found in:

I Classici della Musica Italiana XXVI (Alceo Toni-Società Anonima Notari).

L'Arte Musicale in Italia III (Torchi-Ric).

Antologia di musica antica e moderna per il pianoforte (G. Tagliapietra-Ric) VI.

10 Toccatas (Torchi-Ric). B. Bartók transcribed Nos. 1 and 9 (CF).

6 Toccatas (Boghen-Heugel) in C, a, e, g, B, f.

4 Toccatas are found in *Antichi Maestri Italiani: Toccate* (Boghen-Ric).

10 Correnti for cembalo or organ (Torchi-Ric). Bartók transcribed Nos. 1, 2 and 5 (CF).

GIOACCHINO ROSSINI (1792-1868) Italy

5 Original Pieces (CFP 1952). Selected from his *Sins of Old Age.* Fun pieces, pianistic, large span required. See especially No. 3 Capriccio. Int.

8 Selected Pieces (Rognoni-SZ 1951). Selected from *Quelques riens.* Int. Ischia, Allegretto moderato E♭, Andantino mosso D♭, Allegretto moderato E, Fanfare, Sorrente, Un rien sur le mode enharmonique.

18 Selected Pieces (Heugel). From *Quelques riens,* a collection of autograph albums located at Fondazione Rossini, Pesaro, Italy.

Pieces for Piano (G. Macarini-Carminignani Fondazione Rossini 1954). Vol. 1: 10 pieces. Petit Caprice; Prélude inoffensif; L'innocence italienne — La candeur française, Ouf! Les petits pois; Une caresse à ma femme; Un petit train de plaisir — Comique imitatif; Spécimen de l'ancien régime; Tarantelle pur Sang; Echantillon du chant de Noël à l'italienne; March et réminiscence pour mon dernière voyage.

Fanfare pour Chasse (J. Werner-Curwen). Brilliant, witty, charming.

Une réjouissance (Faber). Probably Rossini's last composition. In waltz style, Neopolitan flavor, some RH glissandi. Dated September 20, 1868.

Piano Pieces (K). 4 volumes.
Vol. 1: 6 pieces. Vol. 2: 3 pieces. Vol. 3: 4 pieces.
Vol. 4: 5 pieces. Broad selection. Int. to M-D.

ALBERT ROUSSEL (1869-1937) France

Roussel is a composer who merits further exploration.

Rustiques Op. 5 (1904-1906) (Durand). Three pieces. D. Advanced pianism for its period. Danse au bord de l'eau. Promenade sentimentale en forêt. Retour de fête.

Suite Op. 14 (1910) (Sal). Four movements requiring thorough pianistic equipment. Prélude: bravura writing; Sicilienne: built on three themes, treated extensively; Bourrée: style of Chabrier; Ronde: a "tour de force", highly effective.

Sonatine Op. 16 (1912) (Durand). Two large sections, each subdivided. Transitional work. D.
Modéré — Vif et très leger: fast moving, thick harmonies.
Très lent — très animé: square chordal textures lead to light, energetic finale.

Petit canon perpétuel (1913) (Durand). Short, lyric. ". . . go back to the da capo, transposing the three voices up an octave and continue thus as far as the range of the keyboard will permit." M-D.

L'Accueil des Muses (1920) (Durand). Lament for Debussy, chordal and broken harmonies, big climax. D.

Segovia Op. 29 (1925) (Durand). Originally for guitar, arranged by Roussel.

Prélude et Fugue (1932-1934) (Durand). Hommage to Bach. The fugue on BACH takes the final "H" up a seventh, an unusual approach. M-D.

Trois Pièces Op. 49 (1933) (Durand).
Toccata C: rhythmic, octaves, driving.
Valse lente F: dainty, two- and three-voice texture.
Scherzo et trio C: brilliant lyric mid-section with large climax, longest of set.

GASPARD LE ROUX (ca. 1660-1707) France

Fuller points out in his introduction that the works of Le Roux "may very well be considered in retrospect as a summing up of the French keyboard traditions and the springboard for the final brilliant and consummate splash of François Couperin himself."

Pieces for Harpsichord (1705) (A. Fuller-Alpeg 1959).
Contains an elaborate introduction with bibliographical and critical notes, facsimiles and translations. Le Roux's style most resembles d'Anglebert. There is a close relationship with French lute music, even in some of the titles, i.e. "Courante luthée." In the usual manner of the French clavecinistes he

gives fanciful titles to some of his pieces, e.g. "Allemande l'Incomparable" etc. His music has an individuality that lifts it above the conventional level of some of his contemporaries. The editor's fine notes are often applicable to the works of other French harpsichordists. 7 suites: d, D, a, A, F, f♯, g. Also contains arrangements of 5 of these pieces for two harpsichords, i.e. *Pièces Pour Deux Clavecins:* Allemande La Vauvert, Gavotte en rondeau, Menuet, Second Menuet, Courante, and a Gigue that does not appear anywhere else in the collection.

HOWARD ROVICS (1936-) USA

3 Studies for Piano (Seesaw Music Corp. 1964-66). For Robert Goldsand.
Well-contrasted. No. 2 uses techniques such as string tapping, plucking, sliding finger on string, etc. Advanced pianism required.

ALEC ROWLEY (1892-1958) Great Britain

Rowley is primarily known for his fine contribution to pedagogical piano music.

Etudes in Tonality (CFP 1937). Prologue, Modal, Pentatonic, Diatonic, Chromatic, Whole-tone, Polytonal, Atonal. Each piece follows the title, clear forms. Int.

Polyrhythms Op. 50 (CFP 1939). 7 Pieces. M-D.

Sonate (Durand 1939). 17 p. D.

Sonata No. 2 D (JWC 1949). 18 p. M-D. 11 minutes.

Suite (Durand 1946). Praeludium, Passepied, Pavana, Siciliana, Toccata.

2 Sonatinas Op. 40 (CFP). Spring-Summer. Easy to M-D.

2 Sonatinas Op. 40 (CFP). Summer-Winter. Easy to M-D.

Sonatina No. 1 F (JWC 1955). M-D.

Sonatina No. 2 G (JWC 1957). M-D.

Toccata (Augener 1934). "The Two Worlds."

Toccata No. 2 (Augener 1935). 3½ minutes.

Recreation Op. 37 (CFP). Easy.

Elves and Fairies Op. 38 (CFP). Easy.

A Chinese Suite Op. 20 (W. Rogers). The Mood River, In the Temple, Dragon Dance.

A Christmas Carol (Swan). 2 parts. Part 1: 4 pieces, Part 2: 5 pieces.

Poetical Studies Op. 41 (Ashdown). Part 1: 16 pieces, Part 2: 8 pieces.

7 Preludes (Augener). On all the intervals. M-D.

MIKLÓS RÓZSA (1907-) Hungary, came to USA 1940

Bagatelles Op. 12 (Br&H 1932). 6 pieces. M-D.
Little March (bitonal), Novellette, Valse Lente, Hungarian (folksong quality), Canzone, Capriccietto. Usable as a group or separately.

Kaleidoscope Op. 19 (AMP 1945). 6 pieces. Int.
MC recital pieces effective as a set or individually. March, Zingara, Musette, Berceuse (easiest), Chinese Carillon, Burlesque.

Sonata Op. 20 (Br&H 1948). D. Strong rhythms and rhythmic ideas. First movement: energetic; Second movement: romantic, pensive Andante; Third movement: vigorous, earthy dance, Bartók influence.

EDMUND RUBBRA (1901-) Great Britain

Introduction and Fugue Op. 19 c (Augener 1942). 8 minutes.

Prelude and Fugue on a theme by Cyril Scott Op. 69 (Lengnick 1950). 5 minutes. The theme is from the slow movement of Cyril Scott's first *Piano Sonata* Op. 66. Romantic treatment of a romantic theme. Fugue, chromatic. M-D.

Children's Pieces (Lengnick 1952). 3 volumes. Easy to Int.

Introduction, Aria and Fugue Op. 104 (Lengnick). For harpsichord. Classic line, chromatic idiom. Rhythmic problems are found in the 3-voice fugue. D.

8 Preludes Op. 131 (Lengnick 1966). M-D.
Prefers low registers, No. 6 especially thick. No. 3 short (16 bars), solemn, charming. See especially Nos. 1 and 6. Some of Rubbra's best piano writing.

See: Michael Dawney, "Edmund Rubbra and the Piano," MR, 31, August 1970, 341-8.

ANTON RUBINSTEIN (1830-1894) Russia

Album de Peterhof Op. 75 (Augener). 12 pieces. Nos. 4, 5, 8, 11 are contained in this collection.

The Ball Op. 14. Fantasy in 10 numbers. No. 1. Impatience (Augener), Nos. 4. Valse and 6. Polka (USSR).

Barcarolle and Allegro Apassionato Op. 30 (Bo&H) (USSR) (Ashdown). The Allegro Apassionato is available separately from (Augener) (K&S).

3 Caprices Op. 21. No. 1 F♯ (USSR).

Album of National Dances Op. 82 (Jurgenson). 6 pieces.
1. Rousskaja et Trepak 2. Lesghinka (Caucase) 3. Mazurka D (Pologne) 4. Czardas (Hongrie) 5. Tarantelle (Italie) 6. Valse (Allemagne). 7. Polka (Bohême).

Etude de Concert C (USSR) "On Wrong Notes."

6 Etudes Op. 23 (CFP) (Ric) (GS) (USSR). Virtuoso writing. Contains the once popular Staccato Etude.

Impromptu, Berceuse and Serenade Op. 16. Impromptu, Berceuse (ABRSM), Serenade (Gerard).

2 Melodies Op. 3 (Augener) (USSR). No. 1 (Schott).

Nocturne G♭ (USSR).

6 Preludes Op. 24. No. 5 G (USSR).

Soirées de St. Pétersbourg Op. 44. 6 pieces. 1. Romance (USSR) (Ashdown) (Augener) (GS). 2. Scherzo (Bo&H) (Ashdown). 3. Preghièra (USSR) (Ashdown) (Augener). 4. Impromptu (Bo&H) (Ashdown). 5. Nocturne (Ashdown) (Durand). 6. Appassionata.

Turkish March from The Ruins of Athens by Beethoven (GS) (Ashdown).

Valse-Caprice E♭ (GS) (USSR) (Augener).

Album (CFP). 11 pieces. M-D.

Album (USSR). All the above listed pieces by this publisher are contained in this album.

Album of Selected Piano Compositions by Anton Rubinstein (EBM). Barcarole f Op. 30/1, Ondine Op. 1, Polka Op. 82, Aubade Op. 75/22, Fourth Barcarole G, Third Barcarole g Op. 50, Valse Caprice E♭, and other works.

See: Charles MacLean, "Rubinstein as Composer for the Pianoforte," PRMA, 39, 1912-13, 129-51.

BERYL RUBINSTEIN (1898-1952) USA

Rubinstein was Director of the Cleveland Institute of Music for many years.

Two Etudes (OUP 1929). M-D.

Ignis Fatuus: *Will o' the Wisp.* Short, presto staccato, double notes.

Whirligig: continuous RH figuration, light, brilliant.

A Day in the Country (CF). Five impromptus, varied moods. Int.

Sonatina c♯ (OUP 1929). Brisk, cheerful opening movement, atmospheric Adagio with French influence in the harmonic treatment, tarantella-like Allegro vivace, brilliant. M-D.

Twelve Definitions (GS 1950).

A set of character pieces portraying the following moods: Gently moving, Animated, Lightly, Decisive, Gay, Lyric, Serene, Spritely, Graceful, Agitated, Expressive, Spirited. Int. to M-D.

Scenes from Alice in Wonderland (Chappell 1951). 19 p.

CARL RUGGLES (1876-1971) USA

Evocations, 4 Chants (AME 1937-43).
Highly dissonant and complex works, profuse chromaticism. Style similar to Charles Ives yet distinctive. Fondness for constantly changing meters, tritone, thick colors, legato melodies. No. 4 is dedicated to Ives. Advanced pianism required.

Organum for Orchestra (NME, Oct. 1947). Arranged for piano by John Kirkpatrick. Sustained sounds, many sequences, tritone and thick textures, many octaves. Dissonance seems to be the main basis for this style. D.

See: Steven E. Gilbert, "The 'Twelve-Tone System' of Carl Ruggles: A Study of the Evocations for piano," Journal of Music Theory, 14/1, Spring 1970, 68-91.

FRIEDRICH WILHELM RUST (1739-1796) Germany

Twelve Sonatas (V. d'Indy-Rouart, Lerolle).
Effective pianistic writing. No. 9 *Sonata* G imitates the Timpanum, Psaltery and Luth and anticipates a few twentieth-century devices, including the RH touching a string while the LH depresses the key. Mainly in 3 movements. These sonatas resemble the pianism of Clementi. Also available separately.

GIOVANNI RUTINI (1723-1797) Italy

Rutini composed about 88 keyboard sonatas, mainly published in sets. Most contain 2 movements, some have 3 and a few have 4 movements. Main ideas incorporate modulatory figuration, fragmentary in character. He is fond of trills, turns and appoggiaturas, runs, arpeggios, alternation and crossing of hands.

18 Sonatas (Hedda Illy-De Santis) Three Books. 6 sonatas in each opus: 3, 5 and 6. Opus 5 appears to be the strongest of the set. See especially No. 3 D in Opus 3. These three sets date from 1757, 1759 and 1760 respectively.

12 Sonatas Op. 1 and Op. 2 *I Classici della Musica Italiana* XXVII and TPA XIII.

See: Bess Hieronymous, "Rutini, the Composer of Pianoforte Sonatas, Together with Thematic Index of the Sonatas," unpub. thesis, Smith College, 1948.

DANIËL RUYNEMAN (1886-1963) The Netherlands

Kleine Sonate (UE 1928). 1 movement. 11 p.
Various tempi changes, not easy but effective.

Marsch-Impressie (B&VP 1936). 3 minutes.

Vijf nocturnes (Donemus 1949). 24 p.

Drie pathematologeën (Alsbach 1915). Hallucination, The Voice from the Past, Impression.

Sonate No. 9 (Donemus 1931). 10 minutes.

Sonatine (Alsbach 1917). 11 minutes.

Sonatine (B&VP). 5 minutes. Three movements, each two pages long. MC, changing meters, no bar lines in second movement, rhythmic drive in last movement. M-D.

S

HANS WOLFGANG SACHSE (1891-1960) Germany

6 Bagatelles Op. 76 (Br&H).
Romantic, subtle, spontaneous. Easy to program. Nos. 1, 3 and 5 toccatalike, No. 2 pastorale, No. 4 nocturnelike melody over ostinato bass. M-D.

PEDRO SAENZ (1915-) Argentina

Saenz studied in his native country as well as with Arthur Honegger, Darius Milhaud and Jean Rivier in Paris. He has held important teaching and administrative positions in Buenos Aires.

Preludio y Fuga á la Manera de J. S. Bach (Gau 1938). 9 minutes.

Tres Piezas Epigramaticas (Gau 1938). 5 minutes. Burlesca, Elegia, Tocata.

Juguetes (Ric 1943). 4 miniaturas. 6 minutes. Int.

Variationes Sobre un Tema Original (Ric 1947). 5 minutes.

Preludio en Fa (EAM 1949). 4 minutes.

Norteña (Ric).

HARALD SAEVERUD (1897-) Norway

5 Capricci Op. 1 (NMO). Post-romantic, M-D.

Sonata g Op. 3 (EMH 1921).

Suite Op. 6 (EMH 1930). Atonal. D.

Siljuslatten Op. 17 (NMO). From "Siljustöl", the name of the composer's home in Bergen. Short character pieces. Int.

Tunes and Dances from "Siljustöl" in 4 volumes (EMH). Expanded tonal usage.
Vol. 1: Op. 21, 5 pieces. Clever, No. 5 most adventurous.
Vol. 2: Op. 22, 5 pieces. 4 charming pieces plus No. 5 "Ballade of Revolt."
Vol. 3: Op. 24, 5 pieces. More contemporary style. "Beware Bear!" is most appealing.
Vol. 4: Op. 25, 5 pieces.

6 Sonatinas Op. 30 (EMH 1948-50). 1 volume. 29 p. Some are 2, some 3 movements. All are short, thin textures. Many moods, MC. Contains fresh teaching material. Int.

CAMILLE SAINT-SAËNS (1835-1921) France

Saint-Saëns was a brilliant pianist with a fine sense of style. He was an excellent craftsman, facile, elegant and well-grounded. His piano writing can always be counted on to glitter and flow without much emotional depth. He has been called the "French Mendelssohn." (Durand) publishes most of Saint-Saëns' works, assumed, unless otherwise noted.

6 Bagatelles Op. 3 (1856). One of the few sets of Bagatelles written at this time.

Mazurka No. 1 g Op. 21 (1868). Also (CF).

Gavotte Op. 23 (1872).

Mazurka No. 2 g Op. 24 (1872).

6 Etudes Op. 52 (1877). 22 minutes. Prélude; Pour l'independance des doigts; Prelude et fugue f; Etude de rythme; Prélude et fugue A; En forme de valse (more Valse influence than Etude) long (422 bars), brilliant. D.

Menuet et Valse Op. 56 (1878).

Mazurka No. 3 b Op. 66 (1883).

Album of 6 pieces Op. 72 (1884). Prélude, Carillon, Toccata, Valse, Chanson napolitaine, Finale. Also published separately. Toccata requires a diligent staccato touch.

Souvenir d'Italie Op. 80.

Les Cloches du soir Op. 85.

Valse canariote Op. 88.

Suite Op. 90 (1892). 4 pieces: Prélude et fugue, Menuet, Gavotte, Gigue.

Thème varié Op. 97 (1894). 6 minutes.

Souvenir d'Ismailia Op. 100.

Valse Mignonne Op. 104.

Valse nonchalant Op. 110. Charming, in the style of Liszt *Valse oubliée*. M-D.

6 Etudes Op. 111 (1899). Tierces majeures et mineures; Traits chromatiques; Prélude et Fugue; Les cloches de Las Palmas; Tierces majeures chromatiques; Toccata d'après le 5ème concerto. D. (virtuoso piece). (IMC) publishes No. 6.

Valse langoureuse Op. 120.

Valse gaie Op. 139.

6 Etudes Op. 152 (1919). D.

6 Fugues Op. 161 (1920). A, E♭, G, g, E, C.

Feuillet D'Album Op. 169 (1921).

Allegro Appassionata c Op. 70 (1884). Arranged by the composer for solo piano from the original, for piano and orchestra. A requirement piece at the Paris Conservatory. Bravura writing. M-D.

Caprice on airs from Gluck's Alceste. Also (GS). One of the composer's most brilliant and most frequently performed works. D.

MARINA SAIZ-SALAZAR (1930-) Panama

Sonata (PAU 1954-55).
First movement: punctuated rhythmic drive, disjunct motion.
Second movement: big sonorities, disjunct writing.
Third movement: thin-textured mid-section before driving opening ideas return. Dramatic ending.
Much dissonance and drive to this work. Neoclassic handling of key centers, chromaticism. Some 12-tone techniques used.

ADOLFO SALAZAR (1890-1958) Spain

3 Preludes (JWC).

Romancillo (ESC). For piano or guitar.

GUSTAVE SAMAZEUILH (1877-) France

Esquisses (Durand 1948). 4 pieces.
Dédicace, Luciole, Sérénade (LH only), Souvenir (RH only).

Le Chant de la Mer (Durand 1919). D.
Imaginative virtuoso program music. Warm impressionist pianism that requires expert use of the sostenuto pedal.
Prélude: full chords over pedal point; Clair de lune au large: evocative; Tempête et lever du jour sur les flots: influence of Ravel and Dukas.

Evocation (Durand).

Naiades au soir (Durand). D.

Nocturne (Durand).

3 Petites inventions (Durand).

Suite en sol (Durand).
Prélude, Française, Sarabande, Divertissement, Musette, Forlane. M-D.

GIOVANNI BATTISTA SAMMARTINI (1698-1775) Italy

Sammartini's sonatas follow the FSF sequence. Textures are homophonic with melodic emphasis and the final movements are usually menuets.

Sonatas (*I Classici della musica italiana*) XXVIII.

Two Sonatas C (Curci 1954).

PIERRE SANCAN (1916-) France, born Morocco

Sancan is a distinguished pianist and member of the faculty of the Conservatoire National in Paris.

Boîte à musique (Durand).

Dusting (Durand).

Mouvement (Durand 1946).

Pièces enfantiles (Durand). 2 volumes; 5 pieces in Vol. 1 and 6 in Vol. 2. Easy to Int.

Suite fantasque (Durand). For harpsichord or piano. D.

Toccata (Durand 1943). D.

DOMINGO SANTA CRUZ (1899-) Chile

Santa Cruz has played a large role in the development of music in Chile.

4 Viñetas (Casa Amarilla 1927). 9 minutes. M-D.
Conceived in the spirit of an early suite.

5 Poemas Tragicas (Casa Amarilla 1929). 14 minutes.
Contains touches of atonality.

Imagenes Infantiles (PIC c. 1960). 2 books. 13 minutes.
Book 1 Op. 13a: 4 pieces
Book 2 Op. 13b: 4 pieces.
All are Int. or above. Varied moods and devices, bitonal preferences.

CLAUDIO SANTORO (1919-) Brazil

Santoro studied with Koellreutter and Boulanger. He used serial techniques in much of his writing up to about 1948. At present he is Director of the School of Music at the University of Brasilia.

2 Dansas Brasileiras (Southern 1951). Int.
Fascinating rhythmic interest, 3-staff notation, No. 1 easiest.

Toccata (Ric 1954). Demands endurance and energy. D.

Sonata No. 3 (Ric 1955). 3 movements FSF. 16 minutes.
Clear textures, buoyant rhythms, influence of Boulanger and Debussy, MC. M-D.

Sonata No. 4 (Ric 1957). Fantasia. 3 movements FSF. 16 minutes.

25 Preludes (Ric).

2 Studies (Ric).

ANDRÉS SÁS (1900-1967) Peru, born France

Sás went to Peru in 1924. His style incorporates impressionism with nationalism.

Melodia y Aire Variado Op. 18 (Southern). M-D.
A north Peruvian love song is the basis for the melody. The variations (on a Peruvian Indian dance) are very rhythmic, use double melodies with inner voices and irregular skips. Dissonant harmony.

Preludio y Toccata (Southern 1952). M-D.
Peruvian folk tune is the basis of the Prelude. Toccata ends softly.

Arrulo y Tondero Op. 39 (EV). M-D.
Opening Lullaby in 5/4 with lovely melody followed by a Creole Dance, a quick Tondero in 6/8, very rhythmic.

Sonata Op. 47 (PIC 1964). 4 movements. M-D.
Much play on bitonal relationships. Second movement is an expressive canon. Third movement is a Vals, fourth movement a humorous skippy Rondo.

Aires y Danzas Indios del Peru (Lemoine). 11 pieces.

Himno y Danza (GS 1942).
Short, chordal procession leads to a driving Danza with ostinato rhythms.

ERIK SATIE (1866-1925) France

Satie's influence on other composers was more important than his music but the music is unique in many ways. An antiquarian quality surrounds some of the early works. After a period of study at the Schola Cantorum his style became more linear and infused with humorous, satirical and cynical overtones. He parodied styles of well-known composers, quoted from their works and deliberately attached comical names to his pieces. Satie despised all Germanic Romantic music and his own compositions negated any kind of sentimentality. Most of the works present no great difficulties.

"The piano pieces are a large segment of his small output and bear all the essential traits of his style; the satirical lampooning with which his name is invariably associated, a transparent texture, simple melodies, fresh harmonies, a complete avoidance of histrionics or involved complexities, in short, a type of music that the pianist can take or leave at his pleasure, just as he would the armchair in his living room. Satie even coined the phrase 'musique d'ameublement' (furniture music) to characterize his aesthetic conception at one period in his life." MFTP, 238.

Ogives (1886) (MCA). Four short pieces, parallel chords.

Trois Sarabandes (1887) (Sal). Published separately. Somber, graceful.

Trois Gymnopédies (1888) (Sal) (GS) (K). Melody supported by slightly dissonant chords.

Trois Gnossiennes (1890) (Sal). No time signatures or bar lines, satiric indications.

Trois Préludes from *Le Fils des étoiles* (1891) (Sal).

Sonneries de la Rose-Croix (1892) (Sal). Three pieces, static chords, modal, melody in octaves. Air de L'Ordre, Air du Grand Maître, Air de Grand Prieur.

Danses gothiques (1893) (Sal).

Quatre Préludes (1893) (Sal). Chordal, fourths, fifths, sevenths, ninths, floating effect.

Fête donnée par des Chevaliers Normands en l'Honneur d'une jeune Demoiselle, Prélude d'Eginhard, ler Prélude du Nazareen, 2me Prélude du Nazareen.

Prélude de la porte héroïque du ciel (1894) (Sal).

Piéces froides (1897) (Sal). Flexible meter, clear textures. Available separately.
1. Airs à faire fuir. 2. Danses de travers.

Prélude en tapisserie (1906) (Sal). Neoclassic in style.

Passacaille (1906) (Sal). Neoclassic in style, chordal.

Véritables préludes flasques (1912) (ESC). Four "Flabby Preludes" with ridiculous Latin directions, delightful.

Descriptions automatiques (1913) (ESC). Alludes to a number of popular songs.

Embryons desséchés (1913) (ESC). Three imaginary crustaceans accompanied by silly descriptions. In No. 2, Chopin's *Funeral March* is parodied and called a "quotation from the celebrated Mazurka of Schubert."

Croquis et agaceries d'un gros bonhomme en bois (1913) (ESC). Three parodies of Mozart, Chabrier and Debussy.

Chapitres tournés en tous sens (1913) (ESC). No. 1, a parody on a wife who talks too much; No. 2, a porter who carries heavy stones; No. 3 uses "Nous n'irons plus au bois," (see Debussy *Jardins sous la pluie*).

Vieux Sequins et Vielles Cuirasses (1914) (ESC). Allusions to Gounod, King Dagobert and "Malbrouck s'en va-t-en guerre."

Menus Propos Enfantines (1913) (ESC). Three sets of children's pieces, for small hand, no thumb crossings, comical commentary.

Heures séculaires et instantanées (1914) (ESC). Three pieces with grotesque narratives: Obstacles vénimeux, Crépuscule matinal (de midi), Affolements grantiques.
In a footnote, Satie forbids the player to read the text aloud during performance.

Trois Valses distinguées d'un précieux dégoûté (1914) (Sal). A collage of quotations from Bruyère, Cicero and Cato, running commentary by Satie, short waltzes involving some bitonality.

Sports et Divertissements (1914) (Sal). Available in a regular edition and a deluxe version, a facsimile of the manuscript with colored drawings by Charles Martin. Twenty brief sketches of fantasy and delicate charm. "I recommend that you turn its pages with a tolerant thumb and with a smile, for this is a work of fantasy. Let no one regard it otherwise. For the "dried-up" and the "stultified" I have written a chorale, sober and suitable. This makes a sort of bitter prelude, a kind of introduction quite austere and unfrivolous. Into it I have put all I know about boredom. I dedicate this chorale to those who do not like me. And I withdraw." (From the preface). The twenty pieces include the following titles: The Swing, Hunting, Italian Comedy, The Bride, Blind Man's Buff, Fishing, Yachting, Bathing, Carnival, Golf, The Octopus, Racing, Puss in the Corner, Picnic, Water Slide, Tango, The Sledge, Flirt, Fireworks, Tennis.

Les Pantins dansent (1914) (Sal).

Avant-dernières Pensées (1915) (Sal). Three short pieces. Aubade à Paul Dukas, Idylle à Debussy, Meditation à Albert Roussel.

Nocturnes (1919) (Sal 1-3, ESC 4-5). Each is a page long.

Premier Menuet (1920) (ESC).

Jack in the Box Op. Posth. (UE). Originally music for a pantomime.

Grimaces Op. Posth. (UE). Five pieces, originally incidental music for a Cocteau production of a Shakespeare play.

Sonatine bureaucratique (1917) (Consortium). Neoclassic, in style of Clementi.

Pages Mystiques (ESC). Three one-page fragments including Prière (choralelike) ; Vexations; Harmonies (sparse chords).

Vexations (Musica Obscura) (ESC). To be played 840 times!

The Piano Music of Erik Satie (AMP). A collection of thirty piano pieces including the famous 1912-1914 piano works.

HENRI SAUGUET (1901-) France

Sauguet described himself as a "traditionalist, though strongly anti-academic." His style is characterized by spontaneous and unpretentious writing which seeks to please rather than to be profound.

3 Françaises (Lerolle 1925). Vol. 1.

3 Nouvelles Françaises (Lerolle). Vol. 2.

Sonata D (Sal 1926). 3 movements. 19 p.
Cheerful writing with a few unconvincing modulations.

Près du bal (Sal). Suite.

Feuillets d'Album (Jobert 1928). 3 pieces: Une valse, Un nocturne, Un scherzo.

Romance C (Jobert).

Suite royale (ESC 1962). 24 p. 19½ minutes.

Pièces poétiques (ESC). 2 volumes. Volume 1 is rather easy, volume 2 more difficult.

A. ADNAN SAYGUN (1907-) Turkey

Since 1946 Saygun has been professor of composition at the Ankara State Conservatory. Although he studied in France, he exploits native folk music extensively.

Sonatina Op. 15 (PIC 1938).
First movement, impressionistic.
Second movement, Adagio con moto, uses ostinati and highly embellished melodic ideas.
Third movement, Horon, a dance from the Black Sea area, brilliant, driving rhythms.

Anadolu'dan Op. 25 (PIC 1945).
3 pieces that emphasize interesting rhythmic patterns.
1. Meseli, 9/8 in 2 2 2 3.
2. Zeybek, 9/4 in 4 5, romantic treatment.
3. Halay, 4/4, 10/8 in 2 3 2 3.

Inci'nin Kitabi (Southern 1934). Inci's Book. Easy to Int. A shortened contemporary "Turkish Album for the Young." 7 character pieces of Turkish origin: Inci, Playful Kitten, A Tale, The Giant Puppet, A Joke, Lullaby, A Dream.

10 Etudes on Aksak Rhythms (Southern c. 1969). 51 p. A fine foreword throws light on these rhythmic studies. All are difficult, unusual works.

12 Preludes on Aksak Rhythms (Southern c. 1969). The term *Aksak* designates a special category of rhythms, a few specimens of which were made known by Béla Bartók under the denomination "Bulgarian rhythm." Comments in the foreword explain the use of the rhythms. Interesting sonorities and rhythmic treatment. M-D.

ALESSANDRO SCARLATTI (1660-1725) Italy

Father of the great and better-known Domenico.

Composizioni per Clavicembalo (A. Longo-Ric). Minuett C, Balletto a, Adagio, Allegretto, Aria alla francese, Corrente (in 4/4 time), 2 Fugues g, a.

Primo e Secundo libro di Toccate in *I Classici Musicali Italiani* XIII (R. Gerlin-Fondazione Eugenio Brevi). Contains 10 toccatas. Sectionalized, virtuoso figuration, modulations.

7 Toccatas for Clavier (R. Nardi-Br).

Variations on "Follia di Spagna" (Tagliapictra-Ric).

See: Julio Esteban, "On the Neglected Keyboard Compositions of Alessandro Scarlatti," AMT, 18, January 1969, 22-3.

John Shedlock, "The Harpsichord Music of Alessandro Scarlatti," SIMG, 6, 1904-5, 160-78, 418-22.

DOMENICO SCARLATTI (1685-1757) Italy, lived mostly in Spain

Opere Complete per Clavicembalo ordinate in Suites di 5 Sonate ciascuna (A. Longo-Ric). The complete edition, 10 volumes plus a supplement, arranged in Suites of five "Sonatas" each, 545 "sonatas." It is not entirely clear whether or not Scarlatti used the term "sonata". Longo's arrangement into suites is an arbitrary one and has no chronological validity. Kirkpatrick renumbered the sonatas in an attempt to establish a reasonable chronology (see below). Division of sonatas by volumes in Longo Edition:
Vol. I. 1-50 II. 51-100 III. 101-150 IV. 151-200 V. 201-250 VI. 251-300 VII. 301-350 VIII. 351-400 IX. 401-450 X. 451-500 Supplementary Volume.
Ralph Kirkpatrick's study, *Domenico Scarlatti,* Princeton University Press, 1953 and his edition of sixty of the sonatas for G. Schirmer are exemplary. These *Sixty Sonatas* with (K) and Longo numbers are listed below.

Music	Kirkpatrick	Longo	Music	Kirkpatrick	Longo
1	3	378	20	133	282
2	7	379	21	175	429
3	16	397	22	140	107
4	18	416	23	208	238
5	28	373	24	209	428
6	29	461	25	215	323
7	44	432	26	216	273
8	46	25	27	238	27
9	54	241	28	239	281
10	57	S.38	29	259	103
11	84	10	30	260	124
12	52	267	31	263	321
13	96	465	32	264	466
14	105	204	33	308	359
15	115	407	34	309	454
16	116	452	35	366	119
17	119	415	36	367	172
18	120	215	37	394	275
19	132	457	38	395	65

Music	Kirkpatrick	Longo	Music	Kirkpatrick	Longo
39	402	427	50	491	164
40	403	470	51	492	14
41	420	S.2	52	493	S.24
42	421	252	53	494	287
43	426	128	54	513	S.3
44	427	286	55	516	S.12
45	460	324	56	517	266
46	461	8	57	518	116
47	470	304	58	519	475
48	471	82	59	544	497
49	490	206	60	545	500

"Music" column above refers to number in the Kirkpatrick edition (GS) of *Sixty Sonatas*. A complete catalogue of 545 sonatas listing Kirkpatrick's chronology along with the chronology of Longo is contained in Appendix II in Kirkpatrick's book, *Domenico Scarlatti*.

Heugel began publication of the first complete edition of the 555 sonatas in 11 volumes in 1971, presented in the chronological order of the Kirkpatrick catalogue, newly engraved and edited from the earliest sources with an introduction, facsimiles and notes by Kenneth Gilbert.

Johnson Reprint Corporation has the *Complete Keyboard Works,* 18 Vols., in facsimile from the manuscript and printed sources, compiled and annotated by Ralph Kirkpatrick.

Separate sonatas in the Longo edition are available from (Ric) and include the following:

No. 10 c
No. 14 D
No. 23 E
No. 33 b
No. 46 B♭
No. 49 g
No. 108 d
No. 114 E♭
No. 142 E♭
No. 239 a
No. 256 c♯
No. 387 G
No. 345 A
No. 413 d Pastorale
No. 422 d Toccata
No. 433 F Pastorale-Siciliana
No. 449 b
No. 463 D Tempo di Ballo
No. 499 g Cat's Fugue

Other editions of the sonatas and some of the separate pieces are:

60 Selected Sonatas (Br&H) Unedited. *20 Selected Sonatas* (Br&H) taken from the 60.

24 Sonatas (Sauer-CFP).

25 Sonatas (Longo-Ric) from the complete edition.

24 Sonatas (J. Friskin-JF 1938, 1945): two volumes, 12 in each, edited and fingered.

150 Sonatas (Keller, Weismann-CFP) Urtext.

10 Sonatas (A. Loesser-Music Press 1947) contains some less familiar Sonatas: L. 46, 49, 131, 203, 204, 212, 289, 380, 405, 416.

35 Sonatas (CF 1947): two volumes, fingered, edited, table of ornaments.

5 Pairs of Sonatas (S. Rosenblum-ECS) contains an excellent preface.

4 Sonatas (Newton-OUP). Fine edition.

36 Sonatas (L. Kartun-UMP). Two volumes, highly edited.

9 Selected Sonatas (I. Philipp-IMC) includes L. 97, 486, 488, 490, 465, 463, 487, 413, 375.

6 Selected Sonatas (I. Philipp-IMC) includes L. 33, 483, 23, 25, 209, 430.

30 Sonatas (Gregg Press 1967). This is a beautiful reprint of a 1739 London edition and contains an interesting selection of Sonatas, the *Essercizi per gravicembalo*.

Ausgewählte Klavierwerke (H. Hubsch-Süddeutscher Musikverlag. 24 Sonatas and a fugue in c, in two volumes. Edited.

10 Sonate brillanti (Montani-Ric).

16 Sonate (Silvestri-Ric). Edited.

10 Sonaten (E. Nielsen-WH) arranged in progressive order.

29 Sonatas (Dunhill-Augener). In two volumes, highly edited.

Sonata-Album (D. Bradley-Bosworth) 8 lesser-known Sonatas.

22 Piano Pieces (Buonamici-GS) Capriccio, Toccata, etc.

Klavierbüchlein (W.Weismann-Litolff). Contains some of the easier pieces.

60 Sonatas (K) in 2 volumes includes the following: L. 366, 388, 378, 390, 367, 479, 379, 488, 413, 370, 352, 489, 486, 387, 374, 397, 384, 416, 383, 375, 363, 360, 411, 495, 481, 368, 449, 373, 461, 499, 345, 104, 463, 338, 128, 180, 447, 465, 340, 290, 282, 205, 433, 175, 260, 430, 395, 343, 432, 266, 497, 500, 283, 188, 475, 396, 235, 103, 490, 263.

26 Sonatas (E. Granados-UME). Two volumes. Highly edited for performance on the piano.

Two Collections of Rare and Unpublished Sonatas critically edited by Robert C. Lee, c/o School of Music, University of Washington, Seattle, Washington 98105.

Vol. I: f♯ K. 142, C K. 143, G K. 144.

Vol. II: g K. 4, E (Granados 13), A (Granados 10), d (K. 41), g Bologna (Lee 8), G (K. 80) has a second movement, Minuet F (K. 94). None of the sonatas in these two collections are included in the editions of Kirkpatrick, Longo, or Gerstenberg. They are of great interest and all appear to be genuine D. Scarlatti.

35 Sonatas (CF) in two volumes after the Longo Edition. Vol. I: L. 104, 187, 188, 256, 331, 338, 345, 368, 375, 407, 413, 422, 424, 490, 498, 499, Supp. 39; Vol. II: L. 23, 33, 58, 128, 263, 324, 370, 381, 396, 416, 429, 430, 433, 434, 465, 475, 486, Supp. 3.

Leichte Tänze und Stücke für Klavier. (K. Herrmann-Hug). Collection of Minuets, Aria, Allegros, etc.

37 Pieces and Sonatas (A. Goldsbrough-ABRSM). Three Volumes. A graded series.

The Graded Scarlatti (M. Motchane-Ric).
A collection of 39 sonatas, good varied selection, edited text.

24 Pieces (Simrock) Two Volumes.

49 Sonatas (Hubsch-Br). Two Volumes.
Vol. I: 25 Sonatas. Vol. II: 24 Sonatas.

37 Sonatas (H. Barth-UE 1901). Two Volumes.
Vol. I: 19 Sonatas. Vol. II: 18 Sonatas. Many dynamic, phrasing, and articulation marks added as well as fingering. Interesting selection.

12 Easy Sonatas (A. Mirovitch-EBM).
Some sonatas only one page long. Excellent collection of the easiest sonatas.

10 Sonatas (W. Georgii-Arno Volk Verlag) including L. 430, 139, 461, 231, 287, 499, 498, 384, 476 and a sonata in D. Sources and performance suggestions are given.

See: Rita Benton, "Form in the Sonatas of Domenico Scarlatti," MR, 13, November 1952, 264-273.

Massimo Bogianckino, *The Harpsichord Music of Domenico Scarlatti.* Kassel: Barenreiter, 1967. Translated from the Italian by John Tickner. Contributi di Musicologia, I.

Kathleen Dale, "Domenico Scarlatti: His Unique Contribution to Keyboard Literature," PRMA, 74, 1947-48, 33-44.

Cecil Hopkinson, "18th-Century Editions of the Keyboard Compositions of Domenico Scarlatti," Edinburgh Bibliographical Society Translations, 3/1, 1948-49, 47-71.

HANS SCHAEUBLE (1906-) Switzerland

Sonata Op. 39 (Bo&Bo 1953-54). 3 movements. 23 p. M-D. Plastic writing, mixed meters, linear, 12-tone influence.

BOGUSLAW SCHÄFFER (1929-) Poland

Since 1963 Schäffer has been a member of the faculty at the State College of Music in Kracow.

Musica per Pianoforte (PMP 1949-1960).
This collection of pieces uses "a graphic notation for portray-

ing sound intensities, proportions of duration, and positioning of notes, through use of analytical geometry and, frequently, red and green colors." BBD, 152. These pieces trace Schäffer's style from conservative to radical.

XAVER SCHARWENKA (1850-1924) Poland

Album (CFP). 2 Menuets Op. 49, 6 Fantasy Pieces Op. 50, Tarantella Op. 51/1, Polonaise Op. 51/2, 2 Sonatinas e, B♭, Op. 52. M-D.

Ballade f♯ Op. 85/1 (Leuckhart). M-D.

Polish Dance Op. 3/1 (Br&H) (GS) (CF). Rhythmic. Int.

Barcarolle Op. 62/4 (GS).

Arpeggio Study (Pauer--Augener).

Mazurka g (Augener).

5 Polish Dances Op. 3 (Augener). e♭, f♯, D, g, B♭.

2 Books of Polish Dances (Augener). Including 19 dances from Op. 9, 16, 29, 34, 40, 47, 58.

PETER SCHAT (1935-) The Netherlands

Schat studied with Seiber and Boulez. He uses both serial and electronic techniques.

Inscripties voor Piano (Donemus 1959). 5 minutes. D.
"The Inscripties for piano contains a 12-tone row that is segmented into 2 asymmetrical parts. Each part is further segmented to correlate with a basic rhythmic pattern, also asymmetrically divided. A distinctive quality is achieved from deviations in asymmetrical note groupings placed in opposition to the almost ostinato repetition of rhythmic motives. A brief opportunity for chance and improvisation is permitted in the second of the three pieces." BBD; 154.

SAMUEL SCHEIDT (1587-1654) Germany

Ausgewählte Werke für Orgel und Klavier (CFP). Dance variations and variations on secular songs. Sweelinck influence.

Görlitz Tabulaturbuch 1650 (CFP). 100 chorales in 4-part harmony.

Song Variations for Clavier (Auler-Schott). 3 sets from his *Tabulatura Nova* (1624) on melodies popular in Scheidt's day.

Variations on the English song "Fortune" (Epstein-UE). 5 contrasting sensitive variations.

ARMIN SCHIBLER (1920-   ) Switzerland

Schibler writes in many styles; neobaroque, late-romantic, expressionistic, 12-tone, etc.

Nobody Knows (Eulenberg). 12 pieces based on Negro Spirituals. Int.

Rhythmisches Kaleidoskop Op. 36 (Kahnt). Int.
The composer advises "much expression and much rubato."

Esquisses de Danse Op. 51 (Simrock).

Aphorismen Op. 29 (Ahn & Simrock 1960). Nine short expressive pieces using "dodecaphonic tonality." He defines the term as tonal equality of the 12 tones without the use of a series.

Ornamente Op. 32 (Ahn & Simrock). 12 tone. M-D.

Dodecaphonic Studies for Pedagogic Use (Kahnt).

Aufzeichnungen Op. 86 (Eulenberg 1967). Eight short pieces. Advanced harmonic idiom. M-D.

KARL SCHISKE (1916-   ) Austria, born Hungary

Schiske's style is basically polyphonic.

Little Suite Op. 1 (OBV 1935).

Theme, 8 Variations and Double Fugue Op. 2 (Dob 1936).

Sonata Op. 3 (Dob 1936). 4 movements. 25 p.
One of the composer's strongest works.

Rhapsody Op. 20 (Dob 1945).

Dance Suite Op. 23 (Dob 1945). 20 p.
Foxtrot, Langsamer Walzer, Tango, Schneller Walzer.

3 Pieces on Folktunes Op. 35 (Dob 1951). M-D.

Sonatina Op. 42 (Dob 1954). 3 movements.
Frequently changing meters, neoclassic style.

JULIUS SCHLOSS (1902-) USA

23 Pieces for Children in 12-Tone Style (PIC c. 1958 and 1965). Easy-Int.
Provides a fine introduction to this technique. Pieces are short and highly musical. Interesting titles.

23 Studies for Children in 12-Tone Style (PIC c. 1962 and 1965).
Slightly more difficult than the above volume. A fine follow-up.

FLORENT SCHMITT (1870-1958) France

Schmitt used only the small forms for his solo piano works. The pianistic lay-out often resembles that of his teacher Fauré but his accompanimental writing is more ample than that of Fauré. His harmony is expressive. Schmitt was a meticulous editor of his own works. Durand publishes a large number of the piano works.

Sept Pièces Op. 15 (Leduc 1928).

Petites musiques Op. 32 (Editions de La Sirène 1907). 8 pieces. 17 p. Int.

Pupazzi Op. 36 (Sal 1909). Petite Suite in 8 movements. Int.

Ombres Op. 64 (Durand 1916-17). 36 p.
J'entends dans le lointain, Mauresque, Cette ombre mon image.

Soirs (Durand 1911). 10 Préludes. MC, M-D. Published separately.

Musiques Intimes Op. 16 (Heugel). 6 pieces, delicate, German-romantic plus impressionistic sounds.

Musiques Intimes Op. 29 (Sal). 6 pieces.

3 Préludes (Sal) Prélude triste, Obsession, Chant de cygnes.

3 Danses Op. 86 (Durand). Montferrine, Bocane, Danse de Corde.

Enfants Op. 94 (Durand). 8 short pieces. Technical requirements vary. Int.

Clavecin obtemperant Op. 107 (Durand). 4 pieces. M-D.

Scènes de la vie moyenne Op. 124 (Durand 1952). 4 pieces. A most attractive suite. La Marche au Marché, Anséanic Dance, Castles in Spain, Saut périlleux du poulet.

Chaîne brisée Op. 87 (Durand 1936). 3 pieces.
Stèle pour le tombeau de P. Dukas, Barcarolle des 7 Vierges, Branle de sortie.

Mirages Op. 70 (Durand). A la mémoire de C. Debussy, La tragique chevauchée.

Suite sans esprit de suite Op. 89 (Durand). 5 movements. M-D.

3 Valses nocturnes (Sal).

ARTUR SCHNABEL (1882-1951) Germany

Piece in Seven Movements (EBM 1947). 33½ minutes. D.
A lengthy, involved work reflecting the influence of Schönberg. Requires the most advanced pianism and mature musicianship. Moderato semplice, Vivace un poco resoluto, Allegretto piacevole, Allegretto agitato, Vivacissimo, Adagio (a variation of No. 1).

JOHANN JEAN SCHOBERT (1720-1767) Germany

In Dr. Burney's *A General History of Music* Vol. II, 957, the author noted that the main merit of Schobert's music was to bring "the symphonic, or modern overture style" to the harpsichord. Nevertheless, his keyboard writing is very pianistic and had some influence on the young Mozart who arranged a movement of a Schobert sonata as the second movement of his concerto K. 39, (1767).

A selection of his compositions is found in DDT, Vol. 39, which also includes a thematic index.

Sonata E♭ Op. 10 in collection *Keyboard Music of the Baroque and Rococo* (Georgii-Volk), Vol. III. Originally for keyboard with accompaniment of a violin and possibly two horns. Schobert was a pioneer in making optional the accompaniment in the accompanied keyboard sonata. Elements of SA design present.

Sonata F Op. 8/1 (Saint-Foix-Senart 1923).

Sonata D (Revue Musicale 1922).

See: Herbert C. Turrentine, "Johann Schobert and French Clavier Music from 1700 to the Revolution," Vols. I and II, unpub. diss., State University of Iowa, 1962.
Johann Schobert: A Reappraisal of his musical style and Historical Significance," AMT, 19, January 1970, 20-2.

OTHMAR SCHOECK (1886-1957) Switzerland

"Schoeck . . . belongs to the conservative contrapuntal tradition that takes its point of departure from Reger . . ." SHKY, 444.

Klavierstücke Op. 29 (Br&H 1919-20). Consolation and Toccata. Toccata much more difficult.

Ritornelle und Fughetten Op. 68 (Symphonia Verlag 1953-55). M-D.

ERWIN CHRISTIAN SCHOLZ (1910-) Austria

Kaleidoscope. American Rhythms for Piano (Dob 1959). 2 books. Book 1 is easy, book 2 Int.

Aller Anfang ist nicht schwer (Dob 1951). 82 short, easy, musical pieces.

Pieces for Children (Dob 1960). Short, original, easy to Int.

Sonata No. 3 Op. 52 (Dob 1954). 3 movements FSF. 38 p. D. Tonal. Last movement meter 5/8 3/8 effectively handled.

Toccata (Dob 1959). Brilliant writing with a contrasting midsection. D.

ARNOLD SCHÖNBERG (1874-1951) Austria

"The piano works of the originator of the method of composing with twelve tones come from periods crucial to his general development. The musical and technical problems are more understandable if studied in relation to other works in his output: the *Chamber Symphony,* Opus 9 (transcription by Edward Steuermann for Piano solo, UE 1950), the *Serenade,* Opus 24, and the string quartets. Several factors ask for special study: the melodies, characterized by wide intervals and apparent discontinuity; the rhythms, using a variety and subtlety of stress that serve to conceal the main beat; the sonorities, that ask for a perfect balance and a very discreet use of the damper pedal to achieve the utmost in clarity. Schönberg's markings are minute to a disconcerting degree. His own explanations of these markings precede several of the works. Metronome indications are often included but must not be followed mechanically. Their function is merely to assist in establishing a satisfactory tempo.

Perhaps least important in the performance of these works is an understanding of the twelve-tone method of composing. A clear delineation of the phrase, the proper adjustment of accompaniment to melody and the careful projection of the polyphony are more important considerations for the performer. All the pieces are difficult, calling for the utmost concentration and the achievement of great precision in pianism and musicianship. It is a humble but useful suggestion to play the melodic content of each piece from beginning to end before embarking on a detailed working out of pianistic problems." MFTP, 286. For a better understanding of the piano works see: T. T. Tuttle, "Schönberg's Compositions for Piano Solo," MR, 18, November 1957, 300-18 and the Edward Steuermann article in *Schönberg,* by Merle Armitage, New York: G. Schirmer, 1937.

A complete edition is presently in progress with Josef Rufer as editor-in-chief. The piano works are contained in Series A, Volume 2, Part 4 (UE and Schott) with Edward Steuermann and Reinhold Brinkmann the editors. This volume contains three early (1894) works for piano, an Andantino, Andantino grazioso and a Presto. All three are short (41 bars, 72 bars, 101 bars) and all employ postromantic techniques, oriented toward Brahms. The three make a fine set played together but could also be performed individually. Also available from Belmont Music Publishers. M-D.

Three Piano Pieces Op. 11 (UE 1908). Extensions of the Romantic character piece with a special kinship to Brahms. No. 3 is the most involved, all but defying analysis. D.
Ferrucio Busoni's interpretation of No. 2 is available from (Belmont) and (UE).

Six Little Piano Pieces Op. 19 (1911) (UE) (Belmont). Least complex of the piano works. They are aphoristic miniatures held together by extreme brevity and concentrated psychological content. Subtle, fleeting sketches. M-D.

Five Piano Pieces Op. 23 (1923) (Belmont) (WH). Difficult interpretative problems. No. 1 is somewhat like a three-part invention; No. 2 is a small three-part form; No. 3 "demonstrates numerous ways for employing a short series as the foundation of an entire piece," BBD, 24, while No. 5 (Walzer) employs, for the first time a twelve-tone row as basis for both linear and vertical content of a composition. D.

Suite for Piano Op. 25 (1924) (Belmont) (UE). Prelude, Gavotte, Musette, Intermezzo, M, G. All movements are built on the same row. More complex treatment than the earlier works. D.

Piano Piece Op. 33a (1932) (UE) (Belmont). More vertically structured, sharp contrasts, both dramatic and lyrical, elaborate use of the row. D.

Piano Piece Op. 33b (1932) (Belmont) (NME).
More lyric. Thinner texture than Op. 33a, extended melodies. D.

See: Patricia Carpenter, "The Piano Music of Arnold Schoenberg," PQ, 41, Fall 1962, 26-31 and 42, Winter 1962-63, 23-9.

Ruth Friedberg, "The Solo Keyboard Works of Arnold Schönberg," MR, 23, 1962, 83-96.

Wolfgang Rogge, *Das Klavierwerk Arnold Schönbergs.* Regensburg: G. Bosse, 1964.

A. DeWayne Wee, "The Twelve-Tone Piano Compositions of Arnold Schönberg," unpub. DM paper, Indiana University, 1968.

STIG GUSTAV SCHOENBERG (1933-) Sweden

Improvisatoriska miniatyrer (NMS).

Sonatin No. 1 (Eriks Musikhandel, Karlavagen 40).

Sma variationer (Eriks Musikhandel).

HAROLD SCHRAMM (1935-1971) USA

Schramm lived in the Far East for a while. He was publisher of The Piano Quarterly, a most useful periodical.

Dance Suite (Gen 1968). Int. 8 p.
Jatisvaram (Toccata): based on ostinati.
Padam (Adagio): melody in LH with a two-voice ostinato in RH.
Varnam (Etude): delightfully brilliant study.
These pieces appear to be based on Indian melodies and/or ragas. They call to mind sounds associated with Hindu music.

Bharata Sangita (MCA 1965). 19 p. 6 pieces. Int.
". . . a set of original piano compositions, conceived as a synthesis of Eastern and Western musical elements: the distinctively colorful Indian scales, rhythms, and forms—and occidental compositional techniques." No. 4 Ragatalamalika is a short seven-movement suite. Unusual, worthwhile.

Vertical Construction (Gen 1968). 4p. M-D.
Highly organized. Preference for fourths and sevenths.

HERMANN SCHROEDER (1904-) Germany

Schroeder's style leans towards neobaroque writing.

Sonata a (Schott 1952). More like suite than sonata. Preference for quartal harmony.
Praeludium, Fuge, Aria, Capriccio.

Minnelieder (Schott 1939). Int. to M-D.
Variations on 5 old German songs.

2 Sonatinas (Simrock).

Sonata No. 2 f♯ (Schott 1953). 3 movements. M-D.
Fluent, facile, thin textures, attractive harmonic and melodic construction, MC.

HEINZ SCHRÖTER (1907-) Germany

Schröter is Director of the Conservatory at Cologne, Germany.

Variationen und Fuge über ein Thema von Reger Op. 6 (Süddeutscher Musikverlag 1941). In the style of Reger's large sets of variations. D.

Alt-Frankfurt Op. 7 (Süddeutscher Musikverlag 1941). 5 pieces, M-D.

Sonatine Op. 8 (Bo&Bo 1955). 3 movements. M-D.

5 Etudes Op. 10 (Schott 1951). D.

FRANZ SCHUBERT (1797-1828) Austria

Great lyric beauty, bold harmonic vocabulary, natural spontaneity, intimate writing, sometimes coupled with large spatial design, characterize Schubert's unique keyboard style. A few of the outer movements in the sonatas may seem long, but as Robert Schumann said, they are of "heavenly lengths." Under no circumstances should any of these movements be cut. D. numbers refer to O. E. Deutsch's *Schubert: Thematic Catalogue of all his Works in Chronological Order*. New York: W. W. Norton, 1951. The piano music falls into three broad categories: dances, piano pieces, and sonatas. Dover Publications has the complete piano music in a one-volume reprint of Vol. V of the critical edition of 1884-1897 (Epstein-Br&H).

DANCES: Approximately 400 short pieces comprising Menuetts, German Dances, Ländler, Waltzes, Ecossaisen, Galops. The easiest are *20 Minuette* (D. 41), *Ländler* (D. 378, 679, 681), 17*Ländler* (D. 145), *Ecossaisen* (D. 421, 511, 529, 299, 781).

Slightly more difficult are the *Waltzes* Op. 9, 18, 33, *Kleine Deutsche Tänze* (D. 722). More difficult are the *34 Valses sentimentales* Op. 50, 16 *Waltzes* Op. 33, 12 *Ländler* Op. 171. Finally, the most difficult of the dance pieces are 6 *German Dances* (D. 820), 12 *Grazer Waltzes* Op. 91, and the 12 *Valses nobles* Op. 77.

EDITIONS OF THE DANCES: *Dances* (P. Mies-Henle) 2 vols. Vol. I: 20 *Menuette* (D. 41), 2 *Menuette* (D. 91), 12 *Little German Dances* (D. 128), *Waltz* c♯ (D. 139), 12 *Waltzes,* 17 Ländler, 9 *Ecossaises* Op. 18 (D. 145), 20 *Easy Waltzes* Op. 127 (D. 146), *Ecossaise* d, (D. 158), 12 *Ecossaises* (D. 299), *Menuette* A, E, D (D. 334-6), 36 *Erste Walzer,* Op. 9 (D. 365), 17 *German Dances* (D. 366), 8 *Ländler* (D. 378), 3 *Menuette* (D. 380), 12 *German Dances* (D. 420).
Vol. II: 6 *Ecossaises* (D. 421), *Ecossaise* E♭ (D. 511), 8 *Ecossaises* (D. 529), *Menuett* c♯ (D. 600), *Trio* (D. 610), *German Dance, Ecossaise* (D. 643), 2 *Ländler* (D. 679), 8 *Ländler* (D. 681), 5 *Ecossaisen* (D. 697), *Variation c on a Waltz of Diabelli* (D. 718), *German Dance* G♭ (D. 722), 16 *Ländler,* 2 *Ecossaises* Op. 67 (D. 734), *Galop,* 8 *Ecossaises* Op. 49 (D. 735), 2 *German Dances* (D. 769), 34 *Valses sentimentales* Op. 50 (D. 779), 11 *Ecossaisen* (D. 781), *Ecossaise D* (D. 782), 16 *German Dances,* 2 *Ecossaises* Op. 33 (D. 783), 12 *Ländler* Op. 171 (D. 790), 6 *German Dances* (D. 820), 2 *German Dances* (D. 841), *Albumblatt* G (D. 844), 12 *Grazer Walzer* Op. 91 (D. 924), *Grazer Galop* (D. 925), 12 *Valse nobles* Op. 77 (D. 969), 6 *German Dances* (D. 970), 12 *German Dances* (D. 971-75), *Cotillon* (D. 976, 8 *Ecossaisen* (D. 977), 4 *Walzer* (D. 978-80), 3 *Ecossaisen* (D. 816), Appendix containing 32 pieces from D. 354, 355, 370, 374, 640, 680, 995.

Dance Album (P. Mies-Henle). 12 *Waltzes* from Op. 18, 9, 67; 18 *Waltzes* from Op. 50, 33, 171; D. 820, Op. 91, D. 610, D. 718.

Dances (Niemann-CFP). 161 dances.

Dances (Pauer-Br&H). 2 Vols. Broad selection.

Dances for the Young (Frey-Schott). A fine selection of the easiest dances.

16 German Dances Op. 33 (Georgii-Schott).

PIANO PIECES: *Impromptus, Moments Musicaux* (Gieseking-Henle). Published with *Drei Klavierstücke* (Badura-Skoda-UE).

4 Impromptus Op. 90 (D. 899).

1. c: Continuous variations on two alternating themes. Many repeated chords for LH. Vienna Urtext contains a pencil sketch for this work.
2. E♭: Calls for brilliant finger work in outer sections with strongly contrasted mid-section and coda. One of the most popular of both sets.
3. G♭: Title given by publisher. Unique melodic and harmonic usage. Requires a beautiful singing legato line.
4. A♭: RH rotation study, lyric mid-section.

4 Impromptus Op. 142 (D. 935). Both Robert Schumann and Alfred Einstein believed this work to be a sonata.

1. f: Lengthy, a combination of rondo and SA designs.
2. A♭: Easiest of the set. A lyric quality permeates the work.
3. B♭: One of Schubert's most beautiful sets of variations; theme and 5 variations.
4. f: Most difficult of the set. Requires even scale-work and a fine staccato.

Drei Klavierstücke (D. 946) (1828) (Mies-Henle) (CFP). Approximate difficulty of the impromptus.

1. e♭: An energetic Allegro assai contrasts with two Andante sections.
2. E♭: 5-part form with two episodes.
3. C: An allegro with sharply accented syncopations and interesting harmonies.

6 Moments musicaux Op. 94 (D. 780) (Henle) with Op. 90 and 142, (CFP).

1. C: Lyric mid-section requires fine legato line.
2. A♭: Lyric, sustained, requires good pacing.

3. f: Pianissimo staccato and careful balance of hands required. Enharmonic modulations.
4. c♯: Clean unaccented RH passage work required. Bachlike.
5. f: Powerful chord and octave figuration.
6. A♭: Poetic, chordal legato required.

10 Variations F on an original theme (D. 156) (1815) (EMT). Varied moods and textures. M-D.

13 Variations on a theme of Anselm Hüttenbrenner a (D. 576) (1817) (Br&H). Theme is from Hüttenbrenner's first String Quartet E Op. 3 published in 1816 or 17. Not as difficult as D. 156.

Variation on a Waltz by Diabelli (D. 718) (1821). Int., short, Schubertian harmonies. In collection *Small Works* (Pauer-Br&H).

Albumblatt G (D. 844) (Pauer-Br&H) *Small Works.* Int. Sometimes listed as *Waltz* G.

Allegretto c (D. 915) (1827). In preceding Pauer collection and *400 Years of European Keyboard Music.* Similar to a *Moment Musical.*

Andante C (D. 29) (1812). Int.

Adagio G (D. 178) (1815). M-D. (O. v. Irmer-Stella) 22 *Klavierstücke.*

Scherzo D (D. 570) (1817?) Int.

2 Scherzi B♭, D♭ (D. 593) (1817) (Schott) (Ric). Int. with the first one easier.

5 Klavierstücke (D. 459) (1816). See *Sonata* E D. 459.

Klavierstück A (D. 604) (1818?). Alfred Einstein suggests this movement was originally written for Sonata D Op. 53 (D. 850) (1825). M-D.

Adagio E (D. 612) (1818). Chromatic vocabulary. M-D.

Adagio and Rondo D♭ E (D. 505-6) Op. 145 (1816?). Deutsch says the association of these two works is spurious. The original form of the Adagio seems to be the second movement of the *Sonata* f (D. 625) (1818). M-D.

March E (D. 606) (1818). Trio in A♭. M-D.

Walzer (R. Strauss-UE c. 1970). A simple waltz Schubert improvised at a wedding. Int.

SONATAS: See SSB, 202-18, including a chart and discussion of 23 partial and completed solo piano sonatas.

EDITIONS OF SONATAS:

(Mies, Theopold-Henle) 2 vols., (E. Ratz-UE) 2 vols., (Dover) a reprint of the (Br&H) 1888 edition, (Pauer-Br&H) 3 vols., (Köhler, Ruthardt-CFP) 2 vols., (K) 2 vols.

1. E (D. 157) (1815) 17 minutes. Planned as a 4-movement work but only three movements exist: Allegro ma non troppo; Andante; Menuetto: Allegro vivace. The Andante is elegiac in mood while the Menuetto is vigorous.
2. C (D. 279) (1815) 15 minutes. Unfinished. 3 movements exist: Allegro moderato; Andante; Menuetto: Allegro vivace. In the opening movement daring modulation and thematic development are important. Recapitulation begins on the sub-dominant rather than the tonic, a device Schubert used in later works.
3. E (D. 459) (1816) 27 minutes. Published as *Fünf Klavierstücke*. The autograph with "Sonate" written on it was discovered later. Allegro moderato; Scherzo: Allegro; Adagio; Scherzo con trio: Allegro; Allegro patetico. Concise first movement, alternation of major and minor, interesting modulations in the development. First Scherzo has more interest but is lengthy. Adagio is the finest movement.
4. a (D. 537) Op. 164 (1817) 17 minutes. Allegro ma non troppo; Allegretto quasi Andantino; Allegro vivace. First movement has an energetic opening, unequal phrase lengths, whimsical development. Second movement appears later in the Sonata A (D. 959) in a more spacious conception.
5. A♭ (D. 557) (1817) 23 minutes. Allegro moderato; Andante; Allegro. Begins A♭, ends E♭. Haydn influence. Original sketches in D♭.

6. e (D. 566) (1817) 16 minutes. Moderato; Allegretto; Scherzo: Allegro vivace; Allegretto moto; D. 506. Published and edited by Kathleen Dale (British and Continental Agencies 1948). Vintage Schubert. Deserves performance.
7. E♭ (D. 568) Op. 122 (1817) 24 minutes. Allegro moderato; Andante molto; Menuetto: Allegretto; Allegro moderato. Light, charming, well unified in mood. Smooth piano writing.
8. f♯ (D. 570-1) (1817?). Scherzo, fragment of Allegro f♯ with the bare possibility that the isolated Andante A (D. 604) supplies the missing slow movement. SSB, 208. Walter Rehberg completed this sonata in 1927 (Steingraber c. 1928) as well as Vernon Duke (Chappell c. 1968).
9. B (D. 575) Op. 147 (1817) 21 minutes. Allegro ma non troppo; Andante; Scherzo: Allegretto; Allegro giusto. A restless feeling permeates this work. Unusual key relationships and abrupt modulations punctuate the first movement. A beautiful Andante that anticipates Mendelssohn encloses a dramatic mid-section. Contrapuntal textures in the Scherzo. Motivic development plays a large part in the final movement.
10. C (D. 613) (1818). Moderato; no tempo indication in final movement. First and last movements complete.
11. f (D. 625, 505) (1818) 19 minutes. Allegro; Scherzo: Allegretto; Adagio (D. 505); Allegro. The first movement stops abruptly at the end of the development section after some bold modulations. The Adagio is highly colored while the final movement has a remarkable energetic drive to it. All 4 movements are not published together. In his edition of the Sonatas (UE) 2 volumes, Erwin Ratz has supplied the recapitulation of the first movement and other short missing passages. Walter Rehberg also completed this sonata (Steingraber c. 1928).
12. c♯ (D. 655) (1819). Contains only a sketch of the first movement.
13. A (D. 664) Op. 120 (1819?) 22 minutes. (Mies, Theopold-Henle). One of the most compact, technically easy, and frequently performed sonatas. Allegro moderato; An-

dante; Allegro. First movement is mainly lyric, with octaves in the development presenting the most technical difficulty. Little contrast in this SA design. Andante uses a persistent rhythm, often found in the faster movements, and characteristic alternation of major to minor and reverse. The finale, in SA design, is the most animated and taxing movement.

14. a (D. 784) Op. 143 (1823) 21 minutes. Robert Schumann considered this one of Schubert's best sonatas. Allegro giusto; Andante; Allegro vivace. The first movement with lean textures, broken octaves and powerful development, make this one of the most original movements in all the sonatas. The songlike Andante is punctuated by curious rhythmic PPP octaves. The finale is constructed around three contrasted figures: a triplet idea, a vigorous rhythmic idea and a lyric tune. All three are worked into a strong concluding movement. The octaves in the final 10 bars present a formidable problem.
15. C (D. 840) (1825) (Reliquie) 34 minutes, with the Krenek completion. Only the first 2 movements are complete. This is probably Schubert's most important unfinished sonata. Armin Knab (1881-1951) completed it (CFP) as well as Ernst Krenek (UE c. 1921) and Walter Rehberg (Steingraber c. 1927). Moderato; Andante; Menuetto: Allegretto; Rondo: Allegro. Moderato is in SA design with the two main ideas not greatly contrasted but spread out spaciously. Andante c, is a rondo with the second episode a recapitulation of the first.
16. a (D. 845) Op. 42 (1825) 31 minutes. (Mies, Theopold-Henle) (Bischoff-WH). Moderato; Andante poco moto; Scherzo: Allegro vivace; Rondo: Allegro vivace. This large-scale work was Schubert's best-known sonata during his life time. The first movement is consistently fine throughout with two highly contrasted ideas that must progress at basically the same tempo. The Andante poco moto, a set of 5 variations, displays some of Schubert's finest contrapuntal writing. A spirited Scherzo with Trio follows. The finale, in sonata-rondo design, exhibits thin textures, varied phrase-lengths, unusual economy of ma-

terial, and calls for most skillful handling of the piano.

17. D (D. 850) Op. 53 (1825) 31 minutes. Allegro vivace, Con moto; Scherzo: Allegro vivace; Rondo: Allegro moderato. Great vitality is characteristic of this work. SA design of the first movement is worked out in a masterly way even though the thematic material is not Schubert's best. Rich texture, spacious lay-out and harmonic interest make this rondo with a returning second episode, one of Schubert's finest slow movements. An energetic Scherzo follows. The happy rondo, with two lengthy episodes has been deservedly called "the crown of the sonata" by Alfred Einstein.
18. G (D. 894) Op. 78 (1826) 29 minutes. (Bischoff-WH). First published under the title of "Fantasie, Andante, Menuetto und Allegretto." Schumann called this Schubert's "most perfect sonata in form and spirit." Molto moderato Cantabile; Andante; Menuetto: Allegro moderato; Allegretto. Attention is called to an effective long crescendo in the development section of the first movement. This provides a needed contrast with the lyric serenity in the rest of the movement. Andante is similar in form to the Sonatas D. 840 and 850. A dancelike Menuetto follows. A spaciously conceived Rondo with two episodes concludes this exciting work.
19. c (D. 958) (1828) 28 minutes. This work, as well as D. 959 and 960 were all composed in less than 4 weeks. They were first published as "Drei grosse Sonaten." This somber work is probably the least known of these three sonatas. Allegro; Adagio; Menuetto: Allegro; Allegro. The stormy opening movement should not go too fast. An "Allegro Moderato" warning appears on the sketch. Adagio is an expressive rondolike design used in D. 840, 850 and 894. A spontaneous and wistful menuetto precedes the SA-like finale.
20. A (D. 959) (1828) 35 minutes. Allegro; Andantino; Scherzo: Allegro vivace; Rondo: Allegretto. First movement opens solemnly with brilliant but controlled passage work. The development is based on a small theme from the codetta. Andantino opens as a barcarolle but soon

moves to more improvisatory section and works to a great climax — one of the most difficult movements in all Schubert. A playful Scherzo leads to the finale, a lengthy and lyrical rondo of great beauty. The rondo theme was used in the Allegretto of D. 537.

21. B♭ (D. 960) (1828) 32 minutes. Molto moderato; Andante sostenuto; Scherzo: Allegro vivace con delicatezza; Allegro ma non troppo. A transcendental work of unique individuality. The Molto moderato is one of the quietest and longest of Schubert's first movements. The slow movement, in the unusual key of c♯, evolves a poetic and religious atmosphere of great beauty. The Scherzo exploits a varied harmonic range and utilizes bold chromaticism. Beethoven's influence is felt in the last movement: the opening is centered on the dominant of c, as in the beginning of the finale of Beethoven's Op. 130 string quarter.

Fantasia C (D. 760) Op. 15 (1822) "Wanderer Fantasia." (Badura-Skoda-UE). This fine edition is based on the autograph and contains an excellent preface. (Georgii-Schott)(Cortot-Salabert) (Bischoff-WH) (Niemann-CFP) (Liszt-Augener). Allegro con fuoco ma non troppo; Adagio; Presto; Allegro. Here Schubert writes for the piano in an orchestral, grandiose style. All themes (except the first subsidiary theme of the Scherzo) are derived from the song "Der Wanderer." Each movement deals with its various transformations anticipating similar procedures in Liszt's *Sonata* b. Virtuoso octave technique is required briefly in this very forward-looking work.

Fantasie C (without D. number) (1818?) "Grazer Fantasie." (Walter Dürr-Br c. 1969). Moderato con espressione; Alla polacca; Moderato con espressione. This work was found in 1962. It is not based on SA design but section follows section until the end when the introduction is repeated, similar to Mozart's *Fantasy* c K. 475. Some stylistic points might possibly tie the work to Anselm Hüttenbrenner or other composers. Dürr does point out similarities to D. 605, 612 and 613. It is a brilliant work and could appeal to contemporary tastes as it did in Schubert's day. Not as difficult as D. 760.

See: Maurice J. E. Brown, *Schubert's Variations.* New York: Macmillan, 1954.
Essays on Schubert, New York: St. Martin's Press, 1966. See especially "Towards an Edition of the Pianoforte Sonatas," 197-216.

James Gibb, "Schubert's Piano Music," Music Teacher and Piano Student, 48, August 1969, 7, 14.

William G. Hill, "The Genesis of Schubert's Posthumous Sonata in B♭," MR, 12, November 1951, 269-78.

Colin Mason, "An Aspect of Schubert's Sonatas," MMR, 76, 1946, 152-57.

E. H. W. Meyerstein, "The Problem of Schubert's E minor Piano Sonata (D. 566, 506)," MS, 1/6, 1949, 183-4.

Olga Samaroff, "The Piano Music of Schubert," MQ, 14, October 1928, 596-609.

James L. Taggart, "Franz Schubert's Piano Sonatas: A Study of Performance Problems," unpub. diss., University of Iowa, 1963.

Harold Truscott, "Schubert's Unfinished Piano Sonata in C (1825)," MR, 18, 1958, 37-44.
"The Two Versions of Schubert's Op. 122," MR, 14, 1953, 89-106.

ERWIN SCHULHOFF (1894-1942) Austria

"As a skilled and remarkably prolific composer (Schulhoff) showed surprising elasticity of style, having been influenced by the most recent tendencies of his time, e.g. by Schönberg, jazz music, Soviet realism, etc." GD, 7, 594.

Boston "Partita" (UE 1922). Period piece. M-D.

5 Jazz Etudes (UE). Charleston, Blues, Chanson, Tango, Toccata on Kitten on the Keys.

Ostinato (UE 1923). Int. Papa, Mama, Da Da, Hop Hop, A A, Trara.

Sonata I (UE).

Sonata II (Artia). 38 p. 4 movements, vigorous. Free conception of tonal relations.

Sonata III (Br 1927). D.

WALTER SCHULTHESS (1894-1971) Switzerland

Schulthess "combines sensitive and piquant harmony of an impressionist nature with tense expression." GD, 7, 596.

3 Klavierstücke Op. 12 (Schott). Capriccio, Aria, Alla tarantella.

6 Little Fantasiestücke Op. 13 (Schott). Int.

SVEND SIMON SCHULTZ (1913-) Denmark

Ravel, the late French impressionists and Carl Nielsen are the major influences on Schultz's writings.

Sonate (SPDM 1939).

Concert-Suite (WH 1947). M-D.
Quasi improvisatione: Capriccio; Aria; Toccata.

Sonatine Nos. 1, 2 (WH). Published separately.

JOHANN ABRAHAM PETER SCHULZ (1747-1800) Germany

Six Pieces Op. 1 (Hillemann-Schott). In the style of C. P. E. Bach.

ADOLF SCHULZ-EVLER (1852-1905) Poland

By the beautiful blue Danube. Concert arabesque (GS). This effective period piece with its virtuoso encore writing still deserves to be mentioned. D.

WILLIAM SCHUMAN (1910-) USA

Three-Score Set (GS 1945). 3 short contrasting pieces. M-D.

Voyage (TP 1954). 5 contrasting pieces: Anticipation, Caprice,

Realization, Decision, Retrospection. More musical than technical demands. Taut, chromatic writing.

3 Piano Pieces (Merion). Lyrical, Pensive, Dynamic. Int.

CLARA SCHUMANN (1819-1896) Germany

Romantic Piano Music Book I (Müller).
3 Preludes and Fugues Op. 16, Variations on a theme of Robert Schumann Op. 20, Romance g Op. 21/3. Op. 16 is a fine study in legato playing.

3 Romances Op. 21 (Br&H).
a, F, g.

See: Adelina de Lara, "Clara Schumann's Teaching," ML 26/3, 1945, 143-7.

ROBERT SCHUMANN (1810-1856) Germany

Schumann was the Romantic composer "par excellence." His creative output for piano has provided some of the most imaginative and touching music in the pianist's repertoire. The first twenty-three opera are devoted to the piano. Throughout his career Schumann was occupied writing character-pieces, and though he wrote in larger forms, he continually favored the character-piece. Characteristic of Schumann's piano writing was his use of fast harmonic rhythm, unusual pedal effects, syncopation and cross rhythms, varied accompanimental figurations, chord doublings, and a unique exploitation of contracting and expanding the pianist's hand. Schumann's metronome is known to have been faulty during his lifetime.

EDITIONS:

(O.v. Irmer-Henle) *Piano Solos* Vol. I; Op. 15, 68, 99, 124. *Piano Solos* Vol. II: Op. 1, 12, 18, 19, 21, 23, 28, 82, 111.

(O.v. Irmer-Henle) has separately: Op. 1, 2, 7, 9, 12, 15, 16, 18, 19, 21, 23, 26, 28, 68, 68 with 15, 82, 99, 111, 124.

(Sauer-CFP) 5 volumes.
I: Op. 15, 18, 19, 28, 68, 82, 99, 124.
II: Op. 6, 9, 12, 16, 21.

III: Op. 1, 2, 4, 5, 7, 8, 13, 17, 20, 26.
IV: Op. 3, 10, 23, 32, 72, 76, 111, 118, 126, 133.
V: Op. 11, 14, 22, 54, 92, 134, Op. Posthumous Scherzo f, Presto g.

(C. Schumann, W. Kempff-Br&H) 7 volumes.
I: Op. 1-8.
II: Op. 9-13.
III: Op. 14-19.
IV: Op. 20-23, 26, 28, 32.
V: Op. 56/58 *Studies and Sketches for pedalpiano,* 68, 72, 76, 82.
VI: Op. 99, 111,118,124,126,133.
VII: Op. 54 *Concerto*

(Cortot-Sal) Op. 1, 2, 6, 7, 9, 11-15, 18-22, 26, 82, published separately.

(Augener) 4 volumes.
I: Op. 68, 15, 124, 118, 99, 18, 19, 32.
II: Op. 82, 12, 21, 1, 23, 28, 4, 5, 126, 133.
III: Op. 2, 6, 9, 16, 26, 3, 10, 13, 7, 8, 72, 76.
IV: Op. 11, 22, 14, 17, 20, works for piano and orchestra 54, 92, 134, Opus Posthumous.

(C. Schumann-K) More of Mme. Schumann's interpretation comes through in this edition than that of her husband.
7 Volumes.
I: Op. 1, 2, 3, 4, 5, 6, 7, 8.
II: Op. 9, 10, 11, 12, 13.
III: Op. 14, 15, 16, 17, 18, 19.
IV: Op. 20, 21, 22, 23, 26, 32.
V: Op. 56, 58, 68, 72, 76, 82.
VI: Op. 99, 111, 118, 124, 126, 133.
VII: works for piano and orchestra.

Many works are available separately in the above complete editions.

(Bischoff-WH) Op. 2, 6, 9, 12, 12/2-3, 13, 15, 18, 21, 26, 68, 124, (Niemann-WH) 82.

(Friedman-UE) Op. 1, 2, 6, 9, 12, 15, 16, 18, 20, 26, 28, 68, 124.

(Pauer-Schott) Op. 2, 9, 12/2-4, 15 (4 pieces), 18, 26, 28/2, 68 (7 pieces), 124/15-17.

(Ric) Op. 1, 2, 7, 9, 11, 12, 13, 15, 16, 17, 18, 21, 22, 26, 28, 32/3, 68, 82, 124.

(Steiglich-Br) (Scheltema-Ashdown) Op. 15.

(Palmer-Alfred) Op. 68. Contains excellent preface with section on nineteenth-century ornamentation. Scholarly edition.

EASIER COMPOSITIONS (the five following collections):

Album for the Young Op. 68 (CFP) has a facsimile edition.

Album Leaves Op. 124/1-3.

Colored Leaves Op. 99/3-4.

Three Sonatas for the Young Op. 118.

A New Album for the Young (Werner-Francis, Day and Hunter). Includes nine unpublished pieces from Op. 68. Nos. 4, 5, and 8 are especially attractive.

SEPARATE WORKS (listed numerically by opus number):

Variations on the name Abegg Op. 1 (1830). Theme on the name of Countess von Abegg, three variations with brilliant finale, effective pianistic figuration in Hummel style.

Papillons Op. 2 (1829-31). Cycle of twelve imaginative dance movements, employs chromatic weaving of inner parts and canonic devices. Work concludes with the "Grossvaterlied" and the clock striking while the dancers disperse.

Six Studies after Caprices by Paganini Op. 3 (1832). Literal transcriptions of the Paganini works originally for violin alone. Schumann included a set of exercises to help solve technical problems and suggested these pieces were written to supply material of more interest than the studies of Czerny, Clementi, Hummel and Kalkbrenner. No. 2 is the most musical and was also set by Liszt. a, E, C, B♭, E♭, g.

Intermezzi Op. 4 (1832). Schumann called these works "longer *Papillons*." Six pieces in ternary form written in a free improvisatory style. No. 2 is most involved. No. 4 consists of parts of three different discarded works. No. 5 has great beauty while No. 6 contains the "Abegg" theme in measure 43. A, e, a, C, d, b.

Impromptus on a theme of Clara Wieck Op. 5 (1833). A second and later version (1850) is superior to the first. This work, a free set of nine variations handled in a fluent and ingenious manner, closes with an extensive fugue.

Davidsbündlertänze Op. 6 (1837). Two versions of this work exist. The second version gives Schumann's final ideas. This cycle of eighteen "characteristic" pieces contains indications that underlie the mood of each piece. Technical problems of special note are LH skips in Nos. 3 and 9, complex LH part in No. 6 and fast chords in No. 13. A fascinating article by Roger Fiske throws unusual insight on this work: "A Schumann Mystery," MT, 105, August 1964, 574-8.

Toccata C Op. 7 (1833). This virtuoso masterpiece of the young Schumann is in SA design. Double-notes and octave passage-work account for much of the difficulty. First written in D then transposed to C.

Allegro b Op. 8 (1831). Uncharacteristic work, shows the influence of Hummel.

Carnaval Op. 9 (1834-35). Variegated suite of twenty-two pieces with the sub-title "Little scenes on four notes." Most of the pieces are variations on the four notes A E♭ C B (A S C H in German) or alternatively A♭ C B, the musical letters in Schumann's name. Opening and closing movements are the most extensive. Special technical problems are encountered in *Papillons, Reconnaissance* (fast thumb repetitions), *Pantalon et Columbine* (finger staccato) and *Paganini* (LH skips).

Six Studies after Caprices of Paganini Op. 10 (1833). More imaginative settings than Op. 3. The *Paganini* movement in *Carnaval* refers to No. 1 in this set. No. 2 was also set by Liszt. A♭, g, g, c, b, e.

Sonata f♯ Op. 11 (1835). Four movements: Introduction and Allegro vivace: frequent tempo and key changes, staccato chords; Aria; Scherzo and Intermezzo: two contrasting subjects alternate in the Scherzo, Intermezzo has an unusual recitative; Finale: loosely organized. Orchestrally conceived and demands much physical stamina. Cyclic overtones permeate this work. Moments of rare beauty throughout.

Fantasiestücke Op. 12 (1837). Eight contrasting pieces with individual descriptive titles, planned as a complete unit. Des Abends D♭ (In the Evening) exploits a cross-rhythm; Aufschwung f (Soaring) requires firm rhythmic control; Warum? D♭ (Why?) needs an even, singing tone; Grillen D♭ (Whims) requires a strong rhythmic drive; In der Nacht f (In the Night) one of Schumann's finest inspirations — a passionate piece that requires sensitive handling of multiple layers of melodic writing in the same hand; Fabel C (Fable) alternates capricious and lyric moods; Traumes Wirren F (Restless Dreams) RH rotation technique and sturdy outside fingers are required; Ende vom Lied F (End of the Song) sturdy chordal writing. No. 9 Feurigst (Fiery) (Werner-Curwen) in this series was discarded by Schumann but is now available. Although characteristically Schumannesque it is not up to the quality of the first eight pieces.

Etudes en forme de variations (Etudes Symphoniques) c♯ Op. 13 (1834). There are actually nine variations on the theme (Etudes 3, 9 and the Finale are not based on the theme). Five additional variations were rejected by Schumann but are contained in the (Br&H) edition. Mood and figuration of each etude varies considerably. Staccato chord technique, wide skips for LH and perpetual motion writing are some of the difficulties encoutered in this highly effective masterpiece.

Sonata f Op. 14 (1835-36). Named "Concerto without Orchestra" by publisher Haslinger. Four movements: Allegro f; Scherzo D♭; Andantino f (four variations on a theme by Clara Wieck); Finale f (Sonata-rondo). The theme of the Andantino provides a motto for the entire cyclic work. This sonata is loosely organized and was revised by Schumann. Nevertheless, it does provide some effective, brilliant and demanding writing.

Kinderszenen (Scenes of Childhood) Op. 15 (1838). Programmatic connotations are contained in each individual title although these were added after the completion of the pieces.

Von fremden Ländern und Menschen G (From foreign lands and people). Cantabile melody plus accompaniment divided between hands.

Curiose Geschichte D (Curious Story). Animated chordal writing.

Hasche-Mann b (Catch Me). An etude in finger staccato.

Bittendes Kind D (Entreating Child). Accompanied melody, same hand.

Glückes genug D (Perfect Happiness). Sensitive phrasing in RH melody and LH imitation required.

Wichtige Begebenheit A (Important Event). Heavy chords.

Träumerei F (Dreaming). Needs flexible phrasing and sensitive legato.

Am Kamin F (By the Fireside). Expressive cantabile. Some rearrangement by voicing is appropriate for a small hand.

Ritter vom Steckenpferd C (Knight of the Rocking-Horse). Syncopated rhythm. Keep arms free.

Fast zu ernst g♯ (Almost Too Serious). Needs good tonal balance between syncopated melody and bass.

Fürchtenmachen G (Frightening). Careful dynamic details, contrasted phrases.

Kind im Einschlummern e (Child Falling Asleep). Imagination needed.

Der Dichter spricht G (The Poet Speaks). Firm control of tempo required.

See: Irwin Freundlich, "Robert Schumann's 'Scenes from Childhood'—A Discussion," PQ, 22, Winter 1957, 15-18, 28.

Kreisleriana Op. 16 (1838). The title refers to Kapellmeister Kreisler, a character in several of the tales by E. T. A. Hoffman. Schumann dedicated this work to Chopin. It consists of eight untitled pieces of widely varying moods, many of them in Da Capo form.

Ausserst bewegt d. Precise melodic slurring will be facilitated by a carefully controlled rotation technique.

Sehr innig und nicht zu rasch B♭. Octave and double-note

legato technique are essential. The two intermezzi require quicker tempi.

Sehr aufgeregt g. Repeated four-note figures move to an animated climax. The mid-section is in a contrasting cantilena style.

Sehr langsam B♭. Calls for sensitive tonal control.

Sehr lebhaft g. Opening subject needs a light touch. Numerous rhythmic repetitions test the performer's interpretive powers.

Sehr langsam E♭. Expressive tonal quality demanded.

Sehr rasch c. Vigorous, energetic, calls for facile, yet strong fingers.

Schnell und spielend g. A light pianissimo touch is appropriate for the opening, great power for the climax.

Fantasia C Op. 17 (1836) Schumann's greatest large-scale piano work is dedicated to Franz Liszt. Its three contrasting movements make the utmost demands on the musical sensibilities and technical equipment of the performer. It constitutes a landmark in 19th-century piano literature.

Durchaus fantastisch und leidenschaftlich vorzutragen C. Modified SA design, requires a special sustained quality, great extremes in the dynamic range.

Mässig, durchaus energisch E♭. A scherzo quality hovers over this movement. A big technique, sensitive approach to the middle section plus ability to manage the unusually difficult skips in the coda are all prerequisites.

Langsam getragen, durchweg leise zu halten C. A flowing poetical piece with two powerful climaxes.

Arabesque C Op. 18 (1839). This cantabile piece is constructed in a rondo form with two contrasting episodes. A reflective coda marked "Zum Schluss" employs new material.

Blumenstück D♭ Op. 19 (1839). A theme remodelled in numerous guises moves through five sections, all in similar mood. The final cadence introduces the opening theme of *Humoresque* Op. 20.

Humoresque B♭ Op. 20 (1839). A long improvisational-like work in a free form. Exploits many features of Schumann's piano style but loose organization and numerous themes make it difficult for the listener to follow. One part asks an "inner voice not to be played."

Noveletten Op. 21 (1838). Schumann described these eight untitled pieces as "longish connected tales of adventure." Dance influence is obvious.

No. 1 F: march in full chords with a lyric contrasting section.

No. 2 D: grateful bravura writing utilizing many thumb repetitions.

No. 3 D: jolly waltz using staccato chords.

No. 4 D: waltz with cross-rhythms and lively syncopations.

No. 5 D: uses polonaise rhythm, staccato chord figuration.

No. 6 A: staccato chords in opening followed by more lyric sections, increasing tempo, short coda.

No. 7 E: brilliant octaves contrasted with cantabile writing.

No. 8 f♯: most effective of the set, two works in one. Contrasting in meter 2/4, 3/4, the two works are linked by a romantic episode "Voice from afar."

Sonata g Op. 22 (1830 Andantino, 1833 first and third movements, 1838 Finale).

Four movements, most tightly organized of the three sonatas. Rotation technique is called for in the first movement, a SA design with coda. Andantino is one of Schumann's loveliest lyrical inspirations. Snappy persistent rhythms are present in the Scherzo. Continuous broken-octaves require some stamina in the Rondo.

Nachtstücke Op. 23 (1839). In their final form these four pieces are untitled but originally they were conceived as "Funeral Procession," "Strange Company," "Nocturnal Carouse," and "Round with Solo Voices."

No. 1 C: detached chords support a marchlike subject that contrasts with legato writing.

No. 2 F: fast chords, monotonous rhythmic repetition needs relief by varied tonal coloring.

No. 3 D♭: scherzo with two trios. RH thumb playing melody presents a legato problem.

No. 4 F: melody is heard at the top of the arpeggiated chords. Tonal balance in the lower register presents a problem.

Faschingschwank aus Wien Op. 26 (1839). (Carnaval Prank from Vienna).

This five-movement suite of character pieces is a direct result of Schumann's visit to Vienna in the interests of his publication the "Neue Zeitschrift für Musik."

Allegro B♭: long, robust movement, main idea contrasted with six episodes.

Romanze g: wistful, florid melody, inconclusive ending.

Scherzino B♭: two-bar rhythmic repetition, no trio.

Intermezzo e♭: the finest movement, passionate and noble, can be performed separately.

Finale B♭: SA design animated, similar problems in opening movement.

Three Romances Op. 28 (1839).

No. 1 b♭: melody is supported by a running figuration divided between hands.

No. 2 F♯: duet, melodic writing in rich register of the piano. Careful pedaling and phrasing required.

No. 3 B: animated rondo infused with too many interesting ideas.

Scherzo, Gigue, Romanze and Fughetta Op. 32 (1838-39).

Scherzo B♭: playful, impetuous, short.

Gigue g: light, whimsical.

Romanze d: a short study. Expressive, soaring melody accompanied by brilliant figuration divided between hands.

Fughetta g: subject is tossed between hands with accompanying chords.

Six Studies for Pedal Piano Op. 56 (1845).

C, a, E, A♭, b, B. All are two-part accompanied canons. See especially the ones in A♭ and b. Four have been arranged for piano (Clara Schumann-Augener).

Four Sketches for Pedal Piano Op. 58 (1845).

c, C, f, D♭. Less use of a pedal part is made here. They are not canonic.

Four Fugues Op. 72 (1845).

d, d, f, F. Skillful contrapuntal treatment, themes from Nos.

2 and 3 are inspired by Bach *Well-Tempered Clavier* I/22 and No. 1 of Chopin's posthumous *Etudes*.

Four Marches Op. 76 (1849).
Eb, g, Bb, Eb. No. 3 titled "Camp Scene." Others untitled.

Waldszenen Op. 82 (1848-49). Nine pieces, about same difficulty as Op. 15, alluding to forest scenes.

Eintritt (Entrance) Bb: asymmetrical phrasing.

Jäger auf der Lauer (Hunter in Ambush) d: spirited, some technical problems.

Einsame Blumen (Solitary Flowers) Bb: balance carefully the two lines in same hand.

Verrufene Stelle (Haunted Spot) d: misterioso, double-dotted chords, staccato phrases.

Freundliche Landschaft (Friendly Landscape) Bb: rubato, poetic.

Herberge (At the Inn) Eb: tonal balance is important.

Vogel als Prophet (The Prophet Bird) g: cross-relations, incomplete phrases, questioning melodic line requires great delicacy.

Jagdlied (Hunting Song) Eb: wrist and arm endurance needed.

Abschied (Farewell) Bb: two against three, melody and accompaniment in same hand; a touching, liedlike conclusion.

Bunte Blätter Op. 99 (1839-49) (Colored Leaves).
A heterogeneous collection of fourteen pieces. Three small works A, e, E. Five were titled "Album Leaves" f♯, b, Ab, eb, Eb. Brahms used theme of the first in his Op. 9 *Variations*. Six other titled pieces: Novelette b, Prelude bb, March d, Evening Music Bb, Scherzo g, Quick March g. Novelette is the most significant work in the set and the five miniature "Album Leaves" are exquisite.

Fantasiestücke Op. 111 (1851).
Three short pieces that continue the same idea as Op. 12 but descriptive titles are dropped here.

No. 1 c: powerful sweep.

No. 2 Ab: lyric, engaging.

No. 3 c: robust, marchlike, graceful middle section.

Three Sonatas for the Young Op. 118 (1853).
Dedicated to Schumann's three daughters. Each is in four movements, some with descriptive titles.
No. 1 G In memory of Julie: G, e, C, G.
No. 2 D In memory of Elisa: D, b, G, D.
No. 3 C Dedicated to Mary: C, F, C, C. Final movement contains a reference to the opening of the first sonata.

Album Blätter Op. 124 (1832-45).
Twenty titled unrelated short pieces written over a period of years. See especially Nos. 4, 5, and 17 that were rejected from *Carnaval.* Also see number 16.

Seven Pieces in Fughetta Form Op. 126 (1853).
a, d, F, d, a, F, a. Over-active subjects and restricted tonal schemes suggest monotony for these pieces. Nos. 1, 4 and 5 have the most interest.

Gesänge der Frühe Op. 133 (1853) (Songs of the Dawn).
Five short pieces: D, D, A, f♯, D. Schumann conceived these pieces as "Characteristic pieces depicting the approach and waxing of the morning but more an expression of feeling than painting."

Variations on an Original Theme (1854) (K. Geiringer-Hin).
Schumann's last piano composition. Theme and five variations. Brahms used the theme for his Op. 23 *Variations for piano duet.*

See: J. Fuller-Maitland, *Schumann's Pianoforte Works.* London: Oxford University Press, 1927.

Ian Parrott, "A Plea for Schumann's Op. 11," ML, 33, January 1952, 55-8.

Linda Siegel, "The Piano Cycles of Schumann and the Novels of Jean Paul Richter," PQ, 69, Fall 1969, 16-22.

WILLY SCHUSTER (-) Germany

Zwei Sonatinen (Möseler).
First sonatina is shorter and easier than No. 2. SA in both first movements. First sonatina, slow movement uses ground-

bass and a lively last movement rounds it off. Second Sonatina contains 2 movements concluding with a Passacaglia finale. Hindemithian influence, linear, economical use of material throughout.

ELLIOTT SCHWARTZ (1936-   ) USA

Schwartz received degrees from Columbia University where he studied composition with Otto Luening and Jack Beeson. He also studied privately with Paul Creston and Henry Brant. Schwartz is presently teaching at Bowdoin College in Brunswick, Maine.

Music for Prince Albert on his 150th Birthday (ms from composer). "A piece for pianist and 2 tape tracks (consisting mostly of piano sounds) to be made *by the pianist* from the source sheet opposite (page B)." Lighting effects (optional) are also called for. A fascinating *avant-garde* piece, highly effective, requiring about 9 minutes. Some traditional writing also appears in the body of the work. D.

VALDO SCIAMMARELLA (1920-   ) Argentina

Since 1965 Sciammarella has served as Chief of the Music Department of the National School of Fine Arts of La Plata, Argentina.

Homenaje á Falla (Ric 1952). 8 minutes.

10 Piezas Breves (Ric 1953). 20 minutes. Attractive writing, Int. to M-D.

CYRIL SCOTT (1879-1970) Great Britain

Three Little Waltzes (Elkin). Short, simple.

Pastorale Suite (Elkin). Courante, Pastorale, Rigaudon, Rondo, Passacaglia. The Passacaglia theme is built on a folklike tune.

Impressions from Kipling's Jungle Book (1912) (Schott). The Jungle, Dawn, Rikki-Tikki-Tavi and the Snake, Morning Song in the jungle, Dance of the Elephants.

Lotus Land Op. 47/1 (CF) (Elkin) (Schott). Atmospheric, pentatonic, sonorous.

Poems (1912) (Schott). A collection of five of Scott's finest short pieces. Poppies, The garden of Soul-Sympathy, Bells, The Twilight of the Year, Paradise-Birds. D.

Sonata Op. 66 (Elkin). One movement, concludes with a fugue, improvisatory, driving climax.

Indian Suite (1922) (Schott). Four pieces. D.

First Album (Elkin). Six pieces.

Second Album (Elkin). Five pieces.

Collection of Eight Selected Works (GS).

Valse Caprice Op. 74/7 (Elkin). Span of ninth required, impressionistic, PP ending. Int.

ALEXANDER SCRIABIN (1872-1915) Russia

Scriabin was an outstanding pianist with a fluent and spontaneous style of playing that was recognized throughout Europe. His early piano works owe much to Chopin and Liszt. The etudes, impromptus, mazurkas, nocturnes, preludes and valses all show an affinity with Chopin in his preference for miniature forms. A chromatic harmonic vocubulary later evolved into a highly individual style, closely related to his mystic-theosophic interests. Almost all of Scriabin's piano music is difficult. A few easier works are Op. 2/1; 8/11; 9/1; 11/3, 9, 10, 14, 17; 32/1; 47 and 57. The piano works generally require a large span and a fine sense of pedaling. Widely-spaced writing, melodic leaps, irregular metric and rhythmic groupings, much use of the trill, and lush sonorities are characteristic of his style.

Complete Piano Works (USSR). Two volumes published. Vol. I: Op. 1-11 and 12 youthful compositions. Vol. II: Op. 12-42.

Selected Piano Works (G. Philipp-CFP). Three volumes.
- I: Etudes Op. 8, 42, 65.
- II: Preludes, Poems and Other Pieces, Part I Op. 11, 27, 32, 47, 56, 72, 73, 74.
- III: Preludes, Poems and Other Pieces, Part II Op. 13, 16, 38, 45, 48, 49, 51, 52, 57, 58, 59, 61, 63, 67, 69, 71.

Sonatas (H. Sheldon-MCA). Op. 6, 19, 23, 30, 53, 62, 64, 66, 68, 70. Published in one volume.

SEPARATE WORKS (listed numerically by opus numbers):

Waltz Op. 1 f (Bayley & Ferguson) (CFP).

Three Pieces Op. 2 Study c♯ (CFP) (GS) (CF); Prelude B (Simrock); Impromptu à la Mazur C (Simrock).

Ten Mazurkas Op. 3 b, f♯ (Augener), g, E, d♯, c♯ (Augener), e, b♭, g♯, e♭.

Allegro appassionato e♭ Op. 4 (Bo&H). Liszt influence.

Two Nocturnes Op. 5 f♯, A. Charming. f♯ (JWC).

Sonata No. 1 f Op. 6 (1892) (Belaieff). Romantic, Chopin influence.

Allegro con fuoco: chordal, dramatic arpeggi gestures, PPPP ending.
No title: slow, improvisatory movement.
Presto: fast octaves in low register, agitated, leads to
Funèbre: pedal point on F, chordal mid-section at PPPP, surprise final bar.

Two Impromptus à la Mazur Op. 7 g♯, f♯ (CFP). Light, chromatic pieces.

Twelve Studies Op. 8 (Belaieff) (IMC). Chopinesque treatment. C♯, f♯, b, B, E, A, b♭, A♭, c♯, D♭, b♭, d♯.
(GS) publishes No. 12, d♯. Belaieff has separately E, D♭, d♯.

Two Pieces for the LH Op. 9 (Bo&H). (GS) (CF) have each separately, (TP) has Prelude.
Prelude c♯: requires sensitive control.
Nocturne D♭: a ravishing, romantic display piece.

Two Impromptus Op. 10 f♯, A (Belaieff).

Twenty-four Preludes Op. 11 (Belaieff) (IMC) (EBM). Through the cycle of keys. Varied moods, Chopin influence, charming. See especially D, f♯, D♭, f, d.

Two Impromptus Op. 12 (Bo&H). F♯, b♭.

Six Preludes Op. 13 (Belaieff). Easier than some of the other Preludes. C, a, G, e, D, b.

Two Impromptus Op. 14 (Bo&H). B, f♯.

Five Preludes Op. 15 (Belaieff). A, f♯, E, E, c♯.

Five Preludes Op. 16 (Belaieff). B, g♯, G♭, e♭, F♯.

Seven Preludes Op. 17 (Bo&H). d, E♭, D♭, b♭, f, B♭, g. E♭ is an octave study, f is a brilliant Prestissimo, B♭ a quiet Andante doloroso, g a nervous Allegro assai.

Concert Allegro Op. 18 b♭ (Belaieff).

Sonata No. 2 Op. 19 g♯ (1892-1897) (Belaieff) (IMC). Subtitled *Sonata-Fantasy*.

Andante: melancholy, melody rises out of widely spaced figuration, reflective.

Presto: constant triplets, sweeping melodies.

Polonaise Op. 21 b♭ (Belaieff).

Four Preludes Op. 22 (GS). Very lyrical. g♯, c♯, B, b.

Sonata No. 3 Op. 23 f♯ (1897) (Belaieff) (IMC). More interesting for the manner in which ideas are developed rather than for the ideas themselves. Four movements. Drammatico; Allegretto; Andante; Presto con fuoco.

Nine Mazurkas Op. 25 (Bo&H).

Two Preludes Op. 27 (GS). g, B.

Fantasy Op. 28 b (IMC). Liszt and Wagner influence. A work of great complexity and subtlety. Virtuoso demands.

Sonata No. 4 Op. 30 F♯ (1903) (Belaieff) (IMC). One of the shortest but one of the most grandiose of the sonatas.

Andante: delicate, shimmering, leads to a

Prestissimo volando: driving, enormous climax that reworks the opening Andante.

Four Preludes Op. 31 (Belaieff). D♭-C, f, E♭, C. Characteristics of early and later styles.

Two Poems Op. 32 (Belaieff) (IMC). F♯ (CF), D (CFP). The second Poem points toward future harmonic and thematic treatment.

Four Preludes Op. 33 E, F♯, C, A♭. A varied, well-balanced set.

Tragic Poem Op. 34 B♭ (Belaieff) (IMC) (K). Liszt influence, use of the ninth with raised fifth used more and more.

Three Preludes Op. 35 D♭, B♭, C. Chopin, Wagner and Schumann influence.

Satanic Poem Op. 36 C (Belaieff) (IMC) (K). Virtuoso writing, terms "riso ironico" and "ironico" suggest mood of the work.

Four Preludes Op. 37 b♭, F♯, B, g. Expressive Mesto, chordal Maestoso, lyric Andante, angry Irato impetuoso.

Waltz Op. 38 A♭ (Belaieff). Advanced harmonies, a favorite with Scriabin.

Four Preludes Op. 39 F♯, D, G, A♭.

Two Mazurkas Op. 40 D♭, F♯. Delicate, elegant.

Poem Op. 41 D♭. Less demanding than other Poems, Liszt influence.

Eight Studies Op. 42 (Belaieff) (IMC) (K). (Belaieff) has separately c♯, No. 5.

Two Poems Op. 44 C, C. 2/4 Lento, 3/8 Moderato. Well-contrasted pieces.

Three Pieces Op. 45 Album Leaf E♭, Poème Fantasque C, Prelude E♭. Delightful set of miniatures.

Scherzo Op. 46 C. 6/8 Presto.

Quasi-Valse Op. 47 F.

Four Preludes Op. 48 (Bo&H). F♯, C, D♭, C. Outstanding set. No. 1, impetuous; No. 2, a delightful 8 bars; No. 3, restless; No. 4, a celebration.

Three Pieces Op. 49 Etude E♭, Prelude F, Reverie C.

Four Pieces Op. 51 Fragilité E♭ has frequent meter changes; Prelude a, sobre; Poème ailé B; Danse languide G, especially appealing.

Three Pieces Op. 53 Poem C, meter changes; Enigma, no definite tonality; Poème languide B.

Sonata No. 5 Op. 53 (1908) (Bo&H) (IMC). One movement, fantasy-like, mystical, orchestrally conceived.

Four Pieces Op. 56 Prelude E♭, Ironies C, Nuances, Etude.

Two Pieces Op. 57 (Bo&H). Désir: many augmented sonorities; Caresse Dansée: delicate. Two of Scriabin's best small works.

Album Leaf Op. 58 3/4 con delicatezza, somewhat similar to *Träumerei.*

Two Pieces Op. 59 Poème, Prélude. Early and late Scriabin characteristics.

Poème-Nocturne Op. 61. Complex harmonic usage, interesting scale passages.

Sonata No. 6 Op. 62 (1911-12). One movement, no key signature, dissonance exploited.

Two Poems Op. 63 Masque, 6/8 Allegretto, Etrangeté, 9/8 Gracieux, Délicat.

Sonata No. 7 Op. 64 (1911) (Bo&H). Subtitled "White Mass." One movement, terms such as "mystérieusement sonore," "menaçant," "impérieux," and "comme des éclairs," point out the mystical element. Technically, the most complex of all the sonatas.

Three Studies Op. 65 (CFP). B♭, C♯, G. In ninths, sevenths and fifths, no key signatures.

Sonata No. 8 Op. 66 (1913) (Bo&H) (CFP). Longest of the sonatas, one movement, two development sections, built on a basic chord, lowered tenth plays an important role, dancelike coda, subtle.

Two Preludes Op. 67 Andante 5/8, Presto 4/8.

Sonata No. 9 Op. 68 (1913) "Black Mass." (CFP) (IMC). Diabolical element is present, markings such as "perfide" and "avec une douceur de plus en plus caressante et empoisonée." Twisting melodies and chords, one of the most successful sonatas.

Two Poems Op. 69 (Simrock). Allegretto 3/4, Allegretto 6/8.

Sonata No. 10 Op. 70 (1913) (IMC) (CFP). A complex structure posing great problems in performance. The trill plays such an important role that the composer referred to this work as his "sonata of insects." Enigmatic.

Two Poems Op. 71 Fantastique (CFP), En rêvant.

Poem vers la flamme Op. 72 (IMC) (K). One chord generates this work, great climax, intense.

Two Dances Op. 73 Guirlandes, built on the opening upward figure; Flammes sombres, descriptive.

Five Preludes Op. 74 (IMC). Douloureux, déchirant; Très lent, contemplatif; Allegro drammatico; Lent, vague, indécis; Fier, belliqueux. Some of Scriabin's finest shorter pieces, intense, highly personal creations.

COLLECTIONS:

Sixteen Preludes (Deis-GS). Op. 15/1-5, 22/1-4, 27/1-2, 35/1-3, 51/2, 56/1.

Album of Twelve Selected Preludes (Philipp-IMC). From Op. 11, 13, 15, 16, 27, 48, 51, 59, 67.

Album of Six Pieces (IMC). Albumleaf Op. 58, Désire Op. 57/1, Etude Op. 2/1, Guirlandes Op. 73/1, Masque Op. 63/1, Poem Op. 59/1, Tragic Poem Op. 34.

Album of Scriabin Masterpieces (Sugarman-EBM). Preludes Op. 11/9, 13, 15, Op. 16/4, Op. 27/2, Op. 45/3, Op. 48/4, Op. 74/2; Etudes 2/1, Op. 8/5, 10, 12, Op. 42/4; Nocturnes Op. 5/2, Op. 9/2 (for LH alone); Poème Op. 32/1, Poème tragique Op. 34, Poème fantasque Op. 45/2, Poème ailé Op. 51/3, Poème Op. 69/2, Feuillet d'Album Op. 45/1, Scherzo Op. 46, Quasi Valse Op. 47, Danse languide Op. 51/4, Ironies Op. 56/2.

Youthful and Early Works of Alexander and Julian Scriabin (D. Garvelmann-MTP).
Foreward by Faubion Bowers. A lavishly produced volume of unknown piano works by father and son. Several manuscript facsimiles are published for the first time. M-D. 157 pp. Includes: Canon (1883), Nocturne A♭ 2 versions, Sonate-Fantasie g♯ (1886), Valse g♯, Valse D♭, Variations sur un thème de Mlle. Egoroff (1887), Mazurka F (1889), Mazurka b (1889), Feuillet d'album (1889), Sonata e♭ 3 movements (1887-89), Allegro appassionato Op. 4 (1892), Fantasy for 2 pianos (1889), Aria from the Opera "Keistut and Beirut" (1891), Fuga (1892), Romance for Voice and Piano (1893), Romance for Waldhorn and Piano (1893), Etude Op. 8/12 alternate version (1894-5), Variations sur un thème populaire russe pour quatuor d'archets (1898), Feuille d'album F♯ (1905). Works by Julian Scriabin, son of Alexander: 3 Preludes, Op. 2 (1918) Op. 3 (1918), The last prelude (1919).

See: Faubion Bowers, *Scriabin,* 2 vols. Tokyo and Palo Alto: Kodansha International Ltd., 1969.
"How To Play Scriabin," PQ, 74, Winter 1970-71, 12-18.

Matthew C. Hughes, "Tonal Orientation in Scriabin's Preludes: an Analysis on the Basis of Information Theory," unpub. thesis, University of Texas, 1965.

A. Eaglefield Hull, "Survey of the Pianoforte Works of Scriabin," MQ, 2, October 1916, 601-14.

M. Montagu-Nathan, *Handbook of the Pianoforte Works of Scriabin.* London: Chester, 1922.

Samuel L. Randlett, "Elements of Scriabin's Keyboard Style," PQ, 74, Winter 1970-71, 20-5; PQ, 75, Spring 1971, 18-23; and PQ, 77, Fall 1971, 24-7. "The Nature and Development of Scriabin's Pianistic Vocabulary," unpub. diss., Northwestern University, 1966. Scriabin's pianistic vocabulary divided into twenty-four devices and the use of each device is traced in detail.

HUMPHREY SEARLE (1915-) Great Britain

Searle worked with John Ireland and R. O. Morris at the Royal College of Music in London. He also studied privately with Webern in Vienna (1937-38). These men, plus Franz Liszt and Arnold Schönberg, have been a major influence on Searle. All of his compositions since 1946 have used the 12-tone technique. Searle and Elisabeth Lutyens were the first English composers to use 12-tone technique.

Vigil Op. 3 (Lengnick 1949). "France, 1940-44." Fine craftsmanship, pianistic sonorities, not technically difficult. 7 minutes. 3 main sections. Thick textures.

Ballade Op. 10 (J. Williams 1943). Liszt influence, strong virtuoso writing.

Threnos and Toccata Op. 14 (Lengnick 1949). 6 minutes. 12-tone. D.

Piano Sonata Op. 21 (OUP 1951). 16 minutes. Based on thematic transformation within the 12-tone system. Great variety of styles are contained in this one-movement architectural structure. Begins with a statement of the row and soon develops to a virtuoso display of romantic exhibitionism. Written in 1951 to celebrate the 140th anniversary of the birth of Franz Liszt. Liszt *Sonata* b is the model.

Suite for Piano Op. 29 (Schott 1965). In album *Contemporary British Piano Music*. Atonal. The third movement presents some serial techniques. D.

Prelude on a Theme of Alan Rawsthorne Op. 45 (Faber & Faber 1965). Rawsthorne theme comes from his *Elegiac Rhapsody*. Searle's piece is short, 12-tone, with varied meters, yet retains the lyrical character of the original theme. M-D.

PIA SEBASTIANI (1925-) Argentina

4 Preludes (Southern 1947). Published separately.
Nos. 1 and 3 are technically and easiest with No. 3 (Lento) more free.
No. 2 is vigorous and rhythmic, ends quietly.
No. 4 is bright, festive. D.

MÁTYÁS SEIBER (1905-1960) Great Britain, born Hungary

Gregorian chant, 16th-century vocal polyphony, folk music, jazz and 12-tone technique all played a part in developing Seiber's style. He was extremely versatile as a musician adapting many musical styles, both past and present, into his own.

3 Hungarian Folksongs (WH). Easy.

Rhythmic Studies (Schott). Easy to Int.

24 Easy Dances (Schott 1937). 2 volumes. 12 pieces each volume. Vol. 1 is easiest.

Scherzando Capriccioso (Schott 1944).

CARLOS SEIXAS (1704-1742) Portugal

Seixas, one of the most important Portuguese keyboard composers of the 18th century, was probably a student of D. Scarlatti. In addition to the collection *Cravistas Portugueses* that contains 12 Toccatas and 12 Sonatas, the following publication makes most of Seixas' keyboard compositions available in a modern edition:

80 Sonatas para Instrumentos de Tecla. Transcribed and edited by M. S. Kastner. Vol. X, *Portugaliae Musica,* Serie A (Fundaçaõ Calouste Gulbenkian, 1965). Also available in 4 volumes: Sonatas 1-18, 19-39, 40-60, 61-80. Excellent editorial commentary in English and French.

See: Elyse Mach, "Rediscovering an Old Master—Carlos Seixas," Clavier, 8, November 1969, 36-7. Also includes a reprint of *Sonata* e No. 14, 24-7.

DAVID SERENDERO (1934-) Chile

Serendero studied at the Modern School of Music in Chile and the National Conservatory of the University of Chile, graduating in violin, composition and musicology. He also had further study in Stuttgart, Germany.

Reinhild: Rapsodia para piano (PAU 1961). Sectionalized by varied tempi and textures. Harmonics and tapping on wood of piano employed. Freely chromatic. Chords of 7ths and 9ths used extensively in concluding section. Requires advanced pianism. D.

TIBOR SERLY (1900-) USA, born Hungary

From a Peasant Village (Sprague-Coleman).
7 short moderately-easy character-pieces, pleasant, each with its own charm.

40 Piano Etudes based on Modus Lascivus (ms). (Composer has ms).
Written as studies (between 1945-1960) to demonstrate the "modus operandi" of "Modus Lascivus", a system of composition Serly has developed over a period of years.

KAZIMIERZ SEROCKI (1922-) Poland

Suite of Preludes for Piano (PWM 1952). 10 minutes.
"The fourth, fifth, and sixth preludes represent the first dodecaphonic post-war writing in Poland. The composer noted that the Suite does not fully comply with the Schönberg practices." BBD, 157.

Sonata na Fortepiano (PWM 1955). 18 minutes.

A Piacere (PWM 1963). Combines serial and aleatory practices, in 3 sections, 10 structures for each section. Preliminary remarks, table of abbreviations and symbols in Polish, English and German. D.

ROGER SESSIONS (1896-) USA

Sessions' music has a weighty philosophic character. He has influenced countless younger composers in this country.

Sonata No. 1 (Schott 1930). Andante; Allegro; Andante; Molto vivace. Involved, neoclassic, connecting movements, substantial. D.

March (CF 1935). Pedagogical work in "Masters of Our Day" series.

Scherzino (CF 1935). From "Masters of Our Day" series.

From My Diary (EBM 1937-1940). Four character pieces in contrasting moods, linear in style. Poco adagio: mainly 3 voices, serious, melodic; Allegro con brio: fast passagework, strong climactic points, peaceful mid-section, quiet close; Larghissimo e misterioso: short, atmospheric, sensitive; Allegro pesante: vigorous, sharp rhythmic chordal accents. M-D.

Sonata No. 2 (EBM 1946). Allegro con fuoco; Lento; Misurato e pesante. Large-scale work, highly chromatic, contains broad ideas and is intellectually complex, wears well. It is a challenge to the finest pianist and is probably one of the most important piano sonatas by an American composer of this century. D.

Sonata No. 3 (EBM 1964-5). Large three-movement work: Adagio e misterioso—Sostenuto; Molto allegro e con fuoco; Lento e molto tranquillo (In memoriam: Nov. 22, 1963). Complex work uses serial organization with the same row used in all movements. The middle movement is the most demanding. Three difficult separate lines must be voiced simultaneously at some places. Of transcendental difficulty.

MORDECAI SETER (1916-   ) Israel, born Russia

Seter studied with Dukas and Boulanger in Paris from 1932-1937. He teaches at the Rubin Academy of Music in Tel Aviv. Recipient of the Prix Italia in 1962.

Chaconne and Scherzo (IMI 1956).
A misty theme, five variations and a scherzo which is a sixth variation. The variations are in turn figurative, florid, in two voices, canonic, etc. Theme reappears at end of Scherzo. The music dissolves at the conclusion. D.

DÉODAT DE SÉVÉRAC (1873-1921) France

Sévérac's piano music is descriptive, mainly of events and local places in his native Languedoc. Elements of improvisation as well as sonorous harmonies and traditional pianism are present.

Chant de la Terre: Poème géorgique (1900) (Sal). 4 movements, impressionist, see especially the Prologue, Intermezzo and the spritely Epilog. The Epilog is in Chabrier style.

En Languedoc (1904) (Sal). A suite of 5 pieces depicting scenes and events in the composer's home town. Movements 1, 2, 3, and 5 are available separately (Sal). An extended work.

Baigneuses au Soleil (1908) (Sal). Varied sonorities, lengthy.

Cerdaña (1910) (Sal). 61 p. 5 extended movements. 4 movements are available separately (Sal).

En Vacances (1912) (Sal). 2 collections of 7 and 3 pieces each. 7 pieces in the first book and 2 pieces in the second book are available separately. Romantic. M-D.

Sous les lauriers roses (1919) (Sal).

Stances de Madame de Pompadour (Sal).

See: Elaine Brody, "The Piano Works of Déodat de Sévérac: A Stylistic Analysis," unpub. diss., New York University, 1964. A helpful work on a lesser-known French contemporary of Debussy and Ravel.

GIOVANNI SGAMBATI (1841-1914) Italy

Sgambati was a virtuoso pianist who studied with Liszt.

Concert Etude Op. 10/2 (Schott).

Gavotte a♭ Op. 14 (Schott) (TP). Exuberant rhythmic vitality.

Vecchio minuetto Op. 18/2 (Schott) (GS). Graceful dance.

Nenia Op. 18/3 (Schott).

Campane a festa (Joy Bells) Op. 12/8 (GS).

Etude mélodique Op. 21/5 (Schott).

Nocturnes Op. 31, 33 (Schott).

Melody (from Gluck's "Orpheus") (Schott) (GS). Effective transcription.

HAROLD SHAPERO (1920-) USA

Three Sonatas (GS 1944). Cast in a modern idiom. Transparent works inspired by principles of the 18th century. No. 3 is the most difficult but all require sensitive pianistic equipment. M-D.

Sonata f (Southern 1948). Large-scale (64 p.) work in three movements, employs bold gestures. The first movement is in clear SA design while movement two is a set of variations ("this movement may be performed separately under the title 'Arioso Variations' "). Third movement is a perpetual motion study with large skips and biting chordal sonorities. Virtuoso technique required. D.

Variations c (Southern 1947). Jagged textures, large gestures, unusual sonorities. D.

Song Without Words (TP). Short, bitonal implications. Int.

Staccato Dance (TP). Spritely, short. Careful articulation required. Int.

RODION SHCHEDRIN (1932-) USSR

Shchedrin's music shows a fine melodic gift and exuberance, coupled with intelligent and sensitive craftsmanship.

Toccatina (MCA). Triplet figuration, chromatic color, pianistic, PP ending. M-D.

Sonata (C. A. Rosenthal-MCA 1962). Displays a smooth technique. D.

Allegro da Sonata: tone clusters, much dissonance.

Variazioni Polifonici: 7 variations, melodic interest resolves around a 5 note theme.

Rondo—Toccata: astringent sonorities, virtuoso writing, taxes both performer and audience. Cacophonous but exciting atonal writing.

24 Preludes and Fugues (USSR 1963-4). 2 volumes. Vol. I, 1-12; Vol. II, 13-24. Contemporary writing, highly pianistic. Shostakovitch influence. Vol. I all in sharp keys. An interesting contribution eminently worth investigating.

VISSARION SHEBALIN (1902-1963) USSR

Three Sonatinas Op. 12 (MCA). Solid construction, contrasting movements, M-D.

I: Moderato; Canzona; Fughetta.
II: Prelude; Aria; March; Rondo. Most attractive of the three.
III: Sinfonia; Burlesca (in 5/8); Meditation; Finale.

ARTHUR SHEPHERD (1880-1958) USA

Gay Promenade (CF 1936). For young pianists. Rhythmic trouble-spots. Easy.

Autumn Fields (CF 1936). For young pianists. 2-part melodic writing. Easy.

Second Sonata f (OUP 1930). Three movements: Moderato, ma deciso; Moderato, cantabile ma semplice; Enfatico ed affrettato — Toccata. Impressionistic influences, well-constructed work. Stamina, brilliant playing and a facile technique are required. M-D.

Eclogue (TP 1956). A romantic character-piece requiring considerable facility. M-D.

Capriccio II (Ric 1954). A large-scale work conventionally written but showing skill and an unusual understanding of the instrument. D.

In Modo Ostinato (TP 1956). 7/4 meter, lyric, on quiet side, ostinato transferred between hands, sophisticated elegance. M-D.

Gigue Fantasque (TP). Mainly 2-part writing, interesting syncopations. Int.

Exotic Dance (OUP 1930). Short, effective. Int.

Lento Amabile (TP 1956).

See: Richard N. Loucks, "Arthur Shepherd," unpub. diss., University of Rochester, Eastman School of Music, 1960.

SEYMOUR SHIFRIN (1926-   ) USA, born Austria

Shifrin studied with William Schuman and Otto Luening.

4 Cantos (Merion 1949). Lento, Allegro, Largo Rubato e Espressivo, Vivace. 12-tone, heavily drenched with accidentals and dissonances. All are short. No. 3 is barless and No. 4 uses clusters.

Trauermusik (CFP 1956). 8 minutes. D.

DMITRI SHOSTAKOVITCH (1906-   ) USSR

3 Fantastic Dances Op. 1 (MCA) (K) (IMC). Early (1922) work. Int.

Aphorisms Op. 13 (MCA 1926-27). 10 short character pieces, clear textures, idiomatic, many ideas.

Sonata No. 1 Op. 12 (1926) (Bo&H) (MCA) (CFP) (K). One movement, brilliant virtuoso writing, highly dissonant, vigorous. Influence of Prokofieff.

Sonata No. 2 b Op. 64 (1943) (Bo&H) (MCA) (CFP) (K). Three movements: Allegretto; Largo; Moderato. Easier on performer and audience than No. 1. Final movement is a set of nine variations with a quiet ending.

24 Preludes Op. 34 (1932-33). (MCA) (CFP) (IMC) (K). Modelled on Chopin's set, Op. 28, uses same key scheme as Chopin. Idiomatic writing, varied moods and difficulty ranging from M-D to D.

24 Preludes and Fugues Op. 87 (1951) (Bo&H) (MCA) 2 volumes; (CFP) (K) 3 volumes. Baroque-inspired, a contemporary 'Well-Tempered Clavier." The MCA edition contains an informative preface by Irwin Freundlich. A few of the Preludes are technically easier than those from Op. 34, otherwise the difficulty is approximately the same.

5 Preludes (MCA c. 1968). Short, technically easier than the Op. 34 set and the Preludes from Op. 87. No. 3 requires a good octave technique.

Doll's Dances (CFP) (MCA). 7 easy pieces.

6 Children's Pieces (MCA). Written for his daughter. Easy miniatures, mainly 2 voices.

Melodic Moments (MCA c. 1969). 8 pieces selected from ballet, operetta and film scores. Beautifully arranged by Denes Agay. An interesting collection, generally easier than Op. 1. Attractive addition to the sparse Shostokovitch pedagogic repertoire.

Album of Selected Piano Works (IMC). 12 Preludes from Op. 34; 3 Fantastic Dances Op. 1; Polka from "The Golden Age" ballet.

JAN SIBELIUS (1865-1957) Finland

Most of the (WH) publications are available separately.

Caprice Op. 24/3 (Br&H).

Idyll Op. 24/6 (AMP).

Andantino Op. 24/7 (Br&H).

Romance D♭ Op. 24/9 (CF) (BMC) (SP). Romantic, effective, pianistic.

Barcarole B♭ Op 24/10 (AMP).

6 Finnish Folksongs (Br&H).

Valsette Op. 40/1 (Br&H). Tuneful, easy.

Rêverie Op. 58/1 (Br&H).

5 Pieces Op. 75 (WH). The Solitary Fir Tree, When the Rowan-tree blooms, The Aspen, The Birch Tree, The Spruce-Pine.

13 Pieces Op. 76 (WH). Esquisse, Etude, Carillon, Humoresque, Consolation, Romanzetta, Affettuoso, Pièce enfantine, Arabesque, Elegiaco, Linnaea, Capriccietto, Harlequinade. (Augener) has 10 pieces from this set.

5 Pieces Op. 85 (WH). Bluebells, The Carnation, The Iris, The Snapdragon, The Campanula.

Gavotte Op. 94/6 (WH).

5 Romantic Compositions Op. 101 (WH). 2. Chant du soir 3. Scène lyrique 4. Humoresque.

5 Characteristic Impressions Op. 103 (WH). 2. The Fiddler 3. The Oarsman 4. The Storm 5. The Mournful Mood.

Rondino g♯ Op. 68/1 (UE).

Album of 12 Selected Pieces (JWC).
Op. 75/1, 3, 4; Op. 76/11, 12, 13; Op. 85/3, 4, 5; Op. 94/1, 2, 3.

See: Eric Blom, "The Piano Music" in *Sibelius, A Symposium,* ed. G. Abraham. New York: Norton, 1947, 97-107.

Erik Tawaststijerna, *The Pianoforte Compositions of Sibelius.* Helsinki: Kustannusosakeyhtio Otava, 1957.

OTTO SIEGL (1896-) Austria

Siegl's style is usually neoclassic with the addition of thick textures.

Form und Ausdruck (Dob 1961). 2 books. 15 polyphonic pieces. M-D.

Partita (Dob 1953).

Unterhaltsame Klavierlehrstücke (Dob 1953). Easy to Int.
Pieces demonstrating various intervals, canon, pentatonic scale, ostinato, etc.

Zwei Sonatinen (Rodenkirchen/Rhein, J. P. Tonger 1961).
Difficulty of Hindemith *Second Sonata.*
No. 1: 3 movements. 13 minutes. 15 p.
No. 2: 3 movements. 14 minutes. 15 p.

ELIE SIEGMEISTER (1909-) USA

American Sonata (EBM 1944). Three movements based on popular American materials. Outside movements are highly rhythmic while the middle movement is lyric. M-D.

Sunday in Brooklyn (EBM 1946). Five Americana scenes: Prospect Park, Sunday Driver, Family at Home, Children's Story, Coney Island. Varied moods and techniques. M-D.

Americana Kaleidoscope (Sam Fox). 19 pieces, varied moods and techniques, suitable for teenage pianists. Int.

Toccata on Flight Rhythms (EBM 1942). From "Air Plane Suite," driving rhythms in 3 plus 3 plus 2 sequence, effective. M-D.

The Children's Day (MCA). Six children's pieces. Easy.

Sonata No. 2 (MCA 1968). One movement (18 p.), dissonant, virtuoso writing. D.

From My Window (Chappell). 7 pieces.

BERNHARD VAN DEN SIGTENHORST-MEYER (1888-1953) The Netherlands

For many years Sigtenhorst-Meyer was professor of piano at the Royal Conservatory in The Hague.

All publications are by Alsbach except noted.

Capri Op. 19 (1923). 3 pieces.

Two Capriccios Op. 42.

De Maas Op. 11 (1920). 3 picccs.

Ancient China Op. 2 (1916). 4 pieces.

Ancient Castles Op. 14 (1920). 3 pieces.

Prélude Op. 16 (Senart).

8 Preludes Op. 17 (1922). All are named after animals: The Camel, The Lion, The Mouse, etc.

Sonata No. 1 Op. 18 (1922). 3 movements.

Sonata No. 2 Op. 23 (1926). 3 movements.

Sonatine No. 1 Op. 30 (1929). 7 minutes.

Sonatine No. 2 Op. 32 (1930). 6 minutes.

Sonatine No. 3 Op. 43 (1948). 8 minutes.

Sprookjeswereld (1928).

Saint Quentin Op. 12 (1920). 2 pieces. 9 minutes. Ruins, Reconstruction.

Van de bloemen Op. 1 (1916).

Van de vogels Op. 4. 3 pieces.

Variations Op. 20 (1924).

6 Views of Fuji Op. 9 (1919). 10 minutes.

OSCAR DA SILVA (1872-1958) Portugal

Da Silva studied with Reinecke in Leipzig and Clara Schumann in Frankfurt. He toured widely in Europe as a concert pianist and lived in Lisbon where he taught and composed.

Estados de Alma (Edicoes Ocidente 1954). 43 p. Int. to M-D. 26 short character pieces in romantic-impressionist idiom. See especially No. 2 Exotisimo, No. 10 Garridice, No. 15 Tristeza and No. 18 Contentamento.

13 Preludios (Published by the composer 1947). 23 p. M-D. No. 1 for LH only. Varied moods, short, post-romantic harmony, some impressionist influence.

Dolorosas: Musique Intime (Sassetti c. 1924).
8 short pieces in romantic harmony. Some inspired writing in this set. Excellent int. pedagogic material.

Imagens Op. 6 (Sassetti). 15 p.
7 pieces in romantic harmonic and melodic idiom. No. 7 Coquetterie would make a good substitute for the over-played "Juba Dance."

6 Bagatelles (Sassetti).
Mazurca, Menuet, Valse, Berceuse, L'Ecureuil, Prélude.

Páginas Portuguesas (Sassetti). 2 books.
I. Quizumba, Malhão, Folia, Valentin.
II. Toada Beirôa, Pirolita, S. João-Chegadinho.

Mazurcas (Published by composer 1948).
4 pieces, romantic harmonies, broad sweeping gestures. M-D.

Romanticas (Published by composer 1948).
Romance; Noctural; Canção Triste. M-D.

Embalos (Published by composer 1948).
I: Tempo di "Berceuse", 6/8. II: Tempo di "Berceuse", 3/4. M-D.

Humuristicas (Published by composer 1948).
2 short character pieces. I. Scherzo-like, II. Brilliant, M-D.

NETTY SIMONS (1913-) USA

Time Groups No. 1 (ACA 1964).
Consists of 84 short sections that can be arranged in a number of different ways. Some unconventional notation and numerous directions for performance. Can be longer or shorter, depending on the arrangement of groups. *Avant-garde.*

ROBERT SIMPSON (1921-) Great Britain

Sonata (Lengnick 1944). 34 p. Three movements.
Well-written, closely knit ideas, traditional style. M-D.

Variations and Finale on a Theme of Haydn (Lengnick 1948).
Theme is a reversible minuet, followed by 12 short variations and a lengthy finale. MC.

See: Wadham Sutton, "Robert Simpson's Piano Sonata," Music Teacher, 50, February 1971, 11.

CHRISTIAN SINDING (1856-1941) Norway

Suite Op. 3 (WH).

Studies Op. 7 (WH).

Con fuoco Op. 25/1 (GS).

Marche grotesque Op. 32/1 (GS) (CFP). Rhythmic, alternating-hand technique, fast scales. M-D.

Rustle of Spring Op. 32/3 (CF) (GS). Effective, arpeggi figuration.

Serenade Op. 33/4 (GS) (CFP).

Caprices Op. 44 (WH).

Six Burlesques Op. 48 (WH). 2 books.

6 Pieces Op. 49 (WH). 2 books.

5 Etudes Op. 58 (WH).

Studies and Sketches Op. 82 (WH). 10 pieces.

Sonata b Op. 91 (c. 1901 WH).

Album for Piano (CFP). Op. 24/3; 31/4, 5; Op. 32/4; Op. 34/1.

NIKOS SKALKOTTAS (1904-1949) Greece

Skalkottas studied with Arnold Schönberg. He used twelve-tone technique strictly from 1925 to 1927 but gradually began to employ this technique much more freely in a personal, expressive manner. For a fine discussion of this development see BBD, 159-161.

15 Little Variations (UE 1927). 6½ minutes. Modified 12-tone technique closely constructed around two chord progressions. M-D.

10 Piano Pieces (UE). These works are from *Music for Piano Solo* (32 pieces for the piano, never completed). Andante Religioso, Rêverie in the Old Style, Rêverie in the New Style. Gavotte, Menuetto, Tango, Romance, Little Peasant March, Marcia Funebra, Greek Folk Dance. The composer emphasized that "The difficulties in these pieces can all be overcome and are nearly always there for the sake of some special virtuoso angle."

Passacaglia (UE 1940). D. Free 12-tone organization. 20 short "variations" greatly contrasted. Impressive climax. Advanced pianism required.

Suite for Piano No. 3 (UE c. 1962). Free serial treatment. 4 movements. D. Minuet and Trio; Variations on a Greek Song; Funeral March; Binary movement in 2/4.

Suite for Piano No. 4 (UE 1941). D. 4 movements. 7 minutes. Free dodecaphonic writing. Contains a bristling Toccata, lyrical Andantino, a clever Polka with Trio and a romantic Serenade.

YNGVE SKÖLD (1899-) Sweden

Ballad No. 1 (NMS).

Ballad No. 2 (NMS).

Ballad No. 3 (NMS).

Liten vaggvisa (GM).

Preludio e fuga quasi una Fantasia Op. 20 (MK).

Skogspromenad (NMS).

Tema med variationer Op. 6 (NMS).

FRITZ SKORZENY (1900-1965) Austria

Sonata (Dob). 4 movements.
Written in a neo-Hindemithian style, all movements have attractive and well-defined ideas. MC without pretentiousness or extravagance.

Tempora mutantur (Dob). 7 pieces, M-D.

Musiquettes (Dob 1962).

JOSIP SLAVENSKI (1896-1955) Yugoslavia

From Jugoslavia: Songs and Dances (Schott 1926). 5 pieces, Int.

From the Balkans (Schott 1926). 4 pieces. No. 4 "Jugoslav Dance" most difficult. Int. to M-D.

Jugoslavian Suite Op. 2 (Schott 1936). 4 movements.

LEWIS SLAVIT (1913-) USA

American Sonatina A♭ (EBM 1933). One movement. 10 p.
Effective, diffuse writing with more technical problems than are immediately apparent.

An American Country Dance (EBM 1942).

ROGER SMALLEY (1943-) Great Britain

Piano Pieces I-V (Faber 1962-65). 11 p.
These 5 short epigrammatic studies are essays in concentrated, concisely thought-out, expressionistic piano writing. Full of technical ingenuity (rhythmic formulae, space-time notation and isorhythm), but technique is at the service of expression. Each parameter is strictly controlled.

See: Stephen Walsh, "Roger Smalley," M&M, 17, June 1969, 37-40. No. 1 and 4 of the above are printed in this issue, the works are discussed.

BEDŘICH SMETANA (1824-1884) Czechoslovakia

The Bedřich Smetana Society has published two volumes of piano works, as well as an excellent facsimile of his *Note-Book of Motifs* (c. 1942). Artia publishes the works listed below.

Six Characteristic Pieces Op. 1.

Six Album Leaves Op. 2. No. 1 "To Robert Schumann" available separately. All are short and romantic. Int.

Sketches Op. 4 and 5 (1858). Four pieces in each opus.

Bagatelles and Impromptus (1844). Eight light character pieces.

Bohemian Dances (K) (CFP).

Four Polkas.

From Bohemia's Woods and Fields.

Concert Study On The Seashore (GS) (1862). Virtuoso work.

Six Rêves (Dreams) (1875). Extended character pieces, octaves, chord playing, fast figuration. M-D.

Sonata g (1849). One long movement.

Three Etudes C, a, C.

Three Polkas Op. 8. E♭, g, A♭.

Trois polkas de salon Op. 7 (1855).

Waltzes (1844).

Wedding Scenes.

Two Album Leaves (Werner-Curwen). Op. 5/7, 22. No. 7 is another version of Scherzo-Polka which is published as No. 1 of *Sketches* Op. 5.

Czech Dances Books I and II. Nationalistic flavor. D.

Pensée fugitive.

Selected Pieces (CFP).
Includes: Sketches Op. 4/1-3, Op. 5/4; Bagatelles and Impromptus; Album Leaves Op. 2/2, 6; Waltzes Nos. 2, 4; Bohemian Dances.

LEO SMIT (1921-) USA

Rural Elegy (Bo&H 1950). 3 pleasing pieces. Int.
Rondel, Toccata Breakdown, Hymn.

Sonata in One movement (Belwin-Mills 1951-5).
In actuality, three short movements played without a break. Neoclassic, contrapuntal lines, direct harmonic and melodic usage. M-D.

Variations G (Bo&H 1954). M-D.
A distinguished large-dimension work. 12 variations including many devices lead to a quiet close.

Fantasy: The Farewell (BB 1957).
Sad, somber introduction, lively farewell and return of introduction. MC.

7 Characteristic Pieces (BB 1959).
Suite of short pieces for concert use. Nos. 1, 3 and 6 are especially interesting.

HALE SMITH (1925-) USA

Smith received his bachelor's and master's degrees in composition from the Cleveland Institute of Music. He is a member of the music faculty at the University of Connecticut.

Evocation (CFP).
"The entire piece derives from the row exposed in the first

stave, and in several places has faint but definite rhythmic affinities with jazz phrasing. This doesn't mean that it's supposed to swing — it isn't, but the affinities are there." From Preface. M-D.

LELAND SMITH (1925-   ) USA

Sonata (ACA 1954). 3 movements.
March, Fast (Rondo), Coda. Serial organization. March displays humor in Prokofieff vein. Mature pianistic equipment required.

4 Etudes (Merion 1952).
Each one page, requires large span, disjunct, pointillistic writing. Preference for fourths, sevenths and ninths.

PADRE ANTONIO SOLER (1729-1783) Spain

Soler, a pupil of Domenico Scarlatti, was the most distinguished eighteenth-century composer of Spain. He wrote many sonatas in a one-movement design similar to those of his famous teacher.

Sonatas, Complete edition (S. Rubio-UME). 120 sonatas in 7 volumes: 1-20 Vol. I, 21-40 Vol. II, 41-60 Vol. III, 61-68 Vol. IV, 69-90 Vol. V, 91-99 Vol. VI, 100-120 Vol. VII.

See: Anthologies and Collections, Spanish.

Sonata G (Barcelona ms: 791/12) (Kastner-Schott).

Sonata B♭ (Barcelona ms: 921/12) (Kastner-Schott).

34 Sonatas (Marvin-Belwin-Mills). 3 volumes.

6 Sonatas (L. Duck-Belwin-Mills). 2 volumes.

Fandango (Marvin-Belwin-Mills) 21 pages of colorful and exciting writing. Remarkable for its time. Wild dance.

See: Frederick Marvin, "An Almost Forgotten Composer," MJ, 18, February 1960, 34-6.

Joaquín Nin, "The Bi-Centenary of Antonio Soler," The Chesterian, 11, January-February 1930, 97-103.

HARRY SOMERS (1925-) Canada

Somers received his musical education at the Royal Conservatory in Toronto. Later he studied in Paris with Darius Milhaud.

3 Sonnets (BMI Canada 1958). Prelude, Lullaby to a Dead Child, Primeval. M-D.
Each piece deals with a single idea. Complex, advanced harmonic idiom. Lullaby is written in 4/4 rather than usual 3/4.

12 X 12 Fugues (BMI Canada 1951). D.
12 short fugues using dodecaphonic technique. No. 1 appears in the album *14 pieces by Canadian Composers.*

Strangeness of Heart (BMI Canada 1947).

ÖISTEIN SOMMERFELDT (1919-) Norway

Sonatina No. 1 Op. 4/1 (NMO c. 1964). 3 movements. 17 p. FSF. Clear textures, solid sonorities, not difficult but some facility required.

Sonatina No. 2 Op. 4/2 (NMO 1961). 3 movements. M-D.
First movement: SA. Second movement: ABA. Third movement: Rondo (scherzo character).
Prefers parallel thirds in bass. Carl Nielsen influence. Attractive.

Sonatina No. 3 Op. 14 (NMO 1968). 12 minutes. Three movements FSF. M-D. Slow movement based on ground bass. Contrapuntal.

Miniature Suite (NMO 1959).

Suite No. 1 Moods (NMO c. 1967). 5 short movements.
Inspired by Norwegian landscape. Highly contrasted are No. 1, folkdance-like, and No. 5, a vigorous dance. Neat fingerwork required in these largely 2-part linearly conceived movements. MC.

Fables Op. 10 (NMO). 5 pieces, 2-part design, freely tonal. M-D.

Fables Op. 15 (NMO). Five movements, contrapuntal throughout. M-D.

KAIKHOSRU SHAPURJI SORABJI (1892-)
Great Britain

Sorabji's piano music presents a complex picture. Polyphonic writing is combined with decorative tendencies that produce music of the utmost difficulty. This, plus the fact that many of his works are unusually long, has made his music almost unplayable. On top of this Sorabji has banned public performance of his works!

Opus Clavicembalisticum (Curwen). In 3 parts, 12 subdivisions, 252 pages. Requires 2 hours to perform. Described by the composer as "the most important work for piano since *The Art of Fugue.*"

Pars prima:

1. Introito
2. Preludio corale
3. Fuga 1
4. Fantasia
5. Fuga a due soggetti

Pars altera:

6. Interludium primum (Thema cum XLIV variationbus)
7. Cadenza 1
8. Fuga a tre soggetti

Pars tertia:

9. Interludium alterum (Toccata: adagio passacaglia cum LXXXI variationbus)
10. Cadenza 2
11. Fuga a quattro soggetti
12. Coda stretta

Three Piano Sonatas (OUP). Many rhythmic intricacies, oriental luxuriance of detail and textural density. Exhausting physical demands are made on the performer. "These works display a command of infinitely varied sonorities, inventive figuration and imaginative decoration as yet unequalled by anyone of any period." Clinton Gray-Fisk, MT, 101, April 1960, p. 232.

Sonata II (JWC 1923).

Prelude, Interlude and Fugue (Curwen 1920).
5 pages of unmeasured sixteenth notes comprise the Prelude. Interlude is written on 3 staves, imitative, full chords require large span. Fugue is made up of thick textures in flexible

meters. Highly individual work, unusually difficult both technically and interpretively.

Fantaisie espagnole (London and Continental Publishing Co., 1922). 32 p.

ENRIQUE SORO (1884-1954) Chile

Andante Appassionato Op. 34 (GS).

Cuatro Piezas (GS).

Cuatro Piezas de Concerto Op. 48 (Ric).

Dos Tonadas Chilenas Op. 50 (Ric).

Sonata No. 1 c♯ (GS 1922).

Sonata No. 3 D (Ric 1923).

LEO SOWERBY (1895-1968) USA

Florida (OUP). A five-movement program suite: River Night, St. Augustine, Cypress Swamp, Sun-Drenched Palms, Pines at Dusk. Varied moods and techniques. Especially demanding are the three middle movements. M-D.

From the Northland (BMC). Five movements in a program suite. Sowerby's impressions of the Lake Superior area converted into musical expression. M-D.

Toccata (Mer 1941). Quartal harmony, driving rhythms, martellato playing required. D.

A Fancy (TP). Modal, clever modulations, no key signature. Int.

LEOPOLD SPINNER (1906-) Austria, born Poland; in England since 1938

Spinner studied with Anton Webern from 1935 to 1938, an influence that is clearly noticeable in his writing. Spinner is active as a teacher and composer.

Sonata Op. 3 (UE 1953). D.
A 3-part work in 12-tone writing. Transparent textures.

Fantasy Op. 9 (Bo&H). D.
A minor serial "tour de force." There is a refreshing humorous quality about this piece, very different from most serial works.

Inventions Op. 13 (Bo&H 1958). 5 pieces. D.
Delicate serial ideas move from one hand to another in complex manner.

ALOJZ SREBOTNJAK (1931-) Yugoslavia

"Alojz Srebotnjak studied music in Yugoslavia, Italy, London, and Paris. His first compositions were marked by neoclassic and expressionistic traits, but Srebotnjak proceeded to adopt serial techniques in the 1960's." BBD, 162.

Invenzione Variata per Pianoforte (Drustvo Slovenskih Skladateljev 1961). 12-tone writing of a markedly individual character. Pointillistic writing, thin and thick textures. "Strong dissonances and driving rhythms suggest a unique combination of Schönberg and Charles Ives." BBD, 162.

EDWARD STAEMPFLI (1908-) Switzerland

7 Piano Pieces (Bo&Bo 1957).
Effective, severe 12-tone writing. D.

ROBERT STARER (1924-) USA, born Austria

Starer has steered clear of current fads. He is thoroughly professional, interesting and, above all, completely himself. He studied with Frederick Jacobi at The Juilliard School and lived many years in Israel. He is currently on the faculty at Brooklyn College and The Juilliard School.

Five Preludes (MCA). Two pages each, atonal, requires facility and some experience in this idiom. M-D.

Five Caprices (PIC 1948). Varied moods, from No. 1 a light scherzando, to No. 5 a burlesque rapid toccata. M-D.

Seven Vignettes (MCA). Short, colorful, easy.

Prelude and Toccata (MCA 1946). Chordal, lyric Prelude. Toccata in perpetual motion with changing meters. M-D.

Sonata (MCA 1949). Large-scale three-movement work: Allegro; Andante; Allegro frivole. The outer movements are strongly rhythmic while the middle movement is lyric. Advanced pianism required. D.

Sonata No. 2 (MCA 1965). A serially-organized one-movement work of three contrasting tempi and ideas. Intervals of minor second and seventh exploited, biting dissonance, vigorous rhythmic drive. Large span required. M-D.

Sketches in Color (MCA). Seven clever works, exploit different 20th century techniques. Int.

Three Israeli Sketches (MCA). Nofiah, Gadya, Mahol, M-D.

Hexahedron (MCA 1971). Six short characteristic pieces, interesting, imaginative. Int.

JOHN STANLEY (1713-1786) Great Britain

10 Voluntaries for organ or harpsichord Op. 5 (Denis Vaughan-OUP).

10 Voluntaries for organ or harpsichord Op. 6 (Denis Vaughan-OUP).

10 Voluntaries for organ or harpsichord Op. 7 Denis Vaughan-OUP).

PETER PINDAR STEARNS (1931-) USA

Toccata (ACA 1961). 5 minutes. D.
ABA design, use of thirty-second notes, effective syncopation, highly chromatic.

Adagio with Variations (ACA 1962). 13 minutes. D.
6 venturous variations, well organized and contrasted, worth exploring.

Partita (AMP 1961). Introduction and 4 variations. D.
Flexible meters, irregular rhythms, large span required, dramatic.

CHRISTOPHER STEEL (1939-   ) Great Britain

Sonatina No. 1 (Nov 1960). 14 p. 7 minutes. Movement called Greek Dance could be performed by itself. Entire work needs fluent pianism.

Sonatina No. 2 (Nov 1962). 11 p. 5½ minutes. Delightful writing. M-D.

Jacobean Suite (Nov 1961).
A pastiche. Fanfare at opening and closing surround some untitled pieces. Lute inspired? Not as pianistic as the two *Sonatinas*.

WOLFGANG STEFFEN (1923-   ) Germany

Sonata Op. 21 (Bo&Bo 1956).
Aggressive free-voiced motion in outer movements. Lyrical mid-section spiced with atonal counterpoint.

Reinhenproportionen Op. 25 (Bo&Bo).

DANIEL GOTTLIEB STEIBELT (1765-1823) Germany

For a thorough discussion of Steibelt's sonatas see SSB, 468-70.

6 Sonatinas Op. 49 (Simonetti-Ric).

25 Studies Op. 78 (Tagliapietra-Ric).

Rondo C (H. Albrecht-K&S). In Organum, Series 5, No. 14.

Rondo E♭ (Rowley-Ashdown).

Etudes Op. 78 (Augener).

Sonatina C (Banks).

GITTA STEINER (1932-   ) USA

Steiner has studied composition with Vincent Persichetti, Elliott Carter and Gunther Schuller.

Sonata (Seesaw Music Corp. 1964).
Tightly knit work built on 12-tone technique. One continuous movement with changing tempi and a rich harmonic palate.

Fantasy Piece (Seesaw Music Corp. 1966).
An essay in variegated splashes of sound. Directions are given for performance and notation. Highly exciting.

Three Pieces for Piano (Seesaw Music Corp. 1961).

WILHELM STENHAMMAR (1871-1927) Sweden

Stenhammar was one of the most distinguished figures in Swedish music. He began as a national romantic in the neoromantic vein but gradually achieved a simplicity, refinement and concentration in his musical language.

Tre Fantasien Op. 11 (WH 1895). Deep emotional undertones permeate these pieces.

Sonat Op. 12 A♭ (WH). 31 p.

Sensommernätter Op. 33 (WH). Books 1 and 2. 5 piano pieces.

Hemmarschen (GM).

Tre sma klaverstycken (ELK).

JOSEF ANTON ŠTĚPÁN (STEFFAN) (1726-1797)
Bohemia, Czechoslovakia

Composizioni per piano solo Vol. 64 MAB (Artia) has an English introduction and contains Divertimentos I-IV, similar to Haydn's Divertimentos for keyboard; multi-contrasting movements; and 9 piano sonatas. Some exceptionally fine writing.

Composizioni per piano solo Vol. 70 MAB (Artia). 8 sonatas.

Menuette für Klavier Vol. 9 MVH (Artia).

Capricci (A. Weinmann-Henle).

ERIC-WALTER STERNBERG (1898-   ) Israel,
born Germany

Sternberg has abjured orientalism and folkloristic influences.

Toccata (IMI 1943).
Bravura piano piece, relentless drive, double notes and skips. D.

EDWARD STEUERMANN (1882-1964) USA, born Poland

Steuermann studied piano with Busoni in Switzerland and Berlin and composition with Schönberg from 1912 to 1914. He gave first performances of all of Schönberg's music for the piano and was the first to record Schönberg's complete works for solo piano. The works are available from Mrs. Edward Steuermann, c/o The Library, The Cleveland Institute of Music, Cleveland, Ohio 44106.

Suite (AMC 1953-54). Prelude, Melody, Misterioso, Chorale, March. D. Many tempo changes, serial writing. This work could only have been written by a first-rate pianist.

Vier Klavierstücke (1934). 18 p. Dedicated to Anton von Webern. Preludium, Fantasie, Tema con variazioni, Reigen. Serial, fascinating sonorities. D.

Sonata (1925-26). 22 p. 2 movements: Deciso; Molto sostenuto. Expressionistic, thick textures, many tempo changes. D.

HALSEY STEVENS (1908-) USA

Stevens has written a great deal for the piano. Folk music, Brahms, Hindemith and the Baroque have all played a part in the development of his style. There is a spontaneous flow to his piano music.

8 Piano Pieces (ACA 1961-62). Prelude, Proclamation, Pompous Parade, Palindrome, Plaintive Poem, Pantomime, Pastorale, Pleasantry.
Pedagogic works. Thin textures, usually 2 or 3 voices, imitation, MC. A few technical problems: triplet divided over a full bar in cut time, span of ninth. Either complete set or a judicious selection could be played.

7 French Folksongs (ACA 1953). 5 minutes. The King of Yvetot, The Little Ship, There was a Shepherdess, Go to Sleep, Margoton, Within My Lady's Garden, Young Rousselle. Attractive, simple settings with interesting treatment of countermelodies.

For Joanna—6 Little Pieces (ACA 1954). Simple, charming, two lines each.

10 Short Pieces (ACA 1945-54). Praeludium, In a Mirror, Piece in Fourths, Scherzino, Unison Melody, Elegy, A Tune, Musette, Minuet, Fugue. More advanced than above. Open harmonies achieved by linear writing. Int.

Christmas Songs from Hungary (ACA 1956). Transcription of 9 Hungarian Christmas songs. All short, 2- or 3-voice textures, modal, arrestingly attractive.

Colinde (ACA 1951). 7 Rumanian Christmas Songs.
These 7 Colinde are taken from Béla Bartók's "Melodien der Rumänischen Colinde" (Weihnachtslieder) and are transcribed for piano or harpsichord. More difficult than listing above, short, span of a tenth required for LH in places.

Swedish Folk Tunes (Helios). 6 simple, attractive, musical settings.

10 French Folksongs (ACA 1959). Int., one page each.

11 Ukrainian Folksongs (ACA 1956). Transcriptions of folksongs from "Ukrainski Narodni Pisni." Easy.

4 Rumanian Folk Tunes (ACA 1953). 5½ minutes. Int.

3 Czech Folktunes (ACA 1958). 2 lines each with imitation.

6 Russian Folktunes (ACA 1955). Short, 2 voices, easy.

3 Hungarian Folksongs (ACA 1957). Arrangements of 3 folksongs collected by Zoltán Kódaly.
Nos. 1 and 3 fast and imitative, No. 2 slow, lyric, modal. Int.

5 Portuguese Folksongs (PIC 1956). Int. to M-D. A fine concert group. Dedicated to Fernando Laires.

Béla Bartók once wrote: "the folksong is a perfect model of how to express a musical thought in the most concise form, with the greatest simplicity of means, freshness and vitality . . ." This seems to be Stevens' philosophy, so aptly exemplified in the many folksong settings listed above.

Sonata No. 3 (AME 1947-48). Linear, imitative writing. 15 minutes. D.

Allegro non troppo: opening three bars contain germs for rest of sonata, bold, venturous harmonies, shifting meters, SA design.

Moderato con moto: calm with one climax, ternary.
Molto vivace: bravura, facile writing, rondo.

Partita for Harpsichord (PIC 1953-4). 14 minutes. Prelude, S, Loure, Rondeau, Sicilienne, Passacaille, G. MC. M-D.

Sonatina No. 1 (second version 1967) (Westwood).

Sonatina No. 2 (second version 1959) (Westwood).

Sonatina No. 5 (Westwood 1954).

Sonatina No. 6 (Westwood 1959).

Music for Ann (Helios 1954). 5½ minutes.

Lyric Piece (Merion 1955).

Ritratti per pianoforte (Westwood 1959-60).

Fantasia (Westwood 1961).

17 Piano Pieces (Westwood 1933-65). Prelude, Bell Sounds, Another Waltz, Hommage à Chopin, Hommage à Honegger, Hommage à Clementi, Night Procession, Night Song, Study in Hemiola, Chaconne, Invention, For LH Alone, Erratic Rhythms, Palindrome II, Legato & Staccato, From a Roman Sketch Book, Finale. Varied moods, styles, technical difficulties, interpretative problems. Easy to M-D.

Study in Bulgarian Rhythms (PIC 1966).

5 Little 5-finger Pieces (Helios). 2 minutes.

Jumping Colts (Helios 1960). 1 minute.

4 Bagatelles (Westwood 1960).

See: Wallace Berry, "The Music of Halsey Stevens," MQ, 54, July 1968, 287-308.

RONALD STEVENSON (1928-) Scotland

Prelude, Fugue and Fantasy on Themes from Doktor Faust Op. 51 (Nov 1949-59). Part of "Virtuoso," a modern piano series edited by John Ogdon, the English pianist. Based on themes from Busoni's *Faust.* Extensive demands are made on performer. Three basic motives from *Doktor Faust* are put to cyclic use. All three are introduced in the Prelude while the Fugue is based on the third motive. Fantasy appears to be a telescoped SA design. The tonal centers (C for the Prelude and Fugue and E for the Fantasia) are the same key relations used in Busoni's piano concerto. This also exists in another version entitled *Piano Concerto No. 1: Faust Triptych.* A 2-piano reduction of this version is published by (Nov).

Passacaglia on D-S-C-H Op. 80 (OUP 1963). 151 p. An 80-minute work built on the subject D E♭ C B. Contains such elements as a Fandango, Pibroch, Triple Fugue, March, Sonata, and Waltz. The subjects of the triple fugue are D S C H, B A C H, and the Dies Irae. Technical demands are not staggering but great stamina on the part of the pianist is required. D S C H (in their German counterpart) form the initials of Dmitri Shostakovitch, to whom the work is dedicated. "This is possibly the most concentrated expression of motif development in the history of music," said Ates Orga in M&M, 17/2, October 1968, 29. Stevenson's creative philosophy is summed up in this article. *Passacaglia* is an attempt to achieve a synthesis of "world music."

A Wheen Tune for Bairns tae Spiel Op. 84 (Schott c. 1967). A suite of four Scottish pieces written for Stevenson's youngest daughter. Influence of Percy Grainger in this miniature "Scottish Mikrokosmos." Easy.

Anger Dance Op. 93 (Schott 1965).

See: Ates Orga, "The Piano Music of Ronald Stevenson," MO, 92, March 1969, 292-5.

WILLIAM GRANT STILL (1895-) USA

Copies of the (JF) publications are available from: Mrs. William Grant Still, 1262 Victoria Avenue, Los Angeles, California 90019.

3 Visions (JF 1936). 11 minutes. Dark Horseman, Summerland, Radiant Pinnacle. Short character pieces in varied moods. M-D.

7 Traceries (JF 1939). 17 minutes. Cloud Cradles, Mystic Pool, Muted Laughter, Out of the Silence, Woven Silver, Wailing Dawn, A Bit of Wit. Somewhat impressionistic. M-D.

Fairy Knoll (MCA) A filigree tinkling scherzo. Int.

Phantom Chapel (MCA). Deep, sonorous, bell-tone qualities. Int.

KARLHEINZ STOCKHAUSEN (1928-) Germany

Stockhausen studied with Darius Milhaud, Olivier Messiaen, and Pierre Schaeffer in Paris. Both Stockhausen and Pierre Boulez were students in Messiaen's class on rhythm. "Association with Boulez brought him prominence in France. Stockhausen became the key figure in the transference of French ideas on total serialization to German soil and his writings on rhythm are among the most penetrating studies on the subject." BBD, 163. The music of Anton von Webern was also a major influence on Stockhausen. In 1954 Stockhausen began a cycle of 21 piano pieces and to this date only 11 have been completed. In many ways the writing is pianistic, usually taking advantage of the entire range of the keyboard and dynamics, using overtones most effectively with subtle pedal effects. It is conceivable that these pieces might eventually be considered twentieth-century piano classics.

Klavierstücke I-IV (UE 1952-54).

"The tempo of each piece, determined by the smallest note-value, is 'as fast as possible.' When the player has found this tempo and determined it metronomically, all the more complicated time proportions . . . can be replaced by changes of tempo."

Klavierstücke V (1954) VI (1955) VII (1954) VIII (1954) (UE c. 1965). No V emphasizes "the great range of the keyboard to heighten the sense of space, and used silence more effectively to accentuate the sense of motion." BBD, 164.

No. VI is extremely complex, 48 pages long.

No. VII might appeal to the very adventurous pianist.

No. VIII contains the fewest technical problems.

Nos. V through VIII are analyzed in "Stockhausen's Piano Pieces," by G. W. Hopkins, MT, 107, April 1966, 331.

Klavierstücke IX & X (UE c. 1967). No. IX is technically the easiest of all the pieces. A single sonority is exploited. No. X is 38 separate pages and contains detailed comments and instructions to the pianist. Requires fist glissandi and fore-arm cluster trills among other virtuoso requirements. This is one of Stockhausen's most important pieces. These first 10 pieces may be played as a cycle, in groups, or separately.

Klavierstück XI (UE 1956). Comes in several versions: one is a cardboard tube with a strip of paper (with or without rack) and 19 sections of music. These sections are to be performed at random but each is to be performed according to directions contained in the preceding section. The work is to end whenever one section has been played for the third time. Tone clusters of different sizes are mixed with regular chords. Both free and rigid methods of notation are employed.

A progressive change of notation takes place throughout these eleven works as Stockhausen continues searching for the "correct" notational form of each piece.

See: Robert Craft, "Boulez and Stockhausen," The Score, 24, November 1958, 54-62.

Roger Smalley, "Stockhausen's Piano Pieces," MT, 110, January 1969, 30-2.

ALAN STOUT (1932-) USA

Sonata Op. 45/1 (ACA 1958). One movement. D.
Serial, frequent tempo and meter changes, unbarred. More idiomatic for the piano than many serial works.

WILLARD STRAIGHT (1930-) USA

Straight is a graduate of the University of Kansas and the Chicago Musical College.

Structure (Bo&H).
Commissioned for the Van Cliburn Competition, 1966. A virtuoso-bravura piece designed to display the pianist's skills. Exciting ending consists of a double glissando, black and white notes together. Pianistic. D.

RICHARD STRAUSS (1864-1949) Germany

5 Klavierstücke Op. 3 (UE). Schumann influence. M-D.

Sonata b Op. 5 (UE 1880-81). 4 movements. Composed when Strauss was 16 years old, in a derivative style that contains some effective writing and some notably romantic melodies (see the Andante cantabile movement). Inspiration from Beethoven and Mendelssohn. M-D.

5 Stimmungsbilder Op. 9 (UE). (Moods and fancies). In Silent Forests, Beside the Spring, Intermezzo, Träumerei, On the Heath. These are the best of the composer's character pieces. No. 4 anticipates certain accompanimental characteristics that Strauss demonstrated more fully in his later songs. Int. to M-D.

HERMAN STRATEGIER (1912-) The Netherlands

Acht danswijsjes (B&VP 1938). 3 minutes.

Bagatella (Bender 1950). 3 minutes.

Elegie (Donemus 1954).

Pavane-Gaillarde-Pavane (Basart). 4 minutes.

Sonate (Donemus).

Sonatine (Donemus 1951). 3 movements. 11 p. Chromatic. In the final movement, Toccata, an Adagio mid-section is uncharacteristic but effective. M-D.

IGOR STRAVINSKY (1882-1971) USA, born Russia

Stravinsky's piano works, while varied and interesting, are not as important as his works in other media.

Four Etudes Op. 7 (1908) (CFP) (IMC) (AMP) (K) (Rahter). c, D, e, F♯. Nos. 1, 2 and 4 are involved with metrical problems. No. 4 is a brilliant perpetual-motion study. M-D.

Piano Rag Music (JWC 1919). Short, percussive, rhythmic, jazz inspired. D.

Les cinq doigts (1921) (Mer) (JWC). Eight easy pieces on five notes.

Trois Mouvements de Petrouchka (1921) (Bo&H). Danse Russe, Chez Petrouchka, La Semaine grasse. Virtuoso paraphrases of three scenes from the ballet. Brilliant orchestral writing for the piano. Highly effective and demanding. D.

Sonata (1924) (Bo&H). Objective, neoclassic model, chamber style. "I have used the term 'Sonata' in its original sense, deriving from the word 'sonare' . . ." Three movements FSF, thin textures. The second movement is a florid Adagietto in baroque style while the concluding movement is a toccatalike rondo. D.

Sérénade en la (1925) (Bo&H). Four movements written in the spirit of the eighteenth-century. Hymne: processional, somber; Romanza: elegant, opening and closing cadenzas; Rondoletto: dry, impersonal; Cadenza finale: quiet, moving eighth notes. D.

Tango (1940) (Schott). Syncopated tango rhythm, romantic trio. Int.

Circus Polka for a Young Elephant (1942) (Schott). Humorous, rhythmic, military march-like. M-D.

See: John Ogdon, "Stravinsky and the Piano," Tempo, 81, Summer 1967, 36-41.

SOULIMA STRAVINSKY (1910-   ) USA, born Switzerland

Stravinsky teaches piano in the School of Music at the University of Illinois. He is the son of Igor.

Sonata B♭ (JWC 1947). 32 p. 13 minutes. M-D.
Cheerful writing that requires much keyboard facility.

3 Inventions (CFP 1962). F, F♯, B♭. M-D.

Art of Scales, 24 Preludes (CFP). M-D. A "modern" Clementi that makes scale practice more interesting.

6 Easy Sonatinas for Young Pianists (CFP 1967). 2 volumes. Int. I: Nos. 1-3. II: Nos. 4-6. Very pianistic.

Piano Music for Children (CFP). 2 volumes. Easy.
I: 19 pieces. II: 11 pieces.

Piano Variations (CFP 1970). 2 series.
First series: 18 p. 12 minutes. Neoclassic in style. Int. Prelude, Forlane, Stanza, Piccolo Divertimento (theme and 3 variations), In Modo Russo (theme and 3 variations), Les Valses (theme and 4 variations).
Second series: 16 p. 13 minutes. 11 Tones (theme and 6 variations), Metrics (theme and 6 variations), 12 Tones (theme and 7 variations), Pavana (theme and 3 variations) and Pavana returns more fully harmonized.

SIEGFRIED STROHBACH (1929-　　) Germany

Die Spieldose (Br&H 1951). Int. to M-D.
An unusual set of 7 pieces. Each piece has a music box imitation at the closing with a fortissimo cadence ending.

Die Spielzeugkiste (Br&H 1952). Int.
Neoclassic in style.

MORTON SUBOTNICK (1933-　　) USA

Subotnick studied composition with Leon Kirchner and Darius Milhaud. He was Director of Electronic Music at the Electric Circus in New York City and is associated with the Intermedia Program at the School of Arts at New York University. The purpose of this program is to bring together artists who specialize in various media—film, theatre, tape, etc.

Prelude No. 4 for Piano and Electric Sounds (MCA 1966).
Some parts are not strictly measured ("beat bars") but are not improvisational either. The notated tape part is a series of cues for coordination. Atonal sonorities are used for color only. Experimental but highly expressive. Sensitive, thought-provoking work.

JOSEF SUK (1874-1935) Czechoslovakia

Suk wrote in a style that employed a rich chromatic harmonic vocabulary, sustained contrapuntal textures, rhythmic elasticity and expansive lyrical lines.

Early Pieces (Polivka-Orbis 1951). Polonaise c, Andante B♭, Adagio-Allegro vivace F, Vivace E♭.

Polish Fantasy Op. 5 (Artia 1950).

Stimmungen Op. 10 (Artia).

Suite Op. 21 (Artia).

Sommereindrücke Op. 22b (Artia). Summer Impressions. 3 pieces.

Von meiner Mutter Op. 28 (Artia). About Mother. 5 pieces. 20 minutes.

Von der Freundschaft Op. 36 (Artia). About Friendship.

Drei Klavierstücke (Artia).

Ländler (Artia).

CARLOS SURINACH (1915-) Spain, came to USA 1950

Three Spanish Songs and Dances (PIC 1951). Colorful harmonies, exacting rhythms, superbly written, effective as a group. Int.

Sonatina (PIC 1943). 19 p. 10 minutes. Three movements, lean textures, excellent concert piece. D.

Acrobats of God: Five Dances (AMP). 12 minutes. Transcribed from his ballet of the same title: Fanfare, Antique Dance, Bolero, Minuet, Spanish Galop. Rhythmic emphasis in the faster movements while the slower ones emphasize much embellishment in the melodic treatment. Int. to M-D.

Tales From the Flamenco Kingdom (AMP 1955). Int. Attractive suite.

I. Pepper King: Use of seconds harmonically and melodically, syncopation, accented dissonance, synthetic scale.

II: Sweet Beauty: chromatic, many minor seconds, wide dynamic range, 4 sixteenths followed by triplet eighths, pedal points.

III: Witch Dance: 3/8 and some use of 3/4, accented rhythmic treatment, gypsy scale.

HEINRICH SUTERMEISTER (1910-) Switzerland

Sutermeister's style is basically diatonic and shows a preference for parallel, moving streams of unrelated harmony.

Sonatina E♭ (Schott 1948). 3 movements. M-D.
Felicitous musical invention in all movements. Irregular meters, healthy contemporary language.

Bergsommer (Schott 1941). 8 little pieces. Int.

Hommage à Arthur Honegger (Schott 1955).

HOWARD SWANSON (1909-) USA

The Cuckoo (MCA 1949). Short scherzo inspired by the cuckoo call. M-D.

Sonata (Weintraub Music 1950). Allegro risoluto; Andante cantabile; Allegro vivo. Linear 2- and 3-part writing, strong rhythmic treatment in outer movements. Arresting, relevant writing. D.

JAN PIETERSZOON SWEELINCK (1562-1621)
The Netherlands

An outstanding performer, teacher and composer, this "maker of German organists" wrote in a style that incorporated both Italian and English characteristics. He made no distinction between pieces intended for harpsichord and organ. His complete keyboard output consists of 13 fantasias, 6 echo-fantasias, 13 toccatas, 24 chorale variations, 7 variations on popular tunes, and 5 variations on popular dances.

Complete Keyboard Works (M. Seiffert-Alsbach). An appendix of 4 fragments is also included. (See *Keyboard and Lute Works* below).

7 Fantasias (Döflein-Schott).

Selected Works (Hellmann-CFP) 2 volumes. Vol. I: 6 Toccatas, 2 Toccatas, 5 Secular Song and Dance Variations. Vol. II: Praeludium, 2 Ricercari, 9 Choral Arrangements.

Variations (Döflein-Schott).

Variations on "Mein junges Leben hat ein End" (CFP).

Works for Harpsichord and Organ, Supplement (Alfons Annegarn-Alsbach). Contains 2 Fantasias, 2 Ricercari and a Fugue.

7 Sets of Variations on Secular Songs (Senart).

Keyboard and Lute Works (Dutch Society for Musicology). Three volumes, prepared by Gustav Leonhart, Alfons Annegarn and Frits Noske (1969). Scholarly, supersedes Seiffert. Vol. I: Fantasias and Toccatas; Vol. II: Settings of Sacred Melodies; Vol. III: Settings of Secular Melodies and Dances (Works for Lute).

See: Alan S. Curtis, *Sweelinck's Keyboard Music: a Study of English Elements in Seventeenth-Century Dutch Composition.* Leiden: University Press, 1969. London: Oxford University Press, 1969.

A. van Gool, "Once More: Sweelinck's Keyboard Music: Organ or Harpsichord?" Tijdschrift de Vereniging voor Nederlandse Muziekgeschiedenis, XIX, 1960-63.

RICHARD SWIFT (1927-   ) USA

Swift studied composition with Leland Smith at the University of Chicago. He is Chairman of the Music Department at the University of California at Davis, California.

Stravaganza II Op. 18 (ms available from composer, 1958). 7 p. Basic sixteenth-note pulse is maintained within the context of frequent meter changes. Span of ninth required, numerous major sevenths, highly chromatic, pointillistic writing, quiet ending. D.

Stravaganza VI (ms available from composer, 1964-5). 7 p. One movement, complex rhythmic relationships, clusters, plucked strings, harmonics, extremes in registers exploited, unusual sonorities. D.

Summer Notes (ms available from composer, 1966). 17 p. Three movements separated by 2 Interludes. Notation directions, clusters and harmonic effects, pointillistic writing, exploits extreme ranges, highly organized, unusual sonorities. D.

WILLIAM SYDEMAN (1928-) USA

Sydeman's music is clearly conceived, colorful and linear. His works are effective, clever and direct.

Sonata (Ione Press). 3 movements. 36 p. 14 minutes. D. Thoughtfully organized. Not always pianistic.

Variations (MCA). Diffuse quasi recitativo theme is thoroughly worked out in 6 variations. Abbreviated return of theme closes the work. Preference for sevenths. M-D.

Prelude (EBM). 3 minutes.

Fantasy Piece for Harpsichord (Seesaw Music Corp).

Three Pieces and a Finale for Piano and Tape (Seesaw Music Corp).

FERENC SZABÓ (1902-1969) Hungary

From 1958 to his death Szabó was Director-General of the Franz Liszt Academy of Music in Budapest.

Toccata (EMB).

Free Melodies (EMB).

2 Piano Pieces (EMB).

3 Sonatas (EMB). Published together. Sonata I (1940): 12 p. Andante, poco rubato; Vivace. Sonata II (1947): 22 p. Poco lento e rubato; Allegro moderato. Sonata III (1957-1961): 36 p. Allegro cantabile; Andante, molto expressivo; Con moto, molto cantabile. Each sonata is progressively more difficult ranging from M-D to virtuoso writing. The 20-year span covered by these pieces unfolds an interesting stylistic development.

Sonatina (EMB 1933).

8 Easy Piano Pieces (EMB 1933).

5 Small Piano Pieces (EMB 1933).

ANTONI SZALOWSKI (1907-) Poland

Suite for Piano or Harpsichord (Augener 1956). 3 movements. Tonal, linear style in clear transparent texture. Classic form filled with contemporary substance.

Sonatina (Augener 1934).

Perpetuum Mobile (Augener 1936).

Study (Augener 1955).

GEORG SZELL (1897-1970) USA, born Hungary

Drei Kleine Klavierstücke Op. 6 (UE c. 1922). Skizze, Sarabande, Capriccio. Written in post-romantic tradition, these M-D pieces are attractive.

ERZSEBET SZÖNYI (1924-) Hungary

Miss Szönyi studied with Messiaen and Boulanger in Paris in 1947. She has been on the faculty at the Franz Liszt Academy of Music since 1948.

Cinque Preludi (EMB 1963). 11 p. Short contrasted works showing solid craftsmanship. Impressionist and contemporary idioms blended. Large span required. 1. Ostinato 2. Maestoso 3. Variazioni 4. Grazioso 5. Dotted eighth-note equals 165.

MARIA SZYMANOWSKA (1789-1831) Poland

Maria Szymanowska was an important precusor of Chopin who wrote romantic salon music. Robert Schumann spoke highly of her in his *Music and Musicians*. Chopin was familiar with her music.

Maria Szymanowska Album (Josef and Maria Mirsy-PWM). Biographical material in Polish. Contains: Polonaise f, Menuet E, Le Murmure, Song Setting, Etude F, Etude E♭, Etude d, a revised version of the d Etude, Etudes in E, C, and E♭. Int. to M-D. Interesting and musical writing.

Nocturne B♭ (PWM). Oriented more toward John Field than Chopin. Int.

KAROL SZYMANOWSKI (1882-1937) Poland

Chopin, Scriabin, Richard Strauss, Debussy and Stravinsky all influenced Szymanowski and yet he was an original composer. In the 1920's Szymanowski began to employ Polish folk elements in his music. Many of his piano works are virtuosic and use most of the resources of the instrument. The later compositions which became very personal and unique in style, dissonant and rhythmically complex, emerged to stamp Szymanowski as one of the most creative artists in the early 20th century. Op. 1, 4, and 10 provide an excellent introduction to his works.

Nine Preludes Op. 1 (1900-1902) (PWM) (UE).
Chromatic, quartal harmony, Chopin and Scriabin influence, varied moods. Nos. 1 and 8 are the most popular. Set is dedicated to Artur Rubinstein.

Theme and Variations b♭ Op. 3 (PWM). 12 variations, rich harmony. D.

Four Etudes Op. 4 (1903) (PWM) (UE). (UE) available separately. Romantic harmony, double notes, octaves, broken-chord figuration. D.

Sonata No. 1 c Op. 8 (1905) (Piwarski). Chopin and Scriabin influence. In 1910 received first prize in a competition organized by the Chopin Centenary Committee at Lwów. Large 4-movement work, closes with a fugue. Dramatic ending.

Variations on a Polish Folk Song Op. 10 (1903) (PWM) (UE). 10 variations, postromantic, elegant, virtuoso writing, brilliant closing. D.

Fantasie F Op. 14 (1905) (Piwarski).

Prelude (1905) *and Fugue* (1909) (PWM). Won a second prize in 1909 in a competition sponsored by the Berlin musical journal *Signale für die Musikalische Welt.*

Sonata No. 2 a Op. 21 (1910) (UE). Reger influence. Climax of the composer's earlier period. Appassionato, followed by variations on a spritely theme, concluded by a fugue. D.

Métopes Op. 29 (1915) (UE). L'isle des Sirènes, Calypso,

Nausicaa. Three mythological poems, florid, impressionist, varied tonalities, orchestrally conceived. D.

Twelve Etudes Op. 33 (1916-1918) (UE). (PWM) publish a facsimile of this work. Short pieces intended to be played as a set. Scriabin and Ravel influence. D.

Masques Op. 34 (1915-16) (UE). Shéhérazade, Tantris le bouffon, Sérénade de Don Juan. Thick textures, complex writing. D.

Sonata No. 3 d Op. 36 (1916-1919) (UE). One movement, episodic, leans towards Scriabin, mature pianism required, delicate Presto opening leads to an Adagio, culminates in a grotesque Fugue, scherzando e buffo.

Twenty Mazurkas Op. 50 (1923-1929) (UE) (PWM). 5 volumes of 4 Mazurkas each. Intense, improvisatory, subtle works that require sensitive pianism. M-D to D.

Four Polish Dances (1926) (OUP) (PWM). Int. to M-D.

Two Mazurkas Op. 62 (1934) (PWM) (ESC). M-D.

See: B. M. Maciejewski, *Karol Szymanowski, His Life and Music.* London: Poets and Painters' Press, 1967.

Kornel Michalowski, *Karol Szymanowski 1882-1937; katalog tematyczny dziel i bibliografia (Karol Szymanowski. Thematic Catalogue of Works and Bibliography).* Cracow: PWM, 1967. 248 p. In Polish; summaries in English and German.

T

GERMAINE TAILLEFERRE (1892-   ) France

Dance rhythms permeate most of Tailleferre's writing.

Pastorale A♭ (1928) (Heugel). Smooth, graceful melody, M-D.

Pastorale D (1919) (ESC).

Pastorale C (1929) (Heugel).

Siciliènne (1928) (Heugel).

Partita (Rongwen).

Fleurs de France (Lemoine c. 1962). 8 short, charming pieces. Int.

MARKO TAJČEVIĆ (1900-   ) Yugoslavia

Tajčević approaches Yugoslavian folk music much like Bartók approaches Hungarian folk music.

Seven Balkan Dances (Schott c. 1957). M-D.
Colorful, contrasted dances, technical problems.

Serbian Dances (Rongwen 1959). Int.
Tuneful, graceful, attractive. Excellent pedagogic material.

Five Preludes (Prosveta Belgrad). M-D.
Allegro tranquillo, Molto animato, Agitato, Molto sostenuto, Presto.

Lieder von der Murinsel (Henle). Folksong settings. Easy to Int.

JENÖ TAKÁCS (1902-) Hungary

Takács is presently a member of the composition faculty of the College-Conservatory of Music of the University of Cincinnati.

From Far and Wide Op. 37 (UE). 20 pieces representing many countries. Folk element permeates some of these. Easy to Int.

Little Sonate Op. 51 (Dob). 7 p. In Hungarian folkmusic style. Int.

Toccata Op. 54 (Dob 1946). Effective bitonal writing. Interesting mid-section cadenza marked Quasi Fantasia. Requires fast fingers.

Doubledozen for Small Fingers (UE 1965). 24 short pieces employing many MC idioms. Very original. Easy to Int.

Partita Op. 58 (Dob 1954).

Sounds and Silences Op. 78 (Dob). Atonal, improvisatory, no bar lines, aleatory. Effective, D.

For Me. Little Recital Pieces Op. 76 (Dob). 22 short pieces, clever. Easy to Int.

4 Epitaphs Op. 79 (Dob). Hommage to 4 composers: Hindemith, Debussy, Berg, Bartók. Characteristics of each composer appear in each piece. M-D.

Humoreske (Dob).

YUJI TAKAHASHI (1938-) Japan

Takahashi studied composition at the Toho School of Music in Tokyo. He also studied with Iannis Xenakis in Berlin during 1963-1965 and came to the USA in 1966. He is considered one of Japan's leading exponents of contemporary piano music. He has taught at the San Francisco Conservatory of Music.

Metathesis (CFP 1968). 5 minutes. "The structure is based on the subgroups of a permutation group of 6 and Order 24, which are applied to the various factors of the tone events for piano, such as the density, the duration, the dynamic form, the tone form (all of them are extratemporal structures). The temporal structures are stochastic.' From record jacket, Mainstream MS/5000, recording of the work by the composer.

Chromamorphe II (CFP).

Rosace II (CFP).

JOSEPH TAL (1910-) Israel, born Poland

Sonata (Israeli Music Publications). Three movements. Thick textures. Theme of bass ostinato in second movement is based on a Rahel song. Final movement is a fast Rondo. M-D.

Dodecaphonic Episodes (IMI 1963). D.
". . . are based on a 12-tone row and use many of the 48 forms. The first episodes also introduce a rhythmic series with its R and I forms. In the second episode the rhythmic row is developed according to Boris Blacher's variable meter system, the form being dependent on the continuous time flow thus created. The third episode features motivic exploitation. The fourth and last permits improvisation which is controlled by the rhythmic proportions derived from the pitch row." BBD, 170.

THOMAS TALLIS (ca. 1505-1585) Great Britain

Most of Tallis' keyboard music was written for the organ, but a good deal of it sounds well on the harpsichord, clavichord and virginal.

Complete Keyboard Works (D. Stevens-Hin 1953).
17 short works in polyphonic and motet style. Useful essay on the composer and the keyboard music. Urtext. 5 Antiphons, 7 Hymns, a Fantasy, 2 Offertories, a Lesson (two parts in one), A Point.

4 Pieces from the Mulliner Book (D. Stevens-Hin).

See: Denis Stevens, "The Keyboard Music of Thomas Tallis," MT, 93, July 1952, 303-7.

LOUISE TALMA (1906-) USA

Talma is a composer of authority and high professional skill whose output for piano is not large but is nonetheless interesting and significant. The style is oriented toward Stravinsky and, in the case of the second Sonata, toward Ravel.

Sonata No. 1 (CF 1943). Serious, large-scale three movement work: Largo-Allegro molto vivace: short introduction leads to a driving rhythmic staccato movement in 6/8, ostinato figuration; Larghetto: serene melody, quartal and quintal harmonic usage, homogeneous texture; Presto: toccata-like rhythmic finale, ostinato, changing meters, dramatic closing. D.

Alleluia in Form of Toccata (CF 1947). Lengthy, cheerful, flexible meters, staccato style, fresh melodies. Requires firm rhythmic control, agility and stamina. D.

Six Etudes (GS 1953-4). Impressive virtuoso writing. No. 3, a sostenuto pedal study is of special interest. D.

Pastoral Prelude (CF).

Sonata No. 2 (1944-1955, available from composer: c/o Music Department, Hunter College, 695 Park Avenue, New York, New York 10021). Effective large-scale work demanding bravura and complete musicianship. A rewarding piece to play. D.

Three Bagatelles (1955, available from composer). No. 3 in (Kurt Stone-Scribner) *100 Pieces for piano.*

Passacaglia and Fugue (1955-1962, available from composer).

ELIAS TANENBAUM (1924-) USA

Sonata (ACA 1959) 25 p.
Dissonant counterpoint, atonal, melodic skips, polyrhythms, harmonics, quiet closing. D.

Music for Piano (ACA 1963). 10 minutes.
Serial, preference for sevenths, use of overtones (depress thick chords silently, sound higher notes), pointillistic.

ALEXANDRE TANSMAN (1897-   ) Poland

Tansman, like his fellow compatriot Frédéric Chopin, has lived most of his life in Paris. His style has varied from early pieces definitely influenced by Chopin to impressionist and neoclassic writing. Jazz also played a large part in some of his music. The piano writing is always idiomatic.

Mazurkas (1918-1928) (ESC). 2 volumes. Vol. I:10 pieces of varied difficulty. Vol. II:9 pieces of varied difficulty. Both volumes contain some of his best works.

Petite Suite (1919) (ESC). 7 short movements, lyric, M-D.

Trois Etudes transcendantes (1922) (Sal). Chromatic, pianistically interesting. M-D to D.

Sonatine (1924) (Sal). Well worked out. M-D.

Cinq Impromptus (1926) (ESC). Varied moods. No. 5 Toccata is most difficult. M-D.

Sonatine transatlantique (1930) (Leduc). Fox-trot; Spiritual and Blues; Charleston. Large span required, attractive jazz improvisation. Tansman said "This work does not propose to realize an 'American Music,' but simply to put down the 're-action' of a European musician to contact with the dance rhythms from across the sea." (Composer's note.) M-D.

Arabesques (1931) (ESC). No. 6 Danza, is the best of the set. Int. to M-D.

Troisième Sonatine (1933) (ESC). Animated Pastorale; chordal Hymne; Rondo: perpetual motion. M-D.

Cinq Impressions (1934) (ESC). Calme, Burlesque, Triste, Animé, Nocturne. Short, varied. Int. to M-D.

Pour les Enfants (1934) (ESC). Four graded collections, 12 pieces in each except the final collection which has 10. Attractive, conventional settings.

Trois Préludes en forme de Blues (1937) (ESC). Uncomplicated, convincing settings. M-D.

Intermezzi (1939-40) (ESC). 4 series. I:1-6, II:7-12, III:13-18, IV:19-24. More dissonant in style. M-D to D.

Les Jeunes au Piano (1951) (ESC). 4 volumes of graded pieces from easy to M-D. I: Mireille et les animaux. II: Marianne devant le kiosque aux journeaux. III: L'Autobus imaginaire. IV: Au télescope.

Four Nocturnes (1952) (UE). Large span necessary, each one page in length. Int.

Suite variée (1952) (UE). 7 short pieces, chromatic, the 4-voice fugue is difficult. Int. to M-D.

Sonata No. 5 (1955) (UE). To the memory of Bartók. Allegro deciso; Lento; Molto vivace; Largo—Allegro con moto. Terse, expressive.

11 Interludes (1955) (ESC). Varied moods and styles. M-D.

Four Impressions (1945) (MCA). Impressionistic. M-D.

Eight Novelettes (ESC). Accessible, moderate length, M-D.

Eight Cantilenas (MCA). Homage to Bach. M-D.

SVEN ERIK TARP (1908-) Denmark

The modern French School has influenced Tarp's style. Tarp is associated with The Society for the Publication of Danish Music.

Trois Improvisations Op. 21 (WH).

Mosaik. 10 easy pieces Op. 31 (WH).

3 Dances Op. 41 (Engstroem & Soedring 1945). Spansk, Siciliansk, Snurrepiberier.

Snap Shots Op. 45 (WH). Easy.

Cirkus Op. 47 (Engstroem & Soedring).

*3 Sonatine*r Op. 48 (Engstroem & Soedring c. 1947). Each three movements. Modal, bitonal. Int.
1. C. 2. c Fantasietta. 3. d.
Fresh sounding, not too difficult. Useful Int. material.

Konfetti. 7 easy pieces Op. 52 (WH).

6 easy pieces Op. 55a (WH).

Easy Suite Op. 55b (WH).

Tema med variationer Op. 43 (WH). M-D.

Sonate Op. 60 (Engstroem & Soedring).

CARL TAUSIG (1841-1871) Germany, born Poland

Rêverie Op. 5 (Musica Obscura).

Ungarische Ziguenerweisen (Musica Obscura).

Halka Fantasy (Musica Obscura).

PETER ILICH TCHAIKOWSKY (1840-1893) Russia

All works for solo piano are contained in volumes 51A and B, 52, 53 of the Complete Edition (USSR).

(CFP) has 3 volumes of piano works:

No. 1: Op. 1/1 Scherzo à la russe; Op. 8 Capriccio; Op. 19/6 Theme and Variations; Op. 21 Six Pieces on a Theme (Suite): Prelude, Fugue, Impromptu, Funeral March, Muzurka, Scherzo; Op. 59 Dumka.

No. 2: Op. 2/1 The Castle Ruins; Op. 2/3 Chant sans paroles; Op. 5 Romance; Op. 7 Valse-Scherzo; Op. 9/2, 3 Polka, Mazurka de salon; Op. 10/1, 2 Nocturne, Humoresque; Op. 19/1, 3, 4 Rêverie du soir, Feuillet d'album, Nocturne; Op. 40/2, 6, 9, 10 Chanson triste, Chant sans paroles, Valse, Danse russe; without opus number: Impromptu—Caprice; Valse—Scherzo; Impromptu; Aveu passionne.

No. 3: Op. 51/2, 4, 5, 6 Polka peu dansant, Nata Valse, Romance, Sentimental Valse; Op. 72/1-4, 8, 9, 12, 13, 15, 16 Impromptu, Cradle Song, Tender Reproaches, Characteristic Dance, Dialogue, Un poco di Schumann, L'Espiègle, Rustic Echo, Un poco di Chopin, Valse á 5/8.

Album for the Young Op. 39 (EBM) (CFP) (GS) (Br&H) (Ric) (K). Twenty-four pieces. *Six Dances* (J. Last-Galliard) from this opus.

The Seasons Op. 37b (CFP) (Br&H) (WH) (GS) (K). Twelve pieces, each titled with the name of a month. More demanding than Op. 39, more effective when performed individually.

Variations F Op. 19/6 (Hin). Thematic development more in evidence than in most of his solo piano works.

Dumka Op. 59 (Philipp-IMC). A Concert Fantasy.

Sonata G Op. 37a (CFP) (Simrock) (USSR) (Rahter). Four movements of thick, heavy writing, some attractive ideas also present. Large-scale, virtuoso technique required.

12 Pieces Op. 40 (Taylor-Nov). M-D.

Sonata c♯ Op. 80 (USSR). Four movements, little contrast, composed 1865.

Album of 12 Pieces (Schott).

17 Selected Pieces (Ric).

14 Pieces (WH).

17 Selected Pieces (GS).

See: A. E. F. Dickinson, "Tchaikowsky, The Piano Music," in *The Music of Tchaikowsky*. Edited by Gerald Abraham. New York: Norton, 1946, 114-23.

ANTONIO TAURIELLO (1931-) Argentina

Toccata (Bo&H).

Polytonal usage blended into fine toccata style. See article and lesson on this piece by Ylda Novik in Clavier, 8, January 1969, 29-31. Toccata is printed 23-8.

4 Sonatinas (Barry 1956).

MC, fond of skips. Fine Int. material. Each sonatina is short enough for all four to be played as a larger "sonata."

ALEXANDER TCHÉRÉPNIN (1899-) USA, born Russia

Toccata d Op. 1 (Belaieff). Bravura writing. D.

Toccata g No. 2 Op. 20 (Simrock).

Nocturne g# Op. 2/1 (Belaieff). Short, poetic, stormy.

Dance Op. 2/2 (Belaieff). Martellato writing, sharp changes of registers.

10 Bagatelles Op. 5 (GS 1913-18). The composer has edited this revised version of these popular works.

Episodes (Heugel). 12 sketches, 1 or 2 pages in length. MC, varied moods, early work.

Dix Etudes Op. 18 (Heugel).

8 Préludes (Heugel 1926). Short, facile, varied.

Deux Novelettes Op. 19 (Heugel).

Quatre Romances Op. 31 (UE 1925). Tart, appealing.

Sonatine Romantique (Durand 1918). 4 movements. M-D.

Sonata a Op. 22 (Heugel 1924). Contrasting 4 movements. Unusual closing movement (Grave).

5 Etudes Op. 52 (Schott). Shadow Play, The Luth, Hommage to China, Punch & Judy, Chant. Available separately. D.

Songs Without Words Op. 82 (CFP 1953). 5 pieces, some require large span, colorful names appear at end of each piece.

12 Préludes Op. 85 (EBM 1956). Some are a page long, all require sensitive musicianship.

Paraphrases on the Theme of "Chopsticks" by Liszt and well-known Russian Composers, revised By A. T. (Belaieff 1959). Easy popular theme but 24 variations and 17 small pieces are Int. to M-D, another world! Clever writing. Some amazing movements are found in this work.

Sonata No. 2 Op. 94 (Bo&H 1961). Three movements. 16 p. Introduction to first movement, Lento, then Animato, fluctuating meters. Rhythmically effective, especially in the last movement. Clean textures. D.

4 Nostalgic Preludes (Heugel). M-D.

5 Arabesques (Heugel).

Neuf Inventions Op. 13 (ESC).

Etude du Piano Sur la Gamme Pentatonique Op. 51 (Heugel). 3 sets: Première Suite; Deuxième Suite; Bagatelles Chinoises. The last set is best-known. Easy to Int.

La Quatrième (Heugel 1948-49). Enigmatic title. March, chromatic, large span required.

Suite for Harpsichord Op. 100 (CFP 1966). 13 p. 9 minutes. D.

8 Pieces Op. 88 (TP). Meditation, Intermezzo, Rêverie, Impromptu, Invocation, The Chase, Etude, Burlesque. Varied moods and difficulties. Chromatic sequential motivic treatment.

Expressions (MCA 1951). 10 neoromantic short pieces, different form and title for each.

Badinage (CFP). D.

Etude de Concert b (Hamelle 1923). 3 minutes.

Message Op. 39 (UE 1926).

Petite Suite (Durand 1923). 6 movements. 7½ minutes.

Entretiens Op. 46 (Durand). M-D.

Feuilles libres (Durand).

Histoire de la petit Thérèse de l'Enfant Jésus. Op. 36 (Durand). Int.

Nocturne e♭ (Durand).

Pour petits et grands (Durand). 2 volumes. Int.

4 Préludes (Durand). D.

Scherzo c Op. 3 (Durand).

Voeux (Durand).

Le Monde en Vitrine Op. 75 (Bo&H c. 1948). The composer's impressions of figurines in a "Show-Case." The Greyhounds and the Cow, The Crabs, The Frogs, The Weasel, The Deer. Varied character-pieces in neoclassic style. Large span required. M-D.

Technical Studies on The Five Note Scale (CFP 1936). D.

GEORG PHILIPP TELEMANN (1681-1767) Germany

Telemann, one of the most prolific composers of all time, was inspired by Couperin, Lully and Rameau. Much of his keyboard writing employs thin textures that contribute to the freshness and charm of his rococo miniatures.

Fantasies pour le Clavesin; 3 Douzaines (BB) (Br). 3 dozen small pieces, each dozen reflects a different national style: German, French and Italian.

12 Fantasies (Keller-CFP).

7 Fantasies (Döflein-Schott).

Klavierbüchlein (von Irmer-Schott). 4 dance suites; 4 separate pieces: Moderato, Cantabile, Aria, Praeludium; 2 fugues a, e, for 2 players (duets).

20 Little Fugues (Upmeyer-Nag).

6 Overtures in Vols. 4 and 5 *German Keyboard Music of the 17th and 18th Centuries* (Fischer and Oberdoerffer-Vieweg). All have the same form: a French Overture with two following movements, slow and fast.

Spielstücke für Klavier. (Degen-Br). 36 pieces from "Getreuen Musikmeister", teilweise für Laute. Also includes works by Weiss, Baron, Kreysing, Haltmeier, Goerner and C. Petzold.

Easy Fugues and Short Pieces (IMC). 6 fugues from the *20 little Fugues* each followed by short homophonic movements.

SIMEON ten HOLT, SEE: HOLT, SIMEON ten

SIGISMOND THALBERG (1812-1871) Austria, born Switzerland

Three Operatic Fantasies (MTP).
Moses Op. 33; Barber of Seville Op. 63; Don Pasquale. Annotated by Daniel L. Hitchcock.

12 Studies Op. 26 (Ric).
Contain many tricks of the trade. Most require a virtuoso technique.

Grand Fantasia on God Save the Queen and Rule Britannia Op. 27 (Cramer). D.

Grande Sonate c Op. 56 (1844) (Musica Obscura).

Home! Sweet Home! Fantasia Op. 72. (Augener). D.

Transcription of Pergolesi's "Three Days My Nina" (Musical Scope Publishers).
Once a repertoire piece of Joseffy and Busoni. M-D.

VIRGIL THOMSON (1896-) USA

Five Two-Part Inventions (EV 1926). Tonal essays in 2-part writing with a spicy contemporary flavor. Int. to M-D.

Sonata No. 2 (AMC 1929). Six pages, 3 movements, mixture of styles, witty. Int.

Sonata No. 3 (TP 1930). Five pages, 4 movements. Int.

Sonata No. 4 (EV 1940). Short, humorous. Int.

Ten Etudes (CF 1943-4). Variegated set of clever pieces designed to work out specific technical problems: Repeating Tremolo, Tenor Lead, Fingered Fifths, Fingered Glissando, Double Glissando, For the Weaker Fingers, Oscillating Arm, Five Finger Exercise, Parallel Chords, Ragtime Bass.

Portraits (GS) in four albums. Eight pieces in each album. "The subject sits for his likeness as he would for a painter. An effort has been made to catch in all cases a likeness recognisable to persons acquainted with the sitter." (From the Preface.) Somewhat humorous, but for more serious moments see the neoclassic portrait of Nicolas de Chatelain in Album 3. Many famous people include from Pablo Picasso (No. 1 Album 1) to Lou Harrison (No. 5 Album 1). Int. to M-D.

Nine New Etudes (CF 1954). Graceful, witty, with unusual results. With Trumpet and Horn, Pivoting on the Thumb, Alternating Octaves, Double-Sevenths, The Harp, Chromatic Major Seconds, Chromatic Double-Harmonies (Portrait of Sylvia Marlowe), Broken Arpeggios, Guitar and Mandoline. M-D.

MICHAEL TIPPETT (1905-) Great Britain

Sonata G (Schott). Written in 1942, large-scale 4 movement work, revised by the composer in 1954. Mature pianism required.

Allegro: Theme, 5 variations, brilliant, vigorous, poco maestoso, scherzando, toccata in alternating octaves, theme returns.

Andante molto tranquillo: unassuming melody followed by contrapuntal treatment, quiet closing.

Presto: octaves, cross rhythms, thin textures, quiet closing.

Rondo giocoso con moto: complete rondo, various difficult pianistic figurations. D.

Sonata No. 2 (1962) (Schott). A one-movement work, mainly lyrical, thoroughly worked out, but little development to speak of. Variation and repetition very important. D.

WILLIAM TISDALE (ca. 1570- ?) Great Britain

Complete Keyboard Works transcribed and edited from the FVB and *John Bull Virginal Book* (H. Ferguson-S&B).

Nothing is known about William Tisdale except his name. His music, complete in this edition, so far as is known, is outstanding for the period, with its rich texture and unusual chromatic inflections. Contains 7 pieces, all dance-types: 2 from *JB Virginal Book* and 5 from the FVB.

Pavana Chromatica: Mrs. Katherin Tregian's Paven. Sadness and great lamentation in this dance. FVB II, 278. Howard Ferguson has a sensitive transcription of this (S&B 1958).

ERNST TOCH (1887-1964) Austria, came to USA in 1934

Toch utilized all tones of the chromatic scale in a free way and emphasized linear writing. In many ways his music reminds one of Hindemith.

Burlesken Op. 31 (Schott 1923). Three scherzi. No. 3 *Der Jongleur* is best known. Facility and rhythmic drive required. M-D.

Three Piano Pieces Op. 32 (Schott 1925). Quiet; Delicate without haste; Allegro moderato. Short, require subtle tonal balance and, in the last one, some bravura playing. M-D.

Five Capriccetti Op. 36 (Schott 1925/1936). Short, require sensitivity and facility. M-D.

Kleinstadtbilder Op. 49 (Schott). *From A Small Town.* 14 small pieces that require subtle phrasing and different kinds of touch. Easy to Int.

Five times ten Studies (Schott 1931). A collection dealing with various facets of contemporary piano writing. The pieces are chromatic and atonal; a wide range of problems are investigated.
10 Concert Studies Op. 55 Two volumes.
10 Recital Studies Op. 56.
10 Studies of Medium Difficulty Op. 57.
10 Easy Studies Op. 58.
10 Studies for Beginners Op. 59.

Sonata Op. 47 (Schott 1928). Quasi Toccata; Intermezzo; Allegro. Variety of techniques from two-part writing to thunderous climax of the last movement. Imaginative. M-D.

Profiles Op. 68 (AMP 1948). A cycle of 6 pieces. Calm: flowing dissonant counterpoint; Moderato: changing meters, free counterpoint; Calm, Fluent, Tender: simple lullaby; Merry: scherzo in 5/4, rhythmic, staccato; Slow, Pensive, Very Tender: flowing melody, thin accompaniment; Vigorous, Hammered: perpetual motion, octaves, strong climax. M-D.

Ideas Op. 69 (MCA). Four short sketches. Calm: free, linear 2- and 3-part writing; A Black Dot Dances in My Closed Eyes:

melody, flowing figuration; Vivo: crisp and legato playing required; Allegro: "each note hammered."

Diversions Op. 78a (MCA 1956). Five pieces. M-D.

Sonatinetta Op. 78b (MCA 1958). Three short movements, clever linear writing. M-D.

Three Little Pieces Op. 85 (Belwin-Mills). No. 1 on black keys; No. 2 on white keys; No. 3 on black and white keys. Dissonant, vigorous. Int. to M-D.

Reflections Op. 86 (Belwin-Mills 1961). Five, one-page pieces. Int.

See: Wilton Mason, "The Piano Music of Ernst Toch," PQ, 41, Fall, 1962, 22-25.

CAMILLO TOGNI (1922-   ) Italy

Tre Capricci Op. 38 (SZ 1964). Twelve-tone. D.

HIDENORI TOKUNAGA (1925-   ) Japan

"Following private instruction, Hidenori Tokunaga studied at the Tokyo Music Academy from 1943 to 1946. The main influences from his exposure to Western Music during this period were the rhythmic ideas of Olivier Messiaen and Béla Bartók and the tone cluster usage of Henry Cowell." BBD, 171.

3 Interludes for Piano (TP 1958).

"... based on a 24- and not a 12-tone series in keeping with Tokunaga's theory as to the importance of considering the row and its retrograde form as a single unit, thereby providing the basis for an inversion principle that affords clarity in serial composition. He considers three acoustical elements: traction, repulsion, and synthesis, as having a fusional relationship within the original 24-tone series." BBD, 171. D.

JOHANN WENZEL TOMÁSCHEK (1774-1850) Bohemia, Czechoslovakia

Sonatina G (NV). Homophonic, melodic, easy.

Tre Ditirambi Op. 65 (MAB Vol. 29). c, E, F.
Early examples of the dramatic character piece.

Ten Eclogues (Augener). F, C, A♭, G, E♭, a, B♭, F, B♭, G.
Poetic, somewhat smaller than the *Ditirambi,* in ternary form and pastorale in character.

Eclogue Op. 63/1 (MAB Vol. 20).

Sonata F Op. 21 (Anthology Series *The Solo Sonata* pp. 98-108).
Adagio—Allegro moderato cantabile.
Only one movement of this work is available in a modern edition. The Adagio serves as introduction. Form is clearcut, moments of brilliant figuration.

Rhapsodia Op. 41/1 (MAB Vol. 20).

Selected Pieces of Piano Music (D. Zahn-Henle).

See: Verne W. Thompson, "Wenzel Johann Tomáschek: His Predecessors, His Life, His Piano Works," unpub. diss., University of Rochester, Eastman School of Music, 1955.

THOMAS TOMKINS (ca. 1572-1656) Great Britain

When Thomas Tomkins died in 1656 the school of English virginalists came to a close. His earlier works are more virtuoso-like while the later compositions are more conservative in style.

Keyboard Music, Musica Britannica V (S. D. Tuttle-S&B 1955).
The definitive complete edition, contains 73 works grouped together by forms: Preludes (1-3), plainsong settings (4-20), fancies (21-33), hexachord settings and other ostinati (34-40), pavan-galliard pairs (41-50), pavans and galliards (51-60), variations (61-64), miscellaneous (65-68), doubtful or fragmentary works (69-73).

English Virginalists Vol. 5 (F. Dawes-Schott). 8 pieces from Tomkins Manuscript.

15 Dances (Tuttle, Dart-S&B).

11 Pieces from the Mulliner Book (S&B).

Pavan a. FVB, II, 51. Somber, expressive, chromatic. Half-step motion produces restlessness. This work also exists in a version for 5 viols.

Robin Hood. No. 63 in *Keyboard Music* (above). A set of ten delightful variations. Tomkins appears to have been the only composer of this period to set this melody.

A Toye. Clever, attractive dance, erroneously ascribed to Giles Farnaby in FVB, II, 421. No. 69 in *Keyboard Music.*

HÉCTOR TOSAR (ERRECART) (1923-) Uruguay

In addition to study in his own country, Tosar spent one year in the United States and three years in France on fellowships. His teachers during these years included Aaron Copland, Arthur Honegger, Darius Milhaud, and Jean Rivier.

Danza Criolla (BB 1947). 4 minutes.
Continuous running eighth notes. A few lyric passages, but rhythmic treatment is most interesting. M-D.

Sonatina No. 2 (Ric 1954). 12 minutes. 3 movements. 28 p. Large atonal work, well defined themes, rousing conclusion. D.

Improvisación (ECIC 1941). Extended, ambling "poco animado," four against three, broken chord figuration, espressivo mid-section. M-D.

GIOVANNI MARIA TRABACI (ca. 1580-1647) Italy

Trabaci was active in Naples, primarily as organist-choirmaster and composer.

12 Ricercate, Monumenti di Musica Italiana (Mischiati, Scarpat, Tagliavini-Br) Series I, III. Contrapuntal style; much beauty in these pieces, especially the inner voices.

See: Roland Jackson, "The Inganni and the Keyboard music of Trabaci," JAMS, 21, Summer 1968, 204-08." Artusi defined an inganno as a type of thematic variant wherein the melodic intervals might differ but the hexachord syllables attached to the notes remain the same. Trabaci identifies a number of inganni as these appear in the ricercari of his two keyboard volumes of 1603 and 1615. These inganni involve (1) a modulation from one hexachord to another during the theme, (2) a substitution of a single note from some other hexachord, (3) a combination of these. (Author.)

EINAR TRAERUP-SARK (1921-) Denmark

Sonatine No. 1 Op. 2 (WH).

Sonatine No. 2 Op. 4 (WH).

Lette klaverstykker Op. 5a (WH).

Deux Humoresques Miniature Op. 5b (WH).

Toccata Op. 6 (WH).

Sma klaverstykker (WH).

HAROLD TRIGGS (1900-) USA

6 Surrealist Afterludes (JF). A suite of 6 light-weight pieces, catchy titles. M-D.

Danza Braziliana (CF 1956). Well-conceived, enthusiastic, powerful. M-D.

LESTER TRIMBLE (1923-) USA

Trimble acquired most of his music education at the Carnegie Institute of Technology, where he studied composition with Nikolai Lopatnikoff. Further study was with Darius Milhaud and Arthur Honegger.

5 Episodes (MCA).
Serial, see especially No. 3. Sweeping, various moods. D.

GILBERT TRYTHALL (1930-) USA

Teaches at George Peabody College, Nashville, Tennessee.

Suite for Piano Op. 20. Commissioned by the Tennessee MTA and the MTNA 1969. 5 p. (Available on loan from MTNA).
Prelude: Largo

Nocturne: Andante
Caprice: Allegro—Lento—Allegro.
Contrasted movements, MC style. More musical than technical problems. Int.

EDUARD TUBIN (1905-) Sweden, born Estonia

Tubin's works are based on the folk music of his native country.

Sonatine (Korlings Forlag 1942). 3 movements. 19 p. Ample dimensions. Above-average pianistic equipment required. M-D.

Ballade (Korlings Forlag).

Quatre chansons populaires (Korlings Forlag).

Sonat (Eriks Musikhandel).

JOAQUÍN TURINA (1882-1949) Spain

Turina spent some time in France and was influenced by impressionism. He has written a large repertoire for the piano. Most of his works are in a semipopular style, always colorful, exhibiting a fine mastery of form. (UME) (Sal) and (ESC) publish a large variety of Turina's compositions.

Miniatures (1930) (Schott). 8 little pieces with impressionistic overtones. Int.

Trois Variations (1926) (ESC). Varied simple harmonizations of a melody. Int.

Préludes (1928) (Heugel). Delicate sounds, based on folk songs, diatonic melodies. Int.

Variations on a theme of Chopin (c. 1961) (Sal). Romantic variations on the Prelude A. M-D.

Danzas Gitanas Op. 55 (Sal). Two volumes, 5 pieces in each. Interesting rhythmically. See especially No. 5 in Vol. I Sacromonte.

Niñerias Op. 21 (Sal). Suite of 8 descriptive pieces, casual, flowing. See Prelude and Fugue No. 1. Int. to M-D. Available separately both sets.

Niñerias Op. 56 (Sal). A second set of 8 pieces. See especially Carnaval des enfants.

Silhouettes Op. 70 (Sal). Five descriptive pieces, available separately. L'aqueduc, La tour de la véla (a light dance), La puerta del sol (2 contrasting moods), La tour de l'or, Le phare de Cadix (brilliant closing piece).

Album de Viaje (IMC). Five descriptive "Travel Impressions." Int. to M-D.

Femmes d'Espagne (Sal). Two volumes, 3 pieces in the first, 5 in the second. Portraits of Spanish ladies.

Jardins d'Andalousie (UME). Suite of 3 pieces.

Cadeña de Seguidillas Op. 41/1 (OUP). Int.

FERDINANDO TURINI (1740-1812) Italy

Newman speaks highly (SCE, 296) of these works and laments the fact that only nine of the twenty-four sonatas attributed to Turini may be extant. Vigorous rhythmic treatment, melodic leaps, scalar writing, rich harmonic vocabulary place Turini in the forefront of pre-Romantic composers.

5 Sonatas, I Classici della Musica Italiana, XXXIII.

Sonata D♭ (CF) found in *Le Maîtres du Clavecin* (Kohler-Litolff).

Presto g (Carisch) in *Italian Harpsichord Compositions,* etude-like, perpetual motion figuration.

Sonata g (Keller-CFP) in *Alte Meister der Klaviermusik,* Vol. 3 (See Anthologies and Collections, General).

DANIEL GOTTLOB TÜRK (1750-1813) Germany

Best known for his well-organized *Klavierschule* 1789. This famous pedagogue published forty-eight sonatas for keyboard between 1776 and 1793. The *Klavierschule* is available in a facsimile edition edited by E. R. Jacobi (Br). Only a few of the sonatas are available in contemporary editions.

Sonatas e, C, A, D, (K&S). Available separately.

Collections of teaching pieces: *29 Easy Pieces* (Döflein-Schott); *46 Pieces for Beginners* (Döflein-Schott); *49 Pieces for Small Hands* 1792 (Auerbach-Nag); *60 Handstücke für angehende Klavierspieler* 1792 (W. Serauky-Litolff); *12 Pieces* (Litolff); *49 Pieces for Beginners* (K); *Pieces for Piano Study* (O. Jonas-SB).

GEIRR TVEITT (1908-) Norway

Tveitt could be considered a nationalist composer greatly influenced by the folk music of Norway, especially Hardanger, his particular province. He is very prolific, having written twenty-nine sonatas, five concerti, etc.

Twelve two-part Inventions (NMO) 4 groups of 3 modes. Easy to M-D.

Sonata No. 29 Op. 129 (NMO 1950). 3 movements. 43 p. D. Second movement is a set of 19 variations. Plenty of ideas but not always well worked through. Virtuoso technique required.

U

FLORO M. UGARTE (1884-) Argentina

5 Preludes (Ric 1947). 18 minutes.
5 moods, MC: Sad, Festive, Romantic, Dramatic, Cheerful. Int. to M-D.

De mi Tierra (Ric). Suite No. 1 (1923). 17 minutes.
Three pieces that pay hommage to the composer's country. Poetic, colorful. Suite No. 2 (1934). 17 minutes.

Ronroncitos (Ric 1952). Cinco expressiones de termura. 8 minutes.

Arrullo (Ric).

Lamento campero (Ric).

Vidala (Ric).

ERNST LUDWIG URAY (1906-) Austria

Thema, Variationen und Fuge (UE 1933). D.
In Brahms-Reger tradition. Especially brilliant fugue.

Sonata breve No. 2 (Dob.)

ERICH URBANNER (1936-) Austria

"Urbanner considers the imagination and improvisatory prowess of the composer to be better stimulated by developing a basic series than extending the serial principles. Personal experience has led him to renounce total serialization, which he regards as sterile and inaudible." BBD, 172. Urbanner teaches at the Vienna Academy.

11 Bagatelles (UE 1959).

Volume I in series *Libelli Dodecaphonic.* Contrasted short pieces, some only one-half page, serial technique, extreme clarity. Designed to introduce varied techniques of contemporary music to younger students. Easier to play than to read.

5 Pieces (A. Peschek 1965). Serial D.

Meditation for Piano (Dob 1966). Serial D.

VLADIMIR USSACHEVSKY (1911-) USA

A Piano Piece (AME 1950).

V

FARTEIN VALEN (1887-1952) Norway

Palestrina, J. S. Bach and Schönberg were major influences on Valen's compositions. Valen developed a 12-tone style similar to Schönberg's but "both Bjarne Kortsen and Humphrey Searle have noted an important distinction between Valen and Schönberg with regard to harmony apparent in the piano music. Valen does not rely on the series as a source of his vertical structure. Homophonic chords are, in fact, infrequent in his work. His use of polyphonic structures does, however, bear some relationship to a tonal style." BBD, 173.

Legende Op. 1 (Lyche).

Sonata No. 1 c♯ Op. 2 (WH). Large three-movement work in Brahms-Reger style. Complex, moments of great beauty. See opening of second movement, Adagio.

4 Piano Pieces Op. 22 (Lyche 1935). Nachtstück, Valse noble, Lied ohne Worte, Gigue. M-D.

Variations Op. 23 (Lyche 1936). 12 serial variations. D.

Gavotte and Musette Op. 24 (Lyche 1936).

Prelude and Fugue Op. 28 (Lyche 1937). 2-voice Prelude, 3-voice Fugue, both atonal. D.

Preludes Op. 29/1, 2, (Lyche 1948). Austere. D.

Intermezzo Op. 36 (Lyche 1939). 6 p. Beautiful, serial. D.

Sonata No. 2 Op. 38 (Lyche 1941). 20 minutes.

See: Bjarne Kortsen, *Fartein Valen: Life and Music.* Oslo: J. G. Tanum, 1965. 3 volumes. Vol. 1 His life, Vol. 2 musical examples from the music, Vol. 3 Valen's works, Op. 1-44.

JAN VAŇHAL (1739-1813) Bohemia, Czechoslovakia

Easy Sonatinas. 16 Little Pieces (Millerova-Artia). Excellent teaching material.

Two Sonatinas (Vol. 17 MAB, Artia). Same level as above. Also contained in this volume are sonatinas by Fr. X. Dussek, Benda, and Worzischek.

SÁNDOR VERESS (1907-) Hungary

Veress studied with Bartók and Kodály. He is Professor of Music at the University of Berne.

7 Danze Ungherese (SZ 1938). Nos. 5 and 6 have most interest. M-D.

15 Kleine Klavierstücke (Magyar Kórus 1936). Easy. In style of Bartók's *For Children.*

Sonatina (SZ 1932). 3 movements. 8 p. 6½ minutes. Refreshing. M-D.
Toccata 1; Minuetto-Musette; Toccata 2.

Fingerlarks (Cserépfalvi 1947). Int.

6 Csárdás (Cserépfalvi 1938). M-D. Best are Nos. 5 and 6.

JOHN VERRALL (1908-) USA

Verrall teaches at the University of Washington in Seattle.

Préludes en Suite (AMC). 7 short pieces, varied moods. Pianistic, requires more effort than appears. Int.

Autumn Sketches (New Valley Press 1956). 14 minutes.

Theme and Variations (ACA 1944). 8 minutes. 10 variations in neoclassic style. Finale consists of last 4 variations in Rondo form. M-D.

4 Pieces for Piano Solo (Univ. of Washington Press 1949). 12 minutes.

Sonata (ACA 1951). 15 minutes.
First movement: many tempo changes; Vivace: 3/4-2/4 meter; Adagio e serioso: movement ends with return to tempo of first movement but slows down to a PPP ending. MC.

Sketches and Miniatures (Valley Music Press 1954). 15 p. 17 minutes. 10 pieces.

LOUIS VIERNE (1870-1937) France

3 Nocturnes Op. 35 (Sal).

12 Préludes Op. 38 (Henn). 2 books.

Solitude Op. 44 (Senart 1918). Poem in 4 parts.

HEITOR VILLA-LOBOS (1887-1959) Brazil

Villa-Lobos was one of the most prolific composers of this century. Volume 3 of *Composers of The Americas,* Pan American Union, Washington, D.C., 1957, lists 727 compositions written by him. Villa-Lobos once told the late Olin Downs, "I compose in the folk style. I utilize thematic idioms in my own way, and subject to my own development. An artist must do this. He must select and transmit the material given him by his people. I have always done this and it is from these sources, spiritual as well as practical, that I have drawn my art." (Marcos Romero, *Composers of the Americas.* Vol. III. Washington, D. C., Pan American Union, 1957, p. 9.) This great Brazilian artist began composing in a post-romantic style, moved to impressionism and folklore, later experimented with classicism, and finally synthesized all these elements. Some works are simple and easily understood while others are abstract and highly complex. It is helpful to remember that this composer wrote for many different publics. His keyboard style often involves a wide dynamic range, complex cross-rhythms, improvisatory sweeps, lush sonorities, and a unique manner of handling the pedals.

This list of works is not complete. Vicente Vitale (Irmaos Vitale Industria e Comercio Ltda, Rua da Quitanda 17-1 andar, Rio de Janeiro) and Arthur Napoleão, (Casa Napoleão, Sampaio Araujo & Cia., 122 Avenida Rio Branco, Rio de Janeiro, Brazil) list many pieces not easily available in this country.

Amazonas (ESC). Bailado indigena brasileira. M-D.

Cirandinhas (ESC). Suite of nine moderately easy pieces based on popular children's themes.

Ciclo Brasileiro (Consolidated Music Publishing 1936-37). M-D.
Native Planting Song: quiet, melody in tenor, widespread chordal figuration in RH.
Minstrel Impressions: lengthy, rich sonorities, waltz, improvisatory treatment.
Jungle Festival: alternating hands, octaves, cross-rhythms, brilliant RH figuration.
Dance of the White Indian: alternating chords and octaves, energetic, bravura.

Bachianas Brasileiras No. 4 (Consolidated Music Publishing 1941). M-D. Brazilian and Bachlike elements combined. Preludio—Introducao; Coral; Aria; Dansa. Dansa is in collection *Latin American Art Music* (GS).

Carnaval das Crianças Brasileiras (Arthur Napoleão 1919-20). Eight pieces. Nos. 2 and 3 published separately by (EBM) and (Consolidated Music Publishing). No. 2 O Chicote do Diabinho (The Devil's Whip), short, light, brilliant, trills, fast, repeated chords, M-D; No. 3. A Manha da Pierette (Pierette's Hands), playful, attractive, Int.

Ten Pieces on Popular Children's Folk Tunes of Brazil (Mer). Two volumes, five pieces in each. Short, simple settings, traditional harmony. Int.

Guia Prático (1932-1935). Eleven collections containing about half a dozen pieces in each. Settings of popular Brazilian children's songs that range in difficulty from Int. to M-D.
Album I (Consolidated Music Publishing). See especially No. 1 Dawn.
Album II (ESC). See No. 4 Samba.

Album III (ESC). See No. 1 Le Petit berger.
Album VI (Mer). See No. 4 Anda a roda.
Album VII (Mer). See No. 5 O Corcunda.
Album VIII (Consolidated Music Publishing). See Nos. 1 O limao and No. 4 Pai Francisco.
Album IX (Consolidated Music Publishing). See No. 3 O ciranda, a cirandinha.
Album XI (Southern). See No. 6 Long Live the Carnival, colorful virtuoso writing.

Francette et Piá (1929) (ESC). Suite of ten pieces based on story of little Brazilian Indian who went to France and met a little French girl. French and Brazilian tune are combined in each piece. Requires imagination. Int.

The Three Maries. (1939) (CF). Short, modal set based on a Brazilian folk story. Int.
Alnitah: requires brilliance and facility.
Alnilam: lyric, short staccato contrasting mid-section.
Mintika: facility, careful tonal balance and free pedaling required.

Cirandas (Arthur Napoleão 1926). Collection of sixteen pieces based on popular Brazilian themes. Int. to M-D.

Prole do Bébé (The Baby's Dolls) (Series I 1918) (EBM) (ESC) (K). This set of pieces came into being as a result of the composer meeting Artur Rubinstein. They are based on Brazilian folklore and are permeated with an imaginative impressionistic flavor. Int. to M-D.
Branquinha (The Porcelain Doll) Bell-like sonorities, pedaling and balance problems.
Moreninha (The Paper Doll) (EBM separately). Cross-rhythms, brilliant, 16th-note tremolos.
Caboclinha (The Clay Doll). Samba rhythm, chordal, steady 16ths.
Mulatinha (The Rubber Doll) (EBM separately). Varied textures and tempi, improvisatory.
Negrinha (The Wooden Doll). Brisk, alternating hands in 16ths.
A Pobrezinha (The Rag Doll). Short, chordal, ostinato har-

monies, melancholy.
O Polichinello (Punch) (Ric separately). Fast alternating hands in 16ths, breathless.
A Bruxa (The Witch Doll). Lengthy, broad scope, varied textures, climatic.

Prole do Bébé (The Little Animals) (Series II 1921) (ESC). More difficult and longer than Series I.
A Baratinha de Papel (The Little Paper Bug). Study in cross accents.
O Gatinha de Papelão (The Little Cardboard Cat). Atmospheric, ostinato figures.
O Camondongo de Massa (The Little Toy Mouse). Brilliant, bravura playing required.
O Cachorrinho de Borracha (The Little Rubber Dog). Slow, moves to sonorous climax, short.
O Cavalinho de Pau (The Little Wooden Horse). Lively, cross-rhythms, FFFF climax, ends softly.
O Boizinho de Chumbo (The Little Tin Ox). Large scope, octaves, double notes, big chords. D.
O Passarinho de Pano (The Little Cloth Bird). Cross rhythms, trills in both hands. D.
O Ursinho de Algodão (The Little Cotton Bear). Lively, alternating hands, double notes. D.
O Lobozinho de Vidro (The Little Glass Wolf). A ferocious toccata, broad sweeps. D.

Suite Floral Op. 97 (Consolidated Music Publishing 1916-17).
Idílio no Rêde (Summer Idyll). Lyric, broken-chord figuration divided between hands.
Camponeza Cantadeira (A Singing Country Girl). Melodic, irregular groupings, quiet close.
Alegria na Horta (Joy in the Garden). Lively, colorful dance, varied textures. D.

Saudades Das Selvas Brasileiras (Brazilian Forest Memories) (ESC).
Two pieces. M-D.
No. 1 Lively mosaiclike melodies over ostinato bass figures, exotic.

No. 2 Brisk, rhythmic, chordal, four against three.

Alma Brasileira-Choros No. 5 (EBM) (ESC). Syncopations, lament over chord and broken-chord accompaniment, rubato, atmospheric. M-D.

Rudepoema (ESC). This "rough poem" is the composer's most extended piano solo. Virtuoso writing throughout. D.

Hommage à Chopin (Merion Music) (ESC). Two pieces.
No. 1 Nocturne: lyric impressionism. M-D.
No. 2 Ballade: broad scope, romantic, brilliant. D.

Petizada (PIC c. 1954). Six delightful 2-page works. Simple tunes, mainly 2 voices. Easy to Int. Published separately.

Poema Singelo (Consolidated Music Publishing 1942). Variations on a simple tune, alternating chordal treatment between hands, vivace chromatic triplets, opening Andantino closes piece. M-D.

Caixinha de Música Quebrada (The Broken Little Music Box). (Consolidated Music Publishing 1931). Syncopated chromatic RH accompaniment over broken-chord figuration in LH, large sweeps, catchy closing. M-D.

Simples Colentânea (Consolidated Music Publishing 1917). Three pieces.
No. 1 Valse Mística: fast, broken melodic figuration, expressive mid-section, FFF closing. M-D.
No. 2 Um Berço Encantado: improvisatory, atmospheric, broad sweeps. M-D.
No. 3 Rhodante: fast triplet figuration, glissandi, repeated notes, double trills, brilliant closing. D.

Brinquedo De Roda (The Toy Wheel) (PIC). Six pieces published separately. Charming realizations based on Brazilian children's tunes, contrasted, clever. Int.

See: Frina Boldt, "A Survey of Selected Piano Works of Heitor Villa-Lobos," unpub. paper, Indiana University, Latin American Music Center, 1966. 25 p.

JAN AUGUSTIN VÍTAŠEK (1770-1839) Bohemia, Czechoslovakia

Drei Vortragsstücke (Artia).

Tanzreigen in Album *I Classici Boemici,* Vol. 14 MAB.

ROMAN VLAD (1919-) Italy, born Rumania

Vlad began utilizing serial techniques in 1939. He studied with Alfredo Casella but his interest in twelve-tone techniques was stimulated after working with Frank Martin and Luigi Dallapiccola.

Studi Dodecafonici per Pianoforte (SZ 1943, revised 1957). Four contrasted 12-tone studies. In these pieces . . . "a segment of the basic row recurs in the transpositions so frequently that it provides a source of structural unity. Vlad frequently creates a complex of two rows; at such times this recurring segment of the basic row is conspicuous." BBD, 176.

Romeo and Juliet Suite (Terry-Ric).

WLADIMIR VOGEL (1896-) Switzerland, born Russia

Vogel was the first Swiss composer to use twelve-tone technique.

Etude-Toccata (Bo&H 1926). Virtuoso writing.

Variétude (Bo&H 1931-2). ". . . contains chaconne-like repetitions of the principle theme, suggestive of a rhythmic series." BBD, 178. D.

Epitaffio per Alban Berg (Ric 1936). D. The tone row is a series of 23 tones using 9 pitches derived from the words "Alban Berg auf's Grab Friede!" and develops in the manner of a passacaglia. The row appears continuously in one or the other voices. Very expressive in spite of strict control. "The brilliance of much of the figuration is typical of Vogel's style. The work is an effective example of application of serial writing to a traditional form." BBD, 178.

Nature vivante (HV c. 1962). 8 p. Expressionistic pieces: Strophe d'album, Prélude gris, Nettement désagreable, Morceau poétique, Lasse et plaintif-Joyeaux. M-D.

JOSEPH VOGLER (1749-1814) Germany

Preludes and Suites (A. Mirovitch-EHM 1954).
Six preludes, three suites, one to three pages long. Unusual pieces. Int.

ALEXANDER VOORMOLEN (1895-   ) The Netherlands

Voormolen studied with Ravel and Roussel in Paris so it is natural that his music reflects both French and Dutch influences. His style of writing changed around 1930 when his music began to developed a more intense expressiveness.

Suite de Clavecin (Alsbach 1921). Ouverture, G, Siciliènne, Toccatina. M-D.

Suite No. 1 (Sal 1916). 3 movements.

Falbalas (Sal 1915). M, S, Gavotte. M-D.

Livre des enfants (Sal 1923-25). 2 vols. Int. 12 pieces.

Tableaux des Pays-Bas (Sal 1919-24). 2 vols. Dutch landscapes pictured in impressionist style.

Sonnet (Sal 1922). 3 minutes.

Scène et danse érotique (Sal 1922). 8 minutes. D.

Sonata (Alsbach 1947). 12 minutes.

Eléphants (Sal 1951). 8 minutes.

Eline (Sal 1951). 8 minutes.

JOHANN HUGO VOŘÍŠEK,
See: JOHANN HUGO WORŽISCHEK

BERNARD WAGENAAR (1894-1971) USA, born The Netherlands, came to USA 1920

For many years on the faculty of The Juilliard School of Music.

Ciacona (EBM 1942). A four-bar chordal phrase varied seven times. Chordal with florid melodies, short, dissonant, dramatic closing. M-D.

Sonata (AMC 1920). Three movements. Broad, large-scale opening movement leads to an atmospheric, lyric Improvisation, followed by closing Rondoletto. Widely-spaced sonorities, complete exploitation of instrument's resources. D.

Saltarello (TP). Polytonal, 2 voices, gay, dancelike. Int.

Six Short Tales (Chappell).

GEORG CHRISTOPH WAGENSEIL (1715-1777) Germany

4 Divertimenti (Nag No. 36). Similar to C.P.E. Bach *Prussian* and *Württemberg* Sonatas. Three and four movements, homophonic, thin textures, pianistic figuration.

Sonata F Op. 4 (Köhler-Litolff). Also in Pauer collection *Alte Meister,* Vol. II.

Das Glockengeläute zu Rom, Dem Vatikan (K. Nemetz-Fiedler, OBV) *Chimes in the Vatican in Rome.*

JOSEPH WAGNER (1900-) USA

Wagner studied with Nadia Boulanger and Alfredo Casella. He is composer-in-residence at Pepperdine College in California.

Sonata b (Southern 1946). 24 p. Three movements. Well-contrasted ideas, shifting accents, quartal and quintal harmonies, some jazz syncopation. Advanced pianism required.

Pastorale and Toccata (Southern 1948). Pastorale is lyric, melodic; Toccata highly rhythmic. M-D.

Four Miniatures (Southern 1959). Preface, S, Berceuse, March. Tonal and polytonal, humorous, clever. M-D.

Two Interludes (Robert B. Brown Music Co.).

Sonatina (Senart 1934).

Four Landscapes (Southern 1936).

RICHARD WAGNER (1813-1883) Germany

Grosse Sonata A (Gerig c. 1960). 3 movements FSF, 28 p. M-D. Dates from 1831 when Wagner was studying with Theodor Weinlig at Leipzig. Not prime Wagner. Many clichés and trite writing abound. The composer tried his hand at fugal writing in the last movement.

Sonata B♭ (Br&H) (Musica Obscura). Four movements, 23 p. M-D. See SSB: 381-3. Dates from 1831. First and last movements make much use of Alberti bass.
Allegro con brio: 4/4 SA design; Larghetto: 3/8; Menuetto and Trio: Bellini-like; Finale-Allegro Vivace: Rondo.

Album-Sonate A♭ (Schott c. 1853) (Musica Obscura). 2 sections, 16 p. Dedicated to Mathilde Wesendonck. Salonlike, restful, sweet, many cliché harmonies. Easier than the above listed works.

Fantasia f♯ (Kahnt c. 1905) (Musica Obscura). 20 p. Sectionalized, recitativo passages, chromatic, quite lovely, many starts and stops. Sounds more like the operatic Wagner.

See: W. S. Newman, "Wagner's Sonatas," Studies in Romanticism, 7/3, Spring 1968, 128-39. A discussion of the circumstances, dates, publication, and content of five known piano sonatas by Richard Wagner, with special reference to Wagner's relation to Liszt and the Wesendonck family.

RUDOLF WAGNER-RÉGENY (1903-1969) Germany, born Hungary

Spinettmusik (UE 1934). Int.

2 Sonatas (UE 1943). Published together.
Sonata I: 4 movements, 9 p.
Sonata II: 3 movements, 10 p. Both are neoclassic in style. M-D.

Hexameron (UE 1943). 6 moderately easy pieces.

Zwei Tänze für Palucca (UE 1950). Clever studies in variable meters. 12-tone. M-D.

Klavierstücke für Gertie (Bo&H 1951). Variable meters. M-D.

5 French Pieces (Bo&Bo 1951). Meter studies. Free 12-tone techniques. D.

7 Fugues (Bo&Bo 1953). Concise. Each one dedicated to a well-known friend whose style is imitated in the writing: Carl Orff, Boris Blacher, G. von Einem, Kurt Weill, Paul Hindemith, Ernst Krenek, Darius Milhaud.

Little Piano Book (UE).

ARNOLD M. WALTER (1902-   ) Canada, born Austria

Walter completed his studies at the Universities of Berlin and Prague. He is Director of the Royal Conservatory of Music of the University of Toronto.

Sonata (G. V. Thompson 1950). 3 movements. 15 minutes. FSF. Adagio introduction to first movement. Second movement is modal, subdued, mournful. Advanced pianism required.

Suite (OUP 1945). 10 minutes. Prelude, Adagio, Fugue. Well-defined ideas, chromatic. Calls for mature musicianship.

ROBERT WARD (1917-) USA

Ward studied composition with Howard Hanson, Frederick Jacobi and Aaron Copland. He is President of the North Carolina School of the Arts in Winston-Salem.

Lamentation (Mer 1948). Somber largo builds to a sonorous climax, quartal harmony, a few brilliant octaves. M-D.

Bagatelle (Highgate Press 1949).

Angels (Highgate Press 1949).

Scherzo (Highgate Press 1950).

DAVID WARD-STEINMAN (1936-) USA

Ward-Steinman teaches at San Diego State College, California.

3 Lyric Preludes (Highgate 1965). For piano or organ. Clear textures, rhythmic interest. M-D.
Moderately Fast; Very Slow; Not too slow: contains a few clusters.

Elegy for Martin Luther King (Galaxy 1969).
Short, poignant processional ode. Uses palm clusters as an accompaniment. Mainly diatonic melody. Part of "We Shall Overcome" is worked in. 3 minutes.

Improvisations on Children's Songs (Lee Roberts).
Contemporary treatment of "Twinkle, Twinkle Little Star", "Happy Birthday" and "Frère Jacques." Int.

3 Miniatures (CFE). Int.

Trois improvisations sur un thème de D. Milhaud (Sal).

BEN WEBER (1916-) USA

Weber's "works lie in the region between atonal chromaticism and the twelve-tone system." ICM, 619.

5 Bagatelles Op. 2 (TP 1938). Short pieces in 12-tone technique. M-D.

3 Piano Pieces Op. 23 (Bomart 1946). Nos. 1 and 2 are freely serial while No. 3 is atonal.

Episodes Op. 26a (CFE 1957). Well-concealed serial technique.

Piano Suite No. 2 Op. 27 (CFE 1948). 4 contrasted movements. 12-tone.

Fantasia Op. 25 (EBM 1946). 8½ minutes. Large-scale set of variations requiring advanced pianism. Weber's most important work for piano solo.

Humoreske (LG 1963). In album *New Music for the Piano.*

Lyric Piece Op. 40a (EBM). In album *American Composers of Today.*

CARL MARIA von WEBER (1786-1826) Germany

Weber's piano works may be considered to be period pieces of charm and imagination showing how well Weber explored the potential of the instrument during his day. A fluent technique is required to perform any of the representative works and a large span is frequently needed. Orchestral influence often shows in Weber's piano writing which is characterized by large skips, brilliant passages in thirds, sixths, octaves, dramatic crescendos and awkward stretches.

Editions:

(CFP) has the complete piano works in three volumes:
- I: Four sonatas Op. 24, 39, 49, 70.
- II: Op. 7, 12, 21, 40, 62, 65, 72, 79. Concert piece, Invitation to the Dance, Polonaise, Rondo, Variations Op. 7 and 40, etc.
- III: Variations and Concertos. Variations: Op. 2, 5, 6, 9, 28, 55. Concertos: Op. 11, 32.

Four Sonatas (Volbach-CFP) (Liszt-Augener) (Durand) (Tagliapietra-Ric) (Riss-Arbeau-Heugel).

No. 1 C Op. 24 (1812). Allegro C; Adagio F; Menuetto: Allegro e, Trio E; Rondo: Presto C. Symmetrical thematic structure and lack of tonal integration hinder effective opening movement. Adagio contains some dramatic moments, variation technique, and an unconvincing formal design. A short and fast Minuet, more like a Scherzo, and the famous Rondo (Perpetual Motion) round off this work. Final movement is available separately from (Durand) (CF) (Ric) (GS) (O. Jonas-Simrock). (Simrock) edition includes a second version by Brahms for LH and a version by Tchaikowsky, also for LH.

No. 2 A♭ Op. 39 (1814-16) (Cortot-Sal).
Allegro moderato con spirito ed assai legato A♭; Andante C-c; Menuetto capriccioso A♭: Presto assai; Rondo: Moderato e molto grazioso A♭. A rich texture is apparent throughout a noble and original opening movement. Orchestrated with highly contrasting figuration, tremolos and arpeggiated chords. Expansive Andante is lyric in conception although a large climax provides strong contrast. A vivacious and whimsical Menuetto capriccio follows. Concluding graceful movement contains some beautifully elided sections.

No. 3 d Op. 49 (1816) (GS).
Allegro feroce d-D; Andante can moto B♭; Rondo: Presto D. This sonata has been sub-titled the "Demoniac," but not by Weber. First movement has Beethoven characteristics, especially the contrast of thematic material. Simple structure and ornamental decoration characterize the Andante con moto. Presto, in 3/8, contains five different ideas, one an elegant waltz rhythm, leads to one of Weber's most effective conclusions. This movement is effective played separately and is also known as "Allcgro di Bravura."

No. 4 e Op. 70 (1819-22).
Moderato e; Menuetto: Presto vivace ed energico e-D; Andante quasi Allegretto, consolante C; Finale (La Tarantella): Prestissimo e. Finest of the four sonatas, this work shows refinement of numerous elements seen in the earlier sonatas. Moderato is built on two contrasting ideas. Leggermente murmurando is called for in the Trio of the Menuetto. A Schubertian quality pervades the third movement which resembles a rondo but is more mosaic in actual design. La Tarantella is a unique piece of virtuoso writing.

Momento capriccioso B♭ Op. 12 (1808) (Cortot-Sal). Sparkling pianissimo staccato study, highly effective.

Grande Polonaise E♭ Op. 21 (1808) (Georgii-Schott) (Seak-Ric). Florid pianistic writing, dotted notes, contrasted second episode.

Rondo Brillante "La Gaieté" E♭ Op. 62 (1819) (Cortot-Sal) (Georgii-Schott) (Kroll-Ric) (Durand) (CF). Inspired by the dance, includes a variety of technical problems, effective.

Invitation to the Dance D♭ Op. 65 (1819) (Cortot-Sal) (Georgii-Schott) (CFP) (Br&H) (CF) (GS) (Durand). Weber's most popular piano work, a rondo design with numerous thematic fragments woven into a successful whole. Brilliant. Exquisite when properly performed.

Polacca Brillante E Op. 72 (1819) (Cortot-Sal) (Georgii-Schott) (Kroll-Ric). Dotted rhythms, similar to Op. 62 but less difficult.

Less interesting are the eight sets of variations. They employ mainly melodic decoration and are highly sectionalized.

Variations on an Original Theme C Op. 2 (1800) (CFP).

Variations on a Theme from Castor and Pollux F Op. 5 (1804) (CFP).

Variations on a Theme from Samori B♭ Op. 6 (1804) (CFP). With violin and cello ad lib.

Variations on Bianchi's 'Vien' quà, Dorina Bella' C Op. 7 (1807) (CFP) (GS).

Variations on an Original Theme F Op. 9 (1808) (CFP).

Variations on a Theme from Méhul's 'Joseph' C Op. 28 (1812) (CFP). More virtuoso.

Variations on "Schöne Minka" c Op. 40 (1915) (CFP).

Variations on a Gipsy Air C Op. 55 (1817) (CFP).

Seven Ecossaises (Werner-Curwen). Excellent teaching material.

Two Waltzes (Werner-Curwen). Tuneful, easy.

Twelve German Dances Op. 4 (1801) (Frey-Schott).

Book of Dances (Wolters-Schott). Contra-Dances, Waltzes, German Dances, Max-Waltz.

Nine German Dances (Beer-HV).

Twenty Easy Dances (Frickert-Mitteldeutscher Verlag). German Dances, Waltzes, Ecossaises, two four-hand German Dances. Attractive format.

Miscellaneous Compositions (Mason-GS).
Op. 12, 21, 62, 65, 72, Les adieux Op. 81, Op. 7, 37 with a biographical sketch.

Pièces Célèbres (Riss-Arbeau-Heugel).

ANTON von WEBERN (1883-1945) Austria

Webern's influence on twentieth-century composition cannot be over emphasized. He is a seminal figure in our century. However, his contribution to piano literature is small. 1924 was the first year Webern used serial technique as advocated by Schönberg.

Sonatensatz (CF 1906). This rondo movement "belongs to a large group of works, written about 1906, that are indicative of the ferment in harmonic concepts soon to lead to the abolition of traditional tonality." From the Preface by Hans Moldenhauer. A key signature is present, more traditional in harmonic and melodic treatment than his later style. M-D.

Satz für Klavier (CF 1906). Fine example of SA design, tonality present although in a very fluid state, chromatic, post-romantic qualities. M-D.

Klavierstück (1925) (UE). Posthumous work, published in 1966. Short minuet, sparse textures, pointillistic writing. M-D.

Kinderstück (1924) (CF). 17 bar work, provides an excellent introduction to serialism. Based on 12-tone row, one of Webern's earliest examples of this technique. Webern had intended to write a series of pieces for children but this was the only one finished. Int.

Variations Op. 27 (1936) (UE). Webern once described this work as "kind of a suite." It is a unique work with the barest sonorities, extreme skips, changeable rhythms, and dynamics. Based on a row, divided into three movements. Mirror canon is constantly in use throughout the piece. Dedicated to Edward Steuermann. D.

See: Walter Kolneder, *Anton Webern, An Introduction to His Works*. Translated by Humphrey Searle. Berkeley: University of California Press, 1968.

Peter Westergaard, "Some Problems in Rhythmic Theory and Analysis", Perspectives of New Music, 1, Fall, 1962, 180-91. "Webern and Total Organization: an analysis of the second movement of the Op. 27 Variations," Perspectives of New Music, 1, Spring 1963, 107-20.

MATTHIAS WECKMANN (ca. 1619-1674) Germany

Collected Works, Das Erbe Deutscher Music, second series, Vol. IV, Braunschweig: H. Litolff, 1942.

See: Anthologies and Collections, General: *Aus Historischen Klavierkonzerten.* (Buchmayer-Br&H) Vols. I, II and III.

KARL WEIGL (1881-1949) Austria

Bilder und Geschichten Op. 2 (UE 1910). Pictures and Tales. 6 pieces.
Late 19th-century approach to folklike tunes. Attractive titles and music. No. 3, "Stork, lanky long-legs" is clever. Int.

28 Variations über ein achttaktiges Thema Op. 15 (UE). Schönberg influence. D.

5 Nachtphantasien Op. 13 (Leuckhart).

LEO WEINER (1885-1960) Hungary

Weiner's works are not "modern" in the sense that we apply the term to his compatriot Bartók. Nevertheless, he is revered in Hungary as a musician who exerted immeasurable influence on an entire generation of musicians.

31 Hungarian Peasant Songs (ZV). Vol. I: 1-19; Vol. II: 20-31. Some are short, others are extended, all have melodic and rhythmic charms.
See especially No. 17. Easy to Int.

Passacaglia Op. 17 (EMB 1937).

Praludium, Nocturne und Scherzo Op. 7 (Rahter). Scherzo is best.

Hungarian Folk Dances. (EMB). 3 pieces.

20 Easy Short Pieces (EMB 1948).

6 Hungarian Peasant Songs Op. 19 (EMB).

6 Hungarian Peasant Songs Op. 19b (EMB).

LOUIS WEINGARDEN (1943-) USA

Weingarden studied with Miriam Gideon and Elliot Carter. He was winner of the Prix de Rome in 1968.

Triptych (AMC 1969).
Abraham and Isaac.
David the Shepherd: a spiritual etude.
The Three Marys Lamenting and the Angel Describing the Resurrection. Large-scale virtuoso work, freely atonal, ample romantic structures, serious in intent, of imposing dimensions. Well worth exploring, for mature pianists. D.

JOHN WEINZWEIG (1913-) Canada

Weinzweig introduced twelve-tone technique to Canada in 1939. He teaches at the University of Toronto.

Berceuse (OUP 1950). Serial, a 5-note series. M-D.

Toccata Dance (OUP 1950). 12-tone.

Conversation Piece (OUP 1950). 12-tone.

FLEMMING WEIS (1898-) Denmark

16 Short Pieces for Piano Students (SM).

Variations and Fugue on a Theme by W. A. Mozart Op. 2 (SM). Neoclassic.

Suite for klaver (WH c. 1947). 22 p. Hymne, Arabeske, Elegie, Finale. D.
Neoclassic design. Requires big octave and chord technique à la Rachmaninoff. Exploits large range of the keyboard.

ADOLPH WEISS (1891-) USA

Weiss was the first to introduce Schönberg's twelve-tone technique in the United States.

12 Preludes (NME 1927). Serial.

Pulse of the Sea (CFE 1950). 5 minutes. Impressionistic and expressionistic influences. Etude for piano.

EGON WELLESZ (1885-) Austria, living in England since 1939

Drei Skizzen Op. 6 (Dob 1911). Similar to the Schönberg Op. 11. Requires subtle shading.

Epigramme Op. 17 (UE 1914). Danse, Capriccio, Vision, Notturno, Elégie fantastique. More accessible style than Op. 6. M-D.

Idyllen Op. 21 (UE 1917). 5 pieces, impressionist style. Beautiful melodic writing. M-D.

Zwei Studien Op. 29 (Dob 1921). 3 minutes. Atonal.

1. Langsam: restricted dynamic range, study in tonal balance.
2. Sehr ruhig: repeated notes, chords and octaves, light. Requires a supple wrist.

Fünf Tanzstücke Op. 42 (UE 1927). Harsh dissonances. No. 4 is most appealing. D.

5 Piano Pieces Op. 83 (Simrock 1962). Skillful miniatures. Int.

Triptychon Op. 98 (UE 1967). 4 minutes. Grazioso, Cantabile, Appassionata. Atonal, but accessible. The last is most difficult.

Studien in Grau Op. 106 (Dob). Five serial studies. D.

FREDERICK WERLÉ (1914-) USA

Werlé is a product of the Curtis Institute, Cincinnati Conservatory and the Eastman School of Music. He studied composition with Rosario Scalero in Italy and with Nadia Boulanger in Paris. He is Associate Dean of the Mannes College of Music in New York City.

Sonata brevis No. 2 (Rongwen). 11 p. M-D.
Based on short opening motive of D C♯ G♯. Changing tonalities. Formally balanced by eight different tempo sections. Economy of material. Large span required.

Toccata (Rongwen 1949). Neoromantic style, impressionist treatment, Ravel influence, dramatic closing. M-D.

Pastorale (TP). 2 p. Int.
Melody in thirds, rocking rhythmic motion, tonal, pianistic.

CHRISTOPHER ERNST FRIEDRICH WEYSE (1774-1842) Denmark

Sonate g (1818) (WH facsimile). 16 p.
Allegro agitato; Grave; Allegro assai.
Interesting writing, well worth reviving. Classic in style, some daring modulations, especially in the second movement. M-D.

JOHN WHITE (1937-) Great Britain

White studied composition with Bernard Stevens at the Royal College of Music and privately with Elizabeth Lutyens. He has composed thirty-six piano sonatas.

First Sonata (Leduc 1961). Three movements FSF, 15 p. M-D.
Striking opening. Thin textures, clear ideas, expressive slow movement. Semi-ostinato forms basis of final movement. Not overly difficult, highly concentrated work.

Fifth Sonata (Leduc 1961). One movement. D.
Numerous tempo changes, keen sense of keyboard sonorities and contrapuntal textures. Fondness for low sonorities. Big technique required.

See: Brian Dennis, "The Music of John White," MT, 112, May 1971, 435-7.

IAN WHYTE (1901-1960) Scotland

An Edinburgh Suite (Ascherberg 1949). 22 p. 3 pieces. M-D. St. Giles: hints at metrical psalmody; Holyrood; Princes Street: contains an Irish reel.
Serious work, displays fine sense of keyboard writing.

CHARLES MARIE WIDOR (1844-1937) France

Fugue on H A Y D N (Durand 1910).

Suite b Op. 58 (Hamelle). 9½ minutes.
Moderato assai: Theme and variations; Scherzo: Trio cantabile; Recordare; Finale.

Valse oubliée (Hamelle 1904). 6 p.

En route (Quintard 1904). 4 p.

JEAN WIENER (1896-) France

Wiener's style exhibits a facile technique strongly influenced by jazz.

Sonatine Syncopée (1923) (ESC). Three movements: Lourd; Blues; Brillant. Extended work employing stylized jazz. D.

Sonate (1925) (ESC). Three movements, requires a facile pianism, juxtaposed sonorities. D.

Deuxième Sonatine (1928) (ESC). Popular style, involved, jouncing finale. M-D.

Quatre petites pièces Radio (Jobert). Popular style, attractive. Int.

Polka (Heugel).

Java (Heugel).

Tango (Heugel).

ADOLF WIKLUND (1879-1950) Sweden

3 Pianostycken Op. 3 (WH). Restrained romantic style. M-D. Fantasistykke; Vid Solofjorden; Melodi.

Allegro energico (AL).

Fran mitt fonster (NMS).

CAROL WILLIAMS (1939-) USA

Williams is a graduate of the American Conservatory of Music and has studied composition with Robert Kelly and Stella Roberts.

Bells. Commissioned by the Illinois MTA and the MTNA, 1969. 5 p. M-D. (Available on loan from MTNA).
Quartal and quintal harmonic usage. ABA design with corresponding tempo changes. Large climax at close. Requires a fine legato control and balance of line. Unusual pedal effects. Parallelism.

A *Piano Sonata* and some teaching pieces are available from the composer: 1961 Coral Ave., Aurora, Illinois 60506.

DAVID R. WILLIAMS (1932-) USA

Piano Sonata No. 2 (AMC). 3 movements, FSF. M-D. MC style throughout, pianistic.

5 Pieces for Harpsichord (AMC).

Piano Sonata No. 3 (AMC).

Piano Sonata No. 5 (AMC).

RALPH VAUGHAN WILLIAMS (1872-1958) Great Britain

The Lake in the Mountains (OUP 1947). 4 minutes.
From the film music for *49th Parallel.* Linear, unusual key changes, atmospheric, quiet. M-D.

Suite of Six Short Pieces (S&B). Prelude, Slow Dance, Quick Dance, Slow Air, Rondo, Pezzo ostinato. Unpianistic. M-D.

Hymn Tune Prelude on Gibbons Song 13 (OUP 1936). 3½ minutes. Legato is a problem. Int.

MALCOLM WILLIAMSON (1931-) Great Britain, born Australia

Williamson studied with Eugene Goossens, Elisabeth Lutyens and Erwin Stein. "He is in manner an eclectic, a virtuoso in a dozen different styles ranging from austere serialism to pop tunes modelled on Richard Rodgers." Andrew Porter, "Some New British Composers," MQ, 51, January 1965, 19.

Sonata (Bo&H 1953-55). 3 movements, FSF.
Thin textures, more pandiatonic than chromatic, centers around F in a kind of Stravinskian sense. Eclectic style, witty rhythms, some serialism used in slow movement. One of the finest piano sonatas from the 1950's.

Travel Diaries (Chappell 1961). 5 books. In order of difficulty: Sydney, Naples, London, Paris, New York. Excellent series of pedagogic music. From easy to M-D.

5 Preludes (Weinberger).

DAG WIRÉN (1905-) Sweden

Wirén admits that his first desire is to please and entertain, so his music is easy on the listener. He studied in Paris for three years and his work shows fine craftsmanship.

Theme and Variations Op. 5 (GM 1949). 15 p.
Theme, 9 variations, and return of theme. Facile writing. M-D.

Ironiska smastycken Op. 19 (NMS 1942). Suite in 5 movements. Fun is poked at the waltz.

Improvisationer Op. 35 (GM c. 1960). 5 pieces. M-D.
Suitelike, varied moods.

KARL WOHLFART (1874-1943) Sweden

Klockorna Op. 16 (NMS).

Oktavetyder Op. 27 (NMS).

Svit Op. 30 (NMS c. 1933). Character-pieces. Traditional harmonic idiom.
Preludium; Dans; Intermezzo; Tarantella.

Sonata D Op. 35 (NMS).

ERNST WILHELM WOLF (1735-1792) Germany

Zwei leichte Sonaten d, E (Organum Vol. 7 K&S).

Zwei leichte Sonaten G, B♭ (Organum Vol. 21 K&S).

Zwei leichte Sonaten c, F (Organum Vol. 25 K&S).

CHRISTIAN WOLFF (1934-) USA, born France

Wolff received a Ph.D. in comparative literature from Harvard in 1963. He studied with John Cage for a short time and was associated with a group who espoused the Cage philosophy. Anton Webern exerted a major influence on Wolff. "With Webern as a point of departure, and using Cage's concept of rhythmic structure based on proportional sequences, Wolff established a musical form on the basis of rhythmic continuity. He felt that multiplication of a basic rhythmic series by its components successively provides an additional series which is comparable to the transformation of a tone-row; the number of components determine the number of sequences, or phrases, and the number of sections. Further, the sum of the components in the initial series constitutes the square root of the total structure." BBD, 186.

For Piano I (CFP 1952). "The pitches, durations, and dynamics are each based on a pattern of 9 components, repeated with such re-ordering and over-lapping as is necessary to compensate for a structural length of 16 beats." BBD, 186. An extract of this work is found in M&M, 17, May 1969, 42-3.

Suite No. 1 for Prepared Piano (CFP 1954). This work requires 6 screws, 2 bolts (small), a strip of tin (from a tin can cover) about 2″ x ½″, a penny, a small stick of wood, 3 strips of jar rubber and 3 rubber wedges. D.

For Prepared Piano (NME 1951). Wolff tells performer more how to play than what to play. He also notes how to listen.

See: Christian Wolff, "Taking Chances," M&M, 17, May 1969, 38-40. "On Form," Die Reihe, 7, 1965, 26-31. "On Movement," Die Reihe, 2, 1959, 61-3.

H. A. WOLLENHAUPT (1827-1863) Germany

5 Morceaux caractéristiques en forme d'Etudes Op. 22 (GS). A certain charm about these pieces still makes them welcome in the pianist's repertoirc. None are easy.

Collection (B. Tour-Nov). Contains 11 separate pieces.

Etude A♭ Op. 22/1 (CF).

STEFAN WOLPE (1902-1972) Germany, in USA since 1939

Wolpe is a powerful musician who has strongly influenced many American composers.

Early Pieces for Piano (McGinnis & Marx 1924). MC with improvisatory character. Content stretched.

Dance (Arrow). In the form of a chaconne. Short, rhythmic vigor, percussive. D.

Pastorale (MCA). In *U.S.A.* Vol. II.

Zemach Suite (Hargail 1949).

Form (Tonas Verlag 1959). Serial, harmonic experimentation, restless. D.

2 Studies for Piano (Part 2) (McGinnis & Marx 1955). Two-part structure, difficult rhythmic procedures, full use of keyboard. D.

Suite Im Hexachord (AMC 1964). 4 movements: Sostenuto; Pastorale; Fugue; Adagio. D.

Passacaglia (AMC). A major work of virtuoso proportions on a theme utilising all the intervals. Powerful, demanding.

JAMES P. WOODARD (1929-   ) USA

Woodard studied piano with James Friskin at The Juilliard School and composition with Carlisle Floyd and John Boda at Florida State University. He teaches at Southern Illinois University.

Partita. Commissioned by the Kentucky MTA and the MTNA, 1969. 45 p. D. (Available on loan from MTNA).
Overture, A, C, S, G. Neoclassic in style, effective chromatic virtuoso pianistic writing, employing broad gestures throughout. Advanced pianism required.

JOHN W. WORK (1901-1967) USA

Appalachia (Three Fiddle and Game Tunes) (SP 1945).
Three demanding pieces. Advanced pianism required.

JOHANN HUGO WORŽISCHEK (VOŘÍŠEK) (1791-1825)
Bohemia, Czechoslovakia

Piano Works (Volume 52 MAB Artia).
Contains a biography and excellent comments on the music in English, Two Rondos Op. 18, Two Impromptus, Eclogue, Ie plaisir Op. 4, Le désir Op. 3, Variations Op. 19.

Sonata b♭ Op. 20 (Volume 4 MAB Artia). See SSB 224-5.
Three movements, his best known work, keys up to seven sharps and five flats. Beethovenian characteristics.

Six Impromptus Op. 7 (Artia). First examples of the title. Ideas repeated rather than developed.

Two Rhapsodies (Artia). From the twelve Rhapsodies that comprised Op. 1.

Rhapsodie g Op. 1/9 (UE). See Anthologies and Collections, General: in album *Viennese Masters from the Baroque, Classical and Biedermeier Periods* (Voříšek).

Selected Pieces of Piano Music (D. Zahn-Henle).

BOLESLAW WOYTOWICZ (1899-   ) Poland

10 Studies (PMP c. 1960). 12-tone. D.

FRIEDRICH WÜHRER (1900-) Austria

18 Studies on Chopin Etudes In Contrary Motion (Süddeutscher Musikverlag 1958). 65 p. Devised to promote equal facility in both hands. D.

CHARLES WUORINEN (1938-) USA

Wuorinen studied composition with Otto Luening, Jack Beeson and Vladimir Ussachevsky.

Piano Variations (McGinnis and Marx 1963). 17 p.
A highly dramatic work but the variation technique is not easy to follow. Webernesque in spirit. Constantly changing meters, a few extra-musical effects such as stopping, plucking strings, clusters. Difficult to read and perform. Virtuoso technique required.

Piano Sonata (ACA). 13 minutes. One movement, dissonant, changing meters, synthetic scales, effective use of rests (one is 16 bars long), clusters, harmonics, dynamic extremes. D.

Harpsichord Divisions (ACA). 13 minutes.

ARNOLD VAN WYK (1916-) Union of South Africa

Night Music (Galliard). 24 minutes.
Extensive nocturne, closer to a symphonic rhapsody. Contemporary idiom, virtuoso technique required.

Pastorale e Capriccio (Bo&H 1956). 19 p. 8 minutes. D.
Contrasting, demanding technically and interpretatively.

4 Piano Pieces (Bo&H 1965). 21 p.
Written for the piano examination of the University of South Africa. Displays a wide variety of pianistic techniques. Irregular rhythms. Dumka; Scherzino: march-like; Romanza: many dynamic levels; Toccata: 5/8 meter.

RUTH SHAW WYLIE (1916-) USA

5 Preludes Op. 12 (Camara Music Publishers).
Contrasted, romantic-impressionistic influences in a MC idiom. No. 3 is especially pianistic.

5 Easy Pieces for Piano (Camara).

6 Little Preludes (Camara).

YEHUDI WYNER (1929-) USA, born Canada

Wyner "evolved from Hindemith's kind of neo-classicism to Stravinsky's. He then moved toward a greater involvement with more chromatic materials, and has been most profoundly influenced by Schönbergian music, although he has never used serial techniques. His affinity is for ample instrumental works that display sustained lyricism of an introspective cast." ICM, 606-7. He is presently on the faculty at the Yale School of Music.

Partita (ACA 1952). 5 minutes. 5 movements: Overture, Aria, A, M, G. Neoclassic style. First half of Overture in French Overture rhythm, major-minor sonorities mixed, then an Allegro with ostinato-like bass. Aria is more melodic, use of ninths. Fugal gigue uses 9/8, 10/8, 12/8 and 13/8. M-D.

Sonata per Pianoforte (CFE 1954). 3 movements. 12-tone but tonal orientation. Thin textures in first movement plus much use of ninth, both harmonically and melodically. Lower register used for single note rhythmic punctuation. Second movement juxtaposes major-minor sonorities. Final movement, ninth again prominent. Widespread thin textures and important use of the trill. Striking work. M-D.

Easy Suite: 6 Short Pieces (CFE).

DAVID WYNNE (1900-) Wales

"Wynne was rooted in the classical tradition of Bach and has come stylistically under the influence of Vaughan Williams, Holst and latterly, Bartók." GD, 9, 376.

Sonata No. 1 (University Council of Music, Cardiff, Wales). 3 movements FSF. Contrasted, well-written, appealing. A solid technique required to solve both technical and interpretative problems.

Sonata No. 2 (University of Wales Press, c. 1962). 3 movements. 23 p. 11 minutes. Written in 1956, first movement uses rhythmic clusters interspersed with linear writing. An increased density of sound accumulates in Elegy, the slow second movement. The final movement (Vivo) flies! D.

Suite of 3 Pieces (University of Wales Press c. 1961). 24 p. 13½ minutes. Commissioned by the BBC, Welsh Region, 1969. Three movements, all show a preference for use of seconds, both melodic and harmonic.
Mosaic: Allegretto; Slow Dance: Lento; Capriccio: Vivo.

X

IANNIS XENAKIS (1922-   ) Greece, born Rumania

Xenakis is Associate Professor of Mathematical and Automated Music at Indiana University and at The Schola Cantorum in Paris. He is one of the foremost *avant-garde* composers of our time.

Herma—"Musique symbolique" (Bo&H 1960-61).
Herma means bond, foundation, embryo. *Avant-garde* work, based on logical operations imposed on classes of pitches. A preface describes work. Notation and sound are unusual.

See: Mario Bois, *Iannis Xenakis—The Man and His Music, a Conversation with the Composer and a Description of His works.* New York: Boosey and Hawkes, 1967.

David Jones, "The Music of Xenakis," MT, 107, June 1966, 495-6.

Iannis Xenakis, *Formalized Music.* Bloomington: Indiana University Press, 1971.

Y

YEHUDA YANNAY (1937-   ) Israel, born Transylvania

Yannay studied under A. U. Boscovich at the Rubin Academy of Music in Tel Aviv. He also had further studies at Brandeis University in 1964.

Music for Piano (IMI 1962).
Serial in style. Three short movements oriented toward Schönberg demanding sophistication and knowledge of the style. D.

RICHARD YARDUMIAN (1917-   ) USA

Yardumian's musical development was acquired entirely through self-study. He was encouraged by José Iturbi and Leopold Stokowski.

3 Preludes (EV 1945). The Wind, The Sea, The Sky.
Short, expressive, refined.

Chromatic Sonata (EV 1947). 3 movements. 20 minutes. M-D.
Dancelike first movement. Slow chorale introduces second movement. Third movement employs varied tempo and ends quietly.

Prelude and Chorale (EV 1949). 3 minutes. M-D.
Prelude employs melodic line embedded in accompaniment of sixteenth notes. Chorale in chordal, long sustained sonorities.

Passacaglia, Recitative and Fugue (EV).

Z

HAROLD ZABRACK (1929-   ) USA

Zabrack is an exceptionally fine pianist. The unpublished works are available from the composer: 8147 Delmar Boulevard, St. Louis, Missouri 63130.

Scherzo (Hommage à Prokofieff) (Bo&H).
Bitonal, biting dissonances, Prokofieff-like. This is No. 1 in a set called *Contours for Piano*. The other pieces are:
Dialogue: 12-tone.
Introduction: 12-tone.
Quasi Improvisation: lyric.
Toccata: rhythmic and motoric.

Sonata No. 1 (1965).

Sonata No. 2 (1967). Bravura virtuoso work. The first 2 movements are based on the tone row from *Dialogue* listed above.
Allegro maestoso: SA.
Andante espressivo: song form, cadenza, mixture of styles.
Allegro con brio: Rondo. Introduction, then a fugal subject based on a new row. Thematic material of first movement returns at close.

Variations Op. 1 (1959). Lyric, impressionistic.

3 Dialogues (1960).

Suite (1964).

FRIEDRICH WILHELM ZACHAU (1663-1712) Germany

Werke für Klavier (G. Ochs-Mitteldeutscher Verlag). Includes Capriccio d, Preludien und Fugen C, F, G, G, G. Fuge G, Fantasie D.

Suite b in collection *Hallisches Klavierbüchlein* (W. Serauky-Mitteldeutscher Verlag).

MARIO ZAFRED (1922-   ) Italy, born Trieste

Zafred's compositional goal is the ideal of immediate communicability. He has considerable technical skill.

Third Sonata (Ric 1950). 2 movements. 23 p. MC, M-D.

Fourth Sonata (Curci 1964). 3 movements. Effective writing M-D.

HENRI ZAGWIJN (1878-1954) The Netherlands

Debussy and Schönberg are the major influences on Zagwijn's music.

Suite (Donemus 1945). 20 minutes. Cyclic, polyrhythmic. D.

Suite fantasque (Alsbach 1920).

Sylphes (Alsbach 1921).

Triade (Donemus 1954). 10 minutes.

JULIEN-FRANÇOIS ZBINDEN (1917-   ) Switzerland

3 Préludes Op. 4 (Foetisch).

Jazz Sonatina Op. 11 (Br&H 1949-50). Blues, Improvisation. Zbinden played in a jazz orchestra for a while and readily absorbed the style. M-D.

4 Solitudes Op. 17 (SZ). M-D.
Contrasted, pianistic. No. 2 asks to be played "with desperate energy."

Album pour mon chien Op. 19 (Foetisch). Amusing, rhythmical, Int.

CARL FRIEDRICH ZELTER (1758-1832) Germany

Rondo mit Variationen (K. H. Taubert-R&E). Graceful, in the style of Mozart Variations.

BERND-ALOIS ZIMMERMANN (1918-1970) Germany

Enchiridion (Schott 1949-51). Bartók, Hindemith and Schönberg influence. Great concentration needed for these 13 short pieces. D.

8 Configurations (Schott 1956). D.
Dynamics exploited, clever 12-tone studies.

DOMENICO ZIPOLI (1688-1726) Italy

Although Zipoli called his collection of works sonatas, they are closer to suites. His works are well written and interesting.

Cembalo Works (CFP). 4 suites, b, g, C, and d and Partite a, C (Sonate d'Intavolatura, 1716). Works in *I Classici della Musica Italiana* XXXVI; *L'arte musicale in Italia* III; TPA X.

Pieces for Piano (Cembalo) (Frickert-Leuckhart). Contains Suite d (Canzona, M, C), Aria, Partita (Aria with 12 variations) a.

Sonate d'Intavolatura per Organo e Cimbalo 1716, (L. F. Tagliavini-Süddeutscher Musikverlag) II: *Cembalowerke* containing Suites b, g, C, d, Variations a, C (Partita). Scholarly edition.

Kompositionen für Klavier (Mitteldeutscher Verlag) Suite b, Allegretto e, Canzone e, Preludio d.

Trois Pièces (Leduc). Preludio, C, S.

Fughetten (CFP).

ANTHOLOGIES AND COLLECTIONS

This section is divided into five groupings, each arranged alphabetically by title. "General" (p. 694) includes music from different countries written over a period of one to three centuries. "General: Contemporary" (p. 718) lists collections of piano music primarily of the twentieth century from different countries. The "Tombeau or Hommage" section catalogs those collections written in honor of a composer. The last and largest category consists of collections from "Separate Countries" (p. 722), sometimes divided into pre-twentieth century and twentieth century. The "Bach" section (under "German") lists those collections which include music by more than one member of the Bach family. Single-composer collections are listed under the composer's name in the first section of the book.

The collections are listed alphabetically by title within each division of the "Anthologies and Collections" section.

Initial articles and Arabic numerals (A, An, Das, Der, I, Le, Les, The, 15, 24, 30) are ignored in alphabetization. An index lists all titles of collections included in the Anthologies and Collections section: (p. 758).

GENERAL

Alte Hausmusik (W. Rehberg-Schott). Two volumes.
Works by d'Anglebert, Byrd, Couperin, Frescobaldi, Pachelbel, Rameau.

Alte Meister (E. Pauer-Br&H) *Old Masters,* 6 vols. Overedited.
- Vol. 1: Works by Krebs, Martini, Rameau, Kirnberger, Marpurg, Méhul, sons of Bach, Kuhnau.
- Vol. 2: Krebs, Paradisi, Cherubini, Hässler, Zipoli, Mattheson, Couperin, Wagenseil, Benda.
- Vol. 3: Froberger, Rolle, Sacchini, Hasse, W. F. Bach, Händel, Rameau, Loeillet, Lorenzo di Rossi, Turini.
- Vol. 4: C. P. E. Bach, Graun, Matielli, Grazioli, Mattheson, Schobert, Sarti, Scarlatti, Couperin, Muffat.
- Vol. 5: Couperin, Rameau, Zipoli, Galuppi, Marcello, Paganelli.
- Vol. 6: Rutini, Martini, Paradisi, Pescetti.

Alte Meister der Klaviermusik des 16-18 Jahrhunderts (H. Keller-CFP). Four volumes.

Vol. 1: German Masters: Froberger, Buxtehude, Pachelbel, J. K. F. Fischer, Mattheson, Händel, J. S. Bach, Muffat, Krebs, Kirnberger, W. F. and C. P. E. Bach.

Vol. 2: French Masters: Chambonnières, D'Anglebert, Lully, Le Bègue, F. Couperin, Marchand, Dieupart, Rameau, Dandrieu, Daquin, Duphly.

Vol. 3: Italian Masters: Frescobaldi, Pasquini, Pollarolo, A. Scarlatti, Zipoli, D. Scarlatti, Platti, Martini, Galuppi, Paradies, Vento, Turini.

Vol. 4: English, Dutch, Spanish Masters: Byrd, Farnaby, Johnson, Anonymous, Hooper, Philips, Bull, Purcell, Sweelinck, Reinken, Cabézon, Milan, Soler.

Alte Meister des Klavierspiels (W. Niemann-CFP) *Old Masters of the 17th and 18th Centuries.* Three vols.

Vol. 1: English, French, Italian Masters: 11 pieces by Byrd, Bull, F. Couperin, Daquin, Durante, Frescobaldi, Galuppi, Marchand, Martin, Paradisi.

Vol. 2: German Masters: 19 pieces by Böhm, Fischer, Froberger, Graun, Kerll, Kirnberger.

Vol. 3: German Masters: 15 pieces by Krieger, Kuhnau, Marpurg, Mattheson, Muffat, Pachelbel, Murschhauser, Scheidt.

Alte Musik für Tasteninstrumente (Merseburger 1965).
Contains a well developed Fuga suavissima by Karel Luython (ca. 1557?-1620) from the J. Woltz Tablaturbuch of 1617, and a Toccata by Jacob Hassler (1569-1622).

Alte Programmusik (F. Reuter-Mitteldeutscher Verlag).
Banchieri, La Battaglia; F. Couperin, Les Papillons; Rameau, Tambourin; Byrd, The Battle; Munday, The Tempest; Kuhnau, The Battle Between David and Goliath. An unusually fine collection, not edited.

Alte Tänze des 17. und 18. Jahrhunderts (Dana Setkova-Br).
27 works by Chambonnières, D'Anglebert, Rameau, Dandrieu, Zipoli, Froberger, Pachelbel, Kuhnau, J. S. Bach, Purcell, Croft and Handel.

Antologia di Musica Antica e Moderna (Tagliapietra-Ric c. 1931-32). Eighteen volumes.

This is the second largest anthology of keyboard music and extends from the sixteenth century to the twentieth. Includes bio-bibliographical notes in Italian, French, English and Spanish.

Contents:

Vol. 1: F. Verdelotto, A. Willaert, L. Molan, G. Cavazzoni, A. de Mudarra, M. de Fuenllana, G. Bermudo, C. de Rore, A. Gabrieli, A. de Cabézon, A. Padovano.

Vol. 2: C. Merulo, L. Luzzaschi, W. Byrd, T. Morley, G. Gabrieli, F. Richardson, P. Philips, G. Farnaby.

Vol. 3: J. P. Sweelinck, J. Mundy, J. Bull, J. Titelouze, H. L. Hässler, A. Banchieri, C. Erbach, B. Praetorius, O. Gibbons.

Vol. 4: Giorolamo Frescobaldi: Fiori Musicali, Il primo Libro di Capricci.

Vol. 5: G. Frescobaldi, G. M. Trabani, G. Picchi, A. Gabrieli.

Vol. 6: S. Scheidt, H. Scheidemann, G. B. Fasolo, M. A. Rossi, T. Merula, F. Fontana, J. J. Froberger.

Vol. 7: D. Strungk, W. Ebner, J. E. Kindermann, F. Roberday, J. C. de Chambonnières, H. Dumont, J. A. Reinken, N. Gigault, J. R. von Kerll, J. d'Anglebert, G. B. de Lully, J. Gaultier (le "Vieux").

Vol. 8: A. Poglietti, A. Le Bègue, L. Couperin, G. Muffat, D. Buxtehude, B. Pasquini.

Vol. 9: J. C. Bach, J. Krieger, C. F. Pollaroli, A. Corelli, J. Pachelbel, H. Purcell, A. Scarlatti.

Vol. 10: J. Kuhnau, F. X. A. Murschhauser, J. K. F. Fischer, J. B. Loeillet, F. Couperin, L. Marchand, A. B. Della Ciaja, D. Zipoli, A. Vivaldi, G. Ph. Telemann, J. Mattheson.

Vol. 11: J. Ph. Rameau, J. F. Dandrieu, F. Durante, G. F. Händel, J. S. Bach, D. Scarlatti, B. Marcello, N. Porpora.

Vol. 12: G. Muffat, L. C. Daquin, L. Leo, J. A. Hasse, G. B. Sammartini, G. A. Paganelli, G. B. Pescetti, G. B.

Martini, B. Galuppi, W. F. Bach, P. A. Paradies, J. L. Krebs.

Vol. 13: K. P. E. Bach, F. W. Marpurg, J. P. Kirnberger, G. Benda, J. E. Bach, F. Bertoni, G. P. Rutini, J. Haydn, S. Sacchini, J. C. Bach, J. W. Hässler, F. Turini, G. B. Grazioli, M. Clementi, W. A. Mozart.

Vol. 14: L. Cherubini, J. L. Dussek, F. Pollini, D. Steibelt, L. v. Beethoven, J. B. Cramer, J. N. Hummel, J. Field, F. Ries, K. M. v. Weber.

Vol. 15: F. W. M. Kalkbrenner, K. Czerny, I. Moscheles, F. P. Schubert, J. C. Kessler, F. Mendelssohn, F. F. Chopin.

Vol. 16: R. Schumann, F. Liszt, S. Thalberg, H. Kjerulf, S. Golinelli.

Vol. 17: J. Raff, A. Fumagalli, A. Rubinstein, J. Brahms, G. Sgambati, M. Esposito, G. Martucci, C. Albanesi, N. v. Westerhout, A. Longo, G. Orefice.

Vol. 18: F. Busoni, F. Cilèa, A. Zanella, A. Savasta, D. Alageona, R. Pick-Mangiagalli, L. Perrachio, A. Casella, F. Santoliquido, P. Coppola, A. Voretti, M. Castelnuovo-Tedesco, S. Musella, E. Masetti, M. Pilati.

Anthologie Pianistique (I. Philipp-Heugel, 1920). Four volumes. 100 concert etudes for developing technique. 25 works in each volume. All of these etudes are on the difficult side and each one develops one aspect of piano technique, such as double notes, trills, velocity, bravura playing, chords, etc. Well-known and lesser-known composers are represented; a few of the numerous composers are Czerny, Heller, Mathias, Kohler, Zarembski, Liszt, Mayer, Raff, Pollini, Henselt, Litolff, Moscheles, Steibelt, Alkan, Kalkbrenner, Ries, etc.

Anthology of Music (Karl G. Fellerer-Arno Volk Verlag). This is the English edition of *Das Musikwerk*, a collection of 37 volumes with complete musical examples illustrating the history of music. Volumes of special interest to the pianist are: Vols. 1. 400 Years of European Keyboard Music (Georgii); 6. The Classics (Stephenson); 8. The Character Piece (Kahl); 11. The Variation (von Fischer); 12. Improvisation (Ferand);

15. The Solo Sonata (Giegling); 17. The Toccata (Valentin); 19. The Fugue, I (Adrio); 21. Romanticism in Music (Stephenson); 25. The Solo Concerto (Engel); 26. The Suite (Beck); 27. The Dance (Reichert); 33. The Fugue, II (Müller-Blattau).

An Anthology of Piano Music (Agay-YMP c. 1971).
Comprehensive coverage of the periods. Ranges in difficulty from easy to D. with most material Int.

Vol. I: *The Baroque Period*
Scholarly introduction by Louis L. Crowder, editorial notes, biographical sketches of composers, glossary. Works by d'Anglebert, C. P. E., J. S., and W. F. Bach, Blow, Buxtehude, Byrd, Chambonnières, F. Couperin, Dandrieu, Daquin, Durante, J. K. F. Fischer, Frescobaldi, G. Gabrieli, Gibbons, Graupner, Händel, Hurlebusch, Kinderman, Kirnberger, Krebs, Krieger, Kuhnau, Leo, Loeillet, Lully, Maichelbek, Marcello, Martini, Mattheson, Muffat, Nichelman, J. Pachelbel, Paradisi, Pasquini, Pergolesi, Purcell, Rameau, Rathgeber, D. Scarlatti, Scheidt, Seixas, Soler, Sweelinck, Telemann, Tischer, Trabacci, Walther, Weckmann, Witt, Zipoli. Superb survey of the period.

Vol. II: *The Classical Period*
Scholarly introduction by Louis L. Crowder, biographical sketches of composers, glossary. Works by J. C. and J. C. F. Bach, Beethoven, J. A. Benda, Clementi, Cramer, Diabelli, Dittersdorf, Dussek, Hässler, Haydn, Hüllmandel, Hummel, Kuhlau, Mozart, Reichardt, Türk, Weber. Superb survey of the period.

Vol. III: *The Romantic Period*
Scholarly introduction by Louis L. Crowder, biographical sketches of composers, glossary. Works by Albeniz, Alkan, Brahms, Chopin, Dohnányi, Dvořák, Fauré, Franck, Gade, Glinka, Grieg, Heller, Liszt, MacDowell, Mendelssohn, Moussorgsky, Rachmaninoff, Reger, Schubert, Schumann, Sibelius, Smetana, Tchaikovsky, Volkmann, Wolf. Superb survey of the period.

Vol. IV: *The Twentieth Century*
Scholarly introduction by Louis L. Crowder, biographical sketches of composers, glossary. Works by Antheil, Bartók, Casella, Cowell, Creston, Debussy, Einem, Granados, Gretchaninoff, Hauer, Hindemith, Ives, Jelinek, Kabalevsky, Kadosa, Khatchaturian, Kodály, Krenek, Lutoslawski, Martin, Milhaud, Palmgren, Piston, Prokofieff, Ránki, Ravel, Rebikoff, Rieti, Satie, Schuman, Schönberg, Scott, Shostakovich, Scriabin, Starer, I. Stravinsky, Swanson, Tcherepnin, Toch, Villa-Lobos, Webern.

The Art of the Suite (Yella Pessl-EBM).
Eight suites of dances by 17th and 18th century composers including works by Chambonnières, Froberger, Purcell, J. K. F. Fischer, F. Couperin, Dieupart, Daguin and Gottlieb Muffat. The edition is tastefully done, with biographical notes, essay on the suite, and a table of ornaments.

The Character Piece (W. Kahl-Arno Volk) Vol. 8 of the "Anthology of Music Series."
Includes an aesthetic and historical introduction and notes on the music and sources. Solo keyboard pieces include: Johann Kotter, Carmen in sol; Thomas Mulliner, Since thou art false to me, When shall my sorrowful sighing; Johann J. Froberger, Lamentation faite sur la mort très douloureuse de Sa Majesté Impériale Ferdinand le troisième; J. S. Bach, Prelude b♭, WTC, I; F. Couperin, Les Langueurs tendres; C. P. E. Bach, Les Langueurs tendres, Abschied vom Silbermannschen Clavier in einem Rondeau; J. F. Reichardt, Rondo, after a Poem by Petrarch; A. Hüttenbrenner, Nachruf an Schubert in Trauertönen am Pianoforte; W. Taubert, Minnelied; S. Heller, Wanderstunden, from Op. 80, Präludien e, from Op. 81; A. Jensen, Abendlied; J. Rheinberger, Two Pieces in Canonic Form, Op. 180; F. Liszt, Sonetto 123 Petrarca, Consolation E; R. Strauss, Träumerei; J. Haas, Mummenschanz; E. Sjögren, Elegy; Z. Fibich, Three pieces from Stimmungen, Eindrücke und Erinnerungen, Morgenunterhaltung.

Classic Keyboard Music (E. Sauer-UE).
An album of piano solos by great masters. Contains works

from F. Couperin to F. Chopin. Overedited but contains a broad selection of literature.

Classic Sonatas for Piano (Podolsky-CF).

Vol. I: Sonata g, Arne; Sonata G, Grazioli; Sonata C, No. 3 from Six Easy Sonatas, Hässler; Sonata D, Paradisi.

Vol. II: Sonata A, Op. 1/3, Méhul; Sonata C, No. 1 from Six Easy Sonatas, Hässler; Sonata d, Hasse; Sonata A, Paradisi.

Vol. III: Sonata A, Arne; Sonata D, Galuppi; Sonata A, C. P. E. Bach.

Vol. IV: Sonata f, Scarlatti; Sonata f♯, Rust.

Classics To Moderns in the Early Advanced Grades (D. Agay-CMP).
Volume 47 of *Music for Millions* series. Contains 54 original works from three centuries, Baroque to present. Based on urtext or other reliable scores. Works from Purcell, Rameau, Bach to Bartók, Ravel, Prokofieff and others.

Classics To Moderns in the Intermediate Grades (D. Agay-CMP).
Volume 37 of *Music for Millions* series. Contains 115 original pieces from nearly three centuries. Some unfamiliar and fine works by Pasquini, C. P. E. Bach, Villa-Lobos, Kirnberger, Kodály, Stoelzel, Scriabin and Granados make this a desirable collection.

Clavichord Music of the 17th Century (Thurston Dart-S&B c. 1960).
Contains works by: Anonymous, Froberger and Buxtehude. Fine preface and edition. Format is small notebook type.

Composers for the Keyboard (TP). 4 volumes; 2 easy, 2 Int.
Beethoven to Shostakovich (TP). Easy II. 50 original piano solos, compiled and edited by George Walter Anthony. 72 p.
Byrd to Beethoven (TP). Int. I. 27 original piano solos, compiled and edited by George Walter Anthony. 71 p.
Purcell to Mozart (TP). Easy I. 50 original piano solos, compiled and edited by George Anthony. 72 p.
Schubert to Shostakovich (TP). Int. II. 39 original piano solos, compiled and edited by George Walter Anthony. 72 p.

All 4 volumes contain brief biographies and notes concerning the works. The inside cover pages contain photographs and brief comments about the development of keyboard instruments.

Concertante Variationen 1810-1830 (Gerhard Puchelt-Lienau c. 1969).
Bravura keyboard variations of: Hummel, Op. 21 on "Wilhelmus von Nassauen"; Moscheles, Op. 29 on "The Harmonious Blacksmith"; Moscheles, Cramer, Hummel, Kalkbrenner on "Rule Britannia"; Ries, Op. 82 No. 2, on a Venetian Gondola theme; Herz, Op. 12 on a Tirolerlied; Weber, Op. 28 on a theme from Méhul's "Joseph". Commentary in German and English. D.

Con Sentimento (G. Puchelt-Lienau c. 1970). Two volumes. Klaviermusik Der Deutschen Romantik. Biographical notes. Int. to M-D.

Vol. I: 14 small dances including Ludwig Berger, Polonaise Op. 38/4; Adolf Henselt, Zwei kleine Walzer Op. 28/1-2; Ferdinand Hiller, Gigue Op. 81/4; Stephen Heller, Zwei Walzerträumereien Op. 122/6, 9 and Tarantelle Op. 85/1; Robert Volkmann, Tanzweise Op. 18/5; Carl Reinecke, Fandango from Op. 145 and Polka Op. 57/4; Woldemar Bargiel, Walzer Op. 32/8; Theodor Kirchner, Skizze Op. 11 Book II No. 2; Adolf Jensen, Polonaise Op. 33/19 and Reigen Op. 33/5.

Vol. II: 4 entertaining sonatinas by Carl Reinecke, Op. 47/2; Julius Carl Eschmann, Op. 71/1; Isidor Seiss, Op. 8/1; Theodor Kirchner, Op. 70/1.

Corpus of Early Keyboard Music (American Institute of Musicogoly).
Willi Apel is the general editor for this enormous series. It is designed to include all keyboard music from ca. 1300-1700 not otherwise readily available. Missing volumes not yet available.

Vol. 1: Keyboard Music of the 14th and 15th Centuries (W. Apel).

Vol. 2: Marco Facoli: Intravolatura di balli (1588) (W. Apel).

Vol. 3: Giovanni Salvatore: Collected Keyboard works (B. Hudson).

Vol. 4: Hieronymous Praetorius: Magnificats (C. G. Rayner).

Vol. 5: Bernardo Pasquini: Collected Works for Keyboard in 7 volumes (M. B. Haynes).

1. Capricci (2), Fantasia, Ricercari (2), Canzone (3), Fuga, Sonate (2).
2. Suites, Arias
3. Variations
4. Variations
5. Toccatas

6 and 7. not yet available.

Vol. 6: Joh. of Lublin: Tablature of Keyboard music in 6 volumes (J. White).

1. Organ preambula, organ masses, mass ordinary section.
2. Introits, Sequences, Hymns, Antiphons.
3. Intabulations of Motets and other sacred pieces.
4. French, German and Italian compositions.
5. Dances, Polish songs, untitled and unidentified works.
6. Tones of the Psalms and Magnificats, fundamentum exercises, conclusions, clausulae.

Vol. 7: Bernardo Storace: Selva di varie composizioni d'intavolatura per cimbalo ed organo . . . In Venetia, 1644 . . . (B. Hudson).

Vol. 8: Keyboard Dances from the Earlier Sixteenth Century (D. Heartz). This includes 28 of Attaingnant's transcriptions of chansons for keyboard and 25 dances from Antonio Gardane's Intabolatura Nova, 1551.

Vol. 9: Costanzo Antegnati: L'Antegnata Intavolatura de Ricercari de organo (W. Apel).

Vol. 10: Organ Music from Polish Manuscripts (G. Golos and A. Sutkowski). Four vols.

1. Organ chorales by Peter Hasse (ca. 1617-1672) and one piece by Ewald (unknown).

2. Organ chorales by Heinrich Scheidmann (ca. 1596-1663) and Franz Tunder (ca. 1614-1667).
3. Fantasias from Manuscript 300, P. Vv, 123, Archuvium Wojewodzkie, Gdansk.
4. D. Cato, J. Podbielski, M. Wartecki, P. Zelechawski and anonymous pieces.

Vol. 11: Gregorio Strozzi: Capricci da sonare per cembali et organi (1687) (B. Hudson).
Vol. 12: Ercole Pasquini: Collected Keyboard Works (W. R. Shindle).
Vol. 15: Michelangelo Rossi: Collected Keyboard Works (J. R. White).
Vol. 16: Adam Reincken: Collected Keyboard Works (W. Apel).
Vol. 18: Christopher Gibbons: Keyboard Compositions (C. Rayner).
Vol. 24: Neapolitan Keyboard Compositions (c. 1600) (R. Jackson).
Contains works by Stella, Lambardo, Ippolito, Rinaldo, Fillimarino, Montella, Mayone, Gesualdo.
Vol. 27: Samuel Mareschal: Selected Works (J. Bonhote).

Early Classics for the Piano (Mirovitch-GS).
19 pieces by 14 composers, edited. Works by Barrett, Burton, Galuppi, Hasse, Hässler, Haydn, Keller, Leo, Maris, L. Mozart, Paradisi, Turk, Zipoli. Int.

A First Harpsichord Book (Igor Kipnis-OUP c. 1970).
"This anthology is intended primarily for the new harpsichord owner. It is an introduction to the music which can be played on it and to the problems of interpreting such music." From the preface. Editorial system explained, sources identified. Ten pieces from the 17th and 18th centuries. Works by J. S. Bach, Anonymous, F. Couperin, Byrd, Pasquini, Handel, D. Scarlatti, Daquin, C. P. E. Bach, Rameau.

"Folies d'Espagne" (F. Goebels-Schott).
Three sets of variations based on the *La Folia* theme: Bernardo Pasquini: simple elaboration of harmonic scheme; Alessandro Scarlatti: more brilliant figuration; C. P. E. Bach: finest of the three, some expressive writing.

Four Hundred Years of European Keyboard Music (W. Georgii-Arno Volk). Vol. I of the "Anthology of Music Series". Includes a historical introduction, suggestions on performance, list of sources consulted, over 50 pieces representing 47 composers from Johann Kotter (ca. 1485-1541) to Schönberg. Includes works not often performed and some not easily found in other editions. Some works by Kotter, B. Schmid, Byrd, Bull, Purcell, Couperin, Rameau, Poglietti, Scarlatti, Martini, Galuppi, Paradisi, Froberger, Pachelbel, Kuhnau, Buxtehude, Böhm, Fischer, Muffat, Telemann, Bach, Handel, sons of Bach, Schobert, Wagenseil, Clementi, Sonata A, Op. 50/1; Haydn, Presto D; Mozart, Adagio b; Beethoven, Op. 126/4-5; Weber, Menuet from Op. 24; Schubert, Allegretto c; Schumann Op. 16/1, 4; Mendelssohn Op. 7/1; Brahms, Op. 118/2; Chopin, Op. 68/4; Smetana, Op. 13/1; Mussorgsky, In the Village; Liszt, Provenzal and Christmas Song; Grieg, Norwegian Spring Dance; Debussy, Clair de Lune; Scriabin, Op. 51/4; Reger, Op. 143/3; Hindemith, Sonata I; C. Scott, Rainbow Trout; Schönberg, Op. 19/2.

The Joy of Classics (D. Agay-YMP).
Contains 71 pieces including some time-honored original shorter works from the 18th and 19th centuries: Scarlatti and Purcell to Brahms and Tschaikowsky. Broad range of selections.

Keyboard Music of the Baroque and Rococo (W. Georgii-Arno Volk). Three volumes.

Vol. I: Music Before Bach and Handel. Contains works by Byrd, Bull, Farnaby, Purcell, Sweelinck, Chambonnières, L. Couperin, Le Bègue, Frescobaldi, Pasquini, Poglietti, A. Scarlatti, Froberger, G. Muffat, F. T. Richter, Pachelbel, J. K. F. Fischer, Kuhnau.

Vol. II: Music of Contemporaries of Bach and Handel. Contains works by D. Scarlatti, F. Couperin, Rameau, Daquin, Dandrieu, Telemann and Muffat.

Vol. III: Music After Bach and Handel. Contains works by D. Scarlatti, F. Couperin, Rameau, Méhul, Wagenseil, Schobert, J. C. Bach, W. F. Bach, G. Benda, and J. W. Hässler.

Keyboard Sonatas of the 18th Century (Smart-GS c. 1967).
Contains sonatas by J. C. Bach, Pleyel, Schobert, Platti, G. Berg, von Ferguson, de Nebra, Holder, Bull, Horsley. Unusual collection.

Klaviermusik aus älter Zeit (F. Wührer-Süddeutscher Musikverlag).
Works by Sweelinck, Froberger, Kuhnau, Muffat, Frescobaldi, Chambonnières.

Klaviermusik der Romantik (K. Herrmann-Hug 1960).
19 original works by J. P. E. Hartmann, Heller, Jensen, Kirchner, MacDowell, Raff, Smetana, Mussorgsky.

Klaviermusik des 17. und 18. Jahrhunderts (K. Herrmann-Hug). Three volumes.
Vol. I: Froberger, Kindermann, Richter, Krieger, Kuhnau, Mattheson, Telemann, Krebs, Monn, Kirnberger, Purcell, Chambonnières, L. Couperin, Le Bègue, Loeillet, Lully, d'Anglebert, F. Couperin, Rameau, Daquin, Pasquini, Pergolesi.
Vol. II: Telemann, Muffat, Bach sons, Marpurg, Kirnberger, Byrd, Gibbons, Purcell, Couperin, Rameau, Dandrieu, Duphly, Scarlatti, Martini.
Vol. III: Scheidt, Froberger, Pachelbel, Reutter, Muffat, Eberlin, Frescobaldi, Durante, Scarlatti, Porpora, Paradisi.
Difficulty increases with each volume. Excellent selection, clean edition.

Der Kreis um Telemann (At the Time of Telemann) (Frey-CFP).
28 dance movements (M, Gavotte, Air, Loure, Rigaudon, etc.) by Dieupart, Marchand, Graupner, Grünewald, Krebs, Muffat, Stölzel, J. S. Bach, Telemann. All are short dances, easier to perform than the suites of Bach and Händel. Some of these works appear in no other contemporary collection. Excellent introduction to musical life in the first half of the 18th century.

Leichte Klaviermusik aus Zwei Jahrhunderten (Georgii, Keller, Lampe, Theopold-Henle). Two volumes.
Based on autograph and first editions. Int.

Works by I. Albéniz, C. P. E. Bach, W. F. Bach, Beethoven, Brahms, Chopin, Milo Cipra (1906-), Dvořák, Grieg, Hässler, Heller, Jansen, Liszt, Mendelssohn, Mozart, Mussorgski, Schubert, Schumann, Smetana, Tajčević.

Leichte Klavierstücke des Klassischen und Romantischen Zeitalters (Georgii, Gieseking, Lampe, Keller-Henle). Two volumes. Easy-Int.
Based on autographs, first editions and early impressions. Contains performance suggestions. Works by Beethoven, Brahms, Chopin, Clementi, Hässler, Haydn, Kirchner, Liszt, Mendelssohn, Mozart, Schubert, Schumann, Tschaikowsky, Türk.

Lyrische Klavierstücke der Romantik (W. Kahl-ECo 1926).
Tomaschek, Eklog; Worzischek, Le désir, Impromptu; Cramer, Etude, I pensieri dolenti; L. Berger, Etude; Taubert, Minnelied No. 3, and No. 8; Klengel, Romanze; Boehner, Romanze; Burgmüller, Rhapsody.

Masters of the Rococo (M. Frey-Simrock). Two volumes.
Works by Couperin, Dandrieu, Destouches, Lully, Marais, Rameau and Royer.

Das Menuett, 21 Menuette aus dem 17 und 18 Jahrhunderts (L. Beer-HV 1950).
Contains: Minuets by J. S. Bach, C. P. E. Bach, Georg Benda, Couperin, D'Anglebert, Daquin, J. K. F. Fischer, Handel, Kirchhoff, Kuhnau, Marpurg, Muffat, Murschhauser, Paradies, Purcell and Schaale.

Mitteldeutches Musikarchiv (Br&H 1955-).
A collection of old music published at Wiesbaden by the Musicological Seminary of the Friedrich Schiller University of Jena. Series I: Clavier Music includes: 1. Johann Mattheson, "Die wohlklingende Fingersprache", Fugues and Suite movements. 2. Johann Christoph Graupner, 8 Partitas. 3. and 4. Giovanni Benedetto Platti, 12 Sonatas. 5. Giovanni Battista Martini, 6 Sonatas. 6. Johann Gottfried Müthel, 3 Sonatas. 7. Müthel, 2 Ariosi with 12 Variations.

Music of Early Times (1350-1650) (W. Apel-Schott). Two volumes.

Keyboard works from the Renaissance to early Baroque.
Vol. 1: Germany and Italy: works by 18 composers.
Vol. 2: England, Spain and France: works by 12 composers.

Das Neue Sonatinen Buch (M. Frey-Schott). Two volumes.

Two outstanding collections on the Int. to M-D level. Volume I has 17 sonatinas and 15 single pieces; Volume II contains 8 sonatinas and 18 single pieces or movements. Emphasizes 18th- and 19th-century repertoire.

New Recital Repertoire by Masters of the 17th, 18th, and 19th Centuries (A. Mirovitch-EV).

Contains Telemann, Fantasies D, B♭; J. Pachelbel, Fugues c; F. J. Kuhnau, Prelude b; J. C. Bach, Allegretto from Sonata Op. 5/1 and Tempo di Minuetto from Sonata Op. 5/5; Giovanni Giornovichi (1745-1804), Tempo di Gavotta (arr. for piano by S. Dussek); J. F. Reichardt, Aria; M. Clementi, Waltz No. 24; J. L. Dussek, Larghetto, Quasi Andante and J. Haydn, La Roxolane (Air Varie). An unusual collection of repertoire for Int. level.

Old Masters of the 16th, 17th and 18th Centuries (W. Niemann-K).

Overedited but contains an excellent selection of literature. In two sections: German Masters and Other Masters. German Masters contains: Georg Böhm, Presto; J. K. F. Fischer, Praeludium, Rondeau, Sarabande and Praeludium and Chaconne; Froberger, Suite (Variations) on "Auff die Mayerin", 2 Sarabandes D, d, Toccata d; C. H. Graun, Gigue; J. K. Kerll, Capriccio "Cucu", Canzone; J. P. Kirnberger, Polonaise, Menuet, La Lutine, La Gaillarde, Courante, Gavotte, Gigue, and Allegro for the Musical Clock; J. Krieger, Partita d; J. Kuhnau, Praeludium, Gigue, Bourrée, Gavotte, Presto and the Biblical Sonata "The Battle Between David and Goliath;" F. W. Marpurg, Allemende d, 2 Gigues d, e, Grand Fugue G; G. Muffat, Air, Menuet, Rigaudon; F. X. Murschhauser, Aria pastoralis variata; C. Nichelmann, La Gaillarde, La Tendre, Sarabande, Gigue, Sonata; J. Pachelbel, Fugues on the "Magnificat"; S. Scheidt, Passamezzo-Variationen.

Other Masters contains: J. Bull, The King's Hunting Jigg; W.

Byrd, The Bells; F. Couperin, Rigaudon, Les petits moulins à vent; C. Daquin, Le Coucou; F. Durante, Studio; G. Frescobaldi, 2 Canzonas; B. Galuppi, Sonata D; L. Marchand, Gavotte; G. B. Martini, Gavotte; P. D. Paradisi, Sonata A; A. Poglietti, Aria Allemagna con variazioni; J. P. Rameau, Musette en Rondeau, Rigaudon; D. Scarlatti, Siciliano; D. Zipoli, Praeludium, Aria, Gavotta.

Old Masters of the 17th and 18th Centuries (W. Niemann-CFP). Three volumes.

Vol. 1: England, France, Italy
11 pieces: Byrd, The Bells; Bull, King's Hunting Jigg; Couperin, Little Windmills; Daquin, Cuckoo; Durante, Studio; Frescobaldi, Due Canzone; Galuppi, Sonata D; Marchand, Gavotte; Martini, Gavotte; Paradisi, Sonata A.

Vol. 2: Germany
19 pieces: Böhm, Presto; Fischer, Praeludium and Rondeau, Sarabande, Praeludium and Chaconne; Froberger, Suite (Variations) "Auf die Mayerin", 2 sarabandes, Toccata; Graun, Gigue; Kerll, Capriccio "Cucu", Canzone; Kirnberger, 6 pieces.

Vol. 3: Germany
15 pieces: Krieger, Partita No. 11; Kuhnau, Prelude and Gigue, Bourrée, Gavotte, Presto; Marpurg, Menuet, La Badine, La Voltigeuse; Mattheson, Allemande; Muffat, Air, Menuet; Pachelbel, Fugue on the Magnificat; Murschhauser, Aria pastoralis variata; Scheidt, Passamezzo Variations. M-D.

Organum. Series 5, Piano Music (K&S).
Each number is available separately.

1. Clementi, Muzio. Sonate C.
2. Bach, Carl Philipp Emanuel. Sonata G.
3. Dussek, Johann Ladislaus. Sonata g, Op. 10/2.
4. Clementi, Muzio. Sonata B♭, Op. 10/3.
5. Kozeluch, Leopold Anton. Sonata E♭, Op. 51/2.
6. Dussek, Johann Ladislaus. Sonata E♭ (The farewell), Op. 44.
7. Wolf, Ernst Wilhelm. Two easy Sonatas d, E♭.

8. Hummel, Johann Nepomuk. Variations on a Theme from Gluck's "Armida."
9. Türk, Daniel Gottlob. Sonata e.
10. Cramer, Johann Baptist. Les menus plaisirs.
11. Forkel, Johann Nikolas. Sonata D.
12. Dussek, Johann Ladislaus. Sonata B♭, Op. 45/1.
13. Türk, Daniel Gottlob. Sonata C.
14. Steibelt, Daniel. Rondo C.
15. Clementi, Muzio. Sonata g, Op. 7/3.
16. Clementi, Muzio. Sonata f, Op. 14/3.
17. Forkel, Johann Nikolaus. Sonata d.
18. Clementi, Muzio. Sonata B♭, Op. 14/1.
19. Türk, Daniel Gottlob. Sonata a.
20. Clementi, Muzio. Sonata b, Op. 40/2.
21. Wolf, Ernst Wilhelm. Two easy Sonatas, G, F.
22. Dussek, Johann Ladislaus. Sonata c, Op. 35/3.
23. Kozeluch, Leopold Anton. Sonata d, Op. 51/3.
24. Türk, Daniel Gottlob. Sonata D.
25. Wolf, Ernst Wilhelm. Two easy sonatas c.
26. Hässler, Johann Wilhelm. Two easy sonatas.
27. Bach, Wilhelm Friedemann. Solo-Concerto G.
28. Hässler, Johann Wilhelm. Two easy sonatas.
29. Müthel, Johann Gottfried. Sonata B♭ with six Variations.
30. Hässler, Johann Wilhelm. Two easy sonatas.
31. Bach, Wilhelm Friedemann. Fantasie C.

Petit Gradus Ad Parnassum (I. Philipp-Leduc).
100 varied studies by different composers from easy to difficult. Includes composers such as Kullak, Burgmüller, Clementi, Kalkbrenner, Raff, Farrenc, etc.

The Piano and Its Ancestors (F. Gunther-AMP).
14 selected works from 1563 to 1800 by Scheidt, J. S. Bach, C. P. E. Bach, Bull, Farnaby, Purcell, Rameau, Couperin, Telemann, W. F. Bach, Haydn, Mozart. One page of photographs of early keyboard instruments. Brief biographies and notes about the pieces. Int.

Le piano classique (H. Classens-Consortium Musical). Four volumes.
Vol. I: Old English Masters: Arne, Purcell, Peerson, Byrd,

Bull, Blow, Arnold, Farnaby, Morley, Gibbons.

Vol. II: Old French Masters: Séjan, Hüllmandel, Corrette, Tapray, Beauvarlet-Charpentier.

Vol. III: Old Italian Masters: A. and D. Scarlatti, Grazioli, Frescobaldi, Pescetti, Pasquini, Santelli.

Vol. IV: Old German Masters: Händel, Haydn, L. Mozart, Sons of Bach, Telemann, Kirnberger, Kirchoff, Krebs, Wagenseil, Kuhnau, Marpurg.

Pedagogically oriented, fine text.

Pieces by Pre-Bach Composers of Easy and Medium Difficulty (K). Contains original works, with dynamics, fingering, phrasing and pedal marks added. Interesting Preface. J. E. Kindermann, Ballet; J. J. Froberger, Suite b (A, C, S, G); B. Schultheiss, Sarabande; J. K. F. Fischer, Rondeau, Balet anglois; J. Krieger, Rondeau; J. Pachelbel, Gavotte with 2 Variations; J. Kuhnau, Ciacona, Aria; G. Böhm, Rigaudon; F. W. Zachau, Vom Himmel hoch, da komm ich her; F. X. A. Murschhauser, Variations on Gegruest seyest du, O Jesulein; J. H. Buttstedt, Air; J. J. de Neufville, Sarabande; J. B. Loeillet, Minuet-Rondo; H. Purcell, 2 Hornpipes; d'Anglebert, Gigue; A. Couperin, Sarabande; Le Bègue, Bourée, Puer nobis nascitur; G. Le Roux, Menuet; F. Couperin, Le Dodo; C. Dieupart, Sarabande, Gavotte; L. Marchand, Menuet; Frescobaldi, Corrente, La Frescobalda; B. Pasquini, Partite di Folia; D. Zipoli, Versi (Fugetten), Pastorale; Sweelinck, Pavana Hispanica, Soll es sein. Table of embellishments is also included. Fine collection of literature from this period. Not difficult. This is a reprint of Vol. I of *Das Kleine Klavierbuch* (K. Herrmann-CFP) originally in four volumes. II. Music of Bach's Time; III. The Classic; IV. The Romantic. All (CFP).

Pièces de Clavecin des XVIIme et XVIIIme Siècles (Blanche Selva-Senart).

Compositions by Chambonnières, Dagincourt, Frescobaldi, Froberger, Galuppi, Lully, G. Muffat, Paradies.

Polyphonic Piano Music (W. Frickert-Cranz).

Easy pieces from seventeenth through twentieth centuries. Elementary preliminary exercises in two-part writing are included in preparation for the well-edited repertoire.

Ricercare, Canzonen und Fugen des 17. und 18. Jahrhunderts (Hillemann-Nag).
Works by G. Gabrieli, P. Cornet, Hässler, Erbach, Kerll, Murschhauser, Krieger, Pachelbel and Walther.

Romantisches Jugend Album (A. Schoberlechner-UE).
A fine graded collection of elementary to Int. compositions from the 19th century. Includes works by Schumann, Kirchner, H. Hofmann, Heller, Reinhold, Gade, Jensen, Tschaikowsky, Mendelssohn, Fuchs, Schytte, W. Niemann and Reger.

Das Rondo, neun Klavierstücke aus dem 17. und 18. Jahrhunderts (L. Beer-HV 1950).
Contains: N. LeBègue, Rondeau; F. Couperin, Le petit rien; Rameau, Les tendres plaintes; Dandrieu, La musette; Daquin, L'hirondelle; Duphly (Duflitz), Rondeau; Marpurg, Rondeau; Kirnberger, Fanfare; J. F. Christmann, Rondo.

Selected Piano Sonatas by Classical Composers (W. Georgii-Henle)
Two volumes.
Vol. I: C. P. E. Bach, Prussian Sonata F; Clementi, Sonata G Op. 39/2; Haydn, Sonatas C No. 35, G No. 40; Mozart, Sonatas F (280), G (283), C (545); Beethoven, Op. 49/1-2, Op. 14/1-2.
Vol. II: J. C. Bach, Sonata G Op. 17/4; Clementi, Sonata D Op. 39/3; Haydn, Sonatas D No. 37, E flat No. 52; Mozart Sonatas A (331), F (332); Beethoven Sonatas Op. 2/1, Op. 13, Op. 27/2.

Selected Pre-Classical Sonatas (PWM).
18th century German and Italian compositions which, in the history of the development of the sonata for solo instrument, form a link between one-movement sonatas (e.g. those of D. Scarlatti) and sonatas in cyclic form (of the classical period). All performing indications are the editor's suggestions.
J. C. Bach, Sonata c; M. P. Cherubini, Sonata B♭; B. Galuppi, Sonata; J. Hässler, Sonata a; P. D. Paradies, Sonata D; G. B. Pescetti, Sonata c.

Seventeenth-Century Masters of the Harpsichord and Clavichord (K).
Kindermann, Ballet; Froberger, Suite b (A,C,S,G); Schultheiss,

Sarabande; J. K. F. Fischer, Rondeau, Balet Anglois; Kreiger, Rondeau; Pachelbel, Gavotte, Courante; Buttstedt, Aria; Böhm, Rigaudon; Zachau, Chorale; Murchhauser, Variations on a Chorale; Buttstedt, Aria; Neufville, Sarabande; Loeillet, Minuet-Rondo; Purcell, Hornpipe; D'Anglebert, Gigue; L. Couperin, Sarabande, Le Bègue, Bourrée, Puer Nobis Nascitur; Le Roux, Minuet; F. Couperin, Le Dodo; C. Dieupart, Sarabande; Marchand, Minuet; Frescobaldi, Corrente, La Frescobalda; Pasquini, Partite di Follia; Zipoli, Versi (2 little fugues), Pastorale; Sweelinck, Pavana Hispanica, A German Folk Song.

Silhouetten—Old and new dances for piano solo (F. Hirsch-Br&H). Dance movements from the time of Bach to the Present, including boogie-woogie, rumba, cha-cha-cha, mambo and carioca. Short movements of M-D.

Silva Iberica . . . Easy Keyboard Music of the 16th, 17th and 18th Centuries from Italy, Portugal, and Spain (S. Kastner-Schott c. 1954).

14 pieces by different composers: 7 Spanish, 5 Portuguese and 2 Italians. Music from ca. 1500 to 1800. Preface in Spanish, German and English. Clean edition. Some unusual works. Composers are Mudarra, Cabézon, Valenti, Yepes, da Cruz, Puxol, de Olague, Pasquini, Freixanet, Carvalho, Santo Elias, Lidon and anonymous. Easy to M-D.

Six Keyboard Sonatas from the Classic Era (W. S. Newman-SB c. 1965).

Six little-known sonatas. Urtext edition with critical annotations. Sonata D, Op. 13/3 Heinrich Joseph Riegel (1741-1799); Sonata c, Op. 1/6 Nicolas Séjan (1745-1819); Sonata g, Op. 10/3 Nicolas Joseph Hüllmandel (1756-1823); Sonata d, Op. 3/4 Giovanni Marco Placido Rutini (1723-1797); Sonata IV g, Ferdinando Turini (ca. 1749-ca. 1812); Sonata II g, Ernst Wilhelm Wolf (1735-1792). Int. to M-D.

Slavic Keyboard Music (W. Frickert-Zimmermann). Two volumes.

Vol. I: Tchaikowsky, Song without Words Op. 2/3; Smetana, L'innince; Dvořák, Humoresque; Chopin, Nocturne Op. 9/2; Mussorgsky, Souvenir d'enfance; Medtner, March Op. 51/3; Arensky, Barcarolle; Borodin, Mazurka C.

Vol. II: Fibich, Poem; Rimsky-Korsakov, Novelette Op. 11/2; Balakireff, Berceuse; Liapunoff, Un cheval sur un baton, Ramage des enfants; Chopin, Prelude D♭; Smetana, Souvenir en forme de Polka; Dvořák, Albumleaf f; Tchaikowsky, Valse-Scherzo.

Slowakische Klavierkompositionen 1958 (SHV).
Ivan Hrusovsky, Toccata; Pavol Simai, Pastorela; Ilja Zeljenka, Male variacie; Dezider Kardos, Groteskny pochod; Rudolf Macudzinski, Meditacia; Stefan Nemeth-Samorinsky, Toccata a fuga.

Slowakische Klavierkompositionen 1959 (SHV).
Jozef Rosinsky (1897-), Mala ekloga; Stefan Nemeth-Samorinsky (1896-), Improvizacia; Simon Jurovsky (1912-), Dva tance; Mical Vilec (1902-), Rondo; Dusan Martincek (1936-), Etuda, Op. 4/1-2.
Both collections throw interesting light on stylistic characteristics of contemporary Central European piano literature.

The Solo Sonata (F. Giegling-Arno Volk) Vol. 15 of the "Anthology of Music Series."
Includes a historical survey, list of sources consulted, a checklist of modern editions of sonatas of the 17th and 18th centuries and a bibliography. Works for the piano include: Johann Kuhnau, Suonata Seconda ("Frische Clavierfrüchte" 1696); Francesco Geminiani, Pièce de Clavecin (1762); Domenico Alberti, Sonata F (before 1740); Georg Benda, Sonata IX a (ca. 1780); Anton Eberl, Sonatina Op. 6 C (1796); Wenzel Johann Tomaschek, Sonata Op. 21, F (1806); Robert Schumann, Sonata Op. 118/2 D (1853); Paul Hindemith, Second Sonata (1936).

Sonatas of the Pre-Classic Period (M. Frey-Schott).
Works by Kuhnau, Hasse, K. P. E. Bach, Hässler, Türk, Paradisi and others.

Sonaten alter Meister (O. v Irmer-Birnbach).
Works by Händel, Scarlatti, Benda, J. Chr. Bach, Reichardt, Haydn, Mozart and Beethoven. Clean edition. Int. to M-D.

Style and Interpretation (H. Ferguson-OUP).

Vol. 1: Early Keyboard Music I: England and France
Vol. 2: Early Keyboard Music II: Germany and Italy
Vol. 3: Classical Piano Music
Vol. 4: Romantic Piano Music

These four volumes contain 54 pieces ranging from the 16th to the 19th centuries. They are designed to illustrate the way in which style and interpretation change from century to century, and from country to country. Each volume contains detailed essays on the conventions governing performance, and on the instruments of the periods and countries concerned, as well as a short introduction to each work.

Thirteen Keyboard Sonatas of the 18th and 19th Centuries (W. S. Newman-UNC c. 1947).

A fine collection of unfamiliar sonatas with critical commentaries. Includes sonatas by Jean Barrière (flourished 1720-50), Platti, Alberti, Georg Benda (1722-95), J. J. Agrell (1701-65), C. G. Neefe (1748-98), Manuel Blasco de Nebra (ca. 1750-1784), Dittersdorf (1739-99), Joseph Wölfl (1773-1812), E. T. A. Hoffman (1776-1822), J. F. Reichardt, Loewe, Moscheles.

Three Pavanes on the Same Theme (F. Goebels-Schott).

Antonio Cabezón: Pavane Italiana; written for performance on the harpsichord at the Court of Philip II of Spain.

John Bull: The Spanish Pavan; a fine example of virginal writing.

J. P. Sweelinck and S. Scheidt (teacher and pupil): good example of North German and Dutch Organ art.

This is a concentrated view of 16th- and 17th-century keyboard art. As the editor points out, "each work stands as a key work in the output not only of its composer, but of his environment".

Toccata Album (E. Balogh-GS).

18 Toccatas by Antheil, J. S. Bach, Buxtehude, Czerny, Frescobaldi, Gabrieli, Hoiby, Khachaturian, Padovano, Paradisi, Pollini, Prokofieff, Purcell, Rheinberger, A. and D. Scarlatti, Schumann, Froberger. Points up the variety of forms included in this term.

Le Trésor des Pianistes, compiled by Jacques and Louise Farrenc, is the most complete collection of keyboard music ever assembled. It covers a period from the sixteenth through the nineteenth centuries. About 250 of the works are available separately through (Leduc). A reprint of the series was brought out by (BB) in 1970. The original work consisted of 23 volumes, was published between 1861 and 1872 by (Leduc).

Vol. I: Preliminaries, History of the Piano, Treatise on Ornaments.

Vol. II: Parthenia (1611): 18 pieces by William Byrd (1542-1623), John Bull (1562-1628), Orlando Gibbons (1583-1625).
Various English composers.
Claudio Merulo (1533-1604): Toccatas.
Girolamo Frescobaldi (1583-1643): Three Fugues (spurious), 6 Canzoni, various pieces.
Georg Muffat (1645-1704): 12 Toccatas.
Jacques Champion de Chambonnières (ca. 1602-1672: Pièces de Clavecin, 2 Books.
Jean Henri d'Anglebert (1635-1691): Pièces de Clavecin.

Vol. III: Johann Kuhnau (1660-1722): 7 Sonatas, *Neuer Clavier Ubung,* Toccatas.
Henry Purcell (1658-1695): Collection of pieces.
Johann Jakob Froberger (1616-1667): 5 Capricci, 6 Suites.
Louis Couperin (1626-1661).
Antoine Le Bègue (1631-1702).
Bernardo Pasquini (1637-1710).
Johann Kaspar Kerll (1627-1693).
Alessandro Scarlatti (1659-1725).

Vol. IV: François Couperin (1668-1733): Pièces de Clavecin, 3 Books.

Vol. V: François Couperin: Pièces de Clavecin, Book 4.
George Frederick Handel (1685-1759): Suites, 3 Books; 6 Fugues.

Vol. VI: Domenico Scarlatti (1685-1757): 77 pieces.

Vol. VII: Domenico Scarlatti: 75 pieces.

Vol. VIII: J. S. Bach (1685-1750): 6 Partitas, 6 English Suites.
Jean Philippe Rameau (1683-1746): Pièces de Clavecin, 2 Books.
Nicolo Porpora (1686-1766): 6 Fugues.
Vol. IX: Francesco Durante (1684-1755): 6 Sonatas.
François Dandrieu (1682-1738).
Benedetto Marcello (1686-1739).
Georg Telemann (1684-1740).
Giovanni Pescetti (ca. 1704-1766).
Claude Daquin (1694-1772): Pièces de Clavecin.
Padre Martini (1706-1784). 12 Sonatas.
Johann Ludwig Krebs (1713-1780): 3 Fugues.
Vol. X: Wilhelm Friedemann Bach (1710-1784): 12 Polonaises, Sonata, 8 Fugues, 1 Suite, 4 Fantasies.
Gottlieb Muffat (1690-1770): Collection of pieces.
Christoph Nichelmann (1717-1762): 11 Sonatas.
Vol. XI: Johann Gottlieb Goldberg (ca. 1720-?): Prelude and Fugue.
Johann Ernst Eberlin (1702-1762): 6 Preludes and Fugues.
Johann Mattheson (1681-1764): Various pieces.
Domenico Zipoli (1688-1726): Pieces for Organ and Harpsichord.
John Christopher Smith (1712-1795): 9 Suites.
Chr. Schaffrath (18th cent.): 2 Sonatas.
Vol. XII: C. P. E. Bach (1714-1788): 30 Sonatas.
Vol. XIII: C. P. E. Bach: 35 Sonatas and 4 Rondos.
Vol. XIV: Domenico Paradies (1707-1791): 10 Sonatas.
Duphly (1715-1789): Pièces de Clavecin.
Johann Philipp Kirnberger (1721-1783): 6 Fugues, various pieces.
Johann Buttstedt (1666-1727): 2 Sonatas.
Georg Benda (1722-1795): 6 Sonatas.
Vol. XV: Christoph Friedrich Bach (1732-1795): Sonatas, various pieces.
Joseph Haydn (1732-1809): 10 Sonatas.
J. G. Albrechtsberger (1736-1809): 30 Fugues.
Karl Fasch (1736-1800): 2 Sonatas, 1 piece.

Vol. XVI: Muzio Clementi (1752-1832): 3 Sonatas, Op. 2; 2 Sonatas, Op. 7; 3 Sonatas, Op. 8; 4 Sonatas and a Toccata from Op. 9, 10, 14.
Johann Wilhelm Hässler (1747-1822): 2 Fantasies, 9 Sonatas, 4 Solos.
O. A. Lindemann (1769-1859): Various pieces.
Vol. XVII: W. A. Mozart (1756-1791): 10 Sonatas, Romance.
Vol. XVIII: Johann Christian Bach (1735-1782): 7 Sonatas.
Johann L. Dussek (1760-1812): 3 Grandes Sonatas, Op. 35; Sonata, Op. 64.
J. G. Wernicke (?): 5 pieces.
Johann Schwanenberg (1740-1804): 2 Minuets.
Daniel Steibelt (1765-1823): Grande Sonate, Op. 64.
J. B. Cramer (1771-1858): 3 Sonatas.
Vol. XIX: L. van Beethoven (1770-1827): Sonatas (Op. 2 to Op. 27).
Vol. XX: Beethoven: Sonatas (Op. 28 to Op. 90).
Vol. XXI: Beethoven: Sonatas (Op. 101 to Op. 111); 6 Sets of Variations.
Vol. XXII: Johann Nepomuk Hummel (1778-1837): 7 Sets of Variations; Intro. and Rondo Op. 19; Rondo brilliant, Op. 109; Sonatas, Op. 13, 20, 81; Adagio from Op. 38; Fantasie Op. 18.
Vol. XXIII: Ferdinand Ries (1784-1838): L'Infortunée, Sonata, Op. 26.
Carl Maria von Weber (1786-1826): 4 Sonatas.
Felix Mendelssohn (1809-1847): Rondo capriccioso; 3 Fantasies or Caprices, Op. 16.
Frederic Chopin (1810-1849): 9 Nocturnes.

Viennese Masters from the Baroque, Classical and Biedermeier Periods (H. Kann-UE).
Contains Haydn, Capriccio; Mozart, Rondo K. 511; Schubert, Eccossaises; Fux, Sonata No. 4; Muffat, Fantasia; Wagenseil, Ricercata; Albrechtsberger, Galanterie fuga; Czerny, Set of Variations and a sequence of Waltzes; Voříšek (Woržischek), Rhapsody; and works by Hummel and Froberger. Kann's editorial work is excellent. There are also useful notes about the composers and the music.

GENERAL: CONTEMPORARY

Chester Centenary Album (JWC 1961).

These pieces were written especially for this event by five composers long associated with this publishing house:

Poulenc, Novelette.

Berlekey, Improvisation.

G. F. Malipiero, Variazione.

Goossens, Capriccio on His Hurdy Gurdy Man.

Ireland, Sea Idyll.

All works are reproduced in the composer's manuscript and are also available separately.

Collection Moderne (EBM 1936).

Contains works by: Dohnányi, Villa-Lobos, Longas, Stravinsky, Debussy, Scriabin, Medtner, Shostakovich, Satie, Mignone, Juon, Ravel, Rachmaninoff, Palmgren, Albeniz, and others. A practical collection, some transcriptions but most pieces are original. M-D.

Composer-Pianists (J. W. Schaum-Schaum Publications c. 1971).

Ten compositions in their original form including Gustav Mahler, I Walk With Joy Through the Green Forest; Alec Templeton, Springtime in the Village; Arthur Schnabel, Valse Mignonne; Walter Gieseking, Jazz Improvisation; Leopold Godowsky, Meditation; Emil Sauer, Petite Etude; Eugen d'Albert, Blues; Wanda Landowska, En Route; Ossip Gabrilowitsch, Oriental Melody; Tobias Matthay, Moment Musical. Int. to M-D.

Discovery (Nov).

"This is an international Series of Piano Music of Medium Difficulty to serve as a partner to John Ogdon's 'Virtuoso Series.' *Discovery* will contain much less demanding material technically and will introduce British pianists to music from distinguished foreign composers little known within the United Kingdom. British music will also have a place." From the preface.

Vol. I: Fernando Lopes-Graça, *Album for the Young Pianist.*

Vol. II: Charles Camilleri, *Little African Suite.*

Masters of Today (UE).
19 pieces by Busoni, Casella, Eisler, Krenek, Marx, Milhaud, Pisk, Prokofieff, Rathaus, Reger, Respighi, Scriabin, Strauss, Stravinsky, Szymanowski, Tcherepnin.

Musik der Zeit (UE). Five volumes.
Vol. 1: 19 pieces by Foerster, Borwinsky, Brauenfels, Tcherepnin, Dobrowen, Friedman, Kosa, Rachmaninoff, Szymanowski, Springer, Strauss, Weinberger, Marx.
Vol. 2: 17 pieces by Graener, Willner, Tcherepnin, Scriabin, Hába, Gál, Medtner, Szymanowski, Castelnuovo-Tedesco.
Vol. 3: 15 pieces by Bartók, Kósa, Rieti, Polowinkin, Nowak, Miaskowsky, Scriabin, Wladigeroff, Malipiero, Respighi, Kattnigg.
Vol. 4: 15 pieces by Petyrek, Bartók, Prokofieff, Scriabin, Krenek, Milhaud, Grosz, Rathaus.
Vol. 5: 18 pieces by Casella, Bartók, Wellesz, Pisk, Butting, Hauer, Eisler, Schönberg.

The New Piano Book (Autenrieth, Schleussner-Schott).
62 pieces in 3 volumes.
Vol. 1. Jarnach Stravinsky, Zilcher, Schultheiss, Schmid, Toch, Gretchaninoff, Bartók, Butting, Dushkin, Slavenski, Reutter, Schott, Windsperger, Haas, Bornschein, Hindemith.
Vol. 2: Bartók, Schultheiss, Sekles, Jarnach, Korngold, Scott, Windsperger, Reutter, Poulenc, Bornschein, Gretchaninoff, Milhaud, Toch, Hindemith, Tcherepnin.
Vol. 3: Stravinsky, Slavenski, Jarnach, Haas, Copland, Windsperger, Wiener, Albeniz, Reutter, Scott, Tansman, Beck, Benjamin, Honegger, Toch, Hindemith.

Seventeen Contemporary Dances (Sam Raphling-Mills).
Contains dances by: Albeniz, Bartók, Debussy, Kabalevsky, MacDowell, Raphling, Satie, Scriabin, Shostakovitch, Sibelius, Stravinsky.
Some unusual works make this collection useful.

Virtuoso (Nov). A modern piano series edited by John Ogdon. Published separately.

Includes: Alun Hoddinott, *Sonata* No. 3; Kenneth Leighton, *Nine Variations;* John McCabe, *Variations;* Wilfrid Mellers, *Natalis Invicti Solis;* Alfred Nieman, *Two Serenades;* Ronald Stevenson, *Prelude Fugue and Fantasy on Busoni's "Faust";* Erland von Koch, *Varianti Virtuosi*; Richard Hall, *Suite for Piano.*

Styles in 20th-Century Piano Music (UE).
An outstanding collection of 24 pieces by 24 European composers from the first half of this century. Ranges from Sibelius (Post-romantic) to Schönberg (12-tone). Points up the multiplicity of styles and moods already heard in this century. This is a revised and extended version of a volume published in 1951 on the occasion of the 50th anniversary of the Universal Edition. A note on each composer and some commentary on unusual notation add to the fine qualities of a first rate collection. Difficulty ranges from moderate to concert standard.

Thirty-Six Twentieth-Century Piano Pieces (GS).
A collection of contemporary works for recital and study. Works by Antheil, Barber, Bartók, Bernstein, Bloch, Carpenter, Chavez, Creston, Debussy, Dello Joio, Fauré, Fine, Grainger, Griffes, Kabalevsky, Khachaturian, Krenek, MacDowell, Muczynski, Prokofieff, Rachmaninoff, Ravel, W. Schuman, Scott, Shostakovich, Tcherepnin. Contains some important 20th-century piano works. D.

Treize Danses (T. Harsányi-ESC 1930).
13 mildly contemporary dances by Beck, Delannoy, Ferroud, Harsányi, Larmanjat, Lopatnikoff, Martinů, Migot, Milhaliovici, Rosenthal, Schulhoff, Tansman, and Wiener. Varied influences and styles. The "official" existence of a group of young musicians who resided in Paris in the 1920's known as the "Ecole de Paris" was signalized by the publication of this collection. Each member had a composition included.

Universal Edition Book of Keyboard Music of the 20th-Century (UE c. 1965).
Contains thirty-one compositions by: Apostel, Bartók, Bennett, Blacher, Boulez, Casella, Einem, Hába, Haubenstock-Ramati, Hauer, Jelinek, Kodály, Krenek, Martin, Milhaud,

Paccagnini, Petyrek, Poot, Pousseur, Reger, Schönberg, Skalkottas, Stockhausen, Strauss, Szymanowski, Tcherepnin, Wagner-Régeny, Webern, Wellesz, Wladigeroff.
Broad range of style and difficulty. Clean edition.

The Universal Edition Piano Book (Rutz-UE 1951).
Contains biographies and 28 pieces by Akses, Apostel, Bartók, Blacher, Burkhard, Casella, Doucet, Einem, Hauer, Jelinek, Kodály, Krenek, Larsson, Martin, Milhaud, Petyrek, Poot, Reger, Schönberg, Schulhoff, Sibelius, Szymanowski, Wagner-Régeny, Webern, Wladigeroff.

The World of Modern Piano Music (D. Agay-MCA).
42 easy original pieces by contemporary composers of nine different countries.

TOMBEAU, HOMMAGE

Hommage à Albert Roussel (Supplément de la Revue Musicale, April 1939).
Contains two songs by Delage and Milhaud and six pieces for piano by:
Honegger: Sur le nom d'Albert Roussel
Poulenc: Pièce Brève
Tansman: Berceuse
Ibert: Toccata sur le nom de Roussel (delightful)
Beck: Fox-Trot
Hoerée: Fanfare

Hommage à Willem Pijper (B&VP c. 1950).
Also titled as *Dutch Piano Album No. 3.*
Contains a preface in English and ten compositions for piano by Bosmans, Zagwijn, van Lier, Baaren, Henkemans, van Dijk, K. Mengelberg, Dresden, Escher and Wijdeveld.

Hommage Musical à Gabriel Fauré (Supplément de la Revue Musicale, October 1922) *Sept pièces de piano sur le nom de Fauré.* F fa A la U sol R ré E mi by his students.
Contains: Maurice Ravel, Berceuse for violin and piano; Georges Enescu, Pièce pour piano sur le nom de Fauré; Louis Albert, Moderato; Florent Schmitt, Rapide; Charles Koechlin,

Andante, Calme et trés expressif; Paul Ladmirault, Allegro moderato; Roger-Ducasse, D'une extreme lenteur.
The pieces by Ravel, Schmitt, Roger-Ducasse and Albert are published by (Durand).

Hommage to Paderewski (Bo&H).
Published as a memorial and contains works by Bartók, Britten (Mazurka Elegy for two pianos, issued separately), Castelnuovo-Tedesco, Goossens, Hammond, Labunski, Martinů, Milhaud, Nin-Culmell, Rathaus, Rieti, Schelling, Stojowski, Weinberger, Whithorne.
Also contains photographs of Paderewski at various stages of his career.

Tombeau de Claude Debussy (Durand, 1920).
Ten compositions dedicated to the memory of Debussy.
Piano works: Paul Dukas: La plainte, au loin, du faune. G. F. Malipiero: Hommage. Albert Roussel: L'accueil des muses. Florent Schmitt: Et Pan, au fond des blés lunaires. Other works by: Bartók, de Falla, Goossens, Ravel, Satie, Stravinsky.

Le Tombeau de Paul Dukas (Supplément de la Revue Musicale, May-June 1936).
Florent Schmitt, Lent Op. 86/6; Manuel de Falla, Andante molto sostenuto; Gabriel Pierné, Prélude on the name PAUL DUKAS; J. Guy-Ropartz, Grave; J. Rodrigo, Hommage à Paul Dukas; Julien Krein, Pièce; Olivier Messiaen, Pièce; Tony Aubin, Le Sommeil d'Iskender; Elsa Barraine, Hommage. All are of interest and most are short.

SEPARATE COUNTRIES

AUSTRIAN

Klaviermusik aus Osterreich (H. Kann-UE c. 1965).
Works by Froberger, Fux, Muffat, Wagenseil, Monn, Haydn, Capriccio G; Albrechtsberger, Fugue F; Mozart, Rondo a, K. 511; Hummel, Rondo Op. 11; Woržischek, Rhapsody Op. 1/9; Czerny, La Ricordanza Op. 33, Valses di Bravura Op. 35; Schubert, Klavierstück A, Ecossaises. Preface and notes about the composers in English, German, French and Italian. Con-

tains unusual and well-known pieces. Clean text and attractive collection.

Styrian Composers: Works for Piano (Marckhl-OBV). Three volumes. Six sonatas and two sets of pieces by contemporary Austrian composers:
Vol. 1: Waldemar Bloch, Max Haager, H. F. Aigner.
Vol. 2: Karol Haidmayer, Gunther Eisen, Walter Kainz.
Vol. 3: Evany Mixa, Erich Marchl.

BELGIAN

Les Classiques Belges: Oeuvres des Clavecinistes Belges du XVIIe Siècle (E. Closson-Durand).
Contains J. B. Loeillet, Allemande; J. H. Fiocco, L'inconstante, La legère; D. Raick, Allemande (prelude de la première suite), Deux gavottes; C. F. van Meert, Fugato; J. J. Robson, La galeuse.

Clavecinistes Flamands (C. van Elewyck-Schott Frères, c. 1877). Two volumes.
Vol. 1: Mathias van den Gheyn, Op. 3. Six suites pour le clavecin; Divertimenti di Londres; Deux préludes pour orgue; Deux préludes pour carillon.
Vol. 2: Extracts from works by various composers (17 composers in all).

Modern Belgium Piano Music (Dessain).
Richard de Guide, Nocturne; Louis De Meester, Toccata; R. van der Velden, Andante espressivo; William Pelemans, Allegro flamenco.

The Most Beautiful Pages from Belgian Harpsichord Music
P. Montani-Ric 1956).
Jean-Baptiste Loeillet (1653-1728), Allemande; Hector Fiocco (1690-?), L'Inconstante, La Légère; Dieudonné Raik (?-1764), Allemande; C. F. van Meert (?-?), Fugato; Jean-Jacques Robson (?-1785), La Galeuse.

BULGARIAN

Contemporary Bulgarian Piano Music (Otto Daub-Gerig c. 1965). Two volumes.

Introduction and biographical sketches in English. Volume I easier than volume II.

I: Konstantin Iliev (1924-), The Cuckoo, The Hen laid an Egg; Dimiter Nenov (1902-), Melody, Musette, Pastorale; Ljubomir Pipkov (1904-), Spring Dance; Alexander Raitschev (1922-), The Angry Rooster, The Old Water-Mill; Dimiter Tepkov (1929-), Grandfather's Glove. Int. to M-D.

II: Marin Goleminov (1908-), Bulgarian Dance; Bojan Ikonomov (1900-), Horo; Vasil Kasandjiev (1934-), The Jolly Sparrow, Nightmare; Krassimir Kürktschijski (1936-), Elegy; Pantscho Wladigerov (1899-), Lullaby. M-D.

CANADIAN

14 Piano Pieces by Canadian Composers (F. Harris Music Co. 1955).

Works by Fleming, Dolin, Blackburn, Betts, Kasemets, Beckwith, Papineau-Couture, Brott, Weinzweig, Coulthard, Morel, Somers, and Freedman.

Various grades of difficulty. Contains biographical notes.

Contemporary Canadian Music for Young Pianists (Waterloo Music Co.). Two volumes. Each volume contains a long-playing recording.

Vol. I: Pieces and suites by Violet Archer, Jean Coulthard, David Laumes, Arlene A. Street, Nick Slater, Daniel J. Harmer, William K. Rogers, Udo Kasemets, Richard Johnston, Jeannine Vanier, Rhené Jaque. Easy to Int.

Vol. II: Works by Otto Joachin, Ann Southam, Udo Kasemets, Jean Papineau-Couture, Samuel Dolin, George Fiala, Barbara Pentland, M. Kisby Hicks, John Beckwith, Phillip La Marche. Easy to M-D.

CZECHOSLOVAKIAN

Czech Classics (Artia).

Two large series, Musica Antiqua Bohemica (MAB) and Musica Viva Historica (MVH) are available. Volumes of interest to the pianist are:

MAB Vol. 14: *Classici Boemici I* contains works by Benda, Brixi, J. A. Stepan, F. X. Dussek, Kozeluh, Becvarovsky, Vranicky, Cibulka, Jirovec, Held and Vitášek.

MAB Vol. 20: *Classici Boemici II* contains works by J. L. Dussek, Reicha, Tomášek and Voříšek. Both volumes contain biographical and analytical notes in English.

MAB Vol. 17: *Sonatine Boemiche* (Bohemian Sonatinas) Sonatina movements and sonatinas by J. Benda, F. X. Dussek, J. L. Dussek, L. A. Kozeluh, J. Mysliveček, J. B. Vanhal, J. Voříšek.

MVH Vol. 15: *Czech Variations of the 18th Century for Piano* contains works by Stepan, Becvarovsky, Vanhal, Kozeluh, J. L. Dussek, Lipavsky.

MVH Vol. 5: *Ceske Sonatiny* alter tschechischer Meister (Czech Sonatinas) (O. Kredba).

CZECHOSLOVAKIAN, TWENTIETH CENTURY

Album Klavirnich Skladeb (V. Pos-Statni Nakladtelstvi Krasne Literatury, Hudby Umeni, c. 1965).

Fine collection of easy-to-intermediate contemporary Czech teaching pieces.

Contemporary Czechoslovakian Piano Music (Jan Matějček-Gerig c. 1968). Two volumes.

Introduction in English, biographical sketches, volume I easier than volume II.

I: Viktor Kalabis (1923-), About a Fountain; Dezider Kardoš (1914-), Bagatella; Jaroslav Křička (1882-), Scherzino; Bohuslav Martinů (1890-1959), A composition for little Eves; Jan Novák (1921-), Allegretto; Klement Slavický (1910-), A Ballad; Luboš Sluka (1928-), Two Merry Pieces for Piano; Eugen Suchoň (1908-), Arietta; Václav Trojan (1907-), The Bells of Prague. Int. to M-D.

II: Jan Klusák (1934-), Rondo; Marek Kopelent (1932-), For Arnošt Wilde; Juraj Pospíšil (1931-), Monologue; Zbyněk Vostřak (1920-), Essay; Ilja Zeljenka (1932-), Three Pieces for Piano. M-D to D.

Klavir 1947. Piano Album of Czech Composers (Artia).
Preface and biographical notes in English; in two volumes of 19 and 17 pieces. Contains works by: L. Janáček (1854-1928), Vitězslav Novák (1870-1949), Josef Suk (1874-1935), Václav Kaprál (1889-1947), Vilém Petrželka (1889-), Karel B. Jirák (1891-), Jaroslav Kvapil (1892-1958), Frantisek Picha (1893-), Pavel Bořkovec (1894-), Vladimir Polivka (1896-1948), Alois Hába (1893-), P. Haas (1899-1944), Karel Janeček (1905-), Isa Krejčí (1904-), František Bartoš (1905-), Václav Dobiáš (1909-), Vitezslava Kapralova (1915-1940).
An excellent cross section of 20th century Czech piano music.

DUTCH

Dutch Keyboard Music of the 16th and 17th Centuries (Vol. III of Monumenta Musica Nederlandica, A. Curtis-Nederlandse Muziekgeschiedenis c. 1961).
Contains the only surviving 16th-century source of Netherlands keyboard music, printed in its entirety for the first time, together with three 17th-century Dutch manuscripts, heretofore unknown: Van Soldt mss (before 1599), Leningrad mss (after 1650), Camphuysen mss (17th century), Gress mss (17th century). Excellent editorial comment in English plus unusual repertoire.

Klavierboek Anna Maria van Eijl (1656-?) (Vol. II of Monumenta Musica Nederlandica, Frits Noske-Nederlandse Muziekgeschiedenis c. 1959).

Preface in Dutch and English includes a discussion of the composers and works. This collection contains something of the spirit of the time, and points out the important use of variation form in keyboard teaching then in use. Contains 33 works of Steenwich, Berff, Froberger, Scheidemann, Kerll, Broeckhuisen; some works are not identified.

The Most Beautiful Pages from Dutch Harpsichord Music (P. Montani-Ric 1969).
J. P. Sweelinck, Capriccio a; Heinrich Weissenburg, Suite g; Elias Bronnemüller, Toccatina and Fugue d; R. P. van Oevering, Suite IV; Christian F. Ruppe (1753-?), Sonata.

DUTCH, TWENTIETH CENTURY

Anthology of Music from the Netherlands 1890-1960 (Eduard Reeser-Nederlandse Muziekgeschiedenis, 1966).
Volume II in this series. Contains in addition to other works, the following piano compositions: Hendrik Andriessen (1892-), first movement of Sonata (1934), Pavane (1937); Oscar van Hemel (1892-), first and second movements of Sonata No. II (1945); Willem Pijper (1894-1947), Sonatine No. 3 (1925), Fragment of Concerto for piano and orchestra (1927), Second movement of Sonata (1930); Alexander Voormolen (1895-), Sonnet (1922); Henriette Bosmans (1895-1952), Vieille Chanson (1943); Anthon van der Horst (1899-1965), Fragment of Teme con variazioni in modo conjuncto (1950); Hugo Godron (1900-), Nocturne No. 3 (1953); Karel Mengelberg (1902-), Notitia sui (1954); Geza Frid (1904-), Fragment of Variaties op een Nederlands volkslied, Op. 29a (1949); Leon Orthel (1905-), three movements from Epigrammen, Op. 17 (1938), Sonatina No. 4 (1954), Hommage à Ravel, No. 2 Deux Hommages en forme d'étude, Op. 40 (1958); Piet Ketting (1905-), Praeludium (1940); Kees van Baaren (1906-1970), Sonatina (1948), Muzikaal Zelfportret (1954); Bertus Van Lier (1906-), Dans (1943). A superb survey of Dutch piano music of this century with introduction and biographical notes in Dutch and English.

Dutch Piano Album No. 2 (B&VP).
13 compositions by H. Andriessen, W. Andriessen, Felderhof, de Groot, Hengeveld, Meenwisse, Mul, Mulder, Stokvis, Strategier, Van Der Bilt, Van Hemel.

Dutch Piano Album No. 3 (Homage to Willem Pijper) (B&VP).
10 pieces by Van Baaren, Bosmans, Dijk, Dresden, Escher, Henkemans, Van Lier, Mengelberg, Wildeveld, Zagwijn.

Muzikale Zelfportretten (Alsbach c. 1954).
Piano works by 14 contemporary Dutch composers. Contains Henk Badings, Adagio; Oscar van Hemel, Capriolen; Kees van Baaren, untitled one page piece; Rudolf Mengelberg, Allegretto; Hendrik Andriessen, The Convex Looking Glass; Karel Mengelberg, Notitia sui; Cor de Groot, Galop 1954; Daniel Ruyneman, Nocturne No. 4; Alexander Voormolen, Domanda e Risposta; Herman Strategier, Rondino; Leon Orthel, 4th Sonatine voor piano; Ton de Leeuw, Danse Lente; Sem Dresden, Come Fu; Jurriaan Andriessen, L'Azione Finta. Range from easy (Orthel's Sonatine) to M-D, (K. Mengelberg's Notitia Sui).

ENGLISH, TWENTIETH CENTURY

Contemporary British Piano Music (Schott c. 1956).
Works by Don Banks, P. Racine Fricker, Iain Hamilton, and Humphrey Searle.

ENGLISH VIRGINALISTS

At The Court of Queen Anne (Fuller-Maitland-JWC).
Contains smaller pieces by many of the composers listed in *Contemporaries of Purcell* (Fuller-Maitland-JWC). Trumpet Tunes, Minuets, Marches, Aires, a Serenade and two song transcriptions by the composers W. Croft, J. Clarke, John Blow, John Barrett, Richard Jones. Highly edited but contains some delightful literature.

Clement Matchett's Virginal Book (1612) (T. Dart-S&B).
12 pieces by Byrd, Bull, Wilby and others, from a manuscript written by a young musician in 1612. Excellent scholarly editorial notes.

Contemporaries of Purcell (Fuller-Maitland-JWC). Seven volumes.
Vols. I/II: works of John Blow (1648-1708).
Vols. III/IV: works of William Croft (1678-1727).
Vol. V: works of Jeremiah Clarke (ca. 1675-1707).
Vol. VI/VII: various composers. Vol. VI: works by Benjamin Rogers (1614-1698), Mark Coleman, Gerhard Diesner, Robert King, Daniel Purcell, John Eccles.
Vol. VII: works by Francis Piggott (? -1704), William Turner (1651-1740), John Barrett (1674-1735), and Anonymous.

Contemporaries of Purcell (K. Herrmann-Hin).
Contains 16 short works, mainly dance forms by Purcell, Blow, Clarke, Eccles, Loeillet and others. Int.

The Dublin Virginal Manuscript (1583) (J. Ward-Wellesley Edition c. 1954).
This is number 3 of the Wellesley College Editions. It contains 30 compositions of 16th-century dance-tunes and popular songs, probably compiled by an Englishman named John Taylor. Also includes an excellent introduction to this unusual field. Critical notes and commentary with sound editing and text. All pieces are untitled and most are anonymous.

Early English Keyboard Music (H. Ferguson-OUP). Two volumes.
Scholarly notes on the music, ornamentation, rhythmic conventions, interpretation. No editorial phrasing, dynamics or fingering added. Arranged in order of technical difficulty.
Vol. I: 19 pieces by Tallis, Newman, Byrd, Tavener, Farnaby, Bull, Munday, etc.
Vol. II: 23 pieces by Tomkins, Gibbons, Locke, Purcell (both Henry and Daniel), Clarke, etc.

15 pieces from Elizabeth Rogers' Virginal Book (1656) (F. Dawes-Schott c. 1951).
By Anonymous: Nanns maske, Almaygne, The nightingale, Almaygne, Corrant, Selebrand, A maske, The chestnut, Corrant, Selebrand, Mock-Nightingale, Corrant, Phill Porters Lamentation; by Beare: Selebrand; by Robert Johnson (Orlando Gibbons): Almaygne.

See: George Q. Sargent, "An Edition of Elizabeth Rogers' Virginal Book," unpub. diss., Indiana University, 1965. This work furnishes the complete musical text, 81 pieces for virginals, and 19 songs. Names have been assigned to 16 more pieces. Although ERVB is a virginal book, the interest of the music is not as important to the history of the virginalist school as to the more popular songs and dances of the 17th-century.

Elizabethan Virginal Music (Hans Redlich-UE).
17 works by 10 composers (3 Anonymous) from the FVB and *My Layde Nevells Booke.* Works by William Byrd, Peter Philips, Orlando Gibbons, John Munday, Giles Farnaby, John Bull. Contains editor's note and brief biographies. Overedited.

The English Virginalists and Harpsichordists (Montani-Ric).
Works by Bull, Morley, Munday and Purcell.

English Virginalists 1500-1656 (F. Dawes-Schott). Five volumes.
Vol. 1: 10 pieces by Hugh Aston and others (Royal Appendix 58, British Museum).
Vol. 2: 12 pieces from Mulliner's Book (ca. 1555).
Vol. 3: 7 early 17th-century virginal pieces (from British Museum Add. 30486).
Vol. 4: 8 pieces from Tomkins Manuscript.
Vol. 5: 15 pieces from Elizabeth Roger's Virginal Book (1656).
Fine urtext edition.

Fitzwilliam Virginal Book (Fuller-Maitland and Barclay Squire-Br&H). Reprint, Dover, 1964. Two volumes.
The most comprehensive and extensive collection of keyboard music from this period (1550-1620); contains 297 compositions by practically every composer of the virginal school. The majority of works are represented by four composers:
72 pieces by Byrd
52 pieces by Farnaby
45 pieces by Bull
19 pieces by Peter Philips
Contains over 130 dances, 46 arrangements of 40 songs, 9 arrangements of madrigals, 22 fantasias, 19 preludes, 6 sets of hexachord variations, 7 fancy pieces descriptive or otherwise.

This is one of the great keyboard collections of all times and is a very inexpensive "best buy" in the Dover reprint.

The Most Beautiful Pages of The English Virginal and Harpsichord Composers (P. Montani-Ric).
Works by Tallis, Byrd, Morley, Richardson, Bull, Farnaby, Gibbons, Mundy, Blow and Arne.

The Mulliner Book (D. Stevens-S&B c. 1954) Volume I of *Musica Britannica.*
The manuscript of this work was compiled around 1550 and contains works by John Tavener, Richard Farrant, John Redford, Thomas Tallis and others. In the introduction Stevens says: "The Mulliner Book alone runs the whole gamut of 16th-century music. Latin motets, English anthems, arrangements of part-songs, transcriptions of consort music, plainsong, fantasias for organ, dance music for clavichord or virginals, music for cittern and gittern". See his *The Mulliner Book: A Commentary.* London, Stainer and Bell, 1952. (CFP) has a selection of *Pieces from The Mulliner Book.*

Musick's Hand-Maid (T. Dart-S&B).
First published in 1663. Contains approximately eighty miniatures, including works by Locke, Purcell and others. Represents some of the finest harpsichord music of the period. Scholarly edition.

Parthenia (K. Stone-BB c. 1951), (T. Dart-S&B c. 1960).
When first printed in 1611 this collection was called "Maydenhead of the first Musicke ever printed for the Virginals". It contained 21 pieces by Bull, Byrd and Gibbons.

Parthenia In-Violata or Mayden-Musicke for the Virginalls and Bass-Viol (CFP).
This facsimile of the original copy is published by the New York Public Library and contains 17 pieces by Bull, Edmund Hooper, John Coperario, and others. The viol part can be omitted without great damage, some sources do omit it, and these pieces are well suited to the piano. A practical edition is also available (T. Dart-CFP).

25 Pieces for Keyed Instruments from Benjamin Cosyn's Virginal Book (Fuller-Maitland, B. Squire-JWC).
Works by Bull, Byrd, Cosyn, Gibbons and Anonymous. Cosyn's collection dates from ca. 1605-1622.

24 Pieces from the Fitzwilliam Virginal Book (T. Dart-S&B).

15 Pieces from the Fitzwilliam Virginal Book and Parthenia (T. Dart-S&B 1956). Scholarly edition.
All are works by William Byrd: Galiardas, Corantos, A Gigg, La Volta, Pavan: the Earle of Salisbury, Alman G, Rowland, Callion.

Selected Pieces from the Fitzwilliam Virginal Book (Fuller-Maitland, B. Squire-Br&H). Two volumes.
21 pieces by Byrd, Morley, Bull, Giles Farnaby, Munday, Peerson, Philips, Robert Johnson and Anonymous.

Selections from the Fitzwilliam Virginal Book (M. H. Glyn-British and Continental Music Co.).
Does not duplicate any of the above, fine edition except embellishments have been omitted.

Sixteen Pieces from Priscilla Bunbury's Virginal Book (J. L. Boston-S&B).
Most composers remain anonymous, as was the custom of the time, in this early English collection. Quaint titles. Modal and often highly ornamented. Dates from about 1630. The complete work contains 35 pieces with a few by Gibbons, Byrd, Randall Jewett, Robert Hall. Every note and chord was fingered for Mrs. Bunbury and this gives us a fine addition to our knowledge of performance practice in this period.

Tisdale's Virginal Book (A. Brown-S&B).
This book contains two Lachrymae Pavans in keyboard arrangements by J. Dowland; Pavans and Galliards by Randall, Marchant, Byrd, Morley and others, an Orlando Lassus Chanson in keyboard arrangement, a Medley by Edward Johnson, a Pavan by Robert Johnson, and short pieces by Tisdale. First-rate edition.

30 Virginal Pieces by Various Composers (M. H. Glyn-S&B).
Works by Cosyn, Dowland, Holborne, Edmund Hooper, John and Robert Johnson, Lawes, Peerson and Tomkins.

FRENCH

L'Album des Six (ESC c. 1920).
Durey, Romance sans paroles; Honegger, Sarabande; Poulenc, Valse; Milhaud, Mazurka; Auric, Prelude; Tailleferre, Pastorale.
This collection proclaimed the existence of the French group known as "Les Six", although they never had identical aesthetic views or artistic aims.

à l'Exposition (Sal c. 1937).
Contains eight piano works by: Auric, Delannoy, Ibert, Milhaud, Poulenc, Sauguet, Schmitt, Tailleferre.
Wide scope of idioms and difficulty.

L'Ecole Française de Piano 1784-1845 (M. Cauchie-l'OL c. 1957).
This fine collection gives an excellent account of French piano repertoire from this period. Brief biographies are given in French. Contains 12 works: Nicolas Séjan (1745-1819), Pièces dans le genre gracieux, gai Op. 11/1-2 (1784); Charles Bonjour, Prélude en sol mineur, Op. 8/8 (around 1791); G. P. Repichet, Première Sonate, Op. 1/1 (around 1795); Hyacinthe Jadin (1769-1802), Andante de la dixième Sonate, Op. 4/1 (around 1795), Dix-septième sonate, Op. 6/2 (around 1800); Alexandre Boëly (1785-1858), Caprice No. 5/2 (around 1810); Leon Kreutzer (1817-1868), Valses, Op. 3 (1830 or 31); Ambroise Thomas (1811-1896), Fantaisie sur un air ecossais, Op. 5 (1835), Valse caractéristique No. 6 Op. 4 (1835); Felix le Couppey (1811-1887) Troisième étude de salon (1842); Emil Prudent (1817-1863), Scherzo, Op. 19/2 (1845).

L'Ecole Moderne du Piano (From Bizet to Ravel) (I. Philipp-Durand c. 1926). Four volumes.
Shows the development of French piano writing over an eighty-year period; contains some fine literature but also has much that has justifiably dropped from the repertoire.

I: Works by Chapuis, Debussy, Büsser, Bizet, Godard, Durand, Lutz, Aubert, Vuillemin, de Castillion, Widor, Staub.
II: Lacombe, Boëllmann, Lavignac, Philipp, Lazzari, Falkenberg, Bachelet, Saint-Saëns, Grovlez, Schmitt.
III: Saint-Saëns, Oswald, Ravel, deFalla, Chapuis, Godard, Debussy, Fauré, Tcherepnin, Baton, Emmanuel, Saint-Saëns.
IV: Caplet, Aubert, Fairchild, Debussy, Saint-Saëns, Philipp, Tcherepnin, Dukas, Roussel, Roger-Ducasse, Pierné.

Parc d'Attractions (Esposition c. 1937) (ESC).
14 pieces by Tcherepnin, Martinů, Mompou, Rieti, Honegger, Halffter, Tansman, Mihalovici, and Harsányi.

Pièces de Concert (Editions Rideau Rouge c. 1967).
Contains 6 concert pieces by 3 French contemporary composers: Jean-Michel Damase (1928-), Tarentelle, Carillon; Pierre Max Dubois (1930-), Ritournelle, Aubade; Jean Guillou, Nocturne, Impromptu. Excellent examples of contemporary French piano writing. The two pieces of Guillou show the most contrast and originality.

FRENCH CLAVECINISTS

Les Clavecinistes Français (L. Diemer, Saint-Saëns and others-Durand) Four Volumes.
Vol. 1: 20 pieces by Couperin, Daquin, Rameau.
Vol. 2: 20 pieces by Dagincourt, Dandrieu, Daquin, Lully.
Vol. 3: 20 pieces by Couperin.
Vol. 4: 20 pieces by Rameau, Chambonnières, and others.

Early French Keyboard Music (H. Ferguson-OUP). Two volumes. Scholarly introduction that includes a discussion of complete editions of some of the composers included, as well as a table of ornaments by 7 different composers spanning the years 1670 to 1724. Contains 50 pieces by Attaingnant, Chambonnières, L. Couperin, d'Anglebert, de la Guerre, F. Couperin, Marchand.

Early French Masters Miniatures (O. v. Irmer-GS).
Works by d'Anglebert, F. Couperin, Dandrieu, Daquin, Loeillet, Lully, Marchand, de Neufville, Rameau. Smaller and easier works, often selected from larger works. Includes a brief section on ornaments and their realization.

French and Belgian Masters of the 17th and 18th Centuries (Philipp-IMC).
Balbastre, Romance; Couperin, Gavotte, La Fleurie, La Bersan, Soeur Monique; Dandrieu, La Gemissante; Daquin, Le Coucou, La Tendre Sylvie; Loeillet, Gigue, Sarabande; Lully, Air Tendre; Rameau, L'Egyptienne, La Villageoise; Schobert, Allegro; van den Gheyn, Fughetta. Overedited but unusual collection of literature.

French Baroque Music for the Young Pianist (P. Zeitlin-EBM).
21 pieces by 9 French Composers of the 17th and 18th centuries. Editorial markings are distinguished from composer's text. Execution of ornaments indicated in footnotes, variety of styles demonstrated in various pieces. The same fifteen keys that J. S. Bach used in the *Inventions* are represented in this volume. Brief biographies. Easier works by Chambonnières, Louis and François Couperin, Le Bègue, d'Anglebert, Rameau, Dandrieu, Boismortier, and Daquin.

French Piano Music of the 18th Century (W. Georgii-Arno Volk).
Contains mainly excerpts from Couperin's 6th, 8th and 11th ordres, examples from Rameau's *Nouvelles Suites de Pièces de Clavecin*, and also works by Daquin and Dandrieu.

Les Maîtres Français du Clavecin des XVII et XVIII Siècles (P. Brunold-Senart).
Along with some of the better-known composers from this era are included lesser masters such as Le Roux and Le Bègue.

The Most Beautiful Pages from French Harpsichord Music (P. Montani-Ric c. 1956).
Chambonnières, L'Entretien des Dieux; F. Couperin, Le Reveille-Matin, Le Carillon de Cythère, Le Rossignol en amour, Soeur Monique; Jean F. Dandrieu, Les Fifres; Rameau, Tambourin, La Poule, Le Rappel des Oiseaux; Dagincourt, L'Etourdie; Daquin, Le Coucou; J. Duphly, La Victoire.

Le Petit Claveciniste (Motte, Lacroix-Delrieu).
Contains 24 pieces by Händel, Rameau, Dandrieu, Couperin. No distinction between composer's markings and those of the editor.

Les Plus Belles Pièces de Clavessin (G. Grovlez-JWC).
This new edition combines volumes 1 and 2 of old edition, edited by G. J. Aubry. Contains 21 pieces by Chambonnières, Le Bègue, Marchand, Couperin, Dandrieu, D'Anglebert, Daquin, Dornel, Clerambault, Dagincourt, Rameau, Duphly, Corrette.

GERMAN

Aus Historischen Klavierkonzerten (R. Buchmayer-Br&H c. 1927).
Five volumes.
Vol. 1: Matthias Weckmann: Toccata e, Kanzone c, Suite b, Variations a, Organ Toccata d.
Vol. 2: Matthias Weckmann: Toccata a, Kanzone C, d, Suite c, Fantasia d, Chorale Komm heiliger Geist. Franz Tunder: Prelude and Fugue g.
Vol. 3: Matthias Weckmann: Suite a. Johann Reinken: Toccata G, Fugue g. Franz Tunder: Prelude and Fugue g.
Vol. 4: Johann Reinken: Variations on a ballet e. Georg Böhm: Prelude, Fugue, Postlude g, French Suite D.
Vol. 5: Christian Ritter: Suite f♯, Sonatina d. Georg Böhm: Suites E♭, c, a.

Bach-Händel (F. Oberdörffer-Lienau c. 1947).
A fine urtext collection with only fingering added of M-D literature containing:
Bach: Arioso S. 590 (from Pastorale for Organ); Andante S. 989 (four variations from Aria variata all'maniera italiana); Fantasia c (S. 919); Prélude, S and G S. 823; Prélude S. 818a; Suite E♭ S. 819 A, C, S, B, M I & II; M, S, 843.
Händel: Suite d (No. 15 in the 16 Suites) A, C, S, G; M with three variations (from Suite No. 10); Allegro, S, M (from Suite No. 7); Preludio et Allegro g; Sonatina d.

Deutsche Klaviermusik, aus dem Beginne des 18. Jahrhunderts (Nag c. 1927, 1938) Vol. 3.

Suite and sonata movements by Gottfried Kirchoff and other composers.

Early German Keyboard Music (H. Ferguson-OUP c. 1970). Two volumes.
Scholarly introduction that includes a discussion of early sources of German keyboard music, four different systems of notation found in early German keyboard music, forms, tempo, the interpretation of preludes and fugues, ornamentation, rhythmic conventions, and a table of suggested ternary-rhythm interpretation of binary-rhythm gigues. 30 pieces by Anonymous, Kotter, Ammerbach, Paix, Sweelinck, Scheidt, Froberger, Kerll, Buxtehude, Johann Christoph Bach, Krieger Muffat, Pachelbel, Kuhnau, Böhm, J. K. F. Fischer, Telemann.

German Keyboard Music of the 17th and 18th Centuries (H. Fischer, F. Oberdoerffer-Vieweg). Nine volumes. Urtext edition.
1: Easy pieces of both centuries. Includes works by Speer, Krieger, Kindermann, Richter, Pachelbel, Telemann, Hurlebusch, Kuhnau, Graun, Benda, Krebs, Zachau, Buttstedt, Tischer, Maichelbek.
2: Composers of the 17th century, including Froberger, Muffat, Schultheiss, Pachelbel, Krieger, Speth, Murschhauser, J. K. F. Fischer, Buttstedt, Kuhnau.
3: Composers of the 18th century, including Telemann, Maichelbek, Kellner, Tischer, Hasse, Binder, Benda.
4: Telemann: Overtures Nos. 1-3.
5: Telemann: Overtures Nos. 4-6.
6: Benda: 12 Sonatines, 1 sonata.
7: C. P. E. Bach: 3 Sonatas in A, e, C, with violin and cello ad lib.
8/9: Music in Berlin at the Time of Frederick the Great, including works by Graun, Nichelmann, C. P. E. Bach, Schaffrath, Fasch.

Hallisches Klavierbüchlein (W. Serauky-Mitteldeutscher Verlag).
Sources are quoted and identified, unusual collection of works by composers associated with the city of Halle, Germany.
Friedrich Wilhelm Zachow: *Suite* b, A, C, S, Fuga Finalis.
Georg Frederich Händel: *Suite* d: Ouverture, A, C, S, Ciacona.

Johann Gotthilf Ziegler: *Suite* D: Les Allemans Anciens, Les Modernes, Les Français, Les Anglais, Les Polonis.

Gottfried Kirchoff: A from *Suite* g; 2 movements from *Sonata* E, first untitled, second, Presto.

Daniel Gottlob Türk: *Sonata* d: Allegro non tanto, Larghetto tranquillamente, Allegro di molto.

Johann Friedrich Reichardt: *Ein Klavierstück über eine Petrarchische Ode 43.* Sections are Adagio, Andantino, Adagio of 2 bars, Allegretto.

Klavierbüchlein der Maria Christina Roehr 1776 (E. Frerich-HV c. 1943).

32 pieces from very easy to moderately-easy from the second half of the 18th century up to 1776, when this collection was put together. Notes on each piece in German.

Klaviermeister des Barock (G. Ochs-Mitteldeutscher Verlag).

Works by Johann and Johann Philipp Krieger, Murschhauser.

Klaviermusik von Heute (Br&H c. 1962).

8 pieces by 8 composers. Contains Fidelio F. Finke, Zwei Bagatellen; Hans Eisler, Klavierstück; Otto Reinhold, Tanzstück; Fritz Geissler, Ironie und Melancholie; Leo Spies, Canzonetta; Joh. Paul Thilman, Invention; Walter Draeger, Passacaglia. Varied styles and difficulty. Some are good examples of German piano music of the 1960's. A few were written earlier.

Leipziger Klavierbuch (Br&H c. 1965).

In honor of the 800th Anniversary of the founding of the city of Leipzig (1165-1965) this collection is written by contemporary German composers, all, either born in or near Leipzig or educated there. Max Dehnert (1895-), Kleiner Marsch, Elegie; Maxmilian Schwartz (1899-), Klavierstück; Erhard Ragwitz (1933-), Vier kleine Stücke; Hansgeorg Muhe (1929-), Sonatine für Sabine; Siegfried Thiele (1934-), Tokkata; Fred Lohse (1908-), Fantasie; Peter Mai (1935-), Sonatine; Arnold Matz (1904-), Drei Klavierstücke; George Trexler (1903-), Bagatellen, "Vier Temperamente"; Fritz Geissler (1921-), Sonatine; Carl-Heinz Pick (1929-), Vier tanzerische Stücke. Various styles and difficulties, brief biographies in German, all pieces written in the 1960's.

Leipziger Klaviermusik (CFP c. 1965).
This is a collection of music by musicians who have been associated with Leipzig from Ammerbach (1530-97) to Günter Raphael (1903-60). Compiled in honor of the 800th anniversary of the city of Leipzig (1165-1965). Wide range of difficulty.

The Most Beautiful Pages from the German Harpsichordists (P. Montani-Ric).
13 pieces: by Froberger, Toccata d; J. K. Kerll, Capriccio Cucu; Buxtehude, Suite e, A, C, S, G; Murchhauser, Aria pastoralis variata; Muffat, Rigaudon; Graun, Giga; J. K. F. Fischer, Preludio; Kirnberger, Polonaise, La birichina; Pachelbel, Fuga.

New Music for Harpsichord (F. Goebels-Br).
Contains works of Bialas, Driessler, Hessenberg, Marx, Distler and Schafer. Preface in English and German. Emphasis on contrapuntal style. M-D.

GERMAN: BACH FAMILY

Bach (K. Geiringer-Harvard Univ. Press c. 1955).
27 compositions by 14 different Bachs. Includes biographies, bibliographies and source notes. Scholarly edition.

The Bach Family 1604-1845 (K. Geiringer-UE c. 1936).
Contains 14 pieces by 12 members of the Bach family (1604 to 1845). The earliest Bachs, Chorales and a Rondeau; J. S. Bach, Capriccio on the Departure of His Beloved Brother; W. F. Bach, Polonaise; C. P. E. Bach, Farewell to My Silbermann Clavier; J. E. Bach, The Bees; J. C. Bach, Sonata Op. 5/6; W. F. E. Bach, Waltzes. This collection not only reveals the development of the Bach family but also the progress of music within two centuries. Scholarly edition.

The Best Pages from the Works of the Bach Family (Montani-Ric).
Interesting selection of varied works. Johann Christoph, Sarabanda variata (12 variations); Wilhelm Friedemann, Capriccio

and Fuga d; Karl Philipp Emanuel, Rondo G; Johann Ernst, Fantasia and Fuga F; Johann Christian, Sonata B♭ Op. 17/6.

Sons of Bach (W. Newman-TP c. 1957).
J. C. Bach, Sonata B Op. 17/6; C. P. E. Bach, Sonata g, No. 65 (Wotquenne's Catalogue); W. F. Bach, Sonata E. Fine text with excellent editorial preface.

The Sons of Bach (W. Rehberg-Schott).
13 works (sonatas, single movements and pieces) by W. F., C. P. E., J. C. F., and J. C. Bach. Also contains suggestions for practising.

Teachers and Pupils of J. S. Bach (K. Herrmann-Hug).
Two fascinating volumes with fine introductions and prefaces.
Vol. I: Teachers: Works by Froberger, Reinken, Buxtehude, J. K. F. Fischer, Pachelbel, Kuhnau, Böhm, Frescobaldi, Nivers, F. Couperin, C. Dieupart, N. Grigny, Clérambault, Le Roux.
Vol. II: Pupils: Works by W. F. Bach, C. P. E. Bach, J. C. F. Bach, Krebs, Nichelmann, Agricola, Goldberg, Müthel, Kirnberger.

GREEK

Contemporary Greek Piano Music (G. Becker c. 1967). Two volumes, biographical sketches.
Fine survey of younger Greek composers.
I: Michael Adamis (1929-), Epitymbio; Stephanos Gazouleas (1931-), Piano Piece; Jannis Joannidis (1930-), Little Fantasia; Georgios Léotsakos (1935-), Sérenade; Jannis A. Papaioannou (1910-), Oraculum; Yorgo Sicilianos (1922-), Miniature No. 7, Op. 23/7, Nikos Skalkottas (1904-1949), Little Peasant March. Int. to M-D.
II: Theodor Antoniou (1935-), Syllables; Arghyris Kounadis (1924-), Three Idiómela; Jannis Konstantinidis (1903-), Greek Island Dance No. 2; Dimitri Mitropoulos (1896-1961), Piano Piece I; Georges Poniridy, (1892-), Movement from Sonata 1961; Georges S. Tsouyopoulos (1930-), Toccata III. M-D to D.

HUNGARIAN

Forty-Four Little Piano Pieces on Hungarian Folk Tunes by Nine Composers (A. Reschofsky-ZV).
Vol. 1: 1-23. Vol. II: 24-44.
All are short, similar to Bartók's *For Children,* but some are much easier. Composers represented include: Bartók, Kokai, Molnar, Viski, Horusitzky, Szollosy, Gardonyi, Weiner and Reschofsky.

Hungarian Piano Music (M. Szavai-EMB).
A collection of short pieces by 20th-century Hungarian composers. Contains works by Zoltan Gardonyi, Mihaly Hajdu, Pal Kadosa, Istvan Lang, György Ranki, Tibor Sarai, Rezso Sugar, Erzsebet Szonyi, and Béla Tardos. Folksong influence in many of the pieces.

Musica Hungarica (Bo&H c. 1958).
Piano Pieces by Hungarian Composers.
Contains: Bartók, An Evening in the Village, Bear Dance, Rumanian Dance, Op. 8a/1; Dohnányi, Capriccio, Op. 28/6, Ruralia Hungarica, Op. 32/3, 7; Kodály, 9 Piano Pieces, Op. 3/2, 9, Valsette; Liszt, Csárdás Macabre, Bagatelle sans Tonalité, Sunt Lacrymae Rerum; Leo Weiner, 3 Hungarian Rural Dances.

Piano Sonatas of Hungarian Composers of the 18th Century (F. Brodszky-ZV c. 1962).
Anonymous, Suite; Jozsef Csernak, Partita; Pantaleon Roskovszky, Divertimento; Anonymous, Sonata; Ferenc Pokorny, Sonata, Aria; Anonymous, Suite; Ferenc Ninger, Three organ pieces.

Szonatina Albuma (EMB c. 1963).
10 Sonatinas by contemporary Hungarian composers. Unusually fine collection. Int.

IRISH

Six Irish Pieces (Breen-ESC).
A collection of works from the 17th and 18th centuries.

ITALIAN

Antichi Maestri Italiani. Partite (Boghen-Ric).
A collection of five Partitas by B. Pasquini and one by D. Zipoli.

Antichi Maestri Italiani. Toccate (Boghen-Ric).
An unusual collection of Toccatas, overedited, but the original version is also given. Toccatas by Merulo, Frescobaldi, M. Rossi, Pasquini, Stradella, A. Scarlatti, D. Scarlatti, Zipoli, Della Ciaja, Durante, Marcello, Clementi, Pollini, and Pietro Scarlatti.

L'Arte Musicale in Italia (L. Torchi-Ric 1897-1908?).
Vol. III: keyboard works by 16th-, 17th- and 18th-century composers including Cavazzoni, Frescobaldi, A. and G. Gabrieli, B. and E. Pasquini, Porpora, M. Rossi, Zipoli, A. Valente, Pellegrini, C. Merulo, G. Diruta, G. M. Trabaci, Bencini and others.

Balli Antichi Veneziani (K. Jeppesen-WH).
A collection of early 16th-century Venetian dances transcribed for keyboard by Knud Jeppesen. Illustrated with Renaissance prints. Contains 39 short pieces, many with picturesque titles. The author suggests embellishing the repeats in accordance with the practice of the period.

Cembalisti Italiani del Settecento (Benvenuti-Ric c. 1926).
Includes 18 sonatas by Bertoni, Galuppi, Manfredini, Paganelli, Paladini, Paradies, Peroti, Pescetti, Rutini, Sales Pampeo, Sammartini, Serini.

I Classici della Musica Italiana (Società Anonima Notari, 1919-).
This collection of Italian classics (including operatic, vocal and instrumental works by well-known composers from the 16th to the 19th century) was issued under the general editorship of Gabriele d'Annunzio. Of the 36 volumes issued, the following are of most interest to the pianist: 8. M. Clementi, Sonatas; 11. F. Durante, Sonatas; 12. G. Frescobaldi, Assortment of Pieces; 18. G. B. Martini, Sonatas; 22. P. D. Paradisi, Sonatas; 25. N. A. Porpora, Sonatas; 26. M. Rossi, Compositions; 27. G. Rutini, Sonatas; 28. G. B. Sammartini, Sonatas;

29. P. G. Sandoni and Serini, Sonatas; D. Scarlatti, Compositions; 32. G. Tartini, Sonatas; 33. F. Turini, Sonatas; 36. Zipoli, Compositions.

Classici Italiani dell' Organo (I. Fuser-GZ c. 1955).
36 works from Antico (1517) thru Martini (1784). Has an unusual collection of unfamiliar composers, such as Guami, Malvezzi, etc. The biographical notes are excellent. Many of these works sound very well on the piano.

Clavicembalisti Italiani (Montani-Ric).
16 pieces by Galuppi, Zipoli, Vento, Leo De Rossi, Alberti, Pescetti, D. Scarlatti, Paradisi.

Early Italian Keyboard Music (Bedbrook-Schott).
Vol. 1: 4 Toccatas by Claudio Merulo (1553-1604).
Vol. 2: 2 French Chansons and a Ricercar by Marco Antonio di Bologna (ca. 1490-1569).

Early Italian Keyboard Music (H. Ferguson-OUP). Two volumes.
35 pieces ranging from anonymous music of the 16th century to Domenico Scarlatti. Ferguson provides notes on ornamentation, rhythmic conventions, and other points of interpretation. Includes works by Cavazzoni, Della Ciaja, Facoli, Frescobaldi, A. and G. Gabrieli, Luzzaschi, Merulo, Picchi, Poglietti, Rossi, A. and D. Scarlatti, Trabaci and others.

Early Italian Piano Music (Esposito-OD c. 1906).
Works by E. Pasquini, Frescobaldi, M. Rossi, B. Pasquini, A. Scarlatti, C. F. Pollarolo (about 1650-1722), D. Scarlatti (19 Sonatas and The Cat's Fugue), F. Durante, B. Marcello, N. Porpora, Zipoli, Martini, Galuppi, Paradies, Turini, Grazioli, and Clementi. Also contains a discussion of early keyboard instruments, and biographical sketches. Overedited but contains a wide scope of literature from about 250 years of Italian music.

Easy Pieces from Old Italian Masters, See: *Pezzi Facilissimi per Pianoforte di Vecchi Maestri Italiani.*

Eighteenth-Century Italian Keyboard Music (G. F. Malipiero-TP c. 1952).
6 works including sonatas by Sacchini, Sarti, Galuppi, minuets

by Rutini, and anonymous composers. Heavyhanded editing. All the pieces are easy to play.

Fughe per Clavicembalo o Pianoforte di Antichi Maestri Italiani (F. Boghen-Ric).
Overedited but contains a fine collection of fugues by Frescobaldi, Pasquini, Bencini, Pollaroli, Della Ciaja, D. Scarlatti, Durante, Porpora, Martini and Clementi. English preface by Arnaldo Bonaventura.

Intavolatura Nova di Balli (W. Oxenburg, T. Dart-S&B).
Dated 1551 in Venice, this is a collection of 25 various dances of the 16th century: Passamezzi, Gagliards, Pavanes, etc. Interesting from a musical and historical view. None of the composers are named.

Istituzioni dell' Arte Musicale Italiana. Nuova Series (Ric 1956). Vol. 2: edited by Fausto Torrefranca. *G. B. Platti e La Sonata Moderna* (c. 1963).
A scholarly work with 211 pages of introduction and all extant 18 sonatas for the cembalo (188 pages). A handsome work, with index, 413 pages.

18 Italian Compositions for Clavicembalo (Silvestri-Ric).
Compositions from the 18th century including 6 pieces by Scarlatti, Zipoli, 4 pieces by Galuppi, 4 by Pampani, Legati and Croce. Mixture of familiar and unfamiliar works.

Italian Harpsichord Compositions (Vitali-Ric c. 1944). Two volumes.
Vol. 1: Works by Frescobaldi, Grieco, Marcello, B. & E. Pasquini, Pescetti, Pollaroli, Scarlatti, Zipoli.
Vol. 2: Works by Rutini, Durante, Grazioli, Galuppi, Turini, Porpora, Martini, Paradisi.
Good mixture of homophonic and polyphonic styles; embellishments realized and generally overedited.

Italian Masters of the 17th and 18th Centuries (I. Philipp-IMC).
Contains: Galuppi, Sonata; Grazioli, Sonata; Marcello, Toccata on a Song of a Cuckoo; Rossi, Andantino; Zipoli, Suite.

Italian Sonatas of the 18th Century (de Paoli-JWC c. 1939).
Minuet by D. Scarlatti; Sonatas in A♭, D by Galuppi, in B♭

by Paradies, E by Martini and F by Rutini. Excellent introduction by editor, sources listed, biographical notes on each composer. Fine collection of unusual works, tastefully edited.

I Maestri del Clavicembalo (R. Silvestri-SZ c. 1946).
An unusual collection of 21 pieces by Frescobaldi, Pasquini, de Rossi, Grazioli, Galuppi, Couperin, Rameau, Scarlatti, Händel, Daquin, Martini, Paradisi.

Monumenti di Musica Italiana (Mischiati, Scarpat, Tagliavini-Br).
In two series: 1. Organ and harpsichord, II. Polyphonia.
Series I:
Vol. I: Tarquinio Merula (1590-1665). *Composizioni Per Organo e Cembalo* (A. Curtis-1961). Contains Sonata Cromatica, Capriccio Cromatico, Toccata, 5 Canzonas, 3 Intonazione and 1 Canzona for 3 strings and continuo. Also one work by Emanuele Soncino, Cromatica and a Canzona Prima by G. B. Fasolo. Much use of chromaticism, rich harmonic usage. Scholarly edition, all sources quoted
Vol. II: Girolamo Frescobaldi (1583-1643). *Nine Toccatas* (S. D. Libera-1962). Free, rhapsodic out-pourings, amazing music of great beauty. Toccata No. 9 is entitled "Per l'Organo col contrabasso overo Pedale".
Vol. III: Giovanni Maria Trabaci (? -1647). *Twelve Ricercate dal Libro I, 1603* (O. Mischiati-1964). In contrapuntal style; much beauty in these pieces, especially the inner voices.

The Most Beautiful Pages from the Work of Italian Harpsichordists (P. Montani-Ric).
Works by Galuppi, Zipoli, Vento, Leo, de Rossi, Alberti, Pescetti, Scarlatti, Paradisi.

Musiche Clavicembalistiche Italiane (C. Giudici-EC c. 1967).
Contains 20 pieces by Zipoli, D. Scarlatti, L. Leo (Toccata C, would make a fine program opener), Michaelangelo Rossi, G. B. Sammartini, Pescetti, Martini, Paradisi, Rutini, Cimarosa. Highly edited but fingering and articulation are well thought through. Clear printing, well spaced.

Pezzi Facilissimi per Pianoforte di Vecchi Maestri Italiani (G. Bas-EGZ c. 1965).
Easy Pieces from Old Italian Masters (G. Bas-K). Same collection. Excellent collection, easy to intermediate. Contains Zipoli, Sarabande; Corelli, 2 Gavottes, Sarabande; A. Scarlatti, Aria, Minuetto, Tema con Variazoni; B. Pasquini, Canzone Francese; M. Rossi, Andantino; A. Santelli, Prelude. Highly edited.

Il Primo Libra d'Intavolatura di Balli d'Arpicordo di Gio. Maria Rudino (E. M. Harding-W. Heffer & Sons, Ltd).
The First Book of Harpsichord Dances by Maria Radino — 1592, transcribed into modern notation by E. M. Harding. Available through (BB). Contains a Passamezzo with 4 variations, a Galliard derived from the Passamezzo, two Pavanes and four Galliards.

Verses (Kastner-Schott).
A collection of Italian keyboard works of the 16th century.

ITALIAN, TWENTIETH CENTURY

Antologia Pianistica di Autori Italiani Contemporanei (Montani-SZ). Two volumes.
81 pieces by contemporary Italian composers including Casella, Dallapiccola, Petrassi, etc.

Autori Italiani Contemporanei: Composizione Pianistiche (P. Montani-Ric c. 1955).
Piano works by nine contemporary Italian composers: Fuga, Farina, Ghiglia, Gentilucci, Gargiulo, Micheli, Quaranta, Silvestri and Tedoldi. The works by Ghiglia, a 12-tone "Esercizio Per l'Espressione" and "Quaranta (in Modo di Novelletta)" are of special interest.

Composizioni di Autori Contemporanei per Pianoforte (Carisch c. 1959).
Contains Allegretto, F. Ghedini; Ninna-Nanna Campana, J. Napoli; Dancing, E. Porrino; Senza nome, T. Alati; Preludio, B. Bettinelli; Canzonetta, T. Gargiullo; Danza e Notturno, F.

Margola; Il pescatore solitario, G. Piccioli; Ninna-nanna, G. Viozzi. MC and of special interest to intermediate pianists.

Il Pianistica Italiano Moderno (Carisch c. 1944).
Gorini, Perpetuum mobile; Margola, Leggenda; Pick-Mangiagalli, La Ronda d'Ariel; Casella, part of Toccata Op. 59. A curious mixture of styles. Int. to D.

LATIN-AMERICAN

Album Para Piano de Autores Peruanos, 6 Composiciones Para Piano (Ric c. 1952).
Contains works by R. Bracesco (1888-), Aguilar P. Chavez (1899-), Gamarra F. Gonzalez (1890-), Mindreau E. Lopez (1890-), D. A. Robles (1871-1942). Colorful music, not overly difficult; most pieces emphasize rhythmic drive.

Antologia de Musica Argentina para Piano (Ric c. 1962).
Works by Aguirre (1868-1924), Gaito (1878-1945), Troicani (1873-1942), Buchardo (1881-1948), Napolitano (1907-), Ugarte (1884-), Boero (1884-1958), Gilardi (1889-), Sammartino (1890-), Gianneo (1897-). Pieces are of M-D and are generally dancelike in character.

Latin-American Art Music for the Piano (Curt Lange-GS c. 1942).
An anthology by twelve contemporary composers from seven countries, includes preface and biographical data. José María Castro: Cuatro Piezas, de Diez Piezas Brevas; Alberto E. Ginastera: Piezas Infantiles; Roberto García Morillo: Canción Triste y Danza Alegre; Juan Carlos Paz: Balada No. 2 de Canciones y Baladas; Carlos Suffern: Danza; Camargo Guarnieri: Toada Triste; Heitor Villa-Lobos: Dansa (Miudinho) de las Bachianas Brasileiras No. 4; René Amengual: Astaburuaga, Burlesca, Op. 5; Manuel M. Ponce: Deux Etudes pour Piano; Andrés Sás: Hymno y Danza; F. Eduardo Fabini: Triste No. 2; Juan B. Plaza: Sonatina Venezolana.

Musica Nicaraguense (Publicaciones del Ministerio de Relaciones Exteriores Republica de Nicaragua c. 1953).

Includes 4 parts:
I: Musica Folklorica. II: Musica Bailabile (Dance Music). III: Valses de concierto. IV: Musica Clasica.
Composers listed in Part IV include A. V. Matus, Carlos Ramirez, Luis A. Delgadillo, M. A. Sells. Part III of this series is of most interest to the pianist. 24 Preludes and 12 Nocturnes (some quite easy) by Luis A. Delgadillo, dedicated to the memory of Chopin. Many are one page long. This volume also contains Delgadillo's setting of a number of songs and 10 melodies for piano and violin.

Piano Music of Brazil (NME, October, 1942).
Oscar L. Fernandez (1897-1948), Moda; Camargo Guarnieri (1907-), Valsa; Radamés Gnattali (1906-), Choro; H. Villa-Lobos (1887-1959), Melodia Da Montanna, New York Skyline; Francisco Mignone (1897-), Lenda Sertaeja No. 9. Preface and biographical notes by Nicolas Slonimsky.

Piano Music of Brazil (Rio De Janeiro. Universidade do Brazil. Escola nacional de musica c. 1955).
Nine piano compositions by Baptista Siqueira: Carapia Carlos de Almeida, Cantiga da Rua; Domingos Raimundo: Fôlha D'Album; Francisco Braga: Divertimento; Joaquina de Araújo Gomes: Quando eu era Crianca; J. Octaviano: Dois Preludios; Newton Pádua: Valsa No. 1; Octavio Maúl: Chôra No. 1; Virginia Fiuza: Improviso. All are published separately and are for intermediate to moderately advanced pianists.

POLISH

Eight Etudes by Contemporary Polish Composers (PWM c. 1959). Compiled by Zofia Romanszkowa.
Contains works by Grazyna Bacewiczowna, Zafia Iszkowska, Tadeusz Paciorkiewicz, and Tadeusz Szeligowski. Each piece involves a particular problem or set of problems. Most are tonal but are liberally sprinkled with accidentals, adhere to the key signature, and are eminently pianistic.

Polish Contemporary Piano Miniatures 1939-1964 (PMP).
Beautifully printed book of difficult works representing contemporary Polish composer's approach to the keyboard.

PORTUGUESE

Cravistas Portugueses (Kastner-Schott c. 1935, c. 1950).
A collection of old Portuguese keyboard music. Works by Coelho, Correa de Araujo, Seixas, Jacinto, Carvalho.

The Most Beautiful Pages from Portuguese Harpsichord Music (P. Montani-Ric c. 1963).
Padre M. R. Coelho (1583-1633 ca.), Primeiro Tento; J. A. Carlos de Seixas (1704-42), Sonata Prima a, Toccata C, Sonata seconda a; Fra Jacinto (? - ?), Toccata d; J. de Sousa Carvalho (? -1798), Toccata g. Biographical notes in English.

Portuguese and Spanish Keyboard Music of the 18th Century (O. Jonas-SB c. 1958).
Works by Soler, Casanovas, Rodriguez, Angles, Freixanet, M. Albeniz, Galles, Sexias. 12 charming pieces, somewhat in the style of D. Scarlatti. Fine edition. M-D.

SCANDINAVIAN

Ancient Danish Piano Music (E. Winkel-SM c. 1943). Two books.
Works by Johan Foltmar (1714-1794), F. L. A. E. Kunzen (1761-1817), Claus N. Schall (1757-1835), J. A. P. Schulz (1747-1800), J. A. Scheibe (1708-1776).

Musikaliska Konstföreningen (Swedish Society of Musical Art) Stockholm, 1860 —.
The Swedish Society of Musical Art was founded in 1859 for the purpose of printing works by Swedish composers. The following volumes (and date of issue) have most interest for the pianist. (1861) Boom, J. van. Grand sonata; (1867) J. Lindegren, Grand sonata, canon Op. 2; (1871) G. W. Heintze, Grand sonata; (1889) R. Andersson, Sonata Op. 11; (1895) K. Bäck, Theme and variations Op. 2; (1904) E. Sjogren, Sonata No. 2, Op. 44; B. Backman, Om lyckan Op. 10; (1915) L. Lundberg, Sonata Op. 33; (1930) K. Hakanson, 10 variations and fugues Op. 37; (1943) H. Mankell, Andante and variations Op. 57.

New Scandinavian Piano Music (GM).
A collection of 13 Sonatinas composed in 1949-50, including works by Hilding Rosenberg (1892-); Dag Wirén (1905-); Gunnar de Frumerie (1908-); Lars-Erik Larsson (1908-); Erland Von Koch (1910-); Ingvar Lidholm (1921-); Selim Palmgren (1878-1951); Knudage Riisager (1897-); Harald Saeverud (1897-) has two sonatinas in this collection. Finn Hoffding (1899-); Erik Bergman (1911-); Niels Viggo Bentzon (1919-).

Pepparrot (New Scandinavian Piano Music) (B. Nordenfelt-NMS c. 1949).
Forward in English and photograph of each composer plus English biographies. Contains works by Lidholm, K. B. Blomdahl, Bäck, Riisager, Holmboe, Hoffding and Saeverud. The Sonatina by Lidholm is especially appealing and one duet, Minuett, by Hoffding is included. From the Preface: "This collection of modern Scandinavian music is intended for a more or less advanced stage of teaching, to be played *to* the pupils and *by* the pupils themselves."

Pianolyric (Swedish Piano Album) (F. Kjellberg-NMS c. 1949).
Contains works by Erik Alvin, Margit E. Anderson, Tor Bengtson, Nils Björkander, Harry Danielsson, Ejnar Eklöf, Gunnar de Frumerie, Wilhelm Göransson, Axel Hambraeus, Ingemar Liljefors, Carin Malmlof-Forssling, Friedrich Mehler, Gustaf Norqvist, Albert Runbäck, Gerda Söderberg, Gunnar Thyrestam and Rune Wahlberg.

Svenska Albumblad 1962 (Album of Swedish Piano Music) (GM).
Contains works by H. Rosenberg, H. Hallnäs, Dag Wirén, Ingemar Liljefors, Lars-Erik Larsson, Gunnar de Frumerie, Erland Von Koch, Sven-Eric Johanson, Jan Carlstedt, Maurice Karkoff, Hans Edlund and Bo Linde.

Swedish Piano Music (Ingmar Bengtsson-NMS c. 1946).
Forward in English, short biographies of composers in Swedish. Contains works by Gottfrid Berg, K. B. Blomdahl, Bengt Franzen, Gunnar de Frumerie, Hilding Hallnas, Gustaf Heintze, Edvin Kallstenius, Erland von Koch, Hans Leygraf, Ingvar Lidholm, Lennart Luden, Ture Rangström, Hilding Rosenberg. Pieces are one to three pages in length, of moderate difficulty.

SCOTTISH

Early Scottish Keyboard Music (K. Elliot-S&B c. 1967). Second revised edition. Contains 10 keyboard pieces, Pavans, Galliards, etc.; 8 Scottish national airs on folksongs, 5 for cittern and 3 for violin. Most of the keyboard pieces come from Duncan Burnett's music book of about 1610, mainly works by William Kinloch. Excellent and unusual collection with fine historical notes.

SPANISH

Collection Espagnole (Coleccion de obras espanolas e iberoamericanas) from Albéniz to Villa-Lobos (F. Guenther-EBM c. 1941). Works by Albéniz, Chavarri, de Falla, O. L. Fernandez, E. Granados, V. Granados, Isamitt, Lecuona, Longas, Robles, Sandoval, Suffern, Turina, Villa-Lobos.

Mestres de L'Escolania de Montserrat (David Pujol-Monestir de Montserrat). 2 Vols. Works by Miguel Lopez; Narcis Casanovas; Josep Vinyals (1771-1825) Sonata E♭, and others.

The Most Beautiful Pages from Spanish Harpsichord Music (G. Marchi-Ric c. 1955). Edited in accordance with the originals. Padre Vicente Rodriguez (1685-1761), Sonata F; Padre Antonio Soler (1729-1783), Sonatas a, D♭; Padre Felipe Rodriquez (1759-1814), Rondo B♭; Mateo Albéniz (17 ? -1831), Sonata D; Cantallos (1760-), Sonata c; Padre José Galles (1761-1836), Sonatas c, f.

16 Sonatas of Old Spanish Masters (J. Nin-ESC 1925). Sonatas by Soler, M. Albéniz, Cantallos, Serrano, Ferrer.

17 Sonatas of Old Spanish Masters (J. Nin-ESC). Sonatas by V. Rodriguez, Soler, Freixanet, Casanovas, Angles, F. Rodriguez, Galles. All the works in both collections are in one movement and most are moderately easy—Int.

Piano Music from Spain (AMP). Fifteen pieces by Albéniz and Granados.

SWISS

Swiss Piano Music from the Classic and Romantic Era. (W. Frey, W. Schuh-Hug).
Contains Scherzo E, Andante F by X. Schnyder von Wartensee (1786-1868); Toccata, H. G. Naegeli (1773-1836); Finale from Sonata Op. 11 by Theodor Fröhlic.

U. S. A.

American Composers of Today (EBM c. 1965).
Twenty-three original piano works by contemporary American composers; also includes biographical sketches. Int. to M-D. M. Babbitt, Duet; A Berger, Intermezzo; S. Berkowitz, March of the Puppets; M. Castelnuovo-Tedesco, Prelude; N. Cazden, Game; H. Cowell, Toccatina; N. Dello Joio, Night Song; V. Fine, The Small Sad Sparrow; M. Gideon, Walk; L. Harrison, Little Suite for Piano; R. Helps, Starscape; A. Hovhaness, Lullaby; J. Meyrowitz, Noël Far From Home; C. Mills, A Child's Daydream; H. Overton, A Mood; J. Prostakoff, Parade; K. Rathaus, Echo; R. Sessions, Little Piece, Waltz for Brenda; N. Slonimsky, Pastoral; R. Starer. Above, Below and Between; W. Sydeman, Prelude; B. Weber, Lyric Piece.

American Music by Distinguished Composers (I. Freed-TP c. 1964). Two volumes.

I: H. Cowell, Bounce Dance; I. Fine, Lullaby for a Baby Panda; G. Fletcher, A Habanera, Marching Music for Johnny Appleseed; I. Freed, Waltz on White Keys; H. Haufrecht, Song of the Valley; O. Luening, Gay Picture; G. F. McKay, Dance Pastorale. Easy to Int.

II: H. Cowell, Sway Dance; E. Gerschefski, Song of the Mountains; L. Kraft, Perky Pete; R. McBride, School Bus (Stop), Tall in the Saddle; D. Moore, Dance for a Holiday, Prelude; Paul A. Pisk, Dance from the Rio Grande Valley; W. Riegger, Petite Etude; B. Wagenaar, The Flickering Candle. Int.

A Collection of Early American Keyboard Music (McClenny, Hinson-Willis c. 1971).

Contains: Anonymous, Yankee Doodle Arranged with Variations; Raynor Taylor, Rondo G; Christopher Moller, Sonata VIII D; William Brown, Rondo I G; Mr. Newman, Sonata Op. 1/1 C; James Hewitt, Mark My Alford With Variations; Alexander Reinagle, Sonata I, D. Also includes preface, comments on composers and works. Editorial additions in red type. Int. to M-D.

Contemporary American Piano Music (J. Prostakoff-Morris c. 1956).
29 pieces by 19 American composers. Wide range of contemporary idioms and wide range of difficulty. Intermediate to moderately difficult.

Early American Music (A. McClenny, M. Hinson -Belwin-Mills c. 1971).
Reinagle, Hewitt, Carr, Taylor, anonymous dances. Discussion of the works, composers, keyboard instruments. Easy—Int.

Masters of Our Day (Saminsky, Freed-CF c. 1963).
A collection of eighteen pieces in contemporary idiom from series of this same title also published separately a few years ago. This entire series is still available separately. The collection contains: A. Copland, Sunday Afternoon Music, The Young Pioneers; H. Cowell, The Harper Minstrel Sings, The Irishman Dances; I. Freed, Jeneral Jerry's Jolly Jugglers; H. Hanson, The Bell, Dance of the Warriors, Enchantment; D. Milhaud, Touches Blanches. Touches Noir; D. Moore, Careful Etta, Fiddlin' Joe, Grievin' Annie; R. Sessions, March; D. Taylor, The Smugglers; R. Thompson, Little Prelude, Song After Sundown; V. Thomson, A Day Dream. Easy to Int.

New Music for the Piano (J. Prostakoff-LG c. 1963).
24 pieces by 24 contemporary, American composers. A fine collection representing many styles of writing. Pieces range from Int. to D. Samuel Adler, Capriccio; Josef Alexander, Incantation; Milton Babbitt, Partitions; Ernst Bacon, The Pig-Town Fling; Arthur Berger, Two Episodes: 1933; Sol Berkowitz, Syncopations; Mark Brunswick, Six Bagatelles; Norman Caz-

den, Sonata; Ingolf Dahl, Fanfares; Vivian Fine, Sinfonia and Fugato; Miriam Gideon, Piano Suite No. 3; Peggy Glanville-Hicks, Prelude for a Pensive Pupil; Morton Gould, Rag—Blues—Rag; Robert Helps, Image; Alan Hovhaness, Allegro on a Pakistan Lute Tune; Kent Kennan, Two Preludes; Earl Kim, Two Bagatelles; Leo Kraft, Allegro Giocoso; Hall Overton, Polarities No. 1; George Perle, Six Preludes; Paul A. Pisk, Nocturnal Interlude; Mel Powell, Etude; Joseph Prostakoff, Two Bagatelles; Ben Weber, Humoreske.

Piano Music by Distinguished American Composers (I. Freed-TP). Series of 78 separately published compositions from easy to moderately advanced. Many different contemporary compositional techniques are employed. Explanatory editorial notes are given at the beginning of each piece. Composers include Avshalomov, Babbitt, Barati, Binder, Cheney, Cortes, Cowell, Dahl, Diemente, Donovan, Elwell, Fine, Fletcher, Franchetti, Freed, Gershefski, Giannini, Goeb, Haufrecht, Hovhaness, Kerr, Kohs, Koutzen, Kraft, Kubic, Lockwood, Lopatnikoff, Luening, McBride, McKay, Moore, Nordoff, Palmer, Perle, Phillips, Pisk, Porter, Read, Riegger, Rochberg, Rogers, Schuman, Shapero, Siegmeister, Sowerby, Starer, Stein, Stevens, Wagenaar, Weber. A collection of eighteen pieces from this series is titled *American Music by Distinguished Composers* (I. Freed-TP) (see p. 752).

U. S. A. (MCA). Two volumes.
Nine compositions in each volume, all American composers.

I: E. Bacon, Sombrero; P. Creston, Prelude Op. 38/2; A. Fuleihan, To The Young Prince; F. Jacobi, Moods; W. Josten, Dancing Leaves; G. F. McKay, An Outdoor Song; W. Piston, Improvisation; W. G. Still, Marionette; C. Vaughan, Melody. Int. to M-D.

II: G. Antheil, Prelude d; P. Bowles, Dance; T. Chandler, Calm; D. Diamond, Prelude and Fugue No. 4; D. G. Mason, Color Contrasts; C. Maxwell, Dance Caprice; G. Read, Capriccio Op. 27/3; N. G. Scott, Opus Pocus; S. Wolpe, Pastorale. Int. to M-D.

U. S. S. R.

Contemporary Soviet Piano Music (R. Luck-Gerig). Two volumes. Works by Soviet composers since World War I.

I: Devoted to easier pieces for students and amateurs: Arno Babajanian (1921-), Picture No. 4, Intermezzo; Reinhold Glière (1875-1956), Song from the East; Dimitri Kabalevski (1904-), Ball Game Op. 27/4; Aram Khachaturian (1903-), Ljado is Ill; Nodar Mamisashvili, Prelude No. 1, Whole-Tone Scales; Anti Marguste (1931-), The Weasel; Arvo Paert (1935-), Fughetta, Toccatina; Valentin Silvestrov (1937-), Serenade; Georgi Sviridov (1915-), Toccatina; Vladimir I. Tsytovich (1931-), Prelude No. 4.

II: Concert material: Edison Denisov (1929-), Variations; Vitali Godziatski (1936-), Surface Scratches; Alemdar Karamanov (1934-), Prologue, Idea and Epilogue; Alfred Shnittke (1934-), Variations on a Chord; Dmitri Shostakovich (1906-), Aphorisms Op. 13 (10 pieces, 7 included in book).

Educational Series of Russian Music for Piano (JWC). Six volumes.

1. 20 Pieces, Easy, including works by: A. Goedicke, K. Eiges, W. Landstein, W. Rebikov, S. Pantchenko, N. Ladoukhin, V. Selivanov.
2. 13 Pieces, Int., including works by: A. Goedicke, N. Amani, S. Pantchenko, K. Eiges, S. Maykapar, R. Glière, H. Pachulski, N. Ladoukhin.
3. 11 Pieces, M-D, including works by: S. Maykapar, N. Ladoukhin, N. Amani, R. Glière, H. Pachulski, A. Goedicke.
4. 9 Pieces, M-D, including works by: A. Arensky, R. Glière, A. Goedicke, S. Maykapar, H. Pachulski.
5. 10 Pieces, D., including works by: A. Arensky, S. Barmotin, G. Catoire, R. Glière, A. Goedicke, A. Scriabin, B. Zolotarev.
6. 7 Concert Pieces, D., including works by: A. Arensky, G. Catoire, A. Goedicke, N. Medtner, A. Scriabin, B. Zolotarev.

Keyboard Music of Russian and Soviet Masters (Pozniak-CFP). Works by Glinka, Cui, Borodin, Mussorgsky, Scriabin, Tschaikowsky, Liadow, Rubinstein, Rimsky-Korsakov, Glazunov, Spendiarow, Miaskowsky, Alexandrow, Prokofieff, Polowinkin, Ossokin, Gnessina, Kabalevsky, Abassow and Shostakovitch.

Modern Russian Music on Parade (B. Berlin-Thompson). Miaskowsky, Kabalevsky, Kossenko, Rakov, Shostakovich, Prokofieff. MC sounding, appealing works.

Modern Russian Piano Music (C. von Sternberg-OD c. 1915). Two volumes.

Only volume I is presently available and contains works by Akimenko, Aleneff, Alpheraky, Amani, Antipoff, Arensky, Balakireff, Barmotine, Blumenfeld, Cui, Glazounoff, Glière, Glinka, Gretchaninoff, Grodzki, Ilynski, Kalafati, Karagitscheff, Karpoff, Kopyloff, Koretschenko. These pieces do not seem "modern" today but the collection is valuable for access to material almost otherwise impossible to obtain.

Modern Russian Piano Music (Willis c. 1943).

Twenty selected pieces by A. Alexandroff; V. Barvinsky; A. Drosdoff; R. Glière; D. Kabalevsky; N. Miaskowsky; S. Prokofieff; N. Rakoff; W. Schebalin; D. Shostakovitch. See especially the pieces by Barvinsky and Schebalin. Int.

Piano Music of New Russia (EBM).

Selected piano compositions by contemporary composers of the U.S.S.R. including works by: Shostakovitch, Prokofieff, Alexandrov, Birekoff, Dechevow, Feinberg, Kabalevsky, Khrennikov, Miaskowsky, Popov and Schebalin. Some unusual repertoire.

Russian Masters (Elite-Rahter).

Fourteen original piano compositions. Editors: M. Frey, I. Philipp, A. Kleinpaul, O. Singer, E. v. Sauer. Little-known but worthwhile works. M-D.

Russian Music for the Young Pianist (P. Zeitlin, D. Goldberger-MCA c. 1967-68). Six volumes.

Graded literature (Vol. I easiest to Vol. VI most difficult), well-edited, excellent variety of material. Some of the composers included are Rimsky-Korsakov, Prokofiev, Tschaikowsky, Glinka, Shostakovich, Gretchaninoff, Scriabin, Hosenpud, Glière, Laskovsky, Rachmaninoff, Borodin, A. Rubinstein, Liadov, Maykapar, Kabalevsky, Arensky, Cui, A. Tcherepnin, Medtner, Mussorgsky, Rebikov, Gnessina, Khachaturian, Goedicke, Miaskovsky, Shchedrin.

YUGOSLAVIAN

Contemporary Yugoslavian Piano Music (R. Luck-Gerig c. 1966). Two volumes.

Introduction and biographical notes in English. Volume I easier than volume II.

I: Bruno Bjelinsky, Alarm, Fog Creeps Up, Song of the Little Emigrant; Dejan Despić, Duo Pastorale, Fanfare, Waltz; Jakob Jež, The Little Boat is Departing; Ivo Lhotka, Kalinski, Microforms; Božidar Kunc, The Favorite Fairy Tale; Janez Matičić (1926), Pavanc; Dušan Radić (1929-), Rondino; Josip Slavenski (1896-1955), Song from Medjimure; Marco Tajčević (1900-), First Suite. Int. to M-D.

II: Natko Devčic (1914-), Micro-Suite; Ivo Malec (1925-), Dialogues; Slavko Osterc (1895-1941), Arabesque No. 3; Boris Papandopulo (1906-), Dance Study; Primož Ramovš (1921-), Prelude; Branimir Sakać (1918-), Variation. M-D.

Jugoslawisches Album (UE c. 1935).

Contains: Ziga Hirschler (1894-), Sonatina. Three movements: Semplice; Intermezzo; Rondo. Modal; rondo has driving rhythms, D. Bozidar Kunc (1903-), Improvisation on a Folksong Op. 19. Folksong element permeates the writing but not obvious. M-D. Boris Papandopulo (1906-), Reign Op. 14. In Bartók idiom. Fine octave technique required.

TITLE INDEX
TO ANTHOLOGIES AND COLLECTIONS
SECTION (pp. 694-757)

Initial articles and Arabic numerals (A, An, Das, Der, I, Le, Les, The, 15, 24, 30) are placed at end of title and are ignored in alphabetization.

Part II

Bibliography, Appendix, Indexes

PART II

BIBLIOGRAPHY

This section is an extension of the bibliographies which appear after individual composers or single compositions in Part I. The "Bibliography" concentrates on English language books, periodicals and dissertations. These sources are most helpful when used in conjunction with the musical score. Careful attention has been directed toward dissertations, some with annotations. This fast-growing area is adding vast knowledge to all fields. University Microfilms in Ann Arbor, Michigan 48103 has many of these dissertations available in microfilm as well as in xerographically-printed form. As a general rule, biographies have been excluded; however, selected ones focusing on the composer's music have been included. For a more complete list of books related to keyboard pedagogy, accompanying, construction and design and biographies, see Maurice Hinson, *Keyboard Bibliography*. Cincinnati: MTNA, 1968.

Gerald Abraham, "Handel's Clavier Music," M&L, 16/4, 1935, 278-85.
(ed.) *Handel, A Symposium*. London: Oxford University Press, 1954.
Chopin's Musical Style. London: Oxford University Press, 1939. Reprint, Oxford, 1960.

Robert L. Adams, "The Development of a Keyboard Idiom in England during the English Renaissance," unpub. diss., University of Washington, 1960.

Otto E. Albrecht, *A Census of Autograph Music Manuscripts of European Composers in American Libraries*. Philadelphia: University of Pennsylvania Press, 1953. See pages 89-92 for a discussion of Clementi piano sonatas. Of special interest are his observations and conclusions concerning Clementi's performance directions and their relevance to present day performance practices.

Putnam Aldrich, "The Principal Agréments of the Seventeenth and Eighteenth Centuries," unpub. diss., Harvard University, 1942.

Riccardo Allorto, *Le Sonate per pianoforte di Muzio Clementi*. Firenze: Leo Olschki, 1959.

Hilda Andrews, "Elizabethan Keyboard Music," MQ, 16, January 1930, 59-71.

Ruth P. Andrews, "Preferred Editions," AMT, 21/2, November-December 1971, 30.

Willi Apel, *The History of Keyboard Music to 1700*. Bloomington: Indiana University Press, 1972.

"Early Spanish Music for Lute and Keyboard Instruments," MQ, 20, July 1934, 289-301.

"Early German Keyboard Music," MQ, 23, April 1937, 210-237.

Masters of the Keyboard. Cambridge: Harvard University Press, 1947.

"Neapolitan Links between Cabezon and Frescobaldi," MQ, 24, October 1938, 419-37.

Dean Luther Arlton, "American Piano Sonatas of the Twentieth Century: Selective Analyses and Annotated Index," unpub. diss., Columbia University, 1968.

John M. Arnn, "The Harmonic Language of Selected Piano Works by Fauré," unpub. thesis, Indiana University, 1969.

William Austin, "The Music of Robert Palmer," MQ, 42, January 1956, 35-50.

Music in the 20th Century. New York: Norton, 1966. Contains an extraordinary annotated bibliography.

Sol Babitz, "A Problem of Rhythm in Baroque Music," MQ, 38, October 1952, 533-65.

"Modern Errors in Mozart performance," Mozart Jahrbuch, 15, 1967, 62-89. Clear metric accents in performance, with clear articulative silences between unslurred notes and slurred rubato within the beat were characteristic of the Mozart era.

The early style (in Mozart era) aimed at the clarity and expressiveness produced by the use of hand-wrist control, both in violin bowing and keyboard playing. (Author)
"On Using J. S. Bach's Keyboard Fingerings," ML, 43, April 1962, 123-28. Includes a discussion of 'notes inégales', fingerings, ornamentation.

C.P.E. Bach, *Essay on the True Art of Playing Keyboard Instruments.* Translated and edited by William J. Mitchell. New York: Norton, 1949.

Eva Badura- Skoda, "Textual Problems in Masterpieces of the Eighteenth and Nineteenth Centuries," MQ, 51, April 1965, 301-17.

"Clementi's *Musical Characteristics* Opus 19," in *Studies in Eighteenth-Century Music.* New York: Oxford University Press, 1970, 53-67.

Paul Badura-Skoda, "The Fortepiano," Music and Musicians, 17, February 42-3, 70; March 44-5, 78; and April 32-3, 1969.

Joseph Banowetz, "Unfamiliar Liszt Works for the Moderately Advanced Student," AMT, 21, February-March 1972, 28-29, 36.

Philip Barford, "Formalism in Clementi's Pianoforte Sonatas," MMR, 82, October 205-8; November 238-41, 1952.

L. S. Barnard, "Philip Dore's Bach Clavier Lectures," MO, 76, May 1953, 491-93, 557-59; continued in subsequent monthly issues through February 1954. Reports on a series of twenty lecture-recitals entitled "The Clavier Works of J. S. Bach."

Emile Baume, "The Oxford Edition of the Chopin Etudes," MTNA Proceedings, 1940, 388-94.

Gerald S. Bedbrook, *Keyboard Music from the Middle Ages to the Beginnings of the Baroque.* New York: Macmillan, 1949. Reprint, New York: Da Capo, 1968.

Gwilym Beechey, "A New Source of Seventeenth-Century Keyboard Music," ML, 50, April 1969, 278-89. Discusses the Inglis mss in the National Library of Scotland, Edinburgh.

R. Beer, "Ornaments in Old Keyboard Music," MR, 13, February 1952, 3-13.

Rita Benton, "Some Problems of Piano Music Editions," AMT, 6, November-December 1956, 6-7, 21.
"Nicolas Joseph Hüllmandel and French Instrumental Music in the Second Half of the Eighteenth Century," unpub. diss., State University of Iowa, 1961. All of his twelve opera are discussed, all for keyboard, some with violin accompaniment. Also includes an annotated English translation of an article Hüllmadel wrote on the history of the harpsichord.

Oscar Bie, *A History of the Piano and Piano Players.* London: J. M. Dent, 1899. Reprint, New York: Da Capo, 1966.

Joseph Bloch, "Some American Piano Sonatas," JR, 3, Fall 1956, 9-15.

Eric Blom, *The Romance of the Piano.* London: Foulis, 1928. Reprint, New York: Da Capo, 1968.
"The Prophecies of Dussek," MO, 51, 1927-28, 271-73, 385-86, 495-96, 602, 807-8, 990-91, 1080-81. Also reprinted in Blom's *Classics Major and Minor.* London: J. M. Dent, 1958, 88-117.

Dean E. Boal, "A Comparative Study of Existing Manuscripts and Editions of the Robert Schumann Sonata in F Sharp Minor, Opus 11, for Piano," unpub. diss., University of Colorado, 1959.

Kenwyn G. Boldt, "The Solo Clavier Sonatas Attributed to J. S. Bach," unpub. D.M.A. paper, Indiana University, 1967.
"The Solo Piano Ballade in the Nineteenth Century," unpub. D.M.A. paper, Indiana University, 1967.
Discusses Ballades of Chopin, Liszt, Franck, Stanford, Debussy, Brahms, Arensky, Karagitschew, Liadov and Grieg.
"The Solo Piano Variations of Rachmaninoff," unpub. D.M.A. paper, Indiana University, 1967.

David A. Boltz, "The Solo Piano Works of M. Camargo Guarnieri," unpub. paper, Bloomington, Indiana: Indiana University, Latin American Music Center, 1965.

Bonnie Cave Bradley, "The Compositions for Piano Solo by Antonin Dvořák," unpub. thesis, University of Kentucky, 1969.

Joseph Brinkman and Benning Dexter, *Piano Music*. Ann Arbor: University of Michigan Official Publication, 1956. Addenda, 1959.

J. B. Brocklehurst, "A History of Pianoforte Study," unpub. thesis, Great Britain, Sheffield University, 1956.

Nathan Broder, "Mozart and the Clavier," MQ, 27, October 1941, 422-32.

Howard Brofsky, "The Instrumental Music of Padre Martini," unpub. diss., New York University, 1963.

Maurice J. E. Brown, "An Introduction to Schubert's Sonatas of 1817," MR, 12, 1951, 35-44.

Chopin: An Index of His Works in Chronological Order. New York: St. Martin's Press, 1960. Compare "Corrections and Additions," MT, 106, January 1965, 28-30.

Essays on Schubert. New York: St. Martin's Press, 1966. See especially "Towards an Edition of the Pianoforte Sonatas," 197-216.

Schubert: A Critical Biography. New York: St. Martin's Press, 1958.

"Schubert: Discoveries of the Last Decade," MQ, 47, July 1961, 293-314.

"Schubert: Discoveries of the Last Decade," MQ, 57, July 1971, 351-78.

"Schubert's Manuscripts: Some Chronological Issues," MR, 19, August 1958, 180-85.

Schubert's Variations. New York: Macmillan, 1954.

Thomas Alan Brown, "The Aesthetics of Robert Schumann in Relation to His Piano Music 1830-1840," unpub. diss., University of Wisconsin, 1965.

Conrad Bruderer, "A Comparison of the Preludes Found in Common in the *Clavier-Büchlein vor Wilhelm Friedemann Bach, The Well-Tempered Clavier,* and the Forkel Edition of *The*

Well-Tempered Clavier," "The Studies of Charles Ives," unpub. D.M. paper, Indiana University, 1968.

A measure by measure comparison of Bach's 11 preludes. The possibilities of an earlier ms or mss are discussed. Points out the interpretive and editorial problems found in the etudes of Charles Ives and discusses the practicability of their performance. An appendix contains corrected xeroxed copies of the studies. (Author) The *Studies* contain 27 movements, of which some are lost. No. 9: The Anti-Abolitionist Riots; No. 21: Some Southpaw Pitching; No. 22: Twenty-Two; No. 27: Chromatimelôdtune.

Barbara Jeanne Brynie, "The Nineteenth-Century Piano Ballade," unpub. thesis, University of Hawaii, 1968. 19 ballades by 11 different composers are analyzed and reveal elements which serve to differentiate the ballade from other one-movement genre pieces.

Joseph A. Burns, "Neapolitan Keyboard Music from Valenti to Frescobaldi," 2 vols., unpub. diss., Harvard University, 1953.

Ferruccio Busoni, *The Essence of Music and Other Papers.* London: Rockliff, 1957. Reprint, New York: Dover, 1965.

Arthur Byler, "Does Modern Piano Music Require a Special Technique," MTNA Proceedings, 1938, 33-9.

John Cage, *A Year from Monday.* Middletown, Conn.: Wesleyan University Press, 1967. Cage reviews the collected letters of Arnold Schönberg.

Susan Calvin, "The Modern Revolution in Piano Writing," AMT, 18, April-May 1969, 40-42.

Elinor Jane P. Camp, "Temporal Proportion: A Study of Sonata Forms in the Piano Sonatas of Mozart," unpub. diss., Florida State University, 1968.

This study seeks mathematical evidence of proportion in Mozart's sonata-forms, especially in those of the piano sonatas. The kind of proportion sought is temporal proportion, based on musical time and mathematical symmetry.

Robert G. Campbell, "Johann Gottfried Müthel, 1728-1788," unpub. diss., Indiana University, 1966.

Mosco Carner, "Some Observations on Schumann's Sonata Form," MT, 76/1112, 1935, 884-86.

Alfredo Cassella, *Music in My Time: Memoirs*. Translated and edited by Spencer Norton. Norman, Oklahoma: University of Oklahoma Press, 1955.

Alvan D. Cazedessus, "The Study and Performance of Selected Contemporary Piano Sonatinas," unpub. diss., Teacher's College of Columbia University, 1967.

Part I includes an anotated bibliography of ninety-eight sonatinas written between 1900 and 1963, considered suitable for performance by advanced students or concert artists. Part II consists of structural analyses plus comments on performance of nine of these sonatinas.

Mary Helen Chapman, "The Piano Works of John Powell," unpub. thesis, Indiana University, 1968. A survey of Powell's life, emphasizing his political, cultural, and aesthetic values, serves as a background for a stylistic analysis of the complete works for keyboard. (author)

Gilbert Chase, *America's Music*. Revised second edition. New York: McGraw-Hill, 1966.

The American Composer Speaks. Baton Rouge: Louisiana State University Press, 1966.

"Piano Music by Twelve Contemporaries," Inter-American Monthly, 1, September 1942, 32-3.

Abram Chasins, *Speaking of Pianists*. New York: Knopf, 1957.

Jan Chiapusso, "Bach for Purists," MTNA Proceedings, 1940, 380-87.

Ernest Closson, *History of the Piano*. London: P. Elek, 1947.

Elizabeth Cole, "Seven Problems of the Fitzwilliam Virginal Book," An Interim Report. PRMA, 79, 1952-53, 51-64.

Robert Conant, "American Composers and the Harpsichord," The Consort, 22, 1965, 49-53.

Leland A. Coon, "The Distinction between Clavichord and Harpsichord Music," MTNA Proceedings, 1936, 282-91.

Martin Cooper, *French Music from the Death of Berlioz to the Death of Fauré*. London: Oxford University Press, 1951.

Alfred Cortot, *French Piano Music*. London: Oxford University Press, 1932.
Studies in Musical Interpretation. London: Harrap, 1937.

Anthony Cross, "The Significance of Aleatoricism in Twentieth-Century Music," MR, 29, 1968, 305-22.

C. L. Cudworth, "Notes on the Instrumental Works Attributed to Pergolesi," ML, 30, October 1949, 321-28.
"Ye Olde Spuriosity Shoppe," Notes, 12, December 1954, 25-40; September 1955, 533-53.

Kathleen Dale, *Nineteenth-Century Piano Music*. London: Oxford University Press, 1954.
"The Three C's (Clementi, Czerny, Cramer): Pioneers of Pianoforte Playing," MR, 6/3, 1945, 138-48.
"Hours with Muzio Clementi: with a Classified List," ML, 24/3, 1943, 144-54.

Thurston Dart, *The Interpretation of Music*. London, New York: Hutchinson's University Library, 1954. Reprint, New York: Harper & Row, 1963.
"Handel and the Continuo," MT, 106, May 1965, 348-50.
"Performance Practice in the 17th and 18th Centuries: Six Problems in Instrumental Music," in *Report of the Eighth Congress New York 1961*. Ed. by J. LaRue. Vol. I. Kassel: Bärenreiter, 1961, 231-35.

Joan Davies, "Maria Szymanowska," The Consort, 23, 1966, 167-74.

Laurence Davies, "French Piano Music," Music, 3/2, April 1969, 30-2.

Frank Dawes, *Debussy Piano Music*. London: BBC Publications, 1969.

Gail B. Delente, "Selected Piano Music in France Since 1945," unpub. diss. Washington University, 1966. Devoted to the piano works of: Bienvenu, Boutry, Castérède, Constant, Dutilleux, Hugon, Jolivet, and Ohana. Special emphasis is given Dutilleux, Castérède and Jolivet.

Norman Demuth, *French Piano Music. A Survey with Notes on Its Performance.* London: Museum Press, 1959.

J. M. Dent, "The Pianoforte and Its Influence on Modern Music," MQ, 2, April 1916, 271-94.

Otto E. Deutsch, "Cecilia and Parthenia," MT, 100, November 1959, 591-2.
Handel. A Documentary Biography. London: Black, 1955.

Benning Dexter and George Loomis, "Choosing the Best Edition," Clavier, 8, September 1969, 50-2.

Arnold Dolmetsch, *The Interpretation of Music of the XVIIth and XVIIIth Centuries Revealed by Contemporary Evidence.* London: Novello, 1915. Revised edition, Novello, 1946.

Robert Donington, *The Interpretation of Early Music.* London: Faber and Faber, 1963.

John R. Douglas, "The Composer And His Music On Record," Library Journal, 92, March 15, 1967, 1117-21. This is a discography of 115 composers conducting or performing their own works.

Robert S. Douglass, "The Keyboard Ricercar in the Baroque Era," unpub. diss., North Texas State University, 1963.

Olin Downes, "Toscanini Considers Tradition," New York Times, April 7, 1946.

Kenneth Oscar Drake, *The Sonatas of Beethoven as He Played and Taught Them.* Cincinnati: MTNA, 1972.

Stelio Dubbiosi, "The Piano Music of Maurice Ravel, an Analysis of the Technical and Interpretative Problems Inherent in the Pianistic Style of Maurice Ravel," unpub. diss., New York University, 1967.

Raymond Dudley, "Haydn's Knee Pedal Revealed," MJ, 26, February 1968, 33. A more thorough article by the same author is contained in "Harpsichord News," The Diapason, 60, January 1969, 10-11.

Wilgus Eberly, "Some Notes on Seventeenth-Century Piano Music," MTNA Proceedings, 1947, 185-91.

Robert Ehle, "Romanticism in the Avant-Garde: Leon Kirchner's Piano Sonata," AMT, 19, April-May 1970, 30-2, 45.

Mildred Katharine Ellis, "The French Piano Character Piece of the Nineteenth and Early Twentieth Centuries," unpub. diss., Indiana University, 1969.

Alfred Einstein. "Mozart's Handwriting and the Creative Process," in *Papers Read at the International Congress of Musicology,* New York, 1939, 145-53.

Herbert Elwell, "A Composer Evaluates Twentieth-Century Piano Music," MTNA Proceedings, 1950, 42-7.

Keith Fagan, "Music for the Amateur Pianist," MO, 92, May 1969, 404-5.

E. A. Fellowes, "My Ladye Nevells Book," ML, 30, January 1949, 1-7.

Howard Ferguson, "Repeats and Final Bars in the Fitzwilliam Virginal Book," ML, 43, October 1962, 345-50.

John Fesperman, "Rhythmic Alteration in Eighteenth-Century French Keyboard Music," Organ Institute Quarterly, 9, Spring, 4-10; Summer, 13-22, 1961.

Edwin Fischer, *Reflections on Music.* London: Williams and Norgate, 1951. See chapters on interpretation of Mozart, Chopin, Schumann, Beethoven and J. S. Bach.

I. P. Fletcher, "An Analytical Study of the Form and Harmony of the Pianoforte Music of Chopin, Schumann, and Liszt," unpub. diss., Oxford University, 1963.

W. H. Grattan Flood, *John Field of Dublin, the Inventor of the Nocturne: A Brief Memoir.* Dublin: M. Lester, 1921.

Andor Foldes, "Bartók as Pianist," JR, 2, 1955, 18-22.

Lukas Foss, "The State of Piano Playing in the Twentieth Century," MTNA Proceedings, 1948, 158-167.

Irwin Freundlich, "Neglected Works in the Earlier Keyboard Repertoire," PQ, 59, Spring 1967, 12-15.

Philip Friedheim, "Tonality and Structure in the Early Works of Schoenberg," unpub. diss., New York University, 1963.

Russell E. Friedewald, "A Formal and Stylistic Analysis of the Published Music of Samuel Barber," unpub. diss., University of Iowa, 1957.

James Friskin and Irwin Freundlich, *Music for the Piano: A Handbook of Concert and Teaching Material from 1580 to 1952*. New York: Rinehart, 1954.

Thomas Lee Fritz, "The Development of Russian Piano Music as seen in the Literature of Mussorgsky, Rachmaninoff, Scriabin, and Prokofiev," unpub. diss., University of Southern California, 1959.

J. A. Fuller-Maitland, "A Note on the Interpretation of Musical Ornaments," SIMG, 13, 1911-12, 543-51.

Wilhelm Furtwängler, *Concerning Music*. Translated by L. J. Lawrence. New York: Boosey and Hawkes, 1953.

Peter F. Ganz, "The Development of the Etude for Pianoforte," unpub. diss., Northwestern University, 1960.

Rudolph Ganz, *Rudolph Ganz Evaluates Modern Piano Music*. Evanston: The Instrumentalist Co., 1968.

Willis C. Gates, "Mozart's Articulation Signs: A Dilemma for Editors," AMT, 19, September-October 1969, 20-23.

Karl Geiringer, *Haydn, a Creative Life in Music*. New York: Norton, 1946.

Walter Georgii, *Kleviermusik*. Second edition. Zürich: Atlantis-Verlag, 1950.

John Edward Gillespie, *Five Centuries of Keyboard Music.* Belmont: Wadsworth, 1965.
"The Keyboard Sonatas of Félix Máximo López (1742-1821) An Appreciation," in *Studies in Eighteenth-Century Music.* New York: Oxford University Press, 1970, 243-52.

Henri Gil-Marchev, "French Piano Music Since Fauré," AMT, 13, March-April 1964, 10-11, 31-33.

Elfriede Glusman, "The Early Nineteenth-Century Lyric Piano Piece," unpub. diss., Columbia University, 1969.

Margaret Glyn, "The National School of Virginal Music in Elizabethan Times," PRMA, 43, 1916-17, 29-49.
About Elizabethan Virginal Music and Its Composers. London: Reeves, 1924.

Scott Goddard, "The Evolution of the Pianoforte Concert," The Listener (London), 19, 1938, 437.

Theodor Göllner, "J. S. Bach and the Tradition of Keyboard Transcriptions," in *Studies in Eighteenth-Century Music.* New York: Oxford University Press, 1970, 253-60.

Richard Franko Goldman, "The Music of Elliott Carter," MQ, 43, April 1957, 151-70.

Walter Goldstein, "The Rhythmic Tricks of Chopin and Schumann," MTNA Proceedings, 1924, 63-73.

George S. Golos, "Some Slavic Predecessors of Chopin," MQ, 46, October 1960, 437-47.

Katherine Goodson, "English Pianists and the Development of Piano Playing in England," Etude, 29/1, 1911, 9-10.

Glen Hibbard Gould, "A Stylistic Analysis of Selected Twelve-Tone Works by Luigi Dallapiccola," unpub. diss., Indiana University, 1964. Includes the *Quaderno Musicale di Annalibera* for piano, 1953.

Cecil Gray, *The Forty-eight Preludes and Fugues of J. S. Bach.* London: Oxford University Press, 1938.

G. A. Greisinger and A. C. Dies, *Biographische Notizen über Joseph Haydn. Biographische Nachrichten von Joseph Haydn.* Leipzig: Breitkopf and Härtel, 1810. Translated by Vernon Gotwals: *Joseph Haydn, Eighteenth-Century Gentlemen and Genius.* Madison: University of Wisconsin Press, 1963.

"Guide for Selecting Editions," PQ, 56, Summer 1966, 14-36. Most of this issue, compiled by the editors, is devoted to this subject.

Albert L. Hanna, "A Statistical Analysis of some Style Elements in the Solo Piano Sonatas of Franz Schubert," unpub. diss., Indiana University, 1965.

Rosamond E. M. Harding, "The Earliest Pianoforte Music," ML, 13/2, 1932, 194-9.
Origins of Musical Time and Expression. London: Oxford University Press, 1938.
"Experimental Pianofortes and the Music Written for Them," PRMA, 57, 1930-31.

E. Harich-Schneider, *The Harpsichord: An Introduction to Technique, Style and the Historical Sources.* St. Louis: Concordia, 1954.

John Harley, "Ornaments in English Keyboard Music of the Seventeenth and early Eighteenth Centuries," MR, 31, August 1970, 177-200.

Arthur Hedley, *Chopin.* London: J. M. Dent and Sons Ltd., 1947. Revised edition, Dent, 1963.
"Some Notes on Chopin Biography," ML, 18/1, 1937, 42-9.
"Some Observations on the Autograph Scores of Chopin's Works," from *The Book of the First International Musicological Congress* (February 1960) *Devoted to the Works of Frederick Chopin.* Ed. by Zofia Lissa. Warsaw: Polish Scientific Publishers, 1960, 474-77. The article throws fascinating new light on distinctions between Chopin's autographs and Fontana's contemporary copies.

Lennart Hedwall, "Anteckningar kring Wilhelm Peterson-Bergers Pianosviter" (Notes on Wilhelm Peterson-Berger's piano suites), Svensk tidskrift för musikforskning 49, 1967, 41-117. In Swedish: summary in English. While Peterson-Berger's piano miniatures enjoy a widespread popularity in Sweden, his larger-scaled works for the instrument are very little known, although they shed considerable light upon his musical ideas. The author discusses formal and melodic-harmonic features of four suites: I somras (1903), Earina (1917), Italiana (1922), and Anakreontika I-II (1922-23 and 1935). He considers Peterson-Berger's music as a whole: form and style, the composer's manifold inspiration from nature and literature, and his musical "philosophy", characterized by striving to combine "Nordic" and "Southern" traits (often inspired by antiquity) into a sort of Swedish "cultural Synthesis". (Author)

William H. Heiles, "Rhythmic Nuance in Chopin Performances Recorded by Moriz Rosenthal, Ignaz Friedman, and Ignaz Jan Paderewski," unpub. diss., University of Illinois, 1964.

A. M. Henderson, "Paderewski as Artist and Teacher," MT, 97, August 1956, 411-413.
"Old English Keyboard Music (Bryd to Arne)," PRMA, 64, 1937-38.

Karin Heuschneider, *The Piano Sonata of the 18th Century in Italy.* Cape Town: A. A. Balkema, 1966.

Albert G. Hess, "The Transition from Harpsichord to Piano," Galpin Society Journal, 6, 1953, 75-94.

Anna H. Heyer, *Historical Sets, Collected Editions and Monuments of Music: A Guide to Their Contents.* Second edition. Chicago: American Library Association, 1969.

Lloyd Hibberd, "The Early Keyboard Prelude: a Study in Musical Style," unpub. diss., Harvard University, 1941.

Maurice Hinson, *Keyboard Bibliography.* Cincinnati: Music Teachers National Association, 1968.
"Published Piano Sonatas and Sonatinas by American-Born Composers, 1900-1960," AMT, 10, July-August, 1961, 10-11,

14, 35-6.
"Le Trésor des Pianistes," PQ, 72, Summer 1970, 20-21.

Daniel L. Hitchcock, "Sigismund Thalberg 1812-1871, An Evaluation of the Famous Composer-Pianist, on the 100th Anniversary of his Death," PQ, 77, Fall 1971, 12-16.

Jan Holcman,*The Legacy of Chopin.* New York: Philosophical Library, 1954.

Charles A. Horton, "Serious Art and Concert Music for Piano in America in the 100 Years from Alexander Reinagle to Edward MacDowell," unpub. diss., University of North Carolina, 1965.

Louis Horst, *Pre-Classic Dance Forms.* New York: Kamin Dance Publications, 1953.

Richard Albert Hudson, "The Development of Italian Keyboard Variations on the Passacaglio and Ciaccona from Guitar Music in the Seventeenth Century," unpub. diss., University of California at Los Angeles, 1967.

Edwin Hughes, "Expression in Piano Playing," MTNA Proceedings, 1937, 142-50.

Frederick Iliffe, *Ananlysis of Bach's Forty-eight Preludes and Fugues.* London: Novello, 1897.

Oswald Jonas, "On the Study of Chopin's Manuscripts," *Chopin-Jahrbuch 1956* (Internationale Chopin-Gesellschaft). Wien: Amalthea-Verlag, 142-55.

Santiago Kastner, "Parallels and Discrepancies between English and Spanish Keyboard Music of the Sixteenth and Seventeenth Centuries," Annuario Musical, 7, 1952, 77-115.

Edgar Stillman Kelley, *Chopin the Composer, His Structural Art and its Influence on Contemporaneous Music.* New York: G. Schirmer, 1913. Reprint, New York: Cooper Square Publishers, 1969.

Lubov Keefer, "The Influence of Adam Mickiewicz on the Ballades of Chopin," The American Slavic and East European

Review, 5/12-13, May 1946, 38-50.
Baltimore's Music: the Haven of the American Composer. Baltimore: J. H. Furst, 1962.

Alice Kern and Helen Titus, *The Teacher's Guidebook to Piano Literature.* Ann Arbor: J. W. Edwards, 1954. Revised edition, 1964.

Georg Kinsky, *Das Werk Beethovens, thematischbibliographisches Verzeichnis seiner sümtlichen vollendeten Kompositionen.* Completed by Hans Halm. Munich: G. Henle Verlag, 1955.

Frank E. Kirby, *A Short History of Keyboard Music.* New York: The Free Press, 1966. The best work in English on the subject.
"A Typology of Beethoven's Piano Sonatas," PQ, 73, Fall 1970, 12-15.

Leon Kirchner, "A Boo for the Boos of Boulez," New York Times, June 22, 1969.

John Kirkpatrick, "American Piano Music: 1900-1950," MTNA Proceedings, 1950, 35-41.
"The Evolution of Carl Ruggles," PNM, 6, Spring-Summer 1968, 146-66.
"Metre and Rhythm in Performance," Cornell University Music Review, 9, 1966, 14-17.
"United States Piano Music as Recital Literature," MTNA Proceedings, 1941, 70-8.

Ralph Kirkpatrick, "Eighteenth-Century Metronomic Indications," *Papers of the AMS,* 1938, 30-50.

Rudolf Klein, "Chopin's Sonatentechnik," Osterreichische Musikzeitschrift, 22, July 1967, 389-99.

Walter Kolneder, *Anton Webern: An Introduction to His Works.* Translated by Humphrey Searle. Berkeley: University of California Press, 1968.

B'jarn Korsten, *Recent Norwegian Piano Music.* Oslo: Norsk Komponistforening, 1965.

John Lade, "Modern Composers and the Harpsichord," The Consort, 19, July 1962, 128-31.

Christa Landon, "New Schubert Finds," MR, 31, August 1970, 215-31.

Paul Henry Lang, editor, *Problems of Modern Music.* New York: Norton, 1962.

Käbi Laretei, "Hindemith's *Ludus Tonalis:* Play with Animation!" MJ, 29, December 1971, 32, 61, 67-8.

P. Latham, "Piano Interpretation," ML, 32, January 1951, 69-71.

Zofia Lissa, editor, *The Book of the First International Musicological Congress Devoted to the Works of Frederick Chopin.* Warsaw: Polish Scientific Publishers, 1963. This Congress was held in Warsaw February 16-22, 1960. The book is written in six languages, including some articles in English.

Albert L. Lockwood, *Notes on The Literature of the Piano.* Ann Arbor: University of Michigan Press, 1940. Reprint, New York: Da Capo, 1968.

Arthur Loesser, *Men, Women, and Pianos: A Social History.* New York: Simon and Schuster, 1954.
"A Pianist Views Contemporary Piano Music," MTNA Proceedings, 1950, 48-52.

Bobby Hughes Loftis, "The Piano Sonatas of Nicolai Medtner," unpub. diss., West Virginia University, 1970.

Frank E. Lorince, "A Study of Musical Texture in Relation to Sonata-Form as Evidenced in Selected Keyboard Sonatas from C.P.E. Bach through Beethoven," unpub. diss., University of Rochester, 1966. Composers included are C.P.E. Bach, J. C. Bach, Haydn, Mozart, and Beethoven. The appendix (Vol. II) contains formal-textual diagrams and sonority abstracts of the works studied.

Guy A. Marco, "The Alberti Bass before Alberti," MR, 20, May 1959, 93-103.

Frederick H. Martens, "The Modern Russian Pianoforte Sonata," MQ, 5, July 1919, 357-63.

Martha Christine Maas, "Seventeenth-Century English Keyboard Music: a Study of Manuscripts Rés. 1185, 1186, and 1186bis of the Paris Conservatory Library," unpub. diss., Yale University, 1968.

Francis F. McGinnis, "Chopin: Aspects of Melodic Style," unpub. diss., Indiana University, 1968.

Sister Mary de LaSalle McKeon, "Stylistic Tendencies in Mid-Twentieth-Century American Piano Music," unpub. diss., University of Rochester, 1957.

Duncan R. McNab, "A Study of Classic and Romantic Elements in the Piano Works of Mozart and Schumann," unpub. diss., University of Southern California, 1961.

Mischa Meller, "Some Critical Comments on Modern Editions of the Piano Classics," AMT, 4, September-October 1954, 1, 16-17.

Arthur Mendel, "On the Pitches in Use in Bach's Time," MQ, 41, July 1955, 332-54.
editor. *The Passion according to St. John* by J. S. Bach. New York: G. Schirmer, 1951. Important, lengthy introduction by Arthur Mendel discusses performance practice of the period.

Frank Merrick, "Prokofiev's Piano Sonatas One to Five," MT, 86/1223, January 1945, 9-11.
"Prokofiev's Sixth Piano Sonata," MT, 85/1211, January 1944, 9-11.

E. H. W. Meyerstein, "A Note on Schumann's Last Composition," MS, 1/3, May 1948, 61.

Hugh Milton Miller, "Beethoven's Rhythm: Some Observations and Problems," in *Essays in Musicology — A Birthday Offering for Willi Appel.* Bloomington: Indiana University, 1968, 165-74.

Robert P. Morgan, "Towards a More Inclusive Musical Literacy: Notes on Easy 20th-Century Piano Music," Musical Newsletter, January 1971, 8-12.

Robert E. Mueller, "The Concept of Tonality in Impressionistic Music: based on the works of Debussy and Ravel," unpub. diss., Indiana University, 1954.

Israel Nestyev, *Prokofieff*. English translation by Florence Jonas. Stanford: Stanford University Press, 1960.

Paul Nettl, *Forgotten Musicians*. New York: Philosophical Press, 1951. See especially: "Schubert's Czech Predecessors, Johann Wenzel Tomáschek and Hugo Voříšek," pp. 91-109.

Frederick Neumann, "Notes on 'Melodic' and 'Harmonic' Ornaments," MR, 29, November 1968, 249-56.
"The Use of Baroque Treatises on Musical Performance," ML, 48, October 1967, 315-24.

William S. Newman. *The Sonata in the Baroque Era*. Chapel Hill: The University of North Carolina Press, 1959.
The Sonata in the Classic Era. Chapel Hill: The University of North Carolina Press, 1963.
A Selected List of Music Recommended for Piano Students. Chapel Hill: University of North Carolina Extension Service, 1965.
The Pianist's Problems. New York: Harper, 1950. Revised edition, 1956.
The Sonata Since Beethoven. Chapel Hill: The University of North Carolina Press, 1969.
"Beethoven's Pianos Versus His Piano Ideals," JAMS, 23, Fall 1970, 484-504.
"A Definition of Good Music for Piano Students," MTNA Proceedings, 1950, 220-24.
Performance Practice in Beethoven's Piano Sonatas — An Introduction. New York: W. W. Norton & Co., 1971.

The New York Public Library Reference Department: Dictionary Catalog of the Music Collection. 33 vols. and Supplement. Boston: G. K. Hall, 1964-67.

Fritz Oberdoerffer, "Urtext Editions," AMT, 10, July-August 1961, 2, 15-18.

Carl Parrish, "The Early Piano and Its Influence on Keyboard Technique and Composition in the Eighteenth Century, unpub. diss., Harvard University, 1939.
"Haydn and the Piano," JAMS, 1, Fall 1948, 27-34.

Ernst Pauer, *Ernst Pauer's Six Historical Performances of Pianoforte Music . . . April 20, 27, May 4, 11, 18, June 1, 1861 with Comments and Critical Remarks, Biographies, etc.* London: W. J. Golbourn, 1863.

Mildred Pearl, "The Suite in relation to Baroque Style," unpub. diss., New York University, 1957.

Jerry Ross Perkins, "An Examination of the Solo Piano Music Published by the Wa-Wan Press," unpub. diss., Boston University, 1969.

Marion L. Perkins, "Changing Concepts of Rhythm in the Romantic Era: A Study of Rhythmic Structure, Theory and Performance Practices Related to Piano Literature," unpub. diss., University of Southern California, 1961.

Yella Pessl, "Scope and Possibilities of Harpsichord Music," MTNA Proceedings, 1941, 204-9.

Egon Petri, "Principles of Piano Practice," MTNA Proceedings, 1939, 275-83.

C. Vere Pilkington, "A Collection of English 18th Century Harpsichord Music," PRMA, 83, 1956-57, 89-107.

Marc Pincherle, "On the Rights of the Interpreter in the Performance of 17th and 18th Century Music," MQ, 44, April 1958, 145-66.

Saul Podolsky, "The Variation Canzona for Keyboard Instruments in Italy, Austria and Southern Germany in the Seventeenth Century," unpub. diss., Boston University, 1954.

Newman W. Powell, "Early Keyboard Fingering and its Effects on Articulation," unpub. thesis, Stanford University, 1954.

"Rhythmic Freedom in the Performance of French Music from 1650 to 1735," unpub. diss., Stanford University, 1959.

Adolf Prosniz, *Handbuch der Klavier-Literatur 1450 bis 1830*. Second edition. Leipzig: Doblinger, 1908.

Ebenezer Prout, "Dussek's Piano Sonatas," MT, 18, 1877, 422-24, 468-70.

Johann J. Quantz, *On Playing the Flute*. Translated by Edward Reilly. New York: The Free Press, 1966. Contains a fine introduction. This work is one of the best sources for study of performance practices for all instruments in the Baroque era.

Carl H. Reed, "Motivic Unity in Selected Keyboard Sonatas and String Quartets of Joseph Haydn," unpub. diss., University of Washington, 1966. Seventeen movements from the keyboard sonatas and twenty-eight movements from the quartets form the basis of this study. These movements date from the 1760's on into the last decade of the composer's life, giving evidence of his sustained interest in the possibilities of motivic organization.

Eduard Reeser, *The Sons of Bach*. Translated by W. A. G. Doyle-Davidson. Stockholm: The Continental Book Co., 1949.

Rudolph Reti, "The Role of Duothematicism in the Evolution of Sonata Form," MR, 17, May 1956, 110-19.
The Thematic Process in Music. New York: Macmillan, 1951.

Herbert Hugo Riedel, "Recognition and Re-cognition: Bach and *The Well-Tempered Clavier* I," unpub. diss., University of California, Berkeley, 1969.

H. Riley, "Aleatoric Procedures in Contemporary Piano Music," MT, 107, April 1966, 311-12.

Edward Francis Rimbault, *The Pianoforte: Its Origin, Progress and Construction*. London: R. Cocks, 1860.

Alexander L. Ringer, "Leon Kirchner," MQ, 43, January 1957, 1-20.
"Willem Pijper and the Netherlands School of the Twentieth Century," MQ, 41, October 1955, 427-45.

W. Wright Roberts, "The Pianoforte Works of Chabrier," ML, 4/2, 1923, 133-43.

Charles Rosen, "When Ravel Ends and Debussy Begins," HF, 9, May 1959, 42-4.
The Classical Style: Beethoven, Haydn and Mozart. New York: Viking, 1970.

Lydia Rosen, "Guide to the Understanding and Performance of Contemporary Piano Literature of Holland, with Selective Analysis," unpub. diss., Columbia University, 1959.

John Rothgeb, "Another View on Schubert's Moment Musical, Op. 94/1," Journal of Music Theory, 13, Spring 1969, 128-39.

Fritz Rothschild, *Musical Performance in the Times of Mozart and Beethoven.* London: Adam and Charles Black, 1961.
Stress and Movement in the Works of J. S. Bach. London: Adam and Charles Black, 1966. This is the final chapter of *The Lost Tradition in Music* (New York: Oxford University Press, 1953) with additional material, a lengthy Introduction and an Appendix.

John F. Russell, "Mozart and the Pianoforte," MR, 1, 1940, 226-44.

Gyorgy Sandor, "Are Transcriptions Dead?," MJ, 27, October 1969, 22-3.

E. Robert Schmitz, *The Piano Works of Claude Debussy.* New York: Duell, Sloan and Pearce, 1950. Reprints, New York: Dover, 1966 and Westport, Connecticut: Greenwood.

Artur Schnabel, *My Life and Music.* New York: Longmans, 1961.
Music and the Line of Most Resistance. Princeton: Princeton University Press, 1942. Reprint, New York: Da Capo, 1969.

Harold Schonberg, *The Great Pianists.* New York: Simon and Schuster, 1963. From Mozart to the present day.

Leo Schrade, "Charles E. Ives, 1874-1954," Yale Review, 44, June 1955, 535-45.

Hans-Peter Schmitz, *Die Kunst der Verzierung im 18. Jahrhundert.* Kassel: Bärenreiter, 1955.

Erich Paul Schwandt, "The Ornamented Clausula Diminuta in the Fitzwilliam Virginal Book," unpub. diss., Stanford University, 1967.

Humphrey Searle, *The Music of Liszt.* London: Williams & Norgate, 1954. Reprint, New York: Dover, 1966.
"A Plea for Alkan," ML, 18/3, 1937, 276-9.

Rudolph Serkin, "Some Thoughts on Editions for the Artist Student," in *Comprehensive Guide for Piano Teachers.* New York: The Music Education League, 1963, 94-5.

John Shedlock, *The Piano Sonata.* London: Methuen, 1895. Reprint, New York: Da Capo, 1964.
Beethoven's Pianoforte Sonatas; the Origin and Respective Value of Various Readings. London: Augener, 1918.

Joel Leonard Sheveloff, "The Keyboard Music of Domenico Scarlatti: a Re-evaluation of the Present State of Knowledge in the Light of Sources," unpub. diss., Brandeis University, 1970.

Alexander Siloti, *My Memories of Liszt.* London: Methuen Simpson, 1913.

Heinrich Simon, "The Clementi Manuscripts at the Library of Congress," MQ, 28, January 1942, 105-14.

Larry Sitsky, "The Six Sonatinas for Piano of Ferruccio Busoni," Studies in Music, 2, 1968, 66-85. Busoni is established as a figure linking the 19th and 20th centuries, as an individual and essentially mystic personality, and as a great intellect. Analyses are given of Busoni's 6 sonatinas for piano: Sonatina Brevis and Sonatina super Carmen were influenced by Busoni's contact with other composers; Sonatina ad usum infantis, Sonatina 1917, and Sonatina 1910 reflect progressive steps in the development of a sophisticated form of cellular technique; the Sonatina Seconda is the final step in this development and contains elements of tone-row techiques, used in an original and prophetic way. (Author)

Alexander E. Brent Smith, "A Note on Frédéric Chopin," ML 5/2, 1924, 103-8.

Oscar G. Sonneck, *Beethoven: Impressions by his Contemporaries.* New York: G. Schirmer, 1926. Reprint, New York, Dover, 1967.
Early Concert-Life in America (1731-1800). New York: Musurgia, 1949.

Peter Stadlen, "Beethoven and the Metronome," ML, 48, October 1967, 330-49.

Hans Steger, "Scriabin's Musical Principles," Clavier, 11, January 1972, 33-35.

Erwin Stein, *Form and Performance.* London: Faber, 1962.

Leonard D. Stein, "The Performance of Twelve-tone and Serial Music for the Piano," unpub. diss., University of Southern California, 1965. After the consideration of general trends in twelve-tone and serial music, emphasis is centered on the analysis of specific compositions, between 1920 and 1960, which best illustrate characteristic performance problems. Schönberg, Webern, Messiaen, Boulez and Stockhausen are considered.

Eugene Allen Sterling, "A Study of Chromatic Elements in Selected Piano Works of Beethoven, Schubert, Schumann, Chopin, and Brahms," unpub. diss., Indiana University, 1966.

David Stone, "The Italian Sonata for Harpsichord and Pianoforte in the Eighteenth Century (1730-90)," three volumes, unpub. diss., Harvard University, 1952.

Kurt Stone, "Urtext," PQ, 55, Spring 1966, 22-5.
"The Piano and the Avant-garde," PQ, 52, Summer 1965, 14-28.

Frank B. Stratton, "The Clavichord, Then and Now," MTNA Proceedings, 1941, 198-203.

Betty Jean Thomas, "Harmonic Materials and Treatment of Dissonance in the Pianoforte Music of Frederic Chopin," unpub.

diss., University of Rochester, Eastman School of Music, 1963. An objective investigation of the harmonic and non-harmonic materials in Chopin's piano music.

Alf Thoor, "Modern Swedish Piano Music," Musikrevy International, 1954, 16-18.

John Tilbury, "The Contemporary Pianist: An Interview with Michael Parsons," MT, 110, February 1969, 150-2.

Charles W. Timbrell, "Performance Problems of English Virginal Music," PQ, 77, Fall 1971, 20-23.

Hans and Louise Tischler, "Mendelssohn's Style," MR, 8, 1947, 256-73.

Harold Truscott, "Max Reger," MR, 17, May 1956, 134-52. Also see reply by E. Wellesz, MR, 17, August 1956, 272.
"Organic Unity in Schubert's Early Sonata Music," MMR, 89, March-April, 1959, 62-66.
"Brahms and Sonata Style," MR, 25, 1964, 186-201.

Janet E. Tupper, "Stylistic Analysis of Selected Works by Frank Martin," unpub. diss., Indiana University, 1964. Includes the "Ballade pour piano et orchestre", and the "Huit Préludes" for piano (1948).

Alan Tyson, "The First Edition of Beethoven's Opus 119 Bagatelles," MQ, 49, July 1963, 331-38.
The Authentic English Editions of Beethoven. London: Faber, 1963.
"Clementi's Viennese Compositions, 1781-82," MR, 27, 1966, 16-24.
"The Hammerklavier and Its English Editions," MT, 103, April 1962, 235-7.
"John Field's Earliest Compositions," ML, 47, July 1966, 239-48.

John Verrall, "American Composers and the Piano," MTNA Proceedings, 1949, 23-30.

Jacob D. Wagner, "The Keyboard Works of Antonio Caldara," unpub. diss., Washington University (St. Louis), 1966. Contains an extensive discussion of twenty-two fugues and three additional keyboard works: *Proba Organistica, Arpeggio,* and *Capriccio,* almost all of Caldara's keyboard music.

Alan Walker, editor, *Frédéric Chopin: Profiles of the Man and Musician.* New York: Taplinger, 1967. Chapters by Arthur Hedley, Arthur Hutchings, Alan Rawthorne, Paul Hamburger, Robert Collet, Peter Gould, Lennox Berkeley, Bernard Jacobson, Humphrey Searle, Alan Walker and Paul Badura-Skoda.
editor, *Franz Liszt: The Man and His Music.* New York: Taplinger, 1970. Essays by David Wilde, John Ogdon, Humphrey Searle, Robert Collet, Louis Kentner, Arthur Hedley, Christopher Headington and Alan Walker.

Ernest Walker, "The Associated Board's Edition of Beethoven's Pianoforte Sonatas," ML, 13/1, 1932, 11-18.
"The (Beethoven) Pianoforte Sonatas: Some Textual Problems," ML, 8/2, 1927, 211-17.

Helen S. Walker, "Johann Wilhelm Hässler (1747-1822): Eighteenth-Century Solo Keyboard Literature for Amateurs," unpub. thesis, Smith College, 1968. Hässler's keyboard works reveal his awareness of local contemporary styles, the shift from a neatly articulated clavichord idiom to the broader sweep, proportions, and colors of the pianoforte style, and his responsiveness to the needs of his amateur public for short, easy works and effective practice drills. (Author)

Edward N. Waters, "Chopin by Liszt," MQ, 47, April 1961, 170-94.

Bernhard D. Weiser, *Keyboard Music.* Dubuque, Iowa: W. C. Brown Co., 1971.

Hugo Weisgall, "The Music of Henry Cowell," MQ, 45, 1959, 484-507.

Herbert Westerby. *Beethoven and his Piano Works.* London: W. Reeves, 1931.
The History of Pianoforte Music. New York: Dutton, 1924. Reprint, New York: Da Capo, 1971.

Liszt, Composer, and His Piano Works. London: W. Reeves, 1936. Reprint, Westport, Connecticut: Greenwood Press, 1970.

Introduction to Russian Piano Music. London: Reeves, 194-.

Arnold Whittall, "The Sonata Crisis: Schubert in 1828," MR, 30, 1969, 124-30.

Hugh Williamson, "Clementi and the English School of Piano Playing," MTNA Proceedings, 1939, 290-98.

Emanuel Winternitz, *Musical Autographs from Monteverdi to Hindemith.* Princeton: The University Press, 1955. Reprint, New York: Dover, 1965. See especially Volume I, 16, for an account of Beethoven's use of <> sign.

Henry S. Wolf, "The 20th Century Piano Sonata," unpub. diss., Boston University, 1957.

Klaus Wolters, *Handbuch der Klavierliteratur.* Vol. I. *Klaviermusik zu zwei Händen.* Zürich: Atlantis, 1967. The foremost work in its field. An outstanding achievement in thoroughness, detail, scope and organization.

Byron A. Wolverton, "Keyboard Music and Musicians in The Colonies and United States of America before 1830," unpub. diss., Indiana University, 1966. Investigates the earliest known uses of keyboard instruments (harpsichords, clavichords, organs) in the English colonies of North America and traces the development of keyboard music and musicians from that point through 1830.

Guy Wuellner, "The Fitzwilliam Virginal Book," MR, 32/4, November 1971, 326-48. An excellent discussion of textural procedures of the English Virginalists.

Douglas Young, "The Piano Music" (of Aaron Copland), Tempo, 95, Winter 1970-71, 15-22.

William Young, "Keyboard Music to 1600," Musica Disciplina, 16, 1962, 115-50.

APPENDIX OF HISTORICAL RECITAL PROGRAMS

PROGRAMS GIVEN BY ANTON RUBINSTEIN IN 1885-1886 DESIGNED TO EXHIBIT THE SCOPE OF THE LITERATURE OF THE PIANO

PROGRAM 1

William Byrd
- The Carman's Whistle

John Bull
- The King's Hunting Jig

François Couperin
- La Ténébreuse
- Le Réveil-matin
- La Favorite
- Le Bavolet flottant
- La Bandoline

Jean P. Rameau
- Le Rappel des oiseaux
- La Poule
- Gavotte and Variations

Domenico Scarlatti
- Cat's Fugue, Sonata, A

J. S. Bach
- Preludes and Fugues in Cm and D (Well-tempered Clavichord)
- Chromatic Fantasia and Fugue
- Gigue in B♭
- Sarabande
- Gavotte

Georg F. Handel
- Fugue, e
- The Harmonious Blacksmith
- Sarabande and Passacaglia, from g Suite
- Gigue, from Suite in A
- Lied with Variations

Carl P. E. Bach
- Rondo, b
- La Xenophon
- Sybille
- Les Langueurs tendres
- La Complaisante

Joseph Haydn
- Theme and Variations, f

Wolfgang A. Mozart
- Fantasia in c
- Gigue in G
- Rondo

PROGRAM 2

Ludwig van Beethoven
- Seven Sonatas:
  - Op. 27, No. 2
  - Op. 31, No. 2
  - Op. 53
  - Op. 57
  - Op. 90
  - Op. 101
  - Op. 111

PROGRAM 3

Franz Schubert
- Fantasia in C ("Wanderer")
- Moments musicales, Nos. 1-6
- Minuet, b
- Impromptus, c and E♭

Felix Mendelssohn
- Variations sérieuses
- Capriccio in e♭
- Ten Songs Without Words
- Presto and Capriccio

Carl Maria von Weber
- Sonata, A♭
- Momento capriccioso
- Invitation to the Dance
- Polacca brilliant, E

PROGRAM 4

Robert Schumann
- Fantasia, Op. 17
- Kreisleriana, Nos. 1-8
- Etudes symphoniques
- Sonata, f♯
- Des Abends
- In der Nacht
- Traumeswirren
- Warum
- Vogel als Prophet
- Romanza, b♭
- Carnaval, Op. 9

PROGRAM 5

Muzio Clementi
- Sonata, B♭, with the Toccata for closing movement

John Field
- Three Nocturnes, E♭, A, and B♭

Ignaz Moscheles
- Etudes caractéristiques
- Reconciliation
- Juno
- Conte d'enfant

Adolf Henselt
- Poème de'amour
- Berceuse
- Liebeslied
- La Fontaine
- "If I Were a Bird"

Sigismund Thalberg
- Etude, a
- Fantasia on "Don Juan"

Franz Liszt
- Etude, D♭
- Valse caprice
- Consolations in E and D♭
- Au bord d'une source
- Rhapsodies hongroises, Nos. 6 and 12
- Soirées musicales (after Rossini)
- La Gita in gondola
- La Danza

La Regatta
Transcriptions of
  Schubert's Songs:
  Auf dem Wasser zu singen
  Ständchen
  Der Erlkönig
Soirée de Vienne in A
Fantasia on "Robert
  the Devil"

PROGRAM 6

Frédéric Chopin
  Fantasia, f
  Preludes: e, A, A♭, b♭,
    D♭, d
  Barcarolle
  Waltzes: A♭ (the small
    one), a, A♭ (the large
    one)
  Sonata, b♭
  Berceuse
  Impromptus: F♯, G♭
  Scherzo, b
  Nocturnes: D♭, G, c
  Mazurkas: b, f♯, A♭, b♭
  Ballades: g, F, A♭, f
  Polonaises: f♯, c, A♭

PROGRAM 7

Frédéric Chopin
  Etudes: A♭, f, c, e♭,
    E♭, b, A♭, c♯, c
Anton Rubinstein
  Sonata in F
  Theme and Variations
    from Sonata in a
Michael Glinka
  Tarentella
  Barcarolle
  Souvenir de Mazurka
Mili Balakirev
  Scherzo
  Mazurka
  Islamey
Peter Tchaikovsky
  Chant sans paroles
  Valse
  Romance
  Scherzo à la russe
César Cui
  Scherzo-Polonaise
Nikolai Rimski-Korsakov
  Etude
  Novelette
  Valse
Anatol Liadov
  Etude
  Intermezzo
Nicholas Rubinstein
  Feuillet d'album
  Valse

SIX PROGRAMS BY FERRUCCIO BUSONI DEVOTED TO THE PIANO WORKS OF FRANZ LISZT, OCTOBER 31-DECEMBER 12, 1911 BERLIN, GERMANY

PROGRAM 1

Grandes Etudes d'Exécution Transcendante
Fantasie über 2 Motive aus Mozart's Die Hochzeit des Figaro

PROGRAM 2

Années de Pèlerinage, Première Année. La Suisse
Legendes
    St. François d'Assisi. La prédication aux oiseaux
    St. François de Paule marchant sur les flots
Adelaide von Beethoven
Réminiscences de Don Juan

PROGRAM 3

(Italian Pieces)

Années de Pèlerinage, Deuxième Année. Italie
Gondoliera
Tarantella
Sérénade de Rossini
Il Trovatore (Verdi)
Valse a capriccio sur Lucia e Parsina (Donizetti)
Fantasie über Norma (Bellini)

PROGRAM 4

Années de Pèlerinage, Troisième Année
Deuxième Ballade
Bénédiction de Dieu dans la solitude
Valse oubliée
Die Zelle in Nonnenwerth
Polonaise c
Galop chromatique

PROGRAM 5

Variationen über "Weinen, Klagen, Sorgen, Zagen" und das "Crucifixus" aus Bach's H-moll-Messe
Sonate H-moll
Transcriptionen nach Schubert
Erlkönig
Die Forelle
Ungarischer Marshch
Ungarische Rhapsodien
Héroide élégaique
XIII. Rhapsodie
XII. Rhapsodie

PROGRAM 6

Grandes Etudes d'Après les Caprices de Paganini
Transcriptions by Busoni
Fantasie und Fugue über "Ad nos ad salutarem undam"
Mephisto-Walzer
Polonaise E-dur

PROGRAMS GIVEN IN NEW YORK CITY, BOSTON AND CHICAGO BY OSSIP GABRILOWITSCH (1915-1916) SHOWING THE DEVELOPMENT OF PIANO MUSIC FROM THE DAYS OF THE CLAVICHORD AND HARPSICHORD TO THE PRESENT TIME

PROGRAM 1

Clavier-composers of the XVI, XVII and XVIII Centuries

ENGLISH SCHOOL:
William Byrde (1538-1623) (sic)
Pavane, A minor (composed for the Earl of Salisbury)
Henry Purcell (1658-1695)
Minuet from the Suite in G major
FRENCH SCHOOL:
François Couperin (1668-1733)
Les Moissonneurs (The Harvesters)

Claude Daquin (1694-1772)
Le Coucou (The Cuckoo)
Jean Philippe Rameau (1683-1764)
Le Tambourin

ITALIAN SCHOOL:
Padre Michel-Angelo Rossi (1620-1660)
Andantino, G major
Domenico Scarlatti (1683-1757) (sic)
Sonata (Allegro vivace), A major

NORTH-GERMAN SCHOOL:
Johann Sebastian Bach (1685-1750)
Prelude and Fugue, B flat minor (Well-tempered Clavichord, Vol. I, No. 22)
Prelude from 2d English Suite, A minor
Sarabande from 5th English Suite, E minor
Chromatic Fantasy and Fugue, D minor
Georg Friedrich Händel (1685-1759)
Variations (The Harmonious Blacksmith)
Allegro from 2d Suite, F major
Carl Philipp Emanuel Bach (1714-1788)
Rondo in B minor

VIENNESE SCHOOL:
Joseph Haydn (1732-1809)
Sonata No. 2, E minor
Wolfgang Amadeus Mozart (1756-1791)
Variations, F major
Marcia alla Turca (Turkish march)

PROGRAM 2

Ludwig van Beethoven (1770-1827)
Sonata, A major, Op. 2, No. 2
Thirty-Two Variations, C minor
Rondo, G major, Op. 51, No. 2
Sonata, F minor, Op. 57 ("Sonata Appassionata")
Sonata, A flat major, Op. 110

PROGRAM 3

The Romantic Composers

Franz Schubert (1791-1828)
- Moment musical, A flat major, Op. 94
- Menuet, B minor, Op. 78
- Impromptu, B flat major, Op. 142

Carl Maria von Weber (1786-1826)
- Invitation to the Dance

Felix Mendelssohn-Bartholdy (1809-1847)
- Four Songs without Words: E major, Op. 19, No. 1 — A major, Op. 102, No. 5 — E flat major, Op. 53, No. 2 — F major, Op. 53, No. 4
- Variations sérieuses, Op. 54

Robert Schumann (1810-1856)
- Des Abends } from Fantasy-Pieces, Op. 12
- Aufschwung } from Fantasy-Pieces, Op. 12
- Nachtstück, F major, Op. 21, No. 4
- Carnaval, Op. 9

PROGRAM 4

Frederic Chopin (1810-1849)
- Ballade, A flat major, Op. 47
- Etudes: E major, Op. 10, No. 3 — F major, Op. 10, No. 8 — C sharp minor, Op. 25, No. 7 — C major, Op. 10, No. 7
- Sonata, B flat minor, Op. 35
- Twelve Preludes, Op. 28
- Nocturne, G major, Op. 37, No. 2
- Mazurka, B minor, Op. 33, No. 4
- Polonaise, A flat major, Op. 53

PROGRAM 5

Johannes Brahms (1833-1897)
- Variations and Fugue on a Theme by Händel, Op. 24
- Intermezzo, A major, Op. 118
- Intermezzo, E minor, Op. 119, No. 2
- Rhapsodie, E flat major, Op. 119, No. 4

Franz Liszt (1811-1886)
Sonata, B minor
Dance of the Gnomes (Gnomenreigen)
Love-Dream (Liebestraum)
Etude, F minor (from "Etudes d'exécution transcendante")

PROGRAM 6

Modern Composers

César Franck (1822-1890)
Prelude, Choral et Fugue
Edvard Grieg (1843-1907)
Lyrical Pieces: Nocturne, Op. 54, No. 4 — Butterfly, Op. 41, No. 1 — To Spring, Op. 43, No. 6
Edward MacDowell (1861-1908)
To the Sea, Op. 55, No. 1 — Witches' Dance (Hexentanz)
Peter Tschaikovsky (1840-1893)
Chant d'automne, Op. 37, No. 10
Humoresque, Op. 10, No. 2
Anton Rubinstein (1830-1894)
Barcarolle, G minor, Op. 50
Valse, Op. 14
Serge Rachmaninov (born 1873)
Prelude, C sharp minor, Op. 3 No. 2
Alexander Skriabin (1872-1915)
Etude, Op. 42, No. 5
Alexander Glazunov (born 1865)
Gavotte, D major, Op. 49
Theodor Leschetizky (born 1830)
Gigue à l'antique, Op. 44
Ignace Jan Paderewski (born 1859)
Melodie, G flat major, Op. 16
Maurice Moszkowski (born 1854)
Etude de Concert, G flat major, Op. 24
Max Reger (born 1873)
Sarabande, Op. 13, No. 7
Richard Strauss (born 1864)
Intermezzo (from "Stimmungsbilder"), Op. 9

Arnold Schoenberg (born 1874)
  Clavierstücke, Op. 19
Claude Debussy (born 1862)
  Clair de Lune (from "Suite Bergamasque")
  L'Isle joyeuse
Maurice Ravel (born 1875)
  The Fountain (Jeux d'Eau)
Cyril Scott (born 1879)
  A Pierrot-Piece, Op. 35, No. 1
Percy Grainger (born 1884)
  Shepherd's Hey

INDEX I

This index lists composers alphabetically under nationality designations. For composers who lived prior to the Romantic era consult the stylistic period subheadings under the given nationality. The Index also refers to national Anthologies and Collections.

Thalberg
Uray
Urbanner
Webern
Weigl
Wellesz
Wührer

BELGIAN, FLEMISH COMPOSERS
Absil
Baervocts
BELGIAN ANTHOLOGIES AND COLLECTIONS
Boutmy
Fiocco
Gheyn
Helmont
Jongen
Lekeu
Loeillet
Maleingreau
Meulemans
Peeters
Poot
Pousseur
Raick

BOLIVIAN COMPOSERS
Mendoza-Nava

BRAZILIAN COMPOSERS
Carvalho
Fernandez
Guarnieri
LATIN AMERICAN ANTHOLOGIES AND COLLECTIONS
Mignone
Pinto
Santoro
Villa-Lobos

BULGARIAN COMPOSERS
BULGARIAN ANTHOLOGIES AND COLLECTIONS
Eliezer

CANADIAN COMPOSERS
Archer
Bales
Beckwith
Behrens
Betts
Brassard
Callihou
CANADIAN ANTHOLOGIES AND COLLECTIONS
Champagne
Coulthard
Dela
Descarries
Dolin
Duchow
Eckhardt-Gramatté
Fiala
Fleming
Hétu
Jacque
Kasemets
Kenins
Mathieu
Morawetz

VIRGINALISTS
(ca. 1580-1650), and
LATER ENGLISH
COMPOSERS
(17th & 18th centuries)

- Arne
- Avison
- Blow
- Bull
- Byrd
- Chilcot
- Clarke
- Cosyn
- Croft
- ENGLISH VIRGINALISTS ANTHOLOGIES AND COLLECTIONS
- Farnaby
- Gibbons
- Greene
- Hook
- Locke
- Morley
- Munday
- Peerson
- Philips
- Purcell
- Roseingrave
- Stanley
- Tallis
- Tisdale
- Tomkins

FINNISH COMPOSERS

- Bergman
- Kilpinen
- Palmgren
- Rautio
- SCANDINAVIAN ANTHOLOGIES AND COLLECTIONS
- Sibelius

FRENCH COMPOSERS

- Alain
- Alkan
- Amy
- Aubin
- Auric
- Barraine
- Barraqué
- Barraud
- Baudrier
- Bitsch
- Bizet
- Boëly
- Boieldieu
- Bordes
- Boulez
- Bréville
- Casadesus
- Castérède
- Castillon
- Chabrier
- Chaminade
- Charpentier, J.
- Chausson
- Damase
- Debussy
- Decaux
- Delvincourt
- Demarquez
- Dubois, P. M.
- Dubois, T.
- Dukas

Dandrieu
Daquin
Dieupart
Dumont
Duphly
Forqueray
FRENCH CLAVECINISTS ANTHOLOGIES AND COLLECTIONS
Guerre
Marchand
Rameau
Roux, le

GERMAN COMPOSERS
Albert, d'
Baur
Beethoven
Bemetzrieder
Blacher
Brahms
Bruch
Busoni
Cramer
Degen
Distler
Egk
Eisler
Erbse
Feuchtwanger
Fortner
Frommel
Genzmer
GERMAN ANTHOLOGIES AND COLLECTIONS
Gieseking
Henselt
Henze
Herz
Hindemith
Hoffmann
Jacobi, W.
Jensen
Kahn
Kalkbrenner
Karg-Elert
Kempff
Klebe
Koellreutter
Korn
Maler
Mendelssohn-Bartholdy
Orff
Otte
Pepping
Pfitzner
Poser
Raff
Raphael
Reger
Reinecke
Reubke
Reutter
Rust
Sachase
Schnabel
Schroeder
Schröter
Schumann, C.
Schumann, R.
Schuster
Steffen
Steibelt
Stockhausen

Scarlatti, D.
Trabaci
Turini
Zipoli

JAPANESE COMPOSERS
Hachimura
Hayama
Ichiyanagi
Nakada
Okumura
Ozawa
Takahashi
Tokunaga

LATVIAN COMPOSERS
Darzins

MEXICAN COMPOSERS
Bernal-Jimenez
Chávez
Galindo-Dimas
Hernandez-Moncada
Jiménez-Mabarak
Ponce

NORWEGIAN COMPOSERS
Andersen
Cleve
Egge
Grieg
Hovland
Mortensen
Nystedt
Saeverud
Sinding
Sommerfeldt
Tveitt
Valen

PANAMANIAN COMPOSERS
Cordero
Saiz-Salazar

PERUVIAN COMPOSERS
Holzmann
LATIN AMERICAN ANTHOLOGIES AND COLLECTIONS
Malsio
Sás

PHILIPPINE COMPOSERS
Kasilag

POLISH COMPOSERS
Bacevičius
Bacewicz
Bloch, A.
Bury
Chopin
Elsner
Fitelberg
Garścia
Godowsky
Haubenstock-Ramati
Koffler
Lachowska
Lutoslawski
Moszkowski
Paderewski
Palester
Panufnik

Halffter, E.
Halffter, R.
Infante
Lidón
Mompou
Montsalvatge
Narváez
Nebra
Nin
Rodrigo
Salazar
Solèr
SPANISH ANTHOLOGIES AND COLLECTIONS
Surinach
Turina

SWEDISH COMPOSERS

Alfven
Anderberg
Atterberg
Bäck
Bark
Berwald
Björkander
Blomdahl
Broman
Eriksson
Frumerie
Hakanson
Hallnäs
Hambraeus
Haquinius
Helldén
Johnsen
Karkoff
Kempe
Koch
Körling
Larsson
Lidholm
Liljefors
Linde
Lundberg
Mankell
Nilsson
Nordqvist
Peterson-Berger
Rangström
Roman
Rosenberg
SCANDINAVIAN ANTHOLOGIES AND COLLECTIONS
Schoenberg, S.
Sköld
Stenhammar
Tubin
Wiklund
Wirén
Wohlfart

SWISS COMPOSERS

Alessandro, d'
Beck
Blanchet
Bloch
Burkhard
Fischer, E.
Flury
Geiser
Holliger
Honegger
Kelterborn
Lang

Cage
Callinicos
Carpenter
Carr
Carter
Cazden
Chajes
Chanler
Chou
Cooper
Cope
Copland
Cowell
Creston
Crist
Crumb
Cumming
Custer
Dahl
Debusman
Dello Joio
Dett
Diamond
Diemente
Diercks
Dodge
Donato
Donovan
Duke
Elwell
Etler
Evett
Faith
Farwell
Feldman
Fine, I.
Fine, V.
Finney
Flagello
Flanagan
Floyd
Foldes
Foss
Franco
Freed
Fuleihan
Ganz
Gerschefski
Gershwin
Giannini, V.
Giannini, W.
Gideon
Goeb
Goldman
Gottschalk
Gould
Grainger
Grant
Green
Griffes
Gruen
Gutche
Haieff
Hanson
Harris, D.
Harris, R.
Harrison
Hartley
Haubiel
Haufrecht
Heiden
Helfer
Helm
Helps
Hendl
Hensel

Reynolds
Riegger
Rochberg
Rorem
Rovics
Rózsa
Rubinstein, B.
Ruggles
Schloss
Schramm
Schuman
Schwartz
Serly
Sessions
Shapero
Shepherd
Shifrin
Siegmeister
Simons
Slavit
Smit
Smith, H.
Smith, L.
Sowerby
Starer
Stearns
Steiner
Steuermann
Stevens
Still
Stout
Straight
Stravinsky, I.
Stravinsky, S.
Subotnick
Swanson
Swift
Sydeman
Szell
Tanenbaum
Talma
Tcherepnin
Thomson
Toch
Triggs
Trimble
Trythall
U.S.A. ANTHOLOGIES AND COLLECTIONS
Ussachevsky
Verrall
Wagenaar
Wagner, J.
Ward
Ward-Steinman
Weber, B.
Weingarden
Weiss
Werlé
Williams, C.
Williams, D. R.
Wolff
Wolpe
Woodard
Work
Wuorinen
Wylie
Wyner
Yardumian
Zabrack

U.S.S.R., RUSSIAN COMPOSERS

Alexandrow
Arensky
Balakirev

INDEX II

Black Composers and Women Composers (also included in Index I).

BLACK COMPOSERS

WOMEN COMPOSERS

INDEX III: EDITORS, ARRANGERS, TRANSCRIBERS

ADDENDUM: NEW DATES

The following list supplies death dates of composers who have recently died as well as birth and death dates that were not available at the time of the first printing.

Karl Andersen, 1903-1970
Hans Eric Apostel, 1901-1972
Esther Williamson Ballou, 1915-1973
Jean Barraqué, 1928-1973
Boris Blacher, 1903-1975
Arthur Bliss, 1891-1975
Robert Casadesus, 1899-1972
Luigi Dallapiccola, 1904-1975
Sabin V. Dragoi, 1894-1968
Alvin Etler, 1913-1973
Robert Evett, 1922-1975
Samuel Feinberg, 1890-1962
Alois Hába, 1893-1973
Yoshio Hachimura, 1938-
Karel Jirák, 1891-1972
André Jolivet, 1905-1974
Mihail Jora, 1891-1971
Joseph Kaminski, 1903-1972
René Leibowitz, 1913-1972
Gian Francesco Malipiero, 1882-1973
Frank Martin, 1890-1974
John McCabe, 1939-
George Frederick McKay, 1899-1970
Darius Milhaud, 1892-1974
Lev Oborin, 1907-1973
Hall Overton, 1920-1972
André Previn, 1930-
Knudaage Riisager, 1897-1974
Gustave Samazeuilh, 1877-1967
Julius Schloss, 1902-1972
Joseph Wagner, 1900-1974
Egon Wellesz, 1885-1974